Using SVG with CSS3 and HTML5

Vector Graphics for Web Design

Amelia Bellamy-Royds, Kurt Cagle, and Dudley Storey

Beijing · Boston · Farnham · Sebastopol · Tokyo

Using SVG with CSS3 and HTML5

by Amelia Bellamy-Royds, Kurt Cagle, and Dudley Storey

Published by O'Reilly Media, Inc., 1005 Gravenstein Highway North, Sebastopol, CA 95472.

O'Reilly books may be purchased for educational, business, or sales promotional use. Online editions are also available for most titles (*http://oreilly.com/safari*). For more information, contact our corporate/institutional sales department: 800-998-9938 or *corporate@oreilly.com*.

Editor: Meg Foley
Production Editor: Kristen Brown
Copyeditor: Rachel Monaghan
Proofreader: James Fraleigh

Indexer: Amelia Bellamy-Royds
Interior Designer: David Futato
Cover Designer: Karen Montgomery
Illustrator: Rebecca Demarest

November 2017:   First Edition

Revision History for the First Edition

2017-10-17:   First Release
2018-03-09:   Second Release

See *http://oreilly.com/catalog/errata.csp?isbn=9781491921975* for release details.

978-1-491-92197-5

[LSI]

Table of Contents

Table of Contents

Part I.   SVG on the Web

Part II.   Drawing with Markup

Part IV.   Artistic Touches

Part V.   SVG as an Application

Preface

Scalable Vector Graphics (SVG to its friends) has many applications. It is used by graphic designers and by technical drafters. But this book is specifically about its use in web design and development.

Using SVG with CSS3 and HTML5 is, essentially, using SVG on the web. But more than that, it's about using SVG in complex web applications. This is SVG not only as illustrations, but as graphical documents that can be integrated in HTML web pages, and styled with custom CSS. Many chapters will be useful to designers creating images for the web, but the focus is on developers who are adapting designs to add data-based graphics, dynamic styles, interaction, or animation.

A Winding Path

This book traces its origins to 2011, when Kurt started work on a book called *HTML5 Graphics with SVG and CSS3*. At the time, HTML5 and CSS3 were brand new, and SVG was just starting to get decent support in web browsers.

But life, as it often does, got in the way. The book took much longer than planned to complete. And time introduced its own complications.

When Kurt handed off the manuscript to Amelia in late 2014, the state of graphics on the web had changed considerably since when he'd started it. HTML had acquired competely new graphics formats (the Canvas2D API and WebGL), which were completely separate from SVG and CSS. And CSS3 was becoming a bigger and bigger topic every year, quickly outgrowing the one chapter planned for it.

So the decision was made to focus on SVG. However, this book is still all about the intersection of the three web languages—and JavaScript, too! The driving goal for the rewrite was to create a practical guide to using SVG on the web, in complex web pages, with full awareness of the need for cross-browser, multidevice support.

That turned out to be easier said than done. It's taken a few more years (and one more coauthor, Dudley) to complete this manuscript. It's also a considerably larger book than initially planned. We hope it was worth the wait.

The Road Ahead

SVG is a complex topic, but we have tried to arrange this book in a logical progression. Part I begins with the wide view, discussing how —and why—you use SVG in web design:

- The possibilities of SVG as an independent image format, in Chapter 1
- SVG on the web, with a focus on how it interacts with other coding languages, in Chapter 2
- How CSS can be used to style your SVG, and how SVG graphics can be used with CSS to style other documents, in Chapter 3
- Useful software for creating and testing SVG images, as well as some sources of ready-to-use SVG for less artistically inclined web developers, in Chapter 4

The remainder of the book will narrow in on each of the main features of SVG one chapter at a time. Part II concentrates on the core drawing elements in SVG, and how to control their geometry and layout:

- Sizing and positioning basic shapes, in Chapter 5
- Defining custom shapes and lines, in Chapter 6
- Text layout, in Chapter 7

Part III dives into the technical details of how SVG documents are constructed and how vector shapes are positioned:

- Establishing coordinate systems and scale, in Chapter 8
- Redefining coordinate systems when embedding graphics in web pages, in Chapter 9
- Reusing content and embedding images, in Chapter 10
- Transforming coordinate systems to reposition and distort graphics, in Chapter 11

Part IV focuses more on the graphical side of the language:

- Filling the area of shapes and text, including gradients and patterns, in Chapter 12
- Drawing outlines around shapes and text, in Chapter 13
- Adding line markers (repeated symbols on the ends or corners of custom shapes), in Chapter 14
- Clipping and masking of graphics, in Chapter 15
- Filter effects and blend modes, in Chapter 16

Part V looks at how the basic structure of SVG images can be enhanced to create complete web applications, focusing on three main areas:

- Accessibility and metadata, in Chapter 17
- Interactive SVG, links, and event handling, in Chapter 18
- Animation using CSS, XML, or JavaScript, in Chapter 19

Once you have all the pieces in place, Chapter 20 returns to the big picture, discussing best practices for working with SVG.

Before You Begin

This book focuses on "using SVG" in web pages. It assumes that you, the reader, are already familiar with creating web pages using HTML, CSS, and a little bit of JavaScript. When the examples use relatively new features of CSS3 and HTML5, we'll explain them briefly, but we'll assume you know a `<div>` from a `<li>`, and a `font-family` from a `font-style`.

You'll get the most out of the book by working through the code samples as you go. It will help if you have a good code editor that recognizes SVG syntax, and if you know how to use the developer tools in your web browser to inspect the document structure and styles that create the visible result.

About This Book

Whether you're casually flipping through the book, or reading it meticulously cover-to-cover, you can get more from it by understanding the following little extras used to provide additional information.

Conventions Used in This Book

The following typographical conventions are used in this book:

Bold
> Indicates new terms or concepts.

Italic
> Indicates URLs, email addresses, filenames, and file extensions, or simply emphasizes that a word is really important.

`Constant width`
> Used for code listings, as well as within paragraphs to refer to code elements such as elements, attributes, keywords, and function names.

`Constant width italic`
> Shows a variable or other part of code that should be replaced with user-supplied values or by values determined by context, so that `"Hello, Name"` becomes "Hello, Kurt," or "Hello, Dudley," or "Hello, Amelia."

> Tips like this will be used to highlight particularly tricky aspects of SVG, or simple shortcuts that might not be obvious at first glance.

Notes like this will be used for more general asides and interesting background information.

Warnings like this will highlight compatibility problems between different web browsers (or other software), or between SVG as an XML file versus SVG in HTML pages.

In addition, sidebars like the following will introduce complementary topics:

A Brief Aside

"Future Focus" sidebars will look at proposed features that aren't yet standardized, or new standards that aren't widely implemented.

"CSS Versus SVG" will compare the SVG way of designing a web page with the CSS way of achieving a similar effect.

Although these sidebars are not absolutely essential for understanding SVG, they will hopefully add important context when you are planning a complete web project.

Supplementary Material

There is so much to say about SVG on the web, we couldn't fit it all in one book.

We have a couple dozen extra sections, most with extra examples, that go a little deeper into the ideas from the main text. We've also put together reference sections, to make it easier for you to look up syntax details later.

This supplementary material is available online, and also includes the full code for all the examples and figures, and other assets such as JPEG files:

https://oreillymedia.github.io/Using_SVG

Whenever there is extra explanatory or reference material available, a note box like the following will let you know:

More Online

Can't remember if it is `rotate="auto"` or `orient="rotate"`? Good thing we have all the SVG attributes we mention listed for easy reference, in the "SVG Elements and Attributes" guide:

> *https://oreillymedia.github.io/Using_SVG/guide/markup.html*

P.S. It's `orient="auto"` for `<marker>`, and `rotate="auto"` for `<animateMotion>`.

The online supplementary material is also available for download as a zip archive or Git repository:

> *https://github.com/oreillymedia/Using_SVG*

About the Examples

The examples in this book have been tested in common web browsers in mid-2017. Bugs and inconsistencies are noted throughout. Hopefully, some of those bugs will be fixed in the future; web browsers are updated on a monthly basis, and some improvements have occurred even as this book was being edited. However, there are likely other problems that we have overlooked. In addition, other software for manipulating SVG has its own limitations or quirks which are not outlined here. Test early, test often, test in any software your content needs to be displayed with.

The full example code is available for you to experiment with:

- On GitHub, you can download the entire supplementary repo, or can find an individual file and view the code. For SVG files that don't require JavaScript, the GitHub code view also shows you what the graphic looks like.

  > *https://github.com/oreillymedia/Using_SVG*

- On the website, you can test out the working versions of each example in your browser, and use your browser's developer tools (or view-source mode) to see the code.

https://oreillymedia.github.io/Using_SVG

This book is here to help you get your job done. In general, if example code is offered with this book, you may use it in your programs and documentation. You do not need to contact us for permission unless you're reproducing a significant portion of the code. For example, writing a program that uses several chunks of code from this book does not require permission. Selling or distributing a CD-ROM of examples from O'Reilly books does require permission. Answering a question by citing this book and quoting example code does not require permission. Incorporating a significant amount of example code from this book into your product's documentation does require permission.

We appreciate, but do not require, attribution. An attribution usually includes the title, author, publisher, and ISBN. For example: "*Using SVG with CSS3 and HTML5* by Amelia Bellamy-Royds, Kurt Cagle, and Dudley Storey (O'Reilly). Copyright 2018 Amelia Bellamy-Royds, Kurt Cagle, Dudley Storey, 978-1-491-92197-5."

If you feel your use of code examples falls outside fair use or the permission given above, feel free to contact us at *permissions@oreilly.com*.

O'Reilly Safari

 *Safari* (formerly Safari Books Online) is a membership-based training and reference platform for enterprise, government, educators, and individuals.

Members have access to thousands of books, training videos, Learning Paths, interactive tutorials, and curated playlists from over 250 publishers, including O'Reilly Media, Harvard Business Review, Prentice Hall Professional, Addison-Wesley Professional, Microsoft Press, Sams, Que, Peachpit Press, Adobe, Focal Press, Cisco Press, John Wiley & Sons, Syngress, Morgan Kaufmann, IBM Redbooks,

Packt, Adobe Press, FT Press, Apress, Manning, New Riders, McGraw-Hill, Jones & Bartlett, and Course Technology, among others.

For more information, please visit *http://oreilly.com/safari*.

How to Contact Us

Please address comments and questions concerning this book to the publisher:

> O'Reilly Media, Inc.
> 1005 Gravenstein Highway North
> Sebastopol, CA 95472
> 800-998-9938 (in the United States or Canada)
> 707-829-0515 (international or local)
> 707-829-0104 (fax)

We have a web page for this book, where we list errata, examples, and any additional information. You can access this page at *http:// bit.ly/usingSVG_with_CSS3_HTML5*.

To comment or ask technical questions about this book, send email to *bookquestions@oreilly.com*.

For more information about our books, courses, conferences, and news, see our website at *http://www.oreilly.com*.

Find us on Facebook: *http://facebook.com/oreilly*

Follow us on Twitter: *http://twitter.com/oreillymedia*

Watch us on YouTube: *http://www.youtube.com/oreillymedia*

Acknowledgments

A book of this size does not get published without contributions from many people. The authors want to thank the many editors, reviewers, and other production staff who have worked on this book over its many-year gestation.

Special thanks go to former O'Reilly editor Meghan Blanchette, who helped shape the scope and organization of the book; to the final technical reviewers—Ana Tudor, Gabi, and Taylor Hunt—who suggested numerous clarifications for tricky topics (and identified many additional bug warnings); and to the O'Reilly tools and production teams, who crafted numerous custom style and layout features for the print book.

Finally, thanks go to the readers who offered feedback and encouragement based on the early release drafts of the book. In the hyperconnected, fast-paced world of web development, writing a book is still a lonely, long-term endeavor; it is important to be reminded that the explanations and examples we create are helping real human beings working on the web.

Thank you, thank you very much.

additional bug warnings); and to the O'Reilly tools and production teams, who crafted numerous custom style and layout features for the print book.

Finally, thanks go to the readers who offered feedback and encouragement based on the early release drafts of the book. In the hyperconnected, fast-paced world of web development, writing a book is still a lonely, long-term endeavor; it is important to be reminded that the explanations and examples we create are helping real human beings working on the web.

Thank you, thank you very much.

PART I

SVG on the Web

Scalable Vector Graphics (SVG) are drawings and diagrams defined using an open standard of human-readable XML code. SVG can be used in print publishing and even in technical drawings. However, SVG's true potential resides in the web browser. SVG was designed to work with HTML, CSS, and JavaScript, the core languages used to describe, style, and manipulate content on the web.

The following chapters look at SVG as a whole, focusing on how it is created and used on the web, and how it intersects and overlaps other web standards.

CHAPTER 1

Graphics from Vectors

An Overview of SVG

There's a fundamental chicken-and-egg quality to creating SVG that can make teaching it a challenge. Shapes without styles are not terribly attractive; styles without shapes cannot be seen. To work with an SVG, you need to display the graphic on the web; to display a graphic, you need some SVG code to display!

This chapter presents a rough sketch of the chicken *and* the egg, so that subsequent chapters can fill in the details one topic at a time, without making you feel like large parts of the picture are missing.

The chapter starts with a simple SVG graphic and then adapts it to use different techniques and to add new functionality. The examples will introduce many key features of SVG, but will skip over many others. At the end, you should have a good idea of what an SVG file looks like, how the key elements relate to each other, and how you can edit the file to make simple changes.

The graphics in this chapter, and the rest of the book, involve building SVG directly as markup code in a text editor, rather than using a tool such as Inkscape or Adobe Illustrator. There are a couple of reasons for this:

- It helps you focus on building applications with SVG, rather than just drawing graphics—you can always extend these principles to more artistic images. To keep from having pages and pages of SVG markup, the graphics used here are...minimalistic.

- When using graphics editors, it is easy to generate overly complex code that would distract from the key messages of the examples. If you use a code editor to view a file created by these programs, you'll discover many extra attributes and elements identified by custom XML namespaces. These are used internally by the software but don't have an effect when the SVG is displayed in a web browser.

Handcoding SVG from scratch is only practical for simple geometric drawings. Working with the code, however, is essential for creating interactive and animated graphics. For more artistic graphics, a drawing made in a visual editor can be exported to SVG, and then adapted as code.

 Alternatively, some graphics editors, such as Adobe Illustrator, allow you to copy individual shapes (or groups of shapes) from the editor and paste them into your text editor, with the pasted result being the SVG markup for that shape.

To follow along with the examples in this chapter, it will help if you have a basic familiarity with HTML and CSS. If you also know XML —which is similar to HTML, but not the same—you'll be one step ahead. In future chapters, we will also assume that you are familiar with using JavaScript to manipulate web pages. We'll always try to explain the purpose of all the code we use, but we won't discuss the basic syntax of those other web languages.

If you're not comfortable with HTML, CSS, and JavaScript, you'll probably want to have additional reference books on hand as you experiment with SVG on the web.

Defining an SVG in Code

SVG is drawing with code. And that code needs someplace to go. Your SVG exists inside a document, or file, on your computer or on the internet. When testing out the advanced techniques in future chapters, you might start with an existing file that you created in a graphical drawing program or downloaded from a clip-art database. But in this chapter, we're starting from scratch, with an empty file.

We're also going to take it simple, and write markup code.

Markup is the code that actually describes the document that the web browser displays, in a format the web browsers understand. In contrast, lots of code for the web starts in a preprocessor coding or template language, which then gets converted (processed) into markup files by other software (aka the preprocessor). Other websites don't send the web browser the final document, instead sending a bare-bones document with JavaScript instructions for building the rest. We'll have examples of building SVG with JavaScript later.

But for now: we're creating a markup file.

To create that file, you'll need a text editor. Your favorite code editor should work. If you don't have a favorite code editor, we describe some options in Chapter 4. For now, just make sure that your program can save files as plain, unformatted text, with UTF-8 (Unicode) character encoding.

That text file will be parsed (read and interpreted) by a web browser. The browser chooses the correct **code parser** program according to its **file type**. On the internet, file types are defined in the HTTP headers sent with the file. On your computer, file types are defined by the file extension: the last few letters of the filename, after the final . (period or full stop) character.

There are two types of files that can contain SVG markup for the web: SVG files (with filenames like *drawing.svg*) and HTML files (with filenames like *drawing.html*, or sometimes *drawing.xhtml*).

 Depending on your operating system settings, your computer may hide the file extension in your file listings, to prevent you from accidentally changing it when you rename a file. Be careful that you're not unintentionally creating files like *drawing.svg.txt*, which is a plain-text file, not an SVG file.

A *.svg* file is known as a **standalone SVG file**, because the SVG is an entire, independent document. When the browser receives a standalone SVG file, it reads it using the XML parser.

SVG code in a *.html* or *.xhtml* file is known as **inline SVG**, because the SVG code is written directly "in the lines" of the HTML markup.

The difference between *.html* and *.xhtml* is whether the browser will use the HTML parser or the XML parser.[1]

We're going to start with inline SVG in a *.html* file, because we hope you're already somewhat familiar with HTML. Also, the HTML parser is much more forgiving about how it reads your markup.

To get started: open a new, empty file in your text editor. Save it with a *.html* filename. For example, you could call it *my-first-svg.html*. Inside that file type the following code, then save it again:

```
<svg>
```

Congratulations. You now have an HTML file with an inline SVG, defined by the opening tag of an **<svg> element**. That's all you need.

It's not a very *good* HTML file, though. It's a file that takes full advantage of that very-forgiving HTML parser.

If you weren't so lazy, and instead created a *good* HTML file with an inline SVG element, it would look like Example 1-1. This is the basic "boilerplate" code that you can copy and adapt for all the inline SVG examples in this book. This code is so good, you could even save it as a *.xhtml* file, and the much-*less*-forgiving XML parser should read it without error. It would still be inline SVG, though—an SVG element inside an HTML document.

Example 1-1. Defining an inline SVG element in an HTML file

```
<!DOCTYPE html>
<html lang="en">
    <head>
        <meta charset="utf-8" />
        <title>HTML file with Inline SVG</title>
        <style>
        </style>
    </head>
    <body>
        <svg width="400px" height="400px">
        </svg>
    </body>
</html>
```

---

1 Technically, the decision between the XML and HTML parsers is based on the media type, not the file extensions. On the web, media type is determined by the HTTP headers. But on your computer, it's usually determined by the file extension. And most web servers use file extensions to determine the media type HTTP headers, too.

The code in Example 1-1 includes our first **two SVG attributes: width and height**. They set the—surprise, surprise—width and height of the SVG drawing region within our HTML page.

You can also set the SVG dimensions using the CSS width and height properties applied to the <svg> element. The benefit of using attributes is that they set a default value that applies even before CSS is loaded, preventing a "flash of unstyled SVG" (FOUS, for people who like acronyms).

 A lot of examples in this book will use width="400px". There's nothing magical about that number: it just happens to be a round number that is pretty close to the width of a figure in the printed book. Other examples will use width="4in" (four inches), which is exactly the width of a figure in the printed book. When creating examples for the web, however, you might prefer to use width="100%".

So far, we have a valid HTML file with an inline SVG element, but if you open that file in a web browser you'll just see a plain white screen. Time to start drawing.

Simple Shapes

At its most basic, an SVG image consists of a series of shapes that are drawn to the screen. Everything else builds upon the shapes.

Individual SVG shapes *can* be incredibly complex, made up of hundreds of distinct lines and curves. The outline of Australia (including the island of Tasmania) could be represented by a single <path>

shape on an SVG map. For this introductory overview, however, we're keeping it simple. We're using two shapes you're probably quite familiar with: circles and rectangles.

Figure 1-1 is a colored line drawing, such as you might find in a children's book, of a cartoon stoplight. This is the SVG we're going to create.

Figure 1-1. Primary color stoplight graphic

There are four shapes in Figure 1-1: one rectangle and three circles. The layout, sizing, and coloring of those shapes creates the image that can be recognized as a stoplight.

Add the following code between the opening and closing <svg> tags in your file (from Example 1-1) to draw the blue rectangle from Figure 1-1:

```
<rect x="20" y="20" width="100" height="280"
      fill="blue" stroke="black" stroke-width="3" />
```

Save the file in the code editor, and then open the same file in your web browser (or refesh the browser tab, if the earlier version of the file was already open). You should now see a tall blue rectangle with a black outline.

The **<rect> element** defines a rectangle that starts at the point given by the x (horizontal position) and y (vertical position) attributes and has an overall dimension given by the width and height attributes. Note that you don't need to include units on the length attributes. Length units in SVG are pixels by default, although the definition of a pixel (and of every other unit) will change if the graphic is scaled.

"Pixels" when referring to lengths means CSS layout px units. These will not always correspond to the actual pixels (picture elements) on the monitor. The number of individual points of color per px unit can be affected by the type of screen (or printer) and the user's zoom setting.

In software that supports CSS3, all other measurement units are adjusted proportional to the size of a px unit. An in (inch) unit will always equal 96px, regardless of the monitor resolution —but it might not match the inches on your ruler!

The coordinate system used for the x- and y-positions is similar to many computer graphics and layout programs. The x-axis goes from the left of the page to the right in increasing value, while the y-axis goes from the top of the page to the bottom. This means that the default zero point, or origin, of the coordinate system is located at the upper-left corner of the window.

The rectangle is drawn starting 20px from the left and 20px from the top of the window.

If you're used to mathematical coordinates where the y-axis increases from bottom to top, it might help to instead think about laying out lines of text from top to bottom on a page.

The remaining attributes for the rectangle define its presentation, the styles used to draw the shape:

```
<rect x="20" y="20" width="100" height="280"
      fill="blue" stroke="black" stroke-width="3" />
```

The **fill attribute** indicates how the interior of the rectangle should be filled in. The fill value can be given as a color name or a hex color value—using the same values and syntax as CSS—to flood the rectangle with that solid color. The **stroke and stroke-width attributes** define the color and thickness of the lines that draw the rectangle's edges.

The <rect> tag is **self-closed** with a / character, to define a complete rectangle element.

The / (forward slash) at the end of an SVG shape tag is required, even in HTML. You could also use explicit closing tags, like this:

```
<rect attributes ></rect>
```

All SVG elements, even shapes, can have child elements. This means they all must either be self-closing (with />) or have separate closing tags. Both the XML and HTML parsers will make all new SVG elements children of the previous element, until they reach a closing tag. The HTML parser will sometimes automatically close an SVG element, but only if it reaches the closing tag of an earlier element— or the end of the file. The XML parser would report an error in those cases.

With the basic rectangular shape of the stoplight now visible, it is time to draw the lights themselves. Each circular light can be drawn with a **<circle> element**. The following code draws the red light:

```
<circle cx="70" cy="80" r="30"
        fill="red" stroke="black" stroke-width="2" />
```

The first three attributes define the position and size of the shape. The **cx (center-x) and cy (center-y) attributes** define coordinates for the center point of the circle, while the **r attribute** defines its radius. The `fill`, `stroke`, and `stroke-width` presentation attributes have the same meaning as for the rectangle (and for every other shape in SVG).

 If you draw a graphic that looks like our stoplight in a visual editor, then look at the code later, you might not see any `<circle>` elements. A circle, and every other shape in SVG, can also be represented by the more obscure `<path>` element, which we introduce in Chapter 6.

You can probably figure out how to draw the yellow and green lights: use the code for the red light, but change the vertical position by adjusting the `cy` attribute, and set the correct fill color by changing the `fill` presentation attribute. The complete SVG and HTML markup for the stoplight is given in Example 1-2.

Example 1-2. Drawing a primary color stoplight in inline SVG

```
<!DOCTYPE html>
<html lang="en">
<head>
    <meta charset="utf-8" />
    <title>Inline SVG Stoplight</title>
    <style></style>
</head>
<body>
    <svg width="140px" height="320px"> ❶
        <rect x="20" y="20" width="100" height="280"
            fill="blue" stroke="black" stroke-width="3" />
        <circle cx="70" cy="80" r="30"
            fill="red" stroke="black" stroke-width="2" />
        <circle cx="70" cy="160" r="30"
            fill="yellow" stroke="black" stroke-width="2" />
        <circle cx="70" cy="240" r="30"
            fill="#40CC40" stroke="black" stroke-width="2" />
                        ❷
    </svg>
</body>
</html>
```

❶ The `width` and `height` of the SVG have been adjusted to match the drawing.

❷ #40CC40 is a medium green color, defined in hexadecimal RGB notation. It's brighter than the color created by the green keyword (#008800), but not quite as intense as lime (#00FF00). There's actually a limegreen keyword that is a pretty close match, but we wanted to emphasize that you could use hexadecimal notation to customize colors. We'll discuss more color options in Chapter 12.

The shapes are drawn on top of one another, in the order they appear in the code. Thus, the rectangle is drawn first, then each successive circle. If the rectangle had been listed after the circles, its solid blue fill would have completely obscured them.

 If you work with CSS, you know you can change the drawing order of elements using the z-index property. z-index has been added to the SVG specifications, too, but at the time of writing it is not supported in any of the major web browsers.

Inline SVG in HTML files, like this, has many uses on the web. But it is certainly not the only way to use SVG. Sometimes, you want your SVG graphic to be in its own file, which you can embed in any web page—just like you can embed a photograph or video. For those cases and more, you need SVG markup in an SVG file.

Standalone SVG

To create an independent SVG, separate from the HTML, we need an SVG file. Create a new file in your code editor and save it—as unformatted text with UTF-8 encoding—with the *.svg* file extension. In that file, include the following code to define the root SVG element:

```
<svg xmlns="http://www.w3.org/2000/svg" xml:lang="en"
    height="320px" width="140px" >
    <!-- drawing goes here -->
</svg>
```

The **root element** both defines the document as an SVG file and defines the SVG drawing region. All the graphic content will be contained between the starting <svg> tag and the ending </svg> tag.

To confirm that your SVG code is working, copy your `<rect>` and `<circle>` elements from the inline SVG HTML file, and paste them into the SVG file instead of the `<!-- drawing goes here -->` comment. Then save and open up the *.svg* file in your web browser.

The starting tag also contains attributes that modify the SVG element.

The first and most important of the attributes is the declaration of the SVG namespace: `xmlns="http://www.w3.org/2000/svg"`.

An SVG in its own file is always treated as XML. Web browsers will not render (draw) the SVG image without the namespace. The namespace identifier confirms that this is a Scalable Vector Graphics document, as opposed to some custom XML data format that just happens to use the `svg` acronym for its root element.

Many SVG documents have other namespace declarations as well, indicated by an `xmlns:prefix` attribute, where the prefix will be reused elsewhere in the document.

Only one such namespace, `xlink`, is standard in SVG (we'll discuss it in "Repetition Without Redundancy" on page 21). However, you'll often see other `xmlns:prefix` attributes added to SVGs created by software; these define custom namespaces to hold software-specific data.

The root SVG element also has `height` and `width` attributes, here defined in pixel units. Again, including these attributes is important to set a default size for the graphic. We'll discuss all the complexities of SVG width and height in Chapter 8.

You may have noticed that the code has switched from `width` then `height` to `height` then `width`: both are equivalent. The order of attributes does not matter, only their values.

There are a few other differences between HTML files and SVG files. These mostly relate to the fact that standalone SVG files are parsed as XML.

As we've already warned, the XML parser is strict about making sure you close all your tags. It also expects you to quote all your attributes (like `fill="blue"` or `fill='blue'`, but not `fill=blue`). If you forget either of these points, the browser will display an XML error instead of your drawing.

In our examples, we mostly follow the stricter syntax for both SVG-in-HTML and SVG-as-XML. The main difference you'll notice between the two is the `xmlns` attribute.

More Online

There are a few other unique features of XML that you may discover if you look at SVG code created by a software program. This includes **DOCTYPE** and other "prolog" code before the opening **<svg>** in the file.

Read more in "XML Prologs and Document Types":

https://oreillymedia.github.io/Using_SVG/extras/ch01-XML.html

A prolog is not required for SVG if you use a UTF-8 (or UTF-16) character encoding.

The child content of the `<svg>` root element—the code that replaces the `<!-- drawing goes here -->` comment—can be a mix of shape elements, text elements, animation elements, structural elements, style elements, and metadata elements. Unlike in HTML, there is no requirement that you have a `<head>` before a `<body>`. However, it is often useful to put your metadata first, like in HTML.

One metadata element that you should always include is a title, in a **<title> element**. To be recognized as the title of your SVG as a whole, it should be the first child of your `<svg>` element. The following code shows how it is added to the SVG file:

```
<svg xmlns="http://www.w3.org/2000/svg"
     height="320px" width="140px" >
  <title xml:lang="en">Primary Color Stoplight</title>
  <!-- drawing goes here -->
</svg>
```

In graphical SVG editors, you can often set the main title using a "document properties" dialog.

The **xml:lang attribute**, on the `<title>` element, is the XML equivalent to the HTML `lang` attribute. It defines the human language of any text content in the file, so that screen readers and other software can make appropriate adjustments. In this case (and every other case in this book), that language is English, as indicated by the value en. We could specify en-US to clarify that we're using American spelling, if we preferred.

You *don't* need to declare the xml namespace prefix: it is reserved in all XML files.

To make things even simpler, SVG 2 defines a plain lang attribute, without XML prefixes, to replace xml:lang. But keep using the prefixed version for a while, until all software catches up.

The xml:lang attribute can be set on any element, applying to its child content. This behavior is directly equivalent to the lang attribute in HTML. We could have set it on the `<svg>` element, and it would still apply to the title text. Most examples in the book will use this approach. If you have multilingual diagrams, however, you can set the attribute on individual text and metadata elements.

When an SVG `<title>` element is included like this—as the first child of the root `<svg>`—it will be used in the same manner as an HTML `<title>`. The title text is not drawn as part of the graphic, but if you viewed the SVG in a browser, "Primary Color Stoplight" would be displayed in the browser tab bar, as shown in Figure 1-2. Each web browser has a slightly different style, but they all display the document title, whether the document is SVG or HTML. Document titles are also used for browser bookmarks and history listings.

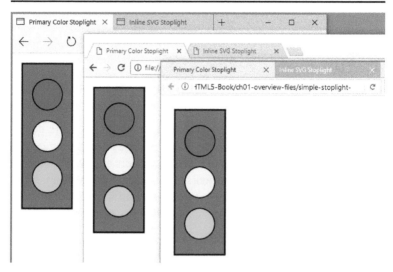

Figure 1-2. SVG and HTML files open in multiple web browser tabs

The SVG `<title>` element is much more flexible than its HTML equivalent; you can add titles to individual parts of a graphic as well, and they'll show up as tooltips. We'll explore titles and other metadata in depth in Chapter 17.

Putting this code together with our shape elements from the previous section, we get the code in Example 1-3. This creates the complete image we saw in Figure 1-1.

Example 1-3. Drawing a primary color stoplight in a standalone SVG file

```
<svg xmlns="http://www.w3.org/2000/svg"
    height="320px" width="140px" >
    <title xml:lang="en">Primary Color Stoplight</title>
    <rect x="20" y="20" width="100" height="280"
        fill="blue" stroke="black" stroke-width="3" />
    <circle cx="70" cy="80" r="30"
        fill="red" stroke="black" stroke-width="2" />
    <circle cx="70" cy="160" r="30"
        fill="yellow" stroke="black" stroke-width="2" />
    <circle cx="70" cy="240" r="30"
```

```
                    fill="#40CC40" stroke="black" stroke-width="2" />
</svg>
```

We've now seen two different ways to draw the same SVG graphic: as inline SVG and as standalone SVG. However, both files used the same drawing elements (shapes) and attributes.

In the next section, we explore other ways of creating the same image with SVG. The graphics will *look* the same, but they will have very different structures in the **document object model (DOM)**: the interconnected software objects that the browser uses to represent the graphic.

Why is that important? If all you care about is the final image, it isn't. However, if you are going to be manipulating the graphic with JavaScript, CSS, or animations, the DOM structure is very important. Furthermore, if you modify the graphic in the future—maybe to change the sizes or styles of the shapes—you will be glad if you used clean and DRY code, where *DRY* stands for Don't Repeat Yourself.

Style and Structure

The drawing code in Examples 1-2 and 1-3 is somewhat redundant: many attributes are the same for all three circles. If you want to remove the black strokes or make the circles slightly larger, you need to edit the file in multiple places.

For a short file like this, that might not seem like much of a problem. But if you had dozens (or hundreds) of similar shapes, instead of just three, editing each one separately would be a headache and an opportunity for error.

You can remove some of the repetition by defining the circles inside a **<g> element**. The <g> or group element is one of the most commonly used elements in SVG. A group provides a logical structure to the shapes in your graphic, but it has the additional advantage that styles applied to a group will be inherited by the shapes within it. The inherited value will be used to draw the shape unless the shape element specifically sets a different value for the same property.

In Example 1-4, the `stroke` and `stroke-width` presentation attributes are specified once for the group containing three circles. The final graphic looks exactly the same as Figure 1-1.

Example 1-4. Grouping elements within an SVG stoplight

```
<svg xmlns="http://www.w3.org/2000/svg" xml:lang="en"
    height="320px" width="140px" >
    <title>Grouped Lights Stoplight</title>
    <rect x="20" y="20" width="100" height="280"
        fill="blue" stroke="black" stroke-width="3" />
    <g stroke="black" stroke-width="2">
        <circle cx="70" cy="80" r="30" fill="red" />
        <circle cx="70" cy="160" r="30" fill="yellow" />
        <circle cx="70" cy="240" r="30" fill="#40CC40" />
    </g>
</svg>
```

Groups have other uses. They can associate a single `<title>` element with a set of shapes that together make up a meaningful part of the graphic. They can be used to apply certain stylistic effects, such as masks (Chapter 15) or filters (Chapter 16) on the combined graphic, instead of the individual shapes. Grouping can also be used to move or even hide a collection of elements as a unit. Many vector graphic drawing programs use layers of graphics that combine to form an image; these are almost always implemented as `<g>` elements in the SVG file.

Why not specify the `cx` and `r` attributes on the group, since they are also the same for every circle? The difference is that these attributes are specific features of circles—describing their fundamental geometry—not shared styles that apply to any shape. Geometric attributes are not inherited; if they aren't specified, they default to zero. And if a circle's radius is zero, it won't be drawn at all.

Using inheritance isn't the only way to reduce the repetition in the `fill` and `stroke` attributes. These attributes, and all other SVG **presentation attributes**, are actually a way of setting **CSS styles** on an element. You can use other CSS notation to set them instead—an inline **style attribute**, or CSS rules in a stylesheet, which can reference **class attributes** on your SVG elements. Example 1-5 uses a mix of both options to set the fill and stroke styles.

Example 1-5. Using CSS styles in the SVG stoplight

```
<svg xmlns="http://www.w3.org/2000/svg" xml:lang="en"
    height="320px" width="140px" >
    <title>CSS-Styled Stoplight</title>
    <style type="text/css">          ❶
        rect, circle {
            stroke: black;
            stroke-width: 3;          ❷
        }
        .light {
            stroke-width: 2;          ❸
        }
    </style>
    <rect x="20" y="20" width="100" height="280"
        style="fill:blue;" />   ❹
    <g>
        <circle class="light" style="fill:red"
            cx="70" cy="80" r="30" />          ❺
        <circle class="light" style="fill:yellow"
            cx="70" cy="160" r="30" />
        <circle class="light" style="fill:#40CC40"
            cx="70" cy="240" r="30" />
    </g>
</svg>
```

❶ The SVG `<style>` element, like its HTML counterpart, defines a stylesheet that applies to the document that contains it. The `type="text/css"` attribute isn't necessary in web browsers (which assume CSS for all stylesheets), but it increases compatibility in other software, like Inkscape and Illustrator.

❷ The first CSS rule applies a 3-unit-wide black stroke to all `<rect>` and `<circle>` elements.

❸ The second CSS rule corrects the `stroke-width` to 2 for elements that have a class of `light`.

❹ The `fill` colors are applied with `style` attributes on the shape elements. `style="fill:blue;"` has the same effect as `fill="blue"`, but it can't be as easily changed by other CSS rules.

❺ In addition to the inline `style` attribute, the `<circle>` elements have the `class="light"` attribute, which allows them to be selected by the `.light {}` CSS rule.

The actual amount of code in Example 1-5 has increased relative to Example 1-4, but again we have each style defined in a single place, so it's easy to update. You could probably imagine more compact ways to style the same elements with inline styles or CSS rules, but one purpose of the example was to demonstrate all the options that can be combined.

Again, the result of this code is exactly the same as Figure 1-1; it has just been rewritten to use CSS format for the styles, instead of presentation attributes. The interaction between CSS and presentation attributes will be discussed in more detail in Chapter 3; for now, think of presentation attributes as default styles to use if CSS styles aren't specified.

The group element is no longer used for styling in Example 1-5, only for structure. However, it could have just as easily been styled with a `style` attribute or a class, so that the styles once again inherited to its children. Just like CSS styles for HTML, many SVG styles —but not all—are by default inherited from a parent element to its children, unless the child element is given a different style.

> You can force inheritance for any CSS property by setting the property's value on the child element to `inherit`. But there's usually a logical reason why certain properties don't inherit.

What about the geometric attributes? As we'll discuss in Chapter 5, SVG 2 allows many geometric attributes to be set with CSS, just like `fill` and `stroke`. However, they still aren't inherited by default.

> Some browsers have started to implement SVG geometry in CSS, but at the time of writing (mid-2017), support is not good enough to rely on it for work on the web. This book therefore always uses attributes for geometry.

Nonetheless, many graphics contain repeated geometric shapes, and those shapes are often much more complicated than simple circles. You cannot (yet) define this shared geometry with a CSS rule, but that doesn't mean you need to copy and paste the same attributes on every element.

Repetition Without Redundancy

SVG has its own approach to avoiding redundant geometry: the **<use>** element. It allows you to reuse graphics that you've already defined once in your file, to draw the same geometry in multiple places.

Example 1-6 uses <use> to reduce the geometric redundancy in the stoplight. The code defines the basic circle once, and then reuses it three times, with different vertical positions and fill colors. To keep the code compact, we've gone back to using presentation attributes, but you could just as easily use CSS here.

Example 1-6. Reusing elements to draw an SVG stoplight

```
<svg xmlns="http://www.w3.org/2000/svg" xml:lang="en"
     xmlns:xlink="http://www.w3.org/1999/xlink"
     height="320px" width="140px" >
    <title>Re-usable Lights Stoplight</title>
    <defs>
        <circle id="light" cx="70" r="30" />
    </defs>
    <rect x="20" y="20" width="100" height="280"
         fill="blue" stroke="black" stroke-width="3" />
    <g stroke="black" stroke-width="2">
        <use xlink:href="#light" y="80" fill="red" />
        <use xlink:href="#light" y="160" fill="yellow" />
        <use xlink:href="#light" y="240" fill="#40CC40" />
    </g>
</svg>
```

Let's break that example down to clearly explain what's going on. The first change is a new attribute on the <svg> itself.

The **xmlns:xlink attribute** defines a second XML namespace, "http://www.w3.org/1999/xlink", which will be identified by the xlink prefix. XLink was a W3C standard (*http://www.w3.org/TR/xlink/*) for defining relationships between XML elements or files. The xlink:href attribute is fundamental to many SVG elements in SVG 1, and other XLink attributes were also adopted to describe hyperlinks. However, XLink isn't really used anywhere else on the web other than SVG, so the namespace and attributes have been deprecated. When browsers fully support SVG 2, you'll be able to use the href attribute without any namespace.

Because a standalone SVG file is XML, you *could* use any prefix you choose to represent the XLink namespace; all that matters is the `"http://www.w3.org/1999/xlink"` namespace URL. However, when you use SVG within HTML files—which don't support XML namespaces—only the standard `xlink:href` attribute name will be recognized.

At the time of writing (early 2017), skipping the namespace altogether (and just using `href`) is supported in Microsoft Edge, Internet Explorer, and recent Firefox and Blink browsers. It isn't supported in WebKit/Safari, or in many older mobile browsers.

The next new feature is the **<defs> element**, which contains definitions of SVG content for later use. Children of a <defs> element are never drawn directly. In Example 1-6, one element is defined in this way: the circle.

```
<defs>
    <circle id="light" cx="70" r="30" />
</defs>
```

The cx and r attributes which were previously repeated for each light are now included only once on this predefined circle. However, the circle has no cy attribute—it will default to zero—and no styles: it will inherit styles whenever it is used.

Most importantly of all, the circle has the **id attribute**, "light". Without an ID, there would be no way to indicate that this is the graphic to be reused later. The SVG id attribute has the same role as id in HTML or xml:id in other XML documents. It should at least match the requirements for the HTML id:

- completely unique within a document
- non-empty (meaning, have at least one character in the value)
- does not contain any whitespace

Ideally, an SVG id should meet the requirements of a valid xml:id:

- start with a letter
- contain only letters, numbers, periods (.), and hyphens (-).

Modern XML software accepts a broad definition of "letter" (any language is OK), but unaccented English letters will have the best support.

The final change to the SVG code in Example 1-6 is that each <circle> in the main graphic has been replaced by a <use> element. Each <use> refers back to the single predefined circle with the **xlink:href attribute**.

```
<use xlink:href="#light" y="80" fill="red" />
```

The element referenced by <use> doesn't have to be inside a <defs>: it could also be a shape that was drawn directly. For example, we could draw one <circle>, then <use> it twice. We use a predefined <circle> (and three <use> elements) because it makes the styling and positioning easier to understand.

The content of xlink:href is always a URI (Universal Resource Identifier). To identify another element in the same document, you use a target fragment: a hash mark (#) followed by the other element's ID value. This is the same format you would use for same-page hyperlinks within an HTML document.

The URI format may make you wonder if it is possible to reuse elements from separate SVG files. The SVG specifications allow it, but there are important browser security and support restrictions, which we'll discuss in Chapter 10.

The <use> elements have other attributes. The **y attribute** tells the browser to shift the reused graphic vertically so that the y-axis from the original graphic now lines up with the specified y-position. A similar x attribute could have been used for a horizontal shift. In both cases, the shifts are in addition to whatever positioning attributes were set on the original element.

Since the circle in the <defs> is defined with its vertical center (cy) as the default zero, the effect of the y attribute is to move the center of the circle to the given value of y. Finally, the fill value specified on each <use> element becomes the inherited fill color for that instance of the circle. Since the predefined circle did not define its own fill color, it is filled with the color inherited from the <use>.

Again, although we've made considerable changes to the document structure, the final graphic still looks the same, as shown in Figure 1-3.

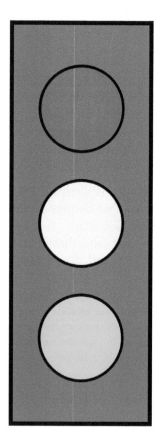

Figure 1-3. Stoplight drawn with reused elements

Exciting, right? Or maybe not. All that fussing with document structure and we've still got the exact same picture. It is important to know that you can draw the same graphic many different ways without changing its appearance. But it is equally important to know how to dress up that graphic with some new styles.

Graduating to Gradients

If your target audience is over the age of 10, you might find the blocks of solid color in Figure 1-3 a tad simplistic. One option for enhancing the graphic would be to draw in extra details with additional shapes. Another option is to work with the shapes we have, but fill them with something other than solid colors.

At first glance, fill would appear to be just another term for color. However, this is a little misleading. You can fill—and also stroke—shapes with gradients or patterns (which we'll discuss more in Chapter 12) instead of solid colors.

The gradients and patterns are defined as separate elements within the SVG code, but they are never drawn directly. Instead, the gradient or pattern is drawn within the area of the shape that references it. In a way, this is similar to a web domain serving up an image for a browser to draw within a specified region of an HTML file. For this reason, the gradient or pattern is known as a **paint server**.

 The server analogy isn't just superficial. In theory, you should be able to put multiple paint servers—gradients or patterns—in an external SVG document, and then reference the file and element with a URI like gradients.svg#metal. However, as mentioned earlier, support for references between files is subject to browser security and support limitations.

Example 1-7 defines four different gradients for the three lights and the stoplight frame. The result is shown in Figure 1-4.

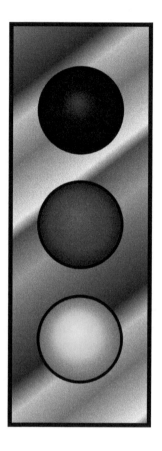

Figure 1-4. Stoplight with gradient fills

Example 1-7. Using gradient fills to enhance a vector graphic stoplight

```
<svg xmlns="http://www.w3.org/2000/svg" xml:lang="en"
    xmlns:xlink="http://www.w3.org/1999/xlink"
    height="320px" width="140px" >
  <title>Gradient-Filled Stoplight</title>
  <defs>
    <circle id="light" cx="70" r="30" />
    <radialGradient id="red-light-off" fx="0.45" fy="0.4">
      <stop stop-color="maroon" offset="0"/>
      <stop stop-color="#220000" offset="0.7"/>
      <stop stop-color="black" offset="1.0"/>
```

```
      </radialGradient>
      <radialGradient id="yellow-light-off" fx="0.45" fy="0.4">
          <stop stop-color="#A06000" offset="0"/>
          <stop stop-color="#804000" offset="0.7"/>
          <stop stop-color="#502000" offset="1"/>
      </radialGradient>
      <radialGradient id="green-light-on" fx="0.45" fy="0.4">
          <stop stop-color="#88FF00" offset="0.1"/>
          <stop stop-color="forestGreen" offset="0.7"/>
          <stop stop-color="darkGreen" offset="1.0"/>
      </radialGradient>
      <linearGradient id="metal" spreadMethod="repeat"
                      gradientTransform="scale(0.7) rotate(75)">
          <stop stop-color="#808080" offset="0"/>
          <stop stop-color="#404040" offset="0.25"/>
          <stop stop-color="#C0C0C0" offset="0.35"/>
          <stop stop-color="#808080" offset="0.5"/>
          <stop stop-color="#E0E0E0" offset="0.7"/>
          <stop stop-color="#606060" offset="0.75"/>
          <stop stop-color="#A0A0A0" offset="0.9"/>
          <stop stop-color="#808080" offset="1"/>
      </linearGradient>
  </defs>
  <rect x="20" y="20" width="100" height="280"
        fill="url(#metal)" stroke="black" stroke-width="3" />
  <g stroke="black" stroke-width="2">
      <use xlink:href="#light" y="80"
           fill="url(#red-light-off)" />
      <use xlink:href="#light" y="160"
           fill="url(#yellow-light-off)" />
      <use xlink:href="#light" y="240"
           fill="url(#green-light-on)" />
  </g>
</svg>
```

The gradients, defined within the <defs> section of the file, come in
two types: <radialGradient> for the circular lights and
<linearGradient> for the frame. Each gradient element has an
easy-to-remember id attribute that will be used to reference it.

The radial gradients also have fx and fy attributes, which create the
off-center effect, while the linear gradient contains spreadMethod
and gradientTransform attributes to control the angle, scale, and
repetition of the gradient. Each gradient contains <stop> elements
that define the color transition. If you absolutely must know more
now, you can jump ahead to Chapter 12 for more details.

Still here? OK, then look at the rest of Example 1-7: the <rect>, <g>, and <use> elements.

It's mostly the same as Example 1-6, except for the fill values. Instead of color names or RGB hash values, each fill attribute is of the form url(#gradient-id).

Why the extra url() notation? Partly, it's because presentation attributes need to be compatible with CSS, and CSS uses url(*reference*). More importantly, it's because fill and stroke and other presentation attributes can be specified as a URL *or* as other data types, and you need to be able to clearly distinguish between them. Without url(), how would you know if #fabdad referred to a paint server element or to a light pink color?

To add a bit of realism, the gradients were defined so that the green light appeared to be lit (bright green), while the red and yellow lights were dim (dark maroon and mustard brown). But a *real* stoplight wouldn't stay green all the time.

It's fairly straightforward to edit the code to switch the stoplight to red: copy the red light gradient, change its id to red-light-on, then change the stop-color values to something brighter. Copy the green light gradient, change its id to green-light-off, then change the colors to something darker. Finally, change the fill values to reference the new gradients. There: you have a red stoplight. But you still don't have a *working* stoplight. For that, you need animation.

Activating Animation

Animation was a core part of the original SVG specifications. Not only was there the option of animating elements with JavaScript, but there was also a way of declaring animations as their own elements.

These animation elements (such as <animate> and <set>) were adapted from another XML language, SMIL, the Synchronized Multimedia Integration Language.

However, Microsoft web browsers don't support the SVG/SMIL animation elements, which means that they aren't used a lot on the web —which means that *other* browser teams don't want to invest a lot of development time on improving their implementations.

Meanwhile, CSS introduced its own animation syntax. CSS animation is not yet a full replacement for the SVG/SMIL animation elements—but for the animations it can handle, it currently has the better browser support.

We'll talk more about your animation options in Chapter 19, or you can pick up Sarah Drasner's *SVG Animations* book for more.[2]

For our animated stoplight, there are a few different ways to approach the problem with CSS. The straightforward approach is to directly animate the fill property. That works fine for solid-color fills. But browsers are currently buggy about animation when the fill value is a url() reference to a paint server. As an alternative, we can create *two* versions of each light, one with the "off" gradient and one with the "on" gradient, layered on top of each other. Then we can animate the visibility of the top layer.

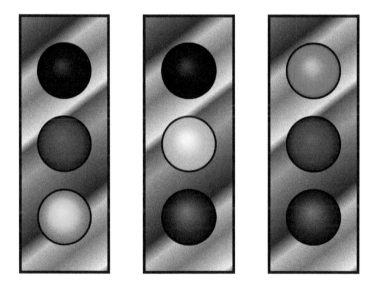

Figure 1-5. Three stages of an animated stoplight with gradient fills

2 Sarah Drasner, *SVG Animations* (Sebastopol, CA: O'Reilly, 2017).

Example 1-8 provides the code for implementing this approach: first the markup for the layered structure, then the CSS code that brings it to life. The CSS code includes **@keyframes rules** for the animation, and also assigns styles by class. Figure 1-5 shows the three states of the stoplight—but to get the full effect, run the code in a web browser!

Example 1-8. Animating the stoplight using CSS keyframes

SVG MARKUP:

```
<svg xmlns="http://www.w3.org/2000/svg" xml:lang="en"
     xmlns:xlink="http://www.w3.org/1999/xlink"
     height="320px" width="140px" >
  <title>Animated Stoplight, using CSS Keyframes</title>
  <defs>
    <circle id="light" cx="70" r="30" />
    <radialGradient id="red-light-on" fx="0.45" fy="0.4">
     <stop stop-color="orange" offset="0.1"/>
     <stop stop-color="red" offset="0.8"/>
     <stop stop-color="brown" offset="1.0"/>
    </radialGradient>
    <radialGradient id="red-light-off" fx="0.45" fy="0.4"> ❶
      <stop stop-color="maroon" offset="0"/>
      <stop stop-color="#220000" offset="0.7"/>
      <stop stop-color="black" offset="1.0"/>
    </radialGradient>
    <!-- More gradients -->                                ❷
  </defs>
  <style>
    /* CSS styles (see below) */    .                      ❸
  </style>
  <rect x="20" y="20" width="100" height="280"
        fill="url(#metal)" stroke="black" stroke-width="3" />
  <g stroke="black" stroke-width="2">
    <g class="red light">                                 ❹
      <use xlink:href="#light" y="80" fill="url(#red-light-off)" />
      <use class="lit"
          xlink:href="#light" y="80" fill="url(#red-light-on)" />
    </g>                                                   ❺
    <g class="yellow light">
      <use xlink:href="#light" y="160"
          fill="url(#yellow-light-off)" />
      <use class="lit" xlink:href="#light" y="160"
          fill="url(#yellow-light-on)" visibility="hidden" /> ❻
    </g>
    <g class="green light">
      <use xlink:href="#light" y="240"
          fill="url(#green-light-off)" />
```

```
<use class="lit" xlink:href="#light" y="240"
     fill="url(#green-light-on)" visibility="hidden" />
  </g>
 </g>
</svg>
```

❶ New radial gradients are added to represent the lit and off states of each light.

❷ But to keep this example short, the repetitive code isn't printed here; all the gradients follow the same structure, just with different colors and different id values.

❸ The `<style>` element can be included anywhere, but it's usually best to keep it before or after the `<defs>`, near the top of the file.

❹ The changed markup replaces each light in the stoplight with a group (`<g>`) containing two different `<use>` versions of the circle. The first one (bottom layer) has the "off" gradient. Each group is distinguished by a class describing which light it is.

❺ The second `<use>` in each group (top layer) has the "on" gradient. It also has the class `lit`, which we'll use to access it from the CSS.

❻ The "lit" layers for the green and yellow lights are hidden by default, using the presentation attribute for the `visibility` property. We use `visibility` (and not `display="none"`) because `display` cannot be animated with CSS. We use presentation attributes (and not inline styles), so that our CSS rules will override them:[3] these are just the default values that apply if CSS animations are not supported.

CSS STYLES:

```
@keyframes cycle {
    33.3% { visibility: visible; }
    100% { visibility: hidden; }      ❶
}
.lit {
    animation: cycle 9s step-start infinite; ❷
```

---

3 CSS animations will actually override inline style attributes—even `!important` styles. But in general, use presentation attributes as fallbacks for CSS overrides.

```
}
.red    .lit { animation-delay: -3s; }
.yellow .lit { animation-delay: -6s; }          ❸
.green  .lit { animation-delay:  0s; }
```

❶ The animation states are defined with an @keyframes block, which names this animation cycle. There are two states in the animation: hidden and visible. The time selectors say that after one-third (33.3%) of the animation cycle, we want the light to be visible, and at the end of the cycle we want it to be hidden.

❷ The animation is assigned to all the layers with class lit using the shorthand animation property. Translated to English, the value means: "use the cycle animation keyframes; advance through all the keyframes in a 9-second duration; for each frame, jump immediately to the new value at the start of each frame's time period; repeat the entire animation infinitely." The step-start value is important for the way we've defined the keyframes: the animation will *start* in the visible state, and switch to the hidden state as soon as the 33.3% time point is past.

❸ All the lights have the same animation keyframes, but we don't want them all to turn on and off at the same time. The animation-delay property staggers the animation cycles for each light. Negative values mean that the animation starts running from a point partway through, when the file loads. The delay offsets are multiples of one-third of the 9-second total cycle time, matching the proportions used in the keyframes.

The animation effect should be visible in most desktop and mobile browsers released since late 2015. Be aware that the animation won't run in many older browsers still in use, or in limited-function mobile browsers such as Opera Mini.

 Although this animation (of visibility) works OK in Internet Explorer (10 and 11), animations of many SVG-specific style properties are not supported.

You *could* increase support in Android and iOS browsers by adding prefixed versions of the animation properties (like -webkit-animation-delay) and by duplicating the keyframes rule and giving it a prefix, too (@-webkit-keyframes). You'll need to decide for yourself whether the number of visitors to your website who use those browsers is worth the duplicated code. If you do decide to add prefixed properties, a CSS processor such as Autoprefixer (*https://github.com/postcss/autoprefixer*) can help you manage them.

For a purely decorative effect, the lack of perfect browser support may be acceptable. You still get a stoplight in the other browsers; it's just stuck on the red light. In other cases, however, the animation is essential to your content, and you will need to use JavaScript to create the animated effect. We'll explore adding JavaScript to the stoplight example in Chapter 2.

Chapter 2 will also have more examples of SVG integrated with HTML, using HTML for text and SVG for graphics. However, text doesn't *have* to be separate from the SVG code: SVG has a <text> element for drawing text as part of your graphic itself.

Talking with Text

Although it may not be immediately obvious, text has a significant role in the realm of graphics, and a surprisingly large amount of the SVG specification is devoted to the placement of and display of text.

When the information in your graphic is essential, you often need to spell it out in words as well as images. Metadata such as the <title> element can help, especially for screen readers, but sometimes you need words on the screen where everyone can see them.

Drawing text in an SVG is done with the creatively named **<text> element**. We'll talk more about text in Chapter 7, but the basics are as follows:

- The words (or other characters) to be drawn are the *child content* of the element, enclosed between starting and ending <text> and </text> tags.

- The text is positioned (by default) in a single line around an *anchor* point; the anchor is set with x and y attributes.

- The text is painted using the fill and stroke properties, the same as for shapes, and not with the CSS color property.

Example 1-9 shows the added or changed code, relative to Example 1-8. Figure 1-6 shows the three states of the animated result.

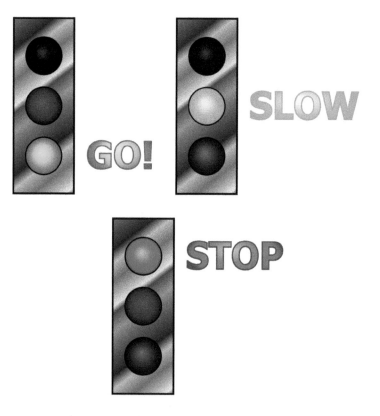

Figure 1-6. Three stages of a labeled, animated stoplight

Example 1-9. Adding text labels to the animated stoplight

CHANGES TO THE ROOT SVG ELEMENT:

```
<svg xmlns="http://www.w3.org/2000/svg" xml:lang="en"
    xmlns:xlink="http://www.w3.org/1999/xlink"
    height="320px" width="400px" > ❶
```

❶ To make room for the labels, the width of the graphic has been increased.

ADDITION TO THE CSS:

```
text {
    font: bold 60px sans-serif; ❶
}
```

❶ A new CSS rule (added to the `<style>` block) assigns font styles to all the `<text>` elements, using the same shorthand `font` property used in CSS text styling for HTML.

CHANGED GRAPHICAL SVG MARKUP:

```
<g stroke="black" stroke-width="2">
  <g class="red light">
    <use xlink:href="#light" y="80" fill="url(#red-light-off)" />
    <g class="lit" fill="url(#red-light-on)">                          ❶
      <use xlink:href="#light" y="80" />
      <text x="140" y="100" stroke="darkRed">STOP</text>               ❷
    </g>
  </g>
  <g class="yellow light">
    <use xlink:href="#light" y="160"
        fill="url(#yellow-light-off)" />
    <g class="lit" fill="url(#yellow-light-on)"
      visibility="hidden" >
      <use xlink:href="#light" y="160" />
      <text x="140" y="180" stroke="darkOrange">SLOW</text>            ❸
    </g>
  </g>
  <g class="green light">
    <use xlink:href="#light" y="240" fill="url(#green-light-off)"/>
    <g class="lit" fill="url(#green-light-on)"
      visibility="hidden" >
      <use xlink:href="#light" y="240" />
      <text x="140" y="260" stroke="darkGreen">GO!</text>
    </g>
  </g>
</g>
```

❶ Each "lit" version of the light has now been grouped together with a matching text label. The class has been moved to the <g> element, so that the entire group will be hidden or revealed as the animation changes the lights. The fill presentation attribute has also been moved to the group: both the shape and the text will inherit the value.

❷ The <text> elements each have an x value that positions them to the right of the stoplight, and a y value that positions the base of the text near the bottom of the circle. The text elements also have a solid-colored stroke assigned directly with a presentation attribute.

❸ The remaining lights follow the same structure, except that the lit layer, including the label, is hidden by default.

The stoplight example now contains shapes, paint servers, text, animation: most of the key features used in SVG clip art, icons, or data visualizations. Of course there's much more to learn—this is only Chapter 1! But by now you should understand enough to start making tweaks and adjustments to a clip art SVG file—or one you created with a drawing program—by editing the code directly.

Equally important, you should be starting to understand how SVG works as a structured graphical document, not simply as a picture. The drawing is divided into meaningful parts, and these parts can be styled or modified independently.

More Online

To understand how SVG balances its dual nature as a document and as an image, it helps to step back and think about how vector graphics work overall. The stoplights we've been drawing so far are all vector graphics, but what does that mean? How do these SVG graphics differ from the bitmap (or *raster*) images that you can create in a basic Paint application?

Read more in "Understanding Vector Graphics":

https://oreillymedia.github.io/Using_SVG/extras/ch01-vectors.html

The SVG Advantage

The basic concept for SVG is simple: use the descriptive power of XML to create overlapping lines, shapes, masks, filters, and text that —when combined—create illustrations. In computer graphics terms, these shapes are either predefined (rectangles, circles, ovals, and so forth), or are constructed by sequences of vector instructions.

The SVG specification, originally finalized in 2002, was complex and extensive. The specifications include more than just the XML markup. They define many new CSS style properties for SVG content (some of which have since been adopted for CSS styling of other content) and a complete set of custom DOM interfaces for manipulating SVG elements.

It has taken time for SVG to reach its potential. Some would argue it is not there yet. Unlike HTML, SVG did not develop in concert with extensive real-world experience from software implementations and web designers.

For the first few years, there were only two implementations of the complete standard: the Adobe SVG viewer, a plug-in for Internet Explorer, and the Apache Batik Squiggle viewer, an open source Java-based tool. Limited implementations of SVG were available in other tools, however, including a version integrated into Mozilla Firefox in 2003.

The Adobe SVG viewer was discontinued after Adobe merged with Macromedia, makers of Flash. Batik remains of limited use, primarily as a component of other Java-based tools. However, by 2009, all major browsers either had or were planning native (no plug-in required) SVG implementations. The browser-based SVG tools have only recently reached the performance and support levels of the old Adobe plug-in.

This delay resulted in a shift in focus: from extending SVG as a standalone dynamic graphics tool to integrating SVG within the rest of the web platform.

Bandwidth availability has improved dramatically since SVG was first proposed. On most broadband networks, the time to download a large raster diagram is comparable to the time for a vector graphics program to calculate how to render a complex image. Nonetheless, many people are accessing the web on mobile networks where large downloads are both slow and costly, so compact file sizes still matter.

The benefits of SVG go well beyond file size:

Familiar syntax
SVG is markup and styles, the same as HTML-based web content. It can be generated by external data feeds and processes on the fly, making it a natural part of web server pipelines. It can also be integrated within other XML document types, which includes the file formats used by major word processing and publishing systems.

Because SVG is XML and CSS, with an established grammar and schema, code-editing tools can check for syntax errors or help fill in values quickly, while also offereing visualization tools to display the SVG even as you type.

Dynamic and interactive
The vector elements in SVG describe not only what the graphics *look like* but also what they *are*. If the elements are modified, their appearance can be recalculated. SVG on the web can be interactive and dynamic, using scripts to manipulate the document in response to user interaction or based on data retrieved from separate files or web services.

Even without JavaScript, SVG can be dynamic: animation elements and CSS selectors can show, hide, or alter content as the user interacts with the graphic. And of course, SVG can be hyperlinked to other documents on the Internet.

Accessible and extendable
SVG supports text-based metadata, not just about the image as a whole, but about individual components within the picture. Maps can internally identify roads, buildings, geographic boundaries, and more; diagrams can provide relevant explanatory and even interactive information; metadata systems can read an SVG document and derive from it a very rich and sophisticated view of the meaning behind the image.

Resolution-independent
SVG, as a vector format, automatically adapts to the capabilities of the display hardware. There is no need to create new files for the latest higher-resolution screens. When working with SVG,

you can apply and undo infinite transformations or filter effects without any irreversible degradation of image quality.

Nonetheless, the biggest advantage for SVG on the web remains the way in which it is integrated with other web platform languages.

Compare it with Portable Document Format (PDF): PDF files can contain PostScript vector graphics code, and are widely available on the internet. But PDF documents exist separate and apart from the websites that link to or embed them.

SVG images, in contrast, are part of the web, and can interact with other web technologies such as HTML, XML, CSS, and JavaScript. Chapter 2 explores the bigger picture of SVG in the context of these other web languages.

Summary: An Overview of SVG

This chapter has breezed through many different features of SVG, and skipped over many more. The intent has been to give you the lay of the land, so you can keep your bearings as we start exploring in detail.

One of the key ideas, beyond the general structure of SVG and its element or attribute names, is that SVG can (and in many cases should) be approached programmatically. There are often multiple ways to create the same picture, but each will differ in how it can be used. Creating effective interactive applications with SVG requires seeing the language as being, like HTML, a complex toolset of inter-connected parts.

While you can use tools such as Adobe Illustrator or Inkscape to draw graphical pieces, the language comes into its own when you treat it as a powerful way to build interfaces—widgets, maps, charts, game controls, and more. Although SVG can replace icons or art that you currently represent as static images (or animated GIFs), the true advantages of SVG are in the ways it is different from any other image type—in particular, in the ways it interacts with other web design languages.

More Online

We hope you find the chapter text and examples easy to read and learn. But we know that you're not going to memorize every last detail. It's always nice to have a reference guide to look up the exact spelling or options for a given feature. MDN (*https://devel oper.mozilla.org/en-US/docs/Web/SVG*) is a fairly good reference, with links to the source specifications. But we've put together our own.

The "SVG Elements and Attributes" guide contains lists of all the SVG elements and attributes we introduce in the book (and a few we haven't had room for):

> *https://oreillymedia.github.io/Using_SVG/guide/markup.html*

You can start with the section "Common Attributes for All SVG Elements", which summarizes the attributes that can be used on any SVG-namespaced element.

CHAPTER 2

The Big Picture

SVG and the Web

In the last few years, a quiet revolution has been taking place in web browsers and operating systems. Solid implementations of SVG have become standard in both desktop and mobile browsers.

As this has happened, web developers and designers have become more confident in using SVG to display content that moves beyond HTML layout. They have also been combining SVG with the power of the newer, efficient, and standardized JavaScript engines to build sophisticated information graphics and interactive games. Anyone working with data visualization on the web is now gaining familiarity with SVG as a tool.

The history of SVG has not been straightforward.

As with HTML, CSS, and the other standards that make up the web, the development of SVG has been a process of back-and-forth compromises between the authors of specifications, the builders of web browsers that implement them, and the designers of web pages that use them. Unlike those other languages, however, the SVG specification did not develop slowly and incrementally—it was created fully formed, as an incredibly complex graphics language.

If you work with HTML and CSS web design, you will find many aspects of SVG familiar—and a few quite different. The SVG standard was built upon other web standards, most notably XML and CSS, and has a complex DOM that can be manipulated with JavaScript. In that way, it is very similar to HTML. But because the primary focus of SVG is graphics, not text, it intersects and connects the parts of the web platform that you usually try to keep separate: content, formatting, and functionality.

This chapter starts with a refresher about the main web languages and their separate roles. It then looks at how SVG interacts with these languages. We adapt the stoplight example from Chapter 1 to show how you can build on a simple SVG to create complete web pages.

SVG and the Web Platform

If you are only interested in SVG as an image format—as a tool to create static, unchanging pictures—you don't need to worry too much about the other web standards. To take full advantage of SVG as a graphical web application, however, you will need to leverage the entire web platform to build and extend your graphics.

More Online

What is the web platform? It is the interconnected set of coding languages that web browsers understand: HTML and XML, HTTP, CSS, and JavaScript. And SVG. Together, these are the foundation on which you can build complex websites.

To make the most of SVG on the web, you'll need to understand what each language adds to the web in general, and to SVG in particular. Read more about the division of responsibilities between web languages in "The Web Platform":

https://oreillymedia.github.io/Using_SVG/extras/ch02-web-platform.html

Where does SVG fit on the web platform? SVG is an XML language, describing a structured document. However, because SVG is a *graphics* format, the structure of the document cannot be separated from its visual presentation. SVG elements represent geometric shapes, text, and embedded images that will be displayed onscreen according to a clearly defined geometric layout. Other markup defines complex artistic effects to be applied to the graphical elements.

SVG exists because not all documents can be displayed with HTML and CSS. Sometimes content and layout are inseparable. In charts and diagrams, the position of text conveys its meaning as much as the words it contains. Other meaning is conveyed by symbols, colors, and shapes—without any words at all. Any complete representation of the content of these documents includes the layout and graphical features.

The same could be said about any image, and images have been part of web pages since the early days of HTML. The W3C even standardized the PNG (Portable Network Graphics) image format, which encodes icons and diagrams in compact files and can be used royalty-free by any software or developer.

But SVG is different. All other image formats on the web are displayed as single, complete entities. SVG, as an XML document, has structured content with a corresponding DOM (document object model). Stylesheets and scripts can access and modify the components of the graphic. Search engines and assistive technologies can read text labels and metadata.

SVG on the web can be used as independent files—as complete web pages or web apps—with hyperlinks and JavaScript-based interaction to connect it to the rest of the web. However, SVG was not designed to display large blocks of text. Nor does it include form-input elements or other specialized features of HTML.

The most effective use of SVG is not as a *replacement* for HTML, but as a complement to it. SVG web applications are nearly always presented as part of larger HTML web pages, either as embedded objects or—with increasing frequency—directly included inline within the HTML markup.

The Changing Web

As SVG has been integrated into web pages, the web pages themselves have changed. The HTML5 specification and the many CSS level 3 (and beyond!) modules have significantly changed the relationship between SVG and the rest of the web platform. The dramatically improved performance of JavaScript since 2009 and the rise of JavaScript-based SVG libraries, such as Snap.svg and D3.js, are smoothing away many of the rough edges between implementations.

This book uses the terms HTML5 and CSS3 fairly generically. One of the main references for HTML, the WHATWG Living Standard (*https:// html.spec.whatwg.org/multipage/*), doesn't use any version numbers; the competing spec at W3C is progressing through version numbers 5.1 to 5.2. These incremental changes can all be thought of as HTML5+.

On the CSS side, the level 3 and 4 modules of existing features are being developed at the same time as level 1 and 2 modules for new features. All of these (essentially, anything beyond the CSS 2.1 specification) can be thought of as CSS3+.

Nonetheless, when working with SVG in the browser, you must always be aware that implementations of the SVG standards are imperfect, incomplete, and frequently changing. This becomes all the more important when you are taking advantage of the features of HTML5 and CSS3 that directly integrate SVG. Cross-browser compatibility is an issue not only as it relates to support of the SVG standard, but also as it relates to support for new features in HTML, CSS, DOM, and JavaScript.

At the time of writing, the best supported version of SVG is 1.1; this specification was created in 2005, without any major new features being added to the original SVG standard. It was republished in 2011 as a second edition, with corrections and a new format, but the same features.

A proposed SVG 2 standard was published in September 2016. It adds many commonly requested features, clarifies numerous details, and improves coordination with HTML and CSS. Other more advanced SVG features are being proposed through additional modules.

There have been other SVG efforts, but these have not had a significant impact on the web. The draft SVG 1.2 standard was ambitious, adding features that would put it in line to replace Microsoft PowerPoint, as well as advanced vector manipulation of graphics. It was abandoned as unworkable when it became clear that the future of SVG would be in the browsers, not specialized software.

A simplified standard, SVG Tiny, was developed for mobile devices. The SVG Tiny 1.2 standard *was* finalized, with some new features from the main SVG 1.2 proposal; however, it fell out of favor as mobile browsers shifted toward displaying standard web pages.

At the time of writing, there is some risk that SVG 2 may be added to this list. Some features have initial browser implementations, but on other features, none of the implementation teams are ready to make the first move.

The other web platform languages have also been revised, in parallel to the SVG work. Figure 2-1 sketches out a rough timeline of the past quarter-century of web standards. At the time SVG 1.1 was finalized, the established standards in other areas of the web included CSS level 2, DOM level 2, and ECMAScript (ES) level 3.

 Many SVG-centric tools, such as Apache Batik and libRSVG, have not significantly updated their CSS implementations since then, nor (in the case of Batik) their DOM and JavaScript implementations.

In contrast, as of SVG 2's publication, the latest web browsers all support DOM level 3 (and much of DOM 4) and ES 5.1 (and some ES 6), as well as many CSS3+ features. And more features are added with every browser update.

This book focuses on SVG in the web browser, and it will often take advantage of the new features from other web specifications. However, many older web browsers and other software are still in use. We will identify areas where you're likely to stumble across backward-compatibility issues, and suggest workaround or fallback options.

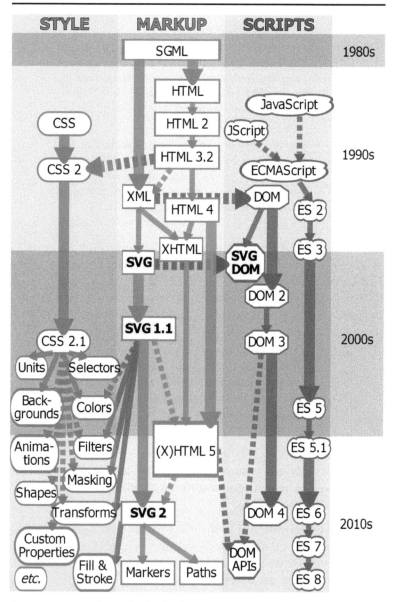

STYLE   MARKUP   SCRIPTS

Figure 2-1. Timeline of web platform standards. Solid arrows indicate direct extensions of existing standards; dashed arrows represent more indirect inspiration. Specifications that were abandoned, such as SVG 1.2 or ECMAScript (ES) 4, are not included.

There is another area of browser support to keep in mind: support for SVG at all.

Every major web browser released since 2012 supports both SVG images and inline SVG. But at the time of writing (mid-2017), some older browsers are still in use. The ones you are most likely to need to worry about:

- Internet Explorer versions 8 and earlier
- the stock browser for Android versions 2.3 and earlier

If any of these make up an important component of your website's audience (based on your user-analytics data), you'll need to consider fallback options.

This book is also very aware of the fact that SVG is still developing. New CSS modules are extending SVG functionality, and SVG 2 introduces a variety of changes. Throughout the book we will highlight these proposed features, which—while not quite ready for production work—are useful to keep in mind as you learn the language. A graphic that is difficult to create now may be much easier with a new tool. The possibilities will be highlighted with "Future Focus" sidebars like the following:

Future Focus
A Crystal Ball

In these boxes, we'll try to predict the future of SVG.

Sometimes the predictions will be clear, because there is wide agreement about what features should be adopted, and it's just a matter of waiting for wider browser support. Other times, the image in our crystal ball will be murky and out of focus, because different proposals are still being debated. But in either case, you should be aware that some of the recommendations and best practices discussed in this book may change as SVG matures and adapts to its role on the web.

While there is still some inconsistency between the various SVG implementations, most browsers now have sufficient support for static scalable vector graphics and JavaScript-based dynamic content that it is possible to build complete graphical web applications with SVG.

JavaScript in SVG

If you've used JavaScript to create a dynamic HTML page, you can use it to create dynamic SVG. SVG elements inherit all the core DOM methods to get and set attributes and styles. The JavaScript itself is parsed and run by the same JS interpreter and just-in-time compiler that runs scripts in your HTML pages.

 That means that you can use modern JavaScript syntax (ES6 and beyond) in modern browsers. However, the examples in this book all use ES5 syntax that should run without error on any browser that supports SVG.

Of course, there are a few complications: SVG is a namespaced XML language, so you need to use namespace-sensitive DOM methods when you're creating elements or setting xlink attributes. This is true even when creating inline SVG elements in an HTML document. Element and attribute names are also always case-sensitive when created via the DOM.

Programmers switching from HTML to SVG often create code like the following, and wonder why nothing is displaying on the screen:

```
var svg = document.createElement("svg");
var use = document.createElement("use");
use.setAttribute("xlink:href", "#icon");
svg.appendChild(use);
document.body.appendChild(svg);
```

This code will create elements that look correct if you inspect them in your browser's developer tools. If you copy and paste the generated markup to a new file, it will even work correctly if you open that file. But that's because your friendly neighborhood HTML parser will read the markup in that file and insert the correct namespaces. The DOM methods don't do that for you.

Creating elements named "svg" and "use" in an HTML document, without setting a namespace, just creates HTMLUnknownElement objects with those names. Doing the same in an SVG document creates generic XML Element objects.

If you're ever unsure of what type of JavaScript object you're working with, you can print its constructor.name property to the console. The constructor property of an object is the function that defined it. And a function's name property is a simple string containing its, well, name.

In the same way, setting an attribute with the name xlink:href creates an attribute with that *literal* name, including the : character.

The following code creates similar-looking elements, but this time with the correct namespaces. It will add an inline SVG icon to the end of the page (assuming you already have another SVG element with id="icon" somewhere in the page):

```
var ns = {svg:   "http://www.w3.org/2000/svg",
          xlink: "http://www.w3.org/1999/xlink"};
var svg = document.createElementNS(ns.svg, "svg");
var use = document.createElementNS(ns.svg, "use");
use.setAttributeNS(ns.xlink, "href", "#icon");
svg.appendChild(use);
document.body.appendChild(svg);
```

It's definitely not ideal. Once again, you have to hardcode XML namespace URLs in your code.

Alternatively, you can use the HTML parser from JavaScript, by setting the **innerHTML property** of an HTML element:

```
var div = document.createElement("div");
div.innerHTML = '<svg><use xlink:href="#icon" /></svg>'
document.body.appendChild(div.firstChild);
```

Much better! But be warned: this only works in an HTML document, which will correctly create an HTMLElement object for the <div>.

The latest versions of web browsers even support innerHTML on SVG elements, but that is a recent addition to the core DOM specs. It isn't supported in older browsers, because innerHTML was previously only defined for HTML elements.

In browsers that support it, setting innerHTML on an SVG element will use either the HTML or XML parser, depending on what type of document the code is running in.

As we discuss in Chapter 4, JavaScript libraries that are designed to work with SVG can take care of this namespace hassle—but JavaScript libraries designed only for HTML can create the same problems as the initial broken code snippet.

Also be aware that some methods you may be familiar with from HTML are *not* part of the core DOM specifications. Some of these, such as the focus() method to control keyboard focus, have been added to SVG elements in SVG 2—but they aren't universally implemented yet.

Even worse, some features, such as className, look similar between HTML and SVG, but are structured differently. Many existing API patterns were ignored by the original SVG DOM definitions. List data types used numberOfItems instead of length, and didn't support JavaScript object [index] access; SVG 2 has added the more familiar patterns, but again—support isn't universal yet.

 Because of these changes, scripts might work well in your browser but stumble in others. At the time of writing, Chrome and Firefox support most of the SVG 2 DOM changes, but Safari/WebKit and Microsoft Edge are a little further behind. And of course, older versions of all browsers may have problems.

As a sort of consolation prize for the missing HTML DOM methods and mismatched patterns, the SVG specifications introduced a variety of SVG-specific methods and properties to make graphical calculations easier. Unfortunately, many of these features were not universally implemented, and some have become obsolete as SVG switches to an animation model more compatible with CSS. Nonetheless, there are still a few useful features that can be relied on in most web browsers.

You can do a lot with these and the core DOM methods that have good support. We'll have numerous simple examples of scripted SVG throughout the book.

More Online

The "Select SVG DOM Methods and Objects" guide has a summary reference of the DOM methods and objects we use in the examples:

https://oreillymedia.github.io/Using_SVG/guide/DOM.html

Which brings up the question: how do you get your JavaScript into your SVG?

If you're working with inline SVG, any script running in your HTML file has access to your inline SVG elements. So you can include an HTML `<script>` element in the page `<head>` or `<body>`, as you usually would.

SVG also has its own **`<script>` element**. To add JavaScript to a standalone SVG file, you can include a `<script>` element anywhere between the opening and closing `<svg>` tags. The SVG `<script>` element is very similar to its HTML counterpart, but they aren't identical.

If you include a `<script>` element as a child of an `<svg>` element that is inline in HTML, the parser will create an `SVGScriptElement`, not an `HTMLScriptElement`.

To include an external JavaScript file with an SVG `<script>` element, use an `xlink:href` attribute (*not* `src` like in HTML) to give the file location.

If you instead include the JavaScript code between the `<script>` tags, remember to wrap it in an XML character data (`CDATA`) block, so that less-than and greater-than operators or ampersands (`<`, `>`, and `&`) do not cause XML validation errors. Combining both types of scripts would look like Example 2-1.

Example 2-1. Adding scripts to a standalone SVG file

```
<svg xmlns="http://www.w3.org/2000/svg" xml:lang="en"
     xmlns:xlink="http://www.w3.org/1999/xlink" >  ❶
  <title>My Standalone D3 Data Visualization</title>
```

```
<script xlink:href="/assets/d3.min.js" />          ❷
<script><![CDATA[  ❸
  if (1 < 0) {
    console.log("Uh oh, math is broken.",
                "But my XML markup isn't.");
  }
  /* more & more JS code */
]]></script>
</svg>
```

❶ Since we're using an xlink:href attribute later, we included the extra namespace declaration on the root <svg> element.

❷ Because this is XML, a <script> tag can be self-closing (with />) if it doesn't have any text content.

❸ The <![CDATA[...]]> structure can be used anywhere in an XML file to indicate that the enclosed text should be treated as plain text, not markup. It's usually required for JavaScript, and can also be used for CSS code that might have special characters in comments.

The CDATA markup *should* also be fine if you copy the SVG code into an HTML file, but *only* if it is inside an inline <svg>, not in a (non-XML) HTML script.

 To be extra sure that your scripts don't break, regardless of XML or HTML parser, you can use JavaScript line comments to hide the CDATA markup:

```
<script>//<![CDATA[
  /* This script will work wherever. */
//]]></script>
```

As in HTML, scripts in an SVG file are executed in the order they appear in the markup. When a script references an external file, the browser waits until the file has downloaded and run before continuing. The SVG <script> element does not yet have an async or defer attribute, equivalent to those added to HTML5. Of course, if you're using inline SVG, you can use asynchronous HTML script elements to manipulate your SVG elements.

There's one other way to get JavaScript into your SVG: on*event* attributes, like `onload` or `onclick`. These work much the same way as in HTML, and—just like in HTML—they are mostly discouraged in the modern web.

We've already alluded to one common use of scripted SVG: cross-browser animation support. Example 2-2 shows JavaScript that could be used to replace the CSS animation from Examples 1-8 or 1-9 from Chapter 1. The code uses classes to select the elements, so it works with either the simple or labeled SVG markup: just remember to remove the CSS animation code from the `<style>` element!

The `<script>` element should be included at the end of the file (right before the closing `</svg>` tag). That way, it won't run until the rest of the file has been parsed.

Example 2-2. Using JavaScript to animate an SVG stoplight

```
<script><![CDATA[
(function(){                                              ❶

    var lights = ["green", "yellow", "red"];             ❷
    var nLights = lights.length;
    var lit = 2;                                         ❸

    function cycle() {                                    ❹
        lit = (lit + 1) % nLights;                       ❺

        var litElement, selector;
        for (var i=0; i < nLights; i++ ) {               ❻
            selector = "." + lights[i] + " .lit";
            litElement = document.querySelector(selector); ❼

            litElement.style["visibility"] =
                (i==lit)? "visible" : "hidden";          ❽
        }
    }

    cycle();
    setInterval(cycle, 3000);                            ❾

})();                                                    ❿
]]></script>
```

❶ The code is contained in an immediately-invoked anonymous function. Although not required, this is good coding practice to avoid conflicts between different scripts on a page. A function creates a closure to encapsulate variables. The "immediately-invoked anonymous" part means we are going to run it immediately after defining it, and don't need a name to refer to it later.

❷ The lights array holds the class names that distinguish each light group. Because the number of lights won't be changing, we can store it in a variable as well.

❸ The red light is initially lit in the markup; this corresponds to index 2 in the lights array (JavaScript array indices start at 0 for the first element).

❹ The cycle() function will change the lights.

❺ To start the cycle, the lit variable is advanced by one; the modulus operator (%) ensures that it cycles back to 0 when it reaches the length of the array.

❻ At each stage of the cycle, each color of light will be modified to either hide or show the "lit" graphic. One of the three won't change, but updating them all keeps the code simple and ensures that it only depends on the lit state, not on knowledge of the current DOM styles.

❼ The "lit" <use> element for each color is retrieved via the querySelector() method; a CSS selector of the form ".red .lit" will select the first element of class lit that is a child of an element with class red.

❽ The visibility style property is set to either visible or hidden according to whether this light should currently be lit. Modifying the style property of an element object has the same effect as setting an inline style. It therefore overrides the presentation attribute in the markup.

❾ The cycle function is run once to turn the light green, and then is called at regular intervals on a 3-second (3,000ms) timer.

❿ The anonymous function is run immediately: the syntax (`function(){ /*...*/ })()` parses and runs the encapsulated code.

Although this isn't a full web application—there is no interaction with the user—it demonstrates how SVG elements can be accessed and modified from a script.

There's nothing SVG-specific about the JavaScript code: it selects elements using CSS selectors and the `document.querySelector()` method, and sets the `visibility` style according to which lit bulb should be displayed. A timer runs the cycle again after every 3-second interval.

 The `querySelector()` method and its sibling `querySelectorAll()` are convenient ways to locate elements. Because they use CSS selectors, they can find elements based on any combination of tag names, class names, and parent-child relationships. However, versions of WebKit and Blink browsers prior to mid-2015 had a bug that prevented them from working for SVG mixed-case tag and attribute names, such as `linearGradient` or `viewBox`, in HTML documents. Related bugs affected the `getElements ByTagName()` methods.

To improve backward compatibility, use classes on these elements if you need to select them in your inline SVG code.

JavaScript and SVG can do more than recreate simple animations, of course.

Scripts can be used to implement complex logic and user interaction. They are also useful for calculating the coordinates of shapes in geometric designs and data visualizations. You *could* even use Java-Script to implement your own form-input elements or wrapped-text blocks in SVG. But it's generally easier to use HTML for that.

The stoplight graphic now cycles through green, yellow, and red lights when you view it in any modern web browser, and even in Internet Explorer 9 (the earliest IE to have SVG support). However, you won't get *any* animation, in any browser, if you reference the SVG from the src attribute of an HTML <img> element!

It's an extra complication when you're dealing with SVG in web pages: the behavior of SVG on the web can be quite different, depending on how the SVG is incorporated in the page.

Embedding SVG in Web Pages

If you're using SVG on the web, you'll usually want to integrate the graphics within larger HTML files. There are three main ways that SVG can be added to web pages:

- SVG as an image
- SVG as an embedded document
- inline SVG

Each embedding mode has advantages and disadvantages.

SVG as an HTML Image

The most straightforward method of combining SVG and HTML is to use a self-contained SVG file as an image in the HTML <img> tag.

Figure 2-2. Sample web page using an SVG image file

Example 2-3 provides the code for a super-simple web page using the CSS-animated SVG stoplight from Example 1-8. Figure 2-2 shows the result.

Example 2-3. CSS-animated stoplight as an image in a web page

```html
<!DOCTYPE html>
<html lang="en">
<head>
    <meta charset="utf-8">
    <title>SVG Images within HTML</title>
    <style>
        body {
            background-color: #222;
            color: white;
            margin: 0; padding: 0;
            font-family: sans-serif;
        }
        header, main {
            border-bottom: dashed yellow;
        }
        header {
            min-height: 12em;
            font-family: serif;
        }
        header h1 {
            margin: 0;
            color: red;
            text-shadow: yellow 0 0 4px, orange 0 0 2px;
            font-size: 500%;
        }
        header img {
            height: 10em;
            float: left;
            margin: 1em 2em;
        }
        p { padding: 0.5em; }
    </style>
</head>
<body>
    <header>
        <img src="../ch01-overview-files/animated-stoplight-css.svg"
            role="img" alt="Traffic light" />
        <h1>Tony's Towing</h1>
    </header>
    <main>
        <p>Main text goes here, but <em>WOW</em>
            look at that image in the header!</p>
    </main>
```

```
</body>
</html>
```

The **`<img>` element** should be familiar to most web developers. The `src` attribute provides the URL of the image file. An `alt` attribute provides text that will be shown if the user has turned off image downloads, or is using a screen reader. It will also be shown in older browsers that can't render SVG.

The `role="img"` attribute would normally be redundant on an `<img>` element. It is required to fix an SVG-specific accessibility bug in Apple's VoiceOver screen reader:

 Without `role="img"`, some versions of WebKit +VoiceOver treat an `<img>` element with an SVG source as an embedded document. The `alt` attribute is ignored, as the browser instead looks for titles in the SVG file.

This is one more reason you should always have a `<title>` in your standalone SVG files. But the title for the SVG might not be a good alternative text for the way you are using it in this web page. So use `role="img"` and `alt` to get consistent alternative text for all users.

In HTML5+, the `<img>` element has a big sister, the **`<picture>` element**, and a new attribute `srcset`. Together, they allow you to give the browser a set of alternative versions of the image to use in different contexts. The most common use is to provide low- and high-resolution versions of a photograph, for different screen sizes and screen resolutions.

With SVG images, you don't need to worry about screen resolution. So you won't need `srcset`. But `<picture>` can still be useful.

A `<picture>` element allows you to provide alternative file *types* as well as alternative file sizes. As a result, it can be used to provide a fallback raster image for SVG.

The `<picture>` element is always used in combination with an `<img>`. It groups that image with the **`<source>` elements** that define alternative files. For SVG fallback, the `<img>` element references your fallback image (a PNG, GIF, or JPEG), and will be used in older browsers. A `<source>` element references the SVG equivalent, and is used in modern browsers. The syntax is as follows:

```
<picture>
  <source type="image/svg+xml" srcset="url-to-graphic.svg" />
  <img src="url-to-fallback.png" alt="Description" />
</picture>
```

Note that you must use `srcset`, not `src`, on a `<source>` element inside a `<picture>`, even though there is only one file in the set.

 Browsers that support SVG but don't support `<picture>` will get the fallback. This includes Internet Explorer 9 to 11, and Safari 4 to 9. All browsers released in 2016 or later (and some released before then) will get the SVG.

If you *really* want users on medium-old browsers to get the SVG instead of the PNG, you can add a JavaScript polyfill like PictureFill (*https:// scottjehl.github.io/picturefill/*). But you have to weigh the benefits of SVG against the cost of the extra JavaScript.

There are a couple other features to emphasize in Example 2-3. First, note that the height of the image is being set in em-units, versus the height of 320px that was set in the SVG file (Example 1-8). Just like other image types, the SVG can be scaled to fit. Unlike other image types, the image will be drawn at whatever resolution is needed to fill the given size. The width of the image isn't set in Example 2-3; since both height and width were set in the SVG file, the image will scale in proportion to the height.

 Or at least, that's how it *usually* works. Internet Explorer scales the width of the image area in proportion to the height you set, but doesn't scale the actual drawing to fit into that area. There's an easy solution, however; it involves the `viewBox` attribute that we'll discuss in Chapter 8.

The second thing to note is that this is the *animated* SVG that is embedded. Declarative animation, including CSS animation and SVG/SMIL animation elements, runs as normal within SVG used as images—in browsers that support that animation type at all.

Or at least, that's how it's *supposed* to work.

MS Edge prior to version 15 (released April 2017) and Firefox prior to version 51 (released end of 2016) will not animate an SVG embedded as an image in a web page, even though CSS animation is supported in other SVG elements *and* SMIL-style animation elements in images are supported in Firefox!

And of course, older browsers do not support CSS animations, in SVG images or otherwise.

Why not use the scripted SVG animation from Example 2-2, which has better browser support? Because scripts *do not* run within images. That's not a bug, it's defined in the HTML spec: for security and performance reasons, files loaded as images can't have scripted content.

There are some other important limitations of SVG used as images:

- SVG in images won't load external files (such as external style-sheets or embedded photos).

- SVG in images won't receive user interaction events (such as mouse clicks or hover movements).

- SVG in images can't be modified by the parent web page's scripts or styles.

The limitations are the same if you reference an SVG image from within CSS, as a background image or other decorative graphic (an embedding option we'll discuss more thoroughly in Chapter 3).

Interactive Embedded SVG

If you want to use an external SVG file without (most of) the limitations of images, you can use an **embedded <object>**, replacing the <img> tag from Example 2-3 with the following:

```
<object data="animated-stoplight-scripted.svg"
        type="image/svg+xml" >
</object>
```

If you try this, you'll note that the graphic doesn't scale to fit like the image did. Again, that can be fixed with a viewBox attribute.

You can also add a fallback for older browsers, by including an <img> element as a child of the <object> element (with the src of the <img> referencing a raster image file), but beware that some older browsers (including most versions of Internet Explorer) will download *both* the SVG and the fallback.

You could also use an <embed> element or <iframe> with much the same effect. There is slightly different support in older browsers and no fallback option. As we discuss in Chapter 8, scaling behavior is also different for <iframe>, and less consistent between browsers.

Embedded objects can load external files, run scripts, and (with a little extra work and some security restrictions) use those scripts to interact with the main document. However, they are still separate documents, and they have separate stylesheets.

 Just like an HTML file in an <iframe>, an embedded SVG object *should* be a fully interactive and accesible part of the main web page. However, they can be a little buggy in browsers. Test carefully, including keyboard interaction and screen reader exposure, if you're embedding interactive SVG as an <object>.

There's another option for fully interactive SVG: inline SVG in the HTML markup. Inline SVG has its own complications, but also many unique features.

Using SVG in HTML5 Documents

Perhaps the biggest step toward establishing SVG as *the* vector graphics language for the web came from the people who work on HTML standards.

When SVG was first proposed, as an XML language, it was expected that developers would insert SVG content directly into other XML documents—including XHTML—using XML namespaces to indicate the switch in content type. But most web authors weren't interested in adopting the stricter syntax of XML when browsers rendered their HTML just fine.

Modern HTML standards have developed after much conflict between the W3C (World Wide Web Consortium), promoting XHTML, and a parallel group, the WHATWG (Web Hypertext Application Technology Working Group), promoting a "living standard" of HTML as developers and browsers used it. Both groups publish competing HTML specifications.

By the time the W3C decided that HTML5 was stable (in 2014), they had long yielded the XML debate. Authors can choose to use XML-compatible markup, but non-XML HTML is the default. Some discord between the two groups remains, but the net effect is that the latest HTML standards are (mostly) reflected in the latest browsers, and have been updated based on plenty of real-world experience.

With HTML developing separately from XML, it could have easily left SVG behind as another too-complicated coding language. Instead, the HTML5 standard (and the WHATWG living standard) welcomed the idea of SVG content mixed in with HTML markup, just without the need for XML namespaces.

By making SVG a de facto extension of HTML, the HTML working groups acknowledged that SVG was a fundamental part of the future of the web. This has had—and will continue to have—a huge impact on SVG.

HTML5 also introduced a number of new elements and attributes. The examples in this book will touch on some of the new HTML features but won't go into too much detail; there are plenty of great resources on using HTML5 out there.

For using SVG, the most important thing to know about HTML5 is the <svg> element.

An <svg> element in HTML represents an SVG graphic to be included in the document. Unlike other ways of embedding SVG in web pages, the graphic isn't contained in a separate file; instead, the SVG content is included directly within the HTML file, as child content of the <svg> element.

The integration isn't one-way. It's also possible to include HTML elements as children of SVG content. The SVG **<foreignObject> element** creates a layout box within an SVG drawing, in which an HTML document fragment can be displayed.

Again, the elements are in the same file, nested in the same DOM. The HTML elements must be marked with proper XML namespaces in a standalone SVG file, but the HTML parser automatically accepts HTML content inside <foreignObject>.

The <foreignObject> was never supported in Internet Explorer, although it is available in Microsoft Edge. Foreign objects in SVG are somewhat quirky in most web browsers, and are best used only for small amounts of content.

There are some key differences to keep in mind between using SVG code in HTML5 documents versus using it in standalone SVG files.

The most common area of difficulty is XML namespaces. The HTML parser ignores them.

If a web page is sent to the browser as an HTML file, namespace declarations have no effect. Namespace prefixes will be interpreted as part of the element or attribute name they precede, except for attributes like xlink:href and xml:lang, which are hardcoded into the parser. If the same markup is parsed by the XML parser (for example, if the web page is sent to the browser as an XHTML file), the resulting document object model may be different.

This book will try to use the most universally compatible syntax for SVG, and to identify any areas where you're likely to have problems.

To further confuse matters, the DOM *is* sensitive to namespaces (as we warned earlier in the chapter). If you are dynamically creating SVG, you need to be aware of XML namespaces regardless of whether or not you're working inside an HTML5 document.

Another important feature of SVG in HTML5 is that the <svg> element has a dual purpose: it is the parent element of the SVG graphic, but it also describes the box within the web page where that graphic should be inserted. You can position and style the box using CSS, the same as you would an <img> or <object> referencing an external SVG file.

Including SVG content within your primary HTML file enables scripts to manipulate both HTML and SVG content as one cohesive document. CSS styles inherit from HTML parent elements to SVG children. Among other benefits, this means that you can use dynamic **CSS pseudoclass selectors**—such as :hover or :checked—on HTML elements to control the appearance of child or sibling SVG content.

Example 2-4 uses HTML5 form validation (*http://www.w3.org/TR/html5/forms.html#constraints*) and the :valid and :invalid pseudoclasses (*http://www.w3.org/TR/selectors4/#ui-validity*) to turn an inline SVG version of the stoplight graphic into a warning light. If any of the user's entries in the form are invalid, the stoplight will display red. If the form is valid and ready to submit, the light will be green. And finally, if the browser doesn't support these pseudoclasses, the light will stay yellow regardless of what the user types.

Example 2-4. Controlling inline SVG with HTML form validation and CSS pseudoclasses

HTML MARKUP:

```
<!DOCTYPE html>
<html lang="en">
<head>
  <meta charset="utf-8" >
  <title>Inline SVG within HTML</title>
  <link rel="stylesheet" type="text/css"
      href="svg-inline-styles.css" >              ❶
</head>
<body>
<form id="contactForm" method="post" >           ❷
  <h1>How can we contact you?</h1>
  <svg width="140" height="320"
      viewBox="20 20 140 320"
      preserveAspectRatio="xMinYMin meet"
      aria-label="stoplight" role="img" >         ❸
    <defs>
      <circle id="light" cx="70" r="30" />
    </defs>
    <rect x="20" y="20" width="100" height="280"
```

```
                 fill="url(gradients.svg#metal) silver"
                 stroke="black" stroke-width="3" />
    <g stroke="black" stroke-width="2">
      <g class="red light" >
        <use xlink:href="#light" y="80"
             fill="url(gradients.svg#red-light-off) maroon" />
        <use class="lit" xlink:href="#light" y="80"
             fill="url(gradients.svg#red-light-on) red"
             visibility="hidden"/>
      </g>
      <g class="yellow light">
        <use xlink:href="#light" y="160"
             fill="url(gradients.svg#yellow-light-off) #705008"/>
        <use class="lit" xlink:href="#light" y="160"
             fill="url(gradients.svg#yellow-light-on) yellow" />
      </g>
      <g class="green light">
        <use xlink:href="#light" y="240"
             fill="url(gradients.svg#green-light-off) #002804" />
        <use class="lit" xlink:href="#light" y="240"
             fill="url(gradients.svg#green-light-on) lime"
             visibility="hidden"/>
      </g>
    </g>
  </svg>
  <label>
    <input type="text" name="CustomerName" required />
    Full Name
  </label>
  <label>
    <input type="email" name="CustomerEmail" required />
    Email Address
  </label>
  <button type="submit" >Send</button>
</form>
</body>
</html>
```

❶ A linked stylesheet contains the CSS, both for the HTML form content and for the inline SVG.

❷ The body of the web page contains a single <form> element. The form contains a heading and the input elements, but also the SVG that will give feedback about the user's entries.

❸ Much of the SVG code should look familiar by now; changes are described next.

The SVG code is a modified version of the stoplight SVG code we used in the CSS-animated and JS-animated versions of the stoplight (Examples 1-8 and 2-2).

The attributes on the `<svg>` element have been changed to fit the new context. For one thing, there is no `xmlns`. For a pure HTML document, no namespaces are required (for XHTML, they would be); the HTML5 parser knows to switch to SVG mode when it reaches an opening `<svg>` tag.

The `width` and `height` attributes provide a default size for the SVG; the final size will be controlled by CSS. Two new attributes (`viewBox` and `preserveAspectRatio`) control the scaling of the graphic; we'll talk more about them in Chapter 8. For now, just trust that these are the magic that make the SVG drawing scale to fit the dimensions we give it within the HTML page.

 The particular attribute values in Example 2-4 also ensure that the graphic will be drawn flush against the top-left edges of the SVG area, making it line up neatly with the heading text.

The **aria-label and role attributes** on the `<svg>` tell screen readers to treat the SVG in the same way as an `<img>` with `alt="stoplight"`; we'll talk more about ARIA in Chapter 17. The actual validation information about the form inputs will be communicated directly to the screen reader by the browser.

Inside the SVG, the main change is that we've removed all the gradient definitions and put them in a separate file, *gradients.svg*. As mentioned in Chapter 1, most browsers do not support this, so you probably would *not* want to do this in production; it's used here so we can focus on the new code.

Here, we use the fact that `fill` can declare **fallback colors**, in case there's a problem with URL references. We'll talk more about the fallback syntax in Chapter 12. Browsers that don't show the gradients use the solid colors instead. It's not pretty, but it's functional.

We've also changed the `visibility` presentation attributes. In other examples, we've left the red light on by default, but now we only want the red light to show if it is meaningful. The `visibility="hidden"` presentation attributes on the red and green lights ensure that they display in the "off" state by default. The yellow light is by default "lit."

The rest of the code describes the form itself. HTML5 form validation attributes have been used that will trigger invalid states:

- Both fields are required, and so will be invalid when empty.

- The second field is of type="email"; browsers that recognize this type will mark it as invalid unless the content meets the standard format of an email address.

 The :valid and :invalid pseudoclass selectors are supported on <form> elements (as opposed to individual <input> elements) in Firefox (versions 13+), WebKit/Safari (version 9+), and Blink browsers (Chrome and Opera, since early 2015). Microsoft Edge (as of EdgeHTML version 15) and older versions of other browsers display the indeterminate yellow light.

For more universal browser support, you could use a script to listen for changes in focus between input elements, and set regular CSS classes on the <form> element based on whether any of the input elements are in the invalid state. The stylesheet would also need to be modified so that these classes also control the SVG styles.

Since this isn't a book about JavaScript, we're not going to write out that script in detail. Once again, nothing about the script would be SVG-specific. The SVG effects are controlled entirely by the (pseudo-)classes on the parent <form>.

The styles that control the appearance of both the form and the SVG are in a separate file, linked from within the HTML <head>. Example 2-5 presents the CSS code that controls the interaction.

Example 2-5. CSS stylesheet for the code in Example 2-4

CSS Styles: *svg-inline-styles.css*

```
@charset "UTF-8";

/* Form styles */
form {
```

```css
    display: block;
    max-width: 30em;
    padding: 1.5em;
    overflow: auto;

    border: double 12px;
    border-radius: 0 2em;
    color: navy;
    font-family: sans-serif;
}
h1 { margin: 0 0 1em; }
label, button {
    display: block;
    clear: right;
    padding: 0 0 3em;
}
input, button {
    float: right;
    min-width: 6em;
    max-width: 70%;
    padding: 0.5em;
    color: inherit;
    border: solid;
}
button { background: silver; }
input:invalid {
    border-color: red;
    box-shadow: none; /* override browser defaults */
}
input:focus, button:focus {
    outline: green dotted;
    outline-offset: 2px;
}
form:invalid button[type="submit"] {
    color: dimGray;
}

/* SVG styles */
form svg {
    float: left;
    width: 6em;
    height: 12em;
    max-width: 25%;
    max-height: 80vh;
    overflow: visible;
}
form:valid .green .lit {
    /* If the validator thinks all form elements are ok,
       the green light will display */
    visibility: visible;
}
```

```
form:invalid .red .lit {
    /* If the validator detects a problem in the form,
       the red light will display */
    visibility: visible;
}
form:valid .yellow .lit, form:invalid .yellow .lit {
    /* If either validator class is recognized,
       turn off the yellow light */
    visibility: hidden;
}
```

The first batch of style rules defines the appearance of the HTML form elements, including using the :invalid selector to style individual inputs that cannot be submitted as-is, and :focus selectors to identify the active field.

The <svg> element itself is styled as a floated box with a standard width and height that will shrink on small screens. The overflow is set to visible to prevent the strokes of the rectangle from being clipped, now that the rectangle has been moved flush against the edge of the SVG.

The remaining rules control the visibility of the lights, taking advantage of the fact that CSS rules override the defaults set with presentation attributes. If the form matches the :valid selector, the bright green light is revealed; if it matches :invalid, the bright red light is displayed. Finally, if *either* of those selectors is recognized by the browser, the illuminated version of the yellow light is hidden. If the selectors aren't recognized (or if the CSS doesn't load), the presentation attributes ensure that only the yellow light is lit.

Figure 2-3 shows the web page in action: when the form is invalid (because of a problem with the email field) versus when it is complete and showing the green light. The screenshots are from Firefox, which at the time of writing is the only browser that supports both the pseudoclasses and SVG gradients from external files.

This demo uses familiar CSS approaches (classes and pseudoclasses) to style SVG in a dynamic way. But this is only the beginning of how SVG and CSS can be integrated.

Figure 2-3. A web page using inline SVG to enhance form validation feedback

Using SVG with CSS3

CSS has also advanced considerably since SVG 1.1 was introduced. The core CSS specification was updated to version 2.1, and finalized in 2011. But already, work had begun on a variety of CSS modules, each focusing on specific topics. There is no single CSS3 specification, but the many modules are collectively known as CSS level 3.

Many of the original CSS3 features are widely implemented in web browsers, and you can use them without problem when designing SVG for the web. SVG tools that still rely exclusively on the SVG 1.1 specifications, however, may not support them. Nonetheless, thanks to CSS's error-resistant syntax, the old software shouldn't break completely; it should just ignore the parts it does not understand.

Some of the newer specifications, although widely implemented, are still not entirely stable. Others are very experimental.

The W3C working group periodically publishes an informal "snapshot" of the state of CSS standards, with links to the modules. The latest version is at *https://www.w3.org/TR/CSS/*.

The new CSS modules include many graphical effects—such as masking, filters, and transformations—that are direct extensions of features from SVG. These standards replace the corresponding SVG definitions, allowing the same syntax to be used for all CSS-styled content. There are no competing chapters in SVG 2. Support for these effects in browsers is more erratic (we'll discuss the details in the relevant chapters); many bugs remain, but they are slowly being squashed.

Not all aspects of CSS3 were developed in collaboration with SVG.

Other new CSS features introduced similar-but-different graphical features that put CSS in direct competition with SVG for some simple vector graphics. Whenever this book discusses a feature of SVG that has a CSS equivalent, we'll highlight the similarities and differences using "CSS Versus SVG" notes like this:

CSS Versus SVG
Style Versus Graphics

In these asides, we'll compare different ways of achieving the same graphical effect, and identify effects that can only be achieved with one language or the other. This should help you, the web designer, decide which tool is best for the job you're trying to do.

The relationship between CSS and SVG is so complex, and so important, that we've given it a separate chapter. Chapter 3 will look at the ways CSS can be used to enhance SVG, and SVG can be used to enhance CSS. It will also consider the ways in which CSS has started to replace SVG for simple graphics like the stoplight example we've been using so far.

Summary: SVG and the Web

This chapter aimed to provide a big picture of SVG on the web, considering both the role of SVG on the web and the way it can complement (and be complemented by) other web technologies.

The web is founded on the intersection of many different coding languages and standards, each with its own role to play. For the most part, web authors are encouraged to separate their web page code into the document text and structure (HTML), its styles and layout (CSS), and its logic and functionality (JavaScript).

SVG redefines this division to support documents where layout and graphical appearance are a fundamental part of the structure and meaning. It provides a way to describe an image as a structured document, with distinct elements defined by their geometric presentation and layout, that can be styled with CSS and modified with JavaScript.

The SVG standard has developed in fits and starts. The practical use of SVG on the web is only just starting to achieve its potential. There are still countless quirks and areas of cross-browser incompatibility, which we'll mention whenever possible in the rest of the book. Hopefully, the messy history of SVG and the interdependent web standards has reinforced the fact that the web, in general, is far from a perfect or complete system, and SVG on the web is still relatively new.

The goal of this book is to help you work with SVG on the web, focusing on the way SVG is currently supported in web browsers, rather than than the way the language was originally defined. In many cases, this will include warnings about browser incompatibilities and suggestions of workarounds. However, support for SVG may have changed by the time you read this, so open up your web browser(s) and test out anything you're curious about.

More Online

The `<script>` and `<style>` elements introduced in this chapter and the previous one are included in our markup reference, under the category "Elements for adding other languages to SVG":

https://oreillymedia.github.io/Using_SVG/guide/ markup.html#integration

The elements for embedding SVG in HTML are summarized in the "Embedding SVG in HTML" guide:

https://oreillymedia.github.io/Using_SVG/guide/embedding.html

CHAPTER 3

A Sense of Style

Working with CSS

On the web, style means CSS. Cascading Style Sheets are used to indicate how the plain text of HTML should be formatted into the colorful diversity of websites and applications that you interact with every day.

SVG and CSS have an intertwined relationship. SVG incorporates CSS styling of decorative aspects of the drawing, but uses a basic layout model completely independent of CSS layout. CSS has been expanded to include so many graphical effects (formerly only available in SVG) that it has become a rudimentary vector graphics language of its own.

This chapter covers how to use CSS styles to modify your SVG graphics, and how to reference SVG images and elements in CSS code used to style HTML. It also discusses the benefits and limitations of using CSS+HTML to create graphics, including its similarities and differences with SVG, and outlines factors for you to consider when deciding between the two.

CSS in SVG

CSS is not required for SVG; it is perfectly possible to define a complete SVG graphic using presentation attributes. However, using CSS to control presentation makes it easier to create a consistent look and feel. It also makes it easier to change the presentation later.

> ## More Online
>
> A complete list of SVG style properties, including their default values, is provided in the "SVG Style Properties" guide:
>
> *https://oreillymedia.github.io/Using_SVG/guide/style.html*
>
> Most properties will be discussed in context throughout the rest of the book.

Style Declarations

There are four different ways to define presentation properties for an SVG element: presentation attributes, inline styles, internal stylesheets (<style> blocks), and external stylesheets.

Presentation attributes

Most style properties used in SVG may be specified as an XML attribute. For the most part, the effect is the same as if CSS were used. Properties that are normally inherited will be inherited, and the inherit keyword can be used to force inheritance on other properties.

Things to note:

- There are no shorthand versions of the presentation attributes (e.g., use font-size, font-family, and so on, not font).

- The XML parser is case-sensitive for property names (must be lowercase) and for some keyword values (although SVG 2 requires presentation attribute values to be parsed the same way as in CSS).

- You cannot include multiple declarations for the same property in order to provide fallbacks for older browsers; you can only have one of each attribute per element.

- You cannot use the !important modifier.

- Values set using CSS take priority over a presentation attribute on the same element. However, presentation attributes supercede inherited style values, even if the inherited value was set with CSS.

Inline styles

All SVG elements can have a **style attribute**. Similar to its HTML equivalent, it accepts a string of CSS `property: value` pairs. Inline styles declared this way supersede both presentation attributes and values from stylesheets, except for `!important` stylesheet values.

A <style> block

You can include an **internal stylesheet** within your SVG document using a `<style>` element, similar to the `<style>` element in HTML.

The element can be placed anywhere, but is usually at the top of the file or inside a `<defs>` section. In addition, when your SVG code is included inline within another document, such as HTML5, any stylesheets declared for that document—or declared in other SVG graphics within the document—will affect your graphic.

The `<style>` block can include any valid CSS stylesheet content, but the main content will be CSS style rules consisting of a **CSS selector** followed, within braces (curly brackets), by a list of `property: value` pairs that will apply to elements matching that selector:

```
selector {
  property1: value;
  property2: value; /* comment */
  property3: value !important;
}
```

The **!important modifier** clobbers the normal CSS cascade rules, and it should only be used as a last resort.

If you're not familiar with CSS and CSS selectors, you'll want to consult a CSS-specific reference guide, such as Eric Meyer's *CSS Pocket Reference* or the CSS-Tricks online almanac (*http://css-tricks.com/almanac/*). Most browsers now support CSS level 3 selectors (and some level 4 selectors), but older browsers and SVG tools that have not been updated since SVG 1.1 may only support CSS 2 selectors.

 Although the SVG `<style>` element works much the same way as its HTML counterpart, HTML introduced additional DOM interfaces that allow you to access and modify the stylesheet using JavaScript, which SVG did not initially match. SVG 2 harmonizes the two, but implementations have not all caught up.

Some other details to consider when using internal stylesheets in SVG files (especially if you're not used to working with CSS in XML):

- The SVG 1.1 specifications did *not* define a default stylesheet type. Although all web browsers will assume `type="text/css"`, other tools (notably Apache Batik and out-of-date versions of Inkscape) will ignore the `<style>` block if the type isn't declared. SVG 2 makes the de facto default official.

- The contents of the `<style>` block can be (but don't have to be) contained in an XML "character data" section. This avoids parsing errors if your comments contain stray `<`, `>`, or `&` characters. The start of the character data region is indicated by `<![CDATA[` and the end by `]]>`, like this:

```
<style type="text/css"><![CDATA[
circle { /* Styles for <circle>s */
    fill: red; /* red & purple are my favorite colors */
}
]]></style>
```

- CSS has its own way of handling XML namespaces, which is completely distinct from any namespace prefixes declared in the XML markup.

More Online

Most web developers have never needed to use XML namespaces in CSS. But when you're working with SVG, namespaced elements and attributes (like `xlink:href`) can trip up your CSS selectors.

Read more in "XML Namespaces in CSS":

https://oreillymedia.github.io/Using_SVG/extras/ch03-namespaces.html

We only use one type of namespaced CSS selector in the examples in this book, and it is to specifically cancel out the distinction between `href` and `xlink:href` in **attribute selectors**.

The `[href]` attribute selector *only* selects `href` attributes without namespaces. To *also* select `xlink:href` attributes, you need to add

*| (asterisk and pipe) ahead of the attribute name, as a wildcard namespace marker. It looks like this:

```
pattern[*|href] /* pattern elements with an
                      href or xlink:href attribute*/
use[*|href="#icon"] /* use elements that clone `icon` */
a[*|href$='.pdf'] /* links to a PDF file */
use:not([*|href^='#']) /* use elements whose cross-references
                          don't start with a `#` target */
```

The issues with `type` and namespaces also apply to external stylesheets.

External stylesheets

Style rules may be collected into external *.css* files so that they can be used by multiple documents.

 External stylesheets (or any external file resources) are never loaded from SVG files that are used as images in web pages (e.g., `<img>` or CSS `background-image`).

There are four ways to include external stylesheets for SVG, all of which allow the stylesheet to be restricted to certain media types:

- An **import rule** at the top of another CSS stylesheet or `<style>` block, like:

  ```
  <style type="text/css">
      @import "style.css";
      @import url("print.css") print;
  </style>
  ```

- An **XML stylesheet processing instruction** in the prolog of an SVG or XML file (the "prolog" being any code before the opening `<svg>` or other root tag), like:

  ```
  <?xml-stylesheet href="style.css" type="text/css"?>
  <?xml-stylesheet href="print.css" media="print"
                   type="text/css"?>
  <svg xmlns="http://www.w3.org/2000/svg">
      <!-- ... -->
  </svg>
  ```

- A **<link> element** in the <head> of an HTML5 document that includes inline SVG, like:

```
<html>
<head>
  <!-- ... -->
  <link href="style.css" rel="stylesheet" type="text/css">
  <link href="print.css" rel="stylesheet"
        media="print" type="text/css">
</head>
<body>
  <!-- ... -->
  <svg>
  <!-- ... -->
```

- An HTML <link> element in a standalone SVG file, using proper XML namespaces (either a prefix or an xmlns attribute on the <link> element itself) to identify it as the HTML element:

```
<svg xmlns="http://www.w3.org/2000/svg"
     xmlns:html="http://www.w3.org/1999/xhtml">
  <html:link href="style.css" rel="stylesheet"
             type="text/css">
  <link xmlns="http://www.w3.org/1999/xhtml"
        href="print.css" rel="stylesheet"
        media="print" type="text/css" />
  <!-- ... -->
</svg>
```

Support for the HTML <link> in SVG files was only officially added in SVG 2. It is supported in every web browser we've tested, but will probably not be supported in other SVG tools.

In all these cases, the first stylesheet (*style.css*) would be used for all media, while the second (*print.css*) would only be used for printing out the graphic.

Overriding Styles

Once the browser has all your different style rules, it **cascades** them together with the default values to create a specified value for each property on each element, and then applies **inheritance** as necessary to create a final used value. For SVG, this works the same as elsewhere in CSS, except that presentation attributes add an extra step to the cascade.

Presentation attributes are treated as an author-level style rule with zero **specificity**. In fact, they have *less* than zero specificity, because the zero-specificity **universal * selector** outranks them.

 There are also a few SVG-specific style defaults that are defined in the SVG specs and applied as browser-level style rules. The most notable one is that overflow is set to hidden on most SVG elements where it has an effect, even though the normal CSS initial value is visible.

More Online

Although CSS in SVG works much the same as CSS in HTML, that doesn't mean it is simple. Even developers who work with CSS every day sometimes get confused by the cascade, selector specificity, or inheritance rules.

Read more about how all these features work—in general and as applied to SVG—in "The Cascade":

https://oreillymedia.github.io/Using_SVG/extras/ch03-cascade.html

CSS cascading and specificity rules can be used to create a stylesheet that completely overrules presentation attributes in the code.

For example, you could use CSS overrides to create a separate set of styles for black-and-white printing. Example 3-1 presents such a stylesheet for the grouped primary-color stoplight from Example 1-4 in Chapter 1. (Other versions of the stoplight could have been used, but this one has short and sweet markup.) The print-preview result is shown in Figure 3-1.

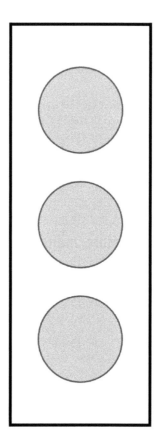

Figure 3-1. A minimalist, monochrome stoplight

Example 3-1. Stylesheet for monochrome printing of an SVG

SVG MARKUP:

```
<?xml-stylesheet media="print"
    href="grouped-stoplight-print-styles.css" ?>        ❶
<svg xmlns="http://www.w3.org/2000/svg" xml:lang="en"
    height="320px" width="140px" >
    <title>Grouped Lights Stoplight</title>
    <rect x="20" y="20" width="100" height="280"
        fill="blue" stroke="black" stroke-width="3" />
    <g class="lights" stroke="black" stroke-width="2">        ❷
```

```
      <circle cx="70" cy="80" r="30" fill="red" />
      <circle cx="70" cy="160" r="30" fill="yellow" />
      <circle cx="70" cy="240" r="30" fill="#40CC40" />
    </g>
</svg>
```

❶ We've used the xml-stylesheet format to include the print stylesheet; an alternative would be to add an HTML-namespaced <link> after the <title>. The media="print" attribute lets the browser know to only use these styles when printing.

❷ The only change to the markup is a class attribute on the <g> group.

CSS STYLES: *grouped-stoplight-print-styles.css*

```
* {                            ❶
    fill: inherit;             ❷
    stroke: inherit;
    stroke-width: inherit;
}
g.lights {                     ❸
    fill: lightgray;
    stroke: dimgray;
    stroke-width: 1;
}
rect {                         ❹
    fill: none;
    stroke: black;
    stroke-width: 2;
}
```

❶ The universal selector (*) is used to reset the styles declared on all elements using presentation attributes.

❷ We use the inherit keyword, instead of setting a value directly on every element, so that style inheritance will work normally.

❸ We give all the lights the same appearance by setting the styles once on the <g> element (using the class added to the markup).

❹ The <rect> is styled separately. Note that, because we reset the stroke and stroke-width presentation attributes for *all* elements, the styles have to be set in the CSS even when, like the black stroke, they have not been changed from the original.

If there are multiple valid stylesheet rules with the same specificity, the final value is used. To determine which value comes last, different stylesheets (both external files and <style> blocks) are concatenated together in the order in which they are included in the document. This allows you to use an external stylesheet for many documents and then modify it for a particular document using a <style> element. It also allows you to specify fallback styles for new features that may not be universally supported.

Conditional Styles

Declaring styles in CSS stylesheets is often simply a convenience compared to using presentation attributes, allowing you to apply the same style rules to many elements (or many files) without repeating your code. However, with CSS, you can create much greater flexibility in your graphic, by using fallback values, media queries, and interactive pseudoclasses to create styles that adapt to the context.

Parser fallbacks

The most basic, and universally supported, conditional CSS is the **fallback value**. CSS error handling rules require browsers to skip any invalid style declarations, and continue reading the rest of the file. If you use a new feature the browser doesn't support, it will ignore the declaration.

In combination with the cascade rules, this means that you can provide fallback values for new property features simply by declaring—earlier in the stylesheet—a more widely supported value for the same property. Browsers will apply the *last* value that they recognize and support. For example, the following code would provide a fallback for a semitransparent rgba() color value (which was introduced in the CSS level 3 Color specification):

```
.stained-glass {
  fill: #FF8888; /* solid pink */
  fill: rgba(100%, 0, 0, 0.5); /* transparent red */
}
```

Fallback styles allow you to use new features while providing alternatives for tools that only support the SVG 1.1 specifications. There are currently only a few such features relevant to styling SVG, such as CSS3 colors and units, and new filter and masking options.

However, the number of inconsistently supported style values will likely increase as new CSS3 and SVG 2 specifications are rolled out.

@supports tests

One limitation of CSS error-handling fallbacks is that they only apply to a single property. Sometimes you need to coordinate multiple property values to provide fallback support for a complex feature. The new **@supports rule** allows this type of coordination. The basic structure looks like the following:

```
.stained-glass {
  fill: #FF0000; /* solid red */
  fill-opacity: 0.5;
}
@supports ( fill: rgba(100%, 0, 0, 0.5) ) {
  .stained-glass {
    fill: rgba(100%, 0, 0, 0.5); /* transparent red */
    fill-opacity: 1; /* reset */
  }
}
```

With this code, the SVG fill-opacity property is used as an alternative to CSS3 transparent colors. Again, thanks to CSS error-handling rules, browsers that don't recognize the @supports rule will skip that entire block.

CSS @supports is supported in all the latest browsers, but older browsers (such as Internet Explorer) will skip over the entire block. Make sure you still have decent fallbacks if "nothing" is supported by the @supports test!

Be aware that @supports only tests whether the CSS parser recognizes a particular property/value combination. It can't test whether that property will be applied when a particular element is being styled.

This is particularly frustrating when you're working with SVG in web browsers. Certain properties (such as filter or mask) may be recognized but only applied on SVG elements, despite applying to all elements in the latest specs. Other properties (such as text-shadow or z-index) may be recognized and applied for CSS box model content, but not for SVG.

Media queries

The @supports rule is a type of **conditional CSS** rule block.

A more established conditional CSS rule is the **@media rule**, more commonly known as a **media query**. A media query applies certain styles according to the type of output medium used to display the document. We already discussed how it is possible to use the media attribute to limit the use of external stylesheets. @media rules allow those same conditions to be included within a single stylesheet or <style> block:

```
@media print {
    /* These styles only apply when the document is printed */
}
```

Originally, CSS used a fixed number of media type descriptions, such as screen, print, tv, and handheld. But this proved limiting.

Handheld devices today are quite different from what they were 15 years ago, and screens come in all shapes and sizes. The only media type distinction that is still relevant is screen versus print. For all other distinctions, use feature-based media queries, which directly test whether the output device is a certain size, or a certain resolution, or able to display full-color images (among other features).

For general information on media query syntax and options, consult a CSS reference. For SVG, there are a couple complications to keep in mind.

The first thing to realize is that the media query is evaluated before any of the SVG code; in other words, before any scaling effects within the SVG change the definition of what a px or a cm is.

The second thing to be aware of, particularly if you're switching between separate SVG files and inline SVG code, is that the media being tested is the window or printed page for the *document* containing the SVG code. If the SVG is inline within HTML5, that means the entire frame containing the HTML web page. However, if the SVG is embedded as an <object> or <img>, it means the specific frame area created to draw the graphic.

In practice, this means that media queries can be a little more predictable with embedded SVG files. You can design around the SVG dimensions directly, without needing to know the rest of the layout.

More Online

See a simple example of how the same media query has different effects on inline versus embedded SVG, in "Media Queries in Embedded Versus Inline SVG":

https://oreillymedia.github.io/Using_SVG/extras/ch03-media-queries.html

It should be clear that a thorough understanding of CSS can help you make the most of your SVG graphics. However, that is not the end of the relationship; it also works the other way.

SVG in CSS

There are two distinct ways in which you can reference SVG files from within a CSS file:

- use the entire SVG file as an image
- use specific SVG elements that apply graphical effects

Complete SVG images can be used like other image types in CSS-styled HTML or XML documents. Theoretically, they can also be used in CSS-styled SVG (for example, as a background-image on the root element), although the practical need is more limited.

SVG element references were initially a feature unique to SVG, for styling other SVG elements; however, many of these properties that use these references (including fill, stroke, filter, mask, and clip-path) are now being expanded to other types of CSS-styled content.

Using SVG Images Within CSS

The ability to reference image files from CSS has existed from the earliest versions of the language. Any HTML element that participates in the document layout flow—that is, anything that takes up space on a web page—has a background. The ability to modify this background was one of the first CSS capabilities implemented in contemporary browsers, and as such is quite robust, fully supported by all popular browsers still in common use.

The **background-image property**, like any CSS property that accepts an image, takes a URL value, contained within the url() function:

```
background-image: url('/images/myImage.jpg');
```

The quotes around the argument in the url() function are recommended, but can often be omitted, so long as the URL only contains ASCII characters with no whitespace.

The URL could be global, starting with a protocol (https://), or at least a double slash (//):

https://www.example.com/images/myImage.jpg

Or it could be local, starting with a single slash (/), meaning it is on the same server as the web page:

/images/myImage.jpg

Or relative to the current web page or stylesheet location:

myImage.jpg
../images/myImage.jpg

 The ../ in that last URL means "go up one level in the file directory, then find the specified folder and file." We use it in the examples, when linking to a file from a different chapter, stored in a different folder in the example repository.

The HTML5 specification, when describing SVG as a required format for images, states that it should also be valid format for background-image in CSS-styled HTML.

This means that if you have an SVG file, such as *myImage.svg*, you can use it in exactly the same manner as you could use a JPEG, GIF, or PNG file, in any modern browser:

```
background-image: url('/images/myImage.svg');
```

If you want to provide fallback images for older browsers that don't support SVG, you have a few options:

- Use a JavaScript tool, such as Modernizr (*http://modern izr.com/*), to test whether SVG images are supported and change the classes (and therefore style rules) on your elements accordingly.

- Use a server script to identify the old browsers and edit your web page to use different style rules.

- Use Internet Explorer conditional comments to include a stylesheet that overrides your main style rules (this doesn't help with older mobile browsers that don't support SVG).

- Use other modern CSS syntax not supported by the older browsers, such as layered background images and CSS gradients, to make the browser ignore the background image declaration that includes SVG, and apply fallback declaration instead.

The layered-image fallback approach looks like the following:

```
background-image: url('/images/myImage.jpg'); /*fallback*/
background-image: url('/images/myImage.svg'),
                  linear-gradient(transparent, transparent);
```

This prevents the SVG file from being downloaded in both old Internet Explorer and old Android browsers.

Although backgrounds are the most common use for images in CSS, there are currently three other well-supported properties that accept image values:

list-style-image
Specifies a custom graphic to replace the bullet or number for a list element (technically, any element with CSS display type list-item).

border-image
Generates decorative frames for elements.

content
Provides content to be used in the ::before and ::after pseudoelements, as a series of text strings and/or images. The images are displayed at their natural size, like a series of inline block elements, so this is best only used for small icons with defined sizes in the SVG file.

New CSS properties, including `mask-image` and `shape-outside`, are extending this list. SVG images are also fairly well supported in the `cursor` property—so long as the image has defined height and width.

In general, if a CSS property takes an image file, it should accept an SVG file.

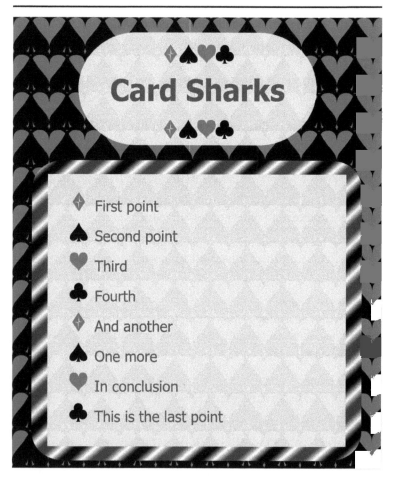

Figure 3-2. A web page using SVG graphics as CSS backgrounds, bullets, and borders

Example 3-2 applies all four properties to an HTML web page, using card suit shapes that we'll learn how to draw in Chapter 6. The (somewhat intense-looking) web page that results is shown in Figure 3-2.

Example 3-2. Using CSS properties that accept an SVG image value

HTML MARKUP:

```
<!DOCTYPE html>
<html lang="en">
<head>
    <meta charset="utf-8" >
    <title>Using SVG in CSS for an HTML page</title>
    <link rel="stylesheet" href="svg-in-css.css" />
</head>
<body>
    <h1>Card Sharks</h1>
    <ul>
        <li>First point</li>
        <li>Second point</li>
        <li>Third</li>
        <li>Fourth</li>
        <li>And another</li>
        <li>One more</li>
        <li>In conclusion</li>
        <li>This is the last point</li>
    </ul>
</body>
</html>
```

CSS STYLES: *svg-in-css.css*

```
body {
    margin: 0 1em;
    font-family: sans-serif;
    color: navy;

    background-color: red;                              ❶
    background-image: url('../ch06-path-files/spade.svg'),
                      url('../ch06-path-files/heart.svg'),
                      url('../ch06-path-files/club.svg');   ❷
    background-size: 40px 40px;
    background-position: 0 0, 20px 0, 20px 20px;        ❸
}
h1 {
    text-align: center;
    border-radius: 2em / 50%;
}
h1::before, h1::after {
```

```
        display: block;
        content: url('../ch06-path-files/diamond.svg')
                 url('../ch06-path-files/spade.svg')
                 url('../ch06-path-files/heart.svg')
                 url('../ch06-path-files/club.svg');        ❹
}
h1, ul {
        background-color: white;
        background-color: rgba(100%, 100%, 100%, 0.85);
        max-width: 70%;
        margin: 0.5em auto;
}
ul {
        padding: 1em;
        padding-left: calc(1em + 10%);
        border: solid #999 1em;
        border-radius: 10%;                                ❺

        border-image-source: url(svg-in-css-border-gradient.svg);  ❻
        border-image-slice:  5% 5%;
        border-image-width:  4.7%; /* = 5% / 105% */
        border-image-repeat: stretch;
}
li {
        line-height: 2em;
}
ul li:nth-of-type(4n+1) {                                  ❼
        list-style-image: url('../ch06-path-files/diamond.svg');
}
ul li:nth-of-type(4n+2) {
        list-style-image: url('../ch06-path-files/spade.svg');
}
ul li:nth-of-type(4n+3) {
        list-style-image: url('../ch06-path-files/heart.svg');
}
ul li:nth-of-type(4n+4) {
        list-style-image: url('../ch06-path-files/club.svg');
}
```

❶ The solid red background color will be visible on any parts of
   the web page not covered by the background images; it will also
   provide a fallback if SVG images are not supported.

❷ For browsers that support SVG and the CSS3 Backgrounds and
   Borders specification, a complex pattern consisting of three
   overlapping images will be used as the background. The backgrounds will be layered top to bottom in the same order they
   are given in the CSS.

❸ A list of values is given for background-position, setting the initial offset for each corresponding graphic in the list of background images. Each shape will have the 40px square size set by background-size. The positions are the initial offset, but each image will repeat in a tiled pattern (set the background-repeat property for a different behavior).

❹ The content property on the pseudoelements of the heading is used to provide a decorative row of icons above and below the heading text.

❺ The <ul> will be surrounded by a decorative border image; however, a solid gray border is defined as a fallback. The border-radius curvature is used to ensure that the padding area will not extend beyond the curved corners of the border image.

❻ The border image consists of a rounded rectangle with a repeating diagonal gradient. The other properties control how the image is divided into edges and corners to fill the border region. CSS border images are a complex topic, with many options, which do not take advantage of any SVG features. You may find it easier to use layered background images to achieve the same effect.

❼ To create a rotating series of custom bullets, the nth-of-type CSS pseudoclass selector is used to assign the different list images. The selector li:nth-of-type(4n+1) will apply to every <li> element that is one more than a multiple of four (when counting all list-item elements that are children of the same parent). In other words, the first, fifth, and ninth item and so on. Unlike JavaScript, CSS does not count the first element in a set as index 0.

The stylesheet presented in Example 3-2 references five separate SVG image files. Each one is only a few hundred bytes in size before compression, but requesting each file from the web server may slow display of the web page.

The HTTP/2 protocol, now available in the latest browsers and many web servers, reduces the
time spent by the browser requesting each new
file. With HTTP/2, you probably wouldn't worry
about having five different image files. But you
might worry about 100.

This is especially true because the server's ability
to compress the file size depends on how much
repetition there is in a single file: repetition that
is divided across many different files cannot be
compressed away.

Making Every File Count

There are various options to reduce the number of file requests
when you have a large number of small SVG graphics:

- Construct a single **sprite image**, with the separate icons
  arranged in a row or grid, to use as a `background-image` file for
  multiple elements. Then use the `background-size` and
  `background-position` properties to position the sprite file in
  such a way that the correct icon is visible.

  This technique has been used for years with raster image sprites;
  there is nothing specific to SVG about it. However, it only works
  for background images—there are no similar size and position
  options to reposition a list image file.

- Create a sprite image as above, but add **<view> elements** that
  describe the target region for each icon. Then specify the ID of
  the relevant view as the target fragment (after the # mark) in the
  URI.

- Create an **SVG stack** file, with your different icons overlapping
  in the same position. Then use the CSS `:target` pseudoclass to
  only display each graphic if it is referenced in the URL target
  fragment.

- Convert each image reference to a data URI, which allows you
  to pass an entire file's contents in the form of a URI value.

We'll discuss SVG views and stacks in Chapter 9. Theoretically, they
should be usable anywhere you use an SVG image file (in CSS or in
HTML), since all the information about position and size is contained in the SVG code and the URL fragment. However, at the time

of writing there are serious limitations on browser support in Web-Kit, and in many older Blink browsers still in use (e.g., on Android).

That last option is worth a longer discussion. It's currently the recommended approach for embedding very small SVG files in a CSS file, such as might be used for custom list bullets or simple background patterns.

A **data URI** is an entire file encoded in a URL string. You can therefore use it anywhere a URL is required, without needing to download a separate file.

 For security reasons, Internet Explorer and Edge do not let you directly open data URIs in a browser tab. IE also doesn't allow them as an `<iframe>` source. However, you can use them almost anywhere else you would use an SVG: `<img>`, `<object>`, or CSS image properties.

To use data URIs, you specify the `data:` file protocol, the media type, optional encoding information, and then the file contents as a URI-safe string. Many browsers allow you to pass a simple SVG file as plain-text markup, with only %, #, and ? characters encoded (since these have special meaning in URIs). However, for cross-browser support, you also need to URL-encode all ", <, and > markup characters and any non-ASCII Unicode characters.

You can guarantee compatibility by using the JavaScript `encodeURIComponent(string)` method to encode your plain-text markup. The result would be entered in the following code to create a data URI:

```
url("data:image/svg+xml,URI-encoded ASCII text file");
url("data:image/svg+xml;charset=utf-8,URI-encoded
        Unicode file");
```

Be sure to use a complete, valid SVG file to create your data URI, including XML namespaces. However, you can *minify* the file as much as possible before encoding, in particular to remove extra whitespace.

Taylor Hunt has discovered that you can keep the encoding URI size smaller by using single-quote characters (') instead of double quotes (") in your markup; the single quotes do not need to be escaped in a URL, so long as the entire string is surrounded by double quotes. His article on SVG data URIs (*https://codepen.io/tigt/post/optimizing-svgs-in-data-uris*) has a more detailed JavaScript function for making optimal data URIs. Jakob Eriksen used the same approach to create a Sass CSS preprocessor function (*https://codepen.io/jakob-e/pen/doMoML*). And Dave Rupert turned it into a copy-and-paste website (*https://codepen.io/davatron5000/pen/owyKJM*), if you're only encoding a few short graphics.

For raster image files—which don't have a plain-text representation—data URIs use the base-64 encoding algorithm. Base-64 encoding converts the raw binary data of a file to a string using 64 URL-safe characters.

Base-64 encoding is not recommended for SVG data URIs in CSS or HTML files, because the end result cannot be compressed (with Gzip or Brotli) as effectively as a URL-encoded text. Even uncompressed, it may be longer than an optimal URI-encoded version.

Nonetheless, base-64 encoding is the best choice for encoding many other file types that you might wish to embed in your SVG file itself. The JavaScript function btoa(*data*) converts file data to base-64 encoding, and there are also lots of online tools that can convert a file. The result is embedded as follows:

```
url("data:image/jpeg;base64,base64-encoded JPEG file");
```

For different file formats, replace the JPEG media type (image/jpeg) as needed.

Using SVG Effects Within CSS

We have already seen, in Chapter 1, how an SVG presentation attribute can reference another SVG element using the url() notation. In that case, it was a fill property referencing a gradient element:

```
<use xlink:href="#light" y="80" fill="url(#red-light-off)" />
```

Other SVG style properties follow the same syntax: you define the details of the graphical effect you want to apply in the SVG markup, and then apply that effect to another element using a url() reference.

For masks, clipping paths, and filters (which we'll discuss in Chapters 15 and 16), these graphical effects can now also be applied to non-SVG content in the latest web browsers. Proposed new CSS modules would also allow SVG gradients and patterns to be used directly as image sources or text fill.

To reference a graphical effect, use a URL that contains a # targeting the reference to a specific element's id.

Theoretically, the URL for most effect properties can reference an element in a different file, either as a local relative URL or an absolute URL (e.g., to a content-delivery network serving up your static image assets). However, browser support for cross-file references varies, and depends on the property.

Even when external files are supported, you can't just reference an SVG filter or mask from someone else's website (a cross-*origin* reference). We talk more about cross-origin issues in "File Management" on page 341.

If the URL is either a local target fragment like url(#filter), or a relative file path like url("../assets/filters.svg#blur"), the URL will be resolved relative to the file that contains the CSS rule. This means that local target fragments can only be used for <style> blocks, inline styles, and presentation attributes—never an external stylesheet, which cannot contain valid SVG elements.

The location of relative URLs, *including* local target fragments, will also be affected by the HTML <base> tag and by xml:base attributes, which instruct the browser to treat all relative URLs as being relative to a different web address.

 SVG 2 and the latest CSS specs propose special rules for URLs that *only* have a target fragment (i.e., they start with a # character), so that they would not be affected by <base> change, and they could be used in external stylesheets. However, browser support isn't consistent yet, and some of the specification details may still change.

With SVG graphical effects, combining many effects into a single file is not a problem: the URL references always target a specific element. Unfortunately, for the time being that file is usually your main web page, not a reusable asset file.

CSS Versus SVG

This chapter has so far emphasized the ways in which CSS and SVG are interdependent and complementary. However, there are also many ways in which the two are contradictory and competitive. As CSS has expanded to include more graphical options, it has included many features that were previously the exclusive domain of SVG, such as gradients, complex shapes, and animation.

Although some of the new CSS graphical effects have been coordinated with work on SVG, others have implemented completely new rules and syntax. As a result, switching between CSS graphics and SVG can be confusing.

Styling Documents Versus Drawing Graphics

The tension between CSS and SVG is driven by their differing goals of formatting documents versus rendering graphics. Both are involved in handling layout; both control the incorporation of images, colors, and patterns; and both determine how text gets rendered. It's easy to get lost in the overlap; some CSS properties work in SVG just the same as in HTML, while others are completely different.

It helps to focus on the different purposes of the two languages.

CSS was designed to describe the presentation of text documents. It assumes that most of the elements in the document contain text. CSS rules define the regions of the web page in which the text should be arranged (layout boxes), the decoration of those boxes, and the styling of the text itself. For the most part, the text is treated as a continuous stream that can be wrapped from one line to another to fit within the layout boxes. When you change the available space for each line, the layout will be rearranged: text wrapping at different points, boxes expanding to fit more or fewer lines of text, and the overall page layout shifting to accommodate them.

In contrast, SVG defines a two-dimensional graphic. There is no single flow of content that can be wrapped to a new line if there isn't enough space on this one. The entire SVG expands or contracts together, preserving the relative positions of all the elements in both horizontal and vertical directions.

The shape and position of SVG elements are a fundamental part of their meaning and purpose. In contrast, the fundamental meaning of HTML elements is contained in their text content and the semantic meaning associated with the HTML tags; the shape and position of the CSS layout boxes is (usually) pure decoration.

When you add a border to a CSS layout box, it takes up extra space around the outside of the box, and the layout adjusts to accommodate it. In contrast, when you add a stroke to an SVG shape, it is positioned exactly centered over the geometric edge of the shape. If that stroke overlaps something else, it's up to you to decide whether to move or resize the shapes to accommodate it; the browser makes no assumptions about why you're drawing graphics in the particular places you specify.

Many other syntax differences come from this difference between styling independent, flexible boxes versus drawing graphics that are explicitly positioned by *x*- and *y*-coordinates. Even for the CSS features that have been adapted from SVG, such as transformations (Chapter 11) or masks (Chapter 15), new rules were required to apply the effects to elements that aren't part of a fixed coordinate system.

Nonetheless, although CSS layout and style properties were created to format text documents, they can just as easily be applied to empty elements in order to construct purely graphical content. It is with this usage that CSS becomes a direct competitor to SVG.

CSS as a Vector Graphics Language

As described in Chapter 1, vector graphics describe where and how a computer should draw an image, rather than describing the pixelated result. In this way, the combination of an HTML document plus CSS stylesheet can be seen as a vector language; together, they describe how the browser should display the web page.

Most web pages do not use the precise coordinate-system layout usually associated with vector graphics. However, CSS absolute positioning can be used to provide coordinate-like positioning, placing elements at a certain point on the page regardless of the flowing layout of the text. CSS also allows you to set the width and height of elements exactly, regardless of the width available or the height required to display their text content.

With these properties—and the many styles available to decorate CSS boxes with borders, backgrounds, and more—CSS can turn a nested series of HTML elements into a vector graphic. Example 3-3 uses CSS and HTML to recreate the original, primary-color stoplight from Chapter 1. Figure 3-3 shows the result, which is very close to Figure 1-1.

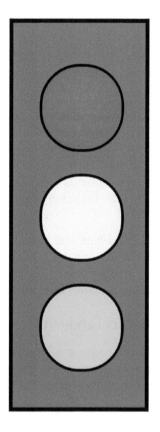

Figure 3-3. The CSS vector graphic stoplight

Example 3-3. Drawing a simple stoplight, with CSS and HTML

HTML MARKUP:

```
<!DOCTYPE html>
<html lang="en">
<head>
    <title>Stoplight Drawn Using CSS Styles</title>
    <style>
        /* Style rules go here (or as an external stylesheet) */
    </style>
</head>
<body>
    <figure aria-label="A stoplight">                        ❶
        <div class="stoplight-frame" >                        ❷
            <div class="stoplight-light red" ></div>          ❸
            <div class="stoplight-light yellow" ></div>
            <div class="stoplight-light green" ></div>       ❹
        </div>
    </figure>
</body>
</html>
```

❶ An HTML5 `<figure>` element is used to group the elements that will be part of the graphic. An `aria-label` attribute adds a text description for accessibility purposes.

❷ The frame and the lights are each `<div>` elements; by default, these will be displayed as independent boxes, but they have no other meaning or default styles. A class attribute is used so that the custom styles can be applied in the stylesheet.

❸ The three elements that will represent the lights are contained inside the element that will represent the frame; unlike SVG shapes, HTML `<div>` elements can be nested, which allows you to position smaller elements relative to the boundaries of larger components.

❹ Each light has been given two class names: one (`stoplight-light`) will be used to assign the common features (size and shape); the other (e.g., `green`) will be used to assign the unique features (color and position).

CSS STYLES:

```css
figure {                              ❶
    margin: 0;
    padding: 0;
}
.stoplight-frame {                    ❷
    margin: 20px;
    width: 100px;
    height: 280px;
    background-color: blue;
    border: solid black 3px;
    position: relative;               ❸
}
.stoplight-light {                    ❹
    width: 60px;
    height: 60px;
    border-radius: 30px;
    border: solid black 2px;
    position: absolute;               ❺
    left: 20px;
}
.stoplight-light.red {                ❻
    background-color: red;
    top: 30px;
}
.stoplight-light.yellow {
    background-color: yellow;
    top: 110px;
}
.stoplight-light.green {
    background-color: #40CC40;
    top: 190px;
}
```

❶ Most browsers inset `<figure>` elements relative to the rest of the text; here, the margin and padding are reset so that positions of the graphic components will be relative to the browser window.

❷ The element with class `stoplight-frame` is offset from the edge of the window using margin spacing, then is given a fixed width and height. It is filled in using `background-color` and given a stroke-like effect with `border`.

❸ The stoplight frame element is also given the `position: relative` property. This does not affect the display of this component, but it defines the component as the reference coordinate system for its absolutely positioned child elements.

❹ All three of the elements representing the lights will share the .stoplight-light styles. The width and height make the element square; then, border-radius rounds it into a circle and border adds a stroke effect.

❺ The light elements are set to use absolute positioning, then the left property sets the horizontal position of each light as an offset from the left edge of the frame element.

❻ Each individual light has its color set according to its class. The vertical position is set with the top property, again as an offset from the frame element.

The example may be simple, but it demonstrates some common features in CSS vector graphics:

- Although CSS elements are by default rectangular, the border-radius feature can be used to create circles or ellipses.
- You can position elements using margin and padding, but it is usually more reliable to position them absolutely.
- You can use one element as the reference frame for absolutely positioning other elements by nesting them in the HTML, by giving it a nondefault position value.

In Chapter 12, we will expand upon this simple stoplight example to recreate the gradient effects from Figure 1-4 using CSS gradients.

Which to Choose?

If you can create vector graphics with CSS, why bother learning SVG? It really depends on what type of graphics you're trying to create.

For advanced graphics, SVG has the undoubted advantage. CSS can create simple rectangles and circles, but other shapes require clipping paths (which aren't well supported) or complex nested structures. There is also much better browser support for graphical effects in SVG, and more flexible options for decorative text.

For graphical decorations on a text document, however, CSS styling may provide a simple solution. For a simple background gradient, styling with CSS is easier than creating a separate SVG file, encoding it, and embedding it as a data URI in your CSS file. By taking advantage of the ::before and ::after pseudoelements available on most elements, you can create moderately complex decorations such as turned-down corners, menu icons, or stylistic dividing rules.

 The ::before and ::after pseudoelements do not apply to "replaced content" such as images, form input elements, or SVG content. They *do* apply to other void (always empty) HTML elements such as <hr/> (horizontal rule), which is rendered using the CSS layout model.

When the CSS graphic requires more than the three layout boxes you can create from a single element, simplicity is compromised. Creating a scaffolding of HTML elements to represent each part of the graphic, as we did in Example 3-3, divides your graphical code between the CSS and the markup. Although the same could be said about inline SVG graphics with external stylesheets, it is generally easier to distinguish SVG graphical markup from the rest of the HTML content of the web page. SVG's <use> element, in particular, makes it easier to organize your graphical markup into a single section of your HTML file.

Compatibility adds another layer of complexity. For the most part, browsers either support SVG or they don't; certain effects may not always render the same, but the geometric structure will be consistent. In contrast, when you're building CSS vectors, the geometric appearance often depends on relatively recent features of the language. Without support for border-radius, the stoplight would have been barely recognizable.

This book focuses on SVG, and so it will for the most part emphasize the SVG way of creating vector graphics. However, this is also intended to be a practical reference for web designers, so the question of CSS versus SVG will be revisited regularly throughout the rest of the book. Whenever an SVG feature is introduced that has a CSS counterpart, the two will be compared and contrasted to highlight the key differences in how they work.

Summary: Working with CSS

CSS and SVG have an interdependent relationship, which has both been enhanced and complicated by the development of level 3 CSS specifications.

CSS3 is big, consisting of more than two dozen different documents representing new functionality beyond what is supported in CSS 2.1. There are specifications covering animations, 2D and 3D transformations, transitions, text to speech, print layout, advanced selectors, and more. Throughout this book, where appropriate, each chapter will cover the CSS capabilities in comparison with SVG features.

It's worth noting that the CSS specifications are a perpetual work in progress. One of the key roles of this chapter was to point out features that were available and relevant to SVG. If you are working with advanced CSS features, it is always worth spending some time looking at the current state of work on CSS specifications at the W3C (*http://www.w3.org/Style/CSS/current-work*) and experimenting to see what is and is not implemented in your target browsers.

When you're using CSS to style SVG content, new CSS features such as media queries can increase the functionality and flexibility of your graphics. Browsers use the same CSS parser and selector-matching implementations for SVG as for HTML. So you can use these new CSS features in your SVG files, in any web browser that supports them, even though they did not exist at the time the SVG 1.1 specifications were finalized. The future-focused CSS error-handling rules allow you to define limited fallback options for software that has not implemented the latest features. The `@supports` rule allows more nuanced control.

SVG has also become an important part of CSS styling for text documents. This chapter has discussed the use of complete SVG images in CSS; other chapters will explore the SVG graphical effects, which can now be used in the latest browsers to manipulate the appearance of HTML content.

At the same time, CSS3 has developed alternatives to many SVG features, so that you can use it to directly create vector graphics from empty elements in your HTML code. This chapter has given a hint of the possibilities. By the end of the book, you should have a clearer understanding of what is possible with CSS and HTML alone, and what is made much easier with SVG.

CHAPTER 4

Tools of the Trade

Software and Sources to Make SVG Easier

The SVG examples in this book were for the most part created "from scratch," with the markup or standard JavaScript being typed into a code editor. However, that's certainly not the only way to work with SVG, nor the most common one.

Most SVG drawings and original art start their life inside some kind of graphical software, created by an artist or designer working with shapes and colors rather than XML tags and attributes.

Most SVG data visualizations are created with JavaScript, and visualization libraries offer different degrees of abstraction between the author and the SVG code.

In most projects, SVG icons are imported from existing icon sets, with the SVG files manipulated entirely by project build scripts.

By showing you the internal components of an SVG, stripped down to their skeletal form, we hope to give you a complete toolset to work with SVG: the skills to modify and extend *any* SVG you work with, no matter how it was created. With this programmatic approach to SVG, you will be better able to manipulate graphics created by others or by software, in order to match your web design or to enable user interaction. But this mental toolset you'll gain by understanding SVG shouldn't detract from the software tools that other developers have created.

Software tools make it easier to create graphics and process files so they are ready to deploy on your web server and display on your pages. The tools discussed in this chapter include:

- graphical editors that emphasize visual components rather than code
- code editors that provide hints and immediate feedback
- libraries that streamline the creation of dynamic graphics with JavaScript
- rendering programs that display the SVG or convert it into other image formats

In addition, we introduce the vast panoply of free and licensable SVG content that can help you quickly enhance your web development process and designs, even if your personal artistic skills don't extend beyond stick figures.

This chapter specifically mentions some of the most popular software and services. These are not the only options, and we don't guarantee they are the best. They are given as examples of what is out there, and of how different options vary from one another. When choosing tools for your own projects, think about the features you need, and the budget you can afford.

Whatever you choose, remember that any standards-compliant SVG file can usually be opened and modified with other SVG tools, so you're not locked into the workflow of a particular product or vendor.

Ready-to-Use SVG

The easiest way to get started with SVG—especially if you're more of a programmer than a graphic designer—is to start with someone else's art. SVG may not be as ubiquitous on the web as other image formats, but it's getting there.

The simplest method is to start searching for your term of interest plus "SVG," which will yield a broad result in most search engines. For more precision, you will want to refine your search: Google Images (*http://images.google.com*) is a good start, although you can refine your search by using the "Search tools" option and choosing "Line Art" or "Clip Art" under the "Type" menu option. Alternatively, typing *"subject* file type:SVG" directly into Google will also work.

Prior to using clip art from a vendor or website, you should ascertain what license it is provided under. Early SVG was mostly produced within open source communities, with graphics often released under a Creative Commons license (*https://creativecom mons.org/*), but today, high-quality SVG artwork is produced by professional artists expecting to be compensated for their work.

Although there are plenty of free-to-use graphics available (some with noncommercial restrictions or attribution requirements), others are offered under paid license systems similar to those used for stock photos or web fonts.

 One benefit of SVG's dual nature as both an image format and an XML format is that it is possible to embed copyright license information directly in the file using a <metadata> block. We'll discuss how you can do this for your own graphics in Chapter 17.

For accessing graphics created by others, remember that creative works are by default "all rights reserved"; the *absence* of a copyright declaration does not mean a work is public domain. Don't use someone else's work unless you are sure that the original creator has offered a license compatible with your intended use.

SVG will never replace JPEG for stock photographs (which can't be efficiently represented in vectors), but it is now a standard option for vector graphic clip art and icons, including those provided by commercial suppliers.

There are a number of tools and libraries that can convert simple SVG art into other vector formats and back again. This can increase the flexibility of the vector graphics: for example, the encapsulated PostScript (EPS) format, long a staple in the realm of clip art, is still dominant in print. For simpler graphics, icon fonts—which allow sets of single-color icons to be distributed as a web font file—are popular because they allow icon size and color to be controlled with familiar CSS properties. Nonetheless, companies that produce clip art, maps, and related graphics for the web are increasingly shifting to SVG for their vector graphic format.

Using a vector graphic as a source file, stock art companies can generate raster images (PNG, JPEG, and GIF) of any size on demand. For a web designer interested in purchasing raster graphics, however, it often makes more sense to license a single SVG and convert it into the required raster format at the needed resolutions yourself, rather than purchasing raster graphics at different scales.

The following sites should help start you on your search for SVG:

Open Clip Art Project
The Open Clip Art Library (OCAL) Project is definitely the oldest, and perhaps the largest, repository of SVG content, all of it available either through Creative Commons or public domain licenses for unrestricted commercial use.

Figure 4-1. Samples from the Open Clip Art Library: on the left, Simple Farm Animals 2 *by user Viscious Speed; on the right, line drawings from Sir Robert Baden-Powell's 1922 book* An Old Wolf's Favourites, *converted to SVG by user Johnny Automatic*

Established in 2004 by Jon Phillips and Bryce Harrington, the OCAL project was created to provide a public commons for clip art, using SVG for encoding primarily because the format typically doesn't have the same type of vendor encumbrances or royalty restrictions as other proprietary formats. Moreover, because the source code for the graphics can be read with a text editor, it's also possible to decompose clip art images into separate pieces, making SVG useful as a way of packaging collections of icons or images in a single file. Figure 4-1 displays some of the diverse artistic styles available.

The project is also integrated with the Flaming Text ImageBot graphics editor (*http://www.flamingtext.com/imagebot/editor*), which allows you to tweak some SVG style properties online.

Wikimedia Commons

The media repository arm of Wikipedia, Wikimedia Commons compiles images, audio, and video in a wide variety of formats. All files are available under some sort of "copyleft" license; some require attribution or are restricted to noncommercial use or to use within similarly licensed work. Detailed license information is available on each file's catalogue page.

Wikimedia is actively pushing their contributors to use the SVG format for diagrams, clip art, icons, and other vector drawings because of its flexibility and ease of editing; their servers then automatically generate raster versions in various sizes. The tagging and cataloguing of files on Wikipedia is often inconsistent, making searching a little difficult. But there is plenty of great SVG content if you take the time to look around. Figure 4-2 displays selections from the SVG Botanical Illustrations category, including a labeled diagram; because SVG files are easily editable, the file is available with labels in many languages.

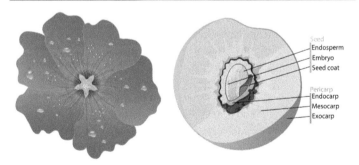

Figure 4-2. SVG from Wikimedia Commons: on the left, a hollyhock flower by user Ozgurel; on the right, a labeled diagram of a peach by Mariana Ruiz Villarreal (aka LadyofHats)

SVG is used for most maps, logos, and diagrams on Wikipedia.

Iconic

Iconic is a commercial SVG icon library, but they offer a set of more than 200 icons completely free to use (MIT license; you must ensure that license information is available in the file). This Open Iconic set includes most common user interface buttons in single-element icons that you style to any color you choose. For their paid offerings, Iconic distinguishes themselves by taking full advantage of all the possibilities of SVG, supporting multicolor styling and using scripts to substitute in more detailed versions of the icons at larger sizes. They even brag about their easy-to-read (and modify) XML markup.

The Noun Project

Another icon-focused library, the Noun Project aims to create a visual language for clear international communication. Access to their entire library is by monthly subscription, but their database includes many public domain and Creative Commons–licensed icons, which users can search by concept using tags in dozens of languages.

 Typically, SVG in the wild is stored as text-based XML files. However, the SVG standards allow for Gzip-compressed SVG—typically having a *.svgz* filename extension—to reduce the file size. This is common for high-quality, photo-realistic SVG files, which can occasionally get to be bigger than their PNG counterparts, and for maps and other complex charts that embed a lot of metadata within the graphics themselves. However, using *.svgz* on the web can be tricky. Even if you get your server configuration correct, browsers can get it wrong if the user then saves the received file.

File compression should nonetheless always be used by a performance-minded web developer (that's you!) to compress an SVG, HTML, or CSS file for transmission from web server to browser—either with Gzip or the newer Brotli algorithm. The compression is usually applied through web server settings, and is indicated via HTTP headers, rather than with a file extension.

Ready-to-use graphics can solve many web design problems. For common interface icons, creating your own graphics may often feel like reinventing the wheel.

But for other projects, or other graphic types, stock art just won't do. You need to create a custom image that perfectly represents a new and unique concept. It takes a little more artistic skill, but there are plenty of tools for creating your own SVG art. After all, that's how most of the graphics in these collections were created in the first place.

Click, Drag, Draw: Graphical SVG Editors

Once upon a time, one of the biggest issues facing adoption of the Scalable Vector Graphics standard was the lack of decent tools for creating SVG graphics. Most SVG needed to be coded by hand, or—if that was too daunting—to be converted from other proprietary graphical standards. This reliance on converted graphics meant that the full features of SVG weren't always used.

On the other side, many vector graphics editors include features that are not part of the standard SVG specification. To ensure that this extra information and features are retained when you save and reload the SVG (a process called "round-tripping"), these programs either have separate, proprietary image formats (like Adobe Illustrator's *.ai* format) or add extra markup to the SVG file (as Inkscape does). To create graphics that will display consistently with other software, these programs also include commands that will "flatten" the extra features into standard SVG 1.1.

If you are creating SVG for the web, always ensure that you export the final version of your graphic in standard SVG. Without this step, the file may be many times larger than the "pure" SVG version. This will slow your site and complicate any future code you try to write.

 You can often fix a bloated, proprietary SVG export with an optimization tool (discussed in "Processing and Packaging" on page 133). But it's always better to make the most of the web-export tools from the original software first.

There are now numerous graphical applications that can export files as SVG; this section lists just a sample.

The common feature of these apps is the visual, what-you-see-is-what-you-get (WYSIWYG) editor, where you can position shapes with your mouse (or stylus, or finger) and select colors from on-screen palettes. They differ in the range of SVG features they support, and in how easy they are to use. We offer some tips and warnings about how to get web-quality output from each.

Adobe Illustrator

Adobe Illustrator is the granddaddy of vector graphics programs, and debuted in 1987. Illustrator not only set the expectations of what a vector graphics program should look like, but has consistently been at the cutting edge of vector graphics support for the past two decades.

Many aspects of SVG were inspired by the capabilities of Illustrator, and Illustrator has long supported export of its graphics to SVG format. However, it's definitely worth remembering that SVG is not a native format for the application (the *.ai* format is). This means that Illustrator must perform a conversion from its internal vector graphics format (built primarily around PostScript) to SVG. For comparatively simple graphics, this is a straightforward process, but it is possible to create Illustrator images that have poor fidelity and large file sizes when rendered to SVG, with the application replacing complex vectors with embedded bitmap images.

The basic save-as-SVG option in Illustrator creates a complex file from which the native graphic can be reconstructed. However, a much more streamlined export-as-SVG option was introduced in Adobe Illustrator CC 2015, which creates a vector graphic optimized for the web.

In the latest (CC, or Creative Cloud) versions of Illustrator, you can also copy individual graphics components from Illustrator and paste them into a text editor; the corresponding SVG code will be pasted. (If it doesn't work, look for the "On Copy: Include SVG Code" option in the "File Handling and Clipboard" settings.) Alternatively, you can select "Copy to SVG" from the right-click context menu of a layer; this is your only option if the selected object is text (copying a text element normally just copies the text content).

Copying and pasting markup for individual elements is useful if you're building a complex application or animation in SVG. You can use the visual editor to draw shapes, without having Illustrator mangle the rest of your markup.

Avoid using "Illustrator filters" in your graphic, as the application doesn't yet translate them well into SVG; use the "SVG filters" instead. Similarly, blending modes (Multiply, Dissolve, etc.) aren't yet translated into SVG-compatible CSS blend modes (as described in Chapter 16). If you use these, remove them before export and then edit the CSS yourself to add them back in. Finally, be sure all stroked shapes use centered strokes, as inside/outside strokes are not yet supported in SVG.

Adobe Photoshop

The most recent (CC) versions of Adobe Photoshop can also export SVG documents. While Photoshop is primarily a bitmap (raster image) editor, it supports vector shapes and text, making this a useful option to be aware of.

To export SVG from Photoshop, name the layer or group with the intended name of the file: for example, *icon.svg*. Then, use File → Generate → Image Assets.

The generated SVG document will be exported into a folder provided with the name of the originating PSD file, with your named SVG documents inside the folder. By default, this folder will appear on your desktop, although you can change this in Photoshop's preferences.

At the time of writing, there are several features of the exported SVG file to keep in mind:

- The exported SVG is responsive (it has a `viewBox` attribute on the root `<svg>` element) but with default sizes (it also has `width` and `height` attributes).

- The `viewBox` is automatically cropped to the edges of the largest vector shape in the current design.

- Elements are given their own unique classes in an embedded style in the SVG.

- Any bitmap images will be turned into inline base-64 data URIs in the SVG.

As an alternative to generating an SVG as an image asset, you can use Photoshop's File → Export options, including setting up preferences to make SVG the default "Quick Export" option. One upside of the image assets approach is that Photoshop will automatically update the exported SVG with any changes made to the original PSD document. It's expected that Adobe Illustrator will offer similar functionality in the near future.

The open-source alternative to Photoshop, GIMP (the GNU Image Manipulation Program) also has some vector features and SVG export of certain graphic components. GIMP's SVG export is optimized for readability, which is great if you're going to be manipulating it in a code editor—but less so if you are worried about minimizing file sizes.

Sketch

Sketch is a Mac-only program that has proved extremely popular with user interface designers. Unfortunately, the SVG export capabilities (at the time of writing) are stuck where Adobe Illustrator was five years ago…although that's not to say that the result can't be improved and cleaned up.

First, Sketch must be informed that a shape can be exported as SVG: you'll find this option at the bottom of the properties panel for a selected shape. Sketch will deliver each shape as its own separate SVG file, unless multiple shapes are merged.

By default, Sketch applies stroke to elements on the inside, which (as previously discussed) SVG does not yet support. The latest versions adjust your path sizes to match the stroke; for more predictable export, ensure that Sketch's preferences are set to stroke paths in their center.

A typical export of SVG code for a simple path will include a lot of extraneous code; Sketch adds its own proprietary code in the output, under the sketch namespace.

To create the cleanest possible SVG output from Sketch, adhere to the same rules we established for Illustrator, with a few additions:

- Create an artboard for each drawing (Insert → Artboard), and one drawing (such as an icon) per artboard.
- Remove any bounding boxes from the drawing.
- Don't attempt to rotate your drawing in Sketch before export, as doing so will (in current versions) significantly distort the SVG export.

Following these rules will eliminate many of the current issues with SVG export from Sketch, but not all of them; you may have more success copying and pasting Sketch drawing objects into another vector application, such as Illustrator.

Inkscape and Sodipodi

Sodipodi was one of the earliest SVG editors, initially developed for Linux systems. It drew its inspiration from Adobe Illustrator, but used SVG natively to store and retrieve content. Inkscape (*http://www.inkscape.org*) started as a branch of Sodipodi, and is now the more actively developed program.

Inkscape has matured into a remarkably sophisticated, feature-rich vector graphics application, while never losing sight of its SVG roots. It is available for Linux, Windows, and Mac, but the Mac version relies on the XQuartz adapter (for running Unix-based software on Mac), and can be difficult to use.

The interface (Figure 4-3) is somewhat crowded with features, but if you put in a little effort to learn all the options it allows for considerable control over the graphic. In addition to supporting most static SVG features, it includes numerous filters and extensions to create graphical effects. There are also controls that allow you to edit nongraphical aspects of the SVG, such as element IDs, alternative text, and even simple JavaScript event handling. You can also inspect the XML file and edit nodes and attributes directly.

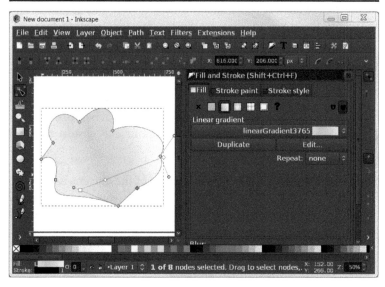

Figure 4-3. The open source Inkscape graphics editor

There are a few features in Inkscape that can make SVG exports easier:

- Use File → "Clean up document" to remove unused `<defs>` elements.

- If you are copying an element for use elsewhere in the same drawing, create a Clone (Edit → Clone), which generates a `<use>` reference to the original element. This reduces output code size and makes later editing far easier.

- Use Path → Simplify to reduce the number of points in an overdrawn element, further reducing file size.

Inkscape uses SVG as its own native format, but with extra application-specific data in its own XML namespaces. In addition, Inkscape implemented some features of SVG 1.2, particularly multiline text boxes, which were never widely supported by browsers; be sure to convert your text boxes to fixed-position SVG text when exporting for the web.

When saving your file, you'll need to be very clear exactly what kind of SVG you are saving from Inkscape: "Inkscape" SVG, with its extra embedded code, or "plain" SVG. Inkscape also has an "Optimized SVG" option.

For the web, you either want the plain version or the optimized version; if you use the optimized option, consider the export settings carefully so you don't accidentally remove content that you need for later styling or scripting.

Draw SVG

Draw SVG (*http://draw-svg.appspot.com/*) is a comprehensive online SVG editor, developed primarily by Joseph Liard. It is under active development, with intent to support SVG 2 features as they become supported by browsers, and performance has significantly improved since we first reviewed it. Figure 4-4 shows the interface.

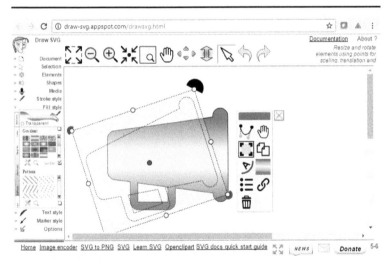

Figure 4-4. The Draw SVG free online SVG graphics editor

Draw SVG implements essentially all the SVG drawing and styling features commonly supported by browsers (except animation). It even supports HTML `<foreignObject>` content for embedding audio, video, or formatted text paragraphs, and multilingual text using the `<switch>` element.

The interface uses standard SVG terminology for attributes and style properties, which is helpful if you will be alternating between using a graphics editor and writing the code yourself. You can add

IDs and classes to elements, and set the language attribute for text, although at the time of writing it does not seem to support alternative text (e.g., <title>). Drawing complex curved shapes can be nonintuitive if you're used to the instant feedback of other drawing tools.

The application also offers tools to create rasterized versions of the SVG, and to encode raster images as embedded data URIs.

There are now many other browser-based online SVG editors, some with more features than others, but all of which use the web browser to convert the code to graphics. We already mentioned the Flaming Text ImageBot editor that is paired with the Open Clip Art Library; the commercial Vecteezy clip art library has their own online SVG editor, which is free to use as a stand-alone SVG editor.

Boxy SVG

A different approach to a browser-based SVG editor, Boxy SVG (*https://boxy-svg.com/*) is a full graphical editor in the form of a Chrome plug-in; in use, it is indistinguishable from a desktop application. A website demo works in any web browser. It has an attractive interface and excellent support for SVG features, including new features such as blend modes. Equally importantly, it is being actively developed.

More Online

Nearly all of the SVG editors described in this section can also convert SVG graphics to raster images, or other vector formats. This can be useful to create fallbacks for old browsers, or to create consistent rendering for print publications.

However, manually saving files in multiple formats from a graphics editor can be tedious. On many web server setups, you can automate the process using dedicated rasterization and conversion tools.

Read more in "SVG Snapshots: Converting Vector to Raster":

https://oreillymedia.github.io/Using_SVG/extras/ch04-rasterizers.html

---

Bringing SVG Alive: SVG in the Web Browser

To see and use the full power of SVG, as more than just an image, you need a dynamic SVG viewer that can update the graphic according to user interaction or timed animations. And if you're building SVG for the web, it's best to test it in web browsers as early and often as possible.

When discussing web browser support for SVG, it helps to group the browsers according to the **rendering engine** (drawing code) that they use. Many of the engines are open source; numerous other tools use the same code. Different applications using the same rendering engines *usually* display web pages and SVG in the same way. For that reason, we focus on the major browser rendering engines (Chrome/Blink, Safari/WebKit, Firefox/Gecko, Internet Explorer, and Microsoft EdgeHTML) in all the browser support warnings in the book.

Knowing the rendering engine also tells you which prefixes were used for experimental CSS features. CSS prefixes are going out of fashion—all the major browsers have pledged not to introduce new prefixed CSS properties for web content—but some features are still only supported in some browsers with a prefixed syntax.

Conversely, some of the most widely used prefixed properties have now been adopted by all new browsers as deprecated synonyms for the standard CSS. Content creators should, of course, use the unprefixed versions.

If you need to add prefixes to support older browsers, use a dedicated software tool to make the conversion. Of course, you should also make sure your designs still function if a feature isn't supported at all—so you may find that prefixes aren't worth the hassle.

New features are now usually enabled with experimental browser modes (or "flags") controlled by the user.

This section reviews the history of the main rendering engines when it comes to SVG, and summarizes major support issues. However— with the exception of Presto and Trident—the browser SVG implementations are all under active development. Feature support may have changed by the time you read this. Consult the version release notes or the issue-tracking databases for the various browsers to determine if a specific feature is now supported.

Gecko for Firefox

The first web browser implementation of SVG was built within the Gecko rendering engine in 2003. Gecko, originally built for Netscape 6, is the basis of the Mozilla Firefox browser as well as numerous niche browsers and tools.

The original SVG implementation was basic, focusing on simple vector shapes. However, it has expanded steadily and continues to improve. Until around 2014, dynamic SVG could be slow and jerky in Firefox; however, significant performance improvements have been made and some animations are now smoother in Firefox than in other browsers.

There are still some areas where Firefox/Gecko does not conform to the SVG specifications in the finer details, particularly around the way `<use>` elements are handled. The rendering engine also did not initially implement many of the style properties that offer nuanced control of the layout of SVG text; some of these features are now (mid-2017) being implemented in coordination with enhancements to CSS-styled HTML text. SVG rendering may also differ slightly between operating systems, as Firefox uses low-level graphical rendering tools from the operating system to improve the performance of some actions.

Experimental CSS features for Gecko used the `-moz-` (for Mozilla) prefix; since mid-2016, Firefox also supports the most common `-webkit-` properties.

WebKit for Safari and iOS Devices

Apple's Safari browser was built upon open source rendering and JavaScript engines originally created for the KDE operating system (for Linux/Unix computers). Apple's branch of the code—known as WebKit—is used in all Apple devices and was also originally the basis for the Google Chrome browser, among many other tools. WebKit is also used in the PhantomJS browser simulator.

WebKit implemented most SVG 1.1 features between 2008 and 2010; many edge cases or areas of poor performance remain, but for most purposes it is a complete implementation. Up until recently, many CSS3 features required a `-webkit-` prefix on Safari and related software, leading to the proliferation of those prefixes in the wild. However, the development team has now committed to transitioning away from prefixes, and Safari 9 and 10 support unprefixed versions of the most commonly used properties, such as those for animations and transforms.

On iOS (the operating system used by iPhone and iPad), *all* web browsers and apps use WebKit, even Firefox and Chrome. It's a requirement of the Apple App Store.

Blink for Newer Versions of Chrome, Opera, and Android Devices

In 2013, Google's Chromium project announced that they would no longer synchronize further development with the WebKit project. The Google Chrome browser at that point used WebKit code to render web pages (and SVG) but had separate code for other functions including JavaScript processing.

The branch of the rendering engine, developed as part of the Chromium project, is now known as Blink. In addition to being used by Chrome, Blink is used in the Opera browser (since version 13) and in native applications on newer Android devices. It is also used by other new browsers, such as Vivaldi and Brave, and by the Samsung Internet browser on Samsung Android devices.

Blink browsers still support `-webkit-` CSS properties, although not necessarily those introduced since the split. They have user settings (flags) to allow developers test out their own new features.

Initial development of the Google Chrome browser (and now Blink in general) was heavily focused on performance; animations are generally fast and smooth (although Firefox has since caught up). Some edge-case features are not supported, particularly in areas where the SVG specifications work differently from CSS and HTML. Blink has removed support for SVG fonts from most platforms, and the development team has indicated that they would eventually like to deprecate SVG animation elements (SMIL animation) in favor of CSS or scripted animations.

Presto for Older Opera Versions and Opera Mini

The Opera browser previously used its own proprietary rendering engine, known as Presto. It is still used for server-side rendering for the Opera Mini browser, converting web pages to much simpler compressed files for transmission to mobile devices with low computing power or expensive and slow internet connections. In Opera Mini, SVG is supported as static images, but not as interactive applications.

Presto supports nearly all of the SVG 1.1 specifications and some CSS3 properties. However, it has not been (and will not likely be) substantially updated since 2013. Furthermore, Opera Mini has intentionally chosen not to implement many decorative CSS effects that require too much memory or computation to recreate on a low-power mobile phone. Opera Mini does support the @supports rule (see Chapter 3), so you can use that to adjust your styles if necessary.

Presto versions of Opera used an -o- prefix for experimental CSS features, but it is unlikely to be useful in modern websites.

Trident for Internet Explorer and Other Windows Programs

Internet Explorer was the last major browser to introduce SVG support. Prior to the development of the SVG standard, Microsoft had introduced its own XML vector graphics language (the Vector Markup Language, or VML), used in Microsoft Office software and supported in Internet Explorer since version 5.

Basic SVG support was introduced (and VML phased out) with Internet Explorer version 9 in 2009. Support for additional SVG features, such as filters, was added in subsequent versions. Nonetheless, older Internet Explorer versions that do not support SVG (particularly Internet Explorer 8) continue to be used because newer versions of the software are not supported on older Windows operating systems. As of the end of 2016, slightly more than 0.6% of global web traffic used Internet Explorer 8, a steady drop from previous years but still a meaningful share for very large commercial websites.[1]

As of Internet Explorer 11 (the final version of the browser), there were a number of small quirks and bugs in SVG support, and some features that were not supported at all. The main area where Internet Explorer does not match the other web browsers is animation: there is no support for either SVG animation elements or CSS

---

[1] Data from *http://gs.statcounter.com*

animation applied to SVG graphics. Another key missing feature is the <foreignObject> element, which allows HTML content to be embedded in an SVG graphic.

The Trident rendering engine used for Internet Explorer is also used in other Microsoft programs and by some third-party software built for Windows devices. It used the -ms- CSS prefix, but there are only a few properties where prefixes make a difference.

EdgeHTML for Microsoft Edge and Windows 10+ Programs

The Microsoft Edge browser developed for Windows 10 uses a new rendering engine, built from a clean codebase to emphasize performance and cross-browser interoperability. The EdgeHTML engine is also used by other software in Windows 10.

Edge supports all the web standards supported in Internet Explorer, and many new ones. Collaboration from Adobe developers helped advance support for a number of graphics and visual effects features. Support for SVG <foreignObject> and CSS animations of SVG content has already been introduced, as has tabindex in SVG. The development team has indicated that they intend to implement many other SVG2/CSS3 features. However, plans to eventually support SVG animation elements were shelved after the Chromium project announced their deprecation plans.

Edge uses two version numbers: one for the application interface version, and one for the EdgeHTML rendering engine. This book uses the EdgeHTML numbers, since those are what affect web standards support.

For backward compatibility, Edge supports -ms- prefixed properties that were supported in Internet Explorer, and also introduced support for some -webkit- prefixes that are commonly used in existing websites. However, you shouldn't normally be adding prefixes for MS Edge support.

Servo

The Mozilla foundation is sponsoring the development of a new browser rendering engine, Servo, that may one day replace Gecko at the core of Firefox. It is being built from scratch in Rust, a programming language optimized for parallel computing environments. At the time of writing, developement work on SVG rendering within Servo is at the very early stages; you can track their open issue to add support (*https://github.com/servo/servo/issues/9998*).

Other Dynamic SVG Viewers

In addition to the web browsers, there are two other dynamic SVG rendering engines that have been important in the development of SVG:

Adobe SVG viewer
As mentioned in Chapter 1, the Adobe SVG viewer—a plug-in for Internet Explorer—was one of the first and most complete SVG environments. Although it has not been developed for years, it can still be downloaded to enable SVG support on older Internet Explorer browsers. To trigger the plug-in, the SVG must be included in the page via either an <object> or an <embed> tag.

Batik Squiggle viewer
The Apache Batik project (*http://xmlgraphics.apache.org/batik/*) is a complete implementation of SVG 1.1 in Java. Batik can be used to generate and display SVG in other Java-based software, and has a rasterizer tool that can be used from the command line (or from command-line scripts). It also comes with its own dynamic SVG viewer called Squiggle for viewing SVG files from your computer or the web.

Squiggle can display SVG animation and can process JavaScript and respond to user events, including following hyperlinks to new files. Batik supports nearly all of the SVG 1.1 specification, but has not been updated for more recent CSS, DOM, and Java-Script methods. It can also be more strict, compared to browser implementations, about requiring common values to be explicitly specified in markup and in scripts.

The web browsers and other dynamic SVG viewers do not merely display an image of the SVG—they present changing, interactive SVG documents. To create such a document, you'll need to use more than the graphical editing programs presented in "Click, Drag, Draw: Graphical SVG Editors" on page 113. You'll need to look inside the SVG, and work with the underlying code.

Markup Management: Code Editors

It is possible to write SVG code in any editor that can save in a plain-text format. You can open up Notepad or something similar; type in your markup, scripts, and styles; save it with a *.svg* extension; and then open the same file in a web browser.

If you typed carefully, and didn't forget any required attributes or misspell any values, your SVG will appear onscreen, ready to be used just as you intended. However, if you're human, chances are—at least some of the time—you'll end up with XML validation errors displayed onscreen, with JavaScript errors printed to the developer's console, or simply with a graphic that doesn't look quite like you intended.

Text editors that are designed for writing code can help considerably. They can color-code the syntax so it's easy to detect a missing quotation mark or close bracket. They can also test for major syntax errors before you save. Many can autocomplete terms as you type. The options for code editors are too numerous to list here; many are available only for specific operating systems. Whatever you choose, be sure to confirm that the editor has—at a minimum—syntax rules for XML, or more preferably specific rules and hints for SVG.

Nonetheless, even the best syntax highlighting and code hints cannot help you *draw* with code. When you're working with complex shapes and graphical effects, it really helps to be able to see the graphical effect of your code as you write it. SVG preview features (often as separately installed extensions) are thankfully becoming more popular in code editors. This section covers only a few of the options.

Once you have tools that allow you to rapidly write and test your code, it becomes easier to think about SVG programmatically. Working with the code forces you to consider the graphic from the perspective of the document object model rather than simply from the perspective of its final appearance.

Atom Plus SVG Preview

A code editor developed by GitHub, Atom (*https://atom.io/*) has a friendly interface that opens up with lots of tips for new coders, but it also has many features for power users, and many more available via extensions.

For standalone SVG files, the SVG Preview extension (*https://atom.io/packages/svg-preview*) will display a live version of the SVG in the editor as you type. The preview image is currently displayed as inline SVG code; this means that minor syntax errors and missing namespaces in a half-finished file do not break the preview. Unfortunately, it also means that external files and stylesheets are not supported, and that `<style>` blocks from one preview affect another. The SVG Preview feature—and the entire editor—uses the Blink rendering engine, via GitHub's Electron framework for creating applications with web technologies. Figure 4-5 shows side-by-side views of the same SVG file in code and preview mode.

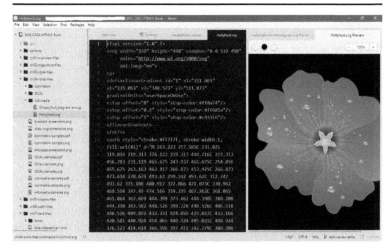

Figure 4-5. The Atom code editor with SVG Preview enabled

Brackets Plus SVG Preview

A code editor developed by Adobe primarily for web developers, Brackets (*http://brackets.io/*) includes a feature whereby you can open the web page you're working on in a browser and have it update as you type in the main editor. At the time of writing (Brackets version 1.8), the live updates only work with HTML and CSS; SVG inline in those pages is displayed, but not updated live. Nonetheless, the integrated local web server can be quite useful for testing. It needs to be started with an HTML file, but you can switch to an SVG file by editing the URL in your browser.

There is an SVG Preview extension (*https://github.com/peterflynn/ svg-preview*) for Brackets. It is independent of the Atom SVG Preview, but has many of the same features. However, it should *only* be used for static SVG images, as script errors in your code can crash the editor. Like the Atom preview, it uses inline code rendered (by Blink) within the HTML5 application, and has the same issues. However, the code for the Brackets SVG Preview is currently injected without sandbox restrictions, and inline scripts can wreak havoc. Unfortunately, there's not an easy way to turn the preview on and off. Figure 4-6 shows the editor with a live preview of SVG icons.

Despite active development of both the core Brackets code and extensions, as of early 2017 there has not been noticeable progress on SVG-focused features for a couple years. Adobe is also developing software (Adobe Extract) to allow users of their commercial design software (e.g., Photoshop) to easily generate matching web code in Brackets; however, at the time of writing this tool primarily focuses on CSS and does not include any features related to SVG or Adobe Illustrator.

Figure 4-6. The Brackets code editor with SVG Preview enabled

Oxygen XML SVG Editor

A commercial XML management program, Oxygen allows you to handle many types of XML-based data and formatting tools. The

SVG editor uses Batik to render graphics, and can render both SVG markup and SVG created via scripts. It is intended primarily for creating SVG as the result of an XSLT (eXtensible Stylesheet Language Transformation) template applied to an XML data file, but can also be used for plain SVG.

Online Live Code Sites

In recent years, numerous web applications have become available that allow you to write web code and see its output in separate frames of the same web page. Because the result is displayed right in your web page, you can use all the latest features supported by your web browser. Most make it easy to import common JavaScript code libraries. However, since you don't control the web server, other external files can often be limited by browser security restrictions.

All these sites currently work with HTML5 documents, including inline SVG elements. As with the live SVG previews for code editors, this means that they are more forgiving of syntax errors than SVG in XML files. Some live code sites worth mentioning include:

- JSFiddle was one of the first sites to offer live execution of web code that you can save to a publicly accessible web link that you can send to collaborators or reference from help forums. The stripped-down interface is best for small test cases and examples.

- CodePen is a more full-featured live code site that also serves as a social media network for web designers; you can explore other coders' work, leave comments, or publish a blog with multiple embedded working examples in each post. A paid "Pro" membership opens up additional collaboration tools and the ability to upload separate image files, scripts, or other resources.

- Tributary is specifically designed for data visualizations and other scripted SVG. By default, it provides you with a blank HTML page containing a single inline <svg> element that you can manipulate with JavaScript. You can also create separate data files accessible from the main script. The interface offers convenient tools such as visual color pickers and GIF snapshots (including animation) of your work.

When you're working on these sites, keep in mind that saving your work usually also means publishing to the web. Some sites, such as

Codepen, automatically apply a very-few-rights-reserved license to work published in this way (you can save work privately and control copyright with a paid CodePen membership).

Because the live code sites support live preview of JavaScript as well as markup, they are particularly useful when you're dealing with dynamic and interactive SVG and when creating data visualizations. If those areas interest you, the next set of tools you'll want to investigate are JavaScript tools to make manipulating the DOM easier.

Ready-to-Use Code: JavaScript Libraries

There are two ways to create an SVG by writing code: writing out the XML markup and attributes, or writing JavaScript to create the corresponding DOM elements dynamically. Scripting is preferred when you have a lot of similar elements or when the geometric attributes should be calculated based on a data file. This book uses both approaches in the examples.

There's actually a third way to code SVG (which we mentioned briefly when discussing the Oxygen XML editor): using an XSLT stylesheet applied to an XML data file.

The XSLT stylesheet is an XML file. It consists of SVG markup templates interspersed with formatting instruction elements that indicate how the data should be processed and inserted into the SVG file. XSLT is therefore another way to create SVG that should correspond with underlying data.

However, unlike with scripting, the XSL transformation can only be applied once, when the file is processed; it cannot be updated with new data or respond to user interactions. With standardized JavaScript being well supported and efficiently implemented in browsers, the use of XSLT to generate SVG is falling out of favor.

The popularity of using JavaScript for the creation and manipulation of SVG has much to do with the availability of open source tools to make this easier. These libraries of JavaScript code provide shorthand methods to perform common tasks, allowing your script to focus on graphics instead of underlying DOM function calls.

The following JavaScript libraries are particularly important for working with SVG. Learning to use these JavaScript libraries is worth a book of its own (and many great books are available). However, they don't replace an understanding of the underlying SVG graphics. It's difficult to effectively manipulate SVG with scripts unless you already know what SVG is (and isn't) capable of.

Raphaël and Snap.svg

The Raphaël library by Dmitry Baranovskiy was important in getting dynamic SVG into production web pages. It provides a single interface that can be used to create either SVG graphics or Microsoft VML graphics, depending on which one the browser supports. The library is therefore essential if you want to provide dynamic vector graphics to users of Internet Explorer 8. The number of features Raphaël supports, however, is limited to the shared features of the two vector graphics languages (SVG and VML).

The terminology used by Raphaël includes a number of convenient shorthands that do not always directly correspond to the standard SVG element and attribute names. The same terminology is used in the newer Snap.svg library, produced by Baranovskiy through his new employer, Adobe. Unlike Raphaël, Snap.svg does not include support for VML graphics. This keeps the size of the library code files down, and allows support for features such as clipping, masking, filters, and even groups, which aren't supported in VML. Snap can also load in existing SVG code, in order to manipulate complex graphics created in WYSIWYG editors. Both Snap and Raphaël have convenient functions to create smooth JavaScript animations, allowing you to animate graphics in any version of Internet Explorer.

D3.js

The D3.js library, originally developed by Mike Bostock, has become the standard tool for creating dynamic SVG data visualizations. D3 is short for *Data-Driven Documents*, and it reflects how the library works by associating JavaScript data objects with elements in the DOM.

The core D3 library is open-ended, allowing you to manipulate groups of DOM elements (SVG or HTML) simultaneously by defining how their attributes and styles should be calculated from the corresponding data objects. Changes in values can be set to smoothly transition over time to create animated effects.

D3 includes a number of convenient functions for calculating the geometric properties of common data visualization layouts, such as the angles in a pie graph. It also includes SVG-specific convenience functions for converting data and geometrical values into the actual instructions you'll use in the attributes of an SVG <path> element. However, D3 does not draw the charts directly; many extensions and add-ons have been developed to make it easier to draw common chart types.

GSAP

An animation-focused commercial library, the GreenSock Animation Platform focuses on making animated HTML and SVG content fast, smooth, and cross-browser compatible. The GSAP library can be freely used on many commercial projects (and most noncommercial ones); a paid license is required if the site's end users pay a subscription or other fees, or to access various extra plug-in scripts. A number of those plug-ins are specifically focused on working with SVG paths, or circumventing browser support issues at the intersection of SVG and CSS3.

SVG.js

SVG.js is a lightweight library for drawing, manipulating, and animating SVG elements. It doesn't offer much new functionality compared to "vanilla JS," but it offers a much friendlier, more compact API for creating elements and setting attributes. It also allows you to create simple animations and transitions.

Processing and Packaging

You have your SVG ready to go, whether it came from a clip art library, was drawn in a graphics editor, or was carefully written as code. There are still a few tools that you may want to use while uploading SVG to your web server. A sample routine, which could be automated, would be to:

- Run your SVG code through an optimizing tool such as SVGO (*https://github.com/svg/svgo*) or Scour (*http://www.coded read.com/scour/*) to eliminate extra markup from graphics tools and to otherwise condense the file (being sure not to use any settings that will remove IDs or classes that you'll use in scripts or stylesheets). SVGO, in particular, has a community of tools built around it, integrating it into most popular web development toolchains.

- Generate raster fallback images for Internet Explorer 8 and Android 2.3 users (using any of the rasterization tools mentioned in *https://oreillymedia.github.io/Using_SVG/extras/ch04-rasterizers.html*).

- Compile a folder full of all individual SVG icons into a single file that can be sent to the user as a whole (the SVGStore Grunt plug-in (*https://github.com/FWeinb/grunt-svgstore*) does this on a Node/Grunt server configuration).

- Use Gzip or Brotli compression to further reduce file size; if you do the compression in advance, instead of dynamically as part of the server request, be sure that your server is set to correctly indicate the compression scheme in the HTTP headers sent with the file.

 Automated optimizing tools like SVGO can be risky, sometimes altering the image in ways that affect the shape of curves. If using an automated tool, stick to the milder optimizations.

Alternatively, there are two online graphical interfaces to SVGO: SVG Editor (*http://petercol lingridge.appspot.com/svg-editor*) and SVG-OMG (*https://jakearchibald.github.io/svgomg/*). Both allow you to adjust options and see the results immediately, while also allowing you to look at the parsed code. SVG OMG has the benefit that, after you have visited the site once, it can run offline through the power of Service Workers.

There are almost certainly many more tools and techniques that can be used, depending on how your website and server are set up, and on how you intend to use the SVG. These examples should get you started.

Summary: Software and Sources to Make SVG Easier

The purpose of this chapter hasn't been to tell you what software or which websites to use, although hopefully it has given you some suggestions if you did not know where to start.

More importantly, the review should have helped you understand the diversity of ways you can create and use SVG. It *also* should have reminded you of the compatibility issues that you must always keep in mind when working on the web. And finally, it should have helped you get some SVG files onto your computer—whether downloaded from a clip-art library or created in an editor—that you can experiment with as you work through the rest of the book.

This chapter has been revised many times since it was first started in 2011, in part due to the dramatic changes in the SVG software landscape. It will surely be the first chapter in the book to become obsolete.

In the past few years, SVG has in many ways become a de facto standard for maps and information graphics on the web, is becoming a commercially viable alternative for clip art, is making its way into graphics usage for component diagrams of everything from houses to aircraft to cars, and is factoring into web interfaces (and even operating system interfaces) in subtle but increasingly ubiquitous ways.

While the example sites and applications given here are a good start, other places to find out more about SVG include infographics and data visualization meetups, or online forums on LinkedIn or Google+ (both of which have a number of active SVG and data visualization groups).

As you're following along with the rest of the book, feel free to use downloaded clip art or SVG you created in a graphics program to experiment with styles and effects. It's what you'll often do in practice. Opening the files in a code editor that highlights the syntax (and particularly one that can "tidy up" or "pretty print" the XML) can help you identify the core structure of group and shape elements in the code. From there, you can add new attributes or CSS classes.

For Part II, however, we will focus on creating graphics entirely with code, defining the raw shapes that make up your image using elements and attributes.

Drawing with Markup

The fundamental structure of an SVG drawing is defined by the elements and attributes that draw content to the screen. These aspects of SVG markup create the shapes and text you see, and control their basic layout. The shapes and layout are defined in a vector language of x and y coordinates that plots out positions on an invisible grid.

The next few chapters describe the SVG elements that create new visible content: basic shapes, custom shapes, and text. Part III examines more closely how those x and y coordinates are measured and manipulated.

CHAPTER 5

Building Blocks

Basic Shapes

Most SVG graphics are built from one or more shape elements. Shapes—along with text and embedded images—provide the basic graphical content that is drawn to the screen. The attributes of each shape element define the geometrical region of that shape; its style properties control *how* that vector region is displayed on the screen (or printed on paper).

SVG defines two different ways of creating a shape. The first is to make use of the predefined shape primitives. In Chapter 1, we introduced two of these: circles and rectangles. The others are `<line>` and `<ellipse>`. These are "quick and dirty" shapes that are useful for fast layout, common operations, and fairly standard interface and graphic design layouts. They can also make your code easier to read, as the element tag names clearly define what shape it is.

However, predefined shapes are limited. For most drawings, you will need to create custom shapes, using `<polygon>`, `<polyline>`, or `<path>`. A `<path>` can be used to replace any of the other shape elements, but is considerably more flexible. SVG paths can be used to draw incredibly complex shapes that are not included in any geometry textbook.

This chapter introduces the basic shapes in detail, discussing how you can specify lengths and positions in SVG. With this information, you will be able to lay out many simple geometric designs. Chapter 6 then explores `<path>` and the other custom shape elements, and the variety of shapes they can create. At the end, you'll have all the information you need to create basic vector icons and line drawings with SVG. In theory, anyway—it takes a lot of practice to really get comfortable with manipulating curved paths!

For now, the shapes will be filled or stroked with solid colors, and they will be drawn at a specific size and position within the graphic. In Part III, we'll explore the ways you can manipulate the geometry of shapes by altering the coordinate system in which the vector shapes are defined. In Part IV, we will discuss the ways in which you can change the appearance of the shapes.

Drawing Lines, from Here to There

The simplest shape in the SVG lexicon is the `<line>`. It represents a straight segment connecting two points. A line's geometry is defined by four attributes: **x1 and y1** give the coordinates of the starting point, while **x2 and y2** give the coordinates of the end point. The following code describes a diagonal line from (0,100) to (100,0):

```
<line x1="0" y1="100" x2="100" y2="0" />
```

 All SVG shapes, even `<line>` and `<polyline>`, are by default styled with `fill: black` and `stroke: none`. This means that, by default, a `<line>` will not be visible. There is no area *inside* a straight line to be filled in.

Use CSS or presentation attributes to give the lines a stroke color. You can also optionally set `fill: none`, although this won't have a visible effect with `<line>`.

As described in Chapter 1, coordinates are (by default) measured from the top-left corner of the graphic. When numbers are given without units, these **user coordinate** lengths are (again, by default) equivalent to CSS px units. Figure 5-1 shows the line with a royal blue stroke 10px wide, in a 1.5in square SVG with a golden yellow background.

Figure 5-1. An SVG line, stroked in blue

CSS background and border properties are supported in web browsers for the root `<svg>` element of an SVG file, in the same way that they apply to an inline `<svg>` in an HTML page. But beware: borders, margin, and padding on that root `<svg>` will mess up sizing and scaling if you use that SVG file in an HTML `<img>` or `<object>`.

If any of the geometric attributes are left out, the corresponding coordinate will default to 0. The following `<line>` is therefore equivalent to the previous one:

```
<line y1="100" x2="100" />
```

In contrast, the following code draws a line from (100,0) to (0,100). Although it will often look exactly the same as the previous lines, some styles (stroke dashes and line markers, which we discuss in Chapters 13 and 14) will distinguish between the start and end points of a line.

```
<line y2="100" x1="100" />
```

The order in which you list the attributes makes no difference, only the attribute names.

In addition to user coordinate values, each attribute can be given as a percentage, or as a length with unit. The units defined in SVG 1.1 are the same as those defined in CSS 2: px, pt, pc, cm, mm, in, em, and ex.

More Online

CSS3 units are supported in some browsers, but not all, and not consistently.

Details and definitions of all the units, are included in the "Units for Measurements" guide:

https://oreillymedia.github.io/Using_SVG/guide/units.html

Example 5-1 uses a simple JavaScript routine to create an arrangement of lines with their start and end points offset at 1-centimeter intervals.

The script uses the document.documentElement property to access the root SVG element. This only works in a *.svg* file. In a *.html* file, the documentElement would be the <html> element, not an <svg>!

To adapt this script for inline SVG, use querySelector("svg") to find the first <svg> element from your markup, or use a class or id.

The code takes advantage of the default coordinates, and does not explicitly set attributes that will always be zero. This is a common trick in SVG coding. The origin is your friend: the more that you can rely upon it, the fewer positioning attributes you need to specify in the SVG markup. Chapters 8 and 11 will discuss how you can control the position of the origin—the (0,0) point—relative to the image region.

Example 5-1. Drawing SVG lines with JavaScript

SVG MARKUP:

```
<svg xmlns="http://www.w3.org/2000/svg" xml:lang="en"
    height="10cm" width="10cm">          ❶
    <title>Line Art</title>              ❷
    <style type="text/css">
        line {
            stroke: purple;
        }
        svg {
            margin: 1cm;                  ❸
        }
    </style>
    <script><![CDATA[                     ❹
        /* script goes here */
]]></script>
</svg>
```

❶ The SVG is given a square drawing region, 10cm wide and tall.

❷ The markup consists only of the title, style rules, and JavaScript.

❸ Although `margin` isn't well defined for standalone SVG, it is supported on the root element in most web browsers.

❹ The entire drawing is created within the `<script>`. The `<![CDATA[` and `]]>` markers ensure that less than/greater than signs within the script are not interpreted as XML markup (don't include them in HTML scripts).

JAVASCRIPT:

```
(function() {
    var size = 10;                       ❶
    var doc = document;
    var svg = doc.documentElement;       ❷
    var svgNS = svg.namespaceURI;        ❸

    if (!(svg.classList && svg.classList.contains("initialized") ))
        draw();                          ❹

    function draw(){
        var l1, l2;                                  ❺
        for (var i = 0; i <= size; i++) {
            l1 = doc.createElementNS(svgNS, "line"); ❻
```

```
        l1.setAttribute("x1", i + "cm" );
        l1.setAttribute("x2", size + "cm" );          ❼
        l1.setAttribute("y2", i + "cm" );
        svg.appendChild(l1);                            ❽

        l2 = doc.createElementNS(svgNS, "line");   ❾
        l2.setAttribute("y1", i + "cm" );
        l2.setAttribute("x2", i + "cm" );
        l2.setAttribute("y2", size + "cm" );
        svg.appendChild(l2);
    }
    if (svg.classList)
        svg.classList.add("initialized");              ❿
    }
})()
```

❶ The size of the drawing region, in centimeters, is stored in a variable to avoid repeating the number 10 multiple times in the code. Once again, the entire script is encapsulated in an anonymous function call.

❷ The documentElement is the root element created in the markup; here, it is the main <svg> element.

❸ Rather than repeat the SVG namespace URI multiple times in the code (and risk a typo), we access it from the <svg> element itself.

❹ In some browsers, if you save a web page that was generated from a script, the saved page will include both the generated elements and the script. When you reopen the saved file, the script runs again, doubling all the generated elements. (Other browsers save the raw source code.) This line tests to see if the SVG has already been initialized, and only draws the graphic if it hasn't. Before using the DOM 3 classList object, it checks to confirm it exists, avoiding errors on older platforms.

❺ Inside the draw() function, a for loop creates the lines, adjusting their start and end points by 1cm at a time, from 0 to 10cm (inclusive).

❻ The first block of code creates the lines for the top-right corner of the graphic, using the methods createElementNS() and setAttribute().

❼ For all of these lines, we leave y1 as the default 0, and set x2 to 10cm. The x1 and y2 attributes are adjusted for each cycle of the for loop.

❽ The appendChild() method adds the newly created <line> element to the SVG, as the last child of the <svg>.

❾ The second batch of instructions is similar, but it now creates lines in the lower left of the graphic. All the lines have x1 of 0 (default) and y2 set to 10cm.

❿ Finally, after drawing is complete, we mark the <svg> element with the initialized class (after again checking that the classList property is supported).

The script (and other scripts in this book) uses what is commonly known as "Vanilla JavaScript." Elements are created, and attributes modified, with the core DOM methods directly supported by the browsers, not with shorthand methods from an imported library or framework. It may *look* more verbose than a JQuery or d3 script, but it's a lot less code from the perspective of the browser's JavaScript parser—and the user's data plan!

As we warned in Chapter 2, you need to use createElementNS with the SVG namespace URI in order to create a valid SVG element. However, the namespace can be accessed from the namespaceURI property of any existing SVG element.

The graphic generated by the script is displayed in Figure 5-2. Mathematically, you could say that the lines create a mesh envelope for the curved region in the center. You may also recognize the pattern as recreating the kind of string-and-peg artwork that was popular in the 1960s.

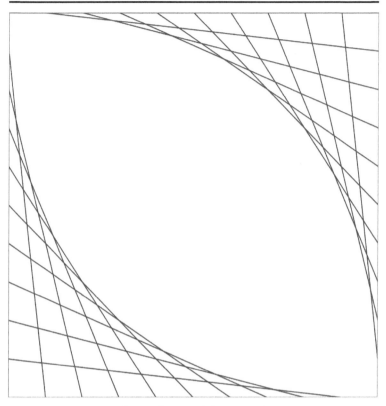

Figure 5-2. String art "curves" created from SVG lines

The code in Example 5-1 includes a `<style>` section that sets the `stroke` property for all line elements. This creates the visible line, drawn centered along the line defined by the vector coordinates.

The exact geometry of a stroke is controlled by a variety of other style properties—`stroke-width`, `stroke-opacity`, `stroke-dasharray`, and so forth—that will be covered in more detail in Chapter 13. For now, it's worth noting that `stroke-width` has a default value of 1; this creates the 1px-wide "strings" in the graphic (Figure 5-2).

Although the lines were created with JavaScript, the final result is an SVG document held in your browser's memory. Example 5-2 shows the markup that describes that SVG document, similar to what you would see in the DOM inspector of your browser's developer tools.

Example 5-2. The SVG document created by the line-art script

```
<svg xmlns="http://www.w3.org/2000/svg" xml:lang="en"
    height="10cm" width="10cm"
    class="initialized">                        ❶
    <title>Line Art</title>
    <style type="text/css">
        line {
            stroke: purple;
        }
        svg {
            margin: 1cm;
        }
    </style>
    <script><![CDATA[                            ❷
        /* the script is still here */
]]></script>
    <line x1="0cm" x2="10cm" y2="0cm"/>         ❸
    <line y1="0cm" x2="0cm" y2="10cm"/>
    <line x1="1cm" x2="10cm" y2="1cm"/>
    <line y1="1cm" x2="1cm" y2="10cm"/>
    <line x1="2cm" x2="10cm" y2="2cm"/>
    <line y1="2cm" x2="2cm" y2="10cm"/>
    <line x1="3cm" x2="10cm" y2="3cm"/>
    <line y1="3cm" x2="3cm" y2="10cm"/>
    <line x1="4cm" x2="10cm" y2="4cm"/>
    <line y1="4cm" x2="4cm" y2="10cm"/>
    <line x1="5cm" x2="10cm" y2="5cm"/>
    <line y1="5cm" x2="5cm" y2="10cm"/>
    <line x1="6cm" x2="10cm" y2="6cm"/>
    <line y1="6cm" x2="6cm" y2="10cm"/>
    <line x1="7cm" x2="10cm" y2="7cm"/>
    <line y1="7cm" x2="7cm" y2="10cm"/>
    <line x1="8cm" x2="10cm" y2="8cm"/>
    <line y1="8cm" x2="8cm" y2="10cm"/>
    <line x1="9cm" x2="10cm" y2="9cm"/>
    <line y1="9cm" x2="9cm" y2="10cm"/>
    <line x1="10cm" x2="10cm" y2="10cm"/>
    <line y1="10cm" x2="10cm" y2="10cm"/>
</svg>
```

❶ The SVG now has the `initialized` class, as the drawing script has completed.

❷ The script code is still part of the DOM, but if the page is reloaded it will only run as far as the point where it checks for the initialized class.

❸ The 22 generated `<line>` elements are appended at the end of the SVG in the order they were created by the script.

The many lines in Example 5-2 may appear to create a single shape, but they don't. Each line is still a separate element in the document. And although they appear to outline a square and also enclose a curved region, you cannot fill in either region as a block of color.

The remaining shape elements, in contrast, allow you to define shapes as you're probably more used to thinking of them—as two-dimensional areas with an inner fill region surrounded by stroked edges.

Future Focus
More Measurements and Calculations

The CSS Values and Units level 3 specification, which was mostly finalized (reached W3C candidate recommendation status) in July 2013, expanded and modified the definition of length units. It introduces two new font-relative units, `rem` and `ch`, plus the four viewport units, `vw`, `vh`, `vmin`, and `vmax`.

Values and Units 3 also introduced the `calc()` function, which allows you to calculate a number or length using arithmetic to combine absolute units, relative units, and percentages; and the `toggle()` function, which allows you to cycle through a list of values by comparing against the inherited value for the same property. (Although support for `toggle()` in browsers is still poor.)

Most modern browsers support the new units and `calc` expressions in all standard CSS properties, including some that can be used in SVG, such as `font-size` (although IE and Edge are buggy here). The new units can also be used to set the `width` and `height` of the `<svg>` element in HTML5.

Support for the new units and functions in SVG-specific style properties (such as `stroke-width`) is inconsistent:

- Firefox (as of 55) supports the new units, but not `calc` expressions.
- Internet Explorer 11 and Microsoft Edge (EdgeHTML 15) accept them both as valid CSS declarations, but when rendering, they do not use a value created with a `calc` expression—meaning that the stroke with that style property was not drawn at all—and a `vw` unit causes Edge 15 to crash completely!

- Chrome/Blink supports CSS units in SVG-related CSS rules (since before version 54), although there may be edge-case bugs.
- WebKit supports `calc` functions as of Safari 9, and the new units as of Safari 10.

In other words, be *very* careful using any of the new units and `calc` yet.

Support for the new units in SVG geometry attributes (such as `cx` or `width`) has been implemented in most browsers over the past few years, but `calc` expressions are still either unsupported or buggy. Blink is the buggy one; as of version 59—and for many versions previous—it uses the first length in a `calc` expression, ignoring the rest of the calculation.

Under SVG 2, all valid CSS3 length expressions—including the new units and `calc` expressions—are valid for style properties and their matching presentation attributes. This includes many geometric attributes, which have been re-defined as presentation attributes for matching CSS properties (more on that later).

For other geometric features of SVG, such as path data, a `calc`-like method may be introduced in the future, but the syntax is not decided.

It's Hip to Be Square (or Rectangular)

Extending the straight line to two dimensions creates the next basic shape, the rectangle. As we saw in Chapter 1, a rectangle is represented in SVG by the **<rect> element**. While lines are defined by the coordinates of two different points, the SVG rectangle follows a slightly different approach. Instead of defining start and end points, a <rect> is defined by one point and a **width and height**. The positioning point is set by **x and y attributes** (*not* x1 and y1 like for a line); this defines the upper-left corner of the rectangle.

 As with <line>, if any of the geometric attributes x, y, width, or height are not specified on a <rect>, they default to 0. However, if either width or height is zero, the rectangle will not be drawn at all—not even the stroke. A negative width or height is invalid.

You can use the `<rect>` element to create a square simply by setting the width and height equal. The following creates a 1-inch square:

```
<rect width="1in" height="1in" />
```

Each attribute is independent, and can have different units—or no units at all. The following code shifts the square 1cm from the left edge of the SVG and 12pt (⅙ inch) from the top edge:

```
<rect x="1cm" y="12pt" width="1in" height="1in" />
```

That square `<rect>`, filled in purple—dark0rchid, to be precise— and added to the line from Figure 5-1, creates Figure 5-3.

Figure 5-3. An SVG rectangle, filled in purple

If you're displaying the preceding square on a screen, and measure it with a ruler, you'll probably discover that it is not exactly 1 inch square.

Browsers that support CSS3 units will always adjust the definition of real-world units (like `in` and `cm`) to maintain a constant ratio to CSS `px` units (96px per inch), while also allowing px layout units to line up neatly with the physical pixels of your screen. When printing, the browser will generally use the real-world inch as the base unit, and adjust px accordingly.

The following describes a rectangle that is 80% of the height and width of the parent `<svg>` and centered in the SVG region (10% off- set from each side):

```
<rect x="10%" y="10%" width="80%" height="80%" />
```

The actual width-to-height ratio of this rectangle will depend on the width-to-height aspect ratio of the SVG itself; it may be a square, but not necessarily.

Simple rectangles may not be very exciting, but there are lots of practical designs that use them. Example 5-3 generates a chess- or checkerboard design from <rect> elements, using JavaScript. The final graphic contains one large rectangle for the edges of the board, then 64 (8×8) smaller black and white squares.

Example 5-3. Creating a checkerboard of SVG rectangles with JavaScript

SVG MARKUP:

```
<svg xmlns="http://www.w3.org/2000/svg" xml:lang="en"
    height="9in" width="9in">               ❶
    <title>Checkerboard</title>
    <style type="text/css">
        .board { fill: saddleBrown; }
        .white { fill: linen; }            ❷
        .black { fill: #222; }
    </style>
    <script><![CDATA[
        /* script goes here */
]]></script>
</svg>
```

❶ The checkerboard will be 9 inches square in total; an 8 × 8 grid of 1-inch-square tiles, with a half-inch border on all sides for the board's frame.

❷ The white and black tiles will be identified by class names, rather than by fill colors set directly in the DOM. This allows us to adjust the actual color used for white and black; in this case, to use a creamy off-white color and a dark charcoal gray.

JAVASCRIPT:

```
(function() {
    var squares = 8;                        ❶
    var doc = document;
    var svg = doc.documentElement;
    var svgNS = svg.namespaceURI;

    if (!(svg.classList && svg.classList.contains("initialized") ))
        draw();
```

```
function draw(){
    var board = doc.createElementNS(svgNS, "rect");        ❷
    board.setAttribute("width", "100%");
    board.setAttribute("height", "100%");
    board.setAttribute("class", "board");
    svg.appendChild(board);

    var square;
    for (var i = 0; i < squares; i++) {
        for (var j = 0; j < squares; j++) {                ❸
            square = doc.createElementNS(svgNS, "rect");
            square.setAttribute("x", (i+0.5) + "in" );     ❹
            square.setAttribute("y", (j+0.5) + "in" );
            square.setAttribute("width", "1in" );
            square.setAttribute("height", "1in" );
            square.setAttribute("class",                   ❺
                        (i+j)%2 ? "black" : "white" );
            svg.appendChild(square);                       ❻
        }
    }
    svg.classList.add("initialized");
    }
})()
```

❶ The script uses the same structure as Example 5-1. In this case, the `squares` variable stores the number of squares in each row and column of the checkerboard.

❷ The first block of the `draw()` function creates the background rectangle that represents the wooden board.

❸ We create the individual tiles using nested `for` loops; the outer loop (with variable `i`) cycles through the rows of the grid, while the inner loop (with variable `j`) cycles through the tiles within each row.

❹ The horizontal and vertical positions of each tile (`x` and `y` attributes) are set from the `i` and `j` variables, adding a half-inch offset for the frame of the checkerboard.

❺ We set the class, either `black` or `white`, by testing whether the sum of the row and column index is even or odd; that is, whether the sum modulus 2 is 1 (truthy) or 0 (falsy). This creates the correct alternating pattern in both the horizontal and vertical directions.

❻ The tiles are all inserted *after* the board, and are therefore drawn on top of it.

Figure 5-4 shows the graphic generated by Example 5-3, scaled down to fit the page. We're not going to print out all 65 generated <rect> elements, but be sure to open the SVG file in a browser and use the developer tools to inspect the DOM, so that you understand how it would look as SVG markup.

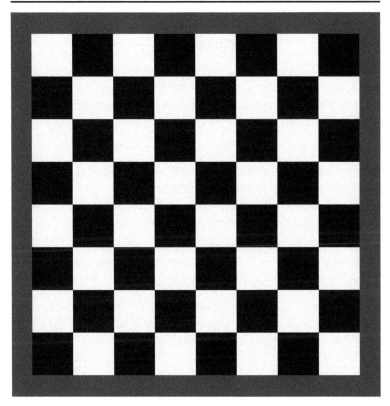

Figure 5-4. A checkerboard of SVG rectangles created with JavaScript

The final checkerboard document includes many very similar elements, and therefore is a candidate for reducing repetition with <use> elements. However, since all these repeated properties are only written once in the original script, it still meets the Don't Repeat Yourself (DRY) principle.

Nonetheless, if you had a much larger number of repeated elements (hundreds or thousands, not just dozens), the size and complexity of the DOM could slow down your browser. For this reason, if you're creating a repeated pattern for decorative effect only—and do not need the individual elements to respond to user events separately—you will want to use a `<pattern>` element, which we'll discuss in Chapter 12.

Future Focus
Geometry as Style

If you're used to CSS layout (and for this book, we're assuming you are), you're used to setting **width** and **height** of elements via CSS properties. If you're creating an SVG layout with a lot of rectangles all the same size (like, for example, a checkerboard), can you set the size once in a CSS rule?

You can't—yet. But that's changing.

In the original SVG specifications, anything that defined a shape's *geometry* was considered a fundamental part of the document structure, and could only be set by attributes in the XML. CSS styles could only be used to control how that shape was painted to the screen, not where or how large.

This proved rather limiting for creating diagrams and charts, where many elements may need to have the same dimensions or the same alignment (without being exact `<use>` copies of each other).

There are other benefits to being able to describe layout with CSS, which didn't exist when SVG was first developed. If layout is set with CSS, you can use CSS media queries to adjust the layout for different screen or page sizes. And if geometry is set with CSS, then you can use CSS animations and transitions to create animated shapes.

With those objectives in mind, the SVG 2 specification (as published in September 2016) defines the following geometry attributes on shapes to also be available as CSS properties:

- **width** and **height**
- **x** and **y**
- **cx** and **cy**

- r, rx, and ry (which we'll introduce in the next section)
- d (which we'll discuss in Chapter 6)

None of the properties inherit by default. At the time of writing (late 2016), both WebKit and Blink rendering engines have partial implementations of SVG geometry properties in CSS.

You may notice that there are some geometric attributes missing from that list. What about x1, x2, y1, and y2 from the <line> element?

There wasn't a clear consensus about what to do with them. Create separate CSS properties for each attribute? Or allow the x and y properties to take multiple values? As we'll discover in Chapter 7, x and y attributes on text elements already take multiple values. The <polyline> and <polygon> elements, however, use a completely different approach to setting multiple points, setting *x* and *y* coordinates in the same (points) attribute.

When geometry is defined in element attributes, each element can have its own attributes. In CSS, however, the same parsing rules have to apply everywhere, and ideally the same property names will be reused.

At present, it isn't really clear how or when the rest of SVG geometry will be integrated into CSS. If you have strong opinions, contribute to SVG standards discussion on GitHub, W3C mailing lists, and web browser issue trackers.

Cutting Corners

The <rect> object is more flexible than it appears at first glance. It has two additional geometric attributes: rx and ry. These parameters are used to create rounded corners on the rectangle. Specifically, they give the horizontal (rx) and vertical (ry) radii of an ellipse (oval) used to draw the rounded corners.

As before, you can use any mix of CSS units you want, or omit the units for px coordinates:

```
<rect x="1cm" y="18pt" width="1in" height="5pc"
      rx="18pt" ry="5mm" />
```

Adding that shape, with deepSkyBlue fill, to our simple example from earlier creates Figure 5-5.

Figure 5-5. An SVG rectangle with rounded corners, positioned atop a regular <rect> and a line

The rx value sets the distance from the left and right edges of the rectangle that should be curved, while ry sets the distance from the top and bottom. These attributes also default to 0 when not specified, making the sharp-cornered rectangles we've seen so far.

Except…the defaults for rx and ry are more complicated than that. If you specify *one* of rx or ry, but not the other, the missing value is automatically calculated to match.

This creates symmetrical, circular corners—even if you use a percentage length, where the same percentage would create a different length in the other direction.

Percentages for the radius, just like percentages for all the other SVG geometry attributes, are measured relative to the SVG coordinate system as a whole: the width for rx, or the height for ry. The percentages don't scale according to the size of the rectangle itself.

However, regardless of how you specify the radius, it will never be more than half the width or height of the rectangle. This means that sometimes a single radius value *won't* create symmetrical corners, after all.

Example 5-4 uses both symmetrical and asymmetrical corner rounding on layered rectangles to create a ripple pattern radiating out from a central shape. Figure 5-6 shows the result.

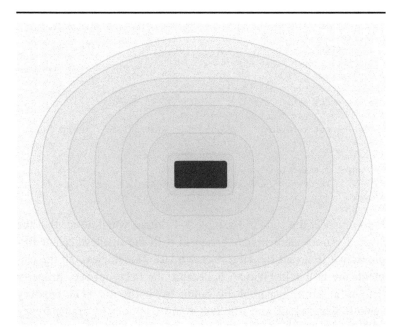

Figure 5-6. A ripple pattern created with rounded rectangles

Example 5-4. Using radiused corners to round rectangles

```
<svg xmlns="http://www.w3.org/2000/svg" xml:lang="en"
    width="14cm" height="11cm">
    <title>Splash!</title>
    <style type="text/css">
        .water {
            fill: paleTurquoise;
        }
        .ripples {
            stroke: lightSeaGreen;
            fill: lightSeaGreen;
            fill-opacity: 0.15;
        }
        .stone {
            fill: darkSlateGray;
        }
    </style>
    <rect class="water" width="14cm" height="11cm" />
    <g class="ripples" >
        <rect x="5.75cm" y="4.75cm" width="2.5cm" height="1.5cm"
            rx="0.25cm" />
        <rect x="5cm"    y="4cm"    width="4cm"   height="3cm"
            rx="1cm"    />
```

```
<rect x="4cm"     y="3cm"    width="6cm"    height="5cm"
      rx="2cm"    />
<rect x="3cm"     y="2.5cm"  width="8cm"    height="6cm"
      rx="3cm"    ry="2.5cm" />
<rect x="2cm"     y="2cm"    width="10cm"   height="7cm"
      rx="4cm"    ry="3cm"   />
<rect x="1cm" y="1cm" width="12cm" height="9cm"
      rx="5.5cm"  ry="4cm"   />
<rect x="0.5cm"   y="0.5cm"  width="13cm"   height="10cm"
      rx="6.5cm"  ry="5cm"   />
</g>
<rect class="stone"
      x="6cm" y="5cm" width="2cm" height="1cm" rx="0.1cm"/>
</svg>
```

If you inspect the code in Example 5-4 closely, you'll notice that the layered `<rect>` elements are arranged with the smallest, center ripple drawn first and the largest drawn last. Nonetheless, all the elements are visible in Figure 5-6, because the `fill-opacity` property defines a semitransparent fill color. We'll discuss `fill-opacity` again in Chapter 12, and will look at more options for transparency and blending colors in Chapters 15 and 16.

CSS Versus SVG
Curved Corners

The CSS `border-radius` property is loosely equivalent to SVG rounded rectangles. However, it is considerably more complex. For starters, you can specify which corner you want to curve with individual style properties for each corner:

```
border-top-right-radius: 4cm 2cm;
    /* the first length is rx, the second ry */
border-bottom-left-radius: 2cm;
    /* only one value is required if they are equal */
```

Alternately, you can specify multiple values in the shorthand `border-radius` property. Multiple values are assigned in clockwise order starting from top left; if two or three values are given, the missing values are taken from the opposite corner. If vertical radii are different, they are specified separately after a slash (/) character:

```
border-radius: 0 4cm 0 2cm / 0 2cm;
    /* same result as the previous two properties */
```

Percentages in **border-radius** are measured against the outside width or height of the border itself. This is different from SVG, where percentages are measured in the same coordinate system used to set the rectangle's width and height. Also unlike in SVG, percentage lengths are always measured against the edge to which they apply, regardless of whether they were specified with the short or full syntax.

The exact shape of the curve is complicated by the fact that borders may have different thicknesses on each side, as may the padding that separates the borders from the content. The border radius (or radii) specified in the CSS defines the *outside* edge of the border curve. The inside edge of the border (the outside edge of the padding), as well as the edge of the content itself, are also rounded but only to the degree required to line up with the start and end of the outside curve.

The following image shows the SVG from Figure 5-6 embedded in HTML as an **<img>**, with 0.5cm of padding, a border that is 1cm thick top and bottom and 0.5cm left and right, and the border radius properties specified in the previous code snippets:

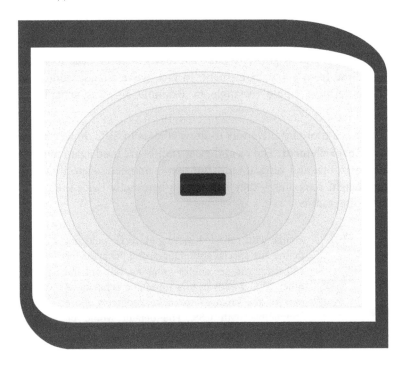

Note that the corners of the image itself are clipped to match the curve. Also notice that while the bottom-left corner is symmetrical on the outer edge, the uneven border width results in asymmetrical inner curves.

The CSS `border-radius` property allows individual corners to be curved up to the full width or height of the element. If the sum of the curves of two adjacent corners is greater than the available space, both are scaled back proportionately until they just fit.

In contrast, there is no way to only round certain corners of an SVG `<rect>`, or to round different corners by different amounts, or to create curvatures greater than half the width or height of the rectangle. You can create these shapes (and many more) with a `<path>` element, but the syntax is very different.

Circular Logic

The next step from rounded rectangles is to create completely rounded shapes: circles and their extended cousins, ellipses.

In Chapter 3, we showed how you can make a rectangular CSS layout box to look like a circle by setting the border radius to half the box's width and height. The same approach *could* be used to create an ellipse from a `<rect>` element. In fact, we've already done that: the outermost ripple rectangle in Example 5-4 was actually an ellipse!

There is a more intuitive way to draw ellipses in SVG, however: the `<ellipse>` element. The rx and ry attributes are used again to specify horizontal and vertical radii, but there's no need to specify width and height separately—they will always be exactly twice the corresponding radius.

 Unlike with rounded rectangles, SVG 1 did not define any special automatic-sizing behavior for ellipses if you set one of rx or ry, but not the other. SVG 2 adds in this automatic behavior as part of the changes to make geometry more compatible with CSS. The default would be equivalent to a new auto keyword.

At the time of writing, auto behavior for ellipses isn't supported in web browsers.

One further difference between rounded rectangles and ellipses is how they are positioned. Rectangles are positioned by the x and y coordinates of their top-left corner, even when that corner is rounded off. Ellipses, in contrast, are positioned by their center point, through the same cx and cy attributes that we used when positioning circles in Chapter 1.

The largest, elliptical ripple <rect> from Example 5-4 was drawn with this code:

```
<rect x="0.5cm"    y="0.5cm"    width="13cm"  height="10cm"
      rx="6.5cm"   ry="5cm" />
```

The exact same size and shape can be drawn as follows:

```
<ellipse cx="7cm" cy="5.5cm" rx="6.5cm" ry="5cm" />
```

The second version is not only DRY-er (because width and height don't need to be set separately from the corresponding radii), it is also much more clear at a glance that it *is* an ellipse.

As with lines and rectangles, if you don't specify a geometric attribute, it defaults to 0; if either rx or ry is 0, the ellipse will not be drawn at all. If rx and ry compute to the same length, the ellipse becomes a circle.

However, if you want a circle, an ellipse isn't your DRY-est option: as we saw in Chapter 1, circles can be drawn more concisely using the <circle> element. A circle uses cx and cy to position the center point, but takes a single radius parameter, r, instead of rx and ry.

Both ellipses and circles are used in Example 5-5, with various units of measurements in the positioning and sizing attributes. (If you're not used to imperial units, it may help to know that there are 72pt in an inch.) The resulting face, Figure 5-7, may not be terribly artistic, but it demonstrates how you can create detailed drawings by layering simple shapes.

Figure 5-7. A funny-looking face making a funny face

Example 5-5. Positioning and sizing circles and ellipses in a drawing

```
<svg xmlns="http://www.w3.org/2000/svg" xml:lang="en"
    width="4.3in" height="4.8in">
    <title>Quizzical Elliptical Face</title>
    <ellipse fill="chocolate"
            rx="55%" ry="60%" cx="50%" cy="50%" />
    <g fill="sienna">
        <ellipse cx="1.1in" cy="1.3in" rx="1in" ry="48pt" />
        <ellipse cx="3.2in" cy="1.3in" rx="1in" ry="40pt" />
        <ellipse cx="50%" cy="55%" rx="8%" ry="22%" />
        <circle cx="45%" cy="71%" r="6%"/>
        <circle cx="56%" cy="68%" r="6%"/>
    </g>
```

```
<g fill="white">
   <ellipse cx="1.1in" cy="1.3in" rx="70pt" ry="38pt" />
   <ellipse cx="3.2in" cy="1.3in" rx="70pt" ry="24pt" />
</g>
<g fill="black"
   stroke="blue" stroke-width="16pt" stroke-opacity="0.6">
   <circle cx="1.6in" cy="1.3in" r="16pt" />
   <circle cx="3.5in" cy="1.3in" r="16pt" />
</g>
<ellipse fill="white"
         stroke="crimson" stroke-width="20pt"
         cx="2.8in" cy="4in" rx="32pt" ry="18pt" />
<g fill="none" stroke="#310" stroke-width="6pt">
  <ellipse cx="45%" cy="22pt" rx="30pt" ry="22pt" />
  <ellipse cx="40%" cy="10pt" rx="30pt" ry="20pt" />
  <ellipse cx="30%" cy="16pt" rx="30pt" ry="22pt" />
  <ellipse cx="20%" cy="16pt" rx="24pt" ry="20pt" />
  <ellipse cx="15%" cy="22pt" rx="22pt" ry="16pt" />
  <ellipse cx="50%" cy="16pt" rx="24pt" ry="22pt" />
  <ellipse cx="55%" cy="22pt" rx="30pt" ry="20pt" />
  <ellipse cx="60%" cy="10pt" rx="30pt" ry="22pt" />
  <ellipse cx="75%" cy="16pt" rx="34pt" ry="18pt" />
  <ellipse cx="80%" cy="12pt" rx="24pt" ry="22pt" />
  <ellipse cx="85%" cy="24pt" rx="22pt" ry="16pt" />
</g>
</svg>
```

Looking at Figure 5-7, you may be surprised to look back at the code and count the number of <circle> elements. There is only one for each eye. The bull's-eye pattern of the iris and pupil is created by a thick, partially transparent stroke.

The example demonstrates two features of strokes that we haven't previously emphasized: they are drawn *centered* over the edge of the shape, and are drawn on *top* of the shape's fill. When you make the stroke partially transparent (by setting the stroke-opacity property, as in the example, or by using a partially transparent color), this creates a two-toned effect; the fill is partially visible through the inner half of the stroke. We'll discuss strokes in more detail in Chapter 13.

There's also a hidden complication in the markup for the "nose" shape, which uses percentages:

```
<ellipse cx="50%" cy="55%" rx="8%" ry="22%" />
<circle cx="45%" cy="71%" r="6%"/>
<circle cx="56%" cy="68%" r="6%"/>
```

Positioning circles and ellipses with percentages (for cx and cy) is fairly straightforward. But sizing them with percentages (in rx, ry, or r) can be nonintuitive, especially for circles.

We mentioned when drawing rectangles that the same percentage value for height and for width might represent different actual lengths. Similarly, an ellipse with rx="50%" and ry="50%" will usually *not* be a circle, because rx is relative to the SVG width while ry is relative to the SVG height. But what happens when you use percentages for r, which is always a single radius value for a circle? Is that relative to width or height?

The answer is neither, and both. Percentage lengths in SVG, if they are neither horizontal nor vertical, are calculated such that they grow and shrink proportional to the length of the *diagonal* of the SVG region.

That doesn't mean that they are percentages *of* the diagonal, however. Instead, they are percentages of the diagonal's length divided by the square root of two ($\sqrt{2}$, approximately 1.41).

More Online

Why the square root of two? Because that way, if the SVG is square —and therefore percentages are equal for width and for height— then the adjusted "diagonal" percentages will match as well.

Read more about how percentage radius values are calculated, and see an example of how it affects a circle in SVGs of different dimensions, in "Perplexing Percentages":

https://oreillymedia.github.io/Using_SVG/extras/ch05-percentages.html

These same "adjusted diagonal" percentages are used for any length in SVG that isn't clearly associated with either the horizontal or vertical direction, including stroke widths and stroke dash lengths.

CSS Versus SVG
Shapes in Stylesheets

As CSS3 has introduced more complex graphical layouts, it has needed a way to define shapes that go beyond `border-radius`.

The CSS Shapes module introduces a series of shape functions that can be used to define geometric shapes as the value of other properties. The same module introduces the `shape-outside` property, which uses these shape functions to control how text wraps around floated objects in the layout. But these functions are also used for other properties, such as `clip-path`.

The syntax for circles and ellipses, which was based on the CSS radial gradient syntax, is designed to be flexible and follow natural language:

```
circle(radius at
       horizontal-position vertical-position)
ellipse(x-radius y-radius at
        horizontal-position vertical-position)
```

Positions and percentages are relative to a reference CSS layout box for the element (for example, the `content-box`, `padding-box`, `border-box`, or `margin-box`). The specific box would be determined by the rest of the CSS property that is using the shape function. The CSS `circle()` function treats a percentage radius using the same method as SVG: relative to the diagonal divided by $\sqrt{2}$.

You can also size CSS circles and ellipses with keyword values in order to create shapes that just fit within the layout box, whatever its aspect ratio: `closest-side` to fit to the first edge encountered, or `farthest-side` to expand to fill the box. Similarly, you can use the keywords `top`, `bottom`, `left`, `right`, and `center` for the position of the center point, using the same syntax as the CSS `background-position` property.

Both the radius parameters and the position parameters are optional; if omitted, the default radius is `closest-side`, while the default position is `center`.

CSS Shapes also supports rounded rectangles, defined with the `inset()` function. It specifies the rectangle's size as an inset from the reference CSS layout box. The inset distances are specified with the same syntax as CSS margins or paddings:

```
inset(inset-distance)
inset(top-bottom-inset right-left-inset)
inset(top-inset right-inset bottom-inset left-inset)
```

You specify rounded corners of an inset box by adding a **round** keyword, and then a set of lengths using any syntax that is valid in the CSS **border-radius** property, such as:

```
inset(inset-distance round corner-radius)
inset(inset-distance
      round horizontal-radius / vertical-radius)
```

The layout box that determines the overall size of the inset shape is not part of the shape function. For **outside-shape** and **clip-path**, it is defined as a separate keyword in the style value. A complete shape declaration could be:

```
img {
    height: 12em;
    border: navy solid 1em;
    float: left;
    margin-right: 1em;
    shape-outside: inset(0px round 0 0 8em) margin-box;
    clip-path: circle(15em at top left);
}
```

 You'd more commonly use the *same* shape for both the clip and the text layout **shape-outside**, but we're trying to show all your options here! We'll talk more about clipping paths (including the better-supported SVG version) in Chapter 15.

With those styles applied to our SVG image from Figure 5-7, and some filler text to show the layout, you have a page that looks like this (in Chrome 57, where both features are supported):

Lorem ipsum dolor sit amet, consectetur adipisicing elit. Odit, quisquam, nostrum. Magni, non tenetur corrupti maxime, provident molestiae voluptas officia atque dolore dolorum quis laudantium! Maiores eveniet atque modi accusantium?

Magni sit dolorem aperiam optio, ut ratione, voluptate id unde sequi omnis consequatur laboriosam blanditiis dignissimos, explicabo earum neque est minima reiciendis sint quo. Dolorum iure modi delectus nobis, repellendus.

Omnis magnam, iste voluptates, deserunt qui error veritatis ipsam quae nostrum odit vero, laborum rem quibusdam veniam! In, dolore. Ipsum inventore perferendis, quod atque dolor, ratione quis eaque quaerat voluptatibus!

Summary: Basic Shapes

The SVG basic shapes are each defined by an element in the markup. Their size, position, and proportions are controlled by individual attributes.

The value of each attribute can be specified as a length, percentage, or number. Numbers are lengths in user units, which are equivalent to px units. Percentages are proportional to the SVG size: its width, its height, or its diagonal divided by √2, depending on whether the measurement is horizontal, vertical, or other.

The `<circle>`, the `<ellipse>`, the `<rect>`, and the `<line>` are the only "standard" shapes of SVG. There is no `<triangle>`, no `<pentagon>`, and no `<semi-circle>` or `<pie-slice>`. At first, this may seem strange—a graphics language with only a handful of shapes doesn't seem like much of a language—but the reality is that these shapes are standard only because rectangles, circles, lines, and ellipses occur often enough that it makes sense to mark them out as special.

Every other shape can be rendered by other means, through the `<polygon>`, `<polyline>`, and—most especially—the `<path>` element.

More Online

The chapter has introduced a large number of elements, attributes, and values. A sorted syntax reference for the shapes markup is available in the "Shape Elements" section of our elements and attributes guide:

https://oreillymedia.github.io/Using_SVG/guide/markup.html#shapes

A separate guide defines all the length units—and percentages:

https://oreillymedia.github.io/Using_SVG/guide/units.html

A reference for CSS shapes is provided in the "CSS Shape Functions" guide:

https://oreillymedia.github.io/Using_SVG/guide/css-shapes.html

CHAPTER 6

Following Your Own Path
Custom Shapes

A complete vector drawing format requires a way to draw arbitrary shapes and curves. The basic shape elements introduced in Chapter 5 may be useful building blocks, but they are no more flexible than CSS layout when it comes to crafting custom designs.

The **<path> element** is the drawing toolbox of SVG. Chances are, if you open up an SVG clip-art image or a diagram created with a graphics editor, you will find dozens or hundreds of kilobytes' worth of <path> statements with only a smattering of <g> elements to provide positional organization. With <path> you can draw shapes that have straight or curved sections (or both), open-ended lines and curves, disconnected regions that act as a single shape, and even holes within the filled areas.

Understand paths, and you understand SVG.

The other custom shapes, <polygon> and <polyline>, are essentially shorthands for paths that only contain straight line segments.

This chapter introduces the instruction set for drawing custom shapes step by step, creating the outline by carefully plotting out each line segment and curve. For icons and images, it is relatively rare to write out the code this way, as opposed to drawing the shape in a graphics editor. With data visualization and other dynamically generated graphics, however, programmatically constructing a shape point by point is common, so learning the syntax is more important.

Even within graphic design, there will be times when you want to draw a simple, geometrically precise shape. Using SVG custom shapes, you can often do this with a few lines of code, instead of by painstakingly dragging a pointer around a screen.

In other situations, you will want to edit or duplicate a particular section of a shape or drawing. By the end of this chapter, you should have enough basic familiarity with how paths work to safely open up the code and start fussing.

If you can't imagine ever drawing a shape by writing out a sequence of instructions, it is safe to skip ahead to future chapters. Regardless of whether an SVG graphic was created in a code editor or in a graphics editor, you manipulate and style it in the same way.

Giving Directions: The d Attribute

A `<path>` may be able to draw incredibly complex shapes, but the attribute structure for a `<path>` element is very simple:

```
<path d="path-data"/>
```

The **d attribute** holds the path instruction set, which can be thought of as a separate coding language within SVG. It consists of a sequence of points and single letter instructions that give the directions for drawing the shape.

 When SVG was first in the development stage, a number of different avenues for paths were explored, including one where each point or curve segment in a path was its own XML element. This was found to be fairly inefficient compared to parsing a string of commands. The chosen approach is also consistent with the philosophy that the shape—not the point—is the fundamental object within SVG.

Understanding how to draw with SVG `<path>` elements is therefore a matter of understanding the path-data code.

To allow paths of any complexity, the `<path>` element lets you specify as many pieces of the path as you need, each using a basic mathematical shape. Straight lines, Bézier curves, and elliptical curves of any length can be specified. Each piece is defined by the *type* of drawing command, indicated by a letter code, and a series of numerical parameters.

The same path instructions are used outside of SVG. The HTML Canvas2D API (for drawing on a <canvas> element with JavaScript) can now accept path-data strings as input. The same code is also used for paths in Android's "vector drawables," which use an XML format that is similar to SVG.

 You can create SVG shapes—in a visual editor or with code—and then copy and paste the path data string, from the d attribute, into your JavaScript or Android code.

The path instructions are written as a single string of data, and are followed in order. Each path segment starts from the end point of the previous statement; the command letter is followed by coordinates that specify the new end point and—for the more complex curves—the route to get there. Each letter is an abbreviation for a specific command: M, for instance, is short for *move-to*, while C is *cubic curve-to*.

More Online

The "Path Commands" guide summarizes the complete instruction set in reference format:

https://oreillymedia.github.io/Using_SVG/guide/path-data.html

There are generally two approaches to rendering the path. In the first approach, path coordinates are given in **absolute** terms, explicitly describing points in the coordinate system. The single letter commands that control absolute positioning are given as uppercase characters: M, L, A, C, Q, and so on. Changing one point only affects the line segments that directly include that point.

The second approach is to use **relative coordinates**, indicated by lowercase command letters: m, l, a, c, q, and so on. For relative commands, the coordinates describe the offset from the end of the previous segment, rather than the position relative to the origin of the coordinate system. You can move around a path defined entirely in relative coordinates by changing the first point.

 Both absolute and relative path commands can be used in the same path.

The shorthand custom shapes, **<polygon> and <polyline>**, only use straight line segments and absolute coordinates. There are no code letters, just a list of points given in the (aptly named) `points` attribute of each shape:

```
<polygon points="list of x,y points"/>
<polyline points="list of x,y points"/>
```

Before getting into the difference between <polygon> and <polyline>, we'll first go back to <path> (which can substitute for either), and consider what it means to draw a shape from a list of points.

Future Focus
Piecewise Paths

Encoding a complex shape in a single element's attributes may be efficient, but it does have its limitations. Sections of shapes cannot be duplicated or manipulated individually. For example, in a map you often have two adjacent regions with the same complex border shared between them; it would be convenient to only have to encode the shape of the border once, and then share it between the two elements.

There have been a few proposals for extensions of SVG that would make it possible to reuse path segments between multiple shapes. This feature is likely to be adopted into the language eventually, but it is not included in SVG 2.

Straight Shooters: The move-to and line-to Commands

The easiest-to-understand path instructions are those that create straight-line shapes. The only numbers you need to include in the directions are the coordinates of the start and end points of the different line segments.

The basic commands you need to know are the M (or m) *move-to* instruction, and the L (or l) *line-to* command. For instance, this code creates a path in the shape of a diamond—technically, a rhombus—centered around the point (10,10):

```
<path d="M3,10 L10,0 L17,10 L10,20 L3,10" />
```

Filled in red, that looks like this:

The directions in the path data can be read as follows:

- M3,10: move to the point (3,10), meaning the point where x=3 and y=10, without drawing any line;
- L10,0: draw a line from the previous point to the position (10,0);
- L17,10: draw another line from there to (17,10);
- L10,20: draw a third line to (10,20); and finally,
- L3,10: draw a line back to (3,10).

Figure 6-1 shows how the five points in the shape would be positioned if they were marked out on graph paper. The final point exactly overlaps the first.

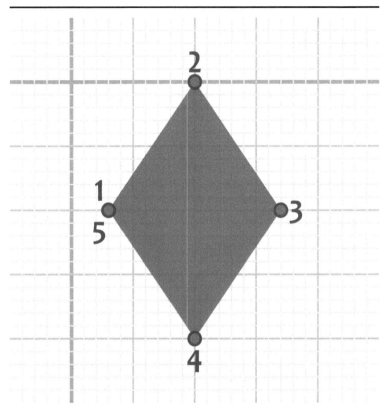

Figure 6-1. A diamond drawn with straight-line path segments

 Because we're focusing on the path data, this chapter uses a lot of short code snippets, instead of complete examples. To follow along, start with the basic inline SVG code (Example 1-1) or standalone SVG code from Chapter 1. Add the `<path>` element, and give it a fill color with presentation attributes or CSS.

You may also want to add a `viewBox` attribute to the `<svg>` element, so that the icons will scale up to a size larger than 20px tall. The versions displayed with the graph-paper grid use `viewBox="-5 -5 30 30"`. We'll explain what those numbers mean in Chapter 8.

Using relative coordinates, you can define the same path with the following code:

```
<path d="m3,10 l7,-10 l7,10 l-7,10 l-7,-10"/>
```

The end result is identical:

In this case, the instructions read:

- m3,10: move 3 units right and 10 units down from the origin;
- l7,-10: draw a straight line starting from the previous point, ending at a new point that is 7 units to the right and 10 units up (that is, 10 units in the negative *y* direction);
- l7,10: draw another line that ends at a point 7 units further to the right and 10 units back down;
- l-7,10: draw a third line moving back 7 units to the left (the negative *x* direction) and another 10 units down; and
- l-7,-10: draw a line moving another 7 units left and 10 units up.

To create the same size diamond at a different position, you would only need to change the initial *move-to* coordinates; everything else is relative to that point.

 All paths must start with a *move-to* command, even if it is M0,0.

The relative *move-to* command in the second snippet may seem equivalent to an absolute M command. Moving *x* and *y* units relative to the coordinate system origin is the same as moving to the absolute point (*x,y*).

However, the *move-to* commands can also be used partway through the path data. In that case, an m command, with relative coordinates, is *not* equivalent to an M command with absolute coordinates. Just like with lines, the relative coordinates will then be measured relative to the last end point.

Unlike with lines, the move command is a "pen up" command. The context point is changed, but no line is drawn: no stroke is applied, and the area in between is not enclosed in the fill region. We'll show an example of move commands in the middle of a path in "Hole-y Orders and Fill Rules" on page 178.

Finishing Touches: The close-path Command

The solid fill that was used in Figure 6-1 disguises a problem with paths created only via *move-to* and *line-to* commands. If you were to add a stroke with a large stroke width, like in Figure 6-2, you would notice that the left corner, where the path starts and ends, does not match the others.

When a path is drawn, the stroke is open-ended unless it is specifically terminated. What that means is that the stroke will not connect the last point and the first point of a region, even if the two points are the same. The strokes will be drawn as loose ends instead of as corners.

We'll discuss more about stroking styles for line ends and corners in Chapter 13. These figures use the default miter corner style.

To close a path, use the **Z or z** *close-path* command. It tells the browser to connect the end of the path back to the begining, drawing a final straight line from the last point back to the start if necessary. The closing line will have length 0 if the two points coincide.

A *close-path* command doesn't include any coordinates, so there is no difference between the absolute Z and relative z versions of the command.

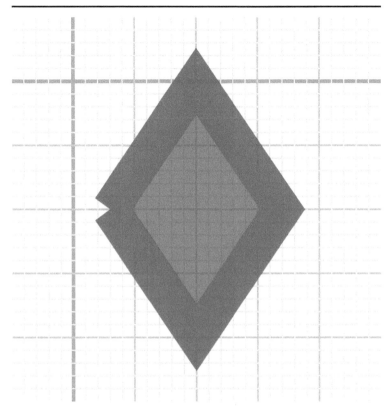

Figure 6-2. An open-path diamond shape, with a thick stroke

The following versions of the diamond each have a closed path; in the second case, it is used to replace the final *line-to* command, which is preferred:

```
<path d="M3,10 L10,0 L17,10 L10,20 L3,10 Z" />
<path d="m3,10 l7,-10 l7,10 l-7,10 z"/>
```

These versions of the path, when stroked using the same styles as before, create the shape shown in Figure 6-3.

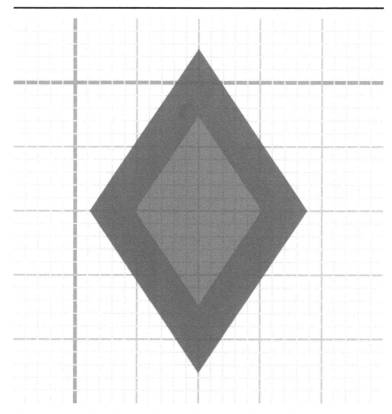

Figure 6-3. A closed-path diamond shape, with a thick stroke

Again, closing a path only affects the stroke, not the fill; the fill region of an open path will always match the closed path, created by drawing a straight line from the final point back to the beginning.

When a path has multiple subpaths created with *move-to* commands, the *close-path* command closes the most recent subpath. In other words, it connects to the point defined by the most recent *move-to* command.

Hole-y Orders and Fill Rules

A useful feature of the "pen-up" *move-to* command is that it allows you to draw several distinct fill regions in the same path, simply by including additional M or m instructions to start a new section. The different subpaths may be spread across the graphic, visually distinct, but they remain a single element for styling and for interaction with user events.

With multiple subpaths—or even with a single subpath that crisscrosses itself—you can also create "holes" within the path's fill region. The following version of the diamond includes cut-away regions to suggest light reflecting off a three-dimensional shape, as demonstrated in Figure 6-4.

```
<path d="M3,10 L10,0 17,10 10,20 Z
         M9,11 L10,18 10,10 15,10 11,9 10,2 10,10 5,10 Z" />
```

Multiple coordinate pairs after a *line-to* command create multiple lines; you don't need to repeat the L each time.

At the default scale, that looks like this:

Figure 6-4 shows how the points are located in the grid. The points are numbered in order, like a connect-the-dots drawing.

Although we haven't mentioned it so far, the outside diamond shape was intentionally drawn in a clockwise direction. The inner cutout is drawn in a counterclockwise direction. By convention in SVG and other vector graphics languages, the counterclockwise path cancels out the clockwise path, returning the center cutout to the "outside" of the path's fill region.

If the inside subpath were also clockwise, or if both subpaths were counterclockwise, then it gets more complicated. By default, the inner path would have *added* to the outside one, and the center region would have still been filled in.

This additive behavior can be controlled with the **fill-rule style property**. The default value is nonzero; if you switch it to evenodd, cutouts will *always* be cut out, regardless of the direction of the path.

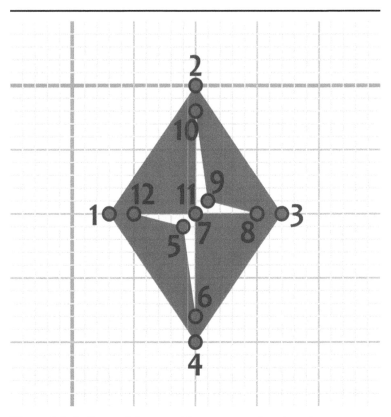

Figure 6-4. A diamond drawn with a cut-out subpath region

Which rule should you use? Which direction should you draw your shapes?

As with most things in programming, it depends.

If both subpaths are drawn in the *same* direction, you can use `fill-rule` to control whether they add together (`nonzero`, the default) or cancel out (`evenodd`). So you'll have flexibility later. It's easier to change a style property than to change your path data.

When a cutout region is drawn in the opposite direction from the main path shape (as in the code for Figure 6-4), it will *always* be a cutout. So you have predictability.

Most visual editors have an option to reverse the direction of a path. Illustrator also automatically reverses paths when you combine them—creating cutout holes—if one of the original paths entirely overlaps the other.

A fill-rule of evenodd forces the shape to alternate between "inside" and "outside" the path every time it crosses an edge, regardless of whether it is clockwise or counterclockwise. That's nice and simple, but it means that *any* overlapping regions are cut out. This can be problematic with complex shapes that have many curves, which might loop around on themselves slightly.

A nonzero fill ensures that these accidental overlaps add together: you have to explictly reverse direction to create a hole.

Although the nonzero fill rule is the default in the SVG specifications, some visual vector graphics programs automatically apply evenodd style rules to their SVG exports.

Inkscape uses evenodd when you draw a shape, but will sometimes switch to nonzero mode if you merge multiple paths or shapes into a single element. You can manually switch the fill-rule in the fill options dialog, and your choice is saved for the next shape.

Illustrator uses nonzero by default, but you can manually switch the mode for compound paths.

Photoshop vector layers always use evenodd mode.

Most vector font formats use nonzero mode.

More Online

Why does fill-rule have to be so complicated? And why are the keywords nonzero and evenodd?

Read more about the **winding order** number of path regions, and how they are calculated, in "The Winding Order of the Fill Rule":

The `fill-rule` style property is inherited. It can be declared once for the entire SVG, or it can be defined for individual shapes.

Following the Grid: Horizontal and Vertical Lines

When you define a line with an `L` (or `l`) command, you specify both horizontal and vertical coordinates (or offsets, for `l`). If either the horizontal or vertical position is staying the same, however, there's a shortcut available.

Precise horizontal and vertical lines can be written concisely with dedicated path commands: **`H` (or `h`) for horizontal lines**, and **`V` (or `v`) for vertical lines**.

These command letters are followed by a single coordinate for the value that is changing. In a horizontal line, the y-value stays the same, so only the x-value is required; in a vertical line, the x-value is constant, so only the y-value is needed.

The following paths therefore both define a 20×10 rectangle with its top-left corner at (10,5) and its bottom-right corner at (30,15). The first path uses absolute coordinates, while the second uses relative offsets:

```
<path d="M10,5 H30 V15 H0 Z" />
<path d="M10,5 h20 v10 h-20 z" />
```

Of course, we already have the `<rect>` element for rectangles. But horizontal and vertical lines show up in many other places. You can create a complete set of gridlines for a chart as a single path with `M`, `H`, and `V` commands. The grids used in the figures in this chapter use a single element for each color and thickness of line:

```
<path id="axes"
      fill="none" stroke="royalBlue" stroke-width="0.3"
      d="M-5, 0H25 M 0,-5V25"/>
<path id="major-grid"
      fill="none" stroke="cornflowerBlue" stroke-width="0.15"
      d="M-5, 5H25 M 5,-5V25
         M-5,10H25 M10,-5V25
         M-5,15H25 M15,-5V25
```

```
        M-5,20H25 M20,-5V25"/>
    <!-- And one more, for the minor grid -->
```

Of course, you can also mix horizontal and vertical with diagonal lines (or curves!) to create all sorts of complex shapes.

The cutout path used for the decorative diamond in Figure 6-4 contains vertical and horizontal lines. After being rewritten to use the shorthand commands, the complete code for the diamond is given in Example 6-1.

Example 6-1. An SVG diamond icon using a multipart path

```
<svg xmlns="http://www.w3.org/2000/svg" xml:lang="en"
    height="20px" width="20px">
    <title>Diamond</title>
    <path fill="red"
        d="M3,10 L10,0 17,10 10,20 Z
           M9,11 L10,18 V10 H15 L11,9 10,2 V10 H5 Z" />
</svg>
```

 To create a larger version of the icon, you can change the height and width, but you'll also need to add a viewBox (as mentioned before). viewBox="0 0 20 20" will create a tight square around the 20-unit-high icon.

Using horizontal and vertical commands helps reduce file size, but more importantly: it helps keep your code DRY. It's easier to change things later if coordinates are not repeated when they don't have to be.

Of course, reducing file size is a common concern of SVG, and path data was designed with that in mind.

Crunching Characters

This book tries to keep path data legible, by using commas to separate *x,y* coordinates for a single point and spaces between separate coordinates or separate commands. However, the path syntax is designed to encourage brevity, allowing the path instructions to be condensed considerably:

- Whitespace and commas are interchangeable, and are only required in order to separate numbers that could be mistaken for a single multidigit value.

- The initial zero in a small decimal number can be omitted. This can be combined with the previous rule, so that a line to the point (0.5, 0.7) could be written as L.5.7: you can't have two decimal places in the same number, so the second . starts a new number.

- The command letter can be omitted when it is the same as the previous path segment, *except* for multiple move-to commands. Multiple coordinates after a *move-to* command will be interpreted as *line-to* commands of the same type (relative or absolute).

Many software export and optimization tools will "uglify" SVG path data in order to cram it into the absolute minimum number of characters. If you will be dissecting the path data later, it may help to turn off path-optimization settings, other than the settings that round decimal numbers.

The following is a valid equivalent to the diamond shape from Example 6-1. It switches between absolute and relative commands, eliminates separators wherever possible, and uses spaces if a separator is required, without regard to keeping coordinate pairs organized:

```
<path d="m3 10 7-10 7 10-7 10zM9 11l1 7V10h5l-4-1-1-7v8H5Z"/>
```

This uses 49 characters to create the same shape that was originally defined in 66 characters plus an indented newline:

```
<path d="M3,10 L10,0 17,10 10,20 Z
         M9,11 L10,18 V10 H15 L11,9 10,2 V10 H5 Z" />
```

That's a savings of more than 25%, which can be significant when you consider that path data often makes up a large portion of SVG file sizes. We highly encourage you to use SVG optimizer tools to condense very large path data strings. But for handwriting code—and reading it later—we'll be sticking with the "pretty" versions.

Short and Sweet Shapes: Polygons and Polylines

There's another, more legible way to simplify straight-line paths: use a `<polygon>` or `<polyline>` element.

Both of these elements allow you to create straight-line shapes simply by giving a list of the corner points in the **points attribute**. The points in a `<polyline>` create an open path when stroked; for `<polygon>`, the shape is closed from the last point back to the first.

The coordinates are always absolute, and can be separated by whitespace or commas, in whichever organization makes sense to you. Here is the basic diamond once again, as a four-point `<polygon>`:

```
<polygon points="3,10 10,0 17,10 10,20" />
```

There are a number of features of SVG that (in SVG 1.1) are only available for `<path>` elements, and not other shapes. This includes text on a path (which we'll introduce in Chapter 7) and the Java-Script functions for accessing the length of a path (which we'll discuss in Chapter 13).

If need be, you can always convert the simple list of points for `<polygon>` to a `<path>` data attribute by inserting an M at the beginning and a Z at the end. For a `<polyline>`, skip the Z to keep the path open-ended.

Another reason to convert polygons to paths is to combine multiple shapes into subpaths of a single complex shape. Polygons and polylines can only have a single, continuous shape.

Even without distinct subpaths, polygons can have "holes" created by criss-crossing edges. Because the edges will all be part of the same continuous shape, the winding order won't change, so the fill rules are simpler than for multipart paths. The overlapping sections will only be treated as holes if you set `fill-rule: evenodd`.

 Fill rules have the same effect for a filled-in `<polyline>` as for `<polygon>`; the two shapes only differ when stroked.

The remaining sections of the chapter focus on curved paths, which means we're focusing exclusively on the `<path>` element, not on `<polygon>` or `<polyline>`.

CSS Versus SVG
Polygon Points

The CSS Shapes specification supports straight-line shapes with the `polygon()` function.

Similar to SVG, the shape is defined by a list of corner points. Unlike SVG, CSS doesn't treat whitespace and commas as interchangeable; CSS syntax uses spaces to separate multipart values, and commas to separate items in a list of repeated values. In this case, that means spaces to separate the x- and y-values, and commas to separate the points.

The CSS syntax to describe the diamond shape would be:

```
polygon(3px 10px, 10px 0px, 17px 10px, 10px 20px)
```

A more significant difference between CSS and SVG polygons is that the coordinates in CSS require units (or percentages). In contrast, SVG polygons, polylines, and paths only accept user coordinate values, *without* units.

CSS polygons also use **evenodd** and `nonzero` to control fill rules. You can optionally specify one of the keywords as the first parameter in the `polygon()` function, separated from the list of points by a comma. As with SVG, the default is **nonzero**, meaning criss-crossing lines *add* to the total shape; **evenodd** must be specified explicitly, as in the following shape:

```
polygon(evenodd,
        0 0, 50% calc(100% - 2em), 100% 0, 50% 0,
        50% 2em, 0 100%, 100% 100%, 50% 2em, 50% 0);
```

The polygon starts at the top left, draws a diagonal down to the center of the screen and almost the bottom, angles back up to the top right, follows the edge of the container to the center top, adjusts down slightly, draws the lower triangle, then connects back up to the top of the screen.

In practice, that looks like the following, where the orange-gold gradient is the polygon and the blue is the background:

Without **evenodd**, the center region would be included in the orange shape.

We created that image by using the **polygon()** function in the **clip-path** property (which we'll discuss more in Chapter 15). Here's the complete code for this CSS vector graphics design:

```
<!DOCTYPE html>
<html lang="en">
<head>
  <meta charset="UTF-8">
  <title>Fill rule and CSS shapes</title>
  <style>
body {
  background: royalblue;
  margin: 0;
}
div {
  height: 100vh;
  background: linear-gradient(tomato, gold);
  clip-path: polygon(evenodd,
      0 0, 50% calc(100% - 2em), 100% 0, 50% 0,
      50% 2em, 0 100%, 100% 100%, 50% 2em, 50% 0);
}
```

```
    </style>
  </head>
  <body>
    <div></div>
  </body>
</html>
```

Curve Balls: The Quadratic Bézier Command

Anyone who has ever put together a connect-the-dots picture knows that straight lines, while useful for getting a general feel for a given shape, are at best a loose approximation of the real world. For a graphics language, the ability to generate curved segments between points is essential.

SVG paths use three types of curves: quadratic Bézier curves, cubic Bézier curves, and elliptical curves. Bézier curves are also available with shorthand smooth-curve commands, and each curve command can be expressed in absolute or relative coordinates. All these options can be a little daunting on first impression, but understanding this breakdown can make the selection of the best curve forms easier.

 Bézier curves are a relatively recent contribution to geometry. In 1962, French industrial engineer Pierre Bézier adapted the graphing algorithms of French mathematician Paul de Casteljau in order to better design car bodies for the Renault automobile company, creating a simpler notation for curves. Bézier defined a curve using "control" points that made it possible to graphically parameterize the equations in early CAD (computer-assisted drafting) applications.

Bézier curves rely on two convenient truths:

- You can express close approximations to most continuous curves by using a series of quadratic or cubic equations (equations where the y position is related to x^2 or x^3, respectively) connected together in a **spline**, such that the curve flows smoothly from one segment to the next.

It's not always a perfect approximation—in equations where more complex mathematical relationships predominate, finding an exact match with a Bézier equation can be difficult at best— but you can always improve the approximation by using a greater number of shorter curve segments, smoothed together.

- You can calculate quadratic and cubic curves over a finite area as a weighted average of multiple *x,y* points: end points for the curve segment and **control points** defining its shape.

Computers can calculate these weighted averages much more efficiently than they can squares or cubes, and many times faster than they can calculate more complicated mathematical relationships.

What does "a weighted average of multiple *x,y* points" mean? Consider Figure 6-5, which is an exact repeat of Figure 5-2 from Chapter 5.

The start points of each line in the top right of the graphic are each a percentage of the distance between (0,0) and the point (10cm, 0); the end points of each line are each positioned at a matching percentage of the distance between (10cm, 0) and (10cm, 10cm). This is a direct result of how the lines were created in the JavaScript loops.

Less obvious is that the same percentages apply to the *apparent* curved line created by the overlapping, intersecting lines. The first line, the one whose start and end points are weighted entirely to the initial positions, sketches out the very beginning of the curve. The second line, which starts and ends 10% of the way along the square's edges, intersects that curve at 10% of *its* (the line's) length. And so on for the rest of the lines: the middle line, which spans from (5cm, 0) to (10cm, 5cm), crosses the curve at its halfway point; the line from (8cm, 0) to (10cm, 8cm) crosses the curve 80% of the way to its end point.

The *apparent* curve created by those intersecting straight lines can be *directly* drawn as a **quadratic Bézier curve**. A quadratic Bézier requires three points: the start point, an end point, and a single con- trol point between them that establishes the farthest extent of the mesh envelope (aka the string art). For the curves created by the lines in Figure 6-5, the start and end points are (0,0) and (10cm, 10cm); the control points are (10cm, 0) for the top half of the curve and (0, 10cm) for the lower half.

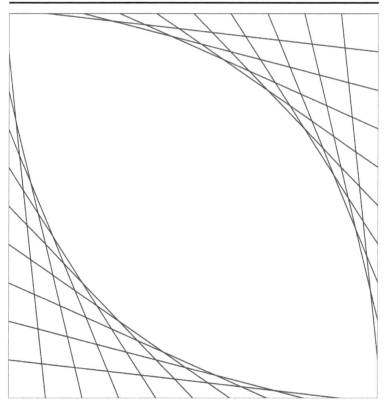

Figure 6-5. String art "curves" created from SVG lines

Figure 6-6 adds those two Bézier curves, as two halves of a filled-in shape, to the SVG. As you can see, the lines perfectly brush the edges of the curved shape.

In SVG path notation, the command letter for quadratic curves is **Q** **(or q for relative coordinates)**. As with all path commands, the start point is taken from the end point of the previous command in the path. That means that a Q is followed by two pairs of *x,y* coordinates: the first pair of numbers describes the control point, and the second pair defines the end point.

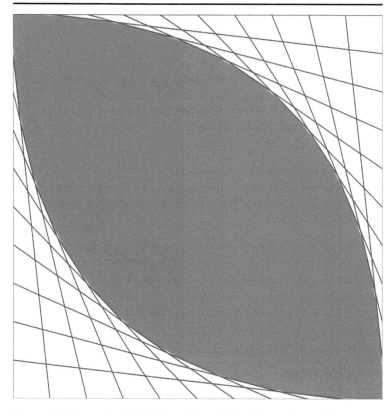

Figure 6-6. A quadratic Bézier path, and the string art mesh that encloses it

Curves shaped like those in Figure 6-6 would be written as follows, in a 10×10 coordinate system:

```
<path d="M0,0 Q 10, 0 10,10
         Q  0,10  0,0 Z" />
```

It starts from the top-left (0,0) point, moves clockwise around the upper curve to the bottom corner, then moves back up along the bottom curve.

In relative coordinates, the curve would be:

```
<path d="m0,0 q 10,0  10,10
           q-10,0 -10,-10 z" />
```

Since the path starts from (0,0), the numbers in the first segment haven't changed; the numbers in the second segment are all relative to the (10,10) point from the end of the first curve.

 When you're using relative coordinates for Bézier curves, both the control points and the end point are relative to the start point of that path segment, not relative to each other.

There's just one more complication. As we briefly mentioned earlier, you cannot use units like cm in path data coordinates; you must use user coordinate numbers. The preceding paths draw shapes *10px* tall and wide, not 10cm.

In Chapter 8 we'll discuss how you can use nested coordinate systems to scale a specific number of user coordinates to exactly match a chosen length. For now, we'll take advantage of the fact that user coordinates are equivalent to CSS px units, and all modern browsers scale real-world units so that there are 96px per in. Since there are 2.54cm per inch—in the real world or in your browser—this means that 10cm is (10*96/2.54) user units, or approximately 377.95 units.

The following path therefore draws the two quadratic curves in Figure 6-6:

```
<path d="M0,0 Q377.95,0 377.95,377.95
         Q0,377.95 0,0 Z"
      fill="royalBlue" />
```

Future Focus
Beyond Simple Coordinates

Although paths are incredibly flexible, they are limited by the requirement that path directions (and also polygon/polyline points) may only use user coordinates, not lengths with units or percentages. It is possible to scale the path as a whole, changing the size of the user coordinates relative to the rest of the graphic. However, it is not currently possible to have some parts of a path scale according to percentage values while other points stay at a fixed offset.

In contrast, the CSS Shapes polygon function allows a mixture of units and percentages. It also allows you to define individual coordinates using calc( )

expressions, so a point can be a percentage plus or minus a fixed offset. (Like `calc(100% - 2em)`, which we used in the clip-path polygon example.)

Future versions of SVG will probably introduce a way to use units, percentages, and arithmetic expressions in path coordinates. However, at the time of writing, there is no accepted proposal for how to do so.

One difficulty is that the condensed path syntax, with letters and numbers following each other, would be confused by having additional letters (units) mixed in. Another issue is the efficiency of the graphical calculations. Currently, when a path is duplicated with `<use>`, its geometrical structure is preserved, and SVG implementations may make use of this to simplify their calculations. If the points of the path included a mix of relative units, absolute units, and percentages, the shape of the path would depend on the context in which it is used.

Smooth Operators: The Smooth Quadratic Command

The two quadratic curves used in Figure 6-6 meet at sharp points. However, earlier we mentioned that you can create continuous curves by connecting multiple Bézier curves *smoothly*.

What makes a smooth connection between curves? A **smooth curve** does not have any sudden changes in direction. In order to connect two curved path segments smoothly, the direction of the curve as it reaches the end of the first segment must exactly match the direction of the curve as it begins the next segment.

Take a look at Figure 6-6 again. The direction of the start of each curve segment is the direction of the line from the start point to the control point. The direction of the end of each segment matches the line from the control point to the end point. Those lines are **tangent** to the start and end of the curve. Line them up so one tangent is a continuation of the other, and your curve will look continuous too.

SVG has a shortcut to make smooth curves easier. The **T (or t) command** creates a quadratic curve that smoothly extends the previous Bézier curve segment. The control point is calculated automatically, based on the control point from the previous segment; the new control point is positioned the same distance from its start point (the previous segment's end point) as the other control point is, but in a straight line on the opposite side.

 Because the control point is implicit, the T is only followed by a single coordinate pair, which specifies the new end point.

Figure 6-7 shows what that looks like. The distance from the control point of the first segment to the mid-point is 3 units right and 5 units down. The reflected control point for the next segment is therefore an *additional* 3 units right and 5 units down. Note that while the control points are reflected, the final shape of the curve is not a mirror reflection. (It could be, but only if the other points were all arranged symmetrically, too.)

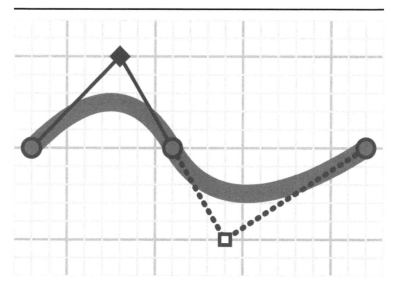

Figure 6-7. A curve made of two quadratic segments, with the control point reflected from the first segment to the second

If the curve segment prior to a T command *wasn't* a quadratic Bézier (smooth or otherwise), the control point for the new segment defaults to its start point. This effectively turns the T segment into a straight line, and turns your smooth connection into a sharp corner.

The smooth curve command is not the only way to smoothly connect Bézier curves. If the second curve should be much deeper or shallower than the previous one, you may need to move the control point to be closer or farther away from the end point, without changing the direction of the tangent line.

To do this, make sure the *slope* of the tangent lines remains the same: the ratio of the change in y-values to the change in x-values. You can also use this calculation to create a curve that smoothly extends from a straight line; the line is its own tangent.

 If you can arrange it so that the tangent lines are perfectly horizontal or perfectly vertical, you can avoid any arithmetic. Simply make sure that the next control point is also on that horizontal or vertical line.

Example 6-2 uses quadratic curves to create a heart icon to match the diamond, with a mix of manual and shorthand smooth connections. The end result should look like this:

Example 6-2. An SVG heart icon using quadratic Bézier curves

```
<svg xmlns="http://www.w3.org/2000/svg" xml:lang="en"
     height="20px" width="20px">
  <title>Heart</title>
  <path fill="red"
        d="M 10,6
           Q 10,0 15,0
           T 20,6
           Q 20,10 15,14
           T 10,20
           Q 10,18 5,14
           T 0,6
           Q 0,0 5,0
           T 10,6
           Z" />
</svg>
```

Figure 6-8 shows the shape, scaled up on the grid. The connect-the-dots numbers have been omitted so we can instead emphasize the positions of the control points. Explicit control points (the ones specified in the code) are marked with solid lines and dark markers; the reflected control points are shown with dotted lines and white square markers.

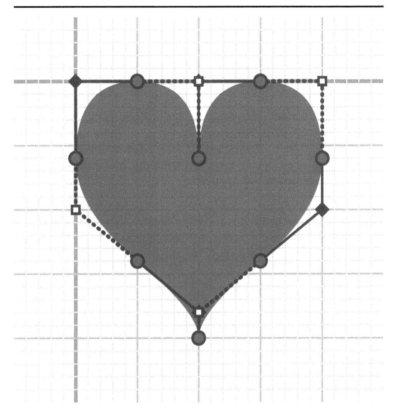

Figure 6-8. A heart drawn with quadratic Bézier curves, showing the control points

The first half of the path directions can be read as follows:

- M 10,6 starts the path at the dimple of the heart, horizontally centered in the 20px width.

- Q 10,0 15,0 creates the first curve segment, tracing the shape of the heart in a clockwise direction. The control point is (10,0) and the end point is (15,0), at the top of the right lobe of the heart.

- `T 20,6` creates a smooth quadratic curve to the far rightmost edge of the heart. The missing control point can be calculated from the previous segment: the tangent line from (10,0) to (15,0) moved 5 units in the x-direction and 0 units vertically; you locate the new control point by repeating that vector, from (15,0) to (20,0).

- `Q 20,10 15,14` manually creates a smooth connection to the next quadratic curve. The ending tangent of the previous segment, from (20,0) to (20,6), was perfectly vertical, so it was easy to position the new control point, (20,10), along the same line. Using that control point, the path segment curves inward to (15,14).

- `T 10,20` smoothly extends the curve, inflecting it back downward to the bottom point of the heart shape. The line from the previous control point (20,10) to the start/end point (15,14) was equal to −5 x units and +4 y units, so the automatically calculated control point will be that same offset again, from (15,14) to (10,18).

The next segment is *not* a smooth continuation of the curve; the bottom of the heart is a sharp point. The rest of the heart is symmetrical to the part drawn so far, reflected around the line $y=10$.

This type of symmetry, it turns out, doesn't make very good use of the automatically calculated control points; in order to recreate the same curves on the other side of the heart, you need to know the control points from the first half. The `Q 10,18 5,14` segment is the reflection of the `T 10,20` segment, but in this case the (10,18) control point needs to be explicitly stated.

With quadratic curves, eight curve segments are required to draw the heart. Each segment can only curve in a single direction, and the start and end points for each segment must be chosen so that a single control point can define both the tangent line that starts the curve and the tangent line that ends it.

To gain more flexibility—to allow the ending tangent of the curve segment to be defined independently from the starting tangent—you need to use cubic curves. But rather than redrawing the heart, the next section uses cubic curves to add a spade to our set of card suit icons.

Paths Beyond SVG

The initial CSS Shapes specification did not include a way to define complex curved paths. This proved limiting as other CSS specifications adopted the use of shapes.

The chosen solution is a `path()` CSS shapes function that accepts a string of SVG path data. Like the `polygon()` function, it would also be possible to specify a fill-rule keyword as an optional first parameter.

This means that any curved shape that can be created with SVG could be used in any CSS property that accepts shape functions. So far, those properties include clip paths, `shape-outside` for curved wrapping around floated images, and motion paths. However, SVG path syntax has its limitations as well: no way to specify coordinates using percentages or relative units, and no easy way (yet) to combine reusable path segments into a single compound path.

This isn't the first time SVG path data has been adopted outside of SVG. As we mentioned briefly earlier, path data strings based on the SVG syntax are used in some HTML canvas drawing functions, and in Android's "vector drawables" XML format.

Wave Motion: The Cubic Bézier Commands

A quadratic Bézier curve is a parabola—useful for creating gentle curves that have a single bend. A **cubic Bézier curve**, on the other hand, is much more flexible.

A cubic curve is defined by *two* control points. The first defines the tangent line from the start point, and the second defines the tangent line to the end point.

If the tangent lines point in opposite directions, a cubic curve segment may have two bends, curving like a letter S in opposite directions. With other control points, the segment may look more like a letter C. A cubic curve may also look not that different from a quadratic curve, with only one gentle bend—or no bend at all, if the two control points fall directly on the line between the start and end points.

Most drawing applications primarily use cubic Bézier curves because they are more flexible than quadratic ones.

Figure 6-9 shows how this flexibility can create curves that no longer feel neat and geometric. The curve consists of two cubic segments, which are smoothly joined with reflecting control points in the middle. But the control points on the ends angle out in completely unrelated directions.

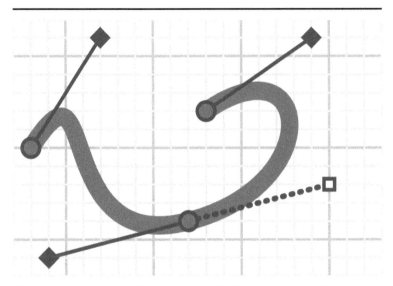

Figure 6-9. A curve made from two cubic Bézier segments, showing the control points

More Online

Geometrically, cubic Bézier curves are created similar to the string art from Figure 6-5, but everything is done twice. It's difficult to picture, but for the computer, it is just a weighted average of weighted averages of all the points.

Read more (and see some best attempts at picturing the construction) in "Calculating Cubic Béziers":

https://oreillymedia.github.io/Using_SVG/extras/ch06-cubic-bezier.html

In the path directions, cubic curves use the letter **C** (or **c**) followed by three sets of coordinates, for the first and second control points and the end point. As always, the start point is taken from the end of the previous command.

Smooth cubic Béziers curves can be used in a similar manner to smooth quadratics. The command letter is **S** (or **s**) and it is followed by two sets of coordinates, for the second control point and the end point. The curve in Figure 6-9 uses the following code:

```
<path d="M 3,10
         C 7,4  4,16 12,14
         S    19,4 13,8 " />
```

The first control point for the smooth segment is calculated automatically.

As with the quadratic smooth curve command, the smooth short-hand only works in certain situations. If you use an S command after a segment that wasn't a cubic Bézier—including after a quadratic Bézier—the automatically calculated control point will default to the curve's start point. This doesn't convert the curve to a *straight line* (as it did for T), since the second control point will still introduce a bend. But it will destroy the smoothness of the connection.

 To smoothly connect quadratic and cubic curves, you can upgrade the quadratic segments to cubic commands by repeating the control point coordinates; a cubic curve where both control points are the same is effectively a quadratic curve.

Example 6-3 continues our series of card suit icons, drawing the following spade shape using cubic Bézier curves:

Example 6-3. An SVG spade icon using cubic Bézier curves

```
<svg xmlns="http://www.w3.org/2000/svg" xml:lang="en"
     height="20px" width="20px">
    <title>Spade</title>
    <path fill="black"
```

```
d="M 9,15
   C 9,20 0,21 0,16
   S 6,9 10,0
   C 14,9 20,11 20,16
   S 11,20 11,15
   Q 11,20 13,20
   H 7
   Q 9,20 9,15 Z" />
</svg>
```

Figure 6-10 shows the scaled-up result with the points marked out on the grid. Again, the solid lines and diamonds mark the explicitly defined control points, while the dotted line and white squares mark the reflected control points. The control points for the cubic and quadratic curves overlap at the stem.

The directions can be read as follows:

- M 9,15 positions the start of the path at the point where the left lobe connects with the stem. As usual, the path will progress clockwise around the shape—direction might not matter if you're not creating cutouts, but it's a good habit to always use clockwise shapes.

- C 9,20 0,21 0,16 draws the entire lower curve of the left lobe. The initial tangent line points directly downward, from (9,15) to (9,20), while the ending tangent line points directly upward, from (0,21) to the end point of (0,16).

- S 6,9 10,0 creates a smooth continuation of the curve, ending with a tangent line from (6,9) to the center point of (10,0).

- C 14,9 20,11 20,16 creates the symmetrical curve: the initial (14,9) control point is the reflection of the (6,9) point from the previous curve, while the second control point (20,11) is the reflection of the point that had been automatically calculated in the previous segment. The (20,16) end point matches the (0,16) point from the initial cubic curve.

- S 11,20 11,15 draws the right lower lobe, reflecting the shape of the left lower lobe.

- Q 11,20 13,20 creates a quadratic curve for the right side of the stem.

- H 7 draws the horizontal line across the bottom of the stem.

- Q 9,20 9,15 Z draws the matching quadratic curve for the opposite edge of the stem, and closes off the path.

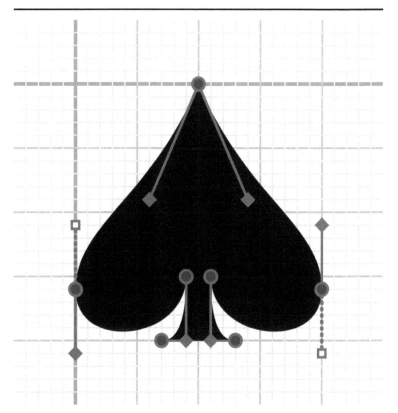

Figure 6-10. A spade drawn with cubic Bézier curves, showing the control points

Using cubic curves, each lobe of the spade was drawn with two path segments, compared to the four quadratic segments required for each lobe of the heart.

Closing Curves

The **Z** *close-path* command, as defined in SVG 1, can only be used to close off a shape using a straight line. To close a curved shape, you need to explicitly repeat the starting coordinate as the ending coordinate of the curve command, and then add a zero-length **Z** command to connect the strokes.

That zero-length **Z** segment is problematic when you use line markers (discussed in Chapter 14) to emphasize every segment. Furthermore, the need to exactly match the starting coordinate can be problematic if your curves use relative coordinates, instead of absolute.

SVG 2 proposes a new approach, where a **Z** (or **z**, doesn't matter) can replace the end point from a curve command. The curve would be drawn as if the missing coordinates were replaced by the starting point of that subpath, and then the ends would be joined without any zero-length connection.

Building the Arcs

In general, cubic Bézier curves can be used to encode nearly any type of shape you might want to draw. However, as mentioned previously, Bézier curves will never *perfectly* match shapes based on mathematical relationships other than quadratic or cubic functions. You can never draw a *perfect* circle or ellipse with a Bézier curve. Because perfect circular arcs are expected in many diagrams, SVG includes a separate command specifically for them.

The final path command in the SVG toolbox is the **arc segment (A or a)**, which creates a circular arc between two points. This is useful for creating circular arcs for pie charts and elliptical arcs for…um, flattened pie charts? It also allows you to create the asymmetrical rounded rectangles that we alluded to in Chapter 5.

The syntax for the arc command is a little more complex than for the Bézier segments. The required parameters are as follows:

```
A rx ry x-axis-rotation large-arc-flag sweep-flag x y
```

The *x* and *y* values at the end of the command are the coordinates of the end point of the arc. These are the only values that differ between absolute (**A**) and relative (**a**) arc commands.

The *rx* and *ry* parameters specify the horizontal and vertical radii lengths of the ellipse from which the arc will be extracted. There's no separate syntax for circular arcs; just set *rx* and *ry* to the same value.

The next number (x-axis-rotation) allows you to rotate the x-axis of the ellipse relative to the x-axis of the coordinate system. The rotation number is interpreted in degrees; positive values are clockwise rotation, and negative values are counterclockwise. For circular arcs, this value is usually 0; rotating a circle has no visible effect on its shape.

The next two parameters tend to confuse people. To fully understand the *large-arc-flag* and *sweep-flag*, it may help to try drawing arcs by hand.

Grab your coffee mug, get a coin out of your pocket, or use a jar, tube, or anything else circular—or elliptical, if you can find an ellipse! Your circular/elliptical design aid, whatever it is, has a fixed radius in both directions. If it's elliptical, try to hold it at a fixed angle, too. Try out this exercise:

1. Take a piece of paper, and mark two points on it for your arc's start point and end point. Don't make them too far apart.

2. Set your coin/coffee mug down on the paper and adjust it until it touches both points.

3. Trace a curve around your circular object to connect the points.

4. Then, trace another curve around the other side of your circle.

5. Take your circle and shift it so that its center point is on the opposite side of the straight line between your start and end points. Readjust it so that it just touches the start and end points.

6. Trace around the circle to connect up the points again, from both directions.

7. Remove your coin/coffee mug. You should have a drawing that looks vaguely like Figure 6-11.

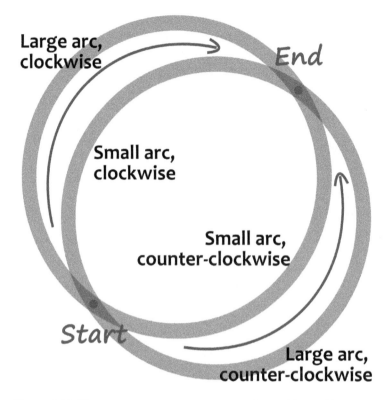

Large arc, clockwise

End

Small arc, clockwise

Small arc, counter-clockwise

Start

Large arc, counter-clockwise

Figure 6-11. *The many ways to connect two points with a coffee mug stain*

Each of the four arcs in Figure 6-11 has been labeled by (a) whether it goes around the longer route (large arc) or the shorter route (small arc), and (b) whether the path from start to end goes around the circle clockwise or counterclockwise. These are the parameters that you specify with the *large-arc-flag* and *sweep-flag*. These parameters are **flags**, meaning that they are "true" (value 1) if the arc should have that property, and "false" (value 0) otherwise.

The *sweep-flag* could be called the *clockwise-flag*, but that would only confuse things once we start transforming the coordinate system. Transformations can create mirror-reflected situations where clockwise isn't clockwise anymore.

If this seems overly confusing, it is. The elliptical arc is one of those commands that gives up in legibility more than what it gains in flexibility. In order to integrate arcs into continuous paths, they need to be defined by precise start and end points, which isn't how arcs are usually defined in geometry.

 If you don't need *perfect* arcs, you can often create a good approximation with quadratic or cubic curves.

The code to draw Figure 6-11 is provided in the online supplementary material. The four arcs are all the same except for the 0 or 1 values in the flag parameters:

```
<path d="M100,350 A180,180 0 1 1 350,100" />
<path d="M100,350 A180,180 0 0 1 350,100" />
<path d="M100,350 A180,180 0 0 0 350,100" />
<path d="M100,350 A180,180 0 1 0 350,100" />
```

Make sure you know which one is which!

Using arcs, we can complete the card suit icon set. The code for this club icon is given in Example 6-4:

Example 6-4. An SVG club icon using arcs

```
<svg xmlns="http://www.w3.org/2000/svg" xml:lang="en"
    height="20px" width="20px">
    <title>Club</title>
    <path fill="black"
        d="M 9,15.5
            A 5,5 0 1 1 5.5,7.5
            A 5,5 0 1 1 14.5,7.5
            A 5,5 0 1 1 11,15.5
            Q 11,20 13,20
            H 7
            Q 9,20 9,15.5 Z" />
</svg>
```

All three arcs are "large," and the entire shape is drawn in a clockwise direction, so both flags are set to 1 for each A command. The stem is the same as for the spade in Example 6-3.

Figure 6-12 shows the enlarged figure, including the complete circles from which the arcs are extracted.

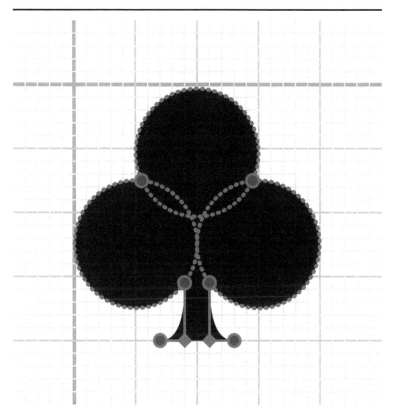

Figure 6-12. A club drawn with path arc commands, showing the underlying geometry

SVG 2 introduces a new path command, which provides a different way to interpret path directions.

The **B** or **b** command will allow you to change the *bearing* (direction) of the path axis, rotating the definition of a horizontal line. A bearing command on its own would not draw anything, but all relative coordinates for other path commands would be calculated relative to current bearing angle, as would the arc-rotation angle in relative arc commands. The bearing would not affect absolute-coordinate commands.

The relative bearing command, **b**, would rotate the bearing angle relative to the tangent direction—rather than the end point—of the previous path segment.

Another proposed extension would provide a different way of defining curves. A **R** or **r** spline curve command would allow you to connect a series of points with a continuous smooth curve. The shape will be calculated by the Catmull-Rom algorithm, which adjusts the curve of a segment between each pair of points so that it visually connects to the previous and subsequent points. The exact syntax has not been settled at the time of writing; it will be included in a future SVG Paths module.

Summary: Custom Shapes

The core concept of SVG (and vector graphics, in general) is that drawings can be described through a set of precise mathematical instructions. With the exception of the few common shape elements described in Chapter 5, most SVG shapes are drawn point by point, using `<polygon>`, `<polyline>`, or the infinitely flexible `<path>`.

While `<polygon>` and `<polyline>` elements can be described by a simple list of points, the `<path>` uses its own language to describe what type of line to draw and how.

Drawing a shape is the first step in creating a piece of artwork, and the tools that SVG provides here are extremely robust. The next step is to be able to position and manipulate those shapes within the vector coordinate system.

The basic shapes `<line>`, `<rect>`, `<circle>`, and `<ellipse>`, while limited in geometry, are incredibly flexible in size because each geometric attribute can be set independently with user coordinates, units, or percentages. In contrast, `<path>`, `<polygon>`, and `<polyline>` allow complete customization of the shape, but all the points must be defined relative to the user coordinate system. To create flexibility in their position and size, you need to manipulate the coordinate system directly, something we'll explore in Part III.

Before we get there, however, we have one final set of SVG shapes to discuss: letters! And numbers! And emoji! In other words, text—the topic of Chapter 7.

More Online

The new elements and attributes introduced in this chapter are included in the "Shape Elements" section of our markup guide:

https://oreillymedia.github.io/Using_SVG/guide/markup.html#shapes

The "Path Commands" guide is a reference for the syntax for path data:

https://oreillymedia.github.io/Using_SVG/guide/path-data.html

A reference for CSS shapes is provided in the "CSS Shape Functions" guide:

https://oreillymedia.github.io/Using_SVG/guide/css-shapes.html

---

CHAPTER 7

The Art of the Word

Graphical Text Layout

Text in SVG is treated very similarly to shapes. Individual letters can be positioned anywhere in the graphic and can be filled or stroked (or both). Instead of using geometric attributes to define this "text shape," you use the text content of the element itself, combined with font-selection style properties and a few SVG-specific text layout attributes and properties.

The font-selection properties in SVG are entirely borrowed from core CSS. If you're familiar with styling text with CSS (and we're assuming you are) you are halfway to styling SVG text. You can even use web fonts declared with an @font-face rule, although external font files—like external stylesheets—are restricted in some SVG contexts.

SVG text layout, in contrast, does *not* reuse CSS layout. When used to style HTML, CSS lays out text by dividing the page into boxes and then wrapping streams of text within them. If you change the styles of a section of HTML text so that it takes up more space, the rest of the text is pushed out of the way, or wraps to a new line. SVG text doesn't (yet) work like that.

In SVG, each <text> element is independent, positioned exactly where you place it, even if it overlaps other content. There are ways to make SVG text flow in continuous streams, but it takes much more work than the equivalent CSS layout. SVG text is therefore best reserved for its intended purposes: figure labels and short snippets of precisely positioned decorative text.

Better support for large blocks of automatically wrapping text has long been a requested feature for SVG. A few programs, such as Inkscape, implemented a proposal from the SVG 1.2/SVG Tiny 1.2 specifications, but it is not supported on the web.

A new proposal, with better CSS integration, is part of SVG 2 but has not been implemented in mainstream browsers (as of mid-2017).

There are numerous complexities to SVG text layout, and—unfortunately—numerous areas where browser implementations are incomplete or inconsistent. If you are interested in all the details, we have written a complete book on the subject.[1]

This chapter briefly introduces the three main types of SVG text layout:

- short labels positioned around a single anchor point
- precise character-by-character positioned graphical text
- text arranged on a path

The features described here are relatively well-supported in web browsers, at least for Western languages. If you are using right-to-left languages such as Hebrew or Arabic, or scripted languages that use complex text shaping (changing or re-arranging the appearance of characters based on their context), beware of browsers making a mess of your text when using character positioning or text on a path.

The original SVG specifications also included a way to define entire custom fonts as SVG graphics; however, SVG fonts aren't supported in most browsers and can't be relied upon for their original purpose of providing consistent, cross-application text rendering.

---

1 Amelia Bellamy-Royds and Kurt Cagle, *SVG Text Layout* (Sebastopol, CA: O'Reilly, 2015).

SVG fonts are not part of the SVG 2 specification. Instead, the SVG in OpenType specification aims to integrate SVG graphics into OpenType, the most commonly used format for defining font metadata.

We're not going to talk about designing your own fonts here, but we do have some tips on working with web fonts and fallback system fonts.

When Text Isn't Text

There are many benefits to using SVG for decorative text that you can't easily create with regular CSS. But those benefits come with some qualifications and complications.

Before starting with SVG text, it's important to understand *how* the text will be used on the page, since that will determine the techniques you use to produce the final result. Images behave very differently from objects or inline SVG.

If you embed an SVG with text elements into a web page with a <img> tag, or if you use it as a CSS background image, you should be aware of a few restrictions:

No web fonts
Browsers prevent external file downloads with SVG used as an image, so any @font-face references to web fonts will be ignored.

Loss of accessibility
Text in the image won't be read by screen readers; you must provide an accessible equivalent using the <img> element's alt attribute (or ARIA attributes).

No text selection
Text in the image can't be selected or copied by the user. This means users cannot easily look up or translate unfamiliar words, and text can't be searched with browser "Find" commands.

Lowered editability

You won't be able to edit the text directly when working with the HTML; you'd have to make changes in the SVG document, upload the file, and refresh the HTML page that references it. There is also no way to update the text via script.

Due to these limitations, when an SVG will be used as an image, it's fairly common to convert text inside it into paths in the shape of the letters. Converting text to paths is particularly useful for logos, where the text must be rendered in exactly the right way every time.

The conversion process must be done by an application that has access to the desired font: in Adobe Illustrator, for example, the option is called "Create Outlines" under the Type menu. Newer versions also allow you to apply the conversion in the SVG export process. In Inkscape, use "Object to Path" in the Path menu.

Naturally, this dramatically alters the editability of the text: with paths, you can move points and change stroke and fill, but can no longer treat the shapes as actual text.

 When converting text to paths, always save a separate copy of the graphic with the editable text, in case you need to change it later.

Converting text to paths can also change the sizing of gradients or patterns, as we'll discuss in Chapter 12.

In contrast, when SVG markup containing `<text>` elements is placed inline as part of an HTML page, the disadvantages associated with text-as-image disappear: the text is editable, uses `@font-face` settings, is fully accessible, and can be copied by users or found with browser page-search features.

The accessibility improvements should also apply for SVG files embedded as interactive `<object>` or `<embed>` elements, although browsers have a tendency to be buggy with accessibility of SVG content inside an embedded object—so test carefully! The SVG text remains in a separate file, of course, so must be edited separately from the main web page. Whether this is an advantage or disadvantage depends on whether the test is reused on many pages (logos or advertisements), or specific to the current page (like decorative headings).

Whether inline, image, or object, SVG text retains a number of advantages. Compared to bitmap images of text (which were once commonly used for decorative headings on the web), SVG text remains crisp at any scale, so is accessible to those that need higher magnification. Compared to bitmaps or to text converted to paths, it is easily editable if you need to change it later. These benefits remain even when the text uses highly convoluted layouts, or is enhanced with decorative filters, masks, or gradients.

Working with Web Fonts

Real SVG text requires real fonts to tell the browser how to draw each letter. You have three options:

- Use only common fonts that will be available on most systems.
- Use web font files that are linked by a CSS `@font-face` rule.
- Use web font data embedded in your SVG.

In the first two cases, you need to think carefully about fallbacks to use if your chosen font isn't available. If you're using a graphics editor, they won't add fallbacks for you. You'll need to open up your file in a code editor and edit the styles to change the `font-family` list.

If you're using web fonts, you'll also need to add an **@font-face rule** for each typeface. The format of the `@font-face` rule is the same as for CSS-styled HTML. Place the rule where you need it:

- If you're using inline SVG, it automatically shares the `@font-face` rules that apply to the rest of the page.
- If you're sharing web fonts between your SVG objects and the rest of the website, you can link your existing stylesheet (using the methods discussed in "External stylesheets" on page 79, in Chapter 3).
- Otherwise, create a `<style>` element in your SVG, and add the `@font-face` there.

If fallback fonts are a design problem, embedding the font data in the SVG can be an attractive option. It means that the complete drawing instructions are contained in a single *.svg* file, which still uses real, accessible text.

Embedding was one of the goals behind SVG fonts, which defined font data through SVG `<font>`, `<glyph>`, and related elements, which could be included in the same file. But SVG fonts had other problems and are now deprecated, with very poor browser support.

Instead, the best approach to embedding fonts today is to use an OpenType font format (such as WOFF), converted to a data URI.

More Online

Data URI fonts should not be your default choice. If used carelessly or excessively, they can considerably limit performance.

Read more about data URI fonts, when to use them, and how to create them, in "Creating Embeddable Fonts as Data URIs":

https://oreillymedia.github.io/Using_SVG/extras/ch07-dataURI-fonts.html

The browser's final choice of typeface for each character is based on a complicated font-matching and fallback algorithm. However, this algorithm is the same for SVG as it is for other CSS-styled text.

Typewriter Text

The bare minimum for SVG text, as we showed in Chapter 1, is a **`<text>` element** with **x and/or y attributes**. It can be quickly enhanced with CSS rules or presentation attributes to define styles.

Unlike HTML, SVG will not automatically render text simply typed into the document; text in SVG *must* appear inside a `<text>` element.

Example 7-1 shows the basic markup to style some text and include it in an SVG; Figure 7-1 is the output. We'll discuss the attributes one at a time.

Some Test SVG Te:

Figure 7-1. SVG text, with minimal style and layout

Example 7-1. Defining basic text in an SVG

```
<svg xmlns="http://www.w3.org/2000/svg" xml:lang="en"
     width="500" height="80">
    <text x="1em" y="60"
          font-size="64" font-weight="bold"
          font-family="Brush Script MT, Brush Script,
                       Segoe Script, cursive">
        Some Test SVG Text
    </text>
</svg>
```

The *x,y* position you specify is—by default—the position of the **baseline** of the first letter in the text. The baseline is the invisible line that letters "sit" on, lining up the bottoms of most of the letters. The browser then "types" the rest of the text in a straight line from there.

 As with the geometric attributes for basic shapes, SVG text positioning attributes can have different units, or no units at all. The font-relative em unit is particularly useful for text.

Note that SVG does *not* wrap text when it runs out of room: words in a <text> element that extend outside the SVG dimensions simply disappear. (Or overflow, if you're using inline SVG with overflow: visible.)

Disappearing text can also be an issue if you omit the y attribute of a <text> element, as it defaults to 0. In a simple SVG like this, this means your text would be drawn so it is sitting on the top edge of your SVG frame, with only the descenders (the tails of letters like *p* and *y*) visible.

Under most circumstances, the y value of a `<text>` element should be at least (or almost) as large as its `font-size`, to ensure that the text is seen.

Starting in Chapter 8, we will introduce another solution: change the coordinate system so 0 isn't right at the top!

As with HTML text, extra spaces in the markup for an SVG `<text>` element are normally ignored, and collapse to a single space. Spaces at the beginning or end of an element, however, have more complicated collapsing rules and inconsistent behavior cross-browser, both of which can sometimes throw off your layout.

It often helps to put your start and end tags right up next to the text content:

```
<text x="50%" y="3em">like this</text>
<text x="50%" y="5em" font-family="long family name"
    >or like this</text>
```

The remaining attributes used in Example 7-1 are presentation attributes for standard CSS font properties: `font-size`, `font-weight`, and `font-family`.

The SVG `font-family` attribute uses the same cascading fallback as the CSS `font-family` property. Other properties, like `font-weight` (for boldness) and `font-style` (for italics), are similarly familiar.

When specified in a presentation attribute, `font-size` can be given as a plain number and is assumed to be measured in pixels (this is what we did in Example 7-1). In CSS, however, the px must be specified explicitly. Like all other measurements in SVG, font size scales along with the coordinate system, so the actual used font size will depend on how large or small the SVG is drawn.

These presentation attributes map directly to their CSS equivalents. It's often more efficient to write them in CSS format, as in Example 7-2 (which looks identical to Figure 7-1 when displayed).

Example 7-2. Using CSS rules to style text in an SVG

```
<svg xmlns="http://www.w3.org/2000/svg" xml:lang="en"
    width="500" height="80">
    <title>Sample SVG Text, styled with CSS</title>
    <style>
        text {
            font-family: Brush Script MT, Brush Script,
                        Segoe Script, cursive;
            font-size: 64px;
            font-weight: bold;
        }
    </style>
    <text y="60" x="1em">Some Test SVG Text</text>
</svg>
```

If you're using CSS (but *not* if you're using presentation attributes), you can also use the font shorthand to set all these properties. The styles in Example 7-2 could be replaced by one declaration:

```
text {
    font: bold 64px Brush Script MT, Brush Script,
                Segoe Script, cursive;
}
```

In inline SVG, all the font properties inherit from the surrounding page. For standalone SVG, the browser's default font settings are used if you don't change them.

 A declared font-size (in absolute units) is recommended for standalone SVG files: older WebKit and Blink browser versions unfortunately applied a default font size of 0 (i.e., infinitely small) in SVG images, with unpredictable results.

Future Focus
Positioning Text with CSS

In both SVG 1.1 and SVG 2, the x and y values cannot be set with CSS properties: they must be written as attributes.

In Chapter 5, we mentioned how the x and y attributes on <rect> and other elements are redefined in SVG 2 as geometry properties that can be controlled in CSS. However, text elements use a different syntax for these attributes (as we'll see in the section "Adjusting the Typewriter" on page 234), and so the spec couldn't include them in the same property without changing its syntax for all elements. One proposed option is to create separate `text-x` and `text-y` properties, but no decision has been made.

Colorful Language

An important difference between CSS-styled HTML text and SVG text is that `color` does not change the color of text in SVG. Instead, SVG text uses `fill`, as either an attribute or a CSS property:

```
text { fill: red; }
```

To coordinate inline SVG text with the color of surrounding text, use `fill: currentColor`. This sets the `fill` value to match the inherited `color` value.

 The same trick doesn't work with embedded images or objects: style values from the main page do not inherit into the external file!

Text can also be stroked in SVG, achieving an effect that cannot yet be reliably recreated in CSS cross-browser:

```
text { fill: red; stroke: black; stroke-width: 2px; }
```

When those additional styles are added to the code from Examples 7-1 and 7-2, the result is Figure 7-2.

Figure 7-2. SVG text, filled in red and stroked in black

As we showed in Chapter 1, the `fill` and `stroke` values can instead reference gradients or other SVG paint server effects, the same as for filling and stroking SVG shapes.

Simple typewriter-style text layout like this may not be particularly artistic, but it still has an important role in graphics. The next section looks at SVG text for labels in a figure or diagram.

Responsive Text Scaling

To demonstrate how SVG text can be used to label a figure, we're going to add labels to a photograph. Unlike labels that are added directly to a photo with Photoshop or other editors, the SVG labels will remain accessible, easy to edit, and crisp at any scale. But in case that's not enough, we're going to expand the show off one of SVG text's superpowers, using CSS to make the labels responsive.

A photograph in an SVG? But of course!

We'll talk more about the `<image>` element in Chapter 10. For now, just trust that it is similar to the HTML `<img>` element, and allows you to embed another image file in your SVG document.

The photograph we're using is of a Lynskey 2017 Vialé bicycle; we'll label it to highlight product features. Example 7-3 gives the code for importing the photograph into an SVG, and adding the `<text>` labels on top. The original photograph is 1,000×586 pixels, so those are the dimensions we've used for the SVG (the image is then set to take up 100% of the SVG dimensions). Figure 7-3 shows the labeled result.

Figure 7-3. The labeled photograph

Example 7-3. Using SVG text to label a photograph

```
<svg xmlns="http://www.w3.org/2000/svg" xml:lang="en"
    xmlns:xlink="http://www.w3.org/1999/xlink"
    width="1000px" height="586px" id="lynskey">
    <title>Lynskey 2017 Vialé Technical Details</title>
    <style>
        svg text {
            font: 20px sans-serif;
            fill: darkBlue;
        }
    </style>
    <image width="100%" height="100%" xlink:href="viale.jpg" />
    <text x="360" y="520">DTSwiss TK540/X.9 Wheelset</text>
    <text x="80" y="120">Selle Italia X1 Flow Saddle</text>
    <text x="420" y="200">Titanium frame</text>
    <text x="80" y="570">SRAM Apex rear dérailleur</text>
</svg>
```

Figure 7-3 shows the result when the SVG file from Example 7-3 is viewed directly. To add it to a web page, you would need to embed it either by copying the code inline, or by using an HTML <object>. (Or <embed>. Or <iframe>. They are functionally much the same as <object>.)

Using an HTML <img> isn't an option. As we've already mentioned earlier in this chapter, the text labels wouldn't be accessible in an image. But in this case, there's an even greater reason: the photograph won't be shown at all if the SVG is displayed as an <img>, because it's an external asset file, and external files aren't loaded when SVG is used as an image.

If we're going to embed the graphic in a web page, we probably want to be able to control its size, so it can scale down on mobile devices. That means adding a viewBox attribute (which we'll talk more about in Chapter 8). In the simplest version of a viewBox, the width and height in pixels are used as the third and fourth values in the viewBox attribute:

```
<svg xmlns="http://www.w3.org/2000/svg" xml:lang="en"
     xmlns:xlink="http://www.w3.org/1999/xlink"
     viewBox="0 0 1000 586" id="lynskey">
```

The viewBox creates a responsive SVG that scales to fit the available space. Now the SVG and the photograph inside it will scale to fit within whatever CSS dimensions we set on the HTML <object> (or on the <svg> itself, if we copy the markup directly into the HTML).

Unfortunately, however, the text will *also* scale down. The 20px font size that is clear and easy to read full-screen can become miniscule if the SVG is displayed on a mobile screen, or as a preview in a catalogue page.

For this reason, you may want to adjust the used font-size of SVG text at certain breakpoints to make it more readable. When the available space is *smaller*, the declared font-size (before scaling down) should be *larger*. Assuming the SVG will be used as an <object>, the following media queries can be added to the code:

```
@media (max-width: 600px), (max-height: 342px) {
    svg text { font-size: 28px; }
}
@media (max-width: 400px), (max-height: 235px) {
    svg text { font-size: 36px; }
}
```

As we warned in Chapter 3, the appropriate media queries will be different when the SVG is a standalone document versus when it is inline in an HTML document. With an `<object>`, the media queries are directly related to the SVG dimensions. In inline SVG, you would need to consider the overall layout.

To make the font-size change a little smoother when the size of the SVG embedded object changes, you can add in a CSS transition effect:

```
svg text { transition: font-size 0.5s; }
```

Figure 7-4 shows scaled-down versions of the labeled diagram. On the left is the original scaled-down text, and on the right is the result of adding in the media queries; in this case, the second query is in effect, so the text is at 36px font size, relative to the SVG scale. It's not perfect, because the text now overlaps the dark lines in the photograph, but it is probably still easier to read for many people.

Figure 7-4. The labeled photograph, scaled down, with and without font-size media queries

The *displayed* font size will never be 36px, of course: the media query only kicks in when the entire SVG is drawn at 40% scale or smaller, so the net font size will be 14px or less.

More Online

Being responsive to size changes is only one of SVG text's super-powers, relative to standard image formats. We can also make the text interactive by changing styles or text visibility as the user inter-acts with the web page.

Read more in "Interactive Text", which shows how we can make the labels from Example 7-3 appear and disappear as the user hovers over the figure:

https://oreillymedia.github.io/Using_SVG/extras/ch07-interactive-labels.html

While interaction and media queries can add a lot of functionality to this diagram, the text labels aren't particularly artistic. For a simple labeled figure, that's fine, but not in other cases. Posters, album covers, comic books, and many other graphics need more precise control over lettering. The rest of this chapter looks at the more graphical side of text layout in SVG.

Anchors and Alignment

To demonstrate advanced text layout in a practical setting, the next few sections use text in comic book–style speech bubbles.

Text is, of course, a key aspect of most comic books, and the layout and styles of the text are often used to convey the tone of voice, so we want to get them just right. Many (most) online comic books use bitmap image formats to save the text as part of the drawing, but that means inaccessible text that can't be selected or found in a search. SVG has the ability to provide the necessary layout control with accessible text, but we'll need a few more attributes and style properties to do so.

For starters, comic books will often need multiple lines of text to be aligned into a single speech bubble. As we've mentioned a few times, SVG (version 1.1) doesn't support automatically wrapping text, but you can of course position multiple text lines one after another.

A simple approach is shown in Example 7-4. It uses three separate <text> elements to convey a quote from Herman Melville's *Moby Dick*, with the result displayed in Figure 7-5.

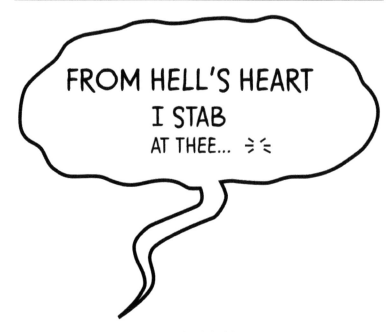

Figure 7-5. SVG text in a comic book bubble

Example 7-4. Positioning graphical SVG text

```
<svg xmlns="http://www.w3.org/2000/svg" xml:lang="en"
    viewBox="0 0 216 175">
    <title>Moby Dick—Comic Book text</title>
    <style>
@font-face {
    font-family: 'SequentialistBB';
    src: url('fonts/SequentialistBB.woff2') format('woff2'),
        url('fonts/SequentialistBB.woff') format('woff');
    font-style: normal;
    font-weight: 400;
}
path {
    fill: #fff;
    stroke: #000;
    stroke-width: 2;
}
text {
```

```
    font-family: SequentialistBB, cursive;
}
.gasp-lines {
    stroke: #000;
    stroke-width: 1px;
}
    </style>
    <path d="...long path data string omitted..." />
    <text font-size="20" y="45" x="30">FROM HELL's HEART</text>
    <text font-size="18" y="65" x="80">I STAB</text>
    <text font-size="14" y="80" x="80">AT THEE…</text>
    <g class="gasp-lines" aria-label="(gasp)">
        <line x1="137" y1="72" x2="140" y2="74" />
        <line x1="144" y1="74" x2="147" y2="72" />
        <line x1="146" y1="76" x2="150" y2="76" />
        <line x1="146" y1="78" x2="150" y2="80" />
        <line x1="137" y1="80" x2="140" y2="78" />
        <line x1="135" y1="76" x2="140" y2="76" />
    </g>
</svg>
```

The graphic uses a "fainting" text effect, with each line smaller than the last, as set by the font-size presentation attributes. However, each <text> element is still a simple typewriter-style label of matching characters in a single line.

In the next section, "Switching Styles with <tspan>" on page 232, we'll show how you can modify font styles within a single line of text, without ruining the layout.

Example 7-4 uses a custom font, included with a CSS @font-face rule. If the web font is downloaded and used, Figure 7-5 is the result. However, if the web font *isn't* used—because of network issues, because the browser doesn't support WOFF fonts, or because the user has turned off font downloads—the font-family rule instructs the browser to use its default cursive font.

Figure 7-6 shows what that will look like in the most common cursive fonts in Windows (Comic Sans, on the left) and in Mac (Apple Chancery, on the right).

Figure 7-6. SVG text in a comic book bubble, displayed in default handwriting fonts

Uh oh. Beyond the stylistic differences caused by the change in typeface, the fallback renderings in Figure 7-6 have some serious layout issues: text is getting cut off, and is overlapping graphical details. We can help fix these issues by improving our font stack, and by changing how we lay out the text.

First, the layout fixes.

So far, we've been laying out text lines by defining the position of the first character. This is the default, but it's not the only option. The *x,y* point we use to layout SVG text is called an **anchor** point. The **text-anchor style property** or presentation attribute lets us change whether that point marks the start (default), middle, or end of the line.

 Why not left, center, and right instead of start, middle, and end? Because SVG text was also designed for vertical and right-to-left text layouts: start and end aren't always left and right.

For a speech bubble effect, you usually want text centered in the middle of the bubble. We can do this by adding text-anchor: middle to the text elements (as a CSS rule or presentation attribute), and adjusting the x attribute accordingly.

For the last line in Example 7-4, however, there's an extra complication: the "breath mark" (signifying a last gasp or sigh) drawn with SVG lines, which should be aligned right after the text. Moving the lines to fit the text would require JavaScript; it's easier to right-align the text to the lines with `text-anchor: end`, so that it never overlaps.

The following changed markup shows those alterations, with the `text-anchor` for each line set with presentation attributes:

```
<text font-size="20" y="45" x="103" text-anchor="middle">
    FROM HELL's HEART</text>
<text font-size="18" y="65" x="103" text-anchor="middle">
    I STAB</text>
<text font-size="14" y="80" x="127" text-anchor="end">
    AT THEE…</text>
```

The x attributes have been adjusted so that there is barely any movement of the text when the web font is used; with our chosen font, it will look almost exactly like Figure 7-5.

Rather than figure out all the changed positions with trial and error, the browser can do the calculations for you. We outline the most important text-related DOM methods in "Measuring the Message" on page 250.

With this new markup, the fallback renderings are improved, as shown in Figure 7-7. The text no longer overlaps the breath mark icon, and it mostly fits in the SVG—although still not completely in the speech bubble!

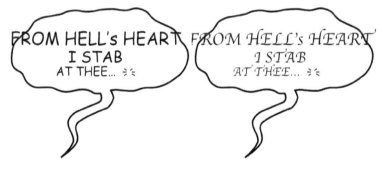

Figure 7-7. SVG text in a comic book bubble, after text anchors are adjusted, displayed in default handwriting fonts

We're going to need some better fallback fonts. The font from the original design, Sequentialist BB, is a relatively condensed (narrow) font, at least as far as capital letters go. It took a bit of experimenting to find similarly condensed fonts among those that come preinstalled on common operating systems.

 There are a number of websites that list operating system fonts and fallbacks for CSS; unfortunately, many are not kept up to date anymore. The two that were most useful for this example were fontfamily.io, which tells you which fonts would be most likely used for a given font-family declaration, and A Padded Cell's "Complete Guide to Pre-Installed Fonts in Linux, Mac, and Windows" (*http://www.apadded cell.com/sites/www.apaddedcell.com/files/fonts-article/final/index.html*), which provides a comparison table of available fonts, with screenshots of their appearance.

The final CSS for the font fallbacks is as follows:

```
text {
    font-family: SequentialistBB,
                 Papyrus-condensed, Impact,
                 sans-serif-condensed, sans-serif;
    font-stretch: condensed;
}
```

If the Sequentialist BB web font is available it will be used. Otherwise, the font-family stack is searched in order:

- Papyrus if it is available in condensed version (it is on most Mac and iPhones);
- Impact (available on all Windows systems, desktop Mac, and in a common font extension for Linux systems);
- sans-serif-condensed, which is a special keyword available in Android that usually matches to Roboto Condensed;
- Otherwise, the default sans-serif font (which is likely to be less extravagant than a cursive font). The font-stretch property ensures that a condensed version of that font is used if available.

The net result, on a standard Windows or Mac desktop, is shown in Figure 7-8.

Figure 7-8. SVG text in a comic book bubble, after text anchors are adjusted and fallback fonts are specified

In other operating systems, there is more variation, but it is usually readable, as shown in the mobile browser screenshots in Figure 7-9.[2]

Figure 7-9. SVG comic book text, with fallback fonts in mobile browsers

There are two more tools you can use to get SVG text to fit:

---

[2] Mobile screenshots generated using the Cross Browser Testing (*https://crossbrowsertest ing.com/*) online service.

- The `font-size-adjust` style property, which adjusts fallback font sizes to match the ex height instead of the em height; unfortunately, it's currently only supported in Firefox.

- The `textLength` SVG attribute, which is best for minor adjustments or for intentionally distorted text; we'll discuss how it works later in the chapter.

Getting good fallback fonts for a graphic isn't easy. It's easy to understand why many designers convert text to paths in their SVG editor, while they still have full control of the fonts. However, for a text-heavy graphic like a comic book, poster, or diagram, having fully accessible, selectable text will be appreciated by many end users.

Switching Styles with <tspan>

Each text element in Example 7-4 uses a different font size. They could have easily also used different font styles or fill colors, just by setting different styles on each element.

In order to change styles—with CSS or with presentation attributes —you need a new element. That was easy enough when we were changing an entire line at a time. But what happens when you only want to style *part* of a line? For example, to emphasize a word with *italic* text, like that?

After all the examples of fallback fonts, you should be wise enough not to try to position separate `<text>` elements side-by-side, pretending to be one continuous line of text. You need a way to switch up the styles without resetting the layout.

The key to this is SVG **<tspan> element**: much like the HTML `<span>` element, `<tspan>` wraps around words, characters, or short phrases to provide a different appearence for part of a `<text>` element. Also like `<span>`, a `<tspan>` makes no difference by itself: some sort of style or attribute must be applied to it to make a change.

A `<tspan>` cannot be used on its own: it must be contained inside a `<text>` element.

Example 7-5 provides the core markup for another comic book bubble, this time containing the "Fe Fi Fo Fum" chant of the giant in *Jack and the Beanstalk*. Some words are made bold or italic via <tspan>, including nested <tspan> elements. Nonetheless, they are all laid out as a single line of text. Figure 7-10 shows the rendering.

Example 7-5. Using <tspan> to modify text styles

```
<svg xmlns="http://www.w3.org/2000/svg" xml:lang="en"
     viewBox="0 0 216 175">
    <style>
        /* omitted */
    </style>
    <path d="M45,5 l20,20 c60-5 120,-5 125,40
             s-70,28 -80,30 -100,0 -100-30 10,-40 35-40Z" />
    <text font-size="28" y="70" x="100" text-anchor="middle">
        Fe <tspan font-style="italic">Fi</tspan>
        Fo <tspan font-weight="bold"
            >Fum<tspan font-style="italic">!</tspan></tspan>
    </text>
</svg>
```

Figure 7-10. Styled SVG text in a comic book bubble

The styles have been excluded from Example 7-5 because they are mostly the same as Example 7-4 (after adding in all the fallback fonts, of course!). To support the different type styles in Example 7-5, an extra @font-face declaration was added to the <style> block, providing the italic version of the font.

An astute observer will note that Example 7-5 actually uses *four* different type-faces: regular, italic, bold, and bold italic. The bold versions are **synthesized** by the browser, essentially by drawing a black stroke around the letters. Synthesized bold type is generally considered a typographic atrocity by designers, but for this particular font family it doesn't look that bad.

Why not use `stroke: black` instead of `font-weight: bold`, if the end result is the same? Because it won't be the same for the fallback fonts: for those, we want the browser to use proper bold typefaces.

We applied the actual bold and italic formatting using presentation attributes. There aren't any semantic (inherently meaningful) text formatting elements in SVG, like `<em>` and `<strong>` in HTML. A `<tspan>` must be used for all formatting changes.

There is actually one element that provides for meaningful markup within an SVG `<text>`, and can be styled accordingly: the `<a>` element for creating hyperlinks, which we'll discuss in Chapter 18.

Of course, the style changes on the `<tspan>` elements could have been assigned with CSS rules, instead of attributes.

Adjusting the Typewriter

So far, we've been positioning SVG `<text>` elements as complete blocks, one line at a time. Individual characters follow from wherever the baseline is set with x and y attributes. Although Example 7-4 created the appearance of multiline text, it was really three independent `<text>` elements, carefully aligned one after another.

However, by adding positioning attributes to a `<tspan>`, it is possible to break a single text element into multiple "chunks" for layout purposes. It's also possible to typeset individual characters to their own positions, which is neccessary for some text special effects that are impossible or very difficult to achieve in standard HTML text.

For <tspan>, the attributes most commonly applied are **dx and dy**, which provide values for a *relative* shift in position (horizontal and vertical, respectively) for the associated text, away from the normal, default position.

In contrast, x and y attributes represent *absolute* positions, measured from the origin of the coordinate system.

You can move the text baseline up and down by wrapping the relevant characters in <tspan> elements with dy values to apply a vertical offset without changing the horizontal flow:

```
<text font-size="28" y="55" x="100" text-anchor="middle">
    Fe <tspan dy="10" font-style="italic">Fi</tspan>
    <tspan dy="10">Fo</tspan>
    <tspan dy="10" font-weight="bold"
        >Fum<tspan font-style="italic">!</tspan></tspan>
</text>
```

The basic y value for the <text> element has been shifted up (relative to Example 7-5), and then each dy value shifts the vertical position of the text down 10 units, as shown in Figure 7-11. The horizontal position, including the text-anchor centering, is not affected.

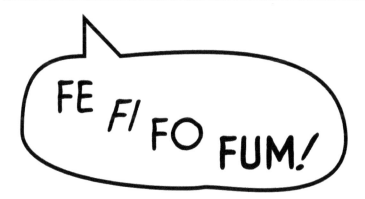

Figure 7-11. Styled and vertically staggered SVG text in a comic book bubble

The dy values are cumulative, even though the <tspan> elements are not nested: the shift in the "typewriter" position persists outside the end of the element with the attribute.

In contrast, the baseline-shift style property is designed for temporary shifts in position that revert to the original baseline after the affected element is closed. Unfortunately, baseline-shift browser support is still poor.

You can use any combination of default positioning, x or y absolute positioning, and dx or dy relative positioning. A common pattern is to use an absolute x value to reset the horizontal position, and then a dy value to shift the text down a line, in effect creating multiline text.

In the days of electric typewriters, hard line breaks were always encoded this way: a "carriage return" (CR) character to reset the horizontal position, followed by a "line feed" (LF) character to shift the print head down. This legacy still haunts us in the discrepancy between text encodings on Windows (two-character, CRLF line breaks by default) versus Linux/Mac (one-character, LF line breaks).

Using this approach, we can combine the three separate <text> elements from Example 7-4 into a single <text> laid out with <tspan> elements:

```
<text font-size="20" y="45" x="103" text-anchor="middle">
    FROM HELL's HEART
    <tspan font-size="18" dy="1.1em" x="103">
    I STAB</tspan>
    <tspan font-size="14" dy="1.1em" x="127" text-anchor="end">
    AT THEE…</tspan>
</text>
```

Each <tspan> in this example has its own alignment anchor, created by the absolute x value, as does the initial line that is positioned with attributes on the <text>. The type of text-anchor (middle versus end) is inherited from the parent <text> element, except where it is explicitly changed on the span.

Automatically Positioned Multiline SVG Text

As mentioned briefly in the chapter introduction, SVG 2 adds proper multiline text support, in three forms:

- Preformatted text, using `white-space: pre` to preserve line breaks, spaces, and tabs from the markup. Each hardcoded line break causes the text position to be reset to the last **x** position, with the **y** position advanced by the value of the `line-height` property. (Or the reverse, for vertical text modes.)

- Simple auto-wrapping text, using the `inline-size` property to define the maximum length of each line of text. If the text extends beyond this length, the browser should automatically insert line breaks, which have the same effect on layout as the preformatted breaks.

- Text in a shape, using the `shape-inside` property to define the shape that the text should fit inside of (as a CSS Shapes function or a `url()` reference to an SVG shape element). The `shape-inside` property is also proposed for use with CSS text layout, in the CSS Shapes level 2 module. Text inside the shape would be laid out like text in CSS layout boxes, with the `text-align` property used for justification and alignment.

At the time of writing (mid-2017), Firefox has implemented the first option, but no browser has implemented automatically-wrapping SVG text.

Full-Control Characters

All this is very well for adjusting the layout of chunks of text. But what if you want to play with the layout of individual characters, like in Figure 7-12?

Figure 7-12. SVG text with staggered letters

Figure 7-12 is a double-shot pop culture reference: The "talking like Shatner…" text and its
wavery layout are directly borrowed from a
frame of the Marvel comic *Deadpool*. These are
real-world text layout requirements!

In order to "stagger" the characters in Figure 7-12 using <tspan>
elements, we'd need to wrap each individual character in its own
<tspan> element, and provide it with a new y or dy value.

Obviously, this can get tiresome, bloating our markup and making it
difficult to read and edit. Thankfully, SVG has a shortcut method to
sequentially affect all of the characters in a <text> or <tspan> element, without adding more markup. The text markup for this is
provided in Example 7-6; styles would be the same as the last few
examples.

Example 7-6. Using multiple values in text positioning attributes

```
<svg xmlns="http://www.w3.org/2000/svg" xml:lang="en"
    viewBox="0 0 550 200">
    <!-- styles and speech-bubble path omitted -->
    <text x="210" y="85" dy="0 0 -5 5 5 0 0 -5 5 0 0 0 -3 5 0 3
                             -3 -3 3 3 -2">
        …TALKING… LIKE
        <tspan x="250" y="120" class="shatner">SHATNER…</tspan>
    </text>
</svg>
```

The first value for the dy attribute operates on the first glyph—the
ellipsis—the second on the *T*, the third on the *A*, and so on. The

count includes spaces used in the final layout, but extra whitespace characters are collapsed before the dy values are assigned.

The <tspan> resets the absolute x and y positions for the second line of text, but still inherits the dy adjustments specified on the parent <text> element, with the dy adjustment for the S applied *after* the y value is changed.

A CSS class applies the remaining style changes; the rest of the styles would be the same as the previous comic-book examples:

```
text {
    font-size: 36px;
}
.shatner {
    font-style: italic;
    font-weight: bolder;
    font-size: 40px;
}
```

You can use per-character list values for any of the positioning attributes: x, y, dx, or dy. However, lists are generally easier to use with dx and dy, because you can always insert a 0 for any character you don't want to change. Any of the attributes can be set on either the <text> element or a <tspan>.

If both a <tspan> element and its parent specify x, y, dx, or dy values for a given character, the child element wins out.

The counting of "characters" uses the same rules as for JavaScript strings, based on UTF-16 blocks. Emoji and other multibyte characters will be assigned two (or sometimes more) positioning values from the attribute, but will only use the first value. The same goes for ligatures (multiple characters drawn with a single combined glyph-shape from the font): they get positioned based on the first character in the block.

While it's not quite as useful as dy (in horizontal text layout), dx can be used to move characters left and right, allowing you to precisely space glyphs exactly where you want and need them. Unlike resetting the x value, dx doesn't break the text into separate chunks for text-anchor alignment.

You *should* also be able to control character spacing with the CSS letter-spacing and word-spacing properties. Unfortunately, Firefox has a long-standing bug[3] such that these properties aren't supported in SVG.

In vertical text, all these rules are swapped: an absolute y value defines the anchor point for (vertically) aligning text with text-anchor, and dy values can be used to control spacing, while x and dx shift characters in the cross-axis.

More Online

Vertical text? Of course!

Well, sort of…SVG 1 defined a complete set of properties to properly format vertical or sideways text, but for a long time browser support has been limited. However, CSS3 has adopted and updated the vertical text properties (in the Writing Modes module), and browsers seem to finally all be on board.

There is one more attribute that can be added to <text> or <tspan> elements to change the position of individual characters: rotate. As you might guess, rotate rotates the character from its normal horizontal position. However, it's only recommended when you are positioning characters one at a time: it doesn't create neat typographical alignment automatically.

Read more about vertical and rotated text in SVG, in "Beyond Horizontal: Rotated and Vertical Text":

> *https://oreillymedia.github.io/Using_SVG/extras/ch07-rotate-vertical.html*

Twists and Turns: The <textPath> Element

As the past few examples have shown, SVG text is about more than just adding words to graphics—it's about using text layout itself as a graphical effect. Informative text on a diagram is often useful, but

---

3 *https://bugzilla.mozilla.org/show_bug.cgi?id=371787*

sometimes text going in a straight line is, well, dull. It's fun to use text as art: to bend and twist and flow text in circles or spirals, perhaps even track it along the edge of a given image.

Smoothly flowing nonlinear text layouts like this can be accomplished with the **<textPath> element**. With <textPath>, you don't control the text layout one character at a time. Instead, you define the overall shape of the *line* of text, and the browser positions the letters along it.

Not only will the letters be positioned along the path, but each letter's base is always tangent to the path itself. This makes it possible to wrap text around a circle, have it spiral inward or outward, jump from one region to another, and otherwise behave in a manner more frivolous and fun than any text has a right to.

 Browsers are currently very buggy and inconsistent when using <textPath> for right-to-left languages, or for languages with letters that change shape according to which letters come before and after.

Placing text on a path currently requires four components as follows:

- A <path> element, which must have a valid id attribute. If you don't want to *draw* the path itself, be sure to include it in a <defs> section of the SVG.

- A <text> element.

- A <textPath> element, which must appear inside the <text> element. The <textPath> must have an xlink:href attribute that links to the id of the <path> you just created.

- Some text inside the <textPath> element.

In code, your basic text-path boilerplate looks like this:

```
<defs>
    <path id="path-for-text" d="M50,100 Q100,0 250,100" />
</defs>
<text><textPath xlink:href="#path-for-text"
            >Text for path</textPath></text>
```

Add that to boilerplate SVG markup (like Example 1-1) and you have Figure 7-13. Change the path's d directions and the text content as required.

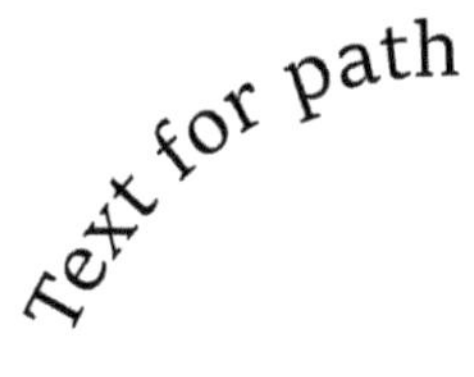

Figure 7-13. Curved text positioned using <textPath>

> You can also have <textPath> inside of <tspan> and <tspan> inside of <textPath>. However, both <textPath> and <tspan> must always be inside a <text>.

The text must *fit* on the path, when written in the selected font and font size. If the text continues past the path end point, excess characters will not being shown. To accommodate differences from fallback fonts, it is often a good idea to make the path longer than required.

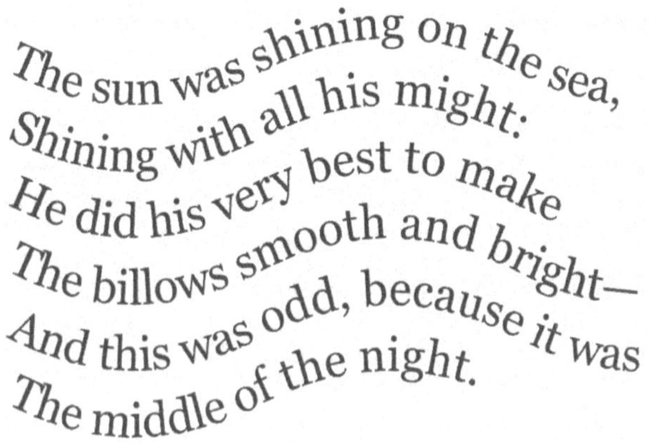

The sun was shining on the sea,
Shining with all his might:
He did his very best to make
The billows smooth and bright—
And this was odd, because it was
The middle of the night.

Figure 7-14. Curved text positioned using multiple <textPath> elements

We're going to create a slightly more creative example for exploring the details of <textPath>. Example 7-7 uses text paths to set the first verse of Lewis Carroll's *The Walrus and the Carpenter* as a series of waves. Each line is a separate <textPath> element, all contained within a single <text>. Figure 7-14 shows the result of the code as written.

Example 7-7. Arranging text using <textPath> elements

```
<svg xmlns="http://www.w3.org/2000/svg" xml:lang="en"
    xmlns:xlink="http://www.w3.org/1999/xlink"
    viewBox="0 0 320 180" >
    <title>The Walrus and the Carpenter—Lewis Carroll</title>
    <defs>
        <path id="wave1" d="M10,35  q50,25 100,0 t100,0 t100,0"/>
        <path id="wave2" d="M10,60  q50,25 100,0 t100,0 t100,0"/>
        <path id="wave3" d="M10,85  q50,25 100,0 t100,0 t100,0"/>
        <path id="wave4" d="M10,110 q50,25 100,0 t100,0 t100,0"/>
        <path id="wave5" d="M10,135 q50,25 100,0 t100,0 t100,0"/>
        <path id="wave6" d="M10,160 q50,25 100,0 t100,0 t100,0"/>
    </defs>
    <rect width="100%" height="100%" fill="azure" />
    <text font-size="18px"
          font-family="Georgia, serif"
          fill="midnightBlue">
        <textPath xlink:href="#wave1"
                  >The sun was shining on the sea,</textPath>
        <textPath xlink:href="#wave2"
                  >Shining with all his might:</textPath>
        <textPath xlink:href="#wave3"
                  >He did his very best to make</textPath>
        <textPath xlink:href="#wave4"
                  >The billows smooth and bright—</textPath>
        <textPath xlink:href="#wave5"
                  >And this was odd, because it was</textPath>
        <textPath xlink:href="#wave6"
                  >The middle of the night.</textPath>
    </text>
</svg>
```

Figure 7-15 shows how it would look if you also drew a stroked version of each path.

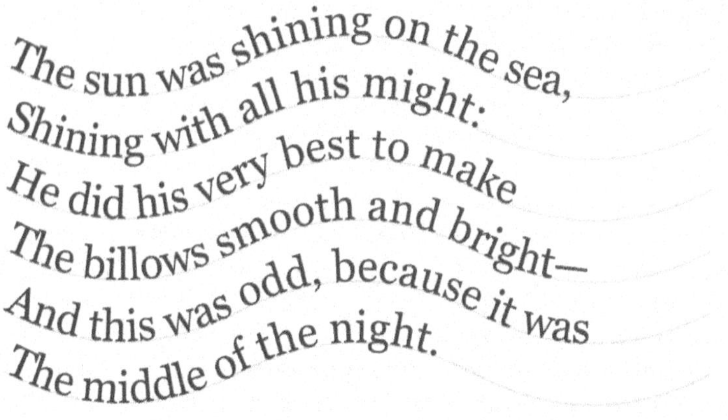

The sun was shining on the sea,
Shining with all his might:
He did his very best to make
The billows smooth and bright—
And this was odd, because it was
The middle of the night.

Figure 7-15. The paths used to position the curved text

Normally, if you were drawing six identical wavy lines at different points in the page (like in Figure 7-15), you would only define the <path> once, and then would use <use> elements to copy it, repositioning each copy with a y attribute. Unfortunately, there are no attributes available on <textPath> to reposition the path when it is used, so reusing a single <path> element for all six <textPath> elements is not so simple.

You *can* use a transform attribute (which we'll discuss in Chapter 11) to reposition separate chunks of text, after aligning them all to the same path, but you cannot transform the <textPath> itself. You would need to separate out each path into a separate <text> element, and transform each <text> into place.

In previous examples, we created multiline text by using dy on a <tspan> to shift the text to a new line. Why not do that here?

We can, but the result will look rather different.

Applying *x* and *y* adjustments on text inside a <textPath> no longer moves letters in simple horizontal and vertical offsets. Instead, dx moves letters *along* the path, and dy moves them *perpendicular to* the path. Similarly, an absolute x resets the text anchor position relative to the start of the path. In vertical writing mode, the x and y relationships are reversed: y and dy values are measured along the path, and dx offsets are perpendicular.

 The SVG specifications do not support absolute y values for characters inside a horizontal writing-mode <textPath>, nor absolute x values for vertical writing mode. Some browsers support it, and some don't.

It's easier to explain with an example. Example 7-8 gives the code for arranging the verse from *The Walrus and the Carpenter* as multiline <tspan> elements, with x and dy creating line breaks. All the lines are contained in a single <textPath> that references a single version of the wavy path. For clarity, the <path> itself is drawn with a visible stroke. Figure 7-16 shows the end result.

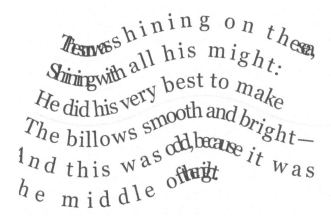

Figure 7-16. Curved text positioned using multiple lines offset from a single <textPath>

Example 7-8. Positioning multiple lines of text above and below the same path

```
<svg xmlns="http://www.w3.org/2000/svg" xml:lang="en"
    xmlns:xlink="http://www.w3.org/1999/xlink"
    viewBox="0 0 320 180" >
    <title>The Walrus and the Carpenter—Lewis Carroll</title>
```

```
<rect width="100%" height="100%" fill="azure" />
<path id="wave" d="M10,90 q50,25 100,0 t100,0 t100,0"
     fill="none" stroke="darkSlateGray" stroke-opacity="0.2"/>
<text font-size="18px"
      font-family="Georgia, serif"
      fill="midnightBlue">
   <textPath xlink:href="#wave">
      <tspan x="0" dy="-3.2em"
             >The sun was shining on the sea,</tspan>
      <tspan x="0" dy="1.4em"
             >Shining with all his might:</tspan>
      <tspan x="0" dy="1.4em"
             >He did his very best to make</tspan>
      <tspan x="0" dy="1.4em"
             >The billows smooth and bright—</tspan>
      <tspan x="0" dy="1.4em"
             >And this was odd, because it was</tspan>
      <tspan x="0" dy="1.4em"
             >The middle of the night.</tspan>
   </textPath>
</text>
</svg>
```

What's happening? As we mentioned, dy moves letters *perpendicular* to the path. That's measured relative to the slope of the path at the particular point. On a curved path like this, the perpendicular lines radiate outward or inward, stretching out or condensing the letters in fan shapes, as they get farther from the original path.

To further complicate matters, you can't add any of the normal text-positioning attributes (x, y, dx, or dy) to the <textPath> itself: they need to be specified on the parent <text> element or a parent or child <tspan>. For better browser support, use a child <tspan>, as we did in Example 7-8.

Sliding Text Along a Path with startOffset

Although <textPath> does not accept the same positioning attributes as <text> and <tspan>, it has a positioning attribute of its own: **startOffset**. This defines the point on the path that should be used as the anchor or origin for the text.

Watch out for the capitalization of startOffset: that's a capital O.

As with other mixed-case attributes in SVG, the HTML parser will correct it for you, but an incorrectly capitalized attribute won't have any effect in XML, or if created from JavaScript.

startOffset is a simple XML attribute, not a presentation attribute. It cannot be set with CSS.

In its simplest application, startOffset can be used to indent text relative to the start of the path, without your having to redefine the path shape:

```
<textPath xlink:href="#wave6" startOffset="1em"
         >The middle of the night.</textPath>
```

Applying startOffset="1em" adjustments like this to every second <textPath> from Example 7-7 (the version of *The Walrus and the Carpenter* with six separate <textPath> elements) results in Figure 7-17.

The sun was shining on the sea,
Shining with all his might:
He did his very best to make
The billows smooth and bright—
And this was odd, because it was
The middle of the night.

Figure 7-17. <textPath> lines adjusted with startOffset

One advantage of startOffset, compared to dx, is that it accepts percentage values that are calculated as a percent of the path length.

Centering text on a path looks like this:

```
<textPath startOffset="50%" text-anchor="middle"
          xlink:href="#p" >...</textPath>
```

To end-align text on a path, use `startOffset="100%"` with `text-anchor: end.`

 Browsers are currently very buggy about the interaction of `startOffset` with absolute x positions on characters inside a `<textPath>`. (It wasn't very well defined in the SVG specifications.) Only use one or the other.

Text paths get a little more complicated if you want to exactly fit text around a *closed* shape. For one thing, you probably no longer want to overestimate the length of the path in order to be sure the text will fit. Instead, you can use the **textLength attribute**—with its value set to the length of the path—to force the browser to exactly fit the text to the shape, regardless of the font used.

 `textLength` is a regular XML attribute, not a style property that can be set in CSS. Its value is always a number, representing a distance in SVG user units (px units).

A matching **lengthAdjust attribute** tells the browser what parts of the text can be tweaked to make the text fit: the default `spacing` value means that letter-spacing is adjusted. The alternate `spacingAndGlyphs` value means that the letters themselves are stretched or compressed.

 Browser support for `textLength` is currently very inconsistent. It really only works reliably in all browsers if used on a plain `<text>` element with no children. Test carefully.

You'll still want to adjust the font size so that it fits nicely in your chosen font, and only use `textLength` for extra enhancement and fallback.

More Online

Getting the correct *path* for the text layout you want also becomes more difficult with closed paths, especially if you're trying to fit the text to a shape that already exists in your drawing. In-browser methods aren't much help, but graphical SVG editors can be, allowing you to convert shapes to paths and change the path start position.

Read more (and see an example of a circular `<textPath>`) in "Perfecting Paths for <textPath>":

https://oreillymedia.github.io/Using_SVG/extras/ch07-textpaths.html

---

Future Focus
More Flexible Text Paths

In SVG 1.1 (and currently, in browsers), a `<textPath>` element *must* reference a `<path>` element. In SVG 2, it instead references any shape element, or uses a `path` attribute to directly include path data in the `<textPath>` element.

For text on basic shapes and also on paths with a single closed subpath, the text would wrap around from the end to the beginning of the path, until it reaches the `startOffset` position again.

SVG 2 also adds the `side` attribute to `<textPath>`; a value of `right` (instead of the default `left`) reverses the directionality of a path for the purpose of text. Using `side` will also allow the application of text on both the outside and inside of rectangles and circles, without forcing you to convert them into paths.

Finally, SVG 2 adds a `path` attribute that would allow you to specify the path data directly on the `<textPath>` element, without needing to create a separate element at all.

And of course—as we've already mentioned elsewhere—SVG 2 allows all `xlink:href` attributes to be replaced with a simple `href`, without namespaces. Most browsers now support simple `href`, but we use the `xlink` version here for compatibility with Safari and older browsers.

Measuring the Message

When figuring out many aspects of SVG text layout, it helps to know how much space that text takes up in the graphic. This is essential when you're dynamically generating text layouts for data charts. Conveniently, the SVG specs define a number of DOM methods that allow the browser to do the calculations for you.

You can use the same methods in your browser's developer console, when rearranging anchor points or setting `textLength` values to ensure better fallback layouts. For creating fallback layouts, use a browser that renders the correct layout, with your preferred fonts installed. Calculate the text positions, then hardcode them to ensure a consistent layout in other browsers or with fallback fonts.

All these DOM methods are available for any of the SVG text-containing elements: `<text>`, `<tspan>`, or `<textPath>`. They are object methods, called with . notation, like *t.method( )*, where *t* is a text element.

The most essential method is `getComputedTextLength( )`. It returns the total displacement (horizontally for horizontal text, or vertically for vertical text) of all the characters in the text element, in user units. The computed text length is measured in the current font, font-size, and other typographic style settings. It also includes dx offsets (dy for vertical text), but not absolute (x or y) repositioning values.

In other words, it's directly comparable to the numbers used in `textLength` attributes:

```
var t = document.querySelector("text");
if (t.getComputedTextLength() > maxLength)
    t.setAttribute("textLength", maxLength);
```

You can also use the computed length to calculate a new absolute anchor (x or y) point when switching from the default `start` text-anchoring to middle or end anchoring:

```
var endX = startX + t.getComputedTextLength(); //end anchor
var midX = startX + t.getComputedTextLength()/2; //middle
```

When dynamically setting text, you'll often want to split too-long text across multiple `<tspan>` lines (instead of squishing it with textLength). The getSubStringLength() method lets you test the computed length of a substring of the text, in order to decide where to add a break. It takes two parameters:

- *charIndex* is the index (using JavaScript character counting) of the first character in the substring, after collapsing whitespace from the element's text content
- *numChars* is the number of (JavaScript) characters in the substring

To get even more positioning data, other methods help you figure out where individual characters are located. This is useful if you have a <textPath> arrangement that you wish to lock in place, by converting it to an absolute layout with x, y, and rotate, or if you're trying to position drawing elements to match individual characters. For details, see *https://oreillymedia.github.io/Using_SVG/guide/DOM.html*.

Finally, for <textPath> elements, you also often want to know the length of the path you're using. A <path> element has a getTotalLength() method that will answer that question.

The getTotalLength() method has many other uses. In Chapter 13, we'll use it to calculate stroke dashing patterns. In Chapter 19, we'll use it to create motion along a path.

Summary: Graphical Text Layout and Fonts

SVG text layout is a hugely complex topic (which this chapter only lightly touches on). At its most basic, SVG text consists of an instruction to the browser to "type this text here." At its most complex, it allows you to carefully position individual letters in geometric patterns, with *nearly* as much control as you position your SVG shapes.

Nearly as much control, but not quite. The individual glyph shapes, their size, and their default spacing are all based on the font. You can provide web fonts, but cannot guarantee they'll be used. A well-designed font stack and careful use of the text-anchoring options—and lots of testing—is required for fallbacks.

Text is one area where SVG used as images are significantly different from inline SVG or embedded objects. Text in images is isolated from user interaction and from assistive tools such as screen-readers. It also cannot access web font files. For this reason, designers commonly convert text into graphical shapes when creating logo images.

When an SVG *is* interactive, then the fun begins: text styles can be updated with JavaScript and CSS. For scripted SVG, a set of unique helper functions can help you calculate the dimensions of dynamic text content, and adjust the layout accordingly.

A key feature of SVG text is that it can be filled and stroked like any SVG shape. In this chapter, we only used solid-color stroke and fill. However, as we explore more graphical effects in Part IV, we will see examples of more decorative text. Before we get there, Part III will explore SVG structure, layout, and coordinate systems in detail.

More Online

A reference to the elements and attributes introduced in this chapter is available in the "Text Elements" section of our markup guide:

https://oreillymedia.github.io/Using_SVG/guide/markup.html#text

The text-related style properties are included in the "SVG Style Properties" guide:

https://oreillymedia.github.io/Using_SVG/guide/style.html

PART III

Putting Graphics in Their Place

In Parts I and II, we described the position and geometry of shapes and text using x and y coordinates. But so far, we have not looked too closely at how those numbers are converted into positions within our SVG drawing.

The x and y coordinates used to position SVG shapes and text are measured relative to an overall coordinate system. By manipulating the coordinate system, you can draw the same shapes at different positions and scales, or even stretched or slanted.

The next few chapters examine the SVG coordinate system more closely, and introduce SVG's structural markup. These structural elements allow you to not only control coordinate systems, but also to duplicate and embed graphical content. Together, these tools allow you to create reusable graphics, such as you would want for an icon set or charting library.

CHAPTER 8

Scaling Up

Defining Coordinate Systems

So far in this book, when talking about the layout of SVG shapes, we have used the word *default* a lot. By *default*, the origin of the coordinate system is in the top-left corner. By *default*, user coordinates are equal to CSS layout px units. By *default*, SVG coordinate systems seem restrictive and arbitrary.

But you don't have to use the default options.

In this chapter, we introduce the ways you can control the coordinate system. Which means we'll introduce the scalable side of Scalable Vector Graphics. By controlling the coordinate system, you control the size of your graphics.

This chapter focuses on defining the initial coordinate systems for your graphic. Defining a coordinate system means setting the origin point, establishing the size of a user unit, and determining the meaning of 100% width or height. All of these are set with the powerful viewBox attribute we've already mentioned multiple times. Other attributes control the size and alignment.

The coordinate system concepts discussed in this chapter will be revisited in the following chapters. The attributes used to define the initial coordinate system of an <svg> are also used in scaling reused content (<use> and <image>), creating local coordinate systems (with nested <svg>), and cropping the graphic during embedding (with <view>).

Another way to modify coordinate systems is by geometrically transforming them, as we'll discuss in Chapter 11. Transformations can also change the origin and the size of a user unit. Transformations *don't* change the meaning of 100% width and height (at least, they don't change it proportional to the size of a user unit). Transformations can also rotate or skew the x and y axes, which is not possible when you're creating coordinate systems with viewBox.

Coordinated Efforts

We've talked about the coordinate system in previous examples. We've had to—it's impossible to draw anything in SVG without defining where to draw it, and how big to draw it, using coordinates.

The SVG coordinate system is a **Cartesian coordinate system**. That means that positions in space are defined relative to an **origin point** and **axes** that are at right angles to each other. The number of axes is equal to the number of dimensions in space. For the two-dimensional space used for SVG, the two axes are the x-axis describing the horizontal distance from the origin and the y-axis describing the vertical distance.

 Axes (pronounced *ax-EEZ*) is the plural of axis (*ax-ISS*), a reference direction in space. Not to be confused with axes (pronounced *AX-ez*), which is the plural of ax, the sharp implement used to chop wood.

Conceptually, you start from the origin point, then measure the distance along one *axis* until you're as close to the desired point as you can get, then turn at a right angle—so that your measuring stick is parallel to the other axis—and measure the distance to the point. Figure 8-1 shows how you could measure out the position where $x = 50$ and $y = 80$. By convention, when talking about 2D points, the horizontal x distance is given first, then the vertical y distance, so this point is also known as (50,80).

The complete coordinate system is defined by (a) the position of the origin point, (b) the direction of the axes, and (c) the scale of units on each axis.

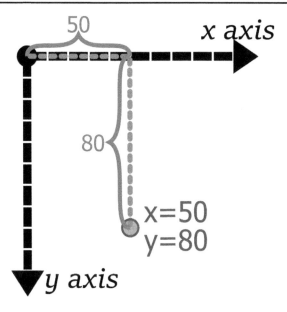

Figure 8-1. Positioning a point in a 2D Cartesian coordinate systems; black lines are the axes, while the orange-red (tomato) line shows how the coordinates are measured

Cartesian coordinates are named after René Descartes, a famous French mathematician and philosopher. Something of a disreputable rogue, Descartes's work on probability theory was inspired by his gambling. The story goes that he developed coordinate geometry while sick in bed, watching ants moving across the walls and ceiling of his apartment.

Those ignominious beginnings led to a breakthrough with profound influence on the development of mathematics, physics, and eventually, computer science—and SVG. Cartesian coordinates merged the then-new disciplines of algebra and calculus to the centuries-old discipline of geometry.

The Cartesian coordinate system that most people learn in high school algebra has an origin—the "zero-point" where both *x* and *y* coordinates are given the value of 0—at the bottom left, or at the center if both negative and positive coordinates are used. Generations of schoolchildren have learned that the x-axis grows toward the right, counting up 0, 1, 2, and so on. Moving left gets you into negative numbers: −1, −2, −3, and so on. The y-axis used in school math textbooks grows from bottom to top: positive numbers above the origin and negative numbers below.

However, the history of computer graphics changed that somewhat. The CRTs used for the original computer monitors had scan guns that swept from left to right and from top to bottom. Because of this, it made sense to use an inverted coordinate system.

The x-axis still goes from left to right (the same as algebra class), but the y-axis starts from the top and increases as it progresses down the screen or page. The origin is typically placed at the upper-left corner of the screen. Figure 8-2 compares the familiar x/y coordinate system from algebra class against the SVG coordinate system, both for the default origin (with only positive coordinates) and a centered origin (both positive and negative coordinates).

This coordinate system is ingrained in most computer graphics systems, with SVG being no exception. The origin is at the top left, x coordinates increase from left to right, and y coordinates increase from top to bottom:

- (150,100) is 150 units to the right and 100 units below the (0,0) origin.
- (−150,−100) will be 150 units to the left and 100 units above the origin.

With the default coordinate system, (−150,−100) would be offscreen. You could move it onto the screen by defining the coordinate system with a different origin, in the center of the graphic or somewhere else. The point (−150,−100) would still be 150 units to the left and 100 units above the origin, wherever that origin is. You can only change the *directions* of the axes using coordinate system transformations, which we'll get to in Chapter 11.

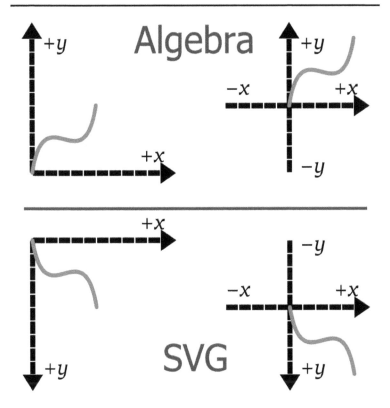

Figure 8-2. Two-dimensional coordinate systems, as they are defined in algebra textbooks (top) versus how they are defined in SVG (bottom); each coordinate system is 100 units wide and 100 units tall, and the orange path is drawn from (0,0) to (50,50) in each.

The final aspect of SVG coordinate systems is not part of purely mathematical Cartesian systems: their width and height. The width and height of the SVG coordinate system are used to determine the meaning of percentage lengths, as discussed in Chapter 5. But the coordinate system's width and height are not firm boundaries: you can still use coordinates that are bigger or smaller than that range.

Framing the View, with viewBox

In theory, the SVG coordinate plane is infinite in extent. Your interest, however, is usually in the fairly confined region that you can display on a screen or print to a page.

This rectangular window into the infinite graphical plane is known as a **viewport**. It defines what you actually see of the graphic.

You experience viewports every time you open a web page that is too big to fit on your screen; the browser knows the position of the rest of the text, but it won't show it to you until you scroll. A more graphical instance of viewports can be found on any digital map. The mapping website or software has information about the whole world, but it only shows you a small rectangle at a time.

On maps, elements are positioned by their longitude and latitude. In SVG, they are positioned by their coordinates. You can tell the browser to draw shapes at any coordinates you choose, but if the resulting shape doesn't overlap the viewport, you won't see it.

 Unlike with HTML web pages, most SVG viewers currently do *not* allow you to scroll or pan to content outside the declared width and height.

An SVG graphic with the root element `<svg width="400px" height="200px">` will create a default viewport with the origin of (0,0) at the upper-left of the box and the point (400, 200) at the lower-right corner of the viewport.

These points are defined in the internal user coordinates or user units, which are always equal to px units, regardless of how the width and height are defined—the fact that the width and height were specified in px is only a convenience. If the coordinates were given as `<svg width="6in" height="4in">`, the user coordinates would still be equivalent to pixels. With 96 pixels to the inch, the lower-right corner would be at the point (576, 384).

Both SVGs in Figure 8-3 have the exact same content: overlapping vertical and horizontal rectangles arranged to create a grid (in plaid!); circles and text elements mark the coordinates of points along the diagonal. In the top part, the SVG is set to 400px by 200px; at the bottom, the dimensions were changed to 6in and 4in.

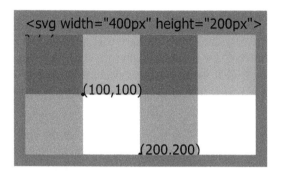

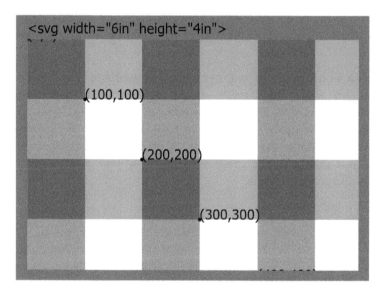

Figure 8-3. A plaid SVG grid, in two differently sized SVG viewports

In total, the grid defined in the SVG file is 1,000 units wide and 1,000 units tall. But in both parts of Figure 8-3, most of the content gets cropped off—including the text that sits above the $y = 0$ baseline. The size of the individual stripes does not change, only how much of them are visible.

By default, when you declare the width and height of an <svg>, the browser calculates how many pixels will fit in those dimensions. It then displays any and all SVG content whose coordinates fit in between (0,0) and the calculated width and height, scaled at 1px per user unit.

But oftentimes, this isn't what you want.

Sometimes, it would be very convenient to have user units scale to a different size. In Chapter 6, we discussed how it would have been much easier (in Figure 6-6) if we could use centimeters, instead of px, to define our curved path to match the lines we already drew using cm units.

Sometimes, it would be convenient to locate the origin of the coordinate system at the visual center of a graphic rather than in the top-left corner.

Most of the time, it would be convenient if your Scalable Vector Graphics would *scale* to fit within a particular region on your web page.

To do all of the above, you use a **viewBox attribute**. The view*Box* specifies which coordinates should be positioned within the view*port* created by the browser window or the web page layout. By defining how many user units, in total, should fit, the viewBox defines the *size* of the default units. By giving exact coordinate values that should fit, the viewBox indirectly sets the *position* of the coordinate system origin.

 Viewports in SVG are similar to but different from the viewport used in CSS viewport units. The SVG viewport used for scaling is created by the CSS layout box for the <svg> element, not by the size of the screen (unless the SVG is set to fill the screen exactly). The CSS vh, vw, vmin, and vmax units follow the CSS meaning, even when you're drawing in SVG.

The number of user units specified by the viewBox is independent of the width and height of the <svg> element (the viewport). The same coordinates of the graphic will be shown, regardless of how large the image is drawn; the graphic scales so that they will fit.

Figure 8-4 takes the plaid grid used in Figure 8-3 and adjusts the attributes on the <svg> again. This time, the width and height create a 4-inch square, but the viewBox ensures that 1,000 units are scaled to fit horizontally and vertically. The text ends up tiny, but it all fits. Well, except for the very first text label, which still ends up on the negative side of the origin and cropped off.

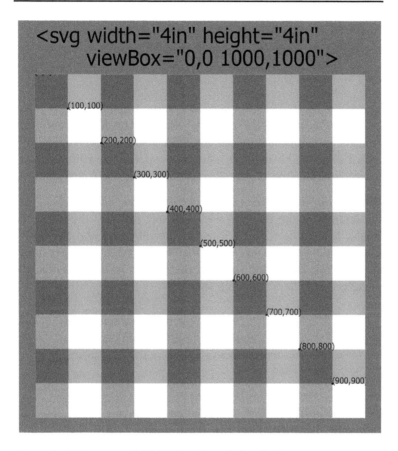

Figure 8-4. The same plaid SVG grid, scaled to fit the viewport using a viewBox attribute

The graphical code within the SVG is the same as in Figure 8-3. The only changes in the code for Figure 8-4 were the attributes on the `<svg>` element: changed width and height, and the new attribute `viewBox="0,0 1000,1000"`.

The value of `viewBox` is a list of four numbers: *min-x*, *min-y*, *width*, *height*. The four numbers can be separated by whitespace or by commas. The first two values give the minimum coordinate, in each direction, that should be included in the viewport region. The width and height values represent the total number of coordinates, in each direction, that should fit within the viewport.

 The width and height values must always be positive numbers. They represent distances, *not* the coordinates at the end of the range.

The minimum coordinates *implicitly* define where the origin of the coordinate system—the (0,0) point—will be. The default coordinate systems are equivalent to using 0,0 for these values. For the SVG with a 400px width and 200px height, the default coordinate system would be equivalent to a viewBox with the values "0,0 400,200".

What if you wanted the origin to be in the center of the SVG? That's the same as saying that you want half that width to the left of the origin, half to the right, and half the height above and half below. The *minimum* coordinates would therefore be negative values equivalent to half the width and half the height. In other words, the viewBox would be "-200,-100 400,200".

 In general: if you want the origin to be positioned *x* units from the left side and *y* units from the top, the first two values in the viewBox are – *x* and –*y*.

Centered coordinate systems are often useful when you're creating geometric diagrams. They can make drawing some shapes easier, but other shapes can be more difficult. Example 8-1 creates an HTML web page with two 400×200 inline SVGs. Both have the same graphical content, but one uses the default coordinate system while the other has a centered coordinate system. Figure 8-5 shows the result.

Figure 8-5. Two SVGs with the same shapes, using (top) default and (bottom) centered coordinate systems

Example 8-1. Using viewBox to create a centered coordinate system

```
<!DOCTYPE html>
<html lang="en">
<head>
    <meta charset="utf-8" />
    <title>Default and centered SVG coordinate systems</title>
    <link rel="stylesheet" href="centered-viewBox.css">        ❶
</head>
<body>
    <svg width="400px" height="200px">                          ❷
        <title>Default coordinates</title>
        <g id="content">
            <rect class="backdrop" width="100%" height="100%" />  ❸
            <g class="target">
```

```
                    <circle r="10" />                      ❹
                    <circle r="30" />
                    <circle r="50" />
                    <circle r="70" />
                    <circle r="90" />
                </g>
            </g>
        </svg>
        <svg width="400px" height="200px"
             viewBox="-200 -100 400 200">                  ❺
            <title>Centered coordinates</title>
            <use xlink:href="#content" />                  ❻
        </svg>
    </body>
</html>
```

❶ The linked styles (not printed here) describe the layout of the page and the coloring of the SVG shapes: dark purple fill for class backdrop and tomato strokes for class target.

❷ The first <svg> is sized with width and height only, no viewBox; the default coordinate system will be used.

❸ The backdrop rectangle is sized to 100% width and height. The x and y attributes aren't specified, so default to 0; this positions the top-left corner of the rectangle in the top-left corner of the SVG, so it completely fills the space.

❹ The set of concentric circles doesn't have cx or cy attributes; these also default to 0. For circles, that means that three-quarters of each circle will be cropped off, because they will be *centered* on the top-left corner.

❺ The second SVG is given a viewBox attribute to center the coordinate system, as described in the text.

❻ The entire content of the first SVG is duplicated into the second one. There are no positioning attributes on the <use> element, so all the shapes will retain their original coordinates. Those coordinates, however, will be positioned in the new coordinate system.

The width and height of the rectangle has not changed in the second SVG. However, it no longer fills the SVG, instead getting cropped at the bottom and right edges. The top-left corner of the rectangle is still positioned at (0,0), but that is now the center of the graphic.

In order to create a rectangle that fills the SVG with a centered coordinate system, you have to set the rectangle's x and y attributes to negative values. The following are two possible ways of doing so:

```
<rect width="100%" height="100%" x="-200" y="-100"/>
<rect width="100%" height="100%" x="-50%" y="-50%"/>
```

In the first case, the positions are in user units and directly match the viewBox offset; in the second case, the value of 50% is calculated against the width or height from the viewBox, and the result is then turned into a negative offset.

In contrast, the circles centered on (0,0) are nicely positioned in the middle of the centered coordinate system, without requiring additional attributes.

 In current web browsers, when you use <use> to duplicate a shape that is defined with percentages, those percentages are calculated based on the *original* coordinate system width and height. In other words, the size of the shape doesn't change, only its position. This was not well defined in the original SVG specs; SVG 2 recommends using percentages from the new context.

In Example 8-1, the width and height of both <svg> elements is the same, so this did not make a difference. In other cases, it's best to avoid mixing percentages with <use>.

In Chapter 10, we'll discuss the <symbol> element, which allows you to duplicate content and have it scale to fit the new context.

Whether a centered coordinate system simplifies your SVG code, or complicates it, will really depend on what you're trying to draw. Positioning "centered" shapes, such as circles and ellipses, can be easier with a centered coordinate system, but shapes and elements that are positioned from the top left, such as rectangles, require extra arithmetic. In Chapter 11, we will see more examples of how controlling the coordinate system origin can simplify your code.

A frequently requested feature in SVG is to have *some* of the graphic scale, but not all. For example, you might want the shapes to get bigger, but not the thickness of the lines. You may want the images to stretch to fit, but not the text. Or you may want the scale of a map or chart layout to increase, but not the size of the individual data marker symbols.

You can achieve some of these effects with nested coordinate systems, which will be discussed in Chapter 9. However, in many cases the only way to make the correct adjustments is to rely on JavaScript to control the scale.

SVG 2 adds `vector-effect` options to reverse scaling of part of a graphic, to create nonscaling stroke and text or symbols. At the time of writing (early 2017), the only value of the `vector-effect` property supported in web browsers is `non-scaling-stroke`, which we'll discuss in "Scaling Shapes Without Scaling Strokes" on page 496 in Chapter 13.

Calibrating the Scales

When you use a `viewBox`, the units you define do not have to match the `px` units used by the web page. If you want 1 unit per inch, instead of 96, all you have to do is say so:

```
<svg width="6in" height="4in" viewBox="0,0 6,4">
```

This code defines a user coordinate system with 6 user units horizontally and 4 user units vertically. It then stretches that coordinate system to fit within a space 6 inches wide and 4 inches tall. As a result, each user unit is 1 inch long, in both directions. Because the first two values of the `viewBox` are both 0, the origin of the coordinate system is in the top left.

You might think that you could now use `in` (inch) units interchangeably with user coordinates. So you might try to add our 1-inch square from Chapter 5 into this SVG:

```
<svg width="6in" height="4in" viewBox="0,0 6,4">
    <rect width="1in" height="1in" />
</svg>
```

But that will draw a square that overflows the SVG, many times over.

When you scale up the coordinate system in SVG, the length units get adjusted accordingly. A px is still equal to a user unit, and an in is still 96px. At this scale, that would be drawn as 96 real-world inches—8 feet!

The ratios between the different length units and user coordinates *never* change when you scale the SVG; all units scale equally.

If you're going to use viewBox to set the scale of your user units, you need to use those user units (i.e., no units at all) in your drawing:

```
<svg width="6in" height="4in" viewBox="0,0 6,4">
    <rect width="1" height="1" />
</svg>
```

If you need a unit (some CSS properties won't accept plain numbers), you can always use px as equal to the SVG user unit.

Scaling to Fit

The viewBox examples so far have all used SVGs of fixed size. In that situation, viewBox is a convenience. It lets us use a coordinate system we choose, independent of the number of pixels.

But this means that we can define our paths and shapes once, then change the width and height later. After all, SVG is *scalable*, right?

It is, if it has a viewBox!

The dimensions that you specify in the viewBox attribute will stretch (or shrink) to fit whatever width and height you set. For example, all the card-suit icons in Chapter 6 were defined as tiny 20px squares. Adding viewBox="0,0 20,20" allows you to redraw the same icon at any size, by setting width and height on the SVG.

For the full-sized figures in Chapter 6, we used viewBox="-5,-5 30,30", to give 5 units of extra room on all sides (including above and to the left of the origin) for drawing grid lines and control points. Changing the viewBox can also be used to pad and crop an image.

The viewBox is most useful when you *don't* know the final size of the SVG. Maybe the SVG is sized to fit a browser window, or maybe it's an icon that adjusts to font-size.

Example 8-2 goes one step further, allowing the *user* to adjust the size. It uses the CSS resize property to create an adjustable <div> element. The <svg> inside is absolutely positioned to completely fill that <div>, whatever its dimensions. The viewBox controls the scale that is used to draw the <path>. Figure 8-6 shows multiple screenshots.

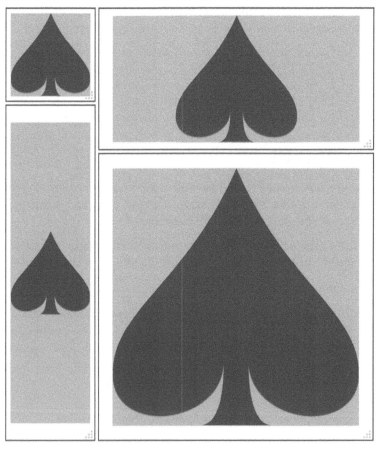

Figure 8-6. Using viewBox to scale a graphic to fit, at various sizes

Example 8-2. Using viewBox to scale a graphic to fit

HTML MARKUP:

```
<!DOCTYPE html>
<html lang="en">
<head>
    <meta charset="utf-8" />
    <title>Scaling with viewBox</title>
    <link rel="stylesheet" href="flex-scale-viewBox.css" />
</head>
<body>
    <div class="wrapper">
        <svg viewBox="0,0 20,20">
            <title>Spade</title>
            <path d="M9,15C9,20 0,21 0,16S6,9 10,0C14,9 20,11 20,16
                     S11,20 11,15Q11,20 13,20H7Q9,20 9,15Z" />  ❶
        </svg>
    </div>
</body>
</html>
```

❶ That's the path data for the spade from Example 6-3 in Chapter 6, just condensed onto fewer lines—more compact, less readable. It still draws the same shape, in the same 20×20 square region, matching the `viewBox` on the `<svg>`.

CSS STYLES: *flex-scale-viewBox.css*

```
html, body {
    height: 100%;
}
.wrapper {
    position: relative;
    height: 10em;
    width: 10em;
    resize: both;
    overflow: hidden;
    border: thin solid;
}
svg {
    display: block;
    position: absolute;
    height: 90%;
    width: 90%;
    top: 5%;
    left: 5%;

    background-color: darkSeaGreen;
```

```
}
path { fill: darkslateblue; }
```

 The CSS `resize` property is not implemented in Microsoft Edge or Internet Explorer, or in many mobile browsers. To see the scaling effect in those browsers, you can set the width and height of the wrapper element with percentages or viewport units, and then rescale your browser window.

The final benefit of using `viewBox` to reset the coordinate system is that you can scale the image according to a coordinate system that makes sense for the data that you are using. For instance, if you were making a map of North America, you might create a coordinate system in degrees latitude and longitude, with a `viewBox` of `"-180,86 130,80"`, corresponding to a map that spans from (180°W 86°N) to (50°W 6°N).

 Directly converting longitude and latitude coordinates into horizontal and vertical coordinates creates an **equirectangular map projection**. It is very convenient for converting geographical coordinates to SVG, but doesn't always create a good map. Because longitude lines (meridians) are not actually parallel—they join together at the North and South Poles—using the longitude as a horizontal coordinate distorts the scale, stretching east-west distances everywhere except the equator.

When using real-world units like this, you need to keep an eye on how big your numbers are—and how small the distances you are trying to graph. Web browsers have limits on how much memory they allocate to each number, and they use approximations for mathematical calculations with large numbers.

For best results, only use real-world numbers if they are fairly close in size to screen pixel values. Aim for no more than 100 px per unit, or 100 units per px.

A Poor Fit (and How preserveAspectRatio Fixes It)

In the theoretical map of North America, the width declared in the `viewBox` was 130 units, and the height was 80 units. Ideally, the width and height attributes on the SVG should have the same width/height ratio, equivalent to 130/80 or 1.625. In other words, if the height is 200 pixels, the width should be 325 pixels.

Now suppose that, for reasons beyond the control of the SVG designer, the aspect ratio—the ratio of width to height—of the SVG on the page or screen has to be something other that 1.625, such as 1.5 or 2.0 or, more likely, some flexible region that will stretch and shrink according to the user's browser size.

There are three possible ways the SVG could scale to fit within this mismatched space:

- The SVG graphic is contorted—stretched or squeezed—to fit the available aspect ratio.
- The whole graphic is fit within the available space, with everything in the right proportions, but with extra blank areas filling the too-large dimension.
- The graphic is scaled to completely fill the space without leaving anything blank, but some parts of the graphic get cut off in the too-small direction.

The choice between these options is controlled by the **preserveAspectRatio attribute** on the <svg> element. This is used to determine how the picture fits into the available space, and has a variety of values. It has no effect unless you define a `viewBox` on the same element. The width and height from the `viewBox` value define the *intrinsic* aspect ratio of your graphic; `preserveAspectRatio` tells the browser what to do when the actual aspect ratio of the SVG region doesn't match.

The simplest property for `preserveAspectRatio` is `"none"`. This is *not* the default; you need to set it explicitly:

```
<svg viewBox="0,0 20,20" preserveAspectRatio="none">
```

In this mode, the graphic will conform to the size of the container, even if that container has a different aspect ratio. One direction will stretch, while the other will compress, until the exact number of units specified in the `viewBox` width and height fit the SVG width and height.

The resulting coordinate units are no longer square—one unit in the *x* direction does not equal one unit in the *y* direction. Your graphic will be distorted to match: circles stretched into ellipses, text looking like it passed through a fun-house mirror, and even the stroke width stretching or compressing depending on which direction it is going.

If you paid attention to the resizable graphic in Example 8-2, you would have noticed that, by default, the aspect ratio *is* preserved. No matter how you change the size of the SVG, the shape is never distorted. To see the difference, edit the `<svg>` to match the preceding snippet.

Then, stretch and squish the icon. The results should look something like Figure 8-7.

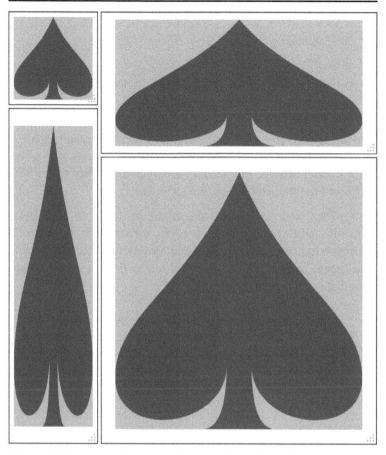

Figure 8-7. Using viewBox to scale a graphic to fit, without preserving the aspect ratio

If that's not the default, what is? What is the opposite of none for preserving aspect ratio?

It isn't that simple. There isn't just one preserveAspectRatio value that tells the software drawing the SVG to preserve the aspect ratio: there are 18. Each variant indicates *how* the software should size and position the graphic within the drawing region, when the aspect ratios don't match.

The general format for these values is as follows:

```
xAlignYAlign meet-or-slice
```

Keywords fill in the parts of that value:

- three options for *xAlign*: xMin, xMid, or xMax
- three for *YAlign*: YMin, YMid, or YMax
- two for *meet-or-slice*: not surprisingly, meet or slice

Multiply those out (3 × 3 × 2), and you get the 18 possible variants.

The *xAlignYAlign* keyword determines how the scaled graphic is positioned in the available space. Specifically, it indicates which point to align between the *viewport* (the region specified by the SVG width and height) and the graphic's viewBox.

A xMinYMin value means that the minimum values in both directions—in other words, the top-left corner—will be aligned; xMinYMax indicates that the lefthand side (xMin) and the bottom edge (YMax) will be aligned; xMidYMid means that the center points, in both directions, will be aligned.

The alignment values are indicated as a single token (word), with no spaces in between. To maintain proper camelCase capitalization, the first letter—the x in the x-alignment value—is lowercase, but the Y is uppercase.

After you define the anchor point with the alignment options, the scale of the graphic depends on the choice between meet and slice.

The meet value indicates that the image is anchored at the alignment point, and then expanded until it *meets* either the horizontal or vertical boundaries of the viewport. This ensures that the whole viewBox image will be displayed, but the SVG may also include areas outside the viewBox. This often means there will be blank space around the graphic.

The slice attribute value, on the other hand, anchors the image, then expands it until both dimensions of the graphic have reached a viewport boundary. This will fill up the entire space of the container, but at the cost of *slicing* off portions of the viewBox dimensions (or causing them to overflow the SVG, for inline SVG with overflow: visible).

The default value for preserveAspectRatio is xMidYMid meet; it fits the entire viewBox region within the drawing area, and centers it in any extra space. This behavior was demonstrated in Figure 8-6.

You can test out the other options by editing the file from Example 8-2. Figure 8-8 shows the same sizes of the graphic, but when preserveAspectRatio is set to xMinYMax slice. The bottom-right corner of the viewBox (minimum *x* and maximum *y*) is always visible—but other parts get sliced off.

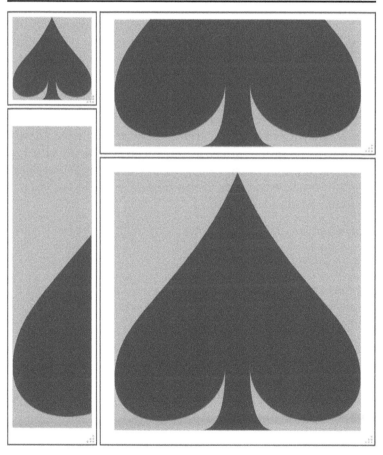

Figure 8-8. A graphic resized with viewBox and slice scaling, with xMinYMax alignment

More Online

If editing markup and refreshing your browser gets boring, you can always write a script for that!

In "Dynamically Changing preserveAspectRatio," we show you how to build an HTML form for the different options, using JavaScript to update the attribute on the SVG:

> *https://oreillymedia.github.io/Using_SVG/extras/ch08-preserveAspectRatio-swap.html*

As you experiment, it should become clear that only one of the alignment options at a time has an effect. The graphic always *exactly* fits one dimension of the available space. Whether it's the *x* or *y* dimension is determined both by the shape of the space, and by `meet` versus `slice`.

The `viewBox` and `preserveAspectRatio` have a huge effect on the final presentation of the graphic. One complication, however, is that the perfect `viewBox` for a graphic can sometimes depend on the specific styles you use. The spade in the previous examples was drawn to *just* fit inside its viewBox. If you added a stroke to the shape, it would extend outside the box.

One option is to adjust the `viewBox` to give a little extra room. However, to make the change dynamically, you'll need to use JavaScript: CSS can't change `viewBox`.

For inline SVG, you can instead use CSS padding to make room for the stroke, setting the `overflow` property to `visible` to allow it to be painted.

When you use SVG as a separate image or object, overflow isn't an option—the image is clipped to its canvas before being inserted in the document. However, you *can* define completely separate alternate `viewBox` parameters, which you can turn on by changing the embedding URL. Chapter 9 will describe how it works.

CSS Versus SVG
Scaling to Fit

CSS has introduced features similar to `preserveAspectRatio`, allowing you to control how an image fits into a box with a different aspect ratio; unfortunately, the CSS terminology does not match the SVG keywords.

The first, and best supported, CSS option applies to background images. The options are supported in any browser that supports layered backgrounds (and a few that don't).

The `background-size` property, instead of specifying a particular size, can use the keyword values `contain` (equivalent to SVG `meet`) or `cover` (equivalent to `slice`). The `background-position` property controls how the scaled image is aligned within the box: min, mid, and max positions can be set by the keywords **left**, **center**, or **right** for horizontal alignment and **top**, **center**, or **bottom** for vertical alignment. The `background-position` can also be specified as a length or a percentage in either direction, allowing for greater control than is currently possible in SVG.

But what about images, video, and other content in the main web page that has a fixed aspect ratio? The CSS Images level 3 module introduces the `object-fit` and `object-position` properties. The syntax for `object-position` is the same as for `background-position`. The `object-fit` property takes one of the following keyword values:

- `fill` (equivalent to the **none** value for `preserveAspectRatio`; this is the default behavior),
- `contain` (same as for `background-size`; equivalent to **meet** for SVG),
- `cover` (same as for `background-size`; like SVG `slice`),
- **none** (meaning no scaling at all, *not* no aspect-ratio control!), or
- `scale-down` (equivalent to `contain` if that is smaller than the intrinsic size, or **none** otherwise).

If you use the `object-fit` property on embedded SVG content, the CSS object scaling is applied first, to create a drawing region size; the SVG is then drawn in this region according to the `preserveAspectRatio` settings. If the two values don't align, this could create unintuitive interactions.

Blink browsers and Firefox have supported `object-fit` and `object-position` for a few years now; Safari has supported fit since version 8, and position starting in version 10. At the time of writing, the properties have just shipped in preview versions of Microsoft Edge; they should be stable in EdgeHTML 16.

Just-Right Sizing

SVG's aspect-ratio control options ensure that the graphic fits neatly in the "frame" you give it. They assume that the size of that frame is controlled by external forces: the screen or page size, or the CSS of the embedding web page.

For small icons and logos, where you know the exact size you want for the graphic, this usually makes sense. Set the `width` and `height` properties on the `<img>`, `<object>`, or (for inline SVG) `<svg>` element in the main web page, and you're good to go.

An SVG file embedded in HTML using `<iframe>` will not always rescale to fit the frame; instead, scroll bars can be added. But browsers are rather inconsistent with SVG scaling and iframes, so use `<object>` if you can.

But often in web design, especially in responsive web design, you want that frame to adjust to match the content. Specifically, you might set a height or width on your SVG container element, and want the other direction to be calculated automatically based on the SVG aspect ratio, without any whitespace gaps or sliced-off bits from the SVG's aspect ratio adjustments.

Raster images in CSS-styled HTML have always had autosizing like this: set *either* `height` or `width` to `auto` (the default), and it will be calculated from the other dimension and the image's aspect ratio.

Unfortunately, this inside-out approach to sizing wasn't fully considered when SVG was originally designed. It has taken a while for web browsers to standardize around a consistent and useful approach to the problem. You may need some hacks to get support in all browsers. How to solve it depends on how you are inserting the SVG into your web page, and on how much information you give the browser to work with.

Autosizing Embedded SVG

The best results, cross-browser, for autosizing occur under the following conditions:

- embedding an independent SVG file in your web page with an `<img>` or `<object>` element;

- the root `<svg>` in the file has a `viewBox` attribute;

- the `<img>` or `<object>` in the web page has *either* `height` or `width` set to an explicit value with CSS, which could be a percentage value.

In this case, scaling the SVG image works pretty much how it does for raster image formats like PNG or JPEG. The `auto` dimension is adjusted to exactly match the aspect ratio of the SVG from the `viewBox`. But unlike with raster images, your graphic will be crisp and clear at any size!

So, for example, if you want an SVG image to always scale to fit the available width, you could use the following CSS code in your web page:

```
img.full-width {
    width: 100%; /* height is auto by default */
}
```

So long as the SVG has a defined aspect ratio (the **intrinsic aspect ratio**), the height of the image will scale to match the width. You won't have to worry about the `preserveAspectRatio` value. Your image will end up not too big and not too small: just right.

 Almost always just right, anyway. Things can get weird with `display: table` or flexbox layout. But that's true for other images, too.

The most reliable way to define an aspect ratio is to use `viewBox`.

You *can* define an aspect ratio using *both* `width` and `height` attributes on the root `<svg>`, without `viewBox`. But it can get buggy.

As mentioned in Chapter 2, when your SVG file has width and height attributes but *not* viewBox, Internet Explorer won't scale the drawing to match the size of the drawing region. However, it *will* still autosize the embedding <img> according to the aspect ratio.

In addition, when you embed with an <object>, the units in an SVG without viewBox will never scale: it will be drawn at exactly the specified width and height.

For these reasons, using width and height without viewBox is only recommended if you have carefully designed your graphic to control scaling yourself—for example, if you position elements entirely using percentages or nested coordinate systems (which we'll talk about in Chapters 9 and 10).

That said: it is often helpful to add width and height, in *addition* to viewBox. These set the default (intrinsic) size for your graphic.

The default size is what will be used if you embed an image in a web page without any CSS sizing instructions—that is, with *both* width and height set to the default auto. For raster images, the default size is the pixel size. For SVG, it is the size set by the width and height attributes on the root <svg> element in the file.

 For consistent autosizing, the width and height aspect ratio should match the viewBox aspect ratio. (They don't need to be the same numbers, just the same ratio.)

If they don't match, height and width take precedence. The viewBox will be used to fit the graphic in the resulting size, with gaps or slices.

If the SVG doesn't have an intrinsic size (no width or height), and the embedding web page doesn't provide any size for the <img> or <object> (*both* width and height are auto), that's when things get buggy.

At the time web browsers first started integrating SVG into web pages, there were two competing sets of instructions about what to do when an SVG didn't have a set size:

- The HTML specs defined a "default object size" of 300px wide and 150px tall.
- The SVG specs said that the width and height attributes had a default of 100% (but then had a whole bunch of text about how these attributes weren't the same as CSS width and height).

Different browsers picked different combinations of these sizes to apply:

- In Internet Explorer, the 100% values are used, but if a percentage height can't be calculated by CSS rules (which is common, because height on web pages isn't usually restricted), the 150px height applied.
- In old Firefox, both the 300px width and 150px height were applied.
- In old WebKit and Blink (Safari and Chrome) browsers, 100% width was used, while height was set to 100% of the screen size (100vh).

Newer browsers have settled on a de facto standard:

- If the SVG has a viewBox, the default size is 100% width and a height based on the aspect ratio.
- Otherwise, the default object size of 300px wide and 150px tall is used.

This isn't quite based in any written standard, or logic for that matter, but is often acceptable enough that it can be easy to forget to apply an explicit width: 100% to your <img> element.

 For consistent results in Internet Explorer, and older versions of other browsers, always include some sizing information for your SVG: either default width and height attributes in the SVG file, or at least one of width or height CSS properties on the <img> or <object>.

So to recap, when creating an SVG file that you'll be embedding in a web page:

- Use a `viewBox` unless you have specifically designed your graphic to work without it.
- Include `width` and `height` values that provide a good default size and match the `viewBox` aspect ratio, unless you know you'll always control the size from the web page. Even then, it rarely hurts to add them.
- If you might be embedding the SVG in such a way that both width and height are constricted (for example, to exactly fit the screen size), decide whether you need a nondefault `preserveAspectRatio` value.

If you're exporting the SVG from a graphical editor like Illustrator or Inkscape, look for options to ensure that `viewBox` is included, and other options to include/remove the `width` and `height` attributes.

Resizing Inline SVG

That was for SVG files embedded as images and objects. What about inline `<svg>`? It should work the same way, right? Just set the `viewBox` attribute and the `width` property, and the height should adjust to match.

It seems logical, but it wasn't obvious when browsers first started implementing inline SVG.

The SVG 1.1 specifications didn't have rules for this situation, and HTML didn't clearly define it, either. Once again, browsers came up with their own defaults for what to do if the width or height of an inline SVG wasn't set explicitly. Not surprisingly, those unstandardized defaults were not consistent with each other.

The situation is getting better: recent browsers (released since 2015) will all happily autosize an inline `<svg>` to match the aspect ratio defined in a `viewBox` attribute, just like they do with `<img>`.

They also all now apply the same de facto standard as for images when *neither* height nor width is set on the `<svg>`: 100% width if it has a `viewBox`; 300px × 150px otherwise.

Safari doesn't update the size of an element with auto width and height when the user resizes the browser. Avoid this by explicitly setting 100% width.

Browsers are also inconsistent about what to do if percentage widths are not defined in the CSS layout context (for example, within inline block or floated boxes, which are sized to their contents). In some browsers, an SVG will scale down to zero width and height in this case.

Unfortunately, at the time of writing (mid-2017), most web developers still have to support older browsers that do not autosize inline SVG based on its aspect ratio.

If you leave the height and/or width of an inline <svg> as auto, Internet Explorer will apply the default size for replaced content, 300px width and 150px height, regardless of the SVG's aspect ratio.

Other older browsers will apply 100% width and 100vh height (i.e., the full height of the viewport).

What can you do to create scale-to-fit inline SVG in older browsers?

If it's possible, the simplest solution is to set both width and height of the inline SVG directly, with units that preserve the aspect ratio.

For icons and other smaller SVGs, use em units. In that way, you can adjust the overall size (e.g., for smaller screens) by changing the font size on the <svg> in a media query, without having to worry about the aspect ratio each time you change the size.

For full-size diagrams that you want to fill the browser window, CSS viewport units can often help. Because viewport units allow you to set height proportional to width, and vice versa, you can set both dimensions while maintaining an aspect ratio:

```
svg.ratio-2-1 {
    width: 80vw;
    height: 40vw;
    max-width: 200vh;
    max-height: 100vh;
}
```

The preceding code will normally size the SVG to 80% of the browser window's width, with a 2:1 aspect ratio. However, the maximum values ensure that the SVG never gets taller than the window's height, while still preserving the 2:1 ratio.

 Viewport units are either buggy or not supported on many older mobile browsers, so you'll also want to add fixed-size fallbacks.

Also, while Internet Explorer 9+ and MS Edge support vw and vh units without problem, they have assorted bugs with vmin and vmax units.

These solutions, however, don't address the most common desire for images: have them size to fit the available width, adjusting the height to maintain the correct aspect ratio. To make that happen cross-browser, you need to get creative with CSS layout rules.

Preserving Aspect Ratios, with CSS Padding

If the older browsers won't allow us to use CSS to scale while using SVG to preserve the aspect ratio, we'll have to use CSS to preserve the aspect ratio instead.

One strategy is to wrap the <svg> in an HTML element (e.g., a <div> or <figure>) that is constrained to the correct aspect ratio, and then use absolute positioning to make the SVG stretch to fit that wrapper.

The absolute positioning approach we've seen before. In Example 8-2, we positioned an SVG to fill the width and height of a resizable HTML element. In that case, we were demonstrating how the SVG adjusts to different aspect ratios. But how do you constrain that container to a *specific* aspect ratio?

You do it by setting the element's padding instead of its height.

In CSS layout, you cannot directly set the height of an element to be proportional to its width, which is what you need for a controlled aspect ratio. However, *padding* set using percentage values is always proportional to the available width, even when it is padding on the top and bottom.[1] This is so that, when you set `padding: 5%`, the padding space will be the same on all sides of the element.

But we can also use it to only set vertical padding, and have that vertical padding be proportional to the width.

 This "padding hack" is also useful for many other cases where you want to control the aspect ratio of a container, such as to scale down embedded videos or to frame a large background image. It also works for SVG embedded with `<iframe>`.

Example 8-3 demonstrates how this approach can be used to create a large inline SVG figure that scales to fill the width of the web page. Figure 8-9 shows what that web page looks like.

---

1 This statement is actually out of date. It *used* to be that percentage padding was *always* proportional to the available width. Flexbox and grid layout have changed that. But if you're using flexbox and grid layout, you don't need this layout hack.

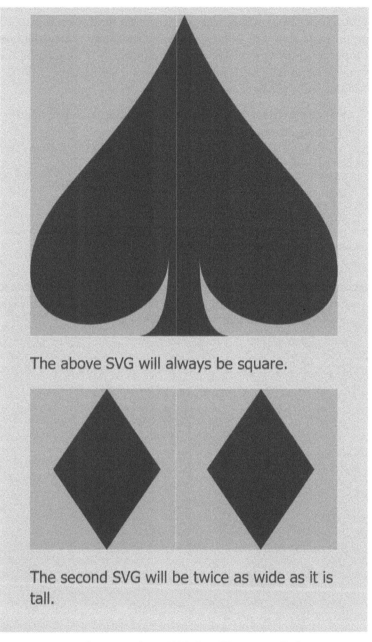

Figure 8-9. A web page with an SVG that fills a controlled aspect ratio container

Example 8-3. Using an HTML element with padding-controlled aspect ratio to scale an SVG evenly in both directions

HTML MARKUP:

```
<!DOCTYPE html>
<html lang="en">
<head>
    <meta charset="utf-8" />
    <title>Scaling inline SVG using a padded wrapper</title>
    <link rel="stylesheet" href="fixed-ratio-wrapper.css" />
</head>
<body>
    <div class="svg-wrapper square">                    ❶
        <svg viewBox="0,0 20,20">                       ❷
            <title>Spade</title>
            <path d="M9,15C9,20 0,21 0,16S6,9 10,0C14,9 20,11 20,16
                     S11,20 11,15Q11,20 13,20H7Q9,20 9,15Z" />
        </svg>
    </div>
    <p>The above SVG will always be square.</p>
    <div class="svg-wrapper ratio-2-1">                 ❸
        <svg viewBox="0,0 40,20">
            <title>Double Diamond</title>
            <path d="m3,10 l7,-10 l7,10 l-7,10 l-7,-10z
                     M20,0 m3,10 l7,-10 l7,10 l-7,10 l-7,-10z" />
        </svg>
    </div>
    <p>The second SVG will be twice as wide as it is tall.</p>
</body>
</html>
```

❶ Each SVG is contained within an HTML element that has classes that will trigger the relevant styles; the `square` class will create a 1:1 aspect ratio.

❷ The aspect ratio defined by the SVG `viewBox` will control how the graphic is drawn in the available space, but it won't affect the layout of the web page as a whole.

❸ The second SVG has a different `viewBox`, but it is the `ratio-2-1` that will adjust the size to match.

CSS STYLES: *fixed-ratio-wrapper.css*

```
/* page styles */
body {
    padding: 0.5em 2em;
    font-family: sans-serif;
```

```
    background-color: lightSteelBlue;
    color: indigo;
}
svg  { background-color: plum; }
path { fill: currentColor; }

/* aspect-ratio control styles */
.svg-wrapper {                           ❶
    position: relative;
    width: 100%;
    height: 1px;                         ❷
    box-sizing: content-box;            ❸
    margin: 0;
    padding: 0;
}
.svg-wrapper.square {
    padding-bottom: 100%;               ❹
    padding-bottom: calc(100% - 1px);   ❺
}
.svg-wrapper.ratio-2-1 {
    padding-bottom: 50%;
    padding-bottom: calc(50% - 1px);    ❻
}
.svg-wrapper > svg {
    display: block;
    position: absolute;                 ❼
    height: 100%;
    width: 100%;
}
```

❶ The wrapper element uses nondefault positioning, so that it will be the reference frame for its absolutely positioned child content.

❷ The wrapper uses up 100% of the available width, but is set to 1px height. We use 1px, and not 0, so that screen readers won't assume that this element is invisible.

❸ The box-sizing property ensures that the specified zero height is only the height of the *content* region of the wrapper; content-box is the default for box-sizing, but many stylesheets override the default, so be sure it is set correctly here. Similarly, margin and padding are cancelled out, just in case.

❹ We control the aspect ratio by setting the padding-bottom property. To make sure it cancels out the shorthand padding set in the previous rule, the selector is a repeat of the previous selector, plus the aspect-ratio class. The `square` class means we need height equal to width, so the padding is 100%, the same value as the wrapper's `width` property.

❺ Except that 1px height will add to the padding. So, to be extra precise, we use CSS `calc()` to cancel it out. But because this code is all about backward compatibility, we keep the basic declaration as a fallback, in case `calc()` isn't supported.

❻ For the 2:1 aspect ratio, the height needs to be half the width. Because the width is 100%, the `padding-bottom` is 50% (minus 1px).

❼ The SVG itself is absolutely positioned within the wrapper. That means that its available width and height *includes* the wrapper's padding region. It takes up 100% of that space, in both directions.

The limitations of this strategy are that you need an extra markup element (the wrapper) whose sole role is to control the layout of the SVG. Furthermore, if you change the dimensions of the SVG, you'll need to change the styles on the wrapper to match, which can make maintainability difficult.

A slightly more streamlined approach is to control the aspect ratio of the inline `<svg>` element directly.

In an HTML page, the top-level inline SVG element is positioned using the CSS box model, which means it can have margins, borders, and padding. Normally, this padding area would not be used to *draw* the SVG content. However, by using a `slice` option for `preserveAspectRatio`, and an `overflow: visible` setting, you can make an inline SVG spill out onto its padding region.

Example 8-4 provides the code for this approach. The result would look exactly the same as Figure 8-9.

Example 8-4. Using sliced SVG scaling, visible overflow, and padding-controlled aspect ratio to scale an SVG evenly in both directions

HTML MARKUP:

```
<!DOCTYPE html>
<html lang="en">
```

```
<head>
    <meta charset="utf-8" />
    <title>Using slice and padding to scale inline SVG</title>
    <link rel="stylesheet" href="fixed-ratio-slice.css" />
</head>
<body>
    <svg class="sliced-svg square" viewBox="0,0 20,20"
        preserveAspectRatio="xMidYMin slice">    ❶
        <title>Spade</title>
        <path d="M9,15C9,20 0,21 0,16S6,9 10,0C14,9 20,11 20,16
                S11,20 11,15Q11,20 13,20H7Q9,20 9,15Z" />
    </svg>
    <p>The above SVG will always be square.</p>
    <svg class="sliced-svg ratio-2-1" viewBox="0,0 40,20"
        preserveAspectRatio="xMidYMin slice">    ❷
        <title>Double Diamond</title>
        <path d="m3,10 l7,-10 l7,10 l-7,10 l-7,-10z
            M20,0 m3,10 l7,-10 l7,10 l-7,10 l-7,-10z" />
    </svg>
    <p>The second SVG will be twice as wide as it is tall.</p>
</body>
</html>
```

❶ The wrapper containers have been eliminated, and the `square`
aspect ratio class is now on the `<svg>` itself. So is the new
`preserveAspectRatio` attribute, which will align the top edge of
the graphic with the top edge of the SVG content box (using a
`YMin` alignment setting), then make it scale to fit the larger
dimension and spill out onto the padding (using a `slice`
setting).

❷ Again, a separate class is required for a separate `viewBox` aspect
ratio, to set the different padding value.

CSS STYLES: *fixed-ratio-slice.css*

```
/* page styles haven't changed */

/* aspect-ratio control styles */
.sliced-svg {
    display: block;
    width: 100%;
    height: 1px;                          ❶
    box-sizing: content-box;
    margin: 0;
    padding: 0;
    overflow: visible;                    ❷
}
.sliced-svg.square {
```

```
    padding-bottom: 100%;
    padding-bottom: calc(100% - 1px);  ❸
}
.sliced-svg.ratio-2-1 {
    padding-bottom: 50%;
    padding-bottom: calc(50% - 1px);
}
```

❶ The 1px height is even more important now; if the SVG is set to
    zero content height, it won't be drawn at all.

❷ The overflow: visible setting ensures that the graphic is visi-
    ble even where it extends beyond the content region. This isn't
    required in all browsers, but it is on Firefox; the HTML and
    SVG specifications differ on whether the padding region should
    be considered overflow.

❸ Again, we control the aspect ratio of the entire layout box using
    padding-bottom to define height as a percentage of the available
    width.

The main benefit of this approach is that all the styles that control
the SVG are assigned to the <svg> element itself. If you have a nonstandard aspect ratio, you could use inline styles to set the padding-
bottom value, so that it is right next to the corresponding viewBox in
your markup.

One limitation is that you cannot use hidden overflow or other
preserveAspectRatio settings to control which parts of your SVG
are visible. If your SVG had shapes that extended outside of the
viewBox (like the circles around the origin in the first half of
Figure 8-5), they will now spill out onto your HTML page.

Both methods (Examples 8-3 and 8-4) depend on the fact that the
percentage used to set padding-bottom, which is always a percentage of the *available* width for the element, is directly proportional to
the 100% *used* width. If you do not want the element to use 100% of
the available width, you will need to either adjust the padding calculation, or add another wrapper element that constrains the SVG to
the width you want.

The HTML5 <figure> element is a good choice for adding another
wrapper element to control layout. It is actually intended for this
purpose: to identify and set off a graphic or other supporting

content that complements your main text. A `<figcaption>` (figure caption) element enclosed within the `<figure>` can be used to add a caption that is recognized by most screen readers and search engines.

Figure 8-10 shows a slightly more realistic example of our SVG in a web page layout, using a `<figure>` containing the `<svg>` (from Example 8-4) and a `<figcaption>`.

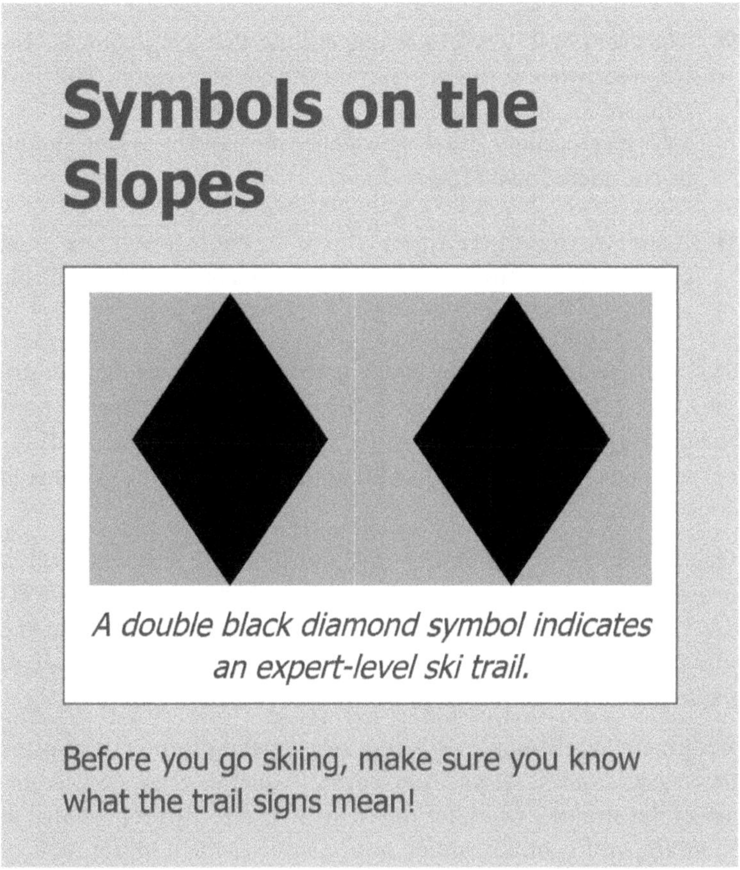

Symbols on the Slopes

A double black diamond symbol indicates an expert-level ski trail.

Before you go skiing, make sure you know what the trail signs mean!

Figure 8-10. A web page with a controlled aspect ratio SVG inside an HTML5 figure

The figure is styled with the following additional CSS:

```css
figure {
    margin: 0.5em 0;
    padding: 4%;
    border: gray thin solid;
    background-color: white;
}
figcaption {
    text-align: center;
    font-style: italic;
    margin-top: 0.5em;
    margin-bottom: -0.35em;
}
```

The `<svg>` continues to take up 100% of the available width, as defined by the content region of the `<figure>`, even if that isn't 100% of the HTML body region.

Future Focus
Aspect-Ratio Control in CSS

Inline SVG isn't the only case in web design where it would be convenient to have a CSS layout box scale to fit the available space, while preserving a set aspect ratio.

The "padding hack" described here was originally proposed by Thierry Koblentz for videos (Flash `<object>` embeds, and later `<video>` elements). For graphical CSS+HTML layouts, such as in headings, advertisements, or some diagrams, JavaScript is often required to determine the correct scale as well as the aspect ratio.

Even for regular images, scaling to fit aspect ratios can be a problem because the browser does not know the aspect ratio until after the image file has downloaded—which can cause the page layout to jump around as it loads.

Multiple suggestions have been made for CSS properties that could set the aspect ratio of an element, or define the height proportional to width, or set a scale factor that is based on available width. One proposal that covers both needs (*https://github.com/w3c/fxtf-drafts/issues/7*) involves making `viewBox` a CSS property and extending it to apply to any element with a block CSS layout.

For SVG developers, `viewBox` in CSS would provide another much-desired feature: the ability to adjust the SVG `viewBox` using CSS media queries, or CSS animations and transitions.

However, there are implementation complexities. For embedded SVG files, the `viewBox` aspect ratio can affect the size of the document used to calculate media queries, so there is a potential to create loops if the media queries can change the `viewBox`. And, as we'll discover in Chapter 9, the `viewBox` used in an embedded SVG file can be affected by the URL target fragment, in a way that isn't easily expressed in CSS.

At the time of writing, there is no complete specification of what a CSS `viewBox` would look like, in all the edge-case details, let alone any commitments from browser teams to implement it.

Summary: Defining Coordinate Systems

Vector graphics are defined by coordinates, and controlling the coordinate system is essential for controlling how SVG appears. When you define the coordinate system of an SVG, you define the scale and reference point used for the graphical content. You also define the intrinsic aspect ratio used when embedding that SVG in other documents.

The coordinate system is established with a `viewBox` attribute, which sets the x and y offset of the coordinate system relative to the top-left corner, and the width and height of the coordinate system in user units. Within the SVG graphic, those user units are equivalent to px units, and all other units are scaled proportionately. The amount of scaling depends on how the width and height defined in the `viewBox` compare with the available width and height.

When the width and height defined in the `viewBox` do not match the aspect ratio of the available drawing space, the `preserve AspectRatio` attribute controls whether the graphic scales to match the too-small dimension or the too-large dimension, or whether it stretches to fit in each direction, ignoring the aspect ratio of the graphic. The same attribute also sets the alignment to be used when the aspect ratio *is* preserved.

Both `viewBox` and `preserveAspectRatio` are important attributes for many of the elements we'll discuss in Chapter 10, controlling the scaling effects to use when content from one SVG coordinate system is inserted into another. They are also fundamental to the SVG views feature that we introduce next, in Chapter 9; we'll also look at nested coordinate systems, using a child <svg> element to redefine a new viewBox for part of a graphic.

Whether defining the original coordinate system on an <svg> or re-defining it with an alternate view, you can significantly alter the final appearance of the graphic using viewBox and preserveAspectRatio.

More Online

A guide to the <svg> element and the attributes described in this chapter is included in the "Document Structure Elements" section of our markup guide:

https://oreillymedia.github.io/Using_SVG/guide/markup.html#structure

CHAPTER 9

A New Point of View

Cropping Embedded SVG Files

This chapter discusses ways to control the coordinate system when you embed the SVG in a web page, changing the graphic's scale or crop, without editing the SVG file. These **SVG view** options allow you to override the SVG file's `viewBox` or `preserveAspectRatio` by modifying the URL you use to access the SVG file.

There are two ways to apply views:

- by using a **target fragment** (the part of the URL after the # or hash character) to reference the `id` of a `<view>` element in the SVG file, or

- by using the **SVG view fragment syntax** to directly set the view information in the URL.

The chapter also covers a related technique, known as **SVG stacks**, which also uses URL fragments to activate different versions of the same SVG file.

These techniques only apply to *embedded* SVG: a separate *.svg* file that is included as an image or object in the HTML, or an image in the CSS. They cannot be used with inline SVG markup that is part of the main HTML document, since inline SVG does not have its own URL. To change the view of an inline SVG, you need to directly edit the `viewBox` and `preserveAspectRatio` attributes, either in the markup or with JavaScript.

Use of these features is currently limited by a number of bugs and restrictions in WebKit/ Safari (*https://bugs.webkit.org/show_bug.cgi? id=91790#c20*). Even in other browsers, support for views arrived later than other SVG features; older browsers may not adjust the SVG to the view, particularly when embedding images via CSS. Finally, because they are not widely used, bugs have a bad habit of slipping through browser QA. Test carefully!

Since we're working with embedded SVG, we'll also be looking a little more closely at your embedding options (`<img>`, `<object>`, and `<iframe>`), and how they differ now that we're working with `viewBox` and *scalable* SVG. Unfortunately, that also includes how they differ from one browser to another.

In the course of discussing these options, we'll also introduce **nested** SVG coordinate systems: `<svg>` inside `<svg>`. Thankfully, nested SVG doesn't have any big browser bugs to warn about.

Alternate Takes, with the <view> Element

The SVG `<view>` **element** defines alternate `viewBox` and `preserveAspectRatio` options for the graphic. The `<view>` element does not directly contain any graphics; instead, its attributes will modify those of its parent `<svg>` element, changing how the rest of the graphic appears within the drawing region.

Views can therefore be used to change the cropping or scaling and alignment of SVG files, according to the needs of the web page using the SVG. But if you're going to use views for cropping, avoid using percentage lengths in your graphic: changing the `viewBox` with a `<view>` also changes the definition of 100% width and height!

Safari/WebKit does not apply views (as of version 10) for cross-origin file embeds, or embeds from unencrypted (`http:`) origins. If your web page and SVG aren't both served from the same HTTPS domain, only use SVG views for nonessential adjustments, where the normal view of the SVG is still an acceptable fallback.

As mentioned in Chapter 3, WebKit and older Blink browsers ignore target fragments on image URLs specified in CSS files. Only use them in CSS background images for nonessential adjustments.

There can be any number of `<view>` elements within an SVG; each is distinguished by its `id` attribute.

The following code defines two views for one of our card-suit icons. The first expands the 20×20 `viewBox` to add an extra unit of padding space (in the scaled coordinate system) on all sides; the second overrides the default aspect-ratio control:

```
<view id="padding" viewBox="-1 -1 22 22" />
<view id="stretch" preserveAspectRatio="none" />
```

Any view attributes *not* specified in the `<view>` element are taken from the `<svg>` itself—or from the default values, if the `<svg>` does not have the attributes either. So, for the padding `<view>`, the `preserveAspectRatio` option won't be changed, and for the stretch `<view>`, the `viewBox` will have the dimensions set for the main SVG.

Or at least, that's how it's supposed to work. A bug in recent versions of Chrome (from approximately version 42 to at least 59) means that you must always specify `viewBox` on the `<view>` element. The second view should therefore be:

```
<view id="stretch" viewBox="0 0 20 20"
      preserveAspectRatio="none" />
```

You use a view by adding a target fragment to the file URL, referencing the ID of the `<view>` element. For example, you could specify the view ID when embedding an SVG image in HTML:

```
<img src="club.svg#stretch" />
```

Alternatively, you could link to the SVG file, so that it will be opened directly in the browser. The following HTML link would open the graphic in the frame with the **browsing context name** `frame1` (if it currently exists in the web page, or as another tab or window) or in a new tab/window otherwise:

```
<a href="club.svg#padding" target="frame1">Show the icon</a>
```

img

iframe

Add padding to the icon in the iframe
Stretch the icon in the iframe

object

Add padding to the icon in the object
Stretch the icon in the object

Figure 9-1. A web page using SVG views, some of which can be changed dynamically

Example 9-1 uses all these snippets to create different views of a single icon file. The resulting web page—as it appears after some of the links have been followed—is displayed in Figure 9-1.

Example 9-1. Using an SVG with multiple views in a web page

SVG FILE: *club-alternate-views.svg*

```
<svg xmlns="http://www.w3.org/2000/svg" xml:lang="en"
    viewBox="0 0 20 20" width="100%" height="200px">      ❶
    <title>Club, with alternate views</title>
    <view id="padding" viewBox="-1 -1 22 22" />           ❷
    <view id="stretch" viewBox="0 0 20 20"
          preserveAspectRatio="none" />
    <path fill="black"
          d="M9,15.5 A5,5 0 1 1 5.5,7.5
             A5,5 0 1 1 14.5,7.5 A5,5 0 1 1 11,15.5
             Q11,20 13,20 H7 Q9,20 9,15.5Z" />           ❸
</svg>
```

❶ We've mixed up the `width` and `height` in the SVG file to be a mix of percentage and absolute values, so you can see all the scaling effects.

❷ The `<view>` elements are as described in the text.

❸ The `<path>` is the one from Example 6-4, but compacted into fewer lines of code.

HTML MARKUP:

```
<!DOCTYPE html>
<html lang="en">
<head>
    <meta charset="utf-8" />
    <title>Different views of an SVG</title>
    <style>
        img, iframe, object {
            display: block;
            width: 90%;
            height: 80px;
            margin: 10px auto;
            background-color: lightgreen;
        }
        h2 { margin: 0.3em 0 0; }
        a  { display: block; }
    </style>
</head>
```

```
<body>
  <h2><code>img</code></h2>
  <img src="club-alternate-views.svg#padding" />
  <img src="club-alternate-views.svg#stretch" />

  <h2><code>iframe</code></h2>
  <iframe name="frame1" src="club-alternate-views.svg">          ❶
  </iframe>
  <a href="club-alternate-views.svg#padding"
     target="frame1">Add padding to the icon in the iframe</a> ❷
  <a href="club-alternate-views.svg#stretch"
     target="frame1">Stretch the icon in the iframe</a>

  <h2><code>object</code></h2>
  <object name="object1" type="image/svg+xml"
          data="club-alternate-views.svg">                      ❸
  </object>
  <a href="club-alternate-views.svg#padding"
     target="object1">Add padding to the icon in the object</a>
  <a href="club-alternate-views.svg#stretch"
     target="object1">Stretch the icon in the object</a>
</body>
</html>
```

❶ The `name` attribute on the `<iframe>` defines the browsing con-
    text name for the embedded document.

❷ The `target` attribute on the links matches the declared name on
    the `<iframe>`.

❸ The `<object>` also has a declared browsing context name, as
    well as a `type` that indicates this object should always contain
    SVG.

If you test out Example 9-1 in multiple web browsers, you will discover a few disagreements (in addition to the Chrome bug that we
already adjusted the code for).

In most browsers (Chrome, Edge, IE, and older versions of Firefox),
the SVG inside the `<iframe>` does not scale to fit the available size of
the frame; instead, it is sized according to the 200px-tall `height`
from the SVG file, and scroll bars are added to the frame. Figure 9-1
shows this result, in Chrome 58.

Safari and recent versions of Firefox (starting with 51) do not use scroll bars on an SVG in an `<iframe>`. Instead, they ignore the width and height from the SVG file, so that an SVG in an `<iframe>` scales just like one in an `object`.

In contrast, when `<object>` has a fixed width and height, like in this demo, an SVG with a `viewBox` will be adjusted to fit within the object; the `height` and `width` attributes on the `<svg>` in the file are always ignored. This is consistent across browsers, and means that SVG in objects scale like SVG in `<img>` tags, so long as a `viewBox` is included.

The improved cross-browser consistency is one reason that this book mostly recommends `<object>` for embedding interactive SVG, instead of `<iframe>`. Unfortunately, for this example, `<object>` has its own browser bug:

Internet Explorer and MS Edge do not support the `name` attribute to create a browsing context name for an `<object>` element (as opposed to an `<iframe>`). The links open in a separate browser tab.

If you need the consistent scaling of `<object>`, but still want links to replace the embedded SVG document, you could use JavaScript to override the normal link activation behavior, directly changing the object's data source. But you'll need to use some very careful browser sniffing if you go this route—while writing up a sample script, I discovered that Chrome (versions 57 to 59, anyway) can freeze completely if you try to change an `<object>` element's data source from JavaScript to point to a `<view>` of the original file!

Another important difference between `<object>` and `<iframe>` is that an `<iframe>` can be sandboxed (restricted) in modern browsers. This can be important if you're embedding documents you don't fully control. Adding a **sandbox attribute** to an `<iframe>` applies a long list of security restrictions on the embedded file. The value of the `sandbox` attribute is a list of permissions that are explicitly granted, like `allow-scripts` or `allow-top-navigation`.

If you are embedding interactive SVG files from other domains that you don't control, using a sandboxed <iframe> may be worth the hassle of dealing with cross-browser scaling inconsistencies.

Rescaling on the Fly, with SVG View Fragments

Alternate views created with a <view> element are known as **predefined views**. The author of the SVG file has specifically defined them within the SVG markup.

However, web page authors can also create **custom views** of an SVG when they embed the SVG, without having to alter the SVG file itself. This view is instead defined with a special URL syntax, called **SVG view fragments**.

The Safari/WebKit limitations on SVG view support also apply to SVG view fragments.

The SVG view fragments are used instead of an element ID in the fragment part of the URL (after the # character). The structure is as follows:

fileURL#svgView(*attributeName*(*value*))

The *attributeName* would be one of the attributes that control the view, such as viewBox or preserveAspectRatio. The *value* would be the value that you would use for that attribute.

To accommodate software that does not support whitespace within URL target fragments, the SVG 1.1 specifications suggested that you use commas (,) to separate parts of the attribute value. This works fine for viewBox, for which the numbers can always be separated by commas instead of whitespace. However, it is problematic for preserveAspectRatio values like xMinYMax slice.

After trying various alternatives (using a comma, using the %20 URL code for the space character, and omitting the spacing entirely), we found that the only option that was supported in all current browsers was using an actual space character in the URL.

In addition to viewBox and preserveAspectRatio, the other allowed attribute names are:

- transform, which adds an extra coordinate system transformation to the SVG element; this value syntax is the same as the attribute we'll discuss in Chapter 11, but browsers have some problematic inconsistencies in how the svgView transformation interacts with transformations and viewBox.
- zoomAndPan, which tells the SVG viewer whether to disable zooming, but has no effect in current web browsers.
- viewTarget, which indicates the id of the element that would be the target, if you weren't busy changing the view; it also has no effect in current browsers.

To specify multiple view attributes in the same fragment, separate them with semicolons, as follows:

`fileURL#svgView(attributeName(value);attributeName(value))`

To show how SVG view fragments can be useful, we're going to adapt Example 9-1 so that it shows the heart icon instead of the club. However, instead of creating a custom SVG file, we'll directly reuse the original 20px-square heart icon file from Example 6-2 in Chapter 6.

We won't reprint all the code here, because it is a simple find-and-replace change from Example 9-1. Wherever the original code referenced "club-alternate-views.svg#padding", the new code uses:

`"heart.svg#svgView(viewBox(-1,-1,22,22))"`

Wherever the original code referenced "club-alternate-views.svg#stretch", the new code uses:

`"heart.svg#svgView(viewBox(0,0,20,20);preserveAspectRatio(none))"`

The resulting web page (after following some of the links) is shown in Figure 9-2.

img

iframe

Add padding to the icon in the iframe
Stretch the icon in the iframe

object

Add padding to the icon in the object
Stretch the icon in the object

Figure 9-2. A web page using SVG view fragments to modify an existing file

As with the `<view>` element, any parameters not specified in the SVG view fragment are taken from the values on the `<svg>` element (or the defaults).

 Blink browsers prior to Chromium version 42 (mid-2015) incorrectly ignored all view attributes from the `<svg>` when an SVG view fragment is used; for consistent cross-browser results, include all the nondefault attributes in the fragment.

In this case, the original file from Example 6-2 did not contain any `viewBox` attributes, so it is always explicitly specified in order to trigger scaling.

As with Example 9-1, the sizing for the `<iframe>` varies by browser: Figure 9-2 is from Chrome, and uses the 20px width and height defined in the original file. The aspect ratio is therefore never distorted, and the padding only adds a single pixel between the heart and the frame.

In contrast, the SVG-as-object fits to the `<object>` element size, once the view fragment gives it a `viewBox`.

Future Focus
Cropping Any Image in a URL

The Media Fragments URI syntax is a proposal for view-based and time-based subsetting of generic media files (images, video, and audio).

So far, the time aspect of media fragments has been more popular. It is used in many JavaScript-based video embedding tools, and is supported in some browsers for directly controlling HTML `<video>` and `<audio>`. SVG 2 adds time-based media fragments to control animations (but that doesn't have support yet).

 The time-based media fragment structure is `#t=start,end`, where *start* and *end* are times represented either as a number of seconds or as *hh*:*mm*:*ss* format. Either the start or end value may be omitted (meaning, the normal start or end of the file is used).

The view-like part of media fragments look like this:

fileURL#xywh=*x,y,width,height*

The meaning of *x, y, width*, and *height* is the same as the equivalent parts of a `viewBox` value. You could therefore use it to crop a PNG or JPEG file in the same way that a view can crop an SVG. For SVG, an `xywh` fragment could be used *instead* of an `svgView` fragment. (But don't, because of browser support.)

You could use a time fragment in combination with an SVG view fragment by separating the values with an **&** (ampersand) character, to create a cropped view of a video or animation.

Interactive Views

The code in Example 9-1 used HTML links to trigger the new views. There is also an `<a>` link element in SVG, which can be used to link out to other files or to link to a targeted view (predefined or via `#svgView()` notation) in the same file. The link reference is indicated with a `xlink:href` attribute, but it is otherwise similar to HTML.

An SVG `<a>` element is a generic grouping element that can contain either text or graphics. We'll discuss more about SVG links in Chapter 18.

By default, an SVG link will update the file that contains it, whether that is inside an `<object>`, `<iframe>`, or the main tab. That means you can link to a `<view>` in the same file without repeating the filename, as in Example 9-2, which creates an SVG that can zoom in on itself—and then back out again. Figure 9-3 shows both views of the drawing.

Figure 9-3. An interactive SVG, before and after being zoomed in to a view

Example 9-2. Using SVG links and views to create interactive zooming

```
<svg xmlns="http://www.w3.org/2000/svg" xml:lang="en"
    xmlns:xlink="http://www.w3.org/1999/xlink" id="top"
    height="200px" width="200px" viewBox="0,0 100,100">  ❶
    <title>Zoomable Interactive SVG</title>
    <style>
    text {
        font: 15px Snap ITC, Ravie, Markerfelt, Impact, sans-serif;
        text-anchor: middle;
    }
    text a { fill: indigo; }
    </style>
    <rect width="100" height="100" fill="lightBlue" />  ❷
    <path fill="palevioletred"
        d="M40,50 C-20,45 15,25 20,20 S45,-20 50,40
                   C55,-20 75,15 80,20 S120,45 60,50
                   C120,55 85,75 80,80 S55,120 50,60
                   C45,120 25,85 20,80 S-20,55 40,50 Z" />  ❸
    <circle fill="gold" stroke="gold" stroke-width="3"
            stroke-dasharray="0.4 3" stroke-linecap="round"
            cx="50" cy="50" r="8" />                        ❹
    <text y="100" dy="-0.5em" x="50">
        <a xlink:href="#zoom">Zoom in!</a></text>           ❺
    <view id="zoom" viewBox="40,40 20,20" />                ❻
    <text y="50" dy="0.5ex" x="50" style="font-size: 3px">
        <a xlink:href="#top">Zoom out!</a></text>          ❼
</svg>
```

❶ The <svg> has a 100×100 viewBox, and the id of top.

❷ The backdrop rectangle (and the rest of the graphic) is sized with absolute lengths, not percentages, so it won't move around when we change the `viewBox` size.

❸ The flower petals are a single `<path>` element. Each petal is a 90° rotation of the previous—so it would have been a lot easier to define if the *bearing* command from SVG 2 was supported anywhere.

❹ The lobed pattern on the center of the flower, in contrast, was created from a simple `<circle>` and a lot of fancy stroke properties—which you'll learn all about in Chapter 13.

❺ The `<a>` link with the "Zoom in!" text points to an element with the `id` of `zoom`.

❻ That `id` is located on the `<view>` element, which defines a new `viewBox` that is 20×20 units, centered around the center of the flower.

❼ That conveniently happens to be where we drew the "Zoom out!" link, in a much smaller `font-size`. This link points back to the root `<svg>` element.

If this SVG were used in an interactive environment (e.g., embedded as an `<object>`), clicking on the "Zoom in!" text would cause the graphic to do just that, switching to the cropped view. Clicking on "Zoom out!" would change the target fragment, cancelling the view —and zooming back to the original scale. Of course, to be interactive, the SVG would need to be embedded in an `<object>` or `<iframe>` (not an `<img>`).

More Online

Interactive effects aren't the only time you might want to switch SVG views. When creating a responsive web layout, you often want to change the view, cropping the image for different screen sizes or orientations.

We've used CSS media queries within SVG to adjust font sizes and stroke thicknesses for different-sized screens. But CSS can't (yet) change the `viewBox` from inside the SVG file.

Instead, you need to change the URL of the file, from the web page that embeds it. The HTML `<picture>` element allows you to do this automatically, based on screen size or other media queries.

Read more about using `<picture>` with SVG views in "Picking the Perfect View":

https://oreillymedia.github.io/Using_SVG/extras/ch09-picture.html

Packaged Deals

The view examples so far have focused on fine-tuning the display of a single graphic. The rest of the chapter looks at ways to pack multiple graphics into a single SVG file—and then use URL fragments to show only one at a time.

The `<view>` element is key to one of the ways to create a single SVG file with many icons within it. As we mentioned briefly in "Using SVG Images Within CSS" on page 87 in Chapter 3, an image **sprite file** is one in which a set of icons is laid out in a neat grid format; you then show only one cell in that grid at a time.

Sprites reduce the number of files the browser downloads from the web server, which can speed up page load times, and allow the Gzip compression algorithm to condense repeated markup from one icon to the next.

Traditional CSS sprites require you to coordinate your sprite layout with CSS properties that crop the image when it is used. With SVG views, you can predefine the cropping coordinates for each icon within the SVG file, and use the sprites anywhere you can use an image URL with a target fragment.

 Sprites don't qualify as "nonessential adjustments" of an image, so you'll need to keep the browser support limitations in mind: use them in `<img>` or `<object>`, not CSS background images, and only if both the SVG and the HTML page will be served from the same secure domain.

With this approach, we can create a single file with all four of the card-suit icons.

If you were drawing the icons in a graphics program, you could use rulers or guidelines to divide up the file into your different icon regions, exactly matching the coordinates you'll use for your views.

Since we already have all our shapes drawn to appear in a 20×20 region, we want to shift them in the main graphic without redefining the coordinates. One way to do this would be to use coordinate system transformations, as we'll show in Chapter 11. For now, we'll take a different approach: defining local coordinate systems with nested <svg> elements.

In an SVG graphic, you can always create a nested coordinate system simply by introducing a new <svg> element. Nested SVGs have x, y, width, and height attributes that define the rectangle in which the new coordinate system will be fit.

The nested <svg> can also have viewBox and preserveAspectRatio attributes to create a custom coordinate system, the same as for a root SVG. All graphical elements contained within the nested <svg> element will be drawn in the new coordinate system.

 By default, x and y are 0, width and height are 100%, and there is no viewBox scaling. So, by default, your nested SVG exactly matches the parent coordinate system.

Some points to consider when using nested SVGs:

- If you don't include a viewBox, a default coordinate system is created in which the length of the user units is the same as for the parent SVG. However, the origin is reset to the top-left corner of the nested SVG (defined by x and y) and percentages are reset to use the nested SVG's width and height.

- If the parent SVG used preserveAspectRatio= "none", the vertical and horizontal units used to establish the new coordinate system may not be equal. The aspect ratio of the new coordinate system will be evaluated according to the length in parent units, not according to the actual displayed aspect ratio.

In other words, it is impossible to "reset" aspect ratio control once it has been turned off.

- By default, any content that extends outside the width and height of the nested <svg> will be clipped. You can change this behavior by setting the CSS overflow property (or presentation attribute) to visible.

 When using <view> elements with nested <svg> elements, do *not* nest the <view> inside the inner <svg> regions. The SVG specifications were not clear about how a <view> within a nested <svg> should be interpreted, and each browser handles it differently.

Instead, use a <view> as a sibling to the <svg>, with its viewBox matching the x, y, width, and height on the paired <svg>. The coordinates in the view's viewBox apply to the top-level SVG, not the nested coordinate system.

As we warned at the top of the chapter, when using views to crop an SVG (changing the viewBox width and height), don't use percentages that depend on the main SVG's dimensions. That means: don't use percentages to lay out your nested <svg> elements. However, you can safely use percentages *inside* the nested coordinate systems, because they have their own viewBox context.

With all that advice in mind, Example 9-3 takes the four suit icons from Chapter 6 and arranges them in a grid within a single SVG file, using nested <svg> elements. For each icon, a <view> element is defined that sets the viewBox so it will show only that icon.

Example 9-3. Using views and nested SVGs to arrange multiple icons in a single file

```
<svg xmlns="http://www.w3.org/2000/svg" xml:lang="en"
    width="400px" height="400px" viewBox="0 0 200 200" >
    <title>Card Suits</title>

    <view id="diamond" viewBox="0 0 100 100"/>
    <svg height="100" width="100" viewBox="0 0 20 20">
        <title>Diamond</title>
```

```
    <path fill="red"
        d="M3,10L10,0 17,10 10,20Z
           M9,11L10,18V10H15L11,9 10,2V10H5Z" />
</svg>

<view id="club" viewBox="100 0 100 100"/>
<svg x="100" y="0" height="100" width="100" viewBox="0 0 20 20">
    <title>Club</title>
    <path fill="black"
        d="M9,15.5A5,5 0 1 1 5.5, 7.5
           A5,5 0 1 1 14.5, 7.5A5,5 0 1 1 11, 15.5
           Q11,20 13,20H7Q9,20 9,15.5Z" />
</svg>

<view id="spade" viewBox="0 100 100 100"/>
<svg x="0" y="100" height="100" width="100" viewBox="0 0 20 20">
    <title>Spade</title>
    <path fill="black"
        d="M9,15C9,20 0,21 0,16S6,9 10,0C14,9 20,11 20,16
           S11,20 11,15Q11,20 13,20H7Q9,20 9,15Z" />
</svg>

<view id="heart" viewBox="100 100 100 100"/>
<svg x="100" y="100" height="100" width="100" viewBox="0 0 20 20">
    <title>Heart</title>
    <path fill="red"
        d="M10,6 Q10,0 15,0T20,6Q20,10 15,14
           T10,20Q10,18 5,14T0,6Q0,0 5,0T10,6Z" />
</svg>
</svg>
```

The default view of the SVG file—with all four icons visible—is shown in Figure 9-4.

The SVG file from Example 9-3 can be used to display the icons in HTML `<img>` or `<object>` elements. You'd display individual icons by adding the target fragment (*#heart*, *#spade*, etc.) to the URL.

Figure 9-4. An SVG icon sprite

Example 9-4 creates a sample website that does just that, using the icons as images in HTML. It uses the icons both as inline icons and as illustrations, adding CSS background, borders, and padding to the <img> element to create a different appearance for the larger figures. Figure 9-5 shows the result.

Card suits

In playing cards, a suit is one of several categories into which the cards of a deck are divided. Most often, each card bears one of several symbols showing to which suit it belongs; the suit may alternatively or in addition be indicated by the color printed on the card. Most card decks also have a rank for each card and may include special cards in the deck that belong to no suit, often called jokers.

The four suits in the standard French deck—also used in most English-speaking countries—are spades or *piques* (♠), hearts or *couers* (♥), clubs or *trèfles* (♣), and diamonds or *carreaux* (♦).

Text adapted from Wikipedia

Figure 9-5. A web page with many images that all come from one image file

---

Example 9-4. Using an SVG view sprite within a web page

HTML MARKUP:

```html
<!DOCTYPE html>
<html lang="en">
<head>
    <meta charset="utf-8" />
    <title>Using SVG Icons from a Sprite Sheet with Views</title>
```

```
    <link rel="stylesheet" href="sprites-suits.css" />
  </head>
  <body>
    <h2>Card suits</h2>
    <figure role="img" aria-label="The four card suits">      ❶
      <img class="icon float big" src="suits-views.svg#spade">
      <img class="icon float big" src="suits-views.svg#heart">
      <img class="icon float big" src="suits-views.svg#club">
      <img class="icon float big" src="suits-views.svg#diamond">
    </figure>
    <p>In playing cards, a suit is one of several categories into
    which the cards of a deck are divided. Most often, each card
    bears one of several symbols showing to which suit it belongs;
    the suit may alternatively or in addition be indicated by the
    color printed on the card. Most card decks also have a rank for
    each card and may include special cards in the deck that belong
    to no suit, often called jokers.</p>
    <p>The four suits in the standard French deck&mdash;also used
    in most English-speaking countries&mdash;are
    spades or <i lang="fr">piques</i>
      (<img class="icon inline" src="suits-views.svg#spade"
            alt="a black spade" width="16" height="16" />),      ❷
    hearts or <i lang="fr">couers</i>
      (<img class="icon inline" src="suits-views.svg#heart"
            alt="a red heart" width="16" height="16" />),
    clubs or <i lang="fr">trèfles</i>
      (<img class="icon inline" src="suits-views.svg#club"
            alt="a black club" width="16" height="16" />),
    and diamonds or <i lang="fr">carreaux</i>
      (<img class="icon inline" src="suits-views.svg#diamond"
            alt="a red diamond" width="16" height="16" />).
    </p>
    <small>Text adapted from
<a href="http://en.wikipedia.org/wiki/Suit_(cards)">Wikipedia</a>
    </small>
  </body>
</html>
```

❶ The role and aria-label on the <figure> element tell the
browser to treat the four graphics as a single image for accessibility purposes—while still allowing us the layout flexibility of
having four separate <img> elements.

❷ The inline images, in contrast, each have their own alt text.

CSS STYLES: *sprites-suits.css*

```css
body {
    font-family: serif;
    background-color: #CDF;
}
figure {
    padding: 0;
    margin: 0;
}
.icon {
    width: 1em;
    height: 1em;
}
.icon.big {
    width: 4em;
    height: 4em;
}
.icon.float {
    display: block;
    float: left;
    clear: left;
    margin: 0 0.5em 0.5em 0;
    padding: 0.2em;
    border: gray solid thin;
    background-color: white;
}
.icon.inline {
    display: inline;
    vertical-align: middle;
    padding: 0.1em;
}
```

There are two different types of icons used in the web page—large floated graphics and the inline icons in the text—but the styling is controlled by a set of logically independent classes.

The position and layout of each icon is controlled by one of the classes inline or float. The float class also adds the border, background, and padding for the illustrations.

The size of each icon is by default 1em square, but is enlarged to 4em square with the big class.

However, the intrinsic size of our SVG, defined by the width and height in our *suits-views.svg* file (Example 9-3) is 400px square. If our CSS doesn't load, that's the size that we'll get. That would be mildly problematic for the floated figures, but it would completely ruin the inline layout. To prevent that, we give the inline images a default width and height of 16 (meaning 16px) in the markup.

 The `width` and `height` attributes on HTML `<img>` elements only accept integer values, for the number of pixels. Just like SVG presentation attributes, they will be overridden by any CSS `width` and `height` properties on the element.

Even if the layout of the web page were much more flexible, you would still usually need to set both width and height on the images, controlling the aspect ratio to match the view.

If you don't, you may find that your helpful sprites turn into troublesome imps, sneaking in where they don't belong.

Example 9-5 gives the code for a (very basic) web page layout where each icon is drawn within a fixed-height image that stretches according to the width of the page. Figure 9-6 shows the result.

Example 9-5. Using an SVG view sprite, without constraining the image dimensions to the aspect ratio

HTML MARKUP:

```
<!DOCTYPE html>
<html lang="en">
<head>
    <title>SVG views, in Flexibly-Sized Images</title>
    <style>
        img {
            display: block;
            width: 90%;
            height: 80px;
            margin: 10px auto;
            background-color: lightgreen;
        }
    </style>
</head>
<body>
    <code>#diamond</code> <img src="suits-views.svg#diamond" />
    <code>#heart</code>   <img src="suits-views.svg#heart" />
    <code>#club</code>    <img src="suits-views.svg#club" />
    <code>#spade</code>   <img src="suits-views.svg#spade" />
</body>
</html>
```

`#diamond`

`#heart`

`#club`

`#spade`

Figure 9-6. An SVG icon sprite used in a web page, without clipping to the icon dimensions

The extra icons appear because the (default) `meet` value for `preserveAspectRatio` creates a view that only takes up *part* of the available drawing space when the aspect ratio doesn't match.

The `viewBox` for each `<view>` ensures that the selected icon will scale to fit the drawing region, and it will be centered within the image. However, it does not clip the content to that view. The CSS `overflow` property doesn't help. Hiding overflow only clips to the drawing region for the <svg>, not to the viewBox.

Ideally, you could use auto sizing to let the browser size the image to match the view. Nearly all browsers support autosizing of SVG in <img> and <object>, using the viewBox to determine the intrinsic aspect ratio of the image when you set height or width but not both. This *should* mean that the browser will automatically clip the image to the specified view.

Unfortunately, this cannot be used reliably in practice:

 When you use an SVG view to reset the viewBox, web browsers currently do *not* update the intrinsic aspect ratio that is used for auto height and width. Instead, they use the aspect ratio from the viewBox on the root <svg> to set the image size, and use the view only for scaling.

In the SVG from Example 9-3, the aspect ratio of the image as a whole (200:200) is equal to the aspect ratio of the individual views (100:100). As a result, for this particular case you *can* safely use views and autosizing in all browsers. With a fixed height and width: auto, each image would become a square, cropped to the correct icon.

But if you know the aspect ratio in advance, you could just set the width to match.

For the more general case, a different approach is needed to ensure that only one icon is displayed at a time.

One option is to space the icons out with lots of whitespace in between: unlike with PNG sprites, this does not add to the SVG file size. However, it is difficult to know in advance how much space you would need, and the extra size can lead to extra memory requirements in some browsers, which rasterize the entire image even if only part is displayed.

The other strategy would be to use the CSS **:target pseudoclass** to only show each graphic when the correct view is targeted. The following CSS code, if added to Example 9-3, would hide the icons unless the correct <view> (the previous sibling in the document) was in effect:

```
view:not(:target) + svg { display: none; }
```

 Older versions of Firefox (prior to 39) did not
apply the :target pseudoclass for <view> element targets.

SVG 1 defined a viewTarget attribute for <view> elements that
would allow you to specify the *logical* "target" element for a view:
that is, the drawing element(s) that are visually emphasized by the
view. The value of viewTarget would be one or more element id
values:

```
<view id="diamond" viewBox="0 0 100 100"
      viewTarget="diamondsvg" />
<svg id="diamondsvg" viewBox="0 0 20 20"
      height="100" width="100">
```

The original specifications suggested that this could be somehow
used directly to style the targeted element. But that was never implemented in browsers; the sibling-selector (+ or ~) approach is the
only one that works.

 Current drafts of SVG 2 have dropped
viewTarget. This reduces some of the semantic
logic of views, but doesn't actually remove any
functionality in browsers.

Showing and hiding graphics with :target styles can also be used
without <view> elements, with a URL that targets the graphical content directly. This is the basis of an SVG stack file.

Flat Pack Stacks

If only one icon will be displayed at any time—because of :target
styles—you don't really *need* to space them out into a sprite grid.
Instead, you can stack them all on top of each other, as layers in the
same coordinate space—an **SVG stack file**.

By stacking all your icons in the same region of your SVG, you avoid
having to change the viewBox to switch from one to the other. But it
means that all the icons need to be drawn to fit in the same viewBox
dimensions.

Of course, you would not normally *see* them stacked together in the browser. The :target style hides nontargeted graphics, so if you open the file in a browser without using a target fragment, you wouldn't see anything at all. But for many designers, it can be easier to work with stacked icons in a graphics program. The software's layers feature can hide or show each icon, so the designer can ensure that they are all neatly aligned in the same width and height.

#diamond

#heart

#club

#spade

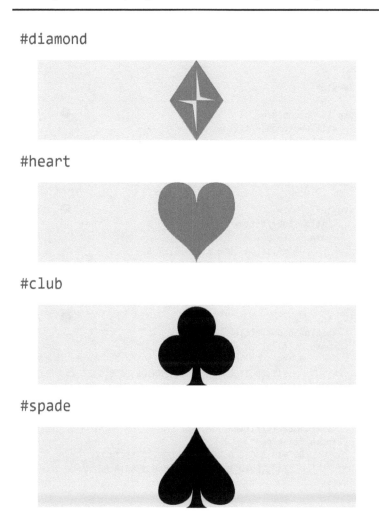

Figure 9-7. An SVG stack used in a web page

Example 9-6 redefines the card-suit set so that it uses the SVG stack structure. Figure 9-7 shows the result when this file is used in the web page from Example 9-5.

Example 9-6. Using :target styles to stack multiple icons in a single file

```
<svg xmlns="http://www.w3.org/2000/svg" xml:lang="en"
    width="100px" height="100px" viewBox="0 0 20 20" >  ❶
    <title>Card Suits</title>
    <style type="text/css">                              ❷
        svg > svg:not(:target) {
            display: none;
        }
    </style>

    <svg id="diamond">                                   ❸
        <title>Diamond</title>
        <path fill="red"
            d="M3,10L10,0 17,10 10,20Z
               M9,11L10,18V10H15L11,9 10,2V10H5Z" />
    </svg>

    <svg id="club">                                      ❹
        <title>Club</title>
        <path fill="black"
            d="M9,15.5A5,5 0 1 1 5.5, 7.5
               A5,5 0 1 1 14.5, 7.5A5,5 0 1 1 11, 15.5
               Q11,20 13,20H7Q9,20 9,15.5Z" />
    </svg>

    <svg id="spade">                                     ❺
        <title>Spade</title>
        <path fill="black"
            d="M9,15C9,20 0,21 0,16S6,9 10,0C14,9 20,11 20,16
               S11,20 11,15Q11,20 13,20H7Q9,20 9,15Z" />
    </svg>

    <svg id="heart">
        <title>Heart</title>
        <path fill="red"
            d="M10,6 Q10,0 15,0T20,6Q20,10 15,14
               T10,20Q10,18 5,14T0,6Q0,0 5,0T10,6Z" />
    </svg>
</svg>
```

❶ The `viewBox` on the parent SVG has been reset to the dimensions of a single icon.

❷ The style rule hides all the nested SVGs *unless* they are the target of a URL fragment.

❸ The id values have been moved to the nested `<svg>` elements.

❹ The x and y attributes have been removed from the subsequent `<svg>` elements, so all the icons appear in the same place.

❺ Similarly, the `height` and `width` attributes have been removed so that each nested SVG takes up the full (100%) space of the parent SVG. In fact, you don't even need to use nested SVGs anymore, since you're not creating nested coordinate systems— the results would be the same with `<g>` elements.

The use of a `:not()` selector ensures that programs that don't recognize the `:target` pseudoclass (such as graphics editors) will display *all* the content. Figure 9-8 shows what the file looks like in Inkscape, with all layers visible.

Figure 9-8. An SVG stack, as it appears in a graphics editor

Although SVG stacks perform better than SVG view sprites in this example, the choice between them is not always straightforward. Here are the main differences:

- SVG view sprites, with each icon arranged in a grid, are easy to work with in a browser, since you can see all the icons at once; stacks require a graphics program that can show and hide individual layers as you work.

- You can also use view sprites with CSS background images, *without* target fragments, by using `background-size` and `background-position` to display the correct portion of the file. This has almost-universal browser support, although you need `width` and `height` in your SVG file, and even then some older WebKit (Android) browsers have bugs with `background-position` and SVG.

  In contrast, stacks do not display anything if target fragments are not supported by the browser, and so cannot reliably be used in CSS.

- In a sprite file, the individual icons can be different sizes or aspect ratios, so long as you don't need the browser to autosize the element based on aspect ratio; stacks use a single `viewBox` for all icons.

- For sprites, you need to externally clip the image to the chosen icon; stacks use `:target` styles to hide the extra content.

Both stacks and sprites are ways to compile multiple icons in a single file, when that file will be used as an image (or embedded object) in a web page. Because they rely on the URL target fragment, they only work when you are embedding SVG by URL reference.

When you're using inline SVG in HTML—or when using icons within a larger SVG file—a different approach is required. Chapter 10 will explore how icons and other content can be reused within a single document.

Summary: Cropping Embedded SVG Files

The SVG `viewBox` and `preserveAspectRatio` options we introduced in Chapter 8 let you control the cropping and alignment of the SVG graphic. But often the exact crop and alignment you need will change each time you use a file. SVG files allow you to dynamically adjust these parameters when you use the SVG, by altering the target fragment of the URL you use to reference the SVG file.

There are two approaches to views: predefined views, created with <view> elements in the SVG file and referenced by ID, or SVG view fragments, where all the view parameters are set in the URL. A related technique is the SVG stack method, which uses URL target fragments to hide or show content using the CSS :target pseudo-class.

There are a number of browser inconsistencies and support limitations to keep in mind when you're using views. The most practical use case is for slight adjustments where the graphic will still look acceptable if the view isn't applied: padding or cropping an image, or changing the preserveAspectRatio alignment.

More complex subsetting of images, using views or :target styles, are currently only recommended where support is good: within <img> or <object> tags, for same-origin embeds on secure domains.

More Online

The <view> element is included in the "Document Structure Elements" section of the markup guide:

*https://oreillymedia.github.io/Using_SVG/guide/
markup.html#structure*

The HTML elements for embedding SVG (with or without views) are summarized in the "Embedding SVG in HTML" guide:

https://oreillymedia.github.io/Using_SVG/guide/embedding.html

CHAPTER 10

Seeing Double

Reusing Content

An SVG file is a structured description of a graphic that can be organized into logical parts and groups. An important consequence of this structure is that you can reuse the same content in multiple contexts without having to repeat all the information used to create that graphic. Symbols, icons, and other repeated motifs can be defined once, then used again and again.

This chapter examines the key structural SVG elements that allow you to copy content defined elsewhere into your graphic.

When it comes to reusing content, there are two distinct strategies used in SVG. On the one hand, you can reuse entire images, embedding the complete graphic in your SVG similar to how an `<img>` element embeds an image in an HTML page. On the other hand, you can reuse individual SVG shapes or groups, from another file or another part of the same file.

With the SVG `<image>` element, you can embed not only SVG files but also raster image formats. This allows an SVG to include photos and other graphics that cannot effectively be represented with vector drawing elements. Regardless of whether an embedded image was originally SVG or not, when you embed it *as* an image, it is treated as an indivisible element. It can be manipulated with graphical effects, but its component parts are inaccessible to styles or scripts from the main document.

In contrast, when you duplicate SVG content with a <use> element, you duplicate the vector graphics *instructions* for that content. The duplicated elements are rendered almost as if they were cloned into the markup, inheriting new styles from the context where they are used.

Reduce, Reuse, Recycle

We introduced the **<use> element** in Chapter 1, but did not explore its full potential. In that chapter, <use> elements were used to duplicate, position, and style the circles in the stoplight graphic.

A quick recap of the basics:

- The <use> element allows you to duplicate SVG graphics without repeating the complete markup.

- The original copy of the graphic is identified with an id value, and the <use> element references it with an **xlink:href attribute**, where xlink is the standard prefix for the namespace *http://www.w3.org/1999/xlink*.

- To prevent the original copy from being drawn directly, you can put it inside a **<defs> element**, indicating that it is a definition for future reuse.

- You can position the duplicated graphics using **x and y attributes** on the <use> element.

- The duplicated graphics inherit style properties from the <use> element.

We've also hinted a few times that the element you're reusing doesn't have to be in the same file. You can use a URL to reference another file, and then a target fragment to reference the element ID, like <use xlink:href="icons.svg#shape" />. But there are limitations, which we'll get to in "File Management" on page 341.

There are a few more things to know about <use> elements, now that we've discussed coordinate systems:

- The content duplicated by a <use> element does not have to be a single shape. It can be a <text> element or a container such as a group (<g> element) or an <svg>.

- The x and y attributes on the <use> element reposition the coordinate system origin for the graphics it duplicates—and also for the <use> element itself, similar to a transform.

The <use> element can also take **width and height attributes**. They allow you to create a scaled, nested coordinate system, but *only* in specific cases:

- If the duplicated element is an <svg> with a viewBox attribute, the copy will scale to fit these new dimensions (respecting any preserveAspectRatio options on the original). The same is true for duplicated <symbol> elements, which we'll introduce in "Symbolic Usage" on page 338.

- The width and height attributes have no effect on other content. They do not create a new coordinate system width and height on their own, meaning they do not affect percentage lengths of duplicated shapes that aren't contained inside an <svg>.

- If a duplicated <svg> has width and height attributes, and the <use> element does not, those dimensions will be used to size the SVG (similar to what would happen if you drew the SVG in an HTML <object>).

- Otherwise, the defaults for width and height are 100%, meaning a duplicated <svg> will scale to fill the current SVG coordinate system, offset by the <use> element's x and y attributes.

- Any x and y positioning attributes on an <svg> will be applied to the duplicate in addition to the x and y values for the <use>, as will transforms.

That last point is also true for duplicated shapes and groups: positioning attributes and transforms on the original elements apply in addition to the attributes and transforms on the <use>. Only width and height on <svg> and <symbol> have the special override behavior.

 Usually, it's easiest if the original graphics are positioned at—or centered around—the origin. That way, the x and y attributes on the <use> element have predictable results.

If you use percentage lengths on shapes inside your reused `<svg>` or `<symbol>`, the percentages will be recalculated according to the width or height of the coordinate system created by the `<use>` element.

In all other cases (that is, if the `<use>` element directly references the shape or a `<g>` group), percentage lengths are best avoided.

 In current web browsers, percentage lengths are not recalculated for reused shapes that aren't part of a nested coordinate system. The original SVG specs were not clear about the correct behavior in this case.

Putting it all together, Example 10-1 reuses the card-suit icons from Chapter 6 to draw complete playing cards. The resulting cards are displayed in Figure 10-1.

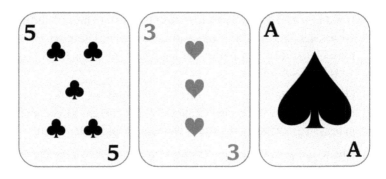

Figure 10-1. Playing card graphics created with reused SVG icons

Example 10-1. Reusing SVG icons to draw playing cards

```
<svg xmlns="http://www.w3.org/2000/svg" xml:lang="en"
    xmlns:xlink="http://www.w3.org/1999/xlink"
    width="400px" height="180px" viewBox="0 0 400 180" >    ❶
    <title>Playing Cards</title>
    <style type="text/css">
        svg:root {
            font-size: 24px;
            font-weight: bold;
        }
```

```
      svg {
          overflow: visible;
      }
      .card {
          stroke: gray;
          fill: linen;
      }
      .diamond, .heart {
          fill: red;
      }
      .club, .spade {
          fill: black;
      }                                                    ❷
</style>
<defs>
      <svg height="20" width="20" viewBox="0 0 20 20"
           id="diamond">                                  ❸
          <title>Diamond</title>
          <path d="M3,10L10,0 17,10 10,20Z
                   M9,11L10,18V10H15L11,9 10,2V10H5Z" />
      </svg>

      <svg height="20" width="20" viewBox="0 0 20 20"
           id="club">
          <title>Club</title>
          <path d="M9,15.5A5,5 0 1 1 5.5, 7.5
                   A5,5 0 1 1 14.5, 7.5A5,5 0 1 1 11, 15.5
                   Q11,20 13,20H7Q9,20 9,15.5Z" />
      </svg>

      <svg height="20" width="20" viewBox="0 0 20 20"
           id="spade">
          <title>Spade</title>
          <path d="M9,15C9,20 0,21 0,16S6,9 10,0C14,9 20,11 20,16
                   S11,20 11,15Q11,20 13,20H7Q9,20 9,15Z" />
      </svg>

      <svg height="20" width="20" viewBox="0 0 20 20"
           id="heart">
          <title>Heart</title>
          <path d="M10,6 Q10,0 15,0T20,6Q20,10 15,14
                   T10,20Q10,18 5,14T0,6Q0,0 5,0T10,6Z" />
      </svg>

      <rect id="card-front" class="card"
            width="120" height="160" rx="20" />         ❹
</defs>

<svg width="140" height="180"
     class="club" id="club5">                            ❺
      <title>5 of clubs</title>
```

```
    <use xlink:href="#card-front" x="10" y="10" />
    <text x="15" y="35">5</text>
    <text x="105" y="160">5</text>
    <use xlink:href="#club" x="40" y="40" />
    <use xlink:href="#club" x="80" y="40" />
    <use xlink:href="#club" x="60" y="80" />
    <use xlink:href="#club" x="40" y="120" />
    <use xlink:href="#club" x="80" y="120" />            ❻
</svg>

<svg x="130" width="140" height="180"
    class="heart" id="heart3">
    <title>3 of hearts</title>
    <use xlink:href="#card-front" x="10" y="10" />
    <text x="15" y="35">3</text>
    <text x="105" y="160">3</text>
    <use xlink:href="#heart" x="60" y="40" />
    <use xlink:href="#heart" x="60" y="80" />
    <use xlink:href="#heart" x="60" y="120" />
</svg>

<svg x="260" width="140" height="180"
    class="spade" id="spadeA">
    <title>Ace of spades</title>
    <use xlink:href="#card-front" x="10" y="10" />
    <text x="15" y="35">A</text>
    <text x="105" y="160">A</text>
    <use xlink:href="#spade" x="30" y="50"
        width="80" height="80" />                       ❼
</svg>

<!-- and many more, to draw the rest of the cards -->
</svg>
```

❶ For this and most of the rest of the examples in the book, we'll
be following our own advice and including *both* width and
height dimensions and a viewBox on our root <svg> elements;
the former define the default size when displaying the graphic
on its own, while the latter ensures it will scale correctly when
displayed at other sizes.

❷ As this is a relatively complex graphic, we've expressed all the
presentation styles CSS using classes; this makes it easier to
change styles later.

❸ The four icons are defined as individual <svg> elements within
a <defs> block. Each icon has both default size attributes (width
and height) and a viewBox.

❹ A rounded `<rect>` is also predefined; it will be used to draw the basic card shapes.

❺ Each card is also contained within a nested `<svg>` to create a self-contained element coordinate system. However, these SVGs are *not* inside the `<defs>`, and so will be drawn.

❻ We construct each card by reusing the basic card shape, using `<text>` elements to write the number or letter in the corners, and then reusing the basic icon as many times as appropriate, positioning it with x and y attributes.

❼ For the number cards, the icons are used at their default (20×20) size; for the ace, we create the large icon by setting width and height attributes on the `<use>` element.

Reusing elements with `<use>` can be recursive. You can reuse a component that contains other reused components—so long as you don't create any circular reference loops!

This means, instead of creating a simple grid of playing cards, you could predefine a complete set of cards, and then code up a card game layout where each card is drawn with a single `<use>` element. For example, an ace of spades would be `<use xlink:href= "#spadeA"/>`. Of course, if you were going to do that, you'd want to go back and remove the x and y attributes from each playing card `<svg>`, so that the cards in your game would be positioned predictably.

Future Focus
The `<use>` Element Shadow DOM

There are a couple minor changes for **`<use>`** elements in SVG 2, and one major change, which should hopefully only have minor effects on most SVG designs.

The minor changes:

- The **xlink** namespace is optional; instead, a simple **href** attribute in the default namespace can be used. This is already supported in most new browsers. But for backward compatibility and support in Safari, you'll need to keep using **xlink** for a while longer.

- You will be able to reuse an entire SVG file, even if the root element does not have an **id** attribute: just reference the file URL without a target fragment (although see "File Management" on page 341 for issues with the **<use>** element and external files).

A more fundamental change to the spec relates to how duplicated content is implemented within the DOM. In HTML, a lot of work is ongoing to make it easier to create modular components and interactive widgets that can be inserted into web pages with simple markup, using what is known as a Shadow DOM. These web components have a number of similarities with SVG **<use>** elements, and Shadow DOM was in part inspired by how **<use>** elements worked.

However, there are also a lot of differences between **<use>** elements and HTML Shadow DOM web components. Each instance of a web component is an independent, modifiable DOM fragment. Once created, it is no longer linked to the template on which it was based. In contrast, **<use>** elements are live copies, always linked to the original.

The SVG 2 specification proposes a set of rules for recreating the **<use>** behavior in the Shadow DOM model. But at the time of writing (mid-2017), browser implementations are quite inconsistent under the hood. Blink and WebKit are partially transitioned to Shadow DOM, IE and Edge still use the SVG 1.1 model (with a couple compatibility tweaks in Edge), and Firefox has its own model that doesn't match any specs (although recent changes fix some of the most problematic inconsistencies).

You're most likely to notice the differences if you try to react to DOM events (like clicks) that start in **<use>** elements, something we'll discuss in Chapter 18.

Symbolic Usage

Creating scalable, reusable icons, as was done in Example 10-1 with nested SVG elements, is a common requirement—so common that SVG has a special element for this purpose: the **<symbol>**.

A **<symbol>** is a compound graphic defined specifically for the purpose of reuse. Similar to a nested **<svg>**, a **<symbol>** can be given **viewBox** and **preserveAspectRatio** attributes so that it will scale to fit the dimensions specified when it is used.

The contents of the <symbol> are never drawn directly; they are only drawn through <use> instances. In this way, a <symbol> is similar to an <svg> inside a <defs> element.

You can place your symbol code inside a <defs> definition block, to maintain a logical organization for your SVG file, but it isn't required.

The <symbol> does not add any extra functionality that you can't achieve with an <svg> inside a <defs>. However, it adds clarity about the purpose of your file. Many SVG icon systems and related tools look specifically for <symbol> elements to identify independent icons. For example, in the latest versions of Inkscape (0.91+), you can import a file of <symbol> elements, and use them in other drawings.

The key differences between <symbol> and <svg> are as follows:

- The <symbol> is never drawn directly.
- There are no x and y attributes on the <symbol>, because it is never directly positioned in the graphic.
- There are no width and height attributes on the <symbol>; its size is controlled entirely by the <use> element.

The last point can sometimes be a limitation; in Example 10-1, switching to <symbol> for the suit icons would require a lot of extra attributes on the <use> elements, most of which currently reproduce the <svg> at its default size.

When you reuse a <symbol> with a <use> element that *doesn't* have width and height specified, the default <use> dimensions apply: 100% of the parent SVG's height and width.

Nonetheless, if we did want to convert the icons to symbols—and future examples will use such symbols—they would look something like this:

```
<symbol viewBox="0 0 20 20" id="diamond"
        style="overflow: visible">
```

```
<title>Diamond</title>
<path d="M3,10L10,0 17,10 10,20Z
         M9,11L10,18V10H15L11,9 10,2V10H5Z" />
</symbol>
```

Because this symbol is intended for reuse as a single-color icon, the color has not been specified in the definition. You would color the diamond using inherited styles defined on the `<use>` element, so you could make it bright red, or crimson, or light purple pink if you chose. Similarly, strokes or other styles could be set at the time of use.

The one style that is included is the CSS `overflow` property. Like the `<svg>` element—and all other elements that can take a `viewBox` attribute—the `<symbol>` is by default set to hide any content that overflows its available width and height. In the case of a `<symbol>`, that's the width and height defined by the `<use>` element (or by the `<use>` element's parent SVG, if it doesn't have specific `width` and `height` attributes).

With the card-suit icon symbols, which exactly touch the boundaries of their `viewBox`, this would mean that any strokes on the shape would be clipped to a square. Setting `overflow: visible` ensures that the symbol can be used with any styles.

Firefox (up until version 56, which will be stable in late 2017) has a number of bugs with respect to CSS styles and reused content. Their style-matching process did not distinguish between the "real" DOM and the hidden, duplicated DOM.

One consequence is that reused instances of `<symbol>` elements instead match style rules for `<svg>` elements. In order to correctly set overflow on symbols, either set the style with attributes or use the following style rule:

```
symbol, use > svg {
    overflow: visible;
}
```

The `use > svg` selector (which matches an `<svg>` that is a direct child of a `<use>`) will not match anything in browsers that conform to the specifications.

Whether you're creating a set of icon symbols or a full set of playing cards, there are many cases where you want to reuse graphics not only within a single SVG, but across multiple web pages. In these cases, it can be much easier to use a separate asset file for the symbol definitions, and then access the same definitions from any page that requires them.

File Management

As we've mentioned a few times, you can `<use>` content from another file. This allows you to create icon library files, with many complex graphics that you can grab one at a time for use in another web page, whether that is a complex SVG application or an HTML file.

There are some important limitations. For starters, most browsers don't support cross-file use when you're viewing SVGs from your own filesystem (`file:` URLs); you'll need to run a local web server or view the examples online. We'll get to why that is in a moment, but first: an illustration of what it looks like when everything works.

Example 10-2 adapts the web page from Example 9-4 in Chapter 9. Instead of using <img> elements to reference views of an external SVG, we use inline SVG and <use> elements to copy the individual icons.

Our icon sprite SVG still uses familiar card-suit icons, but now redefined as <symbol> elements. The final result is shown in Figure 10-2.

Card suits

In playing cards, a suit is one of several categories into which the cards of a deck are divided. Most often, each card bears one of several symbols showing to which suit it belongs; the suit may alternatively or in addition be indicated by the color printed on the card. Most card decks also have a rank for each card and may include special cards in the deck that belong to no suit, often called jokers.

The four suits in the standard French deck—also used in most English-speaking countries—are spades or *piques* (♠), hearts or *couers* (♥), clubs or *trèfles* (♣), and diamonds or *carreaux* (♦).

Text adapted from Wikipedia

Figure 10-2. A web page using external SVG icons as inline code

---

Example 10-2. Using SVG icons from an external file in a web page

SVG SYMBOL FILE: *suits-symbols.svg*

```
<svg xmlns="http://www.w3.org/2000/svg" xml:lang="en"
    xmlns:xlink="http://www.w3.org/1999/xlink"
    width="400px" height="400px" viewBox="0 0 200 200" >
    <title>Card Suit Icons</title>

    <symbol viewBox="0 0 20 20" id="diamond"
        style="overflow: visible">
        <title>Diamond</title>
        <path d="M3,10L10,0 17,10 10,20Z
                M9,11L10,18V10H15L11,9 10,2V10H5Z" />
    </symbol>
    <use xlink:href="#diamond"
        x="0" y="0" width="100" height="100" />         ❶

    <symbol viewBox="0 0 20 20" id="club"
        style="overflow: visible">
        <title>Club</title>
        <path d="M9,15.5A5,5 0 1 1 5.5, 7.5
                A5,5 0 1 1 14.5, 7.5A5,5 0 1 1 11, 15.5
                Q11,20 13,20H7Q9,20 9,15.5Z" />
    </symbol>
    <use xlink:href="#club"
        x="100" y="0" width="100" height="100" />

    <symbol viewBox="0 0 20 20" id="spade"
        style="overflow: visible">
        <title>Spade</title>
        <path d="M9,15C9,20 0,21 0,16S6,9 10,0C14,9 20,11 20,16
                S11,20 11,15Q11,20 13,20H7Q9,20 9,15Z" />
    </symbol>
    <use xlink:href="#spade"
        x="0" y="100" width="100" height="100" />

    <symbol viewBox="0 0 20 20" id="heart"
        style="overflow: visible">
        <title>Heart</title>
        <path d="M10,6 Q10,0 15,0T20,6Q20,10 15,14
                T10,20Q10,18 5,14T0,6Q0,0 5,0T10,6Z" />
    </symbol>
    <use xlink:href="#heart"
        x="100" y="100" width="100" height="100" />
</svg>
```

❶ Since the `<symbol>` elements do not draw anything themselves, a `<use>` copy of each icon draws it to the screen. That way, you

won't see a completely blank file if you open your symbol sheet
directly.

HTML MARKUP:

```
<!DOCTYPE html>
<html lang="en">
<head>
    <meta charset="utf-8" />
    <title>Using SVG Icons from an External File</title>
    <link rel="stylesheet"
        href="../ch09-views-files/sprites-suits.css" />
    <style>
        .icon        { overflow: visible; }
        .icon.float { border-radius: 50%; }
        .black       { fill: #222; }
        .red         { fill: #b00; }
        .big.black   { stroke: gray; }
        .big.red     { stroke: #d33; }
    </style>
</head>
<body>
    <h2>Card suits</h2>
    <figure role="img" aria-label="The four card suits">
        <svg class="icon float big black">
            <use xlink:href="suits-symbols.svg#spade"
                x="10%" y="10%" width="80%" height="80%"/>
        </svg>
        <svg class="icon float big red">
            <use xlink:href="suits-symbols.svg#heart"
                x="10%" y="10%" width="80%" height="80%" />
        </svg>
        <svg class="icon float big black">
            <use xlink:href="suits-symbols.svg#club"
                x="10%" y="10%" width="80%" height="80%" />
        </svg>
        <svg class="icon float big red">
            <use xlink:href="suits-symbols.svg#diamond"
                x="10%" y="10%" width="80%" height="80%" />
        </svg>
    </figure>
    <p>In playing cards, a suit is one of several categories into
    which the cards of a deck are divided. Most often, each card
    bears one of several symbols showing to which suit it belongs;
    the suit may alternatively or in addition be indicated by the
    color printed on the card. Most card decks also have a rank for
    each card and may include special cards in the deck that belong
    to no suit, often called jokers.</p>
    <p>The four suits in the standard French deck&mdash;also used
    in most English-speaking countries&mdash;are
    spades or <i lang="fr">piques</i>
```

```
(<svg class="icon inline black" width="1em" height="1em"
        role="img" aria-label="a black spade">
    <use xlink:href="suits-symbols.svg#spade" /></svg>),
hearts or <i lang="fr">couers</i>
(<svg class="icon inline red" width="1em" height="1em"
        role="img" aria-label="a red heart">
    <use xlink:href="suits-symbols.svg#heart" /></svg>),
clubs or <i lang="fr">trèfles</i>
(<svg class="icon inline black" width="1em" height="1em"
        role="img" aria-label="a black club">
    <use xlink:href="suits-symbols.svg#club" /></svg>),
and diamonds or <i lang="fr">carreaux</i>
(<svg class="icon inline red" width="1em" height="1em"
        role="img" aria-label="a red diamond">
    <use xlink:href="suits-symbols.svg#diamond" /></svg>).
</p>
<small>Text adapted from
<a href="http://en.wikipedia.org/wiki/Suit_(cards)">Wikipedia</a>
</small>
</body>
</html>
```

Let's break that down. Each SVG icon is embedded within its own inline `<svg>` element, replacing the `<img>` elements from Example 9-4. The markup here consists of only the `<svg>` and the `<use>` element:

```
<svg class="icon inline black" width="1em" height="1em"
        role="img" aria-label="a black spade">
    <use xlink:href="suits-symbols.svg#spade" />
</svg>
```

The classes are mostly the same as for the `<img>` version of the icons. However, we've added some extra styles, to reflect the extra styling flexibility that inline SVG gives us.

The `aria-label` attribute replaces the image's `alt`, and `role="img"` tells browsers that this is a noninteractive SVG that should be treated like an image for accessibility purposes. You could also use a `<title>` instead of `aria-label`; we discuss the difference in Chapter 17.

The larger icons are set as 4em square, minus padding, in the CSS, the same as for the images in Example 9-4. However, the `<use>` elements are scaled down inside each `<svg>` (with x, y, width, and height attributes). This gives us room to round off the corners of each `<svg>` with `border-radius` and add strokes to the icons. (We couldn't do that with the `<img>` icons without adding more `<view>` elements to change the scaling.)

The small icons fill up the entire SVG, so the `<use>` elements don't need any attributes—a reused `<symbol>` automatically scales to 100% height and width, allowing you to control the size entirely with styles on the `<svg>`. This is usually preferable when you are reusing SVG icons in HTML.

 In contrast, when we were reusing icons within a larger SVG (Example 10-1), it was preferable to reuse nested `<svg>` elements with default height and width attributes, since we didn't want the icons to take up the entire SVG region.

Nonetheless, just like in Example 9-4, we add default width and height attributes on the inline SVG icons, in case our external style-sheet doesn't load. However, because these are now SVG presentation attributes, the default size can use CSS em units.

Alternatively, we could have shifted the width and height CSS from the external stylesheet to our `<style>` block. The main point is: make sure your small inline SVG icons have a good width and height defined in the same file, to avoid the "flash of unstyled SVG" while waiting for your stylesheet to load.

The final change to the code (relative to Example 9-4) is the new red and black classes that set the fill colors. These also interact with the big class to add matching strokes when there is room.

There are no fill styles at all in the SVG symbol file. The reused icons in Example 10-2 are styled entirely with inherited styles. This allows us to tweak the styles to match our design: the icon colors aren't pure black and red, and the styles are different depending on context.

This is the primary benefit of using icons as inline SVG, instead of images: the web page can control the styling. You can even use CSS pseudoclasses, such as `:hover` or `:focus`, to make those styles dynamic.

However, to be able to style the icons by styling the `<use>` elements, we need to draw the `<path>` elements in the symbols entirely with inherited values. If the <path> (or <symbol>) had a fill attribute, it would be used instead of the inherited color. So you can't set a default fill in your icon file, and then override it from the main web page styles.

 Actually, you *can* set a default fill and override it, too, in recent browsers. But you need CSS variables to do so. We'll have an example of how it works in Chapter 12.

When you reuse content from the same file, any other styles set on the symbols and path are also copied with the cloned graphic. For external-file <use>, it's complicated.

 When you reuse content from an external SVG, browsers currently only clone styles set with presentation attributes or the style attribute. They ignore styles that were defined in the external file via <style> elements and do not download additional stylesheets.

 Some versions of Chrome have a bug where they will not apply patterns and gradients to content reused from external files, regardless of whether the patterns and gradients (or the styles applying them) are defined in the main file or the sprite file.

Despite those bugs, styling <use> icons is still much more flexible than styling image icons, where your only option is a :target style rule in the icon file—or a filter effect applied on the HTML <img>.

Using icons from external files means that your inline SVG code is short and concise—almost as short and concise as an <img>. Furthermore, it allows you to use those icons in many different web pages, and have the user's browser cache the icon file, instead of downloading the data with each HTML page.

However, there are two ways in which this approach is limited in practice.

For starters, some browsers don't support cross-file <use> references at all.

Internet Explorer and older versions of other browsers (including Safari up to version 6) do not allow <use> elements to access content from other files. MS Edge supports external file references starting in version 13.

Some versions of Chrome have a bug where they do not support nested reuse of externally referenced content. That means that if you <use> the content from the external file inside a group or symbol in the current file, and then reference that group or symbol in a second <use>, the external content won't show up in the copy.

However, even in browsers that support cross-file <use>, there is no support for cross-*origin* <use> references. The two files (the one with the <use> and the one with the icon) need to be on the same **origin**:

- served over either HTTP or HTTPS web server, with both URLs using the same protocol
- from the same URL domain, including ports and subdomains (*www.example.com* and *static.example.com* are separate origins)

Cross-origin restrictions like these apply to any "active" content, including files used by scripts. However, most *other* ways of accessing files for websites now support a cross-origin permission system. These **cross-origin (CORS) permissions** (provided in the form of HTTP headers) allow one web origin to request access to files from another origin.

More Online

Why do cross-origin restrictions exist, how do you work around them, and why doesn't that work for SVG **\<use\>**?

Read more in "Understanding CORS and SVG":

https://oreillymedia.github.io/Using_SVG/extras/ch10-cors.html

SVG \<use\> does not—yet—have a way to tell the browser it should request cross-origin permissions. Even if the other web server provides permissions automatically (with HTTP headers), the browser will not use the file.

If you host your images and other asset files on a different web domain than your main web pages, and you want to do the same with your \<use\> assets, you need to work around the restrictions:

- Use JavaScript to download the file with cross-origin headers.
- Inject the markup into your current document, where the SVG renderer can access it.

Conveniently, this is the same approach we use to work around browsers that don't support external file \<use\> references at all.

To get the full benefits of \<use\> elements in a reliable, cross-browser manner, you need to directly define the content in the main HTML or SVG document. However, adding the code for frequently used icons to every file weighs down every web page download. It also causes maintainability problems at the server end, since you need to make sure that every page is updated correctly with the latest versions of the icons.

By using JavaScript to download your icon file (using XMLHttpRequest, or the newer Fetch API), you can access files on other domains so long as the web server provides permission in the CORS HTTP header. Just as importantly, it will work on every browser that supports SVG.

By dynamically copying the DOM of the downloaded file into the DOM of the current document, you make all your icon definitions available to <use> elements in the current document, in every browser that supports SVG.

 Dynamically injecting arbritrary markup into the current document could inject scripts or other active content. Only use this approach for accessing SVG files that you trust and control. To be extra sure, only use it for SVG files you serve over HTTPS connections.

There are ready-made JavaScript libraries designed to take care of this for you. SVG4Everybody by Jonathan Neal (*https://github.com/ jonathantneal/svg4everybody*) is probably the best known. In addition to fetching external file <use> requests for browsers that don't support them, it can replace your inline SVG markup with <img> tags pointing to fallback PNG files, for browsers that don't support SVG at all.

Alternatively, SVGxUse (*https://github.com/Keyamoon/svgxuse*) looks specifically for broken cross-references, regardless of browser, so it also catches <use> requests that fail because of cross-origin references.

More Online

If an existing library does not meet your needs, you can always write the code yourself.

XMLHttpRequest is fairly easy to use if you know exactly which file URL you need. The harder part is automatically identifying the file cross-references from your code, and updating those references once you've imported the SVG markup into the current document.

Read more about XMLHttpRequest, and how to use it to import SVG documents, in "Importing SVG Assets, with AJAX":

https://oreillymedia.github.io/Using_SVG/extras/ch10-ajax.html

---

All this work to use external files may seem overly complicated, compared to using images and image sprite files. The complications come from the fact that graphics duplicated with <use> become live, modifiable parts of your document—and therefore trigger the corresponding browser security precautions.

Of course, if you don't need the flexibility of <use> elements, you *can* embed your external SVG file as an image. Not only can you embed them within HTML with <img>, but you can also embed them within larger SVG documents, using the SVG <image> element.

Future Focus
Enabling Cross-Origin SVG Assets

The original SVG specifications were written before the cross-origin HTTP headers were developed. Now that other web technologies have a standard way of sharing files between domains, it is often frustrating to web developers that SVG cannot do the same.

SVG 2 introduces `crossorigin` attributes for the <image>, <feImage>, and <script> elements, which work the same as the equivalent attributes in HTML: they tell the browser to request the file with cross-origin permissions, with or without using "credentials" (personally identifying data stored as browser cookies). Image embeds normally work cross-origin, but the files they fetch can't be reused in other contexts.

There are also guidelines in SVG 2 and the new CSS/SVG effects specifications for cross-origin file access for `url()` references in style properties (always anonymous, without credentials).

But a similar `crossorigin` attribute for <use> elements was put on hold, as the <use> element implementation model was redefined to work with Shadow DOM. Before browsers can agree on exactly what security processes and permissions are appropriate for cross-origin <use>, they will need to agree on a <use> element implementation.

Picture Perfect: Raster Images in SVG

Loading external images in SVG works much the same way as embedding an image file in HTML. The external file is drawn as a completely independent document. The result is then painted onto a rectangular region of the main graphic, defined by an SVG **<image>** **element**.

As far as the main graphic is concerned, the embedded image is a single object. If it's an SVG image, it has all the same restrictions as SVG used in HTML images: no scripts, and no additional file assets. The elements within it don't respond to user events, and its stylesheets are completely independent from the parent document.

But the primary use of the SVG <image> element isn't to embed other SVG files: it's to embed other image types altogether.

Up until now the focus in this book has been on the use of SVG as a means to handle vector graphics. But SVG is also designed to handle raster images. The SVG <image> tag can be used to embed PNG, JPEG, or any other bitmap images supported by the browser. You can use it combined with filters, patterns, and masks to do things like creating drop shadows, watermarks, color modifications, and other vector effects over photographs.

We've already shown one example of enhancing a photograph with SVG, in Chapter 7, where we used SVG <text> elements to add labels to a product photo (in Example 7-3).

The external image file is specified with an **xlink:href attribute** on the <image> element. The link can be a relative URL to a file on the same web server, but it can also be an absolute URL to any file on the web; there are no security restrictions on embedding images. When you're embedding SVG, the URL can include target fragments to select a view or trigger specific styles, using any of the methods described in Chapter 9.

As with every other use of xlink:href in SVG, most new browsers all support simple href, but keep using xlink for support in Safari and older browsers.

The region in which to draw the image is defined by **x, y, width, and height attributes**. The x and y offsets default to 0; width and height default to 0 in SVG 1.1, but to auto (similar to auto for an

HTML <img>) in SVG 2. If either width or height is 0, the image will not be drawn.

 Although some browsers (Chrome/Blink, at the time of writing) now support auto sizing on SVG <image>, most won't draw an image unless you specify both width and height.

Example 10-3 offers one way in which external images could be used to decorate the face cards in our playing card set; we've only included the new code, relative to Example 10-1. The portraits of Elizabeth I of England and Marie Antoinette of France are photographs of public domain paintings, downloaded from Wikimedia Commons. Figure 10-3 shows the result.

Figure 10-3. Playing card queens using photographs embedded in the SVG

Example 10-3. Using external images in SVG

```
<svg xmlns="http://www.w3.org/2000/svg" xml:lang="en"
    xmlns:xlink="http://www.w3.org/1999/xlink"
    width="400px" height="270px" viewBox="0 0 267 180" > ❶
    <title>Playing Cards</title>
```

```
<!-- Same styles and definitions as before -->                    ❷

<svg width="140" height="180"
    class="diamond" id="diamondQ">
    <title>Queen of Diamonds</title>
    <use xlink:href="#card-front" x="10" y="10" />
    <text x="15" y="35">Q</text>
    <text x="105" y="160">Q</text>
    <use xlink:href="#diamond" x="105" y="20"/>            ❸
    <use xlink:href="#diamond" x="15" y="140"/>
    <image x="35" y="40" width="70" height="100"
            xlink:href="Elizabeth_I.jpg" />              ❹
</svg>

<svg x="130" width="140" height="180"
    class="spade" id="spadeQ">
    <title>Queen of Spades</title>
    <use xlink:href="#card-front" x="10" y="10" />
    <text x="15" y="35">Q</text>
    <text x="105" y="160">Q</text>
    <use xlink:href="#spade" x="105" y="20"/>
    <use xlink:href="#spade" x="15" y="140"/>
    <image x="35" y="40" width="70" height="100"
            xlink:href="Marie-Antoinette.jpg" />
</svg>
</svg>
```

❶ A new `viewBox` and dimensions allow us to reuse the same
    code, while scaling the image to display two cards in a 400px
    width, instead of three.

❷ The styles and icon definitions are exactly the same as for
    Example 10-1, which created the number and ace cards.

❸ The suit is indicated by icons in the corners.

❹ The image is stored in the same folder on the server as the SVG
    code, so all we need is to indicate the filename in the
    `xlink:href` attribute, along with the position and size
    attributes.

There's another use for `<image>`, although it's unofficial: to provide a
fallback image file for inline SVG in HTML.

Most browsers recognize an `<image>` element in HTML as a synonym for `<img>` (to support old, nonstandard web pages). A browser
that doesn't support SVG will therefore treat the `<image>` element as

an HTML image, and look for a src attribute to find the file to download. An SVG-aware browser will see <image> inside <svg>, and look for an xlink:href attribute.

If you include a valid src but an invalid (empty) xlink:href on an SVG <image>, the src fallback image will display in pre-SVG browsers, but won't interfere with your vector graphics in new ones.

 Use an empty xlink:href, instead of omitting the attribute, to avoid a bug where SVG-supporting Internet Explorer versions download the fallback even though they won't use it.

Of course, you can also use this behavior to create a fallback for SVG-enhanced photographs. In that case, src and xlink:href would point to the same image file: modern browsers would show the photograph plus all the SVG annotations, filters, or masking effects. The old browsers would still get the plain photograph.

Smooth Scaling Photographs

Images in SVG might not have been originally designed to autosize, but they were given one feature that HTML images didn't have: the ability to scale without distorting aspect ratios.

A **preserveAspectRatio attribute** on <image> describes what to do if the dimensions of the <image> region don't match the embedded image's intrinsic ratio. You can set it to none to get the stretch-and-squish behavior of <img>, but the default is xMidYMid meet, the same as for <svg>. So your photo will scale to fit, centered inside the width and height you specify.

 As discussed in Chapter 8, the CSS object-fit and object-position properties (in supporting browsers) provide preserveAspectRatio-style control for images and other objects in HTML.

Using an <image> inside inline SVG can be a fallback approach for object-fit.

For the most part, preserveAspectRatio on an image works the same way as for SVGs, as defined in "A Poor Fit (and How preserveAspectRatio Fixes It)" on page 273. There is no viewBox attribute, however: the intrinsic aspect ratio is calculated from the downloaded image data.

The preserveAspectRatio attribute is particularly useful when you are designing an SVG to work with arbitrary image files, where you don't have control over the image dimensions. You can decide whether you want the image to fill the full space, even if it gets cropped (slice) or if you want to scale it down to fit (meet).

If you do know the details of the image, however, you may want to crop it more precisely than min/mid/max options.

If you're embedding an SVG file, you can use #svgView() fragments in the URL to define a custom crop. In the future, you would be able to use #xywh= fragments on other image types to do similar cropping. But until that's supported, you can draw the <image> inside a nested <svg>, using the SVG's hidden overflow to crop parts of the image.

In that approach, the x, y, width, and height on the <svg> are the final dimensions and position for the clipped image; the SVG's viewBox specifies the rectangle you want to display from the image. The <image>'s own width and height should match its natural aspect ratio, in the same units you used for the viewBox. So the following creates a square crop from within a 4×3 photo, offset slightly from the center:

```
<svg width="100" height="100" viewBox="0.8 0 3 3">
    <image width="4" height="3" xlink:href="photo_4x3.jpg" />
</svg>
```

Alternatively, you can use clipping paths (which we discuss in Chapter 15), or even the old clip property. But it's a little harder to control the final position that way.

 Clipping paths are required if you want to create rounded corners on the <image>; there is no border-radius or rx/ry on SVG <image>.

Example 10-4 creates an author profile page for this book. Each author's profile photo has a very different aspect ratio, but the width and height on each photo's <image> element is the same. The example also uses the nested-<svg> cropping technique to crop down an image of the book's cover to focus on the title and illustration.

Figure 10-4 shows the code as written (meet scaling, so each photo fits *within* the <image> dimensions), and then again with preserveAspectRatio changed to xMinYMin slice (so each photo *fills* the <image> dimensions, with cropping). You'll have to play with the online example to see the distortions that result from changing preserveAspectRatio to none.

Figure 10-4. Profile photos with different aspect ratios: (left) with meet aspect ratio options, and (right) slice settings

Example 10-4. Demonstrating preserveAspectRatio options on embedded images

```
<svg xmlns="http://www.w3.org/2000/svg" xml:lang="en"
     xmlns:xlink="http://www.w3.org/1999/xlink"
     width="400" height="600" viewBox="0 0 400 600">        ❶
    <title>The Authors of Using SVG with CSS3 and HTML5</title>
    <style>
```

```
        text {
            font: 20px Tahoma, sans-serif;
            text-anchor: middle;
            fill: darkRed;
        }
        .bird-colors  rect { fill: #5f6cb9; }
        .bird-colors  text { fill: #bbde60; }
        .theme-colors rect { fill: #00aaa9; }
        .theme-colors text { fill: white; }
    </style>
    <svg viewBox="50 5 500 750" width="50%" height="50%">
        <image height="900" width="600"
                aria-label="Using SVG cover image"
                xlink:href="using_svg_cover.png"/>             ❷
    </svg>
    <g class="bird-colors">
        <rect x="50%" height="50%" width="50%" />
        <text x="75%" y="45" dy="-0.5em">Amelia
            <tspan x="75%" dy="1em">Bellamy-Royds</tspan></text>
        <image x="50%" y="80" height="220" width="200"
                preserveAspectRatio="xMidYMax meet"
                aria-label="Amelia in the sunshine"
                xlink:href="Amelia.jpg"/>                      ❸
    </g>
    <g class="bird-colors">
        <rect y="50%" height="50%" width="50%" />
        <text x="25%" y="345">Kurt Cagle</text>
        <image y="380" height="220" width="200"
                preserveAspectRatio="xMidYMax meet"
                aria-label="Kurt in a top hat"
                xlink:href="Kurt.jpg"/>                        ❹
    </g>
    <g class="theme-colors">
        <rect x="50%" y="50%" height="50%" width="50%" />
        <text x="75%" y="345">Dudley Storey</text>
        <image x="50%" y="380" height="220" width="200"
                preserveAspectRatio="xMidYMax meet"
                aria-label="Dudley, re-imagined as a tiny warrior"
                xlink:href="Dudley.jpg"/>                      ❺
    </g>
</svg>
```

❶ The overall SVG layout has a 2×3 (400×600) aspect ratio, which will be divided into quarters (two rows and two columns) with the same aspect ratio.

❷ The cover image is in the correct aspect ratio to fill one quarter (600×900), but it includes the authors' names, which would be slightly redundant in this layout. The viewBox on the nested

`<svg>` defines a custom crop to show only the part we want to feature. Both the `<image>` and the `<svg>` have the correct aspect ratios, so we don't need to worry about "preserving" anything.

❸ After we leave room for the names, the photos all have an almost-square aspect ratio of 200×210.

❹ The xMidYMax meet setting for preserveAspectRatio will position the photos horizontally centered and bottom-aligned in each `<image>` rectangle.

❺ There is no alt attribute on SVG `<image>`. You can either add a child `<title>` element (which will also create a tooltip), or use an aria-label attribute, like we did here.

More Online

To make testing the options a little easier, the "Dynamically Changing preserveAspectRatio" extra (from Chapter 8) provides the code for swapping between **preserveAspectRatio** options with an HTML form and JavaScript:

https://oreillymedia.github.io/Using_SVG/extras/ch08-preserveAspectRatio-swap.html

---

When the `<image>` embeds another SVG file, there is an additional option for preserveAspectRatio. The defer keyword tells the browser to use the preserveAspectRatio value specified in the external file, if it exists. It is specified in combination with a fallback value, which applies if the external file does not specify a value—or is not an SVG. The following code would use xMidYMid meet behavior *unless* different instructions are in the external file:

```
<image xlink:href="overlay.svg"
       preserveAspectRatio="defer xMidYMid meet"
       width="100%" height="100%" />
```

 Based on limited use, the SVG 2 specs proposed removing the defer keyword to make implementations simpler. Test carefully before using.

Easier Embedded Content

As mentioned earlier, SVG 2 adds an **auto** value for height and width, consistent with making these settings presentation attributes for the standard CSS **height** and **width** properties.

Using **auto** would allow the dimensions to be calculated from the image itself, or allow you to specify one dimension and have the other adjust to match. It replaces the default **0** dimensions, which cause an image to be hidden if it doesn't have **height** and **width** attributes.

Another proposal in SVG 2 is to allow HTML **<video>**, **<audio>**, **<iframe>**, and **<canvas>** elements within SVG: these would be the HTML namespace elements, but positioned in SVG via the **x**, **y**, **width**, and **height** CSS properties. This would allow nonbrowser SVG tools to support these features without supporting a full HTML and CSS **<foreignObject>** subtree.

Summary: Reusing Content

A key tenet of computer programming is that you should not have the same information repeated in multiple parts of your code. If you need a value multiple times, assign it to a variable. If you need to perform a calculation multiple times, make it into a function. Keep it DRY: Don't Repeat Yourself.

The specifics are somewhat different with SVG, but the principle is the same. If multiple elements have the same styles, either group them together or use CSS classes so that those styles are only declared once. If an entire shape is repeated, use a <use> element to minimize the repeated markup. Both approaches keep file sizes down, and make it easier to understand and update the code.

Keeping file sizes down also means recognizing when a different image format is required, and the <image> element makes it easy to integrate photographs and other images into the SVG.

The <use>, <symbol>, and <image> elements build upon SVG's scaling mechanisms and the viewBox and preserveAspectRatio attributes introduced in Chapter 8. They will themselves be a fundamental component of many examples throughout the rest of the book.

Images are particularly interesting in the context of masking (Chapter 15) and filters (Chapter 16); many uses of SVG do not include any vector graphic shapes at all, just images manipulated with these graphical effects.

The <use> element will show up in many contexts, including the next chapter—which examines how you can manipulate and distort graphics by transforming the very coordinate system in which they are drawn.

More Online

The new elements and attributes defined in this chapter are included in the "Document Structure Elements" section of the markup guide:

https://oreillymedia.github.io/Using_SVG/guide/ markup.html#structure

CHAPTER 11

Transformative Changes

Coordinate System Transformations

When you define a coordinate system, using the viewBox and preserveAspectRatio attributes introduced in Chapter 8, you create an invisible grid that the browser fits into a rectangular space. When you **transform** a coordinate system, you pick up that grid and move, twist, or stretch it. Any shapes, text, or images drawn in the transformed coordinate system are moved, twisted, or stretched to match.

This chapter introduces the SVG **transform attribute**, and examines the ways in which you can work with the SVG coordinate system to make the most of transformations.

Like the nested coordinate systems created with <svg> and <symbol>, transformations allow you to reposition your origin or change the scale of your units. But transformations don't stop there.

Transformations can change the definition of what "horizontal" or "vertical" means. This means you can draw rectangles and ellipses that don't align with the browser window, without having to use <path> notation and trigonometry.

Furthermore, while new coordinate systems must be defined with a separate <svg> or <symbol> element, a transform can be applied directly—as an attribute—on individual shapes or on groups. This makes transformations incredibly flexible, and they are widely used in SVG.

Since transformations control the geometry of your drawing, transform was originally defined as a core XML attribute. However, transformations are so useful that web designers wanted to use them for non-SVG content. The CSS Transforms module defines how transformations can be set using CSS style rules, for any content controlled by CSS.

This wasn't supposed to be a "CSS versus SVG" situation, however. The new CSS module doesn't compete with SVG, it extends and replaces the original SVG specification. The module upgrades the SVG transform attribute to a presentation attribute, so it can be overridden by CSS. That means that SVG transforms will be controllable with CSS classes, pseudoclasses, and media queries.

But the upgrade process hasn't been easy.

All of the major browsers now implement support for CSS transformations on HTML elements; you can increase support in older browsers by duplicating properties with the -webkit- prefix. But as of early 2017, the same syntax applied to SVG elements is either not supported at all (Microsoft Edge and IE 11) or implemented in inconsistent ways between browsers (Chrome and WebKit versus Firefox).

This book therefore considers CSS transformations in SVG to still be a "future" feature; you can use them, but only as an enhancement, with careful testing and consideration of fallback. Notes throughout the chapter explain the important differences between the well-supported SVG transform attribute and the new CSS transform property.

A Simpler Scale

In Chapters 8 and 10 we discussed scaling your graphics from the perspective of getting them to scale to fit an available drawing region. This is an implicit scale: the browser calculates how much to scale the drawing (up or down) using the difference between the viewBox dimensions and the element's width and height. The final scale is also affected—sometimes extremely so—by the preserveAspectRatio option.

What if you just want to enlarge one copy of an icon to be two or three times the size of another copy? It's possible to use nested coordinate systems to do so. Example 11-1 uses a <symbol> element to define a coordinate system, and then reuses it at different sizes. Figure 11-1 shows the result; note that the elements are listed from largest to smallest in the code, so that the smaller versions are drawn on top of the larger ones.

Figure 11-1. A heart icon at many scales

Example 11-1. Scaling an icon with <symbol> and <use>

```
<svg xmlns="http://www.w3.org/2000/svg" xml:lang="en"
     xmlns:xlink="http://www.w3.org/1999/xlink"
     width="400px" height="400px" viewBox="0 0 80 80" >  ❶
    <title>Scaling with viewBox</title>
    <style type="text/css">
        use                 { fill: darkRed; }
        use:nth-of-type(2n) { fill: lightSkyBlue; }       ❷
    </style>
    <symbol viewBox="0 0 20 20" id="heart" >              ❸
        <title>Heart</title>
```

```
        <path d="M10,6 Q10,0 15,0T20,6Q20,10 15,14
                 T10,20Q10,18 5,14T0,6Q0,0 5,0T10,6Z" />
    </symbol>

    <use xlink:href="#heart" width="80" height="80"/>    ❹
    <use xlink:href="#heart" width="70" height="70"/>
    <use xlink:href="#heart" width="60" height="60"/>
    <use xlink:href="#heart" width="50" height="50"/>
    <use xlink:href="#heart" width="40" height="40"/>
    <use xlink:href="#heart" width="30" height="30"/>
    <use xlink:href="#heart" width="22" height="22"/>
    <use xlink:href="#heart" width="15" height="15"/>
    <use xlink:href="#heart" width="10" height="10"/>
</svg>
```

❶   A viewBox on the <svg> defines the overall coordinate system.

❷   The reused elements are styled with CSS; the :nth-of-type(2n) pseudoclass selector applies to every second sibling element. You could also use :nth-of-type(even), which has the same effect, selecting even-numbered elements (as opposed to odd).

❸   The <symbol> defines the graphic and its coordinate system, but is not drawn directly.

❹   Each use element defines the height and width of the space that the symbol's viewBox should stretch to fit. Because the height and width are always equal, matching the square aspect ratio defined in the viewBox, a consistent scale is achieved.

To scale the icons by a given factor (for example, two or three times as large), you need to define the viewBox width and height for the icon, and then define a drawing region width and height that is that many times larger. You also need to make sure that the aspect ratio is correct; otherwise, the scale will be adjusted to fit. That's a lot of arithmetic, and a lot of attributes to keep synchronized. Not very DRY at all.

In contrast, with coordinate system transformations, if you want one copy of an icon to be two or three times the size of the original, you just say so.

The attribute transform="scale(2)" tells the browser to draw that element twice as large as it normally would. It doesn't matter how much space is available, or what the aspect ratio is. It just makes every unit in the coordinate system twice as large, and draws the shape with those new units.

"Every unit twice as large" is an important distinction. **Scaling** does not change the *number* of units in your drawing. Scaling changes the *size* of the units. A scale factor of 2 means that each unit is now twice as large within the new coordinate system as it was in the old one, giving the appearance of zooming in. A scale factor of 0.5 (one-half) does the opposite—each unit is half as large within the new coordinate system, creating the effect of zooming out.

 As with scaling using viewBox, all the other units (cm, in, pt, em) scale to match the change in size of the basic user units. With transformations, the definitions of 100% width and 100% height also scale.

Example 11-2 creates the exact same image from Figure 11-1, but does it using scale transformations.

Example 11-2. Scaling an icon with transformations

```
<svg xmlns="http://www.w3.org/2000/svg" xml:lang="en"
    xmlns:xlink="http://www.w3.org/1999/xlink"
    width="400px" height="400px" viewBox="0 0 80 80" >  ❶
  <title>Scaling with transformations</title>
  <style type="text/css">
      use                { fill: darkRed; }
      use:nth-of-type(2n) { fill: lightSkyBlue; }
  </style>
  <defs>                                                  ❷
      <path id="heart"
            d="M10,6 Q10,0 15,0T20,6Q20,10 15,14
               T10,20Q10,18 5,14T0,6Q0,0 5,0T10,6Z" />
  </defs>

  <use xlink:href="#heart" transform="scale(4)"/>        ❸
  <use xlink:href="#heart" transform="scale(3.5)" />
  <use xlink:href="#heart" transform="scale(3)" />
  <use xlink:href="#heart" transform="scale(2.5)" />
  <use xlink:href="#heart" transform="scale(2)" />
  <use xlink:href="#heart" transform="scale(1.5)" />
  <use xlink:href="#heart" transform="scale(1.1)" />
  <use xlink:href="#heart" transform="scale(0.75)" />
  <use xlink:href="#heart" transform="scale(0.5)" />
</svg>
```

❶ The base coordinate system, defined on the <svg>, is the same.

❷ Rather than creating a nested coordinate system with a <symbol>, we define a simple <path> for reuse inside a <defs> block.

❸ Each <use> element copies the path, in the main coordinate system, but then scales it by the factor specified in the transform attribute.

Regardless of their size, all the heart icons in Example 11-2 are aligned at the top and left edges. More specifically, they are all aligned at the origin, the (0,0) point in the coordinate system, which does not change when the shape is scaled.

Scaling transformations never change the position of the origin. Every other point is scaled based on its distance to the origin.

Scaling is one of the reasons why it is often convenient to define a centered coordinate system, as we discussed in "Framing the View, with viewBox" on page 260 in Chapter 8.

Example 11-3 changes the layered hearts example to use a centered coordinate system, redefining the heart <path> itself so it is centered on the origin, as shown in Figure 11-2.

Figure 11-2. Scaling a heart icon within a centered coordinate system

Example 11-3. Centering an icon within the coordinate system to control the scaling origin

```
<svg xmlns="http://www.w3.org/2000/svg" xml:lang="en"
    xmlns:xlink="http://www.w3.org/1999/xlink"
    width="400px" height="400px" viewBox="-40 -40 80 80" >     ❶
    <title>Centering the scale effect using coordinates</title>
    <style type="text/css">
        use              { fill: darkRed; }
        use:nth-of-type(2n) { fill: lightSkyBlue; }
    </style>
    <defs>
        <path id="heart"
            d="M0,-4 Q0,-10 5,-10T10,-4Q10,0 5,4
                T0,10Q0,8 -5,4T-10,-4Q-10,0 -5,-10T0,-4Z" />     ❷
    </defs>
```

```
<use xlink:href="#heart" transform="scale(4)"/>              ❸
<use xlink:href="#heart" transform="scale(3.5)" />
<use xlink:href="#heart" transform="scale(3)" />
<use xlink:href="#heart" transform="scale(2.5)" />
<use xlink:href="#heart" transform="scale(2)" />
<use xlink:href="#heart" transform="scale(1.5)" />
<use xlink:href="#heart" transform="scale(1.1)" />
<use xlink:href="#heart" transform="scale(0.75)" />
<use xlink:href="#heart" transform="scale(0.5)" />
</svg>
```

❶ The `viewBox` on the main SVG still defines an 80×80 coordinate system, but it is now offset by 40 units in each direction, so that the origin will be in the center of the drawing.

❷ The original heart icon filled the space from (0,0) to (20,20), meaning it was centered on (10,10). To create a heart icon centered on (0,0), therefore, we subtract 10 from each coordinate. If we'd used relative path coordinates originally, this would have been much easier—only the initial coordinate would need to change!

❸ The `<use>` elements and `transform` attributes are the same, but the result is very different.

We'll return to this example once we start discussing other transformation types, to show other ways in which you can change the center of your coordinate system.

First, there are a few more details about scaling transformations that you should know.

Unbalanced Scales

The `scale()` transformation function has two forms. The simpler version, used in Examples 11-2 and 11-3, applies the same scaling factor to both *x* and *y* coordinates. This is known as *uniform* scaling. The single scaling factor is given as a number in parentheses after the name of the transformation:

```
transform="scale(s)"
```

Mathematically, we can describe the transformation of each point, (*x*,*y*) in the graphic to its transformed position as:

$$(x, y) \Rightarrow (x', y') = (s \cdot x, s \cdot y)$$

The point (x', y') is the position of (x,y) after the transformation, as measured in the *original* coordinate system.

If s is 2, the point (1,3) in the transformed coordinate system would be at the same position as (2×1, 2×3) = (2,6) in the original coordinate system. This should hopefully be what you expect from scaling by a factor of two—but the mathematical approach can be useful as the transformations get more complicated.

 A changed variable in algebra is denoted by an apostrophe or prime symbol after the variable name, like x' (called *x-prime*). Transformations are indicated by an arrow from the original to the final state.

In the second form of scaling transformation, each coordinate axis has its own scaling factor. We indicate this by specifying two numbers within the parentheses; the first is the x-scale, the second the y-scale:

```
transform="scale(sx, sy)"
```

$$(x, y) \Rightarrow (x', y') = (s_x \cdot x, s_y \cdot y)$$

A **nonuniform scale** such as this has the effect of squashing the coordinate system in one direction relative to the other, distorting the shapes of elements.

And distorting more than just the shape: scaling—whether uniform or not—applies to *all* aspects of the graphic, including presentation effects such as strokes. These get scaled and stretched along with the basic geometry.

Example 11-4 draws a series of stroked circles, identical except for their transform attribute. Figure 11-3 shows the resulting scaled shapes, including the stretched effect of an unevenly scaled stroke. Example 11-4 also demonstrates that you can use the transform attribute directly on shape elements, not only on <use> elements.

Figure 11-3. Stroked circles at various scales

Example 11-4. Scaling a stroked shape

```
<svg xmlns="http://www.w3.org/2000/svg" xml:lang="en"
    xmlns:xlink="http://www.w3.org/1999/xlink"
    width="400px" height="400px" viewBox="-40 -40 80 80" >   ❶
    <title>Scaling stroked shapes</title>
    <style type="text/css">
        circle {
            fill: darkSlateBlue;
            stroke: darkSeaGreen;                            ❷
        }
    </style>

    <circle r="10" transform="scale(3)" />                   ❸
    <circle r="10" transform="scale(3.5,1)" />               ❹
    <circle r="10" transform="scale(2,2)" />                 ❺
    <circle r="10" transform="scale(1,3.5)" />
```

```
  <circle r="10" />                              ❻
  <circle r="10" transform="scale(0.5)" />       ❼
</svg>
```

❶ The centered coordinate system ensures that the circles will be centered in the graphic by default.

❷ Specifying a color for `stroke` applies the default `stroke-width` of 1 user unit.

❸ All the shapes in the graphic are (officially) circles with a radius 10; the first (bottom) layer is scaled up three times.

❹ We stretch the next `<circle>` into an elliptical shape by giving it a nonuniform scale.

❺ By explicitly giving the same scale factor for both *sx* and *sy*, you can create a uniform scale with the two-value syntax. In other words, the third `<circle>` is still a circle, doubled in all directions.

❻ The second-smallest circle is the untransformed version, drawn in the base coordinate system created by the `<svg>`.

❼ And finally, the last `<circle>` is drawn half size, with a half-pixel stroke—as measured by the `viewBox` coordinate system.

All the shapes in Figure 11-3 are `<circle>` elements. All the strokes are 1 unit wide, in their transformed coordinate system. The scales result in strokes that range from 0.5 units to 3.5 units in the SVG's coordinate system, including the unevenly scaled strokes on the unevenly scaled shapes.

As we mentioned briefly in Chapter 8, and will discuss more in Chapter 13, you can prevent strokes from scaling with the shape (in most but not all recent browsers) with the `vector-effect` property:

```
vector-effect: non-scaling-stroke;
```

The smallest circle in Figure 11-3 was created by a scale factor of 0.5, which shrunk it to half the original width and height. Scale factors greater than 1 enlarge the graphic, scale factors between 0 and 1 shrink it. When the scale factor is exactly 1, the coordinate system stays the same as before.

A scale factor of 0 will cause your graphic to disappear, collapsing into nothingness. But go a little bit further, and more possibilites open up.

Reflecting on Transformations

Negative scaling factors aren't an error. The same transformation equations apply. If you multiply an (x,y) point by a negative scale factor, positive coordinates end up at negative positions and negative coordinates end up at positive positions. This causes your image to appear flipped, as well as scaled.

When the scale factor in one direction or another is exactly –1, the image stays the same size, but is reflected—it appears as if it were reflected in a mirror placed along the other axis:

- `scale(-1, 1)` will reflect the image onto the other side of the y-axis (the sign of each x coordinate is flipped).
- `scale(1,-1)` will reflect the image onto the other side of the x-axis (each y effectively becomes $-y$).
- `scale(-1,-1)` will reflect around the origin: (x,y) gets shifted to $(-x,-y)$ for each point in the graphic.

Example 11-5 demonstrates all these reflections, using the text "SVG" as our transformed graphic. The example therefore also demonstrates that `<use>` elements can be used to duplicate text for graphical effect. Each copy is drawn in different colors, so you can tell which `transform` creates which reflection. Figure 11-4 shows the result.

Figure 11-4. Mirrored text created with negative scaling factors

Example 11-5. Using negative scaling factors to create reflections of text

```
<svg xmlns="http://www.w3.org/2000/svg" xml:lang="en"
    xmlns:xlink="http://www.w3.org/1999/xlink"
    width="400px" height="200px" viewBox="-40 -20 80 40" >    ❶
    <title>Reflections using scale transformations</title>
    <style type="text/css">
        text {
            font: bold 18px "Times New Roman", serif;
            text-decoration: underline;
            stroke-width: 0.5px;                                ❷
        }
    </style>
    <g fill="lightBlue" stroke="blueViolet">
        <text id="t" x="1.5" y="-5">SVG</text>                  ❸
    </g>
    <g aria-hidden="true">                                      ❹
        <use xlink:href="#t" transform="scale(-1,1)"
            fill="springGreen" stroke="darkSlateGray" />        ❺
        <use xlink:href="#t" transform="scale(1,-1)"
            fill="blueViolet" stroke="lightBlue" />
        <use xlink:href="#t" transform="scale(-1,-1)"
            fill="darkSlateGray" stroke="springGreen" />
    </g>
</svg>
```

❶ Once again, the `viewBox` creates a centered coordinate system, with the origin offset by half the width and half the height.

❷ A half-unit stroke width is sufficient to make a clear outline, given the initial scaling effect created by the `width`, `height`, and `viewBox` attributes.

❸ The original, untransformed, text is positioned in the positive-*x* and negative-*y* quadrant of the graphic, in the top right. It inherits `fill` and `stroke` settings from the surrounding `<g>`, so that its clones will use inherited styles, too.

❹ To prevent screen readers from repeating "SVG" four times, the reflections are contained in a group with the `aria-hidden="true"` attribute, which indicates that this entire branch of the DOM tree is decorative.

❺ The three `<use>` elements duplicate the text—including the underline—and apply the transformations; the first element flips the *x* coordinates (the mirror reflection in the top left of the graphic), the second flips the *y* coordinates (the upside-down text in the bottom right), while the third flips both axes (the upside-down and backward text in the bottom left). The `fill` and `stroke` settings on each `<use>` inherit to the text.

Pay attention to the centered coordinate system in Figure 11-4. The reflected content ends up on the opposite side of the coordinate system origin. If a default origin was used, in the top-left corner, then reflected content would be hidden offscreen.

If you wanted to change the size of the content as well as reflect it, just multiply the −1 reflection factor by the scaling factor. For example, `scale(3,-2)` is the same as scaling to `scale(3,2)` followed by a reflection across the x-axis.

Alternatively, you can list both transformations separately. The `transform` attribute can take a list of whitespace-separated transformation functions, like the following:

```
transform="scale(3,2) scale(-1,1)"
```

The transformations are applied in the order they are listed: the size is adjusted first, and then the content is reflected. In this particular case, the end result would be the same if you used `scale(-1,1)` followed by `scale(3,2)`. However, that isn't true in general; when you're using a mix of transformation types, the order can be very important.

Transforming the transform Attribute

The original SVG syntax for the `transform` attribute is (like much of SVG) very flexible about whitespace and commas. You can use spaces instead of commas to separate the numbers in a transformation function, and you can use commas instead of spaces to separate functions in the list.

CSS, in contrast, has a stricter approach to whitespace and commas. With the adoption of transformations into CSS, a more formal syntax has been developed. Browsers will still use the old rules for parsing the XML `transform` attribute, but only the new syntax can be used in stylesheets. It's therefore best to get used to the new requirements:

- Each transformation is defined with functional notation of the form *name*(*values*); there is no whitespace between the function name and the opening parenthesis.

- Multiple transformations in a list may be separated by whitespace (but not commas).

- The parameters (values) in a function *may* be surrounded by extra whitespace (inside the parentheses).

- If there are multiple parameters to a function, they *must* by separated by a comma (and optionally whitespace before and after it).

The new Transforms module also introduces a number of new transformation functions. For scaling, there is a `scaleX(`*sx*`)` function, equivalent to `scale(`*sx*`,1)`, and a `scaleY(`*sy*`)` function, equivalent to `scale(1,`*sy*`)`.

The new functions should be supported in the attribute form of `transform` as well as the CSS property, but if you're using the attribute, stick with the two-value format for compatibility.

And keep using the attribute, for compatibility.

At the time of writing, support for transforming SVG with CSS properties is incomplete.

Internet Explorer and MS Edge do not apply any transformations defined in CSS to SVG. The latest versions of Chrome/Blink, Safari/WebKit, and Firefox browsers consistently apply simple transformations like these, but older versions of the same browsers disagree about where the default origin point should be for SVG elements. Even in the latest versions (at the time of writing), things are inconsistent once you start using percentage lengths.

For the most reliable results, use the `transform` attribute; for anything else, be sure to test thoroughly.

New Origins

Scaling a coordinate system changes how far each point is from the origin, without moving the origin. However, as we saw with Example 11-3, the origin you used when initially defining your shapes isn't always where you want it to be when you redraw them.

In contrast, a **translation** of a coordinate system moves the origin from one point to another on the drawing canvas, *without* changing the relative positions of different points. In other words, a `translate` operation does not change the size or shape of your graphics, it just moves them around.

The `translate` function used in the `transform` attribute takes two parameters, defining the horizontal and vertical offset in user units:

```
transform="translate(tx, ty)"
```

Mathematically, the transformation can be described as:

$$(x, y) \Rightarrow (x', y') = \left(x + t_x, \; y + t_y\right)$$

As with scaling, multiple transformations can be strung together in a `transform` list. Because the offsets defined by a translation are added together, it doesn't matter which order you use for multiple translations: (a + b) + c is the same as (a + c) + b. However, once you start mixing translation and scale operations, the order becomes relevant: (a + b) × s is *not* the same as (a × s) + b (except for special cases such as a scale of 1 or an offset of 0).

The second parameter to translate() is optional. If you only provide one number, it is used as the *tx* value and *ty* is set to 0. This is in contrast to scaling, where a single scaling factor will apply to both directions equally.

Example 11-6 creates a pattern from the basic club icon, repeated at different translation offsets. Figure 11-5 shows the result; note how the overlapping icons are drawn in exactly the same order that they are specified in the code: left to right, top to bottom.

Figure 11-5. A forest pattern created with translated club icons

Example 11-6. Using translations to position a repeated icon

```
<svg xmlns="http://www.w3.org/2000/svg" xml:lang="en"
     xmlns:xlink="http://www.w3.org/1999/xlink"
```

```
    width="400px" height="400px" viewBox="0 0 40 40" >          ❶
    <title>Translation transformations</title>
    <style type="text/css">
        use {
            fill: darkGreen;
            stroke: seaGreen;
            stroke-width: 0.2;
        }
        use:nth-of-type(2n) {
            fill: lightGreen;                                    ❷
        }
    </style>
    <defs>
        <path id="club"
            d="M9,15.5A5,5 0 1 1 5.5, 7.5
                A5,5 0 1 1 14.5, 7.5A5,5 0 1 1 11, 15.5
                Q11,20 13,20H7Q9,20 9,15.5Z" />                  ❸
    </defs>

    <use xlink:href="#club" transform="translate(-10)"/>        ❹
    <use xlink:href="#club" transform="translate(0)"/>
    <use xlink:href="#club" transform="translate(10)" />
    <use xlink:href="#club" transform="translate(20)" />
    <use xlink:href="#club" transform="translate(30)" />
    <use xlink:href="#club" transform="translate(-10,10)"/>     ❺
    <use xlink:href="#club" transform="translate(0,10)"/>
    <use xlink:href="#club" transform="translate(10,10)" />
    <use xlink:href="#club" transform="translate(20,10)" />
    <use xlink:href="#club" transform="translate(30,10)" />
    <use xlink:href="#club" transform="translate(-10,20)"/>
    <use xlink:href="#club" transform="translate(0,20)"/>
    <use xlink:href="#club" transform="translate(10,20)" />
    <use xlink:href="#club" transform="translate(20,20)" />
    <use xlink:href="#club" transform="translate(30,20)" />
</svg>
```

❶ The 40×40 initial coordinate system has its origin in the top-left
    corner.

❷ Fill and stroke styles are set on the <use> elements; only the fill
    style is reset for the even-numbered elements, so the same
    stroke styles will still apply.

❸ The icon is the basic club shape from Chapter 6.

❹ The first few elements use a translate with a single value; the
    x-position is therefore translated, while the y-position stays the

same. These elements create the first row of icons, staggered along the top of the graphic.

❺ The remainder of the <use> elements use the two-value translate function, to set both *x* and *y* offsets.

Using translations, it is possible to reposition the origin of your graphics prior to adjusting their scale. In other words, you do not have to carefully edit your complex <path> code in order to create a centered path; you can just translate it until it is centered over the origin.

Example 11-7 redraws Example 11-3, but now using translations to center all the scaled icons, instead of redefining the <path> itself. Figure 11-6 shows the result; it should be identical to Figure 11-2.

Figure 11-6. Scaling a heart icon after centering it with translations

Example 11-7. Using translations to center a coordinate system for scaling

```
<svg xmlns="http://www.w3.org/2000/svg" xml:lang="en"
    xmlns:xlink="http://www.w3.org/1999/xlink"
    width="400px" height="400px" viewBox="0 0 80 80" >          ❶
  <title>Centering the scaled effect using translations</title>
  <style type="text/css">
    use                    { fill: darkRed; }
    use:nth-of-type(2n) { fill: lightSkyBlue; }
  </style>
  <defs>
    <path id="heart"
        d="M10,6 Q10,0 15,0T20,6Q20,10 15,14
           T10,20Q10,18 5,14T0,6Q0,0 5,0T10,6Z"
        transform="translate(-10, -10)"/>                        ❷
  </defs>

  <g transform="translate(40, 40)">                              ❸
    <use xlink:href="#heart" transform="scale(4)"/>             ❹
    <use xlink:href="#heart" transform="scale(3.5)" />
    <use xlink:href="#heart" transform="scale(3)" />
    <use xlink:href="#heart" transform="scale(2.5)" />
    <use xlink:href="#heart" transform="scale(2)" />
    <use xlink:href="#heart" transform="scale(1.5)" />
    <use xlink:href="#heart" transform="scale(1.1)" />
    <use xlink:href="#heart" transform="scale(0.75)" />
    <use xlink:href="#heart" transform="scale(0.5)" />
  </g>
</svg>
```

❶ The viewBox on the main SVG defines an 80×80 coordinate system with a default top-left origin.

❷ This is the original heart icon, extending from (0,0) to (20,20), centered on (10,10). The translate(-10,-10) transformation shifts it up and over to center it within its coordinate system.

❸ A <g> grouping element is used to redefine the origin for all the child <use> elements. The translate(40, 40) moves the origin from the top-left corner to the center of the 80×80 drawing region.

❹ The <use> elements draw each copy of the heart within the new, centered coordinate system. Since the <path> element itself is centered over the origin because of its own transform attribute, the hearts are all aligned at the center when the different scales are applied.

In Chapters 1 and 8, we discussed another way to reposition content duplicated with <use>: the x and y attributes. These attributes effectively create a supplemental translation, applied *after* any transformations defined in the transform attribute. The following code:

```
<use xlink:href="#icon" x="50" y="80" transform="scale(2)"/>
```

is directly equivalent to:

```
<use xlink:href="#icon" transform="scale(2)translate(50,80)"/>
```

In other words, the x and y offsets are calculated in the *transformed* coordinate system, after the units are scaled. This is true for geometric attributes on shape elements, too.

All geometric attributes on an element (position as well as size) are applied after that element's coordinate system is transformed.

There is one advantage to using the attributes instead of translations, however: the values for x and y can be lengths with units or percentages. The values for transformations—in SVG 1.1, anyway—must be plain numbers. For translations, those numbers are interpreted as user-unit lengths.

Future Focus
Transformations with Units

For the CSS transform property, the distance to translate the coordinate system *must* be specified as a length with units or as a percentage. In the SVG attribute only, a number without units would still be accepted, as a length in user units.

As with scaling effects created by viewBox, all units are scaled along with the coordinate system. In other words, the px unit is always equivalent to user units, regardless of any transformations that have already been applied.

Percentages, however, have a special meaning in the CSS transform property.

For transformations on CSS layout boxes—including the top-level **<svg>** element—percentages are calculated according to the width and height of the layout box including padding and borders (aka the **border-box**).

Unfortunately, early drafts of the CSS Transforms module only discussed the CSS box layout situation, not SVG. This resulted in inconsistent implementations:

- WebKit/Blink browsers adapted the CSS rules to SVG, so that percentages were relative to the size of the element's fill bounding box (a rectangle based on the fill region).
- Firefox aimed for consistency with SVG; percentages are relative to the coordinate system.

The CSS working group agreed with the Firefox team, but with many web developers already building content specifically for the WebKit/Blink interpretation, those browsers were hesitant to change.

The latest specifications introduced a compromise: the **transform-box** property would allow authors to specify the reference box, for percentages and for determining the origin.

For SVG elements, the default **transform-box** would be **view-box** (note the CSS-style hyphenated, lowercase name), but it could be changed to **fill-box**. That would use a tight rectangle fitting around the unstroked dimensions of the shape. For non-SVG elements, there is currently no option to change the **transform-box** to a value other than **border-box**.

Unfortunately, the current implementation in WebKit/Blink browsers doesn't directly match any of these options, as it uses the **view-box** for origin but the **fill-box** for percentages.

The **fill-box** reference shape used in **transform-box** is equivalent to the **objectBoundingBox** reference shape used in many SVG graphical effects. We'll talk more about object bounding boxes starting in Chapter 12.

Support for **transform-box** ships in Firefox starting in version 55, and the Blink and WebKit teams are working on it. Once those browser teams have implemented a compatible model, expect the Microsoft team to finally add support for CSS transforms for SVG.

Much less controversially, the new CSS Transforms module also introduces `translateX` and `translateY` shorthand functions. These take a single length value, and adjust the coordinate system in the specified direction.

Turning Things Around

Scaling changes the size of units, and translations change the position of the origin, but neither does anything that you can't already do with `viewBox`.

Rotations do something new: they change the directions of the axes. They twist the entire coordinate system as a whole, without changing the size of elements.

As with scaling, rotations are defined relative to the origin of the coordinate system. Rotations use the `rotate()` transformation function, which takes one parameter: the number of degrees to rotate the coordinate system.

Positive rotations are clockwise (deosil, to use the Neo-Pagan terminology) and negative rotations are counterclockwise (or widdershins, another delightful but underused word).

Of course, those directions only apply if you *haven't* flipped the coordinate system with a negative scale. If you've transformed the coordinate system so much that you're not sure which way is which, remember that a rotation from the positive x-axis to the positive y-axis is always +90 degrees.

Rotations are also, like translations, cumulative and commutive on their own. All three of these transformations have the same final result:

```
transform="rotate(120) rotate(60)"
transform="rotate(60) rotate(120)"
transform="rotate(180)"
```

A `"rotate(90) rotate(-90)"` transformation is the same as `transform="rotate(0)"`, which keeps the coordinate system the same as it had been.

There's one exception to these equivalencies: animations. When you animate a set of transformation, each function is animated separately, if possible. In that case, the order of operations matters as much as the final result.

However, once you mix rotations and translations, the order of operations matters: "turn left, then walk 10 steps" will take you to a different point than "walk 10 steps, then turn left."

Example 11-8 applies rotations to a series of spade icons; Figure 11-7 shows the result. Because the spades are not centered on the origin, the rotated icons sweep out a large wreath shape, circling around the coordinate system origin.

Figure 11-7. A wreath of icons created with rotations

Example 11-8. Rotating a graphic around the origin

```
<svg xmlns="http://www.w3.org/2000/svg" xml:lang="en"
    xmlns:xlink="http://www.w3.org/1999/xlink"
    width="400px" height="400px" viewBox="-27 -27 54 54" >   ❶
    <title>Rotations around the origin</title>
    <style type="text/css">
        use                { fill: slateBlue; }
        use:nth-of-type(2n) { fill: lightGreen; }
        use:last-of-type    { stroke: darkSlateGray; }
    </style>
    <defs>
        <path id="spade"
              d="M9,15C9,20 0,21 0,16S6,9 10,0C14,9 20,11 20,16
                 S11,20 11,15Q11,20 13,20H7Q9,20 9,15Z" />   ❷
    </defs>

    <use xlink:href="#spade" transform="rotate(30)"/>      ❸
    <use xlink:href="#spade" transform="rotate(60)"/>
    <use xlink:href="#spade" transform="rotate(90)"/>
    <use xlink:href="#spade" transform="rotate(120)"/>
    <use xlink:href="#spade" transform="rotate(150)"/>
    <use xlink:href="#spade" transform="rotate(180)"/>
    <use xlink:href="#spade" transform="rotate(210)"/>
    <use xlink:href="#spade" transform="rotate(240)"/>
    <use xlink:href="#spade" transform="rotate(270)"/>
    <use xlink:href="#spade" transform="rotate(300)"/>
    <use xlink:href="#spade" transform="rotate(330)"/>
    <use xlink:href="#spade" />                            ❹
</svg>
```

❶ The coordinate system defined by the `viewBox` has a centered origin. The exact number of units was adjusted to fit the graphic neatly.

❷ The spade icon is *not* centered; it will by default (without transformations) be drawn below and to the left of the origin.

❸ Each subsequent icon is drawn rotated 30 degrees clockwise relative to the previous one, with the icons overlapping each other in the order in which they are specified.

❹ After rotating through a complete circle, the last element (which would have had a `rotate(360)` transformation) is equivalent to having no transformation at all. This final, untransformed elemented is highlighted with a dark stroke via the `:last-of-type` selector.

Mathematically, the transformation rotate(*a*) can be defined as follows:

$$(x, y) \Rightarrow (x', y') = ((\cos(a) \cdot x - \sin(a) \cdot y),$$
$$(\cos(a) \cdot y + \sin(a) \cdot x))$$

…which is just the kind of math that makes you glad the browser does it for you!

If you do have to use JavaScript to calculate complex geometry, be aware that the JavaScript trigonometric functions require angles to be given in *radians*, not degrees. To convert between the two, use the Math.PI JavaScript constant in the following helper functions:

```
function rad2Deg(rad){
    return rad * 180 / Math.PI;
}
function deg2Rad(deg){
    return deg * Math.PI / 180;
}
```

If you want the rotations to be relative to a different point, you could use translations to reposition the origin, as we did in Example 11-7. However, SVG also defined an alternative version of the rotate function that allows you to rotate around any point. It uses a three-value rotation syntax:

```
transform="rotate(a, cx, cy)"
```

This has the same effect as a rotation combined with before-and-after translations, as follows:

```
transform="translate(cx, cy) rotate(a) translate(-cx, -cy)"
```

The three-value rotate is *not* valid in the CSS transformation property, which has its own way of changing the center of rotation.

Example 11-9 uses three-value rotations to create a complex pattern with the spade icon rotated around different points. Figure 11-8 shows the result, including two circles used to mark the rotational centers.

Figure 11-8. A complex pattern created by rotating a single icon around two centers

Example 11-9. Rotations around arbitrary points

```svg
<svg xmlns="http://www.w3.org/2000/svg" xml:lang="en"
    xmlns:xlink="http://www.w3.org/1999/xlink"
    width="400px" height="575px" viewBox="-13 -20 46 66" >  ❶
    <title>Rotations around arbitrary points</title>
    <style type="text/css">
        use                   { fill: slateBlue; }
        use:nth-of-type(2n) { fill: lightGreen; }
        use:last-of-type    { stroke: darkSlateGray; }
        circle                { fill: tomato; }
    </style>
    <defs>
        <path id="spade"
              d="M9,15C9,20 0,21 0,16S6,9 10,0C14,9 20,11 20,16
                 S11,20 11,15Q11,20 13,20H7Q9,20 9,15Z" />
    </defs>

    <use xlink:href="#spade" transform="rotate(60,10,0)"/>  ❷
    <use xlink:href="#spade" transform="rotate(120,10,0)"/>
    <use xlink:href="#spade" transform="rotate(180,10,0)"/>
    <use xlink:href="#spade" transform="rotate(240,10,0)"/>
    <use xlink:href="#spade" transform="rotate(300,10,0)"/>
    <use xlink:href="#spade" transform="rotate(360,10,0)"/>
    <use xlink:href="#spade" transform="rotate(90,10,23)"/>  ❸
    <use xlink:href="#spade" transform="rotate(180,10,23)"/>
    <use xlink:href="#spade" transform="rotate(-90,10,23)"/>  ❹
    <use xlink:href="#spade" />                               ❺
    <circle cx="10" cy="0" r="1" />
    <circle cx="10" cy="23" r="1" />                         ❻
</svg>
```

❶ The coordinate system is *not* centered. At first glance, it looks kind of arbitrary. Consider it a reminder that centered origin or top-left origin are not the only options. In this case, it's the result of drawing the graphic first, and then adjusting the viewBox to neatly fit the shapes.

❷ The first six icons are rotated around the point (10,0). This conveniently happens to be the coordinate of the tip of the spade in the original untransformed icon.

❸ The remaining icons are rotated around the point (10,23), which is slightly below the base of the untransformed icon.

❹ A rotation of –90° is equivalent to a rotation of +270°.

❺ Again, the final `<use>` element is untransformed, and will be marked by a dark stroke.

❻ The two tomato-orange circles mark the points of rotation, at (10,0) and (10,23).

Once you have rotated a coordinate system, the x- and y-axes point in new directions. Any subsequent translations are applied in the new directions. So are x and y attributes on shape elements. Text will also be drawn along the rotated x-axis, allowing you to create angled labels on diagrams—but be aware that text in small font sizes on computer-monitor resolutions tends to look pixelated and uneven when written at an angle.

Future Focus
Rotation Units and Adaptable Origins

Rotations in the new CSS transformation syntax must include an angle unit:

- **deg** for degrees
- **rad** for radians
- **grad** for grades or gradians (a sort of metric degree, with 100 grad in a right angle)
- **turn** for a number of full rotations (a right angle is a quarter-turn, or `0.25turn`)

The new CSS Transforms module does *not* include the three-value `rotate` function. Instead, you can control the origin for both rotation and scaling using the `transform-origin` property.

The `transform-origin` property takes a "position" CSS value, similar to that used in the CSS `background-position` property. The value is the horizontal position followed by the vertical position, as a length or percentage, or as keywords: `left`, `center`, or `right` for horizontal, and `top`, `center`, or `bottom` for vertical.

For content that uses a CSS layout model (such as HTML content, or top-level SVG elements), the default origin is `50% 50%`; in other words, scaling and rotations are calculated relative to the center of the reference layout box.

The default origin for SVG content would remain the coordinate system origin. The browsers would apply a default CSS rule of `transform-origin: 0 0` to all SVG elements. However, you should be able to set `transform-origin` yourself to reposition it. This would then affect the origin for rotations and scaling transformations (as well as skews, which we'll get to in the next section).

Setting a `transform-origin` on an element is equivalent to adding supplemental translations before and after the main transformation list: first translate the element by an amount equivalent to the transform origin, then apply the other transformations, then reverse the translation. So the following styles would be equivalent:

```
.transformed {
    transform-origin: 20px 40px;
    transform: rotate(90deg) scale(2);
}

.transformed {
    transform-origin: 0 0;
    transform: translate(20px, 40px)
               rotate(90deg) scale(2)
               translate(-20px, -40px);
}
```

As mentioned previously, implementations of `transform-origin` applied to SVG have been inconsistent. Under the latest specifications, `transform-origin` should be calculated relative to the `transform-box`.

At the time of writing (mid-2017), you get consistent results so long as you don't use percentages—in the latest versions of Firefox, Chrome/Blink, and WebKit Safari, that is. Older versions may be erratic, and IE/MS Edge (at least up to EdgeHTML version 15) have no support at all for CSS transforms on SVG elements.

If possible, ensure compatibility by using the `transform` attribute. You can still create a `transform-origin` effect with before-and-after translations.

Skewed Perspective

Moving up the chain of complexity are **skew transformations**.

Like a rotation, a skew is specified as an angle. While a rotation changes the orientation of both axes relative to the screen, a skew changes the orientation of one axis but not the other. That means that it changes the angle *between* the axes. A skew, therefore, distorts the shape of graphics.

A good way to understand a skew is to envision a box used to pack drinking glasses, with dividers that partition the box into individual cells. If you flatten the box, the entire grid flattens with it. Sections that are normally at right angles get squished at narrower and narrower angles until they are flat against each other. Well, it is never perfectly flat, because the thickness of the cardboard prevents it, but you can get pretty close!

A skew is similar, in that it collapses the angles between the x- and y-axis. However, there is an important difference. In the packing box grid, the length of the cardboard sections remains constant as you flatten the box. As the angles compress, and the ends shift farther out, the opposite sides are drawn together.

Skew works differently, as shown in Figure 11-9. The position of points never changes relative to the axis that *isn't* being skewed. Lines get stretched, shapes get distorted, but the grid doesn't *flatten*. Instead, the image gets stretched out. There is still a limit to a skew, though: eventually the angle between the axes will be zero, and the stretching will be infinite.

The particular skew transform used in Figure 11-9 is skewX(50). The naming of skew transformations is not intuitive: a skewX transformation results in slanted *vertical* lines. However, if you consider the figure again, you'll notice that it's the x coordinates that get shifted sideways, while the y coordinates are unchanged; this is why it is skewX. Similarly, a skewY transform will distort the y positions of the shapes, creating angled *horizontal* lines.

Cardboard

SVG skew

Figure 11-9. Understanding skew: flattening a cardboard grid versus skewing an SVG grid

The value you give to a skewX or skewY function is an angle in degrees; it is the amount by which the angled axis is shifted from its original position. The angle can be positive or negative. However, there isn't an easy clockwise/counterclockwise rule to use. Instead, remember that *positive* skewing angles *increase* the position of points with *positive* coordinates.

(That's assuming you're still using the default SVG (0,0) transform origin. It gets more complicated with other transformation origins.)

A skew of 0 degrees doesn't change anything; a skew of 90° or –90° creates infinite coordinates, which is an error in SVG. Nothing gets drawn in that case.

Mathematically, the transformation skewX(a) can be defined as follows:

$$(x, y) \Rightarrow (x', y') = ((x + \tan (a) \cdot y) , y)$$

The transformation skewY(a) can be defined as follows:

$$(x, y) \Rightarrow (x', y') = (x, (\tan (a) \cdot x + y))$$

In other words, when you skew the x-axis, the amount you change the x-positions depends on the size of the y coordinate. When you skew the y-axis, the amount you change the y-positions depends on the size of the x coordinate. Skews have no effect when the other coordinate is zero.

 Interested in creating the "flattened cardboard" effect from Figure 11-9? That image was created with rotate and translate transformations, neither of which will stretch or distort a shape. The horizontal lines were offset with transformations of the form:

```
transform="rotate(-50) translate(0,y)
           rotate(50)"
```

The formerly vertical lines were positioned and angled with transformations like the following:

```
transform="translate(x,0) rotate(-50)"
```

All the lines start from the origin of their transformed coordinate system.

What use is skew, besides making your graphics strange and distorted? Its primary use is to simulate three-dimensional perspective.

In technical drawings, lines skewed at a consistent angle (usually 30° or 45°) can be used to represent edges that extend at right angles in front of or behind the rest of the drawing. Example 11-10 uses skewed coordinates to draw a projection of an empty box in this style. It uses 45° skews to keep the math simple: the amount of skew offset on the y-axis will be exactly equal to the distance from the origin on the x-axis. Figure 11-10 is the result.

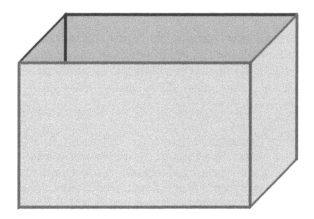

Figure 11-10. A pseudo-3D drawing of a box built from skewed rectangles

Example 11-10. Using skew transformations to simulate three dimensions

```
<svg xmlns="http://www.w3.org/2000/svg" xml:lang="en"
    xmlns:xlink="http://www.w3.org/1999/xlink"
    width="400px" height="300px" viewBox="0 0 40 30" >
    <title>Using skew to create an orthographic projection</title>
    <style type="text/css">
        rect {
            stroke-width: 0.3;
            stroke-linejoin: round;
        }
        .inside {
            fill: burlywood;
            stroke: saddleBrown;
        }
        .outside {
            fill: lightGray;
            stroke: gray;
        }
    </style>
    <g transform="translate(5,10)">                            ❶
        <rect class="inside" width="25" height="15"
```

```
            transform="translate(5,-5)"/>              ❷
    <rect class="inside" width="5" height="15"
            transform="skewY(-45)"/>                   ❸
    <rect class="outside" width="25" height="15" />    ❹
    <rect class="outside" width="5" height="15"
            transform="translate(25,0) skewY(-45)"/>   ❺
  </g>

</svg>
```

❶ The group contains the box as a whole, and a transformation moves it into place. The individual panels are all <rect> elements with their top-left corner at (0,0). The transformation on the group shifts that position away from the very top left of the SVG.

❷ The first rectangle is the back of the box, translated up and to the side.

❸ The next rectangle is the left side; it starts at the same origin as the front, but then is skewed to meet the offset back.

❹ The untransformed rectangle draws the front panel.

❺ The right side is positioned with a translation, then skewed to match the other side.

An important thing to note with the skewed rectangles in Example 11-10 is that the width attribute is the straight-line distance between the two sides, not the distance along the slanted edge.

A technical diagram that uses angled lines to simulate 3D, like this, is known as an orthographic projection (*ortho* meaning right, as in right-angled, and *graphic* meaning drawing).

For more decorative web-based graphics, skew transformations can be useful in simulating shadows. If you have an upright object with a light shining on it from above and to the side, a first approximation of this shadow can be rendered as a skew. This technique is used in Example 11-11, as illustrated in Figure 11-11.

Figure 11-11. Text with a projected shadow created with skew transformations

Example 11-11. Creating a projected shadow effect with skew transformations

```
<svg xmlns="http://www.w3.org/2000/svg" xml:lang="en"
    xmlns:xlink="http://www.w3.org/1999/xlink"
    width="400px" height="140px" viewBox="0 0 400 140">
    <title>Skewed shadows</title>
    <style type="text/css">
        text {
            font: bold 144px Georgia, serif;
        }
    </style>
    <defs>
        <linearGradient id="fadeGray" y2="100%" x2="0%">
            <stop stop-color="gray" stop-opacity="0" offset="0"/>
            <stop stop-color="gray" stop-opacity="1" offset="1"/>
        </linearGradient>
    </defs>
    <g transform="translate(10,120)">
        <use xlink:href="#t" fill="url(#fadeGray)"
            transform="skewX(-45) scale(1,0.7)"
            aria-hidden="true" />
        <g fill="blue" stroke="navy">
            <text id="t">SVG</text>
        </g>
    </g>
</svg>
```

A few additional tricks increase the realism in Example 11-11. The first is the introduction of a linear gradient that fades away from the text itself. The second is scaling the skewed text so that it's slightly smaller than the original, so that the tops of shadow and original are not perfectly aligned.

So the shadow can be styled differently from the original, the <text> itself doesn't have any styles. The `fill` and `stroke` are declared on a surrounding <g>, and inherit to the text—but not to its clone, which inherits the styles from the <use> instead.

Because the shadow needs to be *behind* the text (and because browsers don't support `z-index` for SVG), it comes first in the DOM. However, the shadow is the <use> and the real text is the <text> so that the main text is accessible and selectable in all browsers. Nonetheless, some browsers (Chrome) *do* make <use> copies of text accessible, so `aria-hidden` is used to mark it as redundant.

Older WebKit browsers will not correctly clone an element that is defined later in the document than the <use> element. In this case, that means that you wouldn't see the shadow, which is a reasonable fallback, considering it ensures accessible text in other browsers.

Neither Example 11-10 nor Example 11-11 creates a true 3D drawing environment. The shadow is at best a rough approximation of real shadows, but it's a fairly convincing effect at far less cost. Because skews can be directly calculated from the x and y coordinates and the constant parameter, the computer can rapidly calculate them by applying matrix mathematics to the vector shapes. The same holds true for scaling, rotation, and translation. These are all known technically as **affine transformations**.

Affine transformations convert between coordinate systems in a way that points remain points, straight lines remain straight lines, and parallel lines remain parallel. But true 3D perspective doesn't work like that. When you look at parallel lines on a road stretching out in front of you to the horizon, they appear to angle together towards a single point at infinity. Affine transformations cannot recreate this effect without separate calculations to factor in three-dimensional perspective.

Enter the Matrix

So far, we've described the mathematics behind transformations in terms of functions that convert (x,y) to (x',y'). In the case of translations and scaling functions, the functions that convert x are independent of y, and vice versa. For rotations and skew functions, in contrast, the values of x' and y' depend on both x and y. They also use trigonometry.

These transformation functions may seem like very different types of mathematics, but they can all be described with the same matrix multiplication structure.

If the word *matrix* conjures up a science fiction movie where reality is not what it seems, be assured that it is nothing that insidious. Matrix multiplication is just a structured way of applying mathematical equations to multiple variables (x and y) at the same time.

Warning! There's a bit of math ahead.

The matrices used in 2D affine transformations have the following structure:

$$\begin{bmatrix} a & c & e \\ b & d & f \\ 0 & 0 & 1 \end{bmatrix}$$

The matrix is the basis of the final 2D transformation function: matrix(*a,b,c,d,e,f*). The six variable values from the matrix are specified in column order.

You can create all sorts of interesting transformations with the matrix() function. Try a few numbers and see. For example, Figure 11-12 shows the face drawing from Example 5-5 in Chapter 5, and then shows what it looks like if you group all the drawing code with the following matrix transformation:

```
<g transform="matrix(1,2,3,-1,-2,-3)">
```

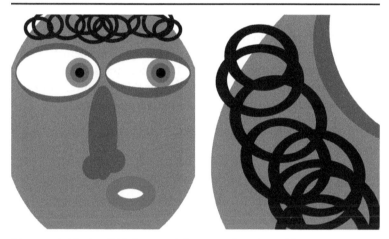

Figure 11-12. An SVG face, and the same drawing with a matrix transformation applied

You may come across matrix transformation functions like this in SVG created by other software (such as Inkscape) or JavaScript libraries (such as Snap.svg). Well, it probably won't be *exactly* like this, but it will be a matrix() function with six numbers.

But how does this seemingly obscure set of numbers relate to the changes you see onscreen?

The matrix expresses scale, rotation, skew, and translation transformations, all at once. If you just throw numbers in the function, you'll get a mix of all of the above.

The universal mapping equation for all the transformations, using matrix multiplication, looks like:

$$\begin{bmatrix} x' \\ y' \\ 1 \end{bmatrix} = \begin{bmatrix} a & c & e \\ b & d & f \\ 0 & 0 & 1 \end{bmatrix} \cdot \begin{bmatrix} x \\ y \\ 1 \end{bmatrix}$$

The preceding matrix equation is the equivalent to the following set of algebraic equations:

(Equation 1) $x' = (a \cdot x) + (c \cdot y) + (e \cdot 1)$
(Equation 2) $y' = (b \cdot x) + (d \cdot y) + (f \cdot 1)$
(Equation 3) $1 = (0 \cdot x) + (0 \cdot 1) + (1 \cdot 1)$

Equation 3 should hold true no matter what you do—it works out as $1 = 1$, so if that fails you might as well give up on mathematics altogether. Equations 1 and 2 describe the actual transformation. You can describe all the 2D transformations in this structure, substituting in constant values—often 0 or 1—for a, b, c, d, e, and f.

For example, in the transformation `translate(5,8)`, the matrix looks like:

$$\begin{bmatrix} 1 & 0 & 5 \\ 0 & 1 & 8 \\ 0 & 0 & 1 \end{bmatrix}$$

The resulting equations therefore look like:

(Equation 1) $x' = (1 \cdot x) + (0 \cdot y) + (5 \cdot 1) = x + 5$
(Equation 2) $y' = (0 \cdot x) + (1 \cdot y) + (8 \cdot 1) = y + 8$
(Equation 3) $1 = (0 \cdot x) + (0 \cdot 1) + (1 \cdot 1) = \quad 1$

This is exactly what the equations for a translation should look like.

For the transformation `skewX(45)`, the matrix looks like:

$$\begin{bmatrix} 1 & \tan(45) & 0 \\ 0 & 1 & 0 \\ 0 & 0 & 1 \end{bmatrix} = \begin{bmatrix} 1 & 1 & 0 \\ 0 & 1 & 0 \\ 0 & 0 & 1 \end{bmatrix}$$

Because $tan(45°)$ equals 1, the equations work out as follows:

(Equation 1) $x' = (1 \cdot x) + (\tan(45) \cdot y) + (0 \cdot 1) = x + y$

(Equation 2) $y' = (0 \cdot x) + (1 \cdot y) + (0 \cdot 1) = y$

(Equation 3) $1 = (0 \cdot x) + (0 \cdot 1) + (1 \cdot 1) = 1$

Again, this is what an x-skew looks like: the x coordinate is adjusted by an amount proportional to the y coordinate, but the y coordinate itself does not change.

Each of the transformation functions affects particular values in the matrix:

- Scaling transformations set the a (x-scale) and d (y-scale) parameters to the matrix.

- Translations use a scale of 1 for a and d, and then adjust the e and f parameters. These are the constants in the equations; they are not multiplied by either x or y.

- Skews also use 1 for a and d, but then set either b (skewY) or c (skewX). These are the parameters that describe how x affects y and how y affects x, respectively.

- Rotations set all of a, b, c, and d.

If a and b are both zero, the final coordinates are not affected by the input x. Similarly, if b and c are both zero, the final coordinates are not affected by the input y. In either case, your 2D drawing collapses into a 1D mathematical concept, and won't be drawn. This is what happens with a scale() where one of the factors is 0.

Why is all this relevant? Why use the matrices at all, when the simplified equations are easier to understand?

The benefit of using matrix mathematics comes when you're applying multiple transformations in sequence. The matrix equation for the transformation translate(5,8) skewX(45) looks like:

$$\begin{bmatrix} x' \\ y' \\ 1 \end{bmatrix} = \begin{bmatrix} 1 & 0 & 5 \\ 0 & 1 & 8 \\ 0 & 0 & 1 \end{bmatrix} \cdot \begin{bmatrix} 1 & 1 & 0 \\ 0 & 1 & 0 \\ 0 & 0 & 1 \end{bmatrix} \cdot \begin{bmatrix} x \\ y \\ 1 \end{bmatrix}$$

The reason this is important is because the two separate transformation matrices can be multiplied together. Multiplying creates a single matrix that describes *both* transformations. It looks like the following:

$$\begin{bmatrix} x' \\ y' \\ 1 \end{bmatrix} = \begin{bmatrix} 1 & 1 & 5 \\ 0 & 1 & 8 \\ 0 & 0 & 1 \end{bmatrix} \cdot \begin{bmatrix} x \\ y \\ 1 \end{bmatrix}$$

Using this consolidated matrix, the browser can apply both transformations simultaneously to any point, in one set of calculations.

Although this example was simple, it doesn't have to be: you can have dozens of nested transformations on an SVG element, including the transformations specified on parent elements and the implicit scaling and translating created by viewBox values. Each of those transformations can be described as a matrix, and all those matrices can be multiplied together. The resulting **cumulative transformation matrix** can then be used to transform individual points.

Even if you never use matrix transformations yourself, it's good to know that the obscure set of numbers is just a condensed list of other transformation functions.

Summary: Coordinate System Transformations

Coordinate system transformations are used throughout SVG to lay out graphics and manipulate their appearance. Rotations and skews allow you to break free of the strict horizontal and vertical coordinate system, while translations and scaling transformations offer a simple way to adjust the coordinate system origin and scale.

In the future, the new 3D transformation options will open up even more possibilities, as will the ability to assign transformations using CSS style rules, including media queries and CSS animations. For now, test carefully when applying CSS transforms to SVG, and use the transform attribute of the same elements to provide an acceptable fallback layout.

With the information in this and the previous few chapters, you have everything you need to create basic vector graphics: you can define coordinate systems, draw shapes within them, transform those coordinate systems, and reuse the shapes in the transformed space. Part IV will explore the options for decorating those shapes, with gradients, patterns, stroke effects, filters, masks, and more.

More Online

A quick reference to the transformation function syntax—including reminders of the differences between the SVG 1 and CSS syntaxes —is provided in the "Transform Functions" guide:

https://oreillymedia.github.io/Using_SVG/guide/transform-functions.html

Artistic Touches

A complete SVG graphic is more than coordinates, shape, and layout. That basic structure must be translated to its final appearance on screen or paper—it must be *rendered*, in computer graphics terminology—through the application of colors, lines, and patterns to the shapes. Other stylistic manipulations can soften the crisp edges or shapes, or otherwise alter the formal mathematical geometry of the SVG structure.

The next few chapters explore the artistic side of SVG: how color is used, how the strokes that outline shape are created and manipulated, and how graphical effects like filters and masks are applied. Many of these graphical effects are being adopted into CSS styling as well, so we'll continue to highlight the similarities and differences.

CHAPTER 12

Filling Up to Full

The fill Property, Gradients, and Patterns

Parts II and III focused on the *geometry* of vector graphics: laying down the lines, curves, and shapes of the design. Such work is necessary; even the most skilled of painters usually work out their rough concepts as drawings first, applying paint only after they've finalized in their mind what they are painting. And as with paintings created with a brush and pigments, an SVG graphic is not truly "complete" until after color has been applied to transform the visual outline into a completed work.

In this chapter, we examine more thoroughly the options you have for filling your graphics with colors and patterns.

The fill style on shape or text determines how the region inside that shape is colored. We've been using fill in examples throughout the book, usually setting its value to a simple color. But SVG shapes and text can also be filled with gradients or patterns. These more complex painting instructions are defined with their own elements and attributes, and then another element uses them with a cross-reference from its fill value.

This chapter briefly reviews your options for declaring colors in SVG—but assumes that you're already familiar with the same options in CSS. It then introduces SVG gradients and patterns. These **paint server elements** are incredibly flexible, and this book isn't going to describe every possible combination.[1] However, by the end of this chapter, you should be able to create simple patterns or gradients, and to understand and adapt the markup created for you by graphics software.

When SVG was first introduced, the only option for patterns or gradients in CSS and HTML was to use repeating background images. Since then, however, CSS has introduced gradient functions, and has greatly increased the flexibility of background images. The syntax differs considerably between CSS and SVG, although the net effect is often similar. This chapter compares the two, to make it easier for you to switch back and forth. It also introduces proposals to adapt the CSS syntax for use in SVG.

Coloring Between the Lines

The `fill` property is one of the simplest to get started with, but one of the most complex in all its possibilities. The next few sections start with the simplest type of fill: colors.

Except it turns out that colors aren't always simple.

The Rainbow Connection

As we've seen in nearly every example so far, the `fill` of a shape can be a simple color. In most of those examples we define the color using a keyword such as `black`, `red`, or `saddleBrown`. These keywords (147 in all) were originally distinguished by their two sources:

- the original HTML color keywords, used in outdated styling attributes like `BGCOLOR` and `VLINK`, and integrated in CSS and then SVG from the beginning

- the X11 color set (used in many open source software programs), which were integrated in the original SVG specifications, but only later adopted by CSS

Any SVG-supporting web browser also supports the X11 color keywords in CSS. There is no need to really distinguish between the two color sets, unless you're defining fallback colors for old browsers.

---

1 If you want more details, we have written an entire book on SVG paint servers, *SVG Colors, Patterns & Gradients* (O'Reilly, 2015), that *does* explore all the options.

However, the mixed origins leave their legacy in inconsistent naming patterns (like `gray` from HTML being darker than `darkGray` from X11).

 Browsers also now support the X11 color keywords in HTML's deprecated presentation attributes, like `bgcolor`. But HTML's color parsing rules also generate (somewhat arbitrary) colors from any other attribute text, too. So... maybe just avoid specifying colors in HTML attributes altogether, OK?

More recent additions to CSS colors (`transparent` and `rebeccaPurple`) can also be used in SVG, but watch for support, particularly in nonbrowser software.

Figure 12-1 shows spot colors for all the named keywords, divided into dark and light, and then arranged with the most intense colors at the edge of the color wheel and darker, lighter, and less saturated colors closer to the middle. It's a two-dimensional visualization of three-dimensional data, but it's enough to make it clear that the named colors aren't evenly distributed in the color space.

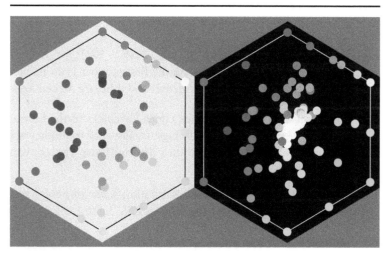

Figure 12-1. Named color keywords recognized in SVG and CSS

Use the keywords for convenience, but do not expect the color names to be systematic or logical. Learn a few combinations of keywords that create nice palettes, and you can quickly whip up a demonstration page or graphic. But for complex design and custom branding, you'll probably want to pick custom colors: colors defined by a triplet of numerical values.

There are multiple CSS custom color formats. For best support in nonbrowser SVG software, stick with the CSS color formats that existed at the time of the original SVG specifications:

- three and six-digit **hex codes**, like `#F00` (red) or `#fabdad` (fabulous pink); each digit is a hexadecimal in the range 0–9 or a–f (or A–F; capitalization doesn't matter)
- integer **RGB functions**, like `rgb(255, 0, 0)` (red again) or `rgb(250, 189, 173)` (that same Fab Dad pink); each value in the function is an integer from 0 to 255
- percentage RGB functions, like `rgb(100%, 0%, 0%)` or `rgb(98%, 74.1%, 67.8%)` (same colors); each value in the function is a decimal percentage

Nonetheless, on the modern web, you can use any colors in SVG that you use in CSS, including those from CSS3. HSL has good support in browsers and newer graphics editors:

- **HSL color functions**, like `hsl(0, 100%, 50%)` for red, or `hsl(12, 89%, 83%)` for `#fabdad`; the first number is an integer for the hue in degrees, and the second and third are percentages

Most graphical SVG editors use hex codes for colors in the output file. However, their color-picking dialogs usually offer multiple ways of expressing the same value. Browser dev tools also can convert from one format to another.

Just be careful: there are a lot of hue/saturation/*something* color systems, where the final value isn't the same as CSS "lightness"!

Future Focus
Controlling Colors, Consistently

CSS Color Module Level 4 introduces a number of new ways of defining colors, based on more scientific models of color perception. It also adds convenient shorthands like `gray(30%)` for `rgb(30%, 30%, 30%)`.

The new color module also introduces a set of color adjustment functions, which take one or two color values as input and calculate a new color from them—inverting, interpolating, or blending with different formulas.

It will be a while before support is good enough to reliably use them on the web, but the proposals are worth keeping an eye on. More natural color functions make it easier to represent light and shadow, or to create attractive color palettes for data visualization.

CSS Color 4 also *re*introduces a feature from the original SVG specifications: color profiles. Color profiles are standard ways of defining the actual output color—that is, not just a percentage of the device's capabilities, but a color that can be consistent from one device to another. They are widely used in commercial printing and in high-quality digital graphics.

By default, colors use the sRGB ("standard" RGB) profile, which is based on the average capabilities of 1990s-era CRT monitors. In reality, few monitors are well calibrated, and colors may appear differently on different computers (or in different lighting conditions).

Modern operating systems (and browsers) already support common colorspaces for displaying digital photographs. Allowing CSS colors (and therefore, SVG colors) to be defined in the same colorspace ensures that you can properly match the colors in the image, on any device.

Each color profile has its own way of defining colors, which may be numeric or keyword-based. It's up to the final output device (printer or monitor and software) to implement a given color profile system. For this reason, both syntaxes for defining profiled colors include a way to specify a fallback color in the standard CSS syntaxes.

The new CSS syntax for profiled colors is quite different from the old SVG syntax. If you are working with printers, you'll need to find out which version (if any) they support. On the web, SVG 1 color profiles were never supported, but the new syntax is expected to start showing up in browsers sometime in 2017.

At the time of writing, browsers are just starting to roll out support for level 4 color features. However, when they are supported, they should be available in SVG properties at the same time as the rest of CSS.

Coordinating Colors

There is another way to define a color in SVG: the `currentColor` keyword. This equates to the current value of the **color property**.

`currentColor` is one of the many SVG features that has been adopted by the rest of CSS. It can now be used in place of any CSS color value, and is the default for many properties, including `border-color` and `text-decoration-color`.

Since `color` isn't otherwise used in SVG, that means it can be used with `currentColor` as a variable to coordinate other color-related properties:

```
<g color="mediumOrchid">
    <circle r="50" stroke="currentColor" />
    <text fill="currentColor">Matching Label</text>
</g>
```

 Yes, you can use `color` as a presentation attribute in SVG, even though it doesn't have a direct effect.

For inline SVG, the `color` property inherits into the SVG from the surrounding text. It can therefore be used to coordinate inline SVG icons with your HTML text color.

When you set an inherited style property to the `currentColor` value, it is *supposed* to inherit as the keyword, not as the computed color value (according to the original SVG specifications and the latest CSS Color modules). That means that child elements use their `color` value, not the `color` value from the element on which the style was set.

In other words, these circles *should* have different fill colors (one orchid-purple, the other pink):

```
<g color="mediumOrchid" fill="currentColor">
    <circle cx="50" r="50" />
    <circle cx="150" r="50" color="deepPink" />
</g>
```

But…don't rely on it:

At the time of writing, most browsers (Safari, Firefox, and IE/Edge) convert currentColor to a specific color value *before* the CSS property is inherited (following the original wording in CSS Color 3). So both of those circles are drawn as mediumOrchid purple.

You need to explicitly set fill: currentColor on the element that has the correct color property.

Using currentColor as a variable is particularly useful with <use> elements in SVG. You can't directly set styles on elements within each copy of a symbol, but you can control the inherited styles, including the color value. That means you can coordinate fill and stroke of different elements within the content.

Example 12-1 shows an example of using currentColor in an icon sprite file to set the color of both fill and stroke. The icons look like this:

In order to create the inset-outline effect, two copies of the triangle are drawn on top of each other. The lower layer has a thick stroke in the same color as the fill; the upper layer is just a thin white stroke and no fill. By using currentColor for the fill and outer stroke, we can do this and still have the background of the icon change to match the text color.

Example 12-1 includes both the icon sprite file and a sample web page, displayed in Figure 12-2.

ACCESSIBILITY WARNING

The markings on the warning icon are always white, so
the inherited color value needs to be dark enough to
ensure contrast.

Figure 12-2. A warning sign with a color-coordinated icon

Example 12-1. Using currentColor in reused SVG symbols

SVG ICON FILE: *warning-icons.svg*

```
<svg xmlns="http://www.w3.org/2000/svg" xml:lang="en"
    xmlns:xlink="http://www.w3.org/1999/xlink">
    <title>Warning Icons</title>
    <defs>
        <path id="triangle" d="M10,4 18,18 2,18 Z"
            stroke-linejoin="round" />                          ❶
        <g id="triangle-sign">
            <use xlink:href="#triangle"
                fill="currentColor"
                stroke="currentColor" stroke-width="4" />       ❷
            <use xlink:href="#triangle"
                fill="none"
                stroke="white" stroke-width="1" />
        </g>
    </defs>

    <symbol id="important" viewBox="0 0 20 20" overflow="visible">
        <use xlink:href="#triangle-sign" />                     ❸
        <text text-anchor="middle"
                fill="white" stroke="none"
                x="10" y="16" font-size="10">!</text>           ❹
    </symbol>
    <rect x="5" y="5" width="40" height="40" fill="lightBlue" />
    <use xlink:href="#important" color="indigo"
        x="5" y="5" width="40" height="40" />                   ❺

    <symbol id="electricity" viewBox="0 0 20 20" overflow="visible">
        <use xlink:href="#triangle-sign" />
        <polygon points="10.5,7.5 8,11.5 10.5,13
                        9.5,16.5 12,12.5 9.5,11"
                fill="white" stroke="none" />                   ❻
```

```
</symbol>
<rect x="55" y="5" width="40" height="40" fill="lightBlue" />
<use xlink:href="#electricity" color="indigo"
    x="55" y="5" width="40" height="40" />

<!-- and more, using similar coloring -->
</svg>
```

❶ The triangle is predefined for use in multiple icons. It's approximately equilateral, with its base along the line $y = 18$. We'll talk more about the stroke-linejoin presentation attribute in Chapter 13; it is used here to give any strokes on the triangle rounded corners.

❷ Two copies of the triangle are grouped together as triangle-sign, and given fill and stroke styles. The thick 4-unit-wide stroke on the lower layer means that the outer edge of the triangle (now with rounded corners) will be 20 units wide, sitting on the line $y=20$.

❸ Each symbol has a 20×20 viewBox (with visible overflow to prevent pixels getting clipped). That exactly fits the copy of the triangle-sign group that is reused inside it.

❹ The important icon has a <text> element drawing an exclamation mark inside it. The text will match the inherited font settings from the web page, except for the font-size, which is adjusted to fit. The fill is set directly, and any inherited stroke is explicitly cancelled out.

❺ The <symbol> is never directly drawn, so to make the sprite file easier to use, <use> copies of each icon are arranged so you can see them if you view the *warning-icons.svg* file directly. A light blue <rect> element makes the full dimensions of each symbol visible, too.

❻ The second icon uses the same triangular backdrop, but creates a lightning bolt out of a <polygon> for the icon itself. Again, the <symbol> created for reuse is also printed to the sprite sheet.

HTML and CSS

```
<!DOCTYPE html>
<html lang="en">
<head>
    <meta charset="utf-8" />
    <title>Warning Notice</title>
    <style>
        .icon {
            width: 1em;
            height: 1em;
            vertical-align: -0.1em;        ❶
        }
        .warning {
            max-width: 30em;
            margin: 0 auto;
            padding: 1em;
            border: double 6px;

            background-color: #eee;
            color: darkRed;                ❷
        }
        h1 {
            font: bold small-caps 200% sans-serif;
            margin: 0 0 0.5em;
        }
        code {
            font: 100% Consolas, monospace;
        }
    </style>
</head>
<body>
    <section class="warning">
        <h1>
            <svg class="icon" role="img">        ❸
                <title>Attention</title>
                <use xlink:href="warning-icons.svg#important" />
            </svg>
            Accessibility Warning
        </h1>
        <p>The markings on the warning icon are always white,
            so the inherited <code>color</code> value
            needs to be dark enough to ensure contrast.
        </p>
    </section>
</body>
</html>
```

❶ The inline SVG elements will have an `icon` class. They are sized to match the surrounding text with `width` and `height` of 1em.

The vertical-align property shifts them slightly, relative to the text baseline, so that they line up more neatly: for Latin letters, part of the 1em height of a line of text is always below the baseline.

❷ The warning class is for the entire warning alert. For this example, the most important part is color: darkRed. The unspecified border color defaults to darkRed as well.

❸ The inline <svg> is contained inside the <h1> heading, so it will inherit the heading's font-size and color. A <title> gives an accessible description, while the role="img" ensures that the entire SVG is treated as a single image—in particular, the exclamation mark in the icon won't be read out as text.

As we warned in Chapter 10, many older browsers do not support <use> references to separate files. You may want to use a JavaScript polyfill to increase support.

Even the browsers that support cross-file <use> references don't currently apply CSS rules from <style> sections inside that file. They only support inline styles or presentation attributes—so that's what we use here.

This is the most heavily nested <use> example we've seen so far. But the styles inherit through all the nesting levels, just like they inherit through nested <div> or <g> elements.

As we warned in Chapter 10, some versions of Chrome (including the latest at the time of writing) have bugs with nested <use> combined with external file <use>. This particular demo works fine, but always test carefully!

The color style applied to the HTML <section> inherits down to the <use> element in the inline SVG, then to the clone of the <symbol> and the elements inside it, including the <use> element that clones the triangle-sign group; the cloned group inherits the color and passes it, finally, to the two different clones of the triangle `<path>` itself.

This example only uses `color` on the `<use>` element, ignoring the inherited `fill` and `stroke`. However, you could of course use all three, with some parts of the icon using inherited `fill` and `stroke` styles and other elements using `currentColor`. To get more options than that, however, you need CSS variables.

Variables for Every Property

Coordinating multiple styles is useful for more than just colors. And it's often useful to have more than one color that you can coordinate to. In other words: `currentColor` is nice, but it's not enough.

CSS custom properties, more commonly known as **CSS variables**, fill in the gap. They allow you to declare your own CSS properties with any value you want, just by giving it a name starting with `--` (two hyphen/minus characters). You can then use those property values in any other property, by referencing your custom property name inside a **var() function**.

 Many people find the `--property` syntax confusing, or ugly. The syntax needed to be compatible with existing CSS parsers, and it also needed to avoid conflicts with popular CSS preprocessors, which usually have their own variable syntax.

Think of the custom property syntax as an extension of the CSS prefixed property syntax, like `-ms-grid-rows` or `-webkit-transform`. But because these are *your* properties, not the browser's, there is no browser prefix between the two hyphens.

At the time of writing, CSS Custom Properties are now supported in the latest versions of every major browser. So they aren't really a "future" feature—you can use them now! Just be careful about creating reasonable fallbacks for older browsers and nonbrowser software.

MS Edge introduced support for CSS variables as of EdgeHTML version 15 (released as stable in April 2017). However, the variable values do not inherit into the <use> element shadow trees. This will hopefully be fixed for the next update.

We can extend our <use> warning icon sprite from Example 12-1 with custom properties. We'll have two properties, to allow the author to set the sign color directly, if desired, and to set the text color to something other than white. In our sprite file, the code for the triangle would look like the following:

```
<g id="triangle-sign">
    <use xlink:href="#triangle"
        fill="currentColor"
        stroke="currentColor" stroke-width="4"
        style="fill: var(--icon-sign-bg, currentColor);
               stroke: var(--icon-sign-bg, currentColor)"/>
    <use xlink:href="#triangle"
        fill="none"
        stroke="white" stroke-width="1"
        style="stroke: var(--icon-sign-text, white)" />
</g>
```

We'd then make similar changes to the rest of the icon code, setting the fill of the <text> and <polygon> elements to var(--icon-sign-text, white).

The presentation attributes are still there, for software that doesn't support CSS variables. For modern browsers, fill and stroke are reset in a style attribute to use var() functions. Each var() has two parameters: the name of a CSS custom property, and a fallback value to use if the browser supports variables but that *particular* variable hasn't been set on the element. The fallbacks for that case are exactly the same as the fallbacks in the presentation attributes.

In the final web page, we can choose to set either --icon-sign-bg (the sign background), --icon-sign-text, or both. For example, if our warning had yellow-gold text on a dark gray background, we might want the sign background to still use currentColor but the markings to be in black:

```
.warning {
    background-color: #222;
    color: gold;

    --icon-sign-text: black;
}
```

However, that leaves us with an issue in browsers that don't support CSS variables: we'll get white markings on gold, which will be almost indistinguishable. To prevent this, we can use a CSS @supports test to adjust the color depending on whether or not CSS custom properties and var() functions are recognized:

```
.warning .icon {
    color: darkGoldenrod;
    /* fallback, if CSS variables aren't supported */
}
@supports (--css: var(--iables) ) {
    .warning .icon { color: inherit; }
}
```

The specific custom property names in the @supports test don't matter; it's just testing the syntax. If the syntax is acceptable, the icon will inherit the gold color value from the rest of the warning sign; otherwise, it will be set to a darker gold to ensure enough contrast against white.

 Because MS Edge 15 recognizes CSS variables, but doesn't use them in SVG <use>, all the fallback methods fail: the @supports test says variables are supported, but the variable value isn't passed to the icon. The icons are barely readable white on gold. Good thing the full meaning is also conveyed by the heading text.

Figure 12-3 shows what the end result would look like in a browser with CSS variable support.

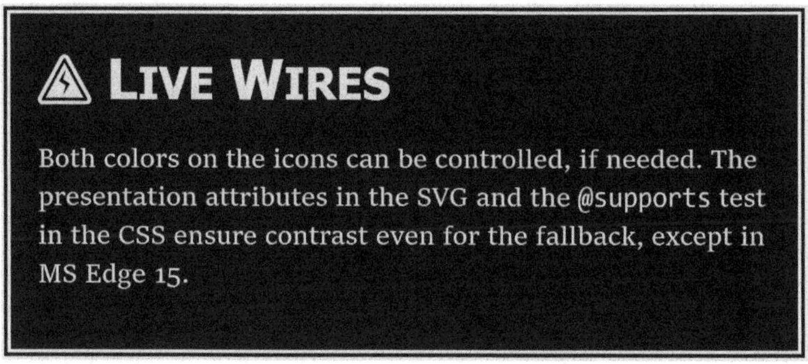

⚠ LIVE WIRES

Both colors on the icons can be controlled, if needed. The presentation attributes in the SVG and the @supports test in the CSS ensure contrast even for the fallback, except in MS Edge 15.

Figure 12-3. A warning sign with color coordination and contrast control

There are limitations to variables as currently specified:

- Default values must be set in every var() function: there's no initial value.

- The CSS parser does not know what type of value should be allowed in your property, so it can't do any type checking or fallbacks for you.

- Similarly, the browser cannot interpolate between custom values in an animation or transition. However, if you change a variable, it will trigger a transition on properties that *use* that variable.

Proposals for future versions of CSS custom properties address these issues, but nothing has been finalized yet. The usefulness of CSS variables for colors will also be considerably enhanced when browsers support the new color-adjustment functions in CSS Color Module Level 4.

Water Colors

If you've worked with color in modern CSS web design, you may also be familiar with the semitransparent color functions. The rgba and hsla color functions take a fourth value, **alpha**, that defines how opaque the color should be. An alpha of 0 creates a perfectly transparent color; an alpha of 1 creates a perfectly opaque (solid) color. Some examples:

- `rgba(0,0,0,0)` is transparent black, equivalent to the `transparent` keyword.

- `hsla(0,0%,100%,0)` is transparent white; in most situations, it would look identical to transparent black, but it can have different effects in gradients or animations.

- `rgba(100%,0%,0%,0.5)` is half-transparent red.

- `hsla(240,100%,50%,1)` is fully opaque blue, equal to `hsl(240,100%,50%)` or #00F.

These alpha color functions were introduced in the level 3 CSS Color module. Although they are now supported in nearly all web browsers that support SVG, they were not part of the original SVG specifications.

Support for semitransparent colors may be limited in nonbrowser SVG software.

There are also a few bugs in browsers related to these colors in SVG: for example, semitransparent colors don't work in gradients in WebKit.

SVG 1 did support semitransparent colors, but in a different way.

SVG has a separate property, **fill-opacity**, to control the opacity of the fill. There are similar opacity properties that pair with other properties in SVG that define a color value: `stroke-opacity`, `stop-opacity` (for gradient stops), and `flood-opacity` (for the <feFlood> filter component). All of these properties can be set using either presentation attributes or CSS.

The overall `opacity` property also adjusts transparency, but in a different way: it applies to the final painted result of the element on which it is applied, even if that element is a group of multiple shapes. `opacity` is discussed in Chapter 15.

Similar to the alpha values in the color functions, the fill-opacity property accepts a value from 0 (completely transparent) to 1 (completely opaque). The other *-opacity properties work the same.

When using fill colors, setting fill-opacity has much the same visual effect as using a color with the equivalent alpha value. A shape with fill: red and fill-opacity: 0.5 would look the same as one with fill: rgba(255,0,0,0.5).

 If you use both fill-opacity and a semitransparent color for fill, the transparency effect is compounded: the net opacity is the two values multiplied together.

Example 12-2 shows all the possibilities, applied to copies of our heart icon (the <symbol> version we created for Example 10-2 in Chapter 10).

The icons in the right column (with x="10") have reduced fill-opacity. The icons in the bottom row (with y="10") have reduced alpha in the fill color. This means the icon in the bottom right has both types of transparency, compounded.

To clearly show the effect of the transparency, the hearts are drawn over the coordinate system grid created for the figures in Chapter 6. Figure 12-4 shows the result.

Figure 12-4. Shapes with and without reduced fill-opacity (right versus left column), and with and without reduced-alpha fill colors (bottom versus top row)

Example 12-2. Creating semitransparent fill in different ways

```
<svg xmlns="http://www.w3.org/2000/svg" xml:lang="en"
    xmlns:xlink="http://www.w3.org/1999/xlink"
    height="400px" width="400px" viewBox="0 0 20 20">
    <title>fill-opacity versus (and with)
            Semi-Transparent Fill</title>
    <use xlink:href="../ch06-path-files/graphing.svg#grid" />        ❶
    <use xlink:href="../ch10-reuse-files/suits-symbols.svg#heart"
        width="10" height="10" />                                   ❷
    <use xlink:href="../ch10-reuse-files/suits-symbols.svg#heart"
        width="10" height="10" x="10" />
    <use xlink:href="../ch10-reuse-files/suits-symbols.svg#heart"
        width="10" height="10" y="10" />                            ❸
    <use xlink:href="../ch10-reuse-files/suits-symbols.svg#heart"
```

```
        width="10" height="10" x="10" y="10" />
    <style>
        [*|href$='#heart'] { fill: magenta; }           ❹
        [x='10'] { fill-opacity: 0.6; }                 ❺
        [y='10'] { fill: rgba(100%, 0%, 100%, 0.6); }   ❻
    </style>
</svg>
```

❶ The #grid in the other file is a `<g>`, not a `<symbol>`. When reused, it is therefore drawn in this SVG's coordinate system using the exact coordinates with which it was originally defined. It was defined to draw grid lines from –5 to +25 in both the *x* and *y* directions; this SVG's viewBox will only show the section of the grid from 0 to +20. The stroke styles are also defined in the other file, as presentation attributes.

❷ The remaining `<use>` elements reference the heart icon `<symbol>`. The width and height attributes constrain them to each use only a 10×10 region of the 20×20 viewBox for this file. The icon code in the sprite file does not define any styles; it will inherit styles set on the `<use>` elements.

❸ The four hearts are positioned in two rows and columns using the x and y attributes on the `<use>` elements.

❹ We could have set the fill and fill-opacity in presentation attributes, but it's good to remind you of all the options CSS opens up. That's the XML-namespace-wildcard version of a CSS attribute selector, which we introduced back in Chapter 3. The dollar sign before the equals ($=) means that it will select elements whose href or xlink:href attribute *ends* with #heart. All four heart icons match that selector, and so they are assigned the fill color magenta.

❺ The `<use>` elements with x="10" are selected with a (much-simpler) CSS attribute selector, and given reduced fill-opacity.

❻ The final selector picks the `<use>` elements with y="10", and overrides the earlier fill setting, to apply an rgba color. The color is a semitransparent version of magenta; the magenta keyword is equal to rgb(100%, 0, 100%) in functional notation.

The effective transparency of the final (bottom right) icon is 0.6×0.6, or 0.36.

 It's good to know that you can play around with CSS selectors, like we did in Example 12-2. But attribute selectors, especially with common attributes like x and y, can easily cause unintended consequences. It's fine for a single small, standalone SVG, but use classes in inline SVG or more complex design systems.

If you're used to working with transparent colors in CSS, it may be tempting to stick with what you know. But there are important benefits of fill-opacity to consider:

- It is supported in nearly all SVG software.
- It can be modified independently from the fill color.
- It allows you to use named color keywords or hex colors—whatever you're already using.
- It also applies to fill paint.

What's fill *paint*? That's when the shape isn't filled with a single color, but instead by complex graphical instructions from a gradient or a pattern.

Future Focus
Percentage Alpha

The SVG 1.1 and CSS Color level 3 specifications only allowed alpha values to be set as a decimal number. However, many graphics programs use percentages to describe alpha: 0% for transparent and 100% for opaque.

SVG 2 and CSS Color level 4 allow a percentage or a number whenever an alpha value is specified. For now, use decimals to ensure browser support.

Filling with More Than Solid Colors

The fill property, as we discovered in Chapter 1, can be set with a url() reference to another element. That other element—the one that describes *how* to fill in this shape—is known as a **paint server**.

There are three paint server elements in SVG 1.1, which can be used to fill (or stroke) shapes or text:

<linearGradient>
A gradient defined by color transitions along a line. The colors are then extended away from that line infinitely on either side.

<radialGradient>
A gradient defined by color transitions along rays extending outward from a point, in all directions, to a circular boundary.

<pattern>
A tiled pattern of the same rectangle of SVG drawing elements, repeated infinitely in rows and columns.

Figure 12-5 shows some of the effects you can create with these elements. We'll explain the code used to create them when we explore the individual elements, later in this chapter.

When you apply a fill-opacity of less than 1 to a shape with a gradient or pattern fill, the entire gradient or pattern is made semitransparent. If parts of it were already transparent, the effect is compounded, in the same way that reducing fill-opacity makes semitransparent colors even more transparent.

The next few sections will discuss some common conceptual features of SVG paint servers, before the rest of the chapter outlines the specific elements and attributes.

Figure 12-5. Linear gradients (top), radial gradients (middle), and patterns (bottom)

Future Focus
Serving Up New Paint

SVG 2 will considerably extend your `fill` options. Unfortunately, at the time of writing, none of the new options are supported in web browsers.

SVG 2 introduces three new paint server elements:

`<solidcolor>`

First proposed in SVG Tiny 1.2, `<solidcolor>` provides a paint-server interface for a single color of paint. That way, you would only need to specify the color value once, and reference it many places. You would also be able to animate the color and have all uses of it update in sync. It remains to be seen whether it ever gets adopted in web browsers: CSS variables provide the same functions, and many more, too.

`<hatch>`

A `<hatch>` defines a pattern as a repeated section of path data. The path data would be repeated to create a continuous path for as long as required to fill up the shape in one direction, and then copies of the path would be repeated side-by-side to fill up the shape in the perpendicular direction. The continuous paths would be better suited to engraving and similar tools than `<pattern>` tiles, and would make common patterns from data visualization and mapping (like repeated wavy or zig-zag lines) much easier to define, for all uses of SVG.

`<meshgradient>`

A `<meshgradient>` is a pattern of continuous color transitions that is defined by a two-dimensional arrangement of color stop points, connected to each other in (possibly curved) paths to create a mesh (a flexible grid) of rows and columns.

All new elements defined in SVG 2 have all-lowercase names, to make them more compatible with the HTML parser. In SVG Tiny 1.2, in contrast, the `<solidcolor>` element was actually `<solidColor>`, with a capital C.

The following examples of mesh gradients were created with the new SVG 2 mesh gradient tool in Inkscape. On the left is a gradient applied to a wide stroke of a circle; on the right is a mesh gradient as fill of a polygon:

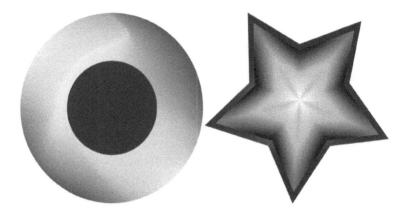

The code for the two graphics combined is just over 16KB as uncompressed, unoptimized SVG code—even with all the Inkscape custom attributes. Adobe Illustrator also creates mesh gradients, but does not yet export to the SVG syntax.

The gradient on the circle's stroke is a mesh of 3×3 stop points, or 2×2 mesh "patches". The stop points are the corners and intersection points of the patches: each patch is defined by four stops and the path edges that connect them. In this case, the edges of the patches are all Bézier curves, with the center point of the mesh pulled off to one side, to create the highlight effect.

The star has a simple radial gradient on the stroke, using the mesh gradient for the fill. The mesh is actually a grid of 10×2 patches, rolled up so all the points along one edge of the mesh are gathered together in the center of the star. The mesh therefore becomes a complex conic gradient. Those stops alternate white and blue-gray; the stops in the next row (the edges between the first and second row of patches) are all the same peachy-gold color; the stops in the final row are positioned on the outer edge of the star and alternate pinky-red and deep blue. Inkscape generates these mesh structures automatically when you apply a mesh to a polygon. SVG 2 also defines a **<mesh>** element that would create a path that exactly matches the outside edges of the patches of a **<meshgradient>**.

SVG 2 also introduces a syntax to allow you to use paint servers without giving them **id** values: you could include the paint server element as a child of the shape, and use the **fill:child(n)** to select it, like this:

```
<path d="M10,0 L 20,10 10,20 0,10 Z" fill="child(1)">
    <linearGradient>
```

```
    <stop stop-color="green" offset="0"/>
    <stop stop-color="lightBlue" offset="1"/>
  </linearGradient>
</path>
```

This avoids the complication of having to create a unique id value for each paint server element. This is important if you're using scripts to generate a large number of elements, especially in inline SVG where there may be other parts of the page that aren't controlled by your script.

Even more options for fill (and stroke) are defined in the newly proposed CSS Fill and Stroke module. We'll describe the changes at the end of the next section.

Fallbacks for Fills

Whenever the fill property (or presentation attribute) is set with a url() value, it can optionally be followed by a color, with white-space separating the two values:

```
fill: url(#gold) #f0b020;
```

The color is used as a fallback, in case there is a problem with the URL reference. Some examples of potential problems:

- No element exists with an id that matches the URL reference.

- The element exists, but it's not a paint server type recognized by the browser.

- The element exists and is a paint server, but it is invalid for some other reason (for example: zero-width pattern tiles that will never fill a shape no matter how many times they are repeated).

- The URL references an element in another file, and the browser doesn't support cross-file references (we saw an example of this in Chapter 2).

- The browser supports cross-file references, but for network reasons or security reasons, it isn't able to access the file.

- The paint server URL is in this file, but the painted shape is reused from another file, and you're using a version of a (Blink) browser that has bugs with this.

Fallback colors can be useful for debugging. They are essential if you're going to use paint servers in other files (as we did, in the interest of code brevity, in Example 2-4 in Chapter 2), and would be even if browser support for this wasn't utterly horrible.

At the time of writing, references to paint servers in other files are only supported fully in Firefox (and other Gecko-based browsers) and Presto-based browsers (old Opera and Opera Mini). MS Edge supports it from *.svg* files only, not from inline SVG.

Even where they are supported, there will be cross-origin restrictions.

Without cross-browser support of cross-file references, your paint server elements have to be copied into every page.

This also means that your CSS rules assigning the fill and stroke values need to be on that page, so the local url(#id) references will be calculated correctly. New rules for #id-only URLs in CSS files have been proposed, but aren't supported reliably yet.

If you're using gradients or patterns as part of an inline SVG icon system, you'll either want to use server-side templating tools to add the markup into every page, or use client-side JavaScript to download the markup and inject it. For the JavaScript approach, you'll want to have fallback colors in place, in case your script fails.

Future Focus
New Fill Effects

The CSS Fill and Stroke module extends the fill and stroke properties so that they also apply to CSS-styled text outside of SVG. So you could set a fill gradient and stroke outline on the text in an HTML heading, without having to include the text in an inline SVG.

The module also proposes changes that will make fill and stroke paint work more like CSS backgrounds:

- Both fill and stroke would take a list of multiple paint values that would be layered together (just like layered background images).

- Instead of an SVG paint server reference, you could use any CSS image data type, including `url()` references to image files (e.g., a JPEG photograph) and CSS gradient functions.

- The `fill` property (and also the `stroke` property) would become a shorthand property, with longhands similar to those for `background`. You'd be able to control the size, positions, and repeat patterns of the images that are used for the paint layers, allowing you to create a basic tiled image pattern without a `<pattern>` element.

For backward compatibility, a `fill-color` specified with a `fill-image` would still be used only as a fallback. To get a solid color layer underneath your pattern, you'd need to add an explicit second layer, with a `none` image value:

```
fill: url(#diamond-pattern) indigo;
 /* diamond pattern with solid indigo as fallback */

fill-color: indigo;
fill-image: url(#diamond-pattern), none;
 /* diamond pattern over top of solid indigo layer */

fill: url(#diamond-pattern), indigo;
 /* the same, using the shorthand: note the comma */
```

Specific details in the module are still being worked out, but there seems to be good browser support for moving forward with it. Recent versions of most browsers already support solid-color fill and stroke on non-SVG text, using the nonstandard `-webkit-text-fill-color` and `-webkit-text-stroke-color` properties; this includes non-WebKit browsers MS Edge and Firefox. The same browsers also support something that *looks* like image or gradient-filled text, with `-webkit-background-clip: text`. The new module would replace these properties with standard CSS options, while also extending SVG paint considerably.

Picturing Paint

"Paint" is the accepted name in SVG for gradients and patterns used to fill (or stroke) a shape, and the elements that define them. But the word is a little misleading.

When you paint something—furniture, a wall, or the shapes in a paint-by-number coloring book—you adjust the paint to fit within the space available. Paint is liquid; it adapts to the space available. You can run your paint brush around the edges, just so.

SVG paint doesn't work that way. SVG paint is more like wallpaper —or fabric. It has its own design that is independent of the shape that you are filling. You need to *clip* the paper or fabric to fit it to a specific shape, like in Figure 12-6.

Figure 12-6. "Painting" a shape in SVG, by cutting it out from a patterned sheet

When you define a gradient or pattern in SVG, you are defining a (theoretically infinite) image of its own. The browser then uses that image as a reference as it fills shape or text.

When the browser **rasterizes** vector shapes, converting it to pixels, it scans across the image row-by-row to figure out which points are in or outside of it. In Chapter 6, when we talked about the fill-rule property, we explained how the direction of each edge is used to determine whether the region on the other side of that edge is inside or outside the fill.

Paint servers are the next step in the process. For every point that is inside the fill, the SVG rendering software looks up a matching point in the paint server image, and uses that image to determine what color the point should be.

This doesn't mean that SVG paint is *completely* independent of the shape being painted, however. The image created by a SVG paint server is a scalable vector graphic in its own way: it's defined by geometric instructions, and those instructions are executed in a scaled coordinate system. The shape being painted helps set the scale.

Scaling Paint Servers

The coordinate system used to scale a pattern or a gradient, like all coordinate systems in SVG, is defined by width, height, an origin point, and a scale (i.e., the size of a px user unit). There are two options for how that coordinate system is calculated, which are expressed in uncomfortably long mixed-case keyword phrases that you're just going to have to memorize:

userSpaceOnUse

With userSpaceOnUse units, the reference coordinate system for the graphical effect is the **user space**, the main coordinate system used to draw the shape or text that has the paint (or other effect) applied.

Or at least, that's how it's *supposed* to work. Unfortunately, most web browsers (WebKit, Blink, and IE/Edge) treat userSpaceOnUse as "user space on definition" when it comes to percentages: they use the coordinate system of the <svg> that contains the pattern or gradient element, instead of the coordinate system of the shape being painted. They transform the basic units to match the scale and transform in the coordinate system on the shape, but they don't change how percentages translate to px.

To get consistent scaling cross-browser, you need to define the paint server in the same <svg> as the shape it is painting. This severely limits the function of many userSpaceOnUse graphical effects with inline SVG icon systems, where you have many independent <svg> elements and you want your effect to scale to 100% for each SVG.

objectBoundingBox
The reference coordinate system is a square 1 unit wide and 1 unit tall—with its origin in the top-left corner—that is scaled to fit the fill bounding box of the shape being painted—that is, a rectangle defining the extent of the shape's fill region.

The reference coordinate system is a 1×1 square, but the bounding box can be any rectangle. That means the scale may be non-uniform, with height and width scaled to different degrees, and a corresponding distortion to the paint-server image, stretching or squishing the gradient or pattern.

The same two scaling options (bounding box and user space) are used in other graphical effects in SVG, notably filters (Chapter 16), clipping, and masking (Chapter 15). So if you take the time to fully understand how objectBoundingBox and userSpaceOnUse work—and to memorize those uncomfortably long keyword phrases—you'll be more comfortable working with any SVG graphical effect.

The keyword phrases must be capitalized correctly (first letter of subsequent words is uppercase). Because these are attribute values—not attribute names—you can't even rely on the HTML parser to fix it for you.

We've already extensively discussed the user coordinates and the SVG coordinate system (in Chapter 8 and subsequently). But bounding boxes require a closer look.

The Boundaries of the Box

The **bounding box** of a shape is the rectangle that tightly fits around it, in its own coordinate system. The *fill* bounding box is the rectangle that exactly fits the fill region, not counting strokes or other effects. In SVG 1.1, it's the only bounding box that is used.

Figure 12-7 shows a variety of SVG shapes (each with a different fill color) and their bounding boxes (the dashed outlines). Regardless of the shape of the element, the bounding box is always a rectangle; however, if you *transform* the shape, the bounding box transforms with it.

You can find the bounding box of any SVG element by selecting it in JavaScript and running the **getBBox() method**. It returns an object with x, y, width, and height properties.

In Firefox, the element has to be currently displayed for the getBBox() method to work.

In general, if you look at every (*x*,*y*) point in the shape, the bounding box would stretch from the minimum to maximum *x* coordinates and from the minimum to maximum *y* coordinates.

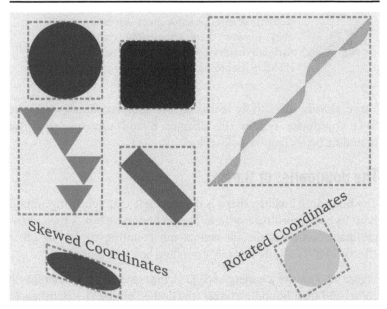

Figure 12-7. Assorted SVG shapes (filled), some transformed, and their bounding boxes (outlines)

Or at least, that's how it's *supposed* to work. Some browsers (WebKit and Blink up to version 62, and Firefox up to version 55 on Mac/Android) use a "fast" calculation for bounding boxes of Bézier curves, which creates a polygon from the points and control points and uses the bounding box of that.

For some shapes, this results in a bounding box that is larger than it should be. And the box that's used for painting may not match the getBBox() result.

The rules are slightly more complicated for <text> elements—and slightly more inconsistent from one browser to another. The key points that are consistent:

- The text bounding box includes the full layout rectangle for each character, even if the drawn glyph only takes up part of that space.

- The bounding box for painting `<tspan>` and `<textPath>` elements is based on the shared bounding box for the entire `<text>`, so that gradients and patterns are continuous from one `<tspan>` to the next.

Because text elements use different bounding boxes than paths do, converting text to paths can cause gradients and patterns to change shape or size. You can reduce the impact by merging the paths for each letter into a single multipart path (depending on the software you use, it might do this already), but it will never be exactly the same.

More Online

For paint servers, one of the most important differences between `objectBoundingBox` and `userSpaceOnUse` is whether the paint looks continuous from one element to the next. But even user-space paint can look discontinuous if you use transformations (or `<use>` with **x** and **y**). And even bounding-box paints can be continuous for text.

Read more—with examples of both effects—in "objectBounding-Box versus userSpaceOnUse":

https://oreillymedia.github.io/Using_SVG/extras/ch12-bounding-boxes.html

---

Great Gradients

Gradients consist of smooth transitions from one color or opacity state to another. We first introduced gradients in Chapter 1, but without dissecting how they are put together. The next few sections look at the elements and attributes that create those gradients, so you can build your own.

Shared Structures

The gradient itself is created by a `<linearGradient>` element or a `<radialGradient>` element. That's the element that has the `id` that you reference from your `fill` (or `stroke`) property. *Inside* the gradient element are `<stop>` elements, which describe the colors.

Here's the simplest structure, with two stops and no extra attributes:

```
<linearGradient id="horizontal" >
    <stop stop-color="gold" offset="0"/>
    <stop stop-color="deepPink" offset="1"/>
</linearGradient>
```

 Technically, you can get simpler than this, and only have *one* color <stop>. But then your gradient isn't a gradient, it's just a solid color paint server, similar to the proposed <solidcolor> element.

The **<stop> elements** are distinguished by three features:

- offset is a number between 0 and 1, or a percentage between 0% and 100%. It defines how far into the gradient this color should occur. It is a regular attribute—it cannot be set with CSS.

  If you don't specify offsets, they will all default to 0, and you won't get a gradient. The <stop> elements must be arranged in order according to their offset values, from smallest to largest; each offset will be adjusted to be no less than the offset of the previous <stop>.

- stop-color sets the color at this offset point in the gradient. It is a presentation attribute, so you can set it with a class or other CSS rule. However, it doesn't inherit (unless you force it by setting stop-color: inherit). A currentColor value would be the color on the <stop> element, *not* on the element you're painting with the gradient.

- stop-opacity (not used in our "simplest" gradient) makes the color stop partially transparent. It is also a presentation attribute, not inherited, and defaults to 1 (opaque).

 For consistent cross-browser results when you're creating partially transparent gradients, use stop-opacity, not semitransparent colors. WebKit completely ignores stop-color transparency. Other browsers disagree on the exact algorithm to use when fading to a semitransparent color.

The <stop> elements in a <radialGradient> work the exact same way. This gradient creates a ring of color, transparent in the middle and the outside, transitioning to opaque in between. It has four stops, each with an offset and a stop-opacity:

```
<radialGradient id="gradient-ring">
    <stop stop-opacity="0" offset="50%" />
    <stop stop-opacity="1" offset="70%" />
    <stop stop-opacity="1" offset="80%" />
    <stop stop-opacity="0" offset="100%" />
</radialGradient>
```

The stop-color isn't specified on any stop, so will default to black. But you could change it with CSS. For example, the following rules would turn that ring to crimson red:

```
#gradient-ring stop { stop-color: crimson; }
```

The <linearGradient> and <radialGradient> elements themselves share common attributes, which we'll describe in the following sections:

• gradientUnits defines whether the gradient is scaled using the objectBoundingBox method (the default) or userSpaceOnUse.

• spreadMethod can be used to create repeating or reflecting gradients (but beware—they aren't currently supported in WebKit/Safari).

• gradientTransform lets you transform the gradient (scale, rotate, skew, or translate) separately from the shape it is painting.

• xlink:href allows you to reference a separate gradient, and have it become a template for this one.

These attributes all have the same options for both types of gradients.

The differences between linear gradients and radial gradients come in how the stop list—which describes a one-dimensional color transition in arbitrary "offset" units—is transformed into the two-dimensional coordinate space of the paint server.

Aligning Linear Gradients

A `<linearGradient>` element creates a gradient defined by the geometry of a line. That line is known as the gradient vector. The stop `offset` values are positioned along that line, and then the colors are extended to infinity on either side.

It therefore might not surprise you that the geometry of a `<linearGradient>` is defined by the same attributes as the geometry of a `<line>` element: **x1, y1, x2, and y2**. Just like with a `<line>`, the four attributes collectively describe the start and end points of the line.

Unlike with a `<line>`, the default value for x2 in a `<linearGradient>` is 100%. The defaults for the other positioning attributes remain 0.

By default, therefore, the line of a `<linearGradient>` runs horizontally left to right across the coordinate space.

That coordinate space is the object bounding box by default. If you set `gradientUnits` to `userSpaceOnUse`, it is the SVG's coordinate system, after any transformations in effect for the shape being painted.

Example 12-3 shows a gradient that uses all four geometric attributes to create a diagonal gradient, but one that doesn't quite reach the opposite corners of the bounding box. Figure 12-8 shows the result, twice: once as defined, and the second time with the vector line and the offsets marked out in crimson-red.

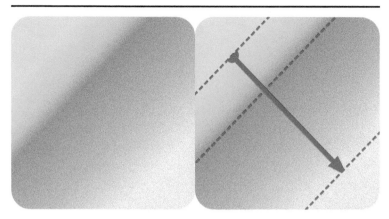

Figure 12-8. A rounded square filled with a diagonal linear gradient, and the same square with the gradient's line vector and stop offsets marked on it

Example 12-3. Drawing a simple linear gradient

```
<svg xmlns="http://www.w3.org/2000/svg" xml:lang="en"
     width="200px" height="200px" viewBox="0 0 200 200">
    <title>Simple Linear Gradient</title>
    <linearGradient id="green-gradient"
                    x1="20%" y1="20%" x2="80%" y2="80%">
        <stop stop-color="mediumSpringGreen" offset="0"/>
        <stop stop-color="forestGreen" offset="0.3"/>
        <stop stop-color="lightBlue" offset="1"/>
    </linearGradient>
    <rect width="100%" height="100%" ry="10%"
          fill="url(#green-gradient)" />
</svg>
```

The shapes in Figure 12-8 have a square bounding box, so the object bounding-box units don't do anything strange to the coordinate system.

In contrast, Figure 12-9 shows how the same gradient is stretched to fit a rectangle that is twice as wide as it is tall. Note how the uneven scale changes the angles of the gradient: they still match the diagonals of the box, even though those diagonals are no longer at right angles to each other.

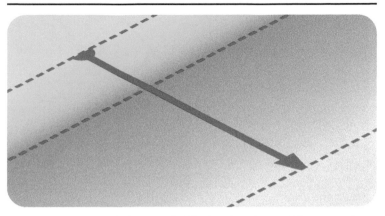

Figure 12-9. A rounded rectangle filled with a diagonal linear gradient, with the line vector and stop offsets marked on it

The corners of the shapes in Figures 12-8 and 12-9, beyond the ends of the gradient vector, are filled with solid colors matching the first and last `<stop>`. There are actually two ways to achieve this effect:

- Make the gradient vector line shorter than the bounding box (as in this example).
- Inset the `offset` values so they don't extend all the way from 0 to 1.

> To create a solid-colored region in the *middle* of a gradient, you need to have two subsequent `<stop>` elements with the same color and opacity. This is a case where it is helpful to set `stop-color` and `stop-opacity` values with a `class`— or even with CSS variables!

The difference between insetting the offsets and insetting the ends of the vector is only revealed when you change the `spreadMethod`. The **spreadMethod attribute** defines how the browser fills in the space beyond the ends of the gradient vector. The default value is `pad`, which pads the space with the nearest `<stop>` value. The other options are `repeat` and `reflect`.

WebKit (as of Safari 10.12) does not support reflecting and repeating SVG gradients. Firefox also lost support for a while when changing graphics libraries—but they've been fine since version 33, in 2015.

Example 12-4 uses a repeating user-space gradient to create gradient stripes. The basic gradient extends from x1=-20 to x2=+20, relative to the user-space coordinate system. In other words, it's a horizontal vector, 40px wide, centered on the origin. Since the SVG has a centered coordinate system, that means the gradient is centered in the graphic, too.

Figure 12-10 shows the result as defined, and with the vector and stops marked on it. The bright cyan annotations in the center are the positions defined by the attributes; the repeats are marked in peachy-yellow.

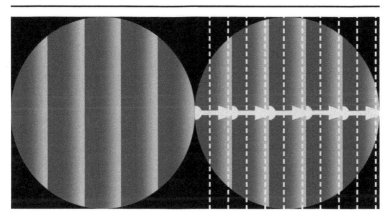

Figure 12-10. A repeating linear gradient in a circle, and the same shape with the gradient's line vector and stop offsets marked on it

Example 12-4. Drawing a repeating linear gradient

```
<svg xmlns="http://www.w3.org/2000/svg" xml:lang="en"
     xmlns:xlink="http://www.w3.org/1999/xlink"
     width="200px" height="200px" viewBox="-100 -100 200 200">
  <title>Repeating Linear Gradient</title>
  <linearGradient id="purple-stripes"
                  gradientUnits="userSpaceOnUse"
                  x1="-20" x2="+20" spreadMethod="repeat">
```

```
    <stop stop-color="purple" offset="0.4"/>
    <stop stop-color="plum" offset="0.9"/>
  </linearGradient>
  <circle r="50%" fill="url(#purple-stripes)" />
</svg>
```

The offset values in Example 12-4 are 0.4 and 0.9, not 0 and 1. This creates solid bands of color at the edge of each stripe, from the start of the vector (the x1 position) to the first <stop>, and then from the second, final <stop> to the end of the vector (x2 position). The stripe repeat length is defined entirely by the x1 and x2 attributes, and isn't affected by the offsets.

Figure 12-11 shows the result if the code in Example 12-4 was modified to change spreadMethod to reflect (instead of repeat). The annotated version shows how we created the very different pattern from the same basic stripe unit, by flipping it back to front in each repetition.

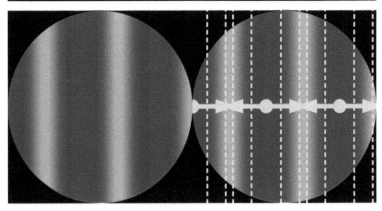

Figure 12-11. A reflecting linear gradient in a circle, and the same shape with the gradient's line vector and stop offsets marked on it

If you wanted to include both the repeating and the reflecting gradients in the same graphic, there's an easy way to reduce your code. One gradient element can cross-reference another with an `xlink:href` attribute.

As with all other `xlink:href` attributes, most modern browsers support simple `href`, but keep using `xlink` for Safari and older versions of other browsers.

Gradient cross-references to other files are only supported in Firefox and MS Edge.

When you use `xlink:href` on gradients, the referenced gradient becomes a template. All gradient-related attributes from the referenced element are used as defaults for the new gradient. They will be used unless the new gradient sets its own value for that attribute.

If the new gradient doesn't have any `<stop>` elements, it uses the template gradient's stops.

You can even create a cross-reference from a `<linearGradient>` to a `<radialGradient>`, and vice versa: the shared attributes and the stops will be copied, while other geometric attributes will have their normal defaults.

Using cross-references, you could define the reflecting gradient as follows:

```
<linearGradient id="purple-reflections"
                spreadMethod="reflect"
                xlink:href="#purple-stripes" />
```

The `<stop>` elements (including their colors and offsets) and the geometric attributes (`gradientUnits`, `x1`, and `x2`) are all copied from the original gradient with id `purple-stripes`. The new gradient then changes the `spreadMethod`.

Transforming Gradients

The x1, y1, x2, and y2 attributes aren't your only options for switching from simple horizontal gradients. There's another way you can reposition a gradient element: the **gradientTransform attribute**. It transforms the entire canvas on which the gradient is drawn, after it has been sized and scaled according to the **gradientUnits**, but before it is actually used to paint the shape.

A **gradientTransform** was used in the shiny metallic gradient for the frame of the stoplight from Chapter 1. The same gradient code was reused for the scissors in Figure 12-6 in this chapter. Both are shown as close-up detail views in Figure 12-12. The gradient markup is as follows:

```
<linearGradient id="metal" spreadMethod="repeat"
                gradientTransform="scale(0.7) rotate(75)">
    <stop stop-color="#808080" offset="0"/>
    <stop stop-color="#404040" offset="0.25"/>
    <stop stop-color="#C0C0C0" offset="0.35"/>
    <stop stop-color="#808080" offset="0.5"/>
    <stop stop-color="#E0E0E0" offset="0.7"/>
    <stop stop-color="#606060" offset="0.75"/>
    <stop stop-color="#A0A0A0" offset="0.9"/>
    <stop stop-color="#808080" offset="1"/>
</linearGradient>
```

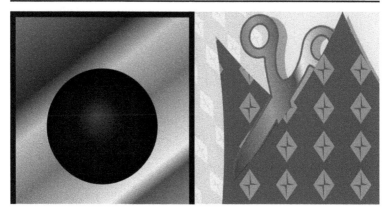

Figure 12-12. Two different shapes, in two different drawings, using the same linear gradient

For the gradient, the eight stops, in oscillating shades of gray, are arranged along the default gradient line, from left to right across the bounding box. The transform takes that pattern, shrinks it slightly, than rotates it 75° clockwise to create a diagonal gradient. The rotation is applied in the distorted bounding-box units, so it's not actually 75°, and the gradient gets stretched out as it rotates, but you still end up with a diagonal gradient that starts in the top-left corner of the bounding box and changes color as you move down and to the right.

The scissors icon was itself drawn with a 100° rotational transform. That transformation applies to the fill gradient, too, rotating the final gradient angle along with the shape (which actually is a <text> ✂</text>).

A `gradientTransform` on a `<linearGradient>` cannot create any unique shapes: no matter how you transform the canvas, the end result is still a linear gradient. However, for many authors, thinking in transforms is easier than dealing with multiple attributes. And you can combine them, of course, adding a transform to slightly tweak an existing gradient.

 According to the CSS Transforms module, you should be able to use the CSS `transform` property to replace a `gradientTransform` attribute. However, that is not supported in browsers yet.

According to the spec, 3D transforms on gradients (and also patterns) should be ignored.

On a <radialGradient>, gradientTransform is even more powerful: skew transformations and nonuniform scales create unique appearances that you cannot create with the basic attributes. Similarly, the patternTransform attribute on the <pattern> element can be used to great effect.

Radiating Radial Gradients

While <linearGradient> elements base their geometry on a <line>, **<radialGradient> elements** use a <circle>. So a <radialGradient> accepts **r, cx, and cy attributes** that define a sizing circle.

Unlike in a <circle> element, the defaults for r, cx, and cy in a <radialGradient> are all 50%.

In object bounding-box units, that means the default circle fits neatly in the box, touching all four sides. With user-space units, the coordinate system might not be square, so the sizing can get complicated: the rules for percentages in r are the same as for <circle>.

The circle defined by the r, cx, and cy attributes defines the position of the <stop> with offset of 1 or 100%. The zero offset is positioned at the **focal point** of the gradient; by default, the focal point matches the center of the circle. The stop offsets are positioned along rays from the focal point to the sizing circle, in all directions. This means that each <stop> becomes a circle.

As we mentioned in "Scaling Paint Servers" on page 437, object bounding-box units can distort the shape of gradients. That means that the circles in an SVG radial gradient can get stretched into ellipses. They can also be stretched or skewed by a gradientTransform.

Example 12-5 uses an r value of 0.2 (equal to 20%, in the scaled object bounding-box units) to create a small radial pattern in the center of the shape, and then uses spreadMethod="repeat" to extend that pattern to fill the rest of the shape. Figure 12-13 shows the result, once as defined and once with geometric annotations. Again, the repeats are annotated in a different color.

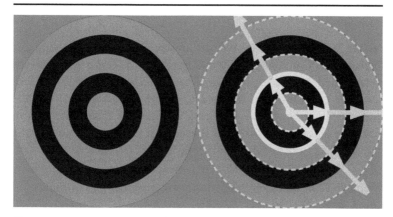

Figure 12-13. A repeating radial gradient with sharp stops, and the same shape with sample rays and the stop offsets marked on it

Example 12-5. Controlling the size of a radial gradient to generate repeated rings

```
<svg xmlns="http://www.w3.org/2000/svg" xml:lang="en"
     xmlns:xlink="http://www.w3.org/1999/xlink"
     width="200px" height="200px" viewBox="-100 -100 200 200">
    <title>Bulls-eye Repeating Radial Gradient</title>
    <radialGradient id="bullseye"
                    spreadMethod="repeat" r="0.2">
        <stop stop-color="tomato" offset="50%"/>
        <stop stop-color="#222" offset="50%"/>
    </radialGradient>
    <circle r="50%" fill="url(#bullseye)" />
</svg>
```

The code in Example 12-5 takes advantage of the fact that using two consecutive <stop> elements with the same offset creates a sharp color change. It also takes advantage of the fact that the first and last <stop> are extended to fill up the entire offset distance, from 0 to 1, and that a repeating spreadMethod can create sharp color changes of its own.

Sharp gradient color transitions like these can look pixelated in many browsers. Gradient rendering code was built for, well, gradients—not stripes or rings. You can smooth the transitions slightly by setting offsets that are a couple pixels apart, or you can redesign your drawing to use shapes instead of gradients, and let the browser anti-alias the edges for you.

As we mentioned earlier, WebKit browsers don't currently support repeating SVG gradients. So they'd just show the center red bull's eye surrounded by black. To make the full concentric-circle pattern available cross-browser, we need to define a gradient that fills the full bounding box, with each ring specified as a separate pair of <stop> elements, one for the inside edge of the ring and one for the outside. The (much less elegant) code is given in Example 12-6.

Example 12-6. Repeating gradient stops to generate rings, without using spreadMethod

```
<svg xmlns="http://www.w3.org/2000/svg" xml:lang="en"
    xmlns:xlink="http://www.w3.org/1999/xlink"
    width="200px" height="200px" viewBox="-100 -100 200 200">
    <title>WebKit-friendly Bulls-eye Gradient</title>
    <style>
        stop.A { stop-color: tomato; }
        stop.B { stop-color: #222; }
    </style>
    <radialGradient id="bullseye" r="0.6">
        <stop class="A" offset="0.1667"/>
        <stop class="B" />
        <stop class="B" offset="0.3333"/>
        <stop class="A" />
        <stop class="A" offset="0.5"/>
        <stop class="B" />
        <stop class="B" offset="0.6667"/>
        <stop class="A" />
        <stop class="A" offset="0.8333"/>
        <stop class="B" />
    </radialGradient>
    <circle r="50%" fill="url(#bullseye)" />
</svg>
```

The radius is now three times as large as before (0.6, or 60% of the bounding box, so the total gradient width is 120% of the box width) and the stop offsets are at multiples of ⅙.

To make the code *slightly* easier to maintain, the `<stop>` elements have classes to distinguish the two colors, so the color values themselves only have to be defined once, in the CSS rules.

Furthermore, the `offset` values have been simplified to take advantage of the fact that a stop offset is never less than the previous offset. When we omit the `offset` on the second `<stop>` at each color change, it defaults to 0 and then will be automatically adjusted to match the previous stop and create a sharp transition, without our having to explicitly repeat the previous value.

 Default `offset` values and `stop-color` set with CSS3 selectors may not be supported in nonbrowser SVG software.

Example 12-6 doesn't work in Inkscape (0.91), for example. In browsers, it also fails in old Android (e.g., version 4.0). You could improve support by repeating the `stop-color` values on every `<stop>` element.

The end result still looks identical to Figure 12-13, in the browsers that rendered Figure 12-13 correctly.

Switching Focus

A `<radialGradient>` has two additional geometric attributes: `fx` and `fy`. These define the focal point of the gradient. If either attribute is unspecified, the value automatically matches `cx` or `cy`, respectively.

Off-center focal points allow radial gradients to go beyond perfect geometric symmetry and provide a sense of three-dimensionality. Although we didn't discuss it at the time, we used this technique to make the stoplights appear three-dimensional in Example 1-7 in Chapter 1. The markup for one of those stoplight gradients is repeated here, including the off-center `fx` and `fy` values:

```
<radialGradient id="green-light-on" fx="0.45" fy="0.4">
    <stop stop-color="#88FF00" offset="0.1"/>
    <stop stop-color="forestGreen" offset="0.7"/>
    <stop stop-color="darkGreen" offset="1.0"/>
</radialGradient>
```

To remind you what that looked like, Figure 1-4 from Chapter 1 is redrawn here as Figure 12-14.

Figure 12-14. Stoplight with gradient fills

Off-center focal points create particularly interesting effects in repeated or reflected gradients. The repetitions as measured in each direction are spaced at the same distance as the spacing between the focal point and that circle in that direction. This means that the repetitions bunch together at one side and spread out in another.

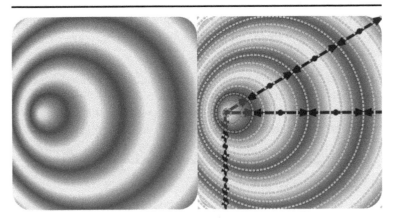

Figure 12-15. A reflecting, off-center radial gradient, and the same shape with the stop offsets and sample rays marked on it

Example 12-7 gives the code for an off-center repeating gradient, shown in Figure 12-15.

Example 12-7. Generating asymmetrical patterns with fx and fy in a reflected radial gradient

```
<svg xmlns="http://www.w3.org/2000/svg" xml:lang="en"
    xmlns:xlink="http://www.w3.org/1999/xlink"
    width="200px" height="200px" viewBox="0 0 200 200">
    <title>Asymmetrical Reflected Radial Gradient</title>
    <radialGradient id="ripples" spreadMethod="reflect"
                    cx="20%" cy="50%" r="10%"
                    fx="15%" >
        <stop stop-color="lightBlue" offset="0.2"/>
        <stop stop-color="lightSlateGray" offset="0.6"/>
        <stop stop-color="darkSlateBlue" offset="1"/>
    </radialGradient>
    <rect width="100%" height="100%" rx="10%"
        fill="url(#ripples)" />
</svg>
```

Note that the offsets always cross each ray at the same proportion (offset distance) along the repeat. However, the repeat distance is different in each direction, matching the distance from the focal point to the original circle in that direction.

Unfortunately, there is no easy way to recreate the asymmetrical-repetition effect in browsers that don't support `spreadMethod`.

CSS Versus SVG
CSS Gradients

The main difference between gradients in CSS and SVG is syntax. SVG gradients are made from markup. CSS gradients are defined as functions that you include in the CSS value, anywhere you could include an image. The stop colors and their offsets are given as parameters, after any geometric parameters:

```
background-image: linear-gradient(to left top,
                                  red 0%, lightBlue 80%);
list-style-image: radial-gradient(lavender 0,
                                  indigo 0.5em);
```

You currently cannot use CSS gradients in SVG fill and stroke. However, as described earlier in the chapter, this would be supported by the new CSS Fill and Stroke module.

There are a number of more subtle differences between SVG and CSS gradients. For starters, the default direction of a CSS linear gradient is vertical, not horizontal. Other differences mean that certain effects are easier to do in one syntax or the other.

Major benefits of the CSS syntax:

- You can apply the same gradient to many elements with a class, but then transition or animate specific instances with another class or pseudoclass. In contrast, to animate SVG gradients, you need to animate the shared markup elements.

- You can use CSS to animate or transition the gradient's geometry, not just its color and opacity.

- For linear gradients, you can set the geometry with keywords (like **to left top**) or with exact angles (**45deg**), without any confusion from object bounding-box units causing nonuniform scaling.

- For radial gradients, you can explicitly set **circle** or **ellipse** geometry, and can size them using keywords (e.g., **closest-side**, **farthest-corner**), percentages (of the image size), or absolute lengths.

- You can mix absolute and relative geometry in the same gradient: for example, position the center of a radial gradient using percentages—which are relative to the image size—but set the radius with absolute units.

- You don't have to specify stop offsets explicitly: if you leave them out, the browser will automatically distribute the stops evenly in the space available.

- Repeating gradients are supported in all recent major browsers (even WebKit).

Benefits of the SVG syntax:

- Reflecting gradient patterns can be created with a single attribute. For CSS gradients, you need to create a reflecting pattern yourself, and then use the repeating gradient functions.

- For radial gradients, you can set the focal point to be off-center. (This had been proposed for CSS, but isn't currently in the CSS Images level 4 spec.)

- With user-space gradients, you can position the gradient geometry relative to the **viewBox** container instead of relative to the size of this particular element, and therefore make gradients that continue from one element to the next.

- The initial and final stop offsets don't need to completely fill the geometry of the gradient that is used to calculate repeats.

- You can have a gradient with a single stop, to create a solid-color layer.

- You can control **stop-color** and **stop-opacity** separately.

- You can use classes to coordinate stop colors in multiple different gradients, or use **xlink:href** cross-references to copy an entire set of stops to a gradient with different geometry. For CSS gradients, you need to use CSS variables to create the same coordination, which means limited support in older browsers.

- You can use transforms to modify the gradient, independently from the element it is used on.

- Support in most browsers goes back further than for CSS gradients, at least for nonrepeating gradients.

Using CSS gradients, we can adapt the CSS stoplight from Example 3-3 (in Chapter 3) to recreate the SVG gradient stoplight (Figure 12-14).

We could recreate the slanted metal gradient on the stoplight frame—which we positioned and sized using **gradientTransform** when drawing it with SVG in Example 1-7—by adjusting the offsets and angle of a CSS **repeating-linear-gradient** function. The following additional style rule creates the effect:

```
.stoplight-frame {
    background-color: silver;
    background: repeating-linear-gradient(-25deg,
        #808080 0, #404040 12%, #C0C0C0 17%,
        #808080 25%, #E0E0E0 35%, #606060 38%,
        #A0A0A0 45%, #808080 50%);
}
```

For the radial gradients, some faking is required.

The original SVG gradients used **fx** and **fy** to create off-center focal points, which are not supported in CSS. To create a similar off-center effect, we can layer two different CSS gradients on each light element, one for the main color transition and one for the off-center highlight. For example, the following code would create off and on versions of the red light:

```
.stoplight-light {
    background-size: 40% 40%, cover;
    background-repeat: no-repeat;
    background-position: 40% 30%, center;
}
.stoplight-light.red {
    top: 30px;
    background-color: #880000;
    background-image: radial-gradient(closest-side,
                      maroon 10%, transparent),
                      radial-gradient(closest-side,
                      maroon, #220000 70%, black);
}
.stoplight-light.red.on {
    background-color: red;
    background-image: radial-gradient(closest-side,
                      orange 10%, transparent),
                      radial-gradient(closest-side,
                      red 80%, brown);
}
```

Each light will always have two background layers: the highlight gradient, which is smaller and off-center, and then the main gradient that completely fills the shape. The highlight gradient is listed first, so it will be drawn on top of the image stack. It transitions from the highlight color to transparent, letting the other gradient show through at the edges. All the gradients are sized via the **closest-side** keyword, so they just fit into the circle we created by radiusing the corners of the layout box.

 For better results on older browsers, the `transparent` keyword used in the gradients could be replaced with an `rgba()` function that matched the highlight color; otherwise, colors may shift to black as they shift to transparent.

For both the **on** and **off** states, a fallback **background-color** is set in case gradients are not supported by the browser.

The complete image looks as follows:

CSS Images Module Level 4 introduces a few new syntax options for CSS gradients, including a shorthand for repeated stops (solid-color sections), and a "color hint" that allows you to shift the mid-point of a color transition to one side or the other. Color hints are supported in all of the latest browsers—but make sure you use fallbacks for older browsers.

Level 4 also adds `conic-gradient()` and `repeating-conic-gradient()` functions. A conic gradient is one in which colors stay constant along a ray extending from a central point, and the colors change as the angle of the ray changes, wrapping around that central point. If you added sharp color changes to a conic gradient, it would look like a pie chart.

Patterns of Possibility

The final paint server you can use to `fill` (or `stroke`) in SVG 1.1 is the **`<pattern>` element**. In simplest terms, a `<pattern>` defines a rectangle, or **tile**, of SVG content. The tile is then repeated in rows and columns, as many times as necessary to paint the shape.

But a `<pattern>`, in practice, is far from simple.

A `<pattern>` can contain any SVG graphics: solid-colored shapes, shapes filled with gradients, shapes filled with other patterns, text (providing it is purely decorative), or embedded images. So the possibilities are as open-ended as SVG itself.

But <pattern> elements are also complex in less inspiring ways. The options for scaling the pattern tiles are so open-ended that they are often confusing. And there are a few unfortunate details in the specifications—and bugs in the implementations—which introduce obstacles for many designs.

The next few sections outline some of the most common structures for SVG patterns.

All the Units to Use

A <pattern>, like a gradient, can be scaled to the object bounding box or to the user-space coordinate system. However, it is more complicated than that. You have *two* attributes to set the scale: patternUnits and patternContentUnits.

The **patternUnits attribute** sets the scale you use for defining the size and position of the initial pattern tile. In other words, it controls the attributes on the <pattern> itself. It defaults to objectBoundingBox units.

The pattern tile attributes affected by patternUnits are **x, y, width, and height**. Set these attributes to percentages or numbers from 0–1 for objectBoundingBox units, or use any SVG lengths if you change patternUnits to userSpaceOnUse.

The **patternContentUnits attribute** sets the scale of the drawing content *inside* the <pattern> element. It defaults to userSpaceOnUse units. You can change it to objectBoundingBox units, *or* you can use a viewBox attribute to define your own scale for each pattern tile. If a viewBox is provided, patternContentUnits has no effect.

Avoid percentages in the pattern contents when using a viewBox or objectBoundingBox content units—they are not relative to the tile size, the viewBox, *or* the bounding box.

Instead, the definition of 100% from the user-space coordinate system is scaled up proportional to the scaling effect on all other units—which is not particularly useful.

You almost never want the default mixed-unit combination of patternUnits and patternContentUnits. You will usually do one of the following:

- Set patternContentUnits="objectBoundingBox" to create a fully scalable pattern that divides the box into an even number of tiles, regardless of box size. Or doesn't divide it: you can create single-tile pattern instead, which fills the shape with a non-repeating graphic.

- Set a viewBox to create a fully scalable pattern with aspect-ratio control and/or easier reuse of content that has been drawn at a scale other than 0–1.

- Set patternUnits="userSpaceOnUse" to create a wallpaper-style fixed-size pattern, where the size of the pattern tiles is consistent regardless of the size of the shape being painted.

- Set patternUnits="userSpaceOnUse" *and* set a viewBox to create a fixed-size pattern (or one scaled to the SVG dimensions, using percentages) with aspect-ratio control or rescaling.

Older versions of Firefox did not handle viewBox in patterns correctly, especially in combination with a patternUnits value of objectBoundingBox (which is the default). It's been fixed since version 40 (mid-2015).

Internet Explorer and MS Edge (up to at least EdgeHTML 15) only apply the *scaling* aspect of viewBox values, not the translation aspect.

To ensure support in Microsoft browsers, only use viewBox values where the first two numbers are zero. To shift the origin of the pattern contents, use a <g> inside the pattern with a translate transformation.

If it weren't for these bugs and the issue with percentages, viewBox patterns would probably be the preferred approach in most cases. As it is, you need to weigh the convenience of defining your own local coordinate system against the bother of working around the bugs.

One final warning about working with patterns: the `<pattern>` contents will always be clipped to the tile. Not only is the default value of `overflow` set to `hidden` for patterns, but no web browser currently supports `visible` overflow. The original SVG specs weren't clear about how visible overflow should work, and so far there hasn't been consensus support from browsers to implement it.

Dividing the Box

In Chapter 5, we drew a checkerboard using a script to generate each individual square (Example 5-3). At the time, however, we noted that a `<pattern>` could be used to generate the same effect if you did not need each square to be an independent, interactive element.

Boards for chess and checkers come in many different sizes, but they always have the same number of squares: eight alternating black and white squares in each row and column. This therefore makes it a perfect example of a pattern that scales to fit the object bounding box. The repeating pattern is not a fixed size relative to the SVG coordinate system, but relative to the size of the board.

To use `objectBoundingBox` units for the pattern contents, we need to convert all the measurements to decimal fractions of the bounding-box width and height. As mentioned in the last section, percentages don't work. Instead of 25%, use 0.25.

Example 12-8 creates the pattern, and then uses it to draw two boards of different sizes, as shown in Figure 12-16.

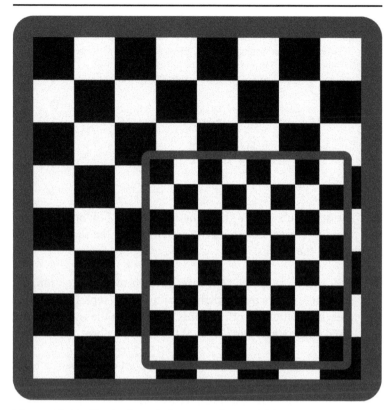

Figure 12-16. Checkerboards drawn with a scalable pattern

Example 12-8. Drawing a checkerboard with a pattern

```
<svg xmlns="http://www.w3.org/2000/svg" xml:lang="en"
     height="9in" width="9in" viewBox="0 0 864 864">
    <title>Checkerboard from a Pattern</title>
    <style type="text/css">
        .board { fill: saddleBrown; }
        .white { fill: linen; }
        .black { fill: #222; }
        .squares { fill: url(#checks); }                    ❶
    </style>
    <pattern id="checks" width="25%" height="25%"
             patternContentUnits="objectBoundingBox">        ❷
        <rect class="white" width="0.25" height="0.25" />    ❸
        <rect class="black" width="0.125" height="0.125" />
        <rect class="black" x="0.125" y="0.125"
              width="0.125" height="0.125" />                ❹
```

```
</pattern>

<g>                                                          ❺
    <rect class="board" width="9in" height="9in" rx="0.5in" />
    <rect class="squares"
          x="0.5in" y="0.5in" width="8in" height="8in" />
</g>
<g>                                                          ❻
    <rect class="board" x="8cm" y="8cm"
          width="13cm" height="13cm" rx="0.5cm" />
    <rect class="squares"
          x="8.5cm" y="8.5cm" width="12cm" height="12cm" />
</g>
</svg>
```

❶ The styles are mostly the same as Example 5-3; an additional class has been added to set the pattern fill on the shape that will hold all the checks.

❷ Although there are eight squares in each row and column, the alternating colors means that the pattern only repeats four times in each direction. In other words, the pattern tile is one-quarter (25%) of the width and height of the bounding box.

❸ Within each pattern tile, we draw a 2×2 set of alternating black and white squares. To reduce the number of elements, the white squares are drawn as a single background <rect> filling up the entire pattern tile.

❹ The two black squares are then drawn on top. They are each 12.5% of the board's width and height, or 0.125 in the scaled object bounding-box coordinates.

❺ The full-size board is drawn with two elements: one for the border and one for the checkerboard pattern.

❻ The second board uses the same structure, but everything is smaller—and measured in metric units.

When using object bounding-box units like this, keep in mind the lessons from "Scaling Paint Servers" on page 437 about the distorting effect of the coordinate system. If the box is not square, the coordinate system will be nonuniform with horizontal and vertical units of different lengths. Circles, text, and images will all be stretched, and rotational angles will be uneven. Also note that *every-*

thing is scaled according to the new units, including stroke widths and font size.

In addition to creating scale-to-fit repeating patterns, object bounding-box units are useful for creating a pattern that fills the entire shape without repeating.

Picture Perfect

By creating a `<pattern>` tile that is too large to repeat, you can remove the "pattern" appearance and create a custom-designed paint server. Since the `<pattern>` can contain any SVG graphics, you can turn any SVG image into paint for other shapes. With the addition of the `<image>` element, you can use any other image type, too.

To create a nonrepeating pattern tile, set the `width` and `height` on the `<pattern>` element to 100%. If using `userSpaceOnUse` units, also set `x` and `y` on the `<pattern>` to match the first two numbers of the SVG's `viewBox`, so that your tile perfectly fills the coordinate system.

The `width` and `height` attributes are still required: they default to 0. A pattern tile with zero width or height is invalid. If you specified a fallback `fill` color, it will be used instead.

You can use a single-tile pattern to fill an SVG element with a photograph or other raster image file, by using an `<image>` element as the content of the `<pattern>`.

As mentioned earlier in the chapter, the CSS Fill and Stroke module will make filling an SVG element with a photograph much easier—you could just use a `url()` reference to the image file.

Until that's supported in browsers, `<pattern>` provides the workaround.

For image fills, you usually don't want the image to be stretched or squished to fit the shape. A `viewBox` pattern, with aspect-ratio control, is preferred. A slice scaling mode ensures that the image completely covers the shape.

Example 12-9 uses a photograph (of clouds over the flat expanse of Lake Ontario) to fill the club shape from our card-suit set. Figure 12-17 shows the result.

Figure 12-17. An SVG shape filled with a photograph

Example 12-9. Using a <pattern> to create a photographic fill

```
<svg xmlns="http://www.w3.org/2000/svg" xml:lang="en"
     xmlns:xlink="http://www.w3.org/1999/xlink"
     width="200px" height="200px" viewBox="0 0 200 200">
    <title>Image Fill using a Pattern</title>
    <pattern id="image-fill" width="1" height="1"
             viewBox="0 0 800 600"
             preserveAspectRatio="xMidYMid slice">    ❶
        <image width="800" height="600"
               xlink:href="lake-ontario.jpg" />          ❷
    </pattern>
    <symbol viewBox="0 0 20 20" id="club"
            style="overflow: visible">
        <title>Club</title>                              ❸
        <path d="M9,15.5A5,5 0 1 1 5.5, 7.5
                 A5,5 0 1 1 14.5, 7.5A5,5 0 1 1 11, 15.5
                 Q11,20 13,20H7Q9,20 9,15.5Z" />
    </symbol>
    <use xlink:href="#club" fill="url(#image-fill)" />  ❹
</svg>
```

❶ The pattern has width and height of 1, equivalent to 100% in object bounding-box units. The viewBox is based on the actual dimensions of the JPEG image file: 800×600. A slice option for preserveAspectRatio ensures that the rectangular photograph will completely cover the shape we're painting.

❷ The JPEG's dimensions need to be repeated in the width and height of the <image> element (since most browsers don't yet support the SVG 2 autosize option). Since the <image> size is set explicitly, we don't need to worry about preserving aspect ratio at this step.

❸ The <symbol> code is directly copied from the sprite file created for Example 10-2 in Chapter 10. The visible overflow won't have an effect in this example, but it will when we use this pattern again with stroked symbols, in Chapter 13.

❹ Because it is a <symbol>, and there are no dimensions on the <use> element, the copy will scale to fit the current SVG's dimensions. A fill presentation attribute assigns the image pattern.

Because the SVG code in Example 12-9 loads an external image file, it would not work if the SVG itself were embedded as an image. Inline SVG or embedded objects only.

To ensure cross-browser support, we copies the <symbol> code directly into the file, instead of referencing the sprite file from Chapter 10 in the <use> element.

The lack of support includes some recent versions of Chrome, which support external <use> references but don't apply paint servers to them.

Since there are no limits to how many <image> elements you can include in your <pattern>, you can use this technique to mimic layered fills. And the layers don't have to be external images: they could be <rect> elements filled with other patterns or gradients. A

<pattern> is therefore also the workaround for layered fills, until browsers support layers set directly in the fill property.

Patterned Prints

The <pattern> designs we've worked with so far aren't exactly what most people think of when they think of patterned fill: fixed-sized patterns that are tiled as many times as necessary to fill up a shape. In this sort of pattern, large shapes get more repeats than small shapes, but the size of the pattern tile doesn't change.

In other words: user-space patterns.

To create such a pattern, you need patternUnits to be userSpaceOnUse, and you need to set the width and height in absolute values (not percentages).

Pattern contents could also be absolute—with the default userSpaceOnUse value for patternContentUnits—or they can be scaled to fit within the pattern tile, with a viewBox.

Example 12-10 uses the viewBox approach to turn our diamond icon (from Chapter 6) into a wallpaper pattern (which we've already seen in figures in this chapter). The pattern is then used to fill a copy of our spade icon. To avoid Chrome bugs with external <use> references, the markup for both card-suit icons has been copied directly into the new file.

A variation on the pattern emphasizes the tile boundaries, and is created by an xlink:href reference to the first. As with gradients, the cross-reference makes one pattern a template for the other. All geometric attributes from the first pattern become defaults for the second.

 If the second pattern *didn't* have any contents, the contents from the template pattern would have been duplicated as part of the template, the same as for the stops of a gradient template.

Figure 12-18 shows the end result of both patterns.

Figure 12-18. A pattern made from a card-suit symbol, used to fill a different suit's symbol

Example 12-10. Defining a classic, fixed-size <pattern> using predefined symbols

```
<svg xmlns="http://www.w3.org/2000/svg" xml:lang="en"
     xmlns:xlink="http://www.w3.org/1999/xlink"
     width="400px" height="200px" viewBox="0 0 400 200">
   <title>userSpaceOnUse Patterns, with re-used symbols</title>
   <pattern id="wallpaper" patternUnits="userSpaceOnUse"
            width="2" height="2" viewBox="0 0 24 24">      ❶
      <rect fill="indigo"
            width="24" height="24" />                      ❷
      <path id="pink-diamond"
            d="M3,10L10,0 17,10 10,20Z
               M9,11L10,18V10H15L11,9 10,2V10H5Z"
            fill="hotPink" transform="translate(2,2)"/>
   </pattern>
   <pattern id="wallpaper2" xlink:href="#wallpaper">       ❸
      <rect fill="indigo" stroke="gold" stroke-width="2"
            x="0" y="0" width="24" height="24" />           ❹
      <use xlink:href="#pink-diamond" />                    ❺
   </pattern>
   <symbol viewBox="0 0 20 20" id="spade"
           style="overflow: visible">
      <title>Spade</title>
      <path d="M9,15C9,20 0,21 0,16S6,9 10,0C14,9 20,11 20,16
               S11,20 11,15Q11,20 13,20H7Q9,20 9,15Z" />
   </symbol>                                                ❻
   <use fill="url(#wallpaper)" xlink:href="#spade" width="200"/>
   <use fill="url(#wallpaper2)" xlink:href="#spade"
```

```
           x="200" width="200" />
</svg>
```

❶   The basic pattern defines 2×2 tiles in the user-space coordinate system, and then defines a 24×24 `viewBox` scale for the contents of each tile, slightly larger than the 20×20 we used when defining our club-suit icons.

❷   The contents consist of an indigo `<rect>` that fills the entire tile, and then a `<path>` copy of the diamond icon, filled in pink. A `transform` attribute on the `<path>` centers it within the tile.

❸   The second `<pattern>` cross-references the first, and does not change any of the geometric attributes.

❹   The contents, however, are altered for the second pattern, to add a gold stroke to the backdrop `<rect>`. The strokes will extend outside the pattern tile and be clipped by the hidden overflow, but the strokes on adjacent tiles will appear to be continuous.

❺   Once we change some of the pattern contents, we have to replace it all. We keep the code DRY by reusing the styled diamond from the previous pattern.

❻   The spade is defined as a `<symbol>`, and then reused twice, filled with each pattern. The `width` and `x` attributes scale and position the `<use>` elements within the main SVG coordinate system.

There are a few complications of patterns and nested coordinate systems hidden in the code in Example 12-10:

- The pattern is applied to the shape in the `<symbol>` element's coordinate system used for drawing the spade `<path>`, not in the main SVG's coordinate system used for scaling the `<use>` elements. The card-suit symbols are defined as being 20px wide and tall, so the 2×2 pattern tiles mean 10 columns of tiles across the width of the spade, even though each spade is drawn 200px wide in the final graphic.

- The `width` and `height` attributes on the `<rect>` inside the pattern contents are set in user units, not as 100%, even though we want the rectangle to completely fill the tile's `viewBox`. A 100% width and height would be interpreted as 100% of the outer

SVG's width and height (400×200px), scaled up according to the local definition of a px. That would make the rectangle many times the size of the pattern tile. For the solid backdrop, the difference would not be obvious—the overflow would still be clipped—but the stroked rectangle would lose half of its strokes.

 The problem with percentages also applies to the default 100% width and height of a reused symbol. For a `<use>` that copies a `<symbol>` inside a `<pattern>`, always include width and height attributes.

When you have a small, repeated pattern like this, it becomes very obvious that the pattern tiles are always arranged in exact rows and columns. If this is too square for your style, a little creativity can help reduce this rectilinear rigidity.

The `patternTransform` attribute is the easiest way to mix things up. Rotations and skews can create diamond or parallelogram tiles out of the simple rectangles in your code.

 Just like with `gradientTransform`, `patternTransform` is merged into the general `transform` property by the CSS Transforms spec—but browsers haven't made the switch yet.

For example, if you add the following attribute to the `wallpaper` pattern in Example 12-10, the end result is as shown in Figure 12-19:

```
patternTransform="rotate(45)"
```

In the version without the extra outlines, the rotated pattern looks almost like a checkerboard of alternating content in rows and columns, because the exactly repeated rows and columns are now actually diagonals.

 You only need to add `patternTransform` to the first of the linked patterns; it will be copied to the second pattern by the `xlink:href` reference.

Figure 12-19. Square pattern tiles, rotated 45°

If you design your pattern tile with the transformation in mind, even more possibilities open up. Figure 12-20 shows the final result if you add the *reverse* transformation to the pink-diamond <path> element:

```
transform="translate(2,2) rotate(-45, 10,10)"
```

The negative rotation on the <use> exactly cancels out the rotation on the pattern tile, so that the diamond icons are drawn upright again. The three-value rotate function is used to ensure that the rotation is centered around the center of the icon.

When you apply transformations to patterns with solid backdrops—like this one—the edges of the pattern tiles sometimes appear in some browsers, because of rounding errors. If this problem shows up in your pattern, one solution is to make your backdrop <rect> slightly larger than the pattern tile.

In future, the solution would be to use a solid-color fill layer underneath the pattern layer, instead of having to include the backdrop in the pattern itself.

Figure 12-20. Square pattern tiles, rotated 45°, containing icons rotated in the opposite direction

Summary: The fill Property, Gradients, and Patterns

It is easy to fall into an analytical, mathematical approach to SVG when working with the markup, drawing using coordinates. But SVG is about graphics as much as it is about vectors. Filling shapes with complex content is the first step to going beyond simple solid-color, flat icons. Of course, *creating* those effects, and controlling them precisely from code, requires diving back in to vector geometry.

The gradients and patterns introduced in this chapter use a structure we'll see again in other SVG graphical effects: dedicated markup elements define an effect, without drawing anything themselves; the effect is applied with a url() reference from a style property of another element.

Simple gradients and patterns can be created with not much markup, but the many attributes for scaling and adjusting the effects create countless possible combinations. The options can seem overwhelming. Browser support limitations don't make it any easier. But if you start from something simple and work up, you can build incredibly complex and creative results.

CSS gradients and repeating backgrounds achieve many of the same effects as SVG gradients and patterns. Many SVG-focused web developers (including us) look forward to the day when the CSS syntax can be used in SVG fill and stroke. However, there are numerous small details and differences that can trip up developers switching from one to the other. Even when the CSS-focused approaches are available in SVG, there will be some effects that require the full markup to recreate.

More Online

A reference for the gradient and pattern elements (and their attributes) is available in the "Paint Server Elements and Markers" section of our markup guide:

https://oreillymedia.github.io/Using_SVG/guide/ markup.html#paint-marker

CHAPTER 13

Drawing the Lines

Stroke Effects

Throughout the book, we have used the `stroke` property to draw outlines around a shape (or text). In this chapter, we will explore the full possibilities of strokes.

At first glance, it may not seem that there are a lot of possibilities for a stroke. It's just an outline, right?

It can be, but it doesn't have to be. A stroke is really a secondary shape, built upon the element that defines it. When that stroke is only a single pixel wide, it is easy to figure out where those pixels should go. But as strokes get thicker, they create multiple options for how the stroke's geometry should relate to the underlying shape's geometry, at corners and at line ends.

You can also change up the geometry of the stroke more directly, by breaking it into a dash pattern. This can be used to create a number of patterns and effects, beyond simple dashed lines.

Once you have a stroke shape (dashed or otherwise), you need to decide how to color it in. Just like with the fill shape, you have a choice of a solid color, semitransparent color, or a complex paint server—gradients and patterns. The options are mostly the same as `fill`, but with a few extra complications.

Different Strokes

In the simple case, a stroke is a continuous outline around the shape, drawn in a single color.

Except…even that isn't always simple. The wider a stroke gets, the more you start to notice the details of how it is constructed.

A Simple Stroke to Start

There are three stroke-related properties that we have introduced so far: `stroke`, `stroke-width`, and `stroke-opacity`. With these, we've drawn solid-colored strokes of various sizes and degrees of transparency. All three can be set as presentation attributes or style declarations, and all three inherit by default.

The **stroke property** controls whether the stroke is painted at all; by default its value is `none`. All other `stroke` values create a stroke, by specifying what it will be painted with.

The syntax is the same as for `fill`: a color value or a `url()` reference to a paint server element. Paint server references can have an optional fallback color:

```
stroke: none;
stroke: rgba(100%, 30%, 50%, 0.7);
stroke: url(#pink-polka-dots) hotPink;
```

The **stroke-width property** controls the thickness of the stroke, expressed as a number of user units, a length with units, or a percentage:

```
stroke-width: 10px;
stroke-width: 0.5em;
stroke-width: 5%;
```

The default `stroke-width` is 1px (scaled to the current user-unit size). A value of 0 would look the same as `stroke: none`, but would create some added complications when you're using markers (Chapter 14) or `pointer-events` (Chapter 18).

Although unitless numbers are valid (`stroke-width: 3`), MS Edge does not currently support them in CSS animations and transitions. Use px units instead.

The **stroke-opacity property** is directly comparable to fill-opacity. It makes the color or stroke paint content transparent. By default, the value is 1, which creates an opaque stroke.

```
stroke-opacity: 1;
stroke-opacity: 0.5;
```

A stroke-opacity of 0 would again *look* like no stroke at all, but would work differently for pointer-events.

We use all three of these properties in Example 13-1, to stroke a circle (with a thick, semitransparent stroke) and a polygon (with a thin, solid stroke). Figure 13-1 shows the result.

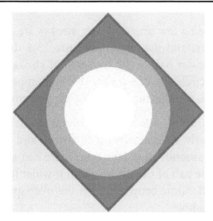

Figure 13-1. Thick and thin strokes on round and square shapes

Example 13-1. Stroking shapes with various styles

```
<svg xmlns="http://www.w3.org/2000/svg" xml:lang="en"
    width="200" height="200" viewBox="-100 -100 200 200"
    style="background-color: lightGreen">
  <title>Stroking Shapes</title>
  <polygon points="-98,0 0,-98 98,0 0,98" fill="royalBlue"
          stroke="crimson" stroke-width="2" />
  <circle r="1.2cm" fill="white"
          stroke="lightGreen" stroke-width="1cm"
          stroke-opacity="0.5" />
</svg>
```

Percentage values for stroke-width are—like percentage values for a circle's radius—proportional to the diagonal of the coordinate system, not either height or width. This is true even when the strokes are being applied to a rectangle or other shape with clear directionality.

More Online

Confused by `stroke-width` percentages? We've got an example of them, in action, in "Perplexing Percentages", the supplementary section from Chapter 5:

https://oreillymedia.github.io/Using_SVG/extras/ch05-percentages.html

As we've discussed a few times already, strokes are *centered* over the edge of the shape, and the circle in Figure 13-1 demonstrates that effectively. The inner half of the transparent stroke, which overlaps the solid white circle fill, has a very different appearance from the outer half, which overlaps the blue fill of the polygon.

A circle—by definition—does not have any corners or dead ends. That makes it fairly straightforward to stroke, and the stroke shape creates a single, smooth ring. However, there can still be complications. If the inside half of the stroke width is wider than the radius, it will overlap itself. Some browsers treat the overlapping inner circle as a cutout donut hole.

 Browsers that use the Skia or AppleCore graphics libraries (all versions of WebKit and Blink, plus Firefox on Mac and Android), will sometimes draw overlapping strokes as cut-outs.

Once you make the shape a little more complex, you start to notice even more complications in the stroke shapes.

Example 13-2 applies the three basic stroke properties to the spade icon from Chapter 6, and the letter A. We apply the properties using a set of independent classes that trigger CSS rules. The results are shown in Figure 13-2.

Figure 13-2. The same shape and text, with varying stroke options

Example 13-2. Using stroke properties to modify the appearance of a reused symbol and text

```
<svg xmlns="http://www.w3.org/2000/svg" xml:lang="en"
    xmlns:xlink="http://www.w3.org/1999/xlink"
    width="410" height="250" viewBox="0 0 410 250">
    <title>Stroking Shapes and Text</title>
    <style type="text/css">
        text {
            font-family: Times New Roman, Times, Georgia, serif;
        }
        .blue { stroke: royalBlue; }
        .pink { stroke: deepPink; }
        .see-through { stroke-opacity: 0.5; }
        .wide { stroke-width: 3px; }
    </style>
    <symbol id="spades-ace" viewBox="0 0 40 20"
            style="overflow: visible">
        <title>Ace Spade</title>
        <path d="M9,15C9,20 0,21 0,16S6,9 10,0C14,9 20,11 20,16
                S11,20 11,15Q11,20 13,20H7Q9,20 9,15Z" />
        <text x="30" y="18" font-size="20"
            text-anchor="middle">A</text>
    </symbol>
    <rect height="100%" width="100%" fill="lavender" />

    <g fill="midnightBlue">
        <use xlink:href="#spades-ace" class="blue"
```

```
                width="200" height="100" x="10" y="10" />
    <use xlink:href="#spades-ace" class="pink see-through"
                width="200" height="100" x="210" y="10" />
    <use xlink:href="#spades-ace" class="pink wide"
                width="200" height="100" x="10" y="135" />
    <use xlink:href="#spades-ace" class="blue wide see-through"
                width="200" height="100" x="210" y="135" />
  </g>
</svg>
```

An important thing to note is that the <symbol> element has an
overflow: visible style rule applied. As we mentioned when discussing symbols, by default symbols have hidden overflow. Since
strokes extend beyond the official edges of a shape, they would be
clipped in this example. The viewBox tightly fits the fill region of the
spade shape on three sides. Figure 13-3 shows a wide-stroked version with hidden overflow, for comparison.

*Figure 13-3. Strokes extending beyond the edge of a symbol with
(default) hidden overflow*

Another important takeaway from Figure 13-2: wide strokes can
completely obscure fine details in shapes and letters. Even the
strokes in the top row—which have the default stroke-width of 1—
are thick relative to the thin lines of the serif letter A. And if those
strokes don't look 1px wide to you, remember that the symbols
define their own coordinate system, within which the icon is 20
units wide and tall, and the text has a font-size of 18px.

The stroke-width is always calculated in the
current coordinate system, including all transformations. As a result, nonuniform scales or
skews can create uneven-width strokes, as we
saw in Example 11-4 in Chapter 11.

On these more complex shapes, the distance from the edge of the shape to the edge of the stroke can vary—and not just in the places where multiple strokes overlap. At the point of the spade, the strokes extend well beyond the point of the fill. At the sharp corners around its base, however, the strokes get cut off tight against the points. The next section will explore why this is so, and the ways in which you can change the behavior.

Future Focus
Layered Lines

In Chapter 12, we mentioned how the CSS Fill and Stroke module introduces a syntax to layer multiple fills. The same possibility will also be supported with strokes, but with even greater potential. Because each stroke can have a different width, even solid-colored strokes can be effectively layered.

There are still a number of open questions (at the time of writing) before the syntax can be finalized, but it will be generally similar to the syntax for CSS layered backgrounds.

In the meantime, to create multiple strokes you need to `<use>` your shape multiple times, with different stroke settings on each copy. We did this in Example 12-1 in Chapter 12, to create a thin inset outline over a thicker stroke that matched the fill.

Making the Connection with Line Joins

The basic geometry of a stroke along a smooth path is straightforward. Imagine a "brush" that is a line `stroke-width` units long. Center it over the edge of the shape, and trace out the path, keeping your line perpendicular to the path at all times. All the points that were touched by the "brush," as you moved it along, are part of your stroke region.

But what happens at sharp corners? If you only included the regions that were directly perpendicular to the stroke segments, you'd get something like Figure 13-4 (which uses a semitransparent stroke to clearly show the underlying fill shape). Every corner has a chip in it.

Figure 13-4. Strokes without line joins

 You can't naturally draw an unjoined stroke, like Figure 13-4, in SVG. It was created with a second `<path>` just for the stroke, with `m0,0` commands inserted between each line segment in the path data. This breaks it into disconnected subpaths, which don't join together. This is similar to the disconnect in the final corner of a `<path>` that doesn't have a `Z` close-path command.

Clearly, you need a way to fill in the gaps to create a continuous shape outline. But how? What shape fills in each chip?

These choices are decided by the **stroke-linejoin property**. It applies anytime a shape has a sharp corner. There are three possible values:

round
> Swivel your "brush" in place, so that the gap between the end of one stroke segment and the start of the next is filled with a circular arc.

bevel
> Trim it off tightly, by connecting the corners of the "chip" with a straight line, creating an angled corner piece.

`miter`

> Extend the outer edge of each stroke segment in a straight line, until they meet in a point.

The value of `stroke-linejoin` may be set as a presentation attribute or style property; like the other stroke properties, it inherits by default.

Figure 13-5 shows how each of those of `stroke-linejoin` styles look when applied to the shape from Figure 13-4.

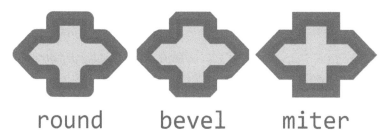

round   bevel   miter

Figure 13-5. Strokes with joined lines, in different stroke-linejoin styles

A `miter` corner is the default. However, it introduces a complication: on really tight corners, you have to extend the strokes for quite a distance, before the two edges meet. For that reason, there is a secondary property: **stroke-miterlimit**. It defines how far you can extend the point when creating a miter corner. The value is a number, measured as a multiple of the current `stroke-width`. If the miter corner would exceed the miter limit, it is replaced by a bevelled corner.

 By default, `stroke-miterlimit` is 4. The value must always be at least 1.

A value of `60` would be enough to guarantee miters for angles as tight as 2°. In general, the miter length of a line join is $(sin(^\theta/_2))^{-1}$, where θ is the angle of the corner.

Example 13-3 applies the three possible `stroke-linejoin` options to the diamond icon from Chapter 6 and the digit 4; it also creates a miter version with `stroke-miterlimit` set to 10. The results are displayed in Figure 13-6.

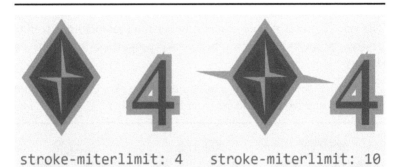

stroke-miterlimit: 4   stroke-miterlimit: 10

Figure 13-6. Shapes and text with mitered corners, at the default settings, and with stroke-miterlimit of 10

Example 13-3. Using stroke-linejoin options

```
<svg xmlns="http://www.w3.org/2000/svg" xml:lang="en"
    xmlns:xlink="http://www.w3.org/1999/xlink"
    width="400" height="160" viewBox="0 0 400 160">
    <title>Stroke Miter Limit Effects</title>
    <symbol id="diamonds-4" viewBox="0 0 36 20"
            style="overflow: visible">
        <title>4 Diamond</title>
        <path d="M3,10 L10,0 17,10 10,20 Z
                M9,11 L10,18 V10 H15 L11,9 10,2 V10 H5 Z" />
        <text x="35" y="20" font-size="20"
                font-family="Times New Roman, Times, Georgia, serif"
                style="font-variant-numeric: lining-nums"
                text-anchor="end">4</text>
    </symbol>
    <rect height="100%" width="100%" fill="lavender" />
    <g fill="indigo" stroke="deepPink"
        stroke-width="2.5" stroke-opacity="0.5">
        <use xlink:href="#diamonds-4"
            width="180" height="100" x="0" y="15"
            stroke-linejoin="miter" />
        <use xlink:href="#diamonds-4"
            width="180" height="100" x="220" y="15"
            stroke-linejoin="miter" stroke-miterlimit="10"/>
    </g>
    <g fill="blueViolet"
        font-family="Consolas, monospace" font-size="16">
        <text x="5" text-anchor="start" y="155"
                >stroke-miterlimit: 4</text>
```

```
    <text x="395" text-anchor="end" y="155"
        >stroke-miterlimit: 10</text>
  </g>
</svg>
```

There are numerous corners of different angles in the figure, in both the inner and outer subpaths of the icon and the digit.

The sharpest angles, in both the diamond and the 4, are on the inner cut-out subpaths. These create the "spikes" sticking out of the diamond with a `stroke-miterlimit` of 10. There aren't matching spikes at the top and bottom, because those miters would have extended more than 10 times the stroke width, and so were cut back completely to bevel corners. It's more subtle, but there are similar spikes at the left and top of the number 4, at both the default and extended miter limits.

Future Focus

New Line-Join Options

SVG 2 and the CSS Fill and Stroke module propose two new `stroke-linejoin` values: `miter-clip` and `arcs`.

The `miter-clip` value would create an effect similar to `miter`, *except* for when the point exceeds the `stroke-miterlimit` ratio. With `miter`, there is a sharp switch to the **bevel** mode, which is usually cropped much more tightly than the limit. In animated sequences, this creates a sudden switch in otherwise fluid motion. It can also create somewhat arbitrary-looking distinctions between long pointed joins on some corners and cropped ones on others. The `miter-clip` value would instead leave in place the part of the mitered corner that is *less* than the limit, and only clip off the parts that extend too far.

 Older versions of Firefox on some operating systems used the `miter-clip` behavior for `miter`, but Firefox has since updated to match the SVG 1.1 specs.

The `arcs` line-join style would create a miter effect when joining *straight* lines, but would create a smoother shape when joining two curves, or a curve with a straight line. It would create a curved point that is the intersection of two elliptical arcs, each of which is a smooth continuation of the curves that make up the strokes. It would not work in all cases: sometimes, smooth continuations of the joined curves would curve away from each other instead of joining in a point. In those cases, the result would be the same as `miter-clip`.

At the time of writing, the exact names for these options are still being debated. There have not yet been commitments from web browser teams to implement them.

Capping It Off with Line Caps

The `stroke-linejoin` effect only applies when two segments of a continuous shape meet. A separate property, **`stroke-linecap`**, controls appearance of open-ended strokes on <line>, <polyline>, or unclosed <path> subpaths. The line cap also applies to dashed strokes, which we'll talk about starting in "A Dashing Design" on page 499.

The `stroke-linecap` also has three options:

`butt`
> The stroke ends exactly where the line does, in a straight perpendicular line

`round`
> The stroke ends in a semicircle that extends beyond the end of the line

`square`
> The stroke extends beyond the official end of the line by half the stroke's width, creating a square around the line ending point

The `butt` value is the default. Like the other stroke settings, it is inheritable and can be set with an attribute or a style declaration.

Although the values do not directly correspond to `stroke-linejoin` options, they can be used to create line endings that harmonize with the joins for your particular shape.

Example 13-4 shows the three line cap options applied to an open path that also includes some line joins. The upper row uses the default `miter` line join, while the bottom row uses line joins that are most complementary to each type of line cap on this zig-zagging shape:

- **bevel** caps with **butt** joins
- **round** caps with **round** joins
- **square** caps with **miter** joins

A narrower version of the stroke (with the default line joins and caps) helps you see the exact dimensions of the path, as displayed in Figure 13-7.

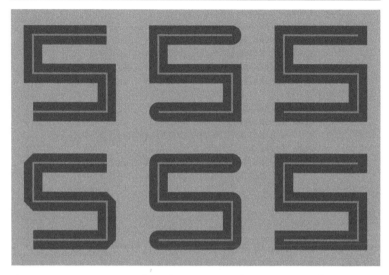

Figure 13-7. An open path with various stroke options: stroke-linecap of butt (left), round (center), and square (right), with stroke-linejoin modifications in the bottom row

Example 13-4. Using stroke-linecap to create line endings that match line joins

```
<svg xmlns="http://www.w3.org/2000/svg" xml:lang="en"
     xmlns:xlink="http://www.w3.org/1999/xlink"
     width="390" height="260" viewBox="0 0 390 260">
    <title>Stroke Linecap Options</title>
    <symbol id="open-path" viewBox="0 0 30 30"
            style="overflow: visible">
        <path id="p" d="M25,5 H5 V15 H25 V25 H5"
            fill="none"/>
        <use xlink:href="#p" stroke="coral" stroke-width="0.5"
            stroke-linecap="initial" stroke-linejoin="initial" />
    </symbol>
```

```
<rect height="100%" width="100%" fill="lightcoral" />

<g stroke="indigo"
    stroke-width="5" stroke-opacity="0.75">
    <g stroke-linecap="butt" >
        <use xlink:href="#open-path"
            width="30%" height="50%" x="1%" />
        <use xlink:href="#open-path"
            width="30%" height="50%" x="1%" y="50%"
            stroke-linejoin="bevel" />
    </g>
    <g stroke-linecap="round" >
        <use xlink:href="#open-path"
            width="30%" height="50%" x="35%" />
        <use xlink:href="#open-path"
            width="30%" height="50%" x="35%" y="50%"
            stroke-linejoin="round" />
    </g>
    <g stroke-linecap="square" >
        <use xlink:href="#open-path"
            width="30%" height="50%" x="69%" />
        <use xlink:href="#open-path"
            width="30%" height="50%" x="69%" y="50%"
            stroke-linejoin="miter" />
    </g>
</g>
</svg>
```

An important thing to note is that the `stroke-linecap` value *only* applies if the subpath actually ends at that point. If you create a U-turn in a single subpath, that will be drawn as a line join, not a line cap. Figure 13-8 shows what happens if you take the code from Example 13-4, but change it to use the following E-shaped path instead of the S-shaped path in the original:

```
<path id="p" d="M25,5 H5 V15 H25 H5 V25 H25"
    fill="none"/>
```

The path consists of a single subpath that creates the *appearance* of an extra line ending by reversing back on itself (`H25 H5`) after drawing the middle stroke of the E.

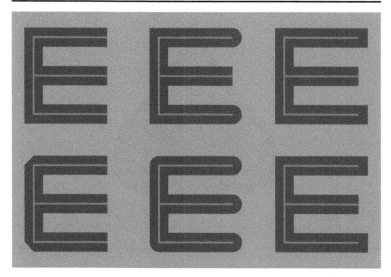

Figure 13-8. An open path with a 180° line join in the middle, and the same stroke-linecap and stroke-linejoin options as Figure 13-7

With a 180° U-turn such as this, a round line join is indistinguishable from a round line cap. A bevel line join looks like a butt line cap, cropped tight against the point. A miter line join in this case will always be converted to a bevelled join, because the hypothetical length of the miter is infinite: no matter how far you extend the "corner," the two edges will never meet in a point.

This may seem like an extreme edge case, drawing a line that backtracks on itself exactly. However, 180° turns (creating a 0° or 360° corner) are more common when you're connecting curved lines. For curves, the angle of the tangents at the line join can coincide even if the curves don't. Figure 13-9 identifies four such U-turns in the spade icon.

Figure 13-9. The 180° turns (circled) between curves in an icon

For line joins like this, both `bevel` and `miter` values of `stroke-linejoin` will crop the stroke exactly at the point of the fill. (A round line join would add a semicircle cap.) Both of the proposed SVG 2 joins, `miter-clip` and `arcs`, would extend the stroke beyond the point in a straight line, to a distance set by `stroke-miterlimit`, before clipping it perpendicular to the stroke direction.

Adjusting Stroke Appearance

You may have figured out by now that SVG strokes can sometimes be frustrating. They don't always line up just where you want. Many options can't yet be controlled by the available stroke styles.

However, there are a few extra style properties that you can use to adjust the appearance of strokes. They even have *fairly* good browser support.

Anti-Anti-Aliasing for Crisp Lines

We've been focusing on *thick* strokes so we can discuss the geometry of line caps and line joins. But *thin* strokes have their own problems.

When drawn on a computer monitor—unless it's *very* high resolution—a thin stroke can look a little blurry. A 1px stroke line will often be positioned so that it is spread across multiple screen pixels. If the stroke is solid black, the actual pixels will be colored in transparent gray.

Consider the following icon, which uses a 1px stroke, in the same darkMagenta color, for both the X and the outline:

Figure 13-10 uses Firefox Dev Tool's color-picker to look at the color of individual pixels when that icon is drawn to the screen. On the left is the standard view, with the 1px stroke blurred across multiple pixels. On the right is the result when every pixel is forced to be either fully colored or not colored at all.

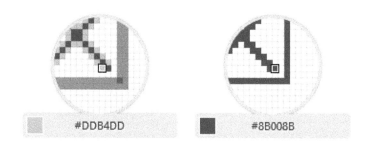

Figure 13-10. Zooming in on a 1px-stroke icon, with anti-aliasing (left) and without (right)

The process of breaking up the diagonal vector lines to exactly match the pixel grid (the right side of Figure 13-10) is called **aliasing** the graphic to the grid. In the early days of computer graphics, that was the normal approach. The blurring effect is called **anti-aliasing**. It smooths out the jagged pixel edges, and is now the standard for vector graphics.

The **shape-rendering property** lets you tell the browser whether anti-aliasing would be a good idea for this element. It has four possible values:

- `crispEdges` turns off anti-aliasing, causing pixels on the edge of a shape to either be fully colored or not at all
- `geometricPrecision` requests anti-aliasing

- `auto` (the default) usually means anti-aliasing in modern browsers

- `optimizeSpeed` will usually be the same as `auto`

The property is inherited, so you can set it once for your `<svg>` as a whole.

`shape-rendering` is one of a series of "rendering hint" properties in SVG. The others either don't have much effect in current browsers, or are being redefined by CSS3 modules. See *https:// oreillymedia.github.io/Using_SVG/guide/ style.html* for their definitions.

Be sure to test your graphic carefully if you change `shape-rendering`. Although "crisp edges" can improve some drawings, they can make others look pixellated and uneven. The exact effect will depend on the browser and the screen resolution.

Swapping Stroke and Fill

One of the basic rules of SVG stroking is that the stroke is painted on top of the fill. As we've seen in a few figures so far, this can often completely obscure details in the geometry of a shape or letter.

In SVG 1.1, you cannot change this ordering.

In SVG 2, you can. The new **paint-order property** allows you to control which goes first, stroke or fill. It also controls the order of line markers (which we'll introduce in Chapter 14). It is an inheritable style property.

Although `paint-order` is now supported in the latest versions of most browsers, it has not yet been implemented in MS Edge, and is not supported in older browsers.

If the effect is essential, duplicate the shape with `<use>` elements to paint the stroke and fill separately, in the order you prefer.

The value of paint-order is a list of the stroke, fill, and markers keywords, ordered the way you want them painted, from bottom to top. You can indicate the default paint-order by using the normal keyword instead.

If the list doesn't include all possible values, the remaining layers will be painted on top, in their usual order. This means that to paint stroke *under* the fill, all you need is:

```
paint-order: stroke;
```

Figure 13-11 shows the result if you apply that style rule to the root `<svg>` element in Example 13-2 from the beginning of the chapter.

Figure 13-11. Shapes and text with various stroke options, when strokes are painted before fill

As you can see, with a solid fill color like this, all the details of the shapes and letters are now clearly visible, over the top of the stroke. However, the strokes now appear to be half as wide as they were, because half of each stroke is obscured behind the fill.

There is not yet any proposal for integrating paint-order with layered fills and strokes in such a way that you can position some stroke layers under the fill and others on top.

Controlling Stroke Position

Using `paint-order` and solid fill, you can make it *appear* that a stroke is entirely on the outside of the shape. But sometimes it would be nice to do that explicitly, even for semitransparent fill. And it would often be nice to have a stroke that instead fits *inside* the exact dimensions of your shape, so it doesn't increase the shape's size.

Inside and outside strokes are supported in most vector graphics tools, including Adobe Illustrator, Sketch, and other software commonly used by web designers. They have long been a requested feature for SVG. Proposals have been bumped from one specification to another, without ever being finalized. The latest is in the CSS Fill and Stroke module.

The `stroke-align` property would allow you to override the default position of the stroke. Instead of centering the stroke over the edge of the shape, you could push the stroke to the outside or inside. However, with custom shapes (paths, polygons, and polylines), the distinction between "outside" and "inside" is not always clear, and decisions have not yet been made about exactly how it will work.

_____

Scaling Shapes Without Scaling Strokes

Another new feature that now has fairly wide support is nonscaling strokes. The idea of a nonscaling stroke is that the stroke width would not be affected by any transforms or `viewBox` scaling on a shape. So a 1px stroke would actually be 1px, regardless of any scaling used to change the size of the shape.

Nonscaling strokes are implemented as part of the **vector-effect property**, which we mentioned in Chapter 8 when discussing the related ability to prevent text or symbols from scaling with the overall coordinate system. At the time of writing, `non-scaling-stroke` is the only vector effect option that is implemented in web browsers.

`vector-effect:` `non-scaling-stroke` is not yet implemented in Microsoft browsers, and isn't supported in older versions of other browsers. Even where it is supported, there can be quirks and inconsistencies in some cases.

If you need consistent rendering, you will need to directly calculate the adjusted `stroke-width` for the current scale. For `viewBox` scaling (but not transforms), you can sometimes approximate nonscaling strokes with percentages or CSS viewport units.

The `vector-effect` property does *not* inherit by default, as this wouldn't make sense for some of the proposed vector effects. To be able to apply `non-scaling-stroke` on a `<g>` or `<use>` element—and actually have an impact on the component shapes—you will need to set `vector-effect:` `inherit` on all the elements in between.

That's the approach used in Example 13-5, which redraws a stroked version of the club-suit icon at various scales, using both transforms and `viewBox` scaling. It then reuses the complete layout, but applies `non-scaling-stroke`. Forced inheritance ensures that the scaling adjustment applies to the individual copies of the path. Figure 13-12 shows the result.

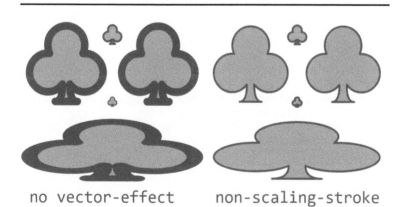

no vector-effect   non-scaling-stroke

Figure 13-12. A 20×20 icon, drawn at various scales, with or without vector-effect: non-scaling-stroke

Example 13-5. Using non-scaling-stroke on icons reused at various scales

```
<svg xmlns="http://www.w3.org/2000/svg" xml:lang="en"
    xmlns:xlink="http://www.w3.org/1999/xlink"
    width="400" height="200" viewBox="0 0 400 200">
  <title>Non-Scaling Stroke Vector Effect</title>
  <style>
      * { vector-effect: inherit; }                         ❶
  </style>
  <symbol id="club-symbol" viewBox="0 0 20 20"
          style="overflow: visible">                        ❷
      <path id="club-path"
            stroke="rebeccaPurple" fill="cadetBlue"
            stroke-width="2"
            stroke-linejoin="round"
            d="M 9,15.5 A 5,5 0 1 1 5.5,7.5
               A 5,5 0 1 1 14.5,7.5 A 5,5 0 1 1 11,15.5
               Q 11,20 13,20 H 7 Q 9,20 9,15.5 Z" />
  </symbol>
  <rect height="100%" width="100%" fill="lightCyan" />
  <g id="layout">
      <use xlink:href="#club-path" x="90" y="10"/>          ❸
      <use xlink:href="#club-symbol"
           width="80" height="80" x="10" y="10"/>           ❹
      <use xlink:href="#club-symbol"
           width="10" height="10" x="95" y="85"/>           ❺
      <use xlink:href="#club-path"
           transform="translate(110,10) scale(4)" />        ❻
      <use xlink:href="#club-path"
           transform="translate(10,110) scale(9,3)" />      ❼
  </g>
  <use xlink:href="#layout" x="200"
       style="vector-effect: non-scaling-stroke" />         ❽
  <g fill="rebeccaPurple"
     font-family="Consolas, monospace" font-size="18">
      <text x="10" text-anchor="start" y="195"
            >no vector-effect</text>
      <text x="390" text-anchor="end" y="195"
            >non-scaling-stroke</text>
  </g>
</svg>
```

❶ A universal CSS selector forces the `vector-effect` to inherit on all elements, unless changed by a more specific CSS declaration.

❷ The club is drawn to just fit within a 20×20 `<symbol>` viewBox. Both the `<symbol>` and the `<path>` it contains are given id values, so they can be reused separately. The path has stroke and fill styles set on it directly, including a 2px `stroke-width`.

❸   The first copy of the club redraws the `<path>` at its natural size.

❹   The second copy scales the `<symbol>` to fit an 80×80 square.

❺   Another copy of the `<symbol>` is scaled down, to fit in 10×10.

❻   A copy of the `<path>` is scaled up and positioned with a `transform`.

❼   The final copy of the `<path>` is also transformed, but this time with an uneven scale.

❽   The entire set of five clubs is then redrawn on the right side of the figure, with a `non-scaling-stroke` for `vector-effect`.

The copy of the club that is drawn at its "natural" size (20×20, in the top center of each side of Figure 13-12) is identical with or without the `vector-effect`. For all the scaled icons, the default (no `vector-effect`) behavior maintains consistent proportions between fill and stroke, even when the entire shape is distorted by an uneven scale. The `non-scaling-stroke` option maintains consistent stroke dimensions in the main SVG's coordinate system.

A Dashing Design

An SVG stroke does not have to be a continuous line. You can introduce breaks in the stroke—without breaking your shape into separate subpaths—to create a dashed line, using the **stroke-dasharray** property.

A Wide Array of Dashes (and Gaps Between Them)

The dash *array* is a list of lengths of alternating dashes (stroked line sections) and gaps (unstroked spaces). The dashes are positioned by measuring along the path, from start to end, turning on and off the stroke as you go. The dash pattern is repeated as many times as necessary to finish stroking the shape.

The value of `stroke-dasharray` is a space- or comma-separated list of lengths, percentages, or numbers of user units. It can be specified as a presentation attribute or in a CSS rule, and is inherited. The default is none, meaning no dashing (solid stroke).

> The comma-separated option is likely to be deprecated by the CSS Fill and Stroke module, in order to better support comma-separated lists of different arrays for different stroke layers. For future compatibility, use spaces as separators in your dash array list.

The *first* value in the dash array list always describes a dash; after that, gaps and dashes alternate. So this array defines long dashes and short gaps:

```
stroke-dasharray: 10px 2px;
```

This looks like the following:

If there is an uneven number of lengths within the dash array, the lengths of dashes and gaps will alternate during each repeat of the pattern. In other words, the following two patterns are equivalent:

```
stroke-dasharray: 1em 10px 1em;
stroke-dasharray: 1em 10px 1em 1em 10px 1em;
```

Either version looks like this if the `font-size` is 16px:

— — — — — — — — — — — — — —

Percentages within a dash array are measured in the same way as percentages for stroke widths: relative to the diagonal of the coordinate system divided by the square root of two.

> Percentage dashes are *not* related to the length of the stroke.

The dash and gap lengths must be positive; negative values are an error. However, any value in the list may be 0 to create a zero-length gap or dash. This can be useful when you're trying to control the dash and gap lengths precisely, instead of in a simple repeating pattern. A `stroke-dasharray` value of 0 0 (or any other number of zeros) should be treated the same as `stroke-dasharray` of none, meaning a solid line.

 Because of unclear language in SVG 1.1, Firefox up to version 40 treated a zero-length dash pattern as a `stroke="none"`, meaning no line at all.

You would normally only use a zero-length dash pattern as the start or end of an animation effect.

The visual effect of a given dash pattern can be quite different depending on the width of the stroke it is applied to. Figure 13-13 repeats the two previous dashing samples, along with a dash array of 3 3 (meaning: 3px-long dashes separated by 3px-long gaps), each on 3px-wide strokes. It then repeats the same three patterns, but on 15px-wide strokes.

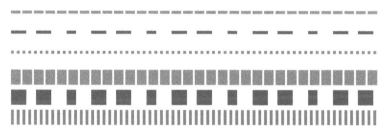

Figure 13-13. Dashed lines with different dash patterns, and (bottom) the same patterns on wider strokes

The 3px dashes on a 3px-wide stroke create a dotted line; on a 15px-wide stroke, however, they create a finely spaced grate.

Unfortunately, there is no way to define a dash pattern that automatically scales with the stroke width. (Although you could hack it—for nontext elements—by defining both properties in `em` units and then scaling the `font-size`.)

On straight lines like those in Figure 13-13, the shape of each dash is, well, straightforward. On more complex shapes there are, well, more complications. To demonstrate the impact, Example 13-6 applies a dash pattern to two of the card-suit icons, as shown in Figure 13-14.

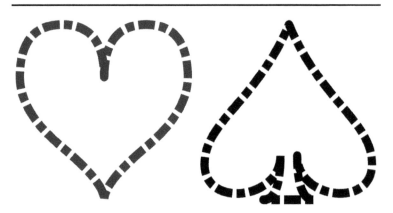

Figure 13-14. Dashed lines on shapes with smooth curves and sharp corners

Example 13-6. Creating dashed lines on curved shapes

```
<svg xmlns="http://www.w3.org/2000/svg" xml:lang="en"
     xmlns:xlink="http://www.w3.org/1999/xlink"
     width="410px" height="205px" viewBox="-1 -1 44 22">  ❶
    <title>Dashing SVG Shapes</title>
    <style type="text/css">
        svg {
            fill: none;
            stroke-linejoin: round;
            stroke-dasharray: 2 0.5 1 0.5;                  ❷
        }
    </style>

    <path id="heart" stroke="darkRed"
          d="M10,6 Q10,0 15,0T20,6Q20,10 15,14
             T10,20Q10,18 5,14T0,6Q0,0 5,0T10,6Z" />
    <path id="spade" stroke="#222" transform="translate(22,0)"
          d="M9,15C9,20 0,21 0,16S6,9 10,0C14,9 20,11 20,16
             S11,20 11,15Q11,20 13,20H7Q9,20 9,15Z" />    ❸
</svg>
```

❶ To leave room for the strokes, the `viewBox` offsets the origin of the icons one unit away from the top-left corner of the SVG. The width and height have been increased to include both this padding and an equivalent amount on the opposite side and in between the shapes.

❷ All the shapes will have `round` line joins and a pattern of alternating long and short dashes with shorter gaps in between. This dash pattern will be applied in the scaled coordinate system, so a half-unit gap will still be clearly visible.

❸ Both shapes were originally designed to just fit within a 20-unit square. With the padding, they each take up 22 units in each direction. The spade is translated horizontally into position.

There are a few things to pay attention to in Figure 13-14. The first is that the dashes follow the curve of the strokes. The start and end of the dash lines are always perpendicular to the path at that particular point—which may not be parallel to the other end of the dash.

Another thing to notice is that the dash pattern continues from one path segment to another, irrespective of any sharp corners. When there is a dash at a corner, the `stroke-linejoin` shape is painted— but if there's a gap at the line join, the tip gets left off. The result can be somewhat unbalanced, as the spade shape certainly demonstrates.

Future Focus
Better References for Dash Lengths

The lengths used in `stroke-dasharray` are always defined in absolute terms or relative to the overall coordinate system, rather than being relative to the shape itself. It would often be preferable to be able to specify dash and gap lengths relative to the stroke width, the total path length, or the current path segment length.

At the time of writing, there are open issues on the CSS Fill and Stroke module to address these options, but no standard yet for a syntax.

Turning Dashes into Dots

Although `stroke-linejoin` shapes do not coordinate well with dashes, `stroke-linecap` can. But it may take a little adjustment to your dash pattern.

The stroke's line cap shape is added to the start and end of every dash.

Example 13-6 used the default `butt` line cap, which does not add anything to the measured end of each dash. However, for `round` and `square` line caps, the cap extends beyond the end of the dash into the gap. If you do not factor this in, it could throw off your gap spacing. In order to have a visible gap, the gap space must be larger than your stroke width.

Line caps can be used to create circular or square dots that automatically adjust to the stroke width. The trick is to use a very small dash length—ideally, less than 1 pixel on the display, after adjusting for the scale of the SVG. Then use a gap length that includes the room required for the dots, which will take up as much space as the stroke is wide. The gaps, unfortunately, will *not* automatically scale to match the stroke width.

Using a zero-length dash, in order to draw perfect circles or squares with just the line caps, is not recommended. Older Blink browsers did not draw the dash line caps at all in this case. In newer Blink, caps are drawn for the zero-length dashes, but they do not rotate with the path direction.

The following styles, when applied to the markup from Example 13-6, create round and square dotted patterns on the heart and spade icons, respectively, with the results shown in Figure 13-15:

```
svg {
    fill: none;
    stroke-dasharray: 0.001 1.999;
}
path[id="heart"] { stroke-linecap: round; }
path[id="spade"] { stroke-linecap: square; }
```

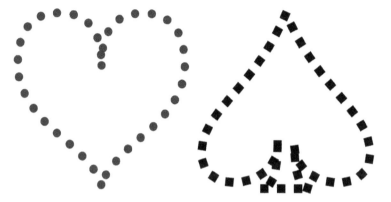

Figure 13-15. Dotted lines created with stroke-linecap

The difference created by the round line caps is obvious, but the square line caps may at first glance appear to be equivalent to a dash pattern of 1 1 with butt line caps. The difference shows up on the strong curves: the dots created by the square line caps remain square, instead of stretching with the path.

CSS Versus SVG
Dashed Borders Versus Dashed Strokes

Dashed stroke patterns in SVG are superficially quite similar to dotted and dashed borders in CSS. The difference, as usual, is that SVG offers greater control at the cost of fewer automated adjustments.

The definitions of these border styles in CSS 2.1 were very open-ended:

dotted
:   The border is a series of dots.

dashed
:   The border is a series of short line segments.

This resulted in some noticeable cross-browser differences. Firefox and Internet Explorer draw dotted borders with circular dots; WebKit and Blink use square dots. Browsers also differ in how long dashes should be, and how much space is in between dots or dashes. The CSS Backgrounds and Borders level 3 module clarifies that dots should be round, while dashes should have square ends. However, it does not prescribe the size or spacing that should be used.

The level 3 guidelines also encourage the use of spacing that creates symmetrical corners. Most browsers now do this to some degree, but the results can be problematic when you mix borders of different widths and styles, or with corners rounded by `border-radius`. Don't expect consistent rendering from one browser to the next.

The other important difference between CSS borders and SVG strokes is that border styles, color, and width can be specified for individual sides of a box (top, right, bottom, left) independent of the others. SVG strokes, in contrast, apply to an entire shape.

More Pleasing Dash Patterns, Made with Math

On symmetrical shapes such as those in Figure 13-15, the lack of symmetry in the dotting or dashing pattern may irritate many designers. To create a symmetrical pattern, you need a dash sequence that evenly matches the length of the stroke.

For a simple rectangle, it is relatively easy to figure out the total length of the stroke around the shape (twice the width plus twice the height) and create a dash pattern to match. For Bézier curves, however, the math is a whole other level of complexity.

Luckily, the browser can do the math for you, using the `getTotalLength()` method that we first introduced when working with <textPath> in Chapter 7. It returns the length of the complete path in user units. By opening up the SVG in a browser, you can use the developer's console to call the method on the chosen path.

In SVG 1.1, `getTotalLength()` was only available on <path> elements, not on other shapes. SVG 2 makes it available on all shapes, but at the time of writing only Blink has implemented the method on the other elements.

The following snippet cycles through all the `<path>` elements in a document:

```
var paths = document.getElementsByTagName("path");
for (var i=0, n=paths.length; i<n; i++){
    console.log(paths[i].getTotalLength(), paths[i].id);
}
```

The code prints out each path's length, as well as its `id` value, so that it is easy to tell which is which. If your paths don't have `id` attributes, you could print something else such as the first part of the path data.

Of course, instead of printing out values and using them in your markup, you could use the results directly in your code, setting styles from a script.

In one version of Firefox, the code printed out the following values for the SVG in Example 13-6:

```
71.2459716796875 "heart"
82.3443603515625 "spade"
```

In other browsers, the calculated path lengths vary by as much as ±0.3 units.

The variation in path lengths is explicitly allowed by the SVG specifications: the math for calculating Bézier curve length is computationally intensive, and the browsers are allowed to use approximations.

To account for discrepancies in the browser's path length calculations, SVG `<path>` elements contain a **pathLength attribute** that allows you to specify the length you *expect* the path to be (in user units). The browser must then adjust many of its calculations on paths, scaling its calculated lengths to match your stated length.

Unfortunately, stroke dashing was *not* one of the areas where the SVG 1.1 specifications explicitly required browsers to adjust for the stated `pathLength`. SVG 2 makes it clear that dashes should be adjusted. Firefox and recent Chrome/ Blink (since 2016) make the adjustments; other browsers don't.

Theoretically, it should be easy to create an even dot pattern for the heart: just set the stated pathLength to twice an even multiple of the dash-array length (2 units), and both halves of the heart will have an even number of repeats, and therefore a matching pattern. Since the measured length of the path was slightly more than 71 units, the closest multiple of 4 units is 72.

However, for these subpixel "dashes," rounding errors add up in Chrome, and most other browsers ignore the pathLength completely. So it only works in Firefox.

Figure 13-16 shows the result (in Firefox) of setting pathLength to 72 on the dotted heart from Figure 13-15. Both the dashes and the gaps scale equally. However, the dash is so small relative to the size of the line caps that the scaling is not visible.

Figure 13-16. Dotted lines after the dash pattern is adjusted with pathLength

To achieve a result similar to Figure 13-16 in the other browsers, you would need to adjust the total dash pattern length yourself, for each shape separately. Instead of a total dash pattern of 2 units, you would want each repeat to total 2 × 71.24 / 72, or 1.9789 units:

```
stroke-dasharray: 0.0089 1.97;
```

With that change (and with the pathLength attribute removed), the heart looks like Figure 13-16 in all browsers. You would still get some *slight* variation between browsers because of the differences in path length approximations, but they are minor.

On a more complex shape, like the spade, the same strategy is not practical. There are too many corners for a simple repeat pattern to look elegant around all of them. You would need to divide the shape into multiple paths, and set separate dash patterns for each.

Future Focus

Greater Control of Dash Position

The CSS Fill and Stroke module introduces two properties that would provide greater control over awkward dashing patterns: `stroke-dash-corner` and `stroke-dash-justify`. Previous SVG draft specs had the same properties under different names; some details may still change.

The `stroke-dash-corner` property would ensure there was always a dash at every corner (line join) in a shape. Its value is the length of the dash that should be centered over the line join—whether that's a sharp corner or a smooth connection between curve segments—and would also be equally divided between the start and end of the path.

If a value other than **none** is used for `stroke-dash-corner`, the dash pattern created by `stroke-dasharray` is used to fill the path segments *in between* corner dashes independently.

The `stroke-dash-justify` property would be used to specify a strategy for adjusting the dashing pattern so that it evenly fits the path, by either increasing or decreasing the length of the pattern. You would be able to specify whether the dashes or the gaps—or both—are adjusted.

Starting Mid-Stride

When trying to place dashes precisely, you can end up wishing you'd defined the shape starting from a different point. For example, the spade icon starts off-center, where the left lobe connects with the stem, instead of at the point. For basic shapes, you don't have any control over the start of the path at all.

Although it wasn't explicitly specified in SVG 1.1, all the major browsers are consistent about where to start stroking a shape. Specifically:

- For rectangles, the "start" of a rectangle is the top-left corner, and then the path continues clockwise. If the corners are rounded, it starts *after* the curve ends.

- For a circle or ellipse, the start is the 3 o'clock position (technically: the point where the shape's edge crosses the cy position, at an x-value greater than the cx position). Again, the path is clockwise.

- Polygons, polylines, and paths follow the values in the points list or d instructions.

- A <line> starts with the (x1,y1) point.

The start point of the stroke in a text character will depend on the font, and isn't guaranteed to be consistent from one browser to the next.

SVG 2 makes these behaviors standard, by defining an "equivalent path" for each shape. However, some SVG tools may use different start points for basic shapes.

By default, the first dash in your dash array starts at this start point.

If that's not what you want, don't worry—you don't have to rewrite all your code just to get greater control over dashing. The **stroke-dashoffset property** allows you to adjust the pattern position directly.

The dash offset is the distance into the dashing pattern at which the start of the path should be positioned. As usual, the length can be specified with or without units, or as a percentage (proportional to the coordinate system diagonal, same as the other stroke properties). The stroke-dashoffset property is inheritable, and can be specified with CSS or as a presentation attribute.

Positive offsets start the dash *before* the path start. Negative offsets start the first dash *after* the path start.

The offset distance isn't an extra gap: the extra space is filled in with more dash array repeats, just at different positions than they would otherwise be.

There are two main uses of stroke-dashoffset: precise position of dashes for geometric effect, and animated dash movement.

Example 13-7 demonstrates the first use case. It uses dashes on a rectangle and a polyline. In both cases, the stroke length can be easily calculated, and the dash pattern is set to repeat an even number of times around the shape. The dash offset is used to make sure the gaps are positioned in the middle of lines instead of at the corners, creating the patterns shown in Figure 13-17.

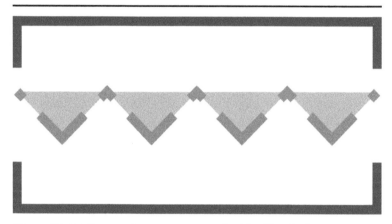

Figure 13-17. Geometric patterns created with offset dashes

Example 13-7. Using stroke-dashoffset to control which parts of a shape are stroked

```
<svg xmlns="http://www.w3.org/2000/svg" xml:lang="en"
    xmlns:xlink="http://www.w3.org/1999/xlink"
    width="410px" height="210px" viewBox="-5 -5 410 210">   ❶
    <title>Stroke Dash Offsets</title>
    <style type="text/css">
        svg {
            stroke-width: 10px;
        }
    </style>
    <rect width="400" height="200"
            fill="none" stroke="indigo"
            stroke-dasharray="500 100" stroke-dashoffset="50" />  ❷
    <polyline points="0,75 50,125 100,75 150,125 200,75
```

```
                    250,125 300,75 350,125 400,75"
        fill="darkSeaGreen" stroke="seaGreen"
        stroke-dasharray="70.71 25 20.71 25"
        stroke-dashoffset="-35.355" />
</svg>
```
❸

❶ The `viewBox` creates a 400×200 drawing region with 5 units of
    padding on each side, to make room for the outer half of the
    thick 10px strokes.

❷ The dash array pattern on the rectangle is 600 units long, so
    there will be exactly two dashes and two gaps around the
    400×200 rectangle. By default, the dash would start at the top-
    left corner and continue until halfway down the right side; the
    `stroke-dashoffset` value positions the starting corner 50 units
    into the dash, so that it is evenly distributed left and right.

❸ Each line segment in the zig-zagging polyline moves 50 units
    right and 50 units up or down. Pythagoras's theorem tells us that
    the length of the line will be $\sqrt{(50^2 + 50^2)}$, or 70.71 units. The
    total dash pattern therefore exactly covers two line segments.
    The offset positions the first long dash to start halfway down the
    first line segment, so that it is evenly balanced around the
    corner.

Figure 13-17 also re-emphasizes that a `<polyline>` creates the fill
region by connecting the end of the path back to the beginning in a
straight line, but that connecting line is not stroked. Dashes don't
change that.

Again, for positioning dashes on more complex shapes, you can use
a `<path>` element's `getTotalLength()` DOM method to calculate the
length of a curve. Unfortunately, there is no easy way to calculate the
length of *part* of a path; you would need to create a new `<path>` element that only includes the relevant path segments. As mentioned
previously, be aware that browsers differ slightly in their path length
calculations.

The second use of `stroke-dashoffset`, to create animated dashes, is
a little more forgiving of these geometric complexities.

In an animation, the specific positions of the dashes are usually less
important than the relative change. By shifting the dash offset by the
exact length of one full repeat of the dash pattern, and then repeat-

ing that animation, you can create smooth movement that appears to cycle the dashes around the entire path.

 MS Edge has the same problem with animations and transitions of unitless numbers in stroke-dashoffset as it does in stroke-width. Use explicit px units if you will be using CSS to animate. Use them anyway, to get in the habit.

Example 13-8 uses CSS animations to cycle a chain of dashes around the heart and spade icons. Figure 13-18 shows the chain-link pattern, but you'll need to run the SVG in a web browser to see the full effect.

Figure 13-18. Chain-link strokes, which could be animated

Example 13-8. Animating dashes with stroke-dashoffset

```
<svg xmlns="http://www.w3.org/2000/svg" xml:lang="en"
    xmlns:xlink="http://www.w3.org/1999/xlink"
    width="410px" height="205px" viewBox="-1 -1 44 22">
    <title>Rotating Dash Links</title>
    <style type="text/css">
        svg {
            fill: none;
            stroke-linejoin: round;            ❶
            stroke-linecap: round;
            stroke-dasharray: 1px 1px;         ❷
            animation: cycle 0.5s 20 linear;   ❸
        }
```

```
            @keyframes cycle {
                from { stroke-dashoffset: 0px; }      ❹
                to   { stroke-dashoffset: 2px; }
            }
        </style>

        <path id="heart" stroke="darkRed"
            d="M10,6 Q10,0 15,0T20,6Q20,10 15,14
                T10,20Q10,18 5,14T0,6Q0,0 5,0T10,6Z" />
        <path id="spade" stroke="#222" transform="translate(22,0)"
            d="M9,15C9,20 0,21 0,16S6,9 10,0C14,9 20,11 20,16
                S11,20 11,15Q11,20 13,20H7Q9,20 9,15Z" />
</svg>
```

❶ Round line caps and line joins create the oval links from each
   dash.

❷ When the line caps are added on to the 1-unit-long dashes, in a
   1-unit-wide stroke, they will just touch across the 1-unit-long
   gaps in the `stroke-dasharray` pattern.

❸ The shorthand `animation` property instructs the browser to
   apply the animation sequence named `cycle` over the course of
   0.5s, to repeat it 20 times, and to transition the values in a linear
   manner, without slowing down or speeding up.

❹ The `@keyframes` rule defines which properties should be
   changed by the `cycle` animation: `from` zero offset, `to` an offset
   equal to the total dash array pattern length.

 Internet Explorer does not support CSS animations of SVG properties like `stroke-dashoffset`
(Microsoft Edge animates it so long as the
lengths have units). Firefox does not correctly
update the `<use>` copy of the shape if the animation is applied directly to the `<path>` instead of
being inherited through the `<use>` itself.

You can increase support in older Webkit and
Blink browsers by duplicating all the animation-
related CSS rules (including `@keyframes`) with a
`-webkit-` prefix.

The same effect could have been created with a nonrepeating animation that changed the `stroke-dashoffset` from 0 to 40 over 10

seconds. By using the minimum repeat, we keep it DRY: to change the total length of the animation, we would only have to update the `animation` rule, and not the `@keyframes`.

Painting Lines

Strokes, as we've briefly mentioned, do not have to use solid colors. The `stroke` property, like the `fill` property, can use a `url()` function to reference a paint server—a gradient or pattern—by its `id` value.

There are two main areas where designers tend to get frustrated when using paint servers for strokes:

- The `objectBoundingBox` units used by paint servers *do not* include the stroke region.
- All paint servers create a rectangle region of paint that is unaffected by the shape or direction of the stroke.

The second point is a conceptual issue, that you will just need to wrap your head around. As much as you may logically think of a "gradient on a stroke" as meaning that the gradient follows the path direction, it doesn't work that way in SVG. The stroke is treated as another shape, not a line drawn with a pen or brush. That stroke shape is clipped from the rectangle of wallpaper-like paint server content.

For straight-line paths, you can create gradients that follow the line by using `userSpaceOnUse` units and matching up the x1, y1, x2, and y2 attributes between the `<line>` and the `<linearGradient>`.

For curved paths, there's no easy solution currently. When `<meshGradient>` is supported in browsers, you could match the path data to the mesh paths.

The misalignment of `objectBoundingBox` units and stroke sizes is more of a mathematical issue—and sometimes the numbers just don't add up.

Many gradients or patterns look fine on a stroke, without modifications. Others, you can fix by tweaking the numbers—maybe a little, maybe a lot. But in some cases, you'll have to redesign your code significantly.

It often depends on the shape you're stroking. Figure 13-19 takes the bull's-eye gradient from Example 12-5 (in Chapter 12) and applies it to the following path:

```
<path stroke="url(#bullseye)" stroke-width="20"
      d="M-100,0 H100 M0,-100 V100
         M-71,-71 L71,71 M-71,71 L71,-71"/>
```

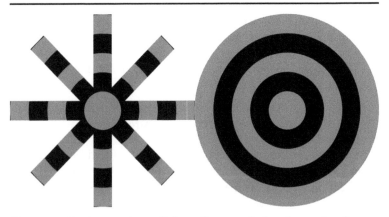

Figure 13-19. A repeating radial gradient applied to the stroke of a path (left) and the fill of a circle (right)

The path draws an 8-point asterisk. As a set of disconnected straight lines, it doesn't have a fill region, but the bounding box is still determined by the maximum and minimum x- and y-values: from (−100,100) to (100,100). In other words, the same fill region as the circle of radius 100 from the original demo (which is redrawn in Figure 13-19 for comparison). The bounding-box gradient is therefore the same size. And because the strokes of the asterisk don't go outside of the bounding box, it looks almost as if it was clipped out of the circle.

The asterisk is a bit of an exception. With most shapes, the stroke extends outside the bounding box. The visual size of the stroked shape doesn't match the size used for bounding-box scaling.

Figure 13-20 applies the linear gradient from Example 12-3 as the stroke on the following `<rect>` element:

```
<rect width="180" height="180" ry="18" x="10" y="10"
      fill="darkSlateGray"
      stroke="url(#green-gradient)" stroke-width="20" />
```

It is then compared with the same gradient on the fill of the rectangle from the original demo:

```
<rect width="200" height="200" ry="20"
      fill="url(#green-gradient)" />
```

Figure 13-20. A repeating radial gradient applied to the stroke of one rectangle (left) and fill of another (right)

In order to have the total—outer—size of both rectangles be equal, the width and height are slightly smaller on the stroked version. If you look closely, you'll see that the distance between color stops has been scaled down to match. But with a smooth, padded gradient such as this, it is hard to tell.

You only *really* start to notice the bounding-box difference when you use a paint server that has been precisely sized to fit the bounding box. In Chapter 12, we did that to create a nonrepeating image fill, in Example 12-9.

Figure 13-21 shows what happens when we apply that same `<pattern>` to the following thick-stroked version of the club icon:

```
<use xlink:href="../ch10-reuse-files/suits-symbols.svg#club"
     fill="none" stroke="url(#image-fill)" stroke-width="5"
     x="20" y="20" width="160" height="160"/>
```

 The 5px `stroke-width` may not seem that thick compared to a 160×160 width and height. But remember: that stroke will be painted in the original `<symbol>` element's 20×20 coordinate system. With 20px scaled up to fill 160px, 5px in the `<symbol>` will be equivalent to 40px in the outer `<svg>`.

For comparison, Figure 13-21 includes a second 160×160 copy of the `<symbol>`, but with the pattern used as a fill, not a stroke.

Figure 13-21. A photographic pattern tile that exactly fills the bounding box, applied to a stroked shape (left), versus the same size shape, filled (right)

The photographic pattern tile is the same size in both elements: scaled to fit in the fill region of the shape. Since half the stroke extends outside the fill, however, that isn't enough. To fill the extra sections of stroke on each side, our "nonrepeating" pattern tile gets repeated on each side.

We're going to need a bigger tile.

Specifically, we need to make the pattern tile large enough that it can cover the entire stroke region without repeats. To do that, we need to adjust the x, y, width, and height of the tile on a copy of the <pattern>:

```
<pattern id="image-stroke" xlink:href="#image-fill"
         x="-12.5%" y="-12.5%" width="125%" height="125%" />
```

Figure 13-22 shows what that looks like, when applied to the stroked icon.

Figure 13-22. A photographic pattern tile that is sized to cover an element including its stroke

This approach is not ideal. The amount by which the attributes on the <pattern> need to be adjusted depends on the ratio of the stroke-width (5px) to the bounding-box dimensions for the original <path> element (slightly less than 20×20). The stroke-width is 25% of the bounding-box width, and *half* of that will extend on each side, so the tile needs to extend 12.5% outside the bounding box, on all sides.

The adjusted <pattern> is therefore not very reusable. You may need to create separately adjusted versions for elements with different dimensions or with different stroke widths.

 This would be slightly easier if you could use CSS calc() in SVG attributes:

```
<pattern id="image-stroke"
         xlink:href="#image-fill"
         x="-5px" y="-5px"
         width="calc(100% + 10px)"
         height="calc(100% + 10px)" />
```

It would be even better with calc() and CSS variables.

SVG 2 says that both should be valid, but it's not supported in browsers yet (and completely breaks the pattern in some of them).

But even this is not the worst problem from using fill-based bounding boxes to scale stroke paint servers.

The worst problem with objectBoundingBox units occurs when you are stroking straight horizontal and vertical lines. In that case, the fill bounding box has zero height or zero width. This means the scale applied to the paint has a factor of 0 in it—and a scale of zero makes graphics disappear.

Using an objectBoundingBox pattern or gradient to stroke a straight horizontal or vertical line is therefore an error. If you specify a fallback color in your stroke declaration, it will be used instead.

The only workaround, currently, is to recreate your bounding-box pattern or gradient in userSpaceOnUse units, with attributes exactly scaled to match the shape you are stroking.

Future Focus
Painting in a Stroke Bounding Box

One of the greatest limitations of using paint servers for strokes is that the object bounding box does not contain the stroke. An often-requested feature is the ability to specify a different bounding-box that includes the stroke region.

SVG 2 defines what a "stroke bounding box" looks like, and makes it available to scripts via options sent to the `getBBox()` DOM method:

```
shape.getBBox({stroke:"true"})
```

 At the time of writing, no browsers have implemented the options for `getBBox()`. They just silently ignore the passed-in parameter, returning the regular bounding box dimensions.

Defining a stroke bounding box is the first step, and getting browsers to implement it is the second, but using it to scale stroke paint is a separate feature. And unfortunately, it's a feature that hasn't been standardized yet.

Ideally, the reference box would be specified at the time the paint server is used, rather than on the pattern or gradient element. This would allow the same gradient or pattern to be used such that it exactly fit the fill bounding box, the stroke bounding box, or any other reference box that makes sense for the shape being painted.

The new longhand `fill` and `stroke` properties in the CSS Fill and Stroke module include properties based on `background-size`, `background-position`, and `background-clip`, which include box-related sizing choices. At the time of writing (mid-2017), the exact details for how these values will map to paint server reference boxes have not been finalized. But the end goal is that you'll have full control over which reference box is used by the paint server element.

Summary: Stroke Effects

Stroking effects are one of the areas of SVG where styles and geometry intersect. The stroke region itself is a type of derived shape, built from the offical shape's geometry according to the many stroke style properties.

The full creative potential of stroking effects comes from the ways in which the different style properties intersect, such as using line caps to change the appearance of dashes. The examples in this chapter have only hinted at all the possibilities.

Nonetheless, there are countless other effects that are currently difficult to create, or require multiple shapes to be layered on top of each other. The new options proposed for SVG 2 and in the CSS Fill and Strokes module will allow much greater control, and therefore much greater creativity. Those changes, and updated implementations, will hopefully one day remove some of the most irritating obstacles to using strokes, especially with paint servers.

More Online

The "SVG Style Properties" guide includes references for all the stroking properties:

https://oreillymedia.github.io/Using_SVG/guide/style.html

"Select SVG DOM Methods and Objects" reviews the DOM methods:

https://oreillymedia.github.io/Using_SVG/guide/DOM.html

CHAPTER 14

Marking the Way

Line Markers

This chapter examines **line markers**, symbols that can be used to accent the points of a custom shape.

Markers can be added to the start and end of every segment in a path (or line, polyline, or polygon), or only to the very beginning or end.

Markers have some similarity to line joins and line caps (which we discussed in Chapter 13). Line joins and line caps can change the appearance of the ends and corners of paths, but maybe not as much as you want. They can't draw line-cap shapes other than circles or squares, and they can't draw anything wider than the stroke itself. That means they can't draw an arrowhead.

Arrowheads are the quintessential use of the `<marker>` element, but there are many other possibilities. Markers can be used to create custom line-join shapes, or to draw symbols on all the points in a line chart.

Markers offer a number of conveniences, compared to line joins, or compared to drawing each marker symbol individually as a `<use>` copy of a `<symbol>`. However, as defined in SVG 1.1, markers are still rather limited. Many things that you might expect to be able to do aren't supported. There are also a number of bugs and inconsistencies that limit the use of markers to the simpler cases.

A few additional marker options are included in SVG 2, but many other advanced features were deferred to a separate SVG Markers module. At the time of writing, it's not clear when further work might happen on those proposals.

Emphasizing Points

A <marker> element is much like a <symbol> in that it defines a small, self-contained icon. Like symbols, markers and their contents are never drawn directly. Unlike symbols, markers are not positioned one at a time, with a <use> element. Instead, they are applied to a path, line, polygon, or polyline.

The browser positions copies of the marker automatically at the line joins or line ends of the shape—any point where a path segment starts and ends (regardless of whether or not there is a visible corner).

As of SVG 1.1, <line>, <path>, <polygon>, and <polyline> are the only shapes that support markers.

SVG 2 makes markers available on the basic shapes (<rect>, <circle>, and <ellipse>), but no web browser supports this at the time of writing.

You assign a marker to a shape using one of the **marker-start, marker-end, or marker-mid properties** or presentation attributes, or the marker CSS shorthand. The value of any of these properties is a url() reference to the id of a <marker> element, or the keyword none (which is the default). All the marker properties are inherited, so you can set them on a group.

The marker-start property assigns a marker to the first point in the path or shape; the marker-end property places the marker on the final point. The marker-mid property adds markers to all the line joins or subpath start or end points in between. Unlike stroke-linecap versus stroke-linejoin, the marker properties only distinguish between the start and end of the overall shape, and not by whether the path has subpaths, or by whether the shape is opened or closed.

Closed shapes will have a start and end marker at the same point.

Line caps for subpaths in the middle of the path will be marked with the "mid" marker, not the start or end version.

The **marker shorthand property** assigns the same marker to every position. In other words, it resets all of marker-start, marker-end, and marker-mid to the same value.

 The shorthand property can only be used in CSS declarations, *not* as a presentation attribute.

By default, the origin (0,0) point of the marker contents is positioned at the exact vertex (corner or end point) of the shape. The simplest `<marker>` markup to create a circle around the marked point would look like this:

```
<marker id="m" overflow="visible">
    <circle r="2.5" />
</marker>
```

 The visible overflow is required, or else the parts of the circle on negative sides of the origin will be clipped, leaving you with a quarter-circle instead of a full one.

We'll discuss other ways to achieve the same effect in "Defining Dimensions" on page 540.

That marker would then be applied with the value url(#m) in one of the marker properties on a markable shape element:

```
<path d="M5,5 Q5,35 35,35" marker-start="url(#m)" />
```

Put those together with some fill and stroke styles on the `<circle>` and the `<path>`, and you get Figure 14-1.

Figure 14-1. A path with a marker on it

Which…is not very exciting. A single marker on a single path isn't a very good use of the `<marker>` element: you can just as easily draw the circle directly.

Markers only really become useful when there are a lot of them, or when the shapes they mark are dynamic. Then, the automatic positioning becomes an advantage.

Example 14-1 uses two markers, a circle and a diamond polygon, to highlight and differentiate the points for two different data lines in a chart. The lines in the chart are `<polyline>` elements, whose points are generated from a script. In a real-world example, that script would grab data from a file or a server; here, the data points are randomly generated. Figure 14-2 shows one possible arrangement of data.

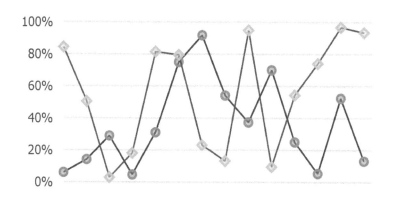

Figure 14-2. A line chart with markers at every data point

Example 14-1. Using markers to annotate a line chart

```svg
<svg xmlns="http://www.w3.org/2000/svg" xml:lang="en"
    width="4in" height="2in" viewBox="-35 -10 240 120">   ❶
    <title>DataPoint Markers on a Data Line</title>
    <path stroke="lightSkyBlue"
        d="M0, 0H200 M0,20H200 M0,40H200
            M0,60H200 M0,80H200 M0,100H200"/>        ❷
    <g text-anchor="end" aria-label="y-axis"
        style="font: 8px sans-serif; fill: navy" >
        <desc>Y-axis tick labels</desc>
        <text x="-7" dy="0.7ex" y="100">0%</text>
        <text x="-7" dy="0.7ex" y="80">20%</text>
        <text x="-7" dy="0.7ex" y="60">40%</text>
        <text x="-7" dy="0.7ex" y="40">60%</text>
        <text x="-7" dy="0.7ex" y="20">80%</text>
        <text x="-7" dy="0.7ex" y="0">100%</text>
    </g>

    <style>
        .dataline {
            fill: none;
            stroke: currentColor;
            stroke-linejoin: bevel;
        }
        .data-marker {
            stroke: currentColor;
            stroke-width: 1.5px;
            fill: currentColor;
            fill-opacity: 0.5;
        }
    </style>
```

```
<marker id="datapoint-1" overflow="visible">
    <circle class="data-marker" r="2.5" color="tomato" />    ❸
</marker>
<polyline id="dataline-1" class="dataline" color="darkRed"
        style="marker: url(#datapoint-1)" >                 ❹
    <title>Team Red</title>
</polyline>

<marker id="datapoint-2" overflow="visible">
    <polygon class="data-marker" points="-3,0 0,3 3,0 0,-3"
            color="mediumSeaGreen" />
</marker>                                                     ❺
<polyline id="dataline-2" class="dataline" color="#364"
        style="marker: url(#datapoint-2)" >
    <title>Team Green</title>
</polyline>
<script><![CDATA[
(function(){
    var datalines = ["dataline-1", "dataline-2"],
        nLines = datalines.length,
        nPoints = 14,
        dx = 15,
        maxY = 100;                                          ❻

    for (var l=0; l<nLines; l++ ) {
        var data = new Array(nPoints),
            points = new Array(nPoints);
        for (var i=0; i<nPoints; i++) {
            data[i] = [i, Math.random()];
            points[i] = [i*dx, maxY * (1 - data[i][1])];     ❼
        }

        document.getElementById(datalines[l])
                .setAttribute("points", points.toString() ); ❽
    }
})()
]]> </script>
</svg>
```

❶ The viewBox of the SVG is defined such that the main chart area
—where the data will be plotted—will be 200×100 units, with
the origin aligned with the y-axis. Extra space outside that
region leaves room for axis labels and for data points that are
close to the edges.

❷ The initial <path> and <text> elements draw the y-axis grid
lines and labels.

❸ The first <marker> will be used for the first data line. It contains a circle centered around the origin. CSS rules for the data-marker class give it a solid stroke and semitransparent fill in the currentColor, which we set in the markup using the color presentation attribute.

❹ We define and style the data lines in the markup, using a class for the shared styles and attributes for the unique ones. We assign the marker with an inline style attribute so we can use the shorthand marker property instead of setting all three presentation attributes to the same value. A child <title> element gives a label for the data series (which browsers use for accessibility and as an automatic tooltip). Despite all the styling, the lines won't be drawn unless the script runs, because the <polyline> elements do not have a points attribute.

❺ The second data line follows the same structure as the first, except that shape inside the marker is now a polygon, which again is centered on the origin. The id, color, and <title> values are also different.

❻ The simplified data visualization script includes references to the id values of the different data lines, as well as constants for how many data points will fit in the plot (14), for how much space to leave between each value on the x-axis (15 units), and for the maximum y-position on the plot (assuming the minimum is 0).

❼ The data for each line is generated as an array where each item is another two-value array, containing an integer x-value and a random y-value between 0 and 1. These data values are then converted into (x,y) points in the drawing coordinate system using our constants. In data coordinates, the y-values increase from bottom to top, but in the drawing they increase from top to bottom.

❽ The points array is transformed into a points attribute for the corresponding <polyline> with the JavaScript array's toString() method, which concatenates all the values in the individual two-value arrays, separating each number with commas. This conveniently happens to be a valid syntax for SVG `points`.

 To avoid style-matching bugs in Microsoft Edge and Internet Explorer, the styles on the marker contents are set directly on the `<circle>` and `<polygon>` (with the class `data-marker`), rather than being assigned with a class on the `<marker>` itself.

By using two different marker shapes, we make it easier to distinguish the two lines, even if the graphic is displayed in black and white—or if the person looking at it is red-green colorblind. However, this example isn't fully accessible to other users: the data values are not exposed to screen readers. You would need to provide the data in another format, such as an HTML table.

When using markers in data visualizations, it is important to realize that they are not independent elements for accessibility, user events, and other interactions. Instead, they are decorations on the main shape element, similar to the graphics inside a `<pattern>`.

Unlike independent elements, the markers cannot have `<title>` elements to create unique tooltips (and accessible names) for each value. (We talk more about `<title>`, accessibility, and tooltips in Chapter 17.) Any mouse or tap events (click or hover) are passed through to underlying shapes.

If you want the individual data markers to be independent and interactive, you'll need to draw them as independent `<use>` elements.

Scaling to Strokes

There are a couple details in Example 14-1 that we've glossed over, creating a simple example without warning you about the hidden complexities. The next few sections explore those complications, and the possibilities they create.

The first important detail that we didn't mention is that the `<polyline>` elements used the default `stroke-width` value of 1. Why is this important? Well, Figure 14-3 shows what happens if you decide to give the line a thicker stroke.

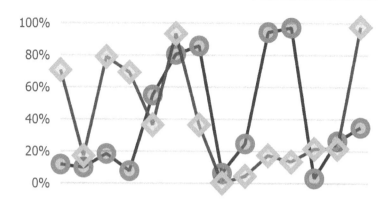

Figure 14-3. A line chart with markers, where the lines are drawn twice as thick

The only change between Figures 14-3 and 14-2 (besides a different set of randomly generated data points) is one extra CSS declaration:

```
.dataline { stroke-width: 2; }
```

But as you can tell from the figures, the stroke on the data lines is not the only thing that has doubled in size. The markers have also been doubled, in their height, width, and stroke width, equivalent to a scale(2) transform.

This is the default behavior for markers: they scale according to the stroke-width of the shape they are marking. It is a useful default when you're drawing arrowheads, but is less useful in this particular example.

You can control the marker scaling with the **markerUnits attribute** on the <marker> element. markerUnits has some similarities to the gradient and pattern *Units attributes we used in Chapter 12, but is not directly equivalent. While gradients and patterns are scaled relative to a reference *box*, markerUnits only applies a single, uniform scaling factor.

The default markerUnits value is strokeWidth; to prevent scaling with the stroke width, switch it to userSpaceOnUse:

```
<marker id="datapoint-2" overflow="visible"
        markerUnits="userSpaceOnUse" >
```

A userSpaceOnUse value for markerUnits only affects the *scale* of the marker, not the origin of the coordinate system—which always gets repositioned to the marked vertex point.

According to the specifications, percentage lengths within markers should be treated the same as any other unit, using the value from the main coordinate system, possibly scaled up for marker Units="strokeWidth".

 Both Internet Explorer and Microsoft Edge treat a <marker> as if it creates its own coordinate system (like a <symbol> or <svg>), so that percentages are relative to the marker size.

In other words, just like for patterns, it is best to avoid percentage lengths inside markers.

The markerUnits setting is an XML attribute, not a style property, so it needs to be set separately on each <marker>. There is no xlink:href attribute for markers, to use one marker as a template for another.

Figure 14-4 shows another version of the chart. The dataline class still has stroke-width of 2, but markerUnits has been set to userSpaceOnUse for both <marker> elements.

Figure 14-4. A line chart with markers, where the lines are drawn twice as thick, but the markers have a fixed size

But maybe you want the data line to be even more visible, and find the markers a bit distracting. By default, markers are painted on *top* of the shape, after the fill and stroke, and in order from start to end of the path.

You can change the layering of the stroke and the markers with the `paint-order` property that we introduced in Chapter 13. The following declaration would paint markers first, then stroke, then fill (if there was any fill):

```
.dataline { paint-order: markers stroke; }
```

Adding that declaration to the `dataline` class in our modified code from Example 14-1 creates a chart like Figure 14-5.

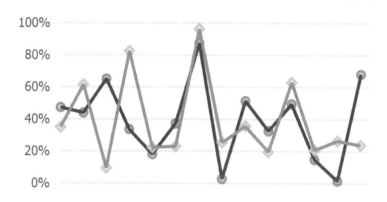

Figure 14-5. A line chart with markers drawn under the line

The two different lines are still drawn separately: markers and line for "Team Green" are drawn on top of the markers and line for "Team Red." If you wanted both lines to be drawn on top of both sets of markers, you would need to <use> separate copies of the <polyline> elements, and apply the markers to the bottom layers and the stroke styles to the top layer.

Multiple <use> layers are also the workaround to create `paint-order` effects in browsers that don't support the property.

The `paint-order` property is not yet supported in Microsoft Edge, and is not supported in many older web browsers still in use. It should therefore only be used for minor design tweaks such as this.

Drawing markers *without* a stroke isn't just for workarounds, though. It can be used if you want to emphasize the points but not the order in which they are connected. Figure 14-6 shows one run of our example code if the `dataline` class is set to have `stroke: none`. The line chart has become a scatterplot.

Figure 14-6. A scatterplot chart drawn as markers on unstroked polylines

Using markers to draw an entire data series with a single element can have an important performance boost for very large data sets. But it comes at a cost: the data values are now completely transparent to mouse and tap events, so you can't add any `:hover` effects or JavaScript event handling, and the `<title>` of the `<polyline>` elements never shows up as a tooltip.

You can make the invisible stroke interactive again by changing the `pointer-events` property, which we'll discuss in Chapter 18. But there is currently no way to make the markers themselves react to pointer events.

Another thing to note: with the default `markerUnits` value, the markers will still scale according to `stroke-width`, even if the stroke is not drawn.

Orienting Arrows

The markers in the data chart examples are all drawn in the same orientation as the main coordinate system (although you can't really tell for the circles). This is the default, and is usually what you want for labeling points, especially if the marker includes text or other content that should stay horizontal regardless of the direction of the line it decorates.

However, we've mentioned a few times that markers are also used for arrowheads. And it would be a pretty strange-looking arrow if the arrowheads always pointed in the same direction, regardless of the angle of the line they are attached to.

The **orient attribute** on the `<marker>` element can be used to control whether markers reorient themselves according to the direction of the line. The default value is 0, which means that all markers are drawn with a 0° rotation, or no rotation at all. Any other numeric value will be treated as a rotation in degrees, relative to the shape's coordinate system.

The `orient` value you are most likely to use is `auto`, which will rotate the shape to match the line, so that the marker's x-axis lines up with the angle of the line (or the line tangent to a curve).

```
<marker id="arrowhead" orient="auto">
```

On corners, autorotation rotates to match the average of the incoming and outgoing line angles.

Browsers are very inconsistent about calculating the orientation angle of markers at the start or end of disconnected subpaths, or markers that are followed or preceded by a zero-length path segment.

Example 14-2 uses the `orient` attribute to create start markers that stay at a fixed angle, and mid and end markers (arrowheads) that rotate to match the line. Figure 14-7 shows the result, applied to paths pointing in various directions.

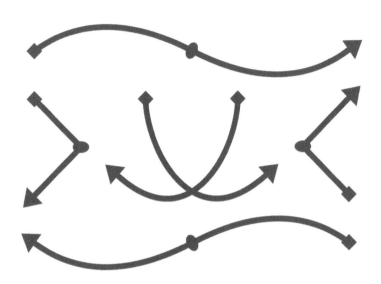

Figure 14-7. Arrows created with line markers on paths

Example 14-2. Drawing arrowheads that rotate with a line—and starting markers that don't—with the orient attribute

```
<svg xmlns="http://www.w3.org/2000/svg" xml:lang="en"
     xmlns:xlink="http://www.w3.org/1999/xlink"
     width="400px" height="300px" viewBox="0 0 400 300">
    <title>Arrow Markers with Automatic and Fixed Orientation</title>
    <style type="text/css">
        .arrow {
            fill: none;
            stroke: darkMagenta;
            stroke-width: 6;
            marker-start: url(#start);        ❶
            marker-end: url(#end);
            marker-mid: url(#mid);
        }
        marker {
            fill: darkMagenta;                ❷
            stroke: none;
            overflow: visible;
        }
```

```
</style>
<marker id="start" orient="45">
    <rect x="-1" y="-1" width="2" height="2" />    ❸
</marker>
<marker id="end" orient="auto">
    <polygon points="0,-2 3,0 0,2" />             ❹
</marker>
<marker id="mid" orient="auto">
    <ellipse rx="1" ry="1.5" />                    ❺
</marker>

<path class="arrow" d="M30,50 Q100,0 200,50 T370,50" />    ❻
<path class="arrow" d="M370,250 Q300,200 200,250 T30,250" />
<path class="arrow" d="M30,100 L80,150 30,200" />
<path class="arrow" d="M370,200 L320,150 370,100" />
<path class="arrow" d="M150,100 C150,150 200,250 280,180" />
<path class="arrow" d="M250,100 C250,150 200,250 120,180" />
</svg>
```

❶ The different markers are assigned to the arrows with the marker-start, marker-end, and marker-mid properties in CSS.

❷ The <marker> elements themselves are also styled, to use a fill color that matches the arrows' stroke.

❸ The start-point marker uses a <rect> element to draw a square centered on the origin, and then uses the orient attribute to rotate that square by 45°.

❹ The end-point marker uses a <polygon> to draw a triangle that points toward the positive x-axis, with its base at the origin. It uses the auto value for orient so that the marker's x-axis—and therefore the triangle's point—will always point in the direction of the line being marked.

❺ The mid-point marker also uses auto orientation. The marker content is an ellipse with a larger ry value than rx; after reorientation, this means that the long axis of the ellipse will be angled *across* the average angle of the lines, and the short axis will go *along* the average angle.

❻ The arrows are drawn as <path> elements with various segment types: smoothly connected quadratic Beziér curves, sharply bent lines, and single-segment cubic curves.

Example 14-2 doesn't use any arc path segments, for a reason: Blink and WebKit browsers convert arcs into a series of cubic Beziér curves, and then draw extra mid markers at the points where those curves connect. For consistent behavior cross-browser, avoid mid-point markers on paths with arcs in them.

The markers in Example 14-2 all use the default (strokeWidth) value of markerUnits. Since the arrows use stroke-width: 6, the markers are drawn six times their defined size. The <rect> in the start marker is therefore not 2px square, but is instead two times the stroke width, or 12px square.

An important thing to note about Example 14-2 is that we had to explicitly style the markers to match the lines. If we had different-colored arrows, we would need different <marker> elements for each color.

Unlike symbols duplicated with <use>, markers do not inherit any styles from the element they are used on. Even if they did, this wouldn't be what we needed, since it is the marker's fill property that needs to match the line's stroke.

Or at least, that's what the specifications say. Internet Explorer incorrectly inherits style attributes from the <path> to the <marker>. To avoid overly large marker shapes, you need to explicitly set stroke: none to override the inherited value.

Microsoft Edge corrects the style inheritance (so marker contents inherit from the <marker> element), but does not completely match the spec for style matching. Avoid selectors like marker > path, which depend on the relationships between the marker and its contents.

Manually coordinating marker and stroke styles is a bother when using solid colors, but it is impossible when using complex paint. Figure 14-8 shows the end result if the solid darkMagenta is replaced by a horizontal, purple-to-magenta linear gradient on both the paths' stroke and the markers' fill.

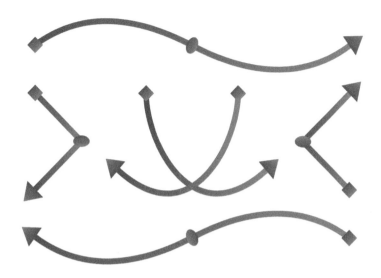

Figure 14-8. Line-marker arrows, where the line and the markers are painted with the same gradient

Each marker shape gets its own copy of the gradient, scaled to fit that shape, independent of the gradient on the path it is marking. Even a `userSpaceOnUse` gradient won't fix matters, since each marker is painted in its own coordinate system, centered on the origin and then rotated into the correct orientation.

Future Focus
Automatically Coordinating Markers with Their Shapes

A much-requested feature for SVG markers is the ability to automatically coordinate markers with the `fill` and/or `stroke` of the shape they are marking.

SVG 2 extends the `fill` and `stroke` properties to support two new keyword values: `context-fill` and `context-stroke`. For markers, these values would reference the fill or stroke in effect for the shape being marked. So for the markers in Example 14-2, we could use:

```
fill: context-stroke;
```

In addition, gradients and patterns referenced with a context keyword would be scaled according to the bounding box and coordinate system of the marked element (the "context element"), rather than by the individual shapes within the marker.

The context keywords are also used in the SVG-in-OpenType specification, to describe how shapes within the font glyphs use the fill and stroke from the text element that is referencing the font. SVG-in-OpenType also defines a generic **context-value** keyword that can be used in any property.

In SVG 2, the context keywords could also be used on shapes within symbols, so that a gradient or pattern applied to a **<use>** copy of that symbol would be applied to the entire symbol continuously, instead of being broken down according to the individual shapes within the symbol.

At the time of writing, no web browser teams have committed to implementing the context paint keywords, other than for fonts. With new work on **fill** and **stroke** being moved to the CSS Fill and Stroke module, it is possible that these features will get left behind, or redefined.

Defining Dimensions

All the marker examples so far have explicitly allowed overflow, using either CSS or presentation attributes to set it to visible. From that, you might have guessed that markers have fixed boundaries, and content that extends outside those boundaries is normally hidden.

So why have we been forcing our markers to overflow?

Because the default position of the marker boundaries isn't particularly useful. But it's only a default, and there are multiple attributes that allow you to control it. Once you know how to control the size and position of the marker boundaries, you can safely let overflow be hidden, without hiding the marker itself.

A <marker> element has a default width and height of 3 units in both directions. The origin (the marked point, by default) is at the top-left corner of this 3×3 square.

Those dimensions are in the scaled units, after the markerUnits attribute is applied. That means that, by default, the marker is a square three times the stroke-width of the marked shape.

If you do not reset overflow, any graphics outside of the marker rectangle are clipped.

In other words, without visible overflow and using all the default attributes, a marker is positioned so the unclipped parts of the marker are off-center, to the left and below the marked point. That's the not-very-useful part.

You can change the size of the marker rectangle using **markerWidth and markerHeight attributes** on the <marker> element. The value can be a number of user units, length with units, or percentage—but all will be affected by any scaling from markerUnits.

Why would you need to set a different markerWidth and markerHeight value when you can simply make overflow visible? Partly because it can make the browser implementation more efficient if it knows that a graphic will be clipped to a certain region. But more usefully, you can use viewBox to create a scaled coordinate system of your choice that fits within the marker region.

With a viewBox, you can turn any symbol or icon you have already created into a marker, and then scale it to your desired markerWidth and markerHeight. If need be, you can also use a preserve AspectRatio attribute to control how the viewBox adjusts to the available space.

We've mentioned a few times that (by default) the origin of the marker's coordinate system is positioned over the corner or end point of the line that you are marking:

- If you have a viewBox, the marker's origin is the origin of the viewBox coordinate system.

- If you *don't* have a viewBox, the origin will be in the top-left corner of the marker rectangle.

So, one option to control the position of your marker is to use the viewBox to adjust the marker's origin.

The other option is to change *which* coordinate gets aligned, using the `refX` and `refY` attributes.

`refX` and `refY` define a **reference point**, in the marker's coordinate system, that will be aligned with the exact vertex point of the shape being marked. They are both 0 by default, which creates the default reference point—the (0,0) origin.

The value of `refX` or `refY` is a length or a number of user units, measured in the scaled marker coordinate system, after it has been adjusted for `viewBox`.

 You can even use `refX` and `refY` values that are outside of the marker dimensions to create a marker label that is offset from the line it is marking.

Example 14-3 uses all of these attributes to modify the code from Example 14-2 in such a way that the marker contents are drawn within the marker boundaries, and `overflow` can remain hidden. The result will still look identical to Figure 14-7.

Example 14-3. Positioning and scaling a marker, without needing visible overflow

```
<svg xmlns="http://www.w3.org/2000/svg" xml:lang="en"
    xmlns:xlink="http://www.w3.org/1999/xlink"
    width="400px" height="300px" viewBox="0 0 400 300">
    <title>Arrow Markers using Size and Position Attributes</title>
    <style type="text/css">
        .arrow {
            fill: none;
            stroke: darkMagenta;
            stroke-width: 6;
            marker-start: url(#start);
            marker-end: url(#end);
            marker-mid: url(#mid);
        }
        marker {
            fill: darkMagenta;                          ❶
            stroke: none;
        }
    </style>
    <marker id="start" markerWidth="2" markerHeight="2"
            refX="1" refY="1" orient="45">              ❷
        <rect width="2" height="2" />
```

```
    </marker>
    <marker id="end" viewBox="0 -2 3 4" orient="auto"
        markerHeight="4">                              ❸
      <polygon points="0,-2 3,0 0,2" />
    </marker>
    <marker id="mid" orient="auto" viewBox="-1 -1.5 2 3">  ❹
      <ellipse rx="1" ry="1.5" />
    </marker>

    <path class="arrow" d="M30,50 Q100,0 200,50 T370,50" />
    <path class="arrow" d="M370,250 Q300,200 200,250 T30,250" />
    <path class="arrow" d="M30,100 L80,150 30,200" />
    <path class="arrow" d="M370,200 L320,150 370,100" />
    <path class="arrow" d="M150,100 C150,150 200,250 280,180" />
    <path class="arrow" d="M250,100 C250,150 200,250 120,180" />
</svg>
```

❶ The overflow: visible style is no longer required.

❷ The start marker uses a default coordinate system in a 2×2
    marker, but then uses refX and refY to change the position of
    the marker relative to the marked point. The <rect> can there-
    fore be positioned at the origin (instead of offset with x and y
    attributes) and still be centered over the end of the line. The
    orient rotation is applied relative to the refX and refY point.

❸ The end marker uses the default (0,0) reference point, but uses a
    viewBox to position that origin point somewhere other than the
    top-left corner (in this case, the center-left edge). A marker
    Height attribute increases the size of the marker to 3×4; without
    it, the arrowhead would be scaled down to fit the 3×3 default
    marker size.

❹ The mid-point marker also uses a viewBox with a centered ori-
    gin to fit around the <ellipse>. The viewBox dimensions are
    2×3, but the marker height and width are left as the default 3×3.
    The default preserveAspectRatio applies, centering the
    viewBox within the available space.

For simple markers like these, you generally only need to use *either* a
viewBox *or* refX and refY, since the viewBox can be used to reposition the origin within the marker clipping region. However, if you
are reusing graphics that have already been drawn for another purpose, they might not be conveniently centered over the origin. In

that case, the viewBox can control the scale while refX and refY control the positioning.

More Online

Using viewBox, refX, and refY, you can easily convert a <symbol> (for example, from an icon set) into a <marker>.

Read more in "Re-purposing Icons as Markers", which *also* has a few more warnings about why markers—particularly auto-oriented markers—sometimes aren't so easy, after all:

> *https://oreillymedia.github.io/Using_SVG/extras/ch14-icon-marker.html*

Future Focus
Expanded Marker Position Options

A wide variety of new features and abilities have been proposed for line markers—so many that the major changes have been separated out into their own SVG Markers module.

A few minor additions are integrated in the SVG 2 specification:

- A new value for the orient attribute, auto-start-reverse would allow the same marker to be used at the start and end of a line, but rotated 180° for the start. So a single arrowhead marker could be used for both the start and end of a line.

  This option is supported in recent versions of WebKit, Blink, and Gecko (Firefox) browsers, but not yet in Microsoft browsers. Unfortunately, since the orientation is set in the markup, not in the style properties, there's no easy way to offer a fallback.

- Fixed-angle orientations could use angle units instead of a number of degrees.

- The refX and refY attributes will accept keyword values: left, right, or center for refX, and top, bottom, or center for refY. These match the equivalent new attributes on <symbol> elements.

- Markers will be positionable on basic shapes (`<rect>`, `<circle>`, and `<ellipse>`) using the standard path equivalents for each shape: circles and ellipses would be constructed from four arcs, starting at the 3 o'clock position and moving clockwise, while rectangles would be made from straight line segments and arcs for rounded corners.

- It will be possible to associate a marker with a shape by making the marker a child element and using the `child` keyword or a CSS selector in the marker style properties, instead of using a `url()` reference to the marker `id`. This will make it easier to build dynamic data visualizations with JavaScript without having to be certain that the `id` value is unique for the entire document.

Much greater changes to markers proposed in the SVG Markers module will apply to how markers are positioned along a path. Currently, markers can only be positioned at end points or joins between line segments; these are called *vertex* markers under the new classification. The SVG Markers module introduces three new types of markers:

- *Segment* or edge markers would be positioned at the mid-point of each line segment.

- *Pattern* markers would be spaced out along the lines using a repeating pattern similar to the `stroke-dasharray` property.

- *Positioned* markers would be placed at specific, author-defined locations along the path, using a new `position` attribute on the `<marker>` element. These markers would have to be child elements to the shape they are associated with. This would, for example, support maps with highway numbers positioned along roadways in such a way that they are always clear to read.

The graphics for positioned markers could be duplicated with an `href` attribute (*not* `xlink:href`, since the `xlink` namespace is being phased out). At the time of writing, the proposal is not as flexible as similar duplications of pattern or gradient content—only the position could be changed each time it is duplicated, not other attributes.

Another new concept, the exact details of which may still change, is the idea of stroke "knock-out" regions around a marker. This would define a certain area on either side of the marker that would not be stroked. Among many other possible effects, this would allow you to create arrowheads with the *point* of the arrow exactly matching the end of the line, instead of its base. Currently, if you try to do this, the stroke will show through behind the point.

Summary: Line Markers

Markers have all the appearance of individual icons, but are positioned within your graphic as decorations on another shape. Like other SVG graphical effects, the marker structure is defined in your SVG markup, and the other shape references the <marker> with a url() reference in a style property.

Attributes on the <marker> element give you considerable flexibility in sizing and positioning the markers relative to the points they mark—which almost makes up for the fact that the default size and position is off-center. However, you currently can only mark the vertex points on a shape, and other than the start and end points, all points are marked the same. This makes markers less useful for annotating lines on a map or creating decorative effects.

Your options for styling the markers, and in particular, styling them to match the shape they are marking, are also currently limited—partly by the SVG 1.1 spec, and partly by browser bugs. Be sure to fully define all styles on the marker contents directly, and to test your graphics thoroughly.

More Online

A reference for the <marker> element is included in the "Paint Server Elements and Markers" section of the markup guide:

https://oreillymedia.github.io/Using_SVG/guide/ markup.html#paint-marker

The marker style properties introduced in this chapter are included in the reference list in the "SVG Style Properties" guide:

https://oreillymedia.github.io/Using_SVG/guide/style.html

CHAPTER 15

Less Is More

Clipping and Masking

The graphical effects we've covered in the past few chapters have applied effects to individual shapes or text elements, changing the way the vectors are painted into pixels. The effects we'll cover in this chapter (clipping and masking) and the next one (filters and blend modes) are **layer effects**: they can apply to single shapes, but also to composited groups, `<image>` elements in SVG, or—with browser support limitations—to non-SVG elements styled with CSS.

This chapter looks at clipping and masking, two methods for removing pieces from a graphic layer, making it partially transparent.

Clipping and masking are often confused. Many visual effects can be achieved by either a clip or a mask. But there are important differences.

Clipping is a vector operation. It uses a **clipping path** that always references a geometrical shape, and creates a cleanly cut result. Parts of the graphic are either inside or outside the clipping path: there are no halfway measures.

Masking is a pixel operation. The **masks** that it uses are variable-strength image layers (typically grayscale) that define the amount of transparency at each point. The variation means that a mask can smooth or "feather" the edges of the transparency effect, creating semitransparent sections and blurred edges.

Both options have well-supported SVG definitions (using the <clipPath> and <mask> elements), as well as newer CSS shorthand approaches. The CSS-only versions were designed as extensions of the SVG methods, not as competitors. Both versions are intended to apply to both SVG elements and CSS-styled HTML elements. However, browser implementations have been erratic, updating the SVG and CSS rendering code separately.

Unfortunately, automatic CSS fallback and @supports tests are not reliable for either property: the CSS parser may recognize a declaration as valid, but that doesn't mean the browser rendering engine will use that style when drawing a particular element.

The best browser support comes from the SVG-defined effects applied to elements within an SVG graphic. For anything other than the all-SVG methods, carefully consider the appearance of your website if the effect is not applied.

Fading Away with the opacity Property

Before we get into clipping and masking, let's take a moment to review the simplest way to make a layer of your graphic partially transparent: the **opacity property**. Opacity changes can be thought of as a uniform mask, making every pixel in that graphic layer transparent by an equal amount.

 The opacity property was one of the first SVG features to cross over into general CSS use. Any web browser that supports SVG will also support opacity applied to HTML elements.

Just like the fill-opacity and stroke-opacity properties, the value of opacity is a number between 0 (completely transparent) and 1 (completely opaque).

Unlike the fill and stroke versions, the core opacity property is a layer effect. If you change the opacity of an <svg>, <g>, or <use> element, the effect does *not* inherit down to the individual shapes. Instead, all the graphics in that container are painted together, and then the final result is made more transparent.

Figure 15-1 shows the difference. It uses three copies of the cartoon face we created in Example 5-5 in Chapter 5, arranged as inline SVG in a web page. The first face is directly copied from the original example, except that the `<svg>` element has been given the `id="face"`. The second and third copies are `<use>` duplicates, with slight style tweaks:

```
<svg><use xlink:href="#face"
          fill-opacity="0.7" stroke-opacity="0.7"/></svg>
<svg><use xlink:href="#face" opacity="0.7"/></svg>
```

Each `<svg>` element has also been given a repeating CSS gradient background, so that the transparency changes are obvious.

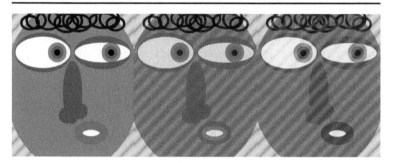

Figure 15-1. An SVG face, and versions of it made transparent with fill-opacity and stroke-opacity (center) or with opacity (right)

With semitransparent fill and stroke, the layered construction of the graphic becomes visible. Each overlapping layer obscures a bit more of the background.

With reduced `opacity`, however, the entire `<use>` element is treated as a single image. Every point becomes equally transparent. The individual shapes don't matter, only the final colors at each point.

 If parts of the original graphic had been partially transparent, the `opacity` change on the parent element would have compounded the transparency. An `opacity` value of 0.7 makes every point 70% as opaque as it otherwise would have been.

There are consequences of the layer-effect behavior of `opacity`. Because it applies to the final, composited (painted) result of that element's child content, it *flattens* effects such as 3D transformations and `z-index` stacking layers. The same is true for clipping, masking, filters, and blend modes, all of which apply an effect to a flattened layer of a graphic.

The Clean-Cut Clip

We've used the term "clipping" informally throughout the book to discuss the `overflow` property: when `overflow` is `hidden` on an `<svg>` or other element with defined boundaries, any graphics outside of the boundary rectangle are not drawn. They are *clipped* off.

Clipping paths work similarly, except that the boundary doesn't have to be a rectangle: it can be any vector shape. When you clip a graphic to a clipping path, only the parts of the graphic that are inside the path will be drawn. Because a clipping path is a binary, on-or-off operation, it operates very fast in terms of rendering and processing overhead.

Figure 15-2 illustrates the process at a conceptual level. We'll look at the different ways to create it with code in the following sections.

The clipping path (triangle) is scaled and aligned to fit over the graphic (photograph). Then all parts of the photograph that don't overlap the triangle are removed.

 The photograph in Figure 15-2 is of an F/A-18 fighter jet passing through the sound barrier, creating a shockwave of condensation behind it. It was taken by Ensign John Gay of the USS *Constellation*, US Navy. You can read more about the photo and science from NASA (*https://apod.nasa.gov/apod/ap010221.html*).

Clipping paths can be somewhat frustrating to debug. If the clipping path does not *intersect* the clipped graphic, the graphic will completely disappear—clipped away to nothing. For the clipped graphic to actually be visible, the clipping path and the graphic must overlap.

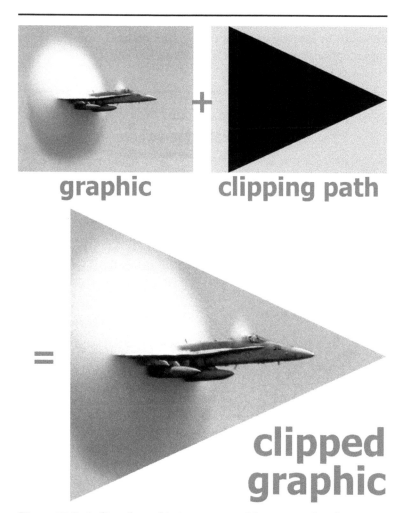

graphic   clipping path

=

clipped
graphic

*Figure 15-2. A clipped graphic is constructed from a graphic (here, a
photograph) and a vector clipping path (here, a triangular polygon)*

 If you're fighting with a completely clipped graphic, try making your clipping-path shape larger and larger, until at least some of it intersects the graphic. Then you can figure out where both shapes are, and—hopefully—why they weren't where you thought they should be.

The examples in this chapter mostly use the well-supported all-SVG approach to clipping paths, but we've also included examples of the newer options created by the CSS Masking module.

Future Focus
Clipping Paths Everywhere

SVG clipping paths, as defined in SVG 1.1, work like most other SVG graphical effects: you define the effect with SVG markup elements, and then apply it with a `url()` cross-reference in another element's style property.

The CSS Masking module adds a syntax for clipping paths defined entirely in CSS, and extends clipping paths (with either syntax) to apply to CSS-styled HTML and XML elements.

The future is *almost* here. You can use these options now, so long as the effect is nonessential, and everything still looks acceptable without the clip.

 At the time of writing, Microsoft browsers have not implemented the new clipping options. WebKit/Safari require the `-webkit-` prefix.

In Firefox, the new options are supported, without restrictions, as of version 54 (stable release mid-2017). Support for SVG clipping paths applied to non-SVG elements has been in Firefox for a couple years.

In Chrome, the basic syntax is supported, but not all the options in the spec.

But test carefully: in addition to the browsers that don't support clipping at all, there are many details and edge cases that are still buggy, or simply aren't well defined in the specs.

Creating a Custom Clipping Path

Clipping paths are applied to a graphic layer with the **clip-path** **CSS property** or presentation attribute. Since clipping is a layer effect, the clip-path property is *not* normally inherited.

In SVG 1.1, the value of clip-path is either none (the default, no clipping) or a url() reference to an **SVG <clipPath> element**.

Note the spelling: the CSS property is clip-path (with a hyphen); the XML element is <clipPath> (capital P, no hyphen).

The <clipPath> element can theoretically be in another file, but—as with most SVG graphical effects—browser support is best if the referenced element is in the same document. If it is in another file, cross-origin restrictions apply.

The only required attribute on the <clipPath> element is an id, so you can reference it in the clip-path property of the other graphic.

A <clipPath> element has one unique attribute: **clipPathUnits**. If you've read Chapter 12, it will look familiar. The options are the same as the *Units attributes for patterns and gradients: objectBoundingBox or userSpaceOnUse.

The default value of clipPathUnits is userSpaceOnUse.

The actual clipping path is defined by shapes included as children of the <clipPath> element. Specifically, a <clipPath> may contain:

- shape elements, normally <rect>, <circle>, <ellipse>, <polygon>, or <path>
- <text> elements (although beware: this text is completely inaccessible!)
- <use> elements that directly copy individual shape or text elements

The triangular clipping path used in Figure 15-2 was defined by a simple three-point <polygon> inside a bounding-box <clipPath>:

```
<clipPath id="clip" clipPathUnits="objectBoundingBox">
    <polygon id="p" points="0.1,0 1,0.5 0.1,1" />
</clipPath>
```

We then apply that clipping path by referencing the <clipPath> element's id in the clip-path presentation attribute of the second copy of the image:

```
<use xlink:href="#image"
     x="20" y="200" width="400" height="320"
     clip-path="url(#clip)" />
```

We could also have applied the clipping directly to an <image> element (instead of a <use> copy), or with a CSS rule instead of a presentation attribute.

The actual clipping path is defined solely by the fill-region geometry of the elements inside the <clipPath>. Strokes, fill, opacity, and most other styles have no effect. For this reason, a <polyline> will behave exactly like a <polygon>, and a straight <line> will have no effect.

The only styles that are relevant inside a <clipPath> are the properties that affect the core geometry of the vector shapes:

- the SVG 2 geometric properties (which correspond to SVG 1.1 geometric attributes)
- the transform property (which also was only available as an attribute in SVG 1.1)
- clip-path clipping
- text layout and font-selection properties
- display and visibility

If any of the <clipPath> child elements has display set to none, or visibility set to hidden, then that element does not contribute to the clipping path. This could be useful if you are animating the clipping path, to show or hide different parts of your graphic.

The fill-rule property affects geometry of a shape, but it *doesn't* affect shapes inside a <clipPath>. Instead, there is a dedicated

clip-rule property that has the exact same options (evenodd versus nonzero) and default (nonzero). It only applies on each shape individually, not the combination of multiple shapes in the clipping path.

Intersecting Shapes

Since the result of a clipping operation is the overlap of two vector graphics, clipping can be used to draw complex shapes that are the *intersection* of simpler shapes. To demonstrate, we'll use a common example of two basic shapes intersecting: a Venn diagram of two overlapping circles.

In a Venn diagram, you use two or three circles to represent two or three different categories, and then overlap the circles to represent items that fit in multiple categories. We'll draw it by predefining a circle in the middle of a centered coordinate system, and then <use>-ing it with different horizontal offsets:

```
<defs>
    <circle id="circle" r="12" />
</defs>
<use xlink:href="#circle" x="-6" fill="royalBlue" />
<use xlink:href="#circle" x="+6" fill="lightGreen" />
```

On their own, these circles look like Figure 15-3.

To turn these overlapping circles into a proper Venn diagram, the area shared between the circles needs to be visibly distinguished. There are many possible ways to achieve this: we could make the circles partially transparent, or use blending modes, so that you could see one circle through the other. But in order to have full control over the appearance of the overlap, we need to draw the "intersection section" of the diagram as its own element.

We *could* do that with a <path> element, figuring out the coordinates for arc segments. But we won't. Instead, we're going to draw the overlap exactly as we defined it: as the region where one circle intersects another. One circle will be our graphic, and the other circle will be our clipping path.

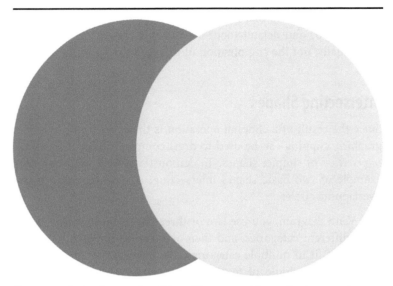

Figure 15-3. An incomplete Venn diagram, without the intersection section

For this example, we are going to *draw* the circle on the right, and then *clip* it to fit within the circle on the left. So in order to keep ourselves straight, we call the clipping path `clip-left`:

```
<clipPath id="clip-left">
</clipPath>
```

We want our clipping path to be defined in terms of the main coordinate system, so we will be able to align the circle in the clipping path with the existing circle in our diagram. This means that the default `userSpaceOnUse` value of `clipPathUnits` is just what we need.

As it's currently defined, if we applied `clip-path: url(#clip-left)` to a graphic, that graphic would disappear. This is an empty `<clipPath>` element: it does not include any shapes to define the actual clipping path. There is nothing for the clipped graphic to intersect with, so the graphic would get clipped away to nothing.

To create a clipping path that clips a graphic to only include the parts that overlap the left circle, we <use> a copy of our predefined circle as a child of the <clipPath> element:

```
<clipPath id="clip-left">
    <use xlink:href="#circle" x="-6" />
</clipPath>
```

The x offset is the same as that for the left circle in the actual drawing.

You *cannot* reuse the <use> element that already has the x offset applied. The SVG specs only allow <use> elements in a <clipPath> if they *directly* reference a shape or <text> element.

Microsoft browsers allow indirect references to other <use> elements, but other browsers don't: they treat it as an empty clipping path, meaning that the graphic gets clipped away to nothing.

SVG 2 suggests that browsers should ignore the clipping path altogether if it has invalid content, but none have implemented it this way yet.

The final step is to draw a circle that overlaps the *right* circle in our Venn diagram, and apply our clip-left clipping path to it.

You might think you could do that with code like this:

```
<use xlink:href="#circle" x="+6" fill="mediumTurquoise"
    clip-path="url(#clip-left)" />
```

But if you did that, you'd get Figure 15-4—which isn't quite what a Venn diagram should look like.

The problem? The x and y attributes on <use> elements are treated as *transformations*. And transformations change the user-space coordinate system. The turquoise copy of the circle is getting clipped to the parts that overlap the blue circle, *before* it gets shifted right to align with the green circle.

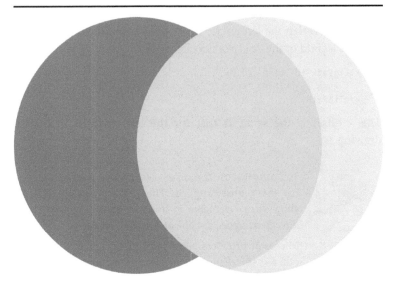

Figure 15-4. A misaligned Venn diagram, caused by clipping a <use> element directly

The solution—for this and most other problems involving transformations messing up `userSpaceOnUse` clipping or masking—is to apply the clipping to a group in the untransformed coordinate system. Then include the transformed element (or in this case, the `<use>` with an x attribute) inside that group:

```
<g clip-path="url(#clip-left)">
    <use xlink:href="#circle" x="+6" fill="mediumTurquoise" />
</g>
```

With that, we finally have a proper Venn diagram: Figure 15-5. The turquoise-colored cat's-eye shape in the middle now correctly matches the intersecting circles on either side.

Now that we have three distinct shapes for the three distinct areas, we can fill those shapes however we like. Example 15-1 compiles all the code snippets together, then adds a stripe pattern (instead of a blended color) to represent the overlap, and some stroke outlines over the top, as shown in Figure 15-6.

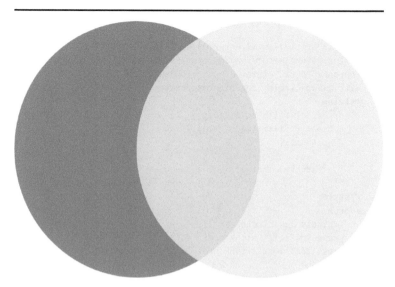

Figure 15-5. A solid-color Venn diagram, created with clipping paths

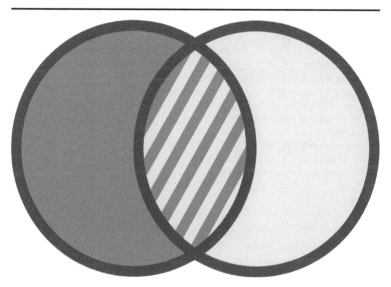

Figure 15-6. A two-circle Venn diagram with a striped pattern fill

Example 15-1. Using clipping paths to draw a patterned Venn diagram

```
<svg xmlns="http://www.w3.org/2000/svg" xml:lang="en"
    xmlns:xlink="http://www.w3.org/1999/xlink"
    height="240px" width="360px" viewBox="-18 -12 36 24">
    <title>Two-Circle Venn Diagram</title>
    <style>
        .left  { fill: royalBlue; }
        .right { fill: lightGreen; }
        .outlines {
            fill: none;
            stroke: indigo;
        }
    </style>
    <defs>
        <circle id="circle" r="11.5" />
        <use id="left" xlink:href="#circle" x="-6"/>
        <use id="right" xlink:href="#circle" x="6"/>
    </defs>
    <clipPath id="clip-left">
        <use xlink:href="#circle" x="-6" />
    </clipPath>
    <pattern id="stripes" patternUnits="userSpaceOnUse"
            width="2" height="100%"
            patternTransform="rotate(30)">
        <rect width="2" height="100%" class="left" />
        <rect width="1" height="100%" class="right" />
    </pattern>
    <use xlink:href="#left"  class="left" />
    <use xlink:href="#right" class="right" />
    <g clip-path="url(#clip-left)">
        <use xlink:href="#circle" x="+6" fill="url(#stripes)" />
    </g>
    <g class="outlines">
        <use xlink:href="#left" />
        <use xlink:href="#right" />
    </g>
</svg>
```

The strokes in Example 15-1 are worth a second look. We can't stroke the *clipped* shape directly. Well, we could, but the stroke would only wrap around the curve that is actually an edge of the circle, not the curve that was created by the clipping path. And we can't just stroke the underlying circles, because those strokes would get hidden by the overlapping layers.

So, instead, the strokes are their own layer: copies of the intersecting circles, drawn with just strokes and no fill.

Finally, because "inside" strokes aren't yet supported in SVG, the overall radius of our predefined circle has been shrunk slightly, so that the outside radius of the circle + stroke is still 12 units.

Clipping a clipPath

With that example accomplished, how would we create a *three-category* Venn diagram? That's a diagram like Figure 15-7, with three circles, all overlapping, including a center section for items that belong in all three categories.

Figure 15-7. A three-circle Venn diagram

The three overlapping sections between *pairs* of circles can be created by the same method as in Example 15-1. The overlap between the top circle and the left circle can be created with the existing `clip-left` clipping path, but you'll also need a `clip-right` path to cut out the overlap on the other side.

But the center section is a little more complicated. It is the intersection of all *three* circles. To create it, we need to draw a circle (for example, aligned with the top circle) and then clip it twice: first to include only the parts that overlap the left circle and then to include only the parts that also overlap the right circle.

The `clip-path` property can't apply two separate clipping paths to the same element. Instead, you have a few choices:

- Use nested <g> groups to apply the two different clipping paths consecutively:

```
<g clip-path="url(#clip-left)">
    <g clip-path="url(#clip-right)">
        <use xlink:href="#circle" y="-10"
            fill="url(#stripes-all)" />
    </g>
</g>
```

- Create a dedicated `clip-both` <clipPath> element, where the shape inside it is the result of clipping the left circle to the right circle. However, because we can't clip a positioned <use> element directly, and because we can't include a <g> element inside a clipping path, that means redefining the <circle> and positioning it on the right with cx:

```
<clipPath id="clip-both">
    <circle r="11.5" cx="6" clip-path="url(#clip-left)"/>
</clipPath>
<g clip-path="url(#clip-both)">
    <use xlink:href="#circle" y="-10"
        fill="url(#stripes-all)" />
</g>
```

- Create a dedicated `clip-both` <clipPath> element, where the shape inside it is one of the circles, and apply a `clip-path` directly to the <clipPath> to clip it to the other circle:

```
<clipPath id="clip-both" clip-path="url(#clip-left)">
    <use xlink:href="#circle" x="6" />
</clipPath>
<g clip-path="url(#clip-both)">
    <use xlink:href="#circle" y="-10"
        fill="url(#stripes-all)" />
</g>
```

Yes, a `<clipPath>` element can have a `clip-path` applied to it. The effective clipping path is then the intersection of the two paths.

All these options *decrease* the size of the final clipped graphic: only the parts that intersect *both* clipping shapes will be drawn.

If you instead wanted a clipping path that clipped to areas that overlap *either* of two shapes, the solution is simpler: include both shapes (or `<use>` copies of them) inside the same `<clipPath>` element.

For example, the following `<clipPath>` would clip an element to the combined shape of both our left and right circles:

```
<clipPath id="clip-either">
    <use xlink:href="#circle" x="-6" />
    <use xlink:href="#circle" x="+6" />
</clipPath>
```

That `<clipPath>`, applied to a gradient-filled rectangle, results in Figure 15-8.

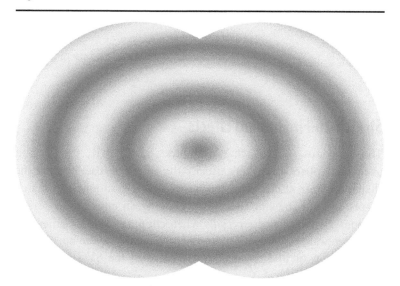

Figure 15-8. A gradient-filled rectangle, clipped to two overlapping circles

Unfortunately, the (rather arbitrary) restrictions on `<clipPath>` contents means that you cannot easily generate a clipping path from an existing `<g>` group of shapes, or from a `<symbol>` or `<svg>`. You need to copy all the shapes individually, and position each one with transformations, without using groups or `viewBox` scaling.

More Online

There's one extra feature of clipping paths (whether shorthand or SVG) that isn't shared with masks. A clipping path clips the *interactive* region of a shape, so that only the unclipped parts will respond to mouse and touch events.

However, beware: Microsoft Edge and Internet Explorer do not clip the interactive region when they clip a graphic. So this can currently only be used as an enhancement, to provide more nuanced user feedback where it is supported.

Read more, including an example of using clipped images to create an interactive image map, in "Clipped Clicks":

https://oreillymedia.github.io/Using_SVG/extras/ch15-imagemap.html

We'll also have more clipping and image-map examples in Chapter 18.

Stretch-to-Fit Clipping Effects

The previous `<clipPath>` examples have used the default `userSpaceOnUse` scaling. It's usually the easiest to use, because the shapes in your `<clipPath>` can be sized and positioned to match shapes in your drawing. But when clipping an entire `<svg>` or an `<image>` element—and *especially* when clipping HTML elements—you often want to define the clipping path relative to the normal size and position of that element, not relative to the SVG coordinate system.

In other words, you will want to change `clipPathUnits` to `objectBoundingBox`.

With `objectBoundingBox` units, the shapes in the clipping path should be defined in units between 0 and 1. Don't use percentages—

just like with patterns, percentages are scaled up by the bounding-box scale and are therefore not useful.

The shapes in your bounding-box clipping path will stretch to fit the graphic being clipped. If the graphic's bounding box isn't square, that stretching effect will be nonuniform, distorting the clipping path. So a <circle> clipping path will be stretched into an ellipse, if it is applied to a rectangular shape.

When a bounding-box clipping path (or other layer effect, such as mask or filter) is applied to a <g>, or <use> element, the bounding box used is the tightest box that fits all the grouped content's bounding boxes, after their sizes and positions have been converted to the parent element's coordinate system.

The bounding box *isn't* affected by any clipping or hidden overflow on the child content.

Bounding-box units can trigger the second type of frustrating clipping-path debugging situation—a clipping path that doesn't appear to have any effect at all! That can be caused if the shapes inside your <clipPath> are too big, completely overlapping the 1×1 bounding-box dimensions, so nothing gets clipped off.

Of course, a lack of clipping *sometimes* just means that a typo in an element or attribute name or id value has prevented the clipping path from being applied at all. So remember to check that, too.

In addition, bounding-box clipping paths have all the same frustrations as bounding-box gradients and patterns: they stretch and distort shapes, they don't include strokes and markers when determining the scale, and they create errors if applied to a straight horizontal or vertical line.

Example 15-2 creates a bounding-box <clipPath> within inline SVG, and then uses it to clip both an SVG <image> and CSS layout boxes within the HTML section of the page. Figure 15-9 shows the resulting web page.

Figure 15-9. HTML elements (and CSS pseudoelements) and an SVG image, all clipped by the same object bounding-box clipping path

Example 15-2. Creating curved boxes, in SVG and HTML, with object bounding-box clipping paths

```
<!DOCTYPE html>
<html>
<head>
    <meta charset='UTF-8'>
    <title>Object Bounding-Box Clipping paths,
        on SVG and HTML elements</title>
<style>
@import url('https://fonts.googleapis.com/css?family=Pacifico');
svg {
```

```
        display: block;
}
body {
    background-color: #432;
    margin: 0.5em;
}
header {
    background: darkSeaGreen;
    position: relative;
    z-index: 0;
    padding: 0.1rem;
}
header::before {
    background: indigo;
    content: "";
    display: block;
    position: absolute;
    z-index: -1;
    top: 0.5rem; bottom: 0.5rem;
    left: 1.5rem; right: 1.5rem;
}
h1 {
    background: plum;
    color: indigo;
    text-align: center;
    padding: 10%;
    margin: 2rem 4rem;
    font-size: 300%;
    font-family: Pacifico, sans-serif;
    font-weight: normal;
}
header, header::before, h1 {
    -webkit-clip-path: url(#wave-edges);
    clip-path: url(#wave-edges);
}
</style></head>
<body>
<header>
  <h1>Curvy Clipping Paths</h1>
</header>
<svg viewBox="0 0 400 300" role="img"
     aria-label="Blue and white violets,
                 in a garden filled with autumn leaves">
    <clipPath id="wave-edges" clipPathUnits="objectBoundingBox">
        <path d="M0.05,0.01
                Q0.15,0.15 0.5,0.05 T0.99,0.05
                Q0.85,0.15 0.95,0.5 T0.95,0.99
                Q0.85,0.85 0.5,0.95 T0.01,0.95
                Q0.15,0.85 0.05,0.5 T0.05,0.01
                Z"/>
    </clipPath>
```

```
<image xlink:href="violets.jpg" width="100%" height="100%"
       preserveAspectRatio="xMidYMid slice"
       clip-path="url(#wave-edges)" />
</svg>
</body>
</html>
```

The stacked outlines in the header in Example 15-2 are created with separate elements (the `<header>` and `<h1>`) and a CSS pseudoelement, all clipped with the same wavy SVG `<clipPath>`. When you clip an element, you clip *all* of it, including SVG strokes and markers, CSS padding and borders, and even shadow and filter effects. So, in order to have a contrasting border for our heading, we needed to draw the contrasting color in a separate element, outside the clipping path.

The three heading layers are all clipped to the same shape, in bounding-box units. However, the clipping path gets stretched and scaled slightly differently for each, so the final curves are not neatly parallel.

The "bounding box" for a CSS layout element is the `border-box`. In contrast, the "user space" for non-SVG elements is not well defined, and may not work how you expect.

Just like the `opacity` property, a `clip-path` has a *flattening* effect. It turns each layer into its own stacking context for CSS `z-index` layering. This means that the `z-index` declarations in Example 15-2 aren't actually required: they are there to ensure that the stacking is correct in browsers that don't support `clip-path` on CSS boxes.

As we mentioned at the start of the chapter, support for SVG clipping paths on non-SVG elements is not universal. At the time of writing, the `-webkit-` prefix is required for support in Safari; Microsoft Edge won't clip the HTML elements at all. However, the fallback layout—with simple layered rectangles for the heading—looks acceptable in Edge and other browsers that don't support `clip-path` outside SVG. And the SVG `<image>` element gets clipped to the curved shape in any browser that supports SVG.

Shorthand Shapes

As we've hinted at previously, the CSS Masking module extends the `clip-path` property in more ways than just applying it on CSS layout boxes.

Instead of defining the clipping path in a SVG `<clipPath>` element, and then using a `url()` reference in the `clip-path` property, you can define the clipping path shape directly in the `clip-path` property with a CSS shape function. For example, a circular clipping path like the one used in the Venn diagram examples earlier in the chapter would look like this:

```
clip-path: circle(12px at -6px center);
```

We introduced the shape functions in Chapters 5 and 6. To recap, they are:

- `circle()` and `ellipse()`
- `inset()` for drawing rectangles and rounded rectangles
- `polygon()`
- `path()`

 The `path()` shape function for creating curved shapes in CSS was defined later than the other shapes. At the time of writing, it is not supported in any web browsers for `clip-path`.

You rarely need to use the `circle()` and `ellipse()` functions in `clip-path` for CSS boxes: you can achieve elliptical clipping—with much better browser support—with `border-radius` combined with `overflow: hidden`. So, for now, CSS shapes and `clip-path` is mostly about the `polygon()` function.

Within a shape function, you can create fixed-size clipping paths with absolute length units, or create a bounding-box effect by using percentages. The exception is the `path()` function, which uses the SVG path syntax, and therefore only accepts user-unit coordinates (not lengths or percentages).

You can also mix percentages with absolute values, using the `calc()` function. This allows you to create clipping paths that scale to the full size of the element and then clip a fixed distance from each edge, something that is not currently possible with SVG <clipPath>.

For example, the following polygon clips a 30px wide and tall triangle from each corner of the box, regardless of the box size:

```
clip-path: polygon(0 30px, 30px 0,
    calc(100% - 30px) 0, 100% 30px,
    100% calc(100% - 30px), calc(100% - 30px) 100%,
    30px 100%, 0 calc(100% - 30px) );
```

Figure 15-10 shows the result if we use that clipping path to replace the wavy <clipPath> in Example 15-2.

Figure 15-10 offers a warning about the limits of "absolute" sizing: the clipping path on the SVG <image> is applied in the scaled SVG coordinate system, so the 30px triangles are much larger than they are for the boxes in the header. (For this example, you could avoid that discrepancy by clipping the <svg> element instead of the scaled <image>.)

According to the latest specs, you should also be able to specify *which* reference box to use for measuring percentages: content-box instead of border-box, for example. For SVG, you could use stroke-box instead of fill-box. An SVG user-space clipping path would be equivalent to using view-box as the reference box.

 At the time of writing, changing the reference box is not supported in Chrome/Blink browsers, or in the -webkit- prefixed property used in Safari/WebKit.

Because a CSS shape's geometry is defined entirely in the clip-path property, you can animate or transition between similar shapes. For example, you could transition a circular clipping path down to zero radius to make an element disappear. To be "similar" enough to transition, shapes must be the same type. For polygon() and path(), they must have the same number of points.

Figure 15-10. HTML and SVG elements clipped to the same CSS polygon clipping path

In contrast, when you animate the shapes inside in an SVG `<clipPath>`, it affects all elements that use that graphical effect. (Also, support is currently poor for animating SVG geometry properties with CSS.)

One *limitation* of using CSS shapes functions, particularly for `polygon()`, is that you can't draw the shapes in a visual software and then copy the generated SVG code: the coordinates need to be in the

CSS syntax. A few tools are currently available to help you draw shapes, especially for clipping image files:

- Clippy (*http://bennettfeely.com/clippy/*), by Bennett Feely, provides a web interface with click-and-drag points, as well as a number of preset polygons for common shapes.
- The Adobe CSS Shapes Editor JavaScript library (*https://github.com/adobe-webplatform/css-shapes-editor*) allows you to add a visual CSS shapes editor into a web page, such as the web interface to a content management system.
- The CSS Shapes Editor (*https://github.com/oslego/chrome-css-shapes-editor*) extension for Chrome (and related browsers), by Razvan Caliman, adds an extra tab to your Developer Tools panel that allows you to edit shape functions for elements in your page using the Adobe JS library. It's currently optimized for use with the `shape-outside` property, but you can copy and paste the code into `clip-path`.

A similar CSS shapes editor will be natively included in Firefox dev tools, starting sometime in late 2017.

As we mentioned in Chapter 5, the `shape-outside` property controls how text wraps around floated elements in CSS layout. It uses the same CSS shapes functions as `clip-path`, so you may find yourself reusing the same value twice, making them a good candidate for CSS variables. However, beware that the two properties have different default reference boxes: if you don't specify the reference box, shapes are measured relative to `border-box` for `clip-path`, but `margin-box` for `shape-outside`.

CSS Versus SVG
clip Versus clip-path

You may be wondering where the long-established CSS `clip` property fits into all of this. The short answer: it doesn't. The `clip` property is considered a legacy feature, kept around only for backward compatibility. `clip-path` is the way of the future.

The longer answer: `clip` was initially proposed with the plan to make it something like what `clip-path` and CSS shapes are now. However, the only value of `clip` that has ever been supported (other than the default `auto`) is a `rect()` function. And the syntax of `rect()` is so inconsistent from all other CSS geometry that CSS Shapes replaced it with `inset()`.

The parameters to `rect()` are the distances to the top, right, bottom, and left edges of the rectangle, as measured from the top/left side of the element.

In contrast, the parameters to `inset()` are always measured from the nearest side.

The `clip` property's other limitation is that it only applies to absolutely positioned elements in CSS. In SVG, it applies to elements that can have hidden overflow (`<svg>`, `<symbol>`, `<pattern>`, `<marker>`), and to `<image>`.

Hiding Behind Masks

Clipping paths are useful for quickly including or excluding specific regions of a graphic, or changing the shape of rectangular elements such as images. But clipping paths are limited. You must be able to define them with simple vector shapes. The final effect is binary: graphics are either inside or outside the path, never in between.

For more subtle effects, you need a mask.

A mask works somewhat differently from a clipping path. Where a clipping path is defined as a vector shape, a mask is defined as a single-channel (e.g., grayscale) image layer. The resulting transparency effect doesn't have a 1-bit, on-or-off value—it has a full 8-bit (1 byte) channel of 256 possible levels. Masks are commonly used in photo-editing applications such as Adobe Photoshop and GIMP, because they operate on pixels, not vectors.

Android browsers did not support SVG masking until version 4.4. Masking is also not supported in some software that is used to convert SVG to raster images or PDF, so if you're creating fallback PNG images with an automated script, double-check that they look correct.

Masks can create stunning visual effects, but going from 1 bit to 1 byte of transparency information adds considerable computational cost. If you can achieve an effect with clip-path instead of mask, it will give you better performance, especially for animated graphics.

The masks defined in SVG 1.1 are known as **luminance masks**. Loosely, that means that the brightness (luminance) of the mask image determines the opacity of the final masked graphic. The mask's image layer is converted to grayscale, it is scaled and positioned as required, and then the grayscale intensity of a given pixel in the mask becomes the alpha factor applied to the corresponding pixel in the graphic that you are masking.

Pure white areas in the mask (100% luminance) correspond to an opacity of 1 (opaque), meaning no masking occurs—the masked graphic has its normal transparency in those sections. Pure black (0% luminance) corresponds to an opacity of 0 (transparent), meaning those sections of the masked graphic will be entirely clipped away, letting the background shine through.

The luminance calculation converts colors to grayscale using a formula the recognizes that yellows and greens are brighter (higher luminance) than equally intense reds and blues.

The same formula is used in filters (but *not* in blend modes!), and in calculating contrast ratios for accessibility.

Figure 15-11 shows a mask in action: the mask is created from black-to-white linear and radial gradients. We'll look at the code to create the effect in the following sections.

The masked version of the photograph is drawn in the regions that are white in the mask, and fades away to transparent (revealing the white page background) in the regions that are black in the mask. The end result is much softer than the sharp lines created when the same photograph was clipped to a triangle in Figure 15-2.

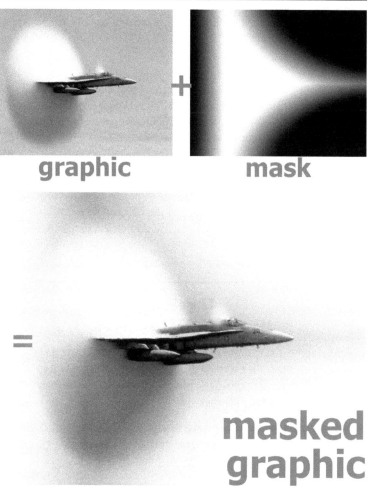

Figure 15-11. A masked graphic is constructed from a full-color graphic (here, a photograph) and a single-channel mask image (here, an arrangement of grayscale gradients)

The luminance levels of the mask are calculated *after* the brightness is scaled down according to the transparency of the mask image itself, as if the mask content were drawn on a black background.

That means that any transparent sections in the mask content are treated the same as black, completely masking that section of the graphic. This can be a problem when you're creating a mask from SVG shapes. Unstyled SVG elements are drawn as black shapes on a transparent background. Within a luminance mask, those black shapes and transparent background are treated equally, turning your masked graphic invisible.

Just like with clipping paths, debugging masks can be frustrating because of graphics that completely disappear. A *white* rectangle inside the mask can make your graphics reappear, and help you figure out the layout issues.

In contrast, in an **alpha mask**, the alpha (transparency) levels in the mask image are used directly to determine the alpha factors for the masking effect. That means that opaque black, white, and color sections in the mask are all treated equally. Alpha masks are included in the CSS Masking module.

Future Focus
More Masks for More Content

It won't surprise you that the CSS Masking module extends masks as well as clipping. Once again, the two main changes are allowing the effect to be used on CSS layout boxes (not only SVG elements), and adding a shorthand version that doesn't require extra SVG markup.

Also once again, browsers have been inconsistent in implementing the new features. Support is currently lagging behind that for the new clipping options, so this book still considers them "future" features.

Microsoft browsers have not yet implemented masking for non-SVG elements, or the new masking syntaxes.

WebKit Safari *and* Chrome/Blink currently require `-webkit-` prefixed properties to use the new syntax, and *only* support them on non-SVG elements. The `-webkit-` version of masking doesn't include SVG masks. So you can't use the CSS-only masks on SVG elements, and you can't use SVG masks on HTML elements.

Firefox, in contrast, has a fairly complete implementation of the CSS Masking module as of version 53 (released in April 2017). Support of SVG masks applied to non-SVG elements has been in Firefox for a couple years.

Again, there are also still some details that might change in the specifications, as feedback is received from early adopters.

Who Was That Masked Graphic?

A mask effect is defined in SVG with a **<mask> element**, and applied to another element with the **mask style property** or presentation attribute.

The mask property works much like the clip-path property—in SVG 1.1, anyway: its value is either none (the default) or a url() reference. But this time, the element in the cross-reference must be a <mask>.

Also like clip-path, mask is a layer effect that flattens graphics, and is not inherited.

Or at least, that's how it's supposed to work. WebKit browsers currently apply the mask *separately* to every drawing operation: every child of the masked element is masked before being layered together, and strokes are masked separately from the fill.

That means you get an incorrect appearance if you are masking a group with more than one element, or if any of the elements you are masking have strokes on them. Unfortunately, there is no easy workaround for the problem.

Like <clipPath>, a <mask> element is a container for other graphics, and it can be scaled to the object bounding box or to the user space. But that's about where their similarities end.

A `<clipPath>` had extensive restrictions on its contents, because those contents needed to be converted into pure vector outlines. A `<mask>` doesn't have those restrictions.

Any valid SVG graphics can be drawn inside the mask, including groups, reused symbols, and embedded images. All the normal SVG styles apply: strokes, markers, fill patterns and gradients, opacity changes: they are all used to draw the image layer, which will then be converted into the luminance mask.

The `<mask>` element's scaling attributes follow the same format as the `<pattern>` element attributes, one for the dimensions and one for the contents:

- `maskUnits` (`objectBoundingBox` by default) controls the scale of the overall mask region, a rectangle defined by **x, y, width, and height attributes** on the `<mask>`.

- `maskContentUnits` (`userSpaceOnUse` by default) controls the scale of the elements inside the mask. There is no `viewBox` to make scaling easier, however: only bounding-box or user-space scale.

The mask region defined by `maskUnits` and x, y, width, and height defines the outer bounds of the mask. Everything outside of that rectangle will be clipped completely. You can *usually* ignore these attributes, and just use the default mask dimensions.

The defaults for the mask dimensions create a mask that covers the object bounding box of the graphic being masked, plus 10% padding on each side. That's good enough for masking images (which fit neatly in their bounding box) and for shapes or text with thin strokes.

The defaults are a problem if the actual dimensions of the graphic are noticeably bigger than its official bounding box:

- shapes or text with thick strokes
- shapes with large markers
- text with large "swash" characters that extend beyond their layout boxes

In those cases, you may need to expand the mask region to completely cover the graphic.

When you use a `<mask>` on an element that is larger than its fill bounding box, x and y on the mask should be *negative*, and width and height should be greater than 100%. This is how the defaults work: x and y default to -10%, and width and height default to 120%.

Adjusting the attributes won't be enough if the fill bounding box of your shape might have zero height or width (e.g., arrows drawn from straight lines). In that case, you'll need to switch maskUnits to userSpaceOnUse, and adjust x, y, width, and height to match.

The choice of maskContentUnits is more of a design decision.

The userSpaceOnUse default means that the shapes inside the mask are measured in the main SVG coordinate system. This makes it easy to size and scale the content, but you're also responsible for making sure your mask content correctly overlaps the shapes you are masking.

If you switch maskContentUnits to objectBoundingBox, then all coordinates in the mask contents are relative to the width and height of the masked graphic's fill bounding box.

Just like with bounding-box clipping paths, this means using lengths scaled from 0 to 1. (Or slightly larger, to cover strokes outside the fill bounding box.) Just like with bounding-box *everything* in SVG, it also means watching out for distorted shapes and errors from zero-height or zero-width bounding boxes.

Just like with patterns, avoid using percentage lengths and lengths with units in the content of bounding-box masks. They are scaled up proportional to the scaling of SVG user units.

In contrast, percentages for x, y, width, and height work as you would expect them to: relative to the bounding-box size when maskUnits is set to objectBoundingBox.

The `<mask>` in Figure 15-11 used bounding-box units to position three gradient-filled rectangles to cover the 1×1 bounding box:

```
<mask id="mask" maskContentUnits="objectBoundingBox">
    <g id="mask-contents">
        <rect fill="url(#fade-left)"
              width="0.2" height="1" />
        <rect fill="url(#fade-top-right)"
              x="0.2" width="0.8" height="0.5" />
        <rect fill="url(#fade-bottom-right)"
              x="0.2" y="0.5" width="0.8" height="0.5" />
    </g>
</mask>
```

The <g> element is there solely so that the contents could be copied with a <use> element to draw them in the figure—like a <pattern> or <symbol>, the <mask> is never drawn directly. But it's also a reminder that <mask>, unlike <clipPath>, lets you use groups in the content.

 Depending on the browser and the size of the SVG, you may detect hairline cracks in the mask, caused by rounding errors that leave a pixel gap (or smaller) between the rectangles. For SVG luminance masks like this, you can usually fix it by making each rectangle slightly larger that it should be, so they overlap by a few pixels.

Because this mask was going to be applied to an <image>, not a stroked shape, we did not need to scale the mask contents to cover any graphics outside the bounding-box rectangle.

Because we're using bounding-box units—by default for the mask boundaries, and explicitly for the mask content—this mask will strech or compress to fit images, or other SVG graphics, of different dimensions. Figure 15-12 shows the mask applied to different versions of the photo, cropped to different aspect ratios.

We created the black-and-white versions of the mask in Figure 15-12 (and Figure 15-11) by copying the mask contents into a <symbol> with a 1×1 viewBox and no aspect-ratio control:

```
<symbol id="mask-image" viewBox="0 0 1 1"
        preserveAspectRatio="none">
    <use xlink:href="#mask-contents" />
</symbol>
```

Figure 15-12. The object bounding-box mask stretches to fit masked images of different dimensions

The symbol is then reused at dimensions matching each bounding box, so that the nonuniform `viewBox` scaling mimics the scaling from `objectBoundingBox` units.

The photos were cropped in a photo editor, and saved as separate files. Normally, you can "crop" a photo dynamically in SVG by putting it inside a nested `<svg>` element with hidden overflow (using `viewBox` to adjust the scale and offset of the visible portion, as we did in Example 10-4 in Chapter 10).

But that hidden overflow is still used to determine the bounding-box size, which would mean that our masks would stretch to cover the full image size, ignoring any cropping. That would be good if the mask had been carefully designed to match the full image. But it's not so useful for demonstrating how masks can stretch to fit different bounding boxes.

Masks aren't just for photos, of course. You can also mask SVG vector shapes or text. Figure 15-13 shows the same mask applied to a `<text>` element (containing the word "SPEED" with solid black fill) to show an all-SVG masking effect.

Figure 15-13. An object bounding-box mask applied to SVG text

If you look closely at the text in Figure 15-13, you'll notice another bounding-box issue, which we briefly mentioned in Chapter 12: text bounding boxes are sized to the layout boxes of the individual characters, not to the visible shapes. The mask isn't perfectly centered over the visible text. It is stretching to cover the space that would be used for lowercase letters that drop below the baseline, or accents that sit above the capitals.

Using a mask this extreme on `<text>` is probably not a good idea—it's hard to tell that the last letter in Figure 15-13 is a D when most of it has been masked away! But if it were included in inline SVG or an embedded SVG object, it would still nonetheless be "real" text that can be selected and copied, or read by screen readers.

In contrast, when you include text inside the `<mask>` itself (or inside a `<clipPath>` or `<pattern>`), that text is just a decorative effect on another element, and is not accessible.

As we mentioned at the start of the section, for performance reasons, you should never use a `<mask>` when a `<clipPath>` will do. That means that most masks will have gradations in brightness. Gradients like those used in Figure 15-12 are one possibility. Another possibility is to use a photograph—not as the masked graphic, but as the mask itself!

Making a Stencil

One of the more interesting applications of masks is to create dynamic duotones out of photographs or other images.

A duotone is an image in which the darkest color in the image is mapped to one color (call it the background), the lightest is mapped to the foreground color, and in-between brightnesses become in-between colors. Depending on the colors you choose, the end result can look like lightly tinted black-and-white photographs, or like psychedelic posters.

You can create duotones by manipulating the colors in an `<image>` directly with filters.[1] But masks require less math.

You create the effect by including the photograph (as an `<image>`) inside a `<mask>`. The mask effectively converts your photograph into a stencil, through which your masked graphics will be painted. The

---

1 For a discussion of how to make duotones with filters, see "Color Filters Can Turn Your Gray Skies Blue," by Amelia Bellamy-Royds, on CSS-Tricks (*https://css-tricks.com/color-filters-can-turn-your-gray-skies-blue/*).

masked "graphic" is normally just a rectangle of solid color, painted on top of a background (unmasked) rectangle of a contrasting color.

The colors in the image are automatically converted to grayscale, based on their luminance. The dark parts in the image become transparent parts in your masked rectangle, so your background color shines through. The bright parts in your image become the parts that are drawn in the color of the foreground rectangle.

To test this effect, we're going to work with the photograph in Figure 15-14. To show off all the color possibilities, we're going to arrange four copies of our duotone image in a figure.

Figure 15-14. The photograph that will be used to create the duotone

So should this mask use `userSpaceOnUse` or `objectBoundingBox` units? It turns out, neither is ideal.

 What we really need is a `viewBox` option, like we used in Chapter 12 for including images inside pattern fills. But that's not yet available for `<mask>`.

An objectBoundingBox mask distorts the mask when the shape being masked isn't square. Since our image isn't square, our duotone rectangles won't be, either.

We could distort the image inside the mask in the reverse direction, drawing it to exactly fit the 1×1 bounding-box region. Then we would make sure that the <rect> dimensions match the correct image ratio, so that the bounding-box scaling exactly cancels out the image scaling. But (depending on the browser implementation), this may mean that the browser applies the scale twice, using up extra processing power and risking lingering distortions in the image.

A userSpaceOnUse mask avoids distortion, but means that we can't rely on the mask to scale our photograph and position it over each masked rectangle. We need to directly size the <image> inside the <mask> to the same size as the rectangles, and we need to position them both in the same position of the coordinate system.

But we want four different copies of the image, in four different positions. Do we need four different masks?

Figure 15-15. Duotone effects created from a photographic mask on SVG rectangles

Thankfully, no. If we use transformations to position the different duotones, we can draw all the rectangles—and the `<image>` in the mask—at the origin, so the mask will align with all of them simultaneously.

Example 15-3 gives the code, and Figure 15-15 shows the final result.

Example 15-3. Creating a duotone photograph with a mask

```
<svg xmlns="http://www.w3.org/2000/svg" xml:lang="en"
    xmlns:xlink="http://www.w3.org/1999/xlink"
    width="4in" height="3in" viewBox="0 0 8 6">
    <title>Duotone Photographs from Masked Rectangles</title>
    <mask id="photo-mask" maskContentUnits="userSpaceOnUse">
        <image xlink:href="lilies.jpg" width="4" height="3"/>
    </mask>
    <g>
        <title>#FFC480 (cream) over #402020 (dark brown)</title>
        <rect width="4" height="3" fill="#402020"/>
        <rect width="4" height="3" fill="#FFC480"
            mask="url(#photo-mask)"/>
    </g>
    <g transform="translate(4,0)">
        <title>#402020 (dark brown) over #FFC480 (cream)</title>
        <rect width="4" height="3" fill="#FFC480"/>
        <rect width="4" height="3" fill="#402020"
            mask="url(#photo-mask)"/>
    </g>
    <g transform="translate(0,3)">
        <title>hotPink over royalBlue</title>
        <rect width="4" height="3" fill="royalBlue"/>
        <rect width="4" height="3" fill="hotPink"
            mask="url(#photo-mask)"/>
    </g>
    <g transform="translate(4,3)">
        <title>3-color radial gradient over indigo</title>
        <radialGradient id="pink-grad" r="0.6">
            <stop offset="0" stop-color="gold" />
            <stop offset="0.4" stop-color="hotPink" />
            <stop offset="1" stop-color="papayaWhip" />
        </radialGradient>
        <rect width="4" height="3" fill="indigo"/>
        <rect width="4" height="3" fill="url(#pink-grad)"
            mask="url(#photo-mask)"/>
    </g>
</svg>
```

The duotone on the upper left uses a dark brown background and cream-colored foreground. Since the foreground paints the bright parts of the mask, the result is a sepia-toned print of the photograph.

The duotone on the upper right reverses the colors. The dark foreground color is preserved in the bright parts of the photo, and the light background color shows through in places where the photo was dark: the final impression is that of an old photographic negative.

The third sample (on the bottom left) slides into psychedelic territory, with pink brights on blue background.

The fourth sample isn't technically a *duo*tone, but it's there to prove a point: once you create the "stencil" from your photograph, you don't have to fill it in with a solid color. Here, we use a radial gradient as the fill on the foreground rectangle.

To make our sepia-toned photograph a little more authentic, we can add a "vignette" effect. Early photographs had a characteristic dark fading or fogging along the outer edges, which were not lit as effectively by the light from the curved lens. This round shadow is now known as a vignette.

To recreate it, we need to combine our photograph mask with a mask that uses a radial gradient. Because the content of a mask can be any SVG graphic, we can most easily create compound masking effects like this by masking the mask contents (the <image> in this case).

Unlike with clipping paths, you cannot apply the mask property to the <mask> element itself: it needs to be on the mask contents.

(But, unlike with clipping paths, you can always group the mask contents in a <g> if you want to apply an effect to all of them!)

In Example 15-4 we create an artificial vignette by using a radial gradient in a bounding-box mask to fade out the corners of the photograph in our duotone mask. The transparent corners of that masked image are treated the same as underexposed (dark) areas when the second mask is used to create a sepia duotone, as shown in Figure 15-16.

Figure 15-16. A sepia photograph, with vignette corners, created with SVG masks

Example 15-4. Creating a duotone photograph with a mask

```
<svg xmlns="http://www.w3.org/2000/svg" xml:lang="en"
    xmlns:xlink="http://www.w3.org/1999/xlink"
    width="4in" height="3in" viewBox="0 0 4 3">
    <title>A Faded Photograph from a Masked Mask</title>
    <radialGradient id="dark-corners" r="0.6">
        <stop offset="0.7" stop-color="white" />
        <stop offset="1" stop-color="#222" />
    </radialGradient>
    <mask id="vignette" maskContentUnits="objectBoundingBox">
        <rect width="1" height="1" fill="url(#dark-corners)"/>
    </mask>
    <mask id="photo-mask">
        <image xlink:href="lilies-large.jpg" width="4" height="3"
            mask="url(#vignette)" />
    </mask>
    <g>
        <rect width="4" height="3" fill="#402020"/>
        <rect width="4" height="3" fill="#FFC480"
            mask="url(#photo-mask)"/>
    </g>
</svg>
```

Future Focus
Easier Image Masks

The shorthand mask syntax introduced in the CSS Masking module allows you to directly reference an image file as a mask, without needing to nest it in a `<mask>` element. Because CSS gradients are treated as image types in CSS, that means you can directly use a CSS gradient function as a mask, too.

But it doesn't stop there. You can layer multiple masks images together, and control their size, position, and repeat patterns, using a syntax directly borrowed from CSS layered backgrounds. That means that the `mask` property is now a shorthand for other properties: `mask-image`, `mask-size`, `mask-repeat`, and so on.

 If you use the *longhand* properties (e.g., `mask-image`) to set a CSS mask, then browsers that don't support the syntax will ignore them and use an SVG `mask` as a fallback. In contrast, if you use a `url()` reference in the `mask` property, CSS parsers will accept that as a valid syntax even if they don't support references to image files.

But here's where it gets confusing: by default (to be consistent with the -webkit- version of the property), image masks in CSS are *alpha* masks, not luminance masks. That means that a white-to-black gradient or a JPEG photograph won't mask anything. You would need a solid-to-transparent gradient or a partially transparent PNG image to have an effect.

So to create the gradient mask from Figure 15-11 with CSS, you would layer three different CSS color-to-transparent gradients as nonrepeating images, and size and position them with percentages so they would fit the image box. The CSS code would be as follows:

```
img {
    mask-image:
        linear-gradient(to right, transparent, red),
        radial-gradient(ellipse 120% 156% at 120% -30%,
            transparent 70%, red),
        radial-gradient(ellipse 120% 156% at 120% 130%,
            transparent 70%, red);
    mask-size: 20% 100%, 80% 50%, 80% 50%;
    mask-position: left top, right top, right bottom;
    mask-repeat: no-repeat;
}
```

 Again, you'll often detect 1-pixel cracks between the sections, caused by browsers rounding the size of each image. Unfortunately, it's not as easy to fix with CSS alpha masks: although you can still make the gradients overlap slightly, this can cause the overlap section to be too opaque.

Applied to any of our fighter jet photos, this would provide the same masking as the all-SVG approach. At the time of writing, the code works as-is in Firefox. To get support in WebKit and Blink browsers, you would need to duplicate all the mask properties with a -webkit- prefix. In Microsoft Edge and in older browsers, you would just see the unmasked image.

Switching from luminance to alpha is easy enough for gradients—although you can't just paint over part of one gradient with another, like you can with SVG masks.

Converting a photograph to an alpha mask is not so simple. Luckily, there's an better solution: the mask-mode property. It allows you to set, for each mask image layer, whether it should be treated as an alpha mask or luminance mask.

The `mask-mode` property has three possible values: `alpha`, `luminance`, or `match-source`. The default is `match-source`, which means alpha masks for image layers and luminance by default for `<mask>` references.

For `<mask>` elements, you would also have the option to change the default when you define the mask. The new `mask-type` style property also takes the values `luminance` (the default) or `alpha`, but it is set on the `<mask>` element itself. The `mask-type` determines the "source" mode when `mask-mode` is set to `match-source`.

An even more interesting new property is `mask-composite`. It allows you to combine multiple mask-image layers (including SVG mask layers) in such a way that they add together, cancel each other out, or interact in other ways. The options are:

- **add**, the default, meaning that solid areas in either mask are solid in the result. It is the same as if the masks were converted to alpha masks and then layered one on top of the other.

- **subtract**, meaning that solid areas in the top mask are cut away from the lower mask layer.

- **intersect**, meaning that only areas that are solid in both mask layers are solid in the result. This is the same as one mask masking the other.

- **exclude**, meaning that only areas that are solid in one mask but *not* the other are solid in the composited result.

So to recreate the vignetted, sepia-toned photograph from Example 15-4, without any SVG markup, we'll need two mask layers: our photo of lilies and a CSS gradient version of our SVG gradient mask. They'll need to be in luminance mode, and they'll need to use **intersect** compositing. We'll also need two overlapping solid-colored CSS layout boxes, with the mask applied to the top layer.

The following CSS code creates that effect with a masked pseudoelement inside a `<figure>` element, using intersecting luminance masks:

```
figure {
    background: #402020; /* dark brown */
    position: relative;
    width: 4in;  /* or create the correct aspect ratio */
    height: 3in; /* using the padding-bottom hack */
    margin: 0;
```

```
}
figure::after {
    content: "";
    position: absolute;
    top: 0; left: 0;
    width: 100%; height: 100%;

    background: #FFC480; /* cream */
    mask-image: url(lilies.jpg),
        radial-gradient(60% 60%, white 70%, #222);
    mask-size: cover;
    mask-mode: luminance, luminance;
        /* the repetition is required for now,
           due to a Firefox bug */
    mask-composite: intersect;
}
```

The end result is a `<figure>` that looks identical to the `<svg>` from Figure 15-16. Or it does in Firefox, anyway. The `-webkit-` version of masking doesn't support luminance masks, so at the time of writing this code doesn't yet work in other browsers. (But try it! Support may have improved by the time you read this.)

When a complete image file is used as a `mask`, it is allowed to be cross-origin. If you reference a same-origin SVG file with a target (#) fragment, the browser will first try to load it as a `<mask>` reference; if that fails, the browser will use the SVG as an image mask.

The CSS Masking module also introduces a `mask-border` property, which has various longhand subproperties inspired by the `border-image` properties. The layout of the mask border images would work equivalently to border images, but then the results would be used as masks. Just like border images, the property is difficult to use (as currently defined) with SVG images or CSS gradients, because it assumes the images are a fixed size measured in pixels.

At the time of writing, there are no implementations of border masks that match the standards (not even in Firefox). WebKit and Blink browsers support a similar, nonstandard `-webkit-mask-box-image` property.

Summary: Clipping and Masking

Both clipping and masking achieve the same broad ends: restricting the user's view to a portion of a element. The element being clipped or masked may be any SVG content, including vector graphics, text, or embedded raster images. In the latest browsers, it can also be any CSS layout box, so you can clip or mask HTML images or video.

The clipping paths and masks are distinguished by the *way* in which they affect elements: a mask is an image layer, and it is applied to the masked element pixel by pixel. Each pixel in the mask is converted into an alpha (transparency) value that can have any intensity from fully transparent to fully opaque. Those values are then used to reduce the opacity of the corresponding pixel in the masked element.

A clipping path is similar to a "1-bit" mask, where every pixel is either fully transparent or fully opaque. However, because clipping paths are defined with vector shapes, they can be much more efficient to implement, and they can affect pointer-events hit testing, changing the interactive region of an element.

Clipping and masking share many similarities with filters, which are the subject of Chapter 16. Clipping, masking, and filters are all layer effects that can apply to a composited group or image, not just to individual vector shapes. But while clipping and masking can only alter that graphic layer to change its transparency, filters can twist and remix the painted pixels in many different ways.

More Online

A quick reference to the elements introduced in this chapter is contained in the "Clipping and Masking Elements" section of the markup guide:

https://oreillymedia.github.io/Using_SVG/guide/markup.html#masking

The `clip-path` and `mask` style properties (and the CSS3 mask longhands) are included with other styles in the "SVG Style Properties" guide:

https://oreillymedia.github.io/Using_SVG/guide/style.html

A reference of the shape functions for `clip-path` is provided in the "CSS Shape Functions" guide:

https://oreillymedia.github.io/Using_SVG/guide/css-shapes.html

CHAPTER 16

Playing with Pixels

Filters and Blend Modes

Vector graphics are defined with mathematics. That tends to mean a very geometric design style. Since SVG is a 2D vector graphics format, it also means a very "flat" design style.

Gradients and masks offered the first steps toward softening those crisp, precise geometric lines. Filters break them down completely.

Filters are instructions for modifying a rendered layer of a graphic or web page by performing calculations on its individual pixel values. When applied to vector shapes or text elements, SVG filters allow you to add blur or jitter to shake up the smooth edges. When applied to embedded images, filters can also dynamically adjust color and contrast.

SVG filters are incredibly powerful. By some measures, they are the most complex aspect of SVG.

Not only are there many possible filter operations to choose from, but there are countless possible combinations. Filter instructions can be chained together, so the result of one filter becomes the input of another. Some filter operations combine multiple inputs, so you can split and recombine the chain of filtered graphic layers in complex flow-chart arrangements.

That complexity has a cost. The SVG filter syntax can make some simple filters unnecessarily obscure. The sheer number of options can scare off some developers who don't know where to start.

The open-ended nature of SVG filters also makes it more difficult for browsers to optimize filter processing. Modern **graphical processing unit (GPU) chips** can perform some filter operations efficiently, but not others, and reading data back from the GPU to the main software can cancel out the performance benefits.

New CSS shorthand functions have been designed to reduce these barriers, making it easier to define simple, easily optimized filter effects. However, the shorthands only represent a slice of what is possible with the full SVG filter syntax.

This chapter introduces the most common SVG filter elements, and compares them with the shorthand filter convenience functions for the same operations. By necessity, it is only a brief overview of what filters can do, focusing on the big concepts and some unique features. The full possibilities of SVG filters are only limited by the creativity of the developer—and the processing speed of the browser.

This chapter also describes the `mix-blend-mode` property. It replaces a feature of SVG filters that was never well supported in web browsers: the ability to alter how the filtered element is combined with its backdrop.

The Filter Framework

Just like masks and clipping paths, filters were defined in SVG as a matching pair of element and style property. The **`<filter>` element** defines a filter effect, which is referenced in the **`filter` style property** or presentation attribute of another element:

```
<filter id="wow">
    <!-- filter contents here -->
</filter>
<style>
    .wow-me { filter: url(#wow); }
</style>
<path d="..." filter="url(#wow)" />
```

Just like masks and clipping paths, the `url()` references can theoretically be to a different file, but browser support isn't great and cross-origin restrictions apply.

Just like masks and clipping paths, filters have expanded from SVG to all of CSS. The Filter Effects module redefines the `filter` property to apply to CSS layout boxes as well as SVG graphics. It also defines the new shorthand functions.

 Just like masks and clipping paths, implementation of the new filter options has been inconsistent. Some browsers implemented SVG filters on HTML elements before they implemented the shorthands, and some implemented the shorthands to apply to HTML elements before implementing them for filtering SVG elements. And some browsers initially only supported prefixed versions.

At the time of writing (mid-2017), filter support in the latest browser versions is as follows:

- Blink/Chrome and WebKit/Safari: both shorthand functions and url() references on HTML elements, only url() references on SVG elements

- MS Edge: only shorthand functions on HTML elements, only url() references on SVG elements

- Firefox: shorthand functions or url() references everywhere, but with a few bugs in the details

These combinations mean that @supports tests are not reliable. It also means that you need to think carefully about fallback, and use different approaches for SVG elements versus CSS layout boxes.

All the latest browsers also support the -webkit-filter prefixed property in the same ways as the unprefixed version. But please, only add prefixes for backward compatibility, and use an automated preprocessor script to do it.

Unlike masks and clipping paths, the content of a `<filter>` element isn't defined with SVG graphic elements. Instead, a `<filter>` contains **filter primitive elements**, which define the individidual processing instructions.

There are 16 different filter primitive elements in SVG 1.1, some of which have their own child elements. This can make filters somewhat overwhelming at first, since each filter primitive has its own attributes to learn, and many of them are defined in very mathematical ways.

All the filter primitive elements have names starting with `fe`, like `<feFlood>` or `<feMerge>`. The `fe` stands for "filter element."

But you don't need to know all the filter primitives. You can get started with just one.

A Basic Blur

One of the most effective single-primitive filters is the **Gaussian blur**. A blur is useful on both vector shapes and photographs. On its own, it creates either an "out of focus" effect or a fast-motion swipe effect. But blurs are also an important first step in more complex filters, including drop shadows and glows.

The "Gaussian" in a Gaussian blur refers to the Gaussian statistical distribution, named after 19th-century German mathematician Carl Friedrich Gauss. You might know the Gaussian distribution as the normal distribution, or the bell curve.

In statistics, a Gaussian distribution represents the probability of achieving different outcomes when there is random and unbiased variation around an expected (or mean) value.

In graphics, a Gaussian blur is one where the color value of each pixel is distributed among neighboring pixels, by amounts that approximate a Gaussian distribution. The "expected" value in this case is that the pixel's color doesn't move at all.

A blur is defined in SVG with the **<feGaussianBlur> element**. The <feGaussianBlur> element must be a child of a <filter> element. It is the <filter> element that gets the id you reference in the filter property:

```
<filter id="blur">
    <feGaussianBlur />
</filter>
```

This is technically a valid filter already. But it won't have a visible effect. You need to tell the browser how *much* blurring to apply. By default, it doesn't apply any.

The amount of blur created by an <feGaussianBlur> element is determined by the **stdDeviation attribute**. Its value is either one or two numbers (separated with whitespace or a comma), which cannot be negative. The default is 0.

 The numbers represent a length in SVG user units (px), but they must be given as unitless numbers, not lengths with units.

If you give a single value for stdDeviation, you will get a uniform blur in all directions. If you give two values, the first is the amount of blur in the horizontal direction and the second is the amount of blur in the vertical direction.

Example 16-1 defines two blur filters: a normal bidirectional blur filter, and a single-direction blur that smears colors in the vertical direction without blurring them horizontally. Both filters are then applied to a photograph and to SVG text, as shown in Figure 16-1.

Figure 16-1. Blur filters applied to SVG text and an embedded photo: (top) unfiltered, (middle) bidirectional Gaussian blur, (bottom) vertical motion blur

Example 16-1. Defining bidirectional and unidirectional blur effects

```
<svg xmlns="http://www.w3.org/2000/svg" xml:lang="en"
    xmlns:xlink="http://www.w3.org/1999/xlink"
    viewBox="0 0 400 360" width="4in" height="3.6in">
    <title>Blur Filters, bi-directional or vertical only</title>
    <filter id="blur">
        <feGaussianBlur stdDeviation="1.5"/>
    </filter>
    <filter id="vertical-smear">
        <feGaussianBlur stdDeviation="0 3"/>
    </filter>

    <text id="t"
        font-size="60px" font-family="Stencil, Stencil Std,
                                        Copperplate, sans-serif"
        fill="#CDB" stroke="#352"
        stroke-width="6px" paint-order="stroke"
```

```
          x="5" y="107" dy="-0.9em" text-anchor="start"
          >Fuzzy
          <tspan dy="0.9em" x="195" text-anchor="end"
                >Text</tspan></text>
    <image id="i"
          x="200" y="10" width="200" height="100"
          xlink:href="sleepy-siamese.jpg"/>

    <use xlink:href="#t" y="120" filter="url(#blur)" />
    <use xlink:href="#i" y="120" filter="url(#blur)" />

    <use xlink:href="#t" y="240" filter="url(#vertical-smear)" />
    <use xlink:href="#i" y="240" filter="url(#vertical-smear)" />
</svg>
```

The bidirectional Gaussian blur (with only one `stdDeviation` value) creates a soft, fuzzy, out-of-focus effect. The vertical-only blur creates the blur effect of something moving quickly up and/or down. This is known as a **motion blur** effect. Although SVG doesn't have a general-purpose motion blur option (you can't create a one-direction blur on an angle other than horizontal or vertical), with careful use of transformations you can use the two-value `<feGaussianBlur>` effect for that purpose.

Be careful with motion blur effects. If the motion blur effect doesn't agree with the actual motion of an element (like here, where the elements aren't actually moving) it sends conflicting messages to your brain, and can trigger vestibular disorders.

In contrast, a motion blur *carefully* applied to an animated item can help smooth the appearance of the animation, making it feel much more natural.

A larger `stdDeviation` value means more blur. A smaller `stdDeviation` is less blur, and of course a 0 value for `stdDeviation` is no blur at all. You can pick a `stdDeviation` value with trial and error in your web browser. But what do the numbers mean?

`stdDeviation` is short for **standard deviation**. In statistics, the standard deviation of a data set is a measure of how much variation there is from the mean. It is measured in the same units as whatever the statistics are measuring. For the Gaussian blur, the statistic is the x- and y-position of the pixel's color value. The standard deviation is a measure of how far away from the initial position that color ends up.

Figure 16-2 shows the normal (Gaussian) distribution as a chart. The x-axis is measured in the number of standard deviations from the mean; the y-axis is the probability. The majority of the values (68%, to be precise) are within one standard deviation from the mean. 95% will be within two standard deviations from it, and 99.7% will be within three standard deviations.

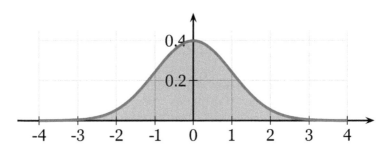

Figure 16-2. The normal distribution, measured as a probability distribution (y) relative to standard deviations offset from mean (x) (adapted from a graphic by Wikimedia commons contributor Geek3)

In a Gaussian blur, that means that 95% of the color from the original pixel will stay within a circle with a radius of two standard deviations, centered on the original pixel. Nearly all of the color will stay within three standard deviations. In fact, most Gaussian blur algorithms don't bother calculating any effects further than three standard deviations.

Of course, you don't usually blur a single pixel. You blur a picture. The final color of each pixel in the blurred result is the sum of the color that didn't get blurred away from the original pixel, plus the color that spilled over from all the neighboring pixels.

The uniform blur in Example 16-1 used `stdDeviation="1.5"`, or 1.5px. That means that most (95%) of the blurring effect is spread within a radius of 3px (two standard deviations) from the original. This is enough spread to make it obviously blurred, without completely obscuring the original shape.

CSS Versus SVG
Blurred Elements Versus Blurred Shadows

Even before the introduction of shorthand filter functions, one type of blur existed in CSS: blurred shadows. The `box-shadow` and `text-shadow` properties both include a "blur radius" value.

The shadow blur radius is *not* the standard deviation. Instead, it is *twice* the standard deviation, and therefore covers *most* of the blurred color.

That said, the exact mathematical definition of the blur radius in the shadows wasn't defined until after browsers had implemented them. There may be slight discrepancies in older browsers.

The CSS shorthand filter functions include a `drop-shadow()` function, which accepts parameters in the same form as `text-shadow`. However, the Filter Effects module was originally unclear about whether the blur-amount value in a drop-shadow filter should be treated as a standard deviation or as a shadow radius. Since an `<feDropShadow>` element was created at the same time, and it *did* use `stdDeviation` explicitly, that's how the browsers implemented it. That means you get *half* as much blurring for `drop-shadow()` as you do for the same values in `text-shadow` or `box-shadow`.

Fast Filters from CSS Alone

Blurs are popular, so it's no surprise that Gaussian blurs are included in the shorthand filter function. The `url(#blur)` filter from Example 16-1 is equivalent to the following shorthand declaration:

```
filter: blur(1.5px);
```

The value inside the `blur()` function is the standard deviation, as a length with units.

There is currently no shorthand function for a nonuniform blur (one with a different standard deviation for the x and y directions). This reflects the fact that uniform blurs are more popular, but also that many GPUs have optimized pathways for uniform blurs (but not for single-direction blurs).

In general, browsers that have implemented the shorthand filters have integrated them with GPU processing where available. Browsers are starting to optimize their SVG filter implementations to use the GPU where possible, but some SVG filters can be noticeably slower than the shorthands in animated web pages.

The shorthand blur() function isn't just less code to write—it also adds new functionality! Because the blur's standard deviation is part of the CSS declaration, it can be animated or transitioned from CSS.

For example, the following code blurs an image within a link until the user hovers over or focuses it, at which point the blur clears up in a smooth transition:

```
img {
    filter: blur(3px);
    transition: filter 0.3s;
}
img:hover, a:focus img {
    filter: none;
}
```

This will be treated as a transition from blur(3px) to blur(0px) in supporting browsers, with the standard deviation changing according to your transition timing function. All of the filter functions have a "none" equivalent that is used for transitioning.

 Short and simple transitions are good, but test carefully before applying significant, ongoing animations with filters, especially to large graphics: they can be huge performance killers! This includes animating the appearance of elements that are being filtered, since the filter results need to be recalculated after each change.

If you want to blur an HTML element like an <img>, you can now get pretty good browser support with just the shorthand (and slightly better if you duplicate it with the -webkit- prefix). But at the time of writing, if you want to blur an SVG element—whether it is inline SVG or in an SVG document—you are better off referencing an SVG <filter> element.

The only exception is the <svg> element that is the root element or a direct child of HTML elements: it has a CSS reference box, and is therefore treated like other CSS layout elements by the browsers that have different filtering support for SVG. (This also means that—for now—you should avoid applying SVG filters on the root <svg> element.)

Unfortunately, you can't just define a set of SVG filters in a separate file and reference them from your CSS. *Theoretically*, that's allowed, but Firefox is the only browser that currently supports it. Similarly, Firefox is the only browser with reliable support for SVG filters specified as data URIs. And Firefox is the one we *don't* need fall-backs for any more.

What's worse: if browsers *cannot* find or apply a filter you specify with url() reference, the filtered element disappears!

Based on SVG 1.1 error-handling rules, most browsers will not draw an element at all if it has a filter that causes an error.

The latest specs instead recommend that the erroneous filter be ignored, and that the element should be drawn without the filter.

So, for best support, when filtering individual SVG elements, use SVG filter markup in the same document.

Older versions of Internet Explorer had a (unprefixed, but nonstandard) filter property. The syntax is completely unlike the new filter shorthands—or any standard CSS syntax, in any property.

The old IE filter isn't supported in any browser that supports SVG filters (that is, IE 10 and later). But it's one more reason why testing for browser support of filters is painfully difficult.

Future Focus
Filtering Images Within CSS

The Filter Effects module also introduces a filter() *function* syntax to CSS. The function would modify a CSS image object being used in another style property.

The filter() function takes two parameters:

- a CSS image (a `url()` of an image file, or a CSS gradient)
- a list of filter effects (shorthand functions or references to SVG filters) to apply to that image

The result is another CSS image, so that `filter()` could be used anywhere an image can be used in CSS.

For example, this code would load a background photo, blur it, make it half-transparent, then layer it over a `mistyRose` background color:

```
background: filter(url(photo.jpg), blur(2px) opacity(0.5))
            0 0/cover mistyRose;
```

The `filter()` image function is not yet supported in browsers.

Mixing Multiple Filter Operations

Beyond browser support issues, why would you use SVG filter markup instead of shorthands? Because the full SVG syntax lets you do things the shorthands can't.

We already mentioned one example: unidirectional motion blurs are currently only available with `<feGaussianBlur>`. Most of the other shorthands are similarly limited to common options for each primitive. This chapter focuses on some of the less common operations. If you need to, you can look up the markup equivalent of a `contrast(150%)` or `saturation(70%)` filter in the Filter Effects spec (*https://drafts.fxtf.org/filters/*).

But the real power of SVG filters comes when you combine multiple filter primitives to create compound effects. Multistep filters can mix, modify, and recombine the vector graphics in surprising ways.

You can find lots of interesting filter examples online, and there are many available as presets in SVG software. The purpose of this chapter is to give you just enough knowledge to start tweaking and remixing those filters to your own needs—and maybe creating new ones from scratch.

If you're using Adobe Illustrator or other software, pay attention to the difference between true SVG filters, which can be exported into standard SVG, versus other effects which need to be converted into images for export.

The Chain of Commands

Filters convert input images to output or result images. Each filter primitive has its own inputs and outputs.

You can **chain** filter primitives together. If you include multiple filter primitive elements as children of the `<filter>`, the output from one is passed (by default) as the input to the next in a straight chain.

The output of the final filter primitive in the filter is the final appearance of the element. Well, not quite final: clipping, masking, and hidden overflow all apply *after* filters.

So the following `blur-desaturate` filter blurs an element (with a 2px standard deviation) and then desaturates the blurred image (to 30% of the original color saturation):

```
<filter id="blur-desaturate">
    <feGaussianBlur stdDeviation="2" />
    <feColorMatrix type="saturate" values="0.3"/>
</filter>
```

Figure 16-3 shows the steps, from the original image to the blur.

For this particular case, the results would look fairly similar if you desaturated first and blurred second, but that's not true in general—the order of operations matters in filters.

Figure 16-3. A two-step SVG filter applied to a photograph: (left) unfiltered, (middle) after the first primitive is applied, (right) final result

The `<feColorMatrix>` element is another of the most common filter primitives. It comes in four `type` variations, each of which has a different `values` requirement:

- `type="saturate"` increases and decreases saturation, while preserving luminance; `values` is a positive number where 1 means no change, 0 means complete desaturation (grayscale), and values greater than 1 increase saturation. There is an equivalent `saturate()` shorthand that takes either numbers or percentages (100% is no change), and also a `grayscale()` shorthand where the values are reversed: 100% is fully gray and 0% is no change.

- `type="hueRotate"` spins every color around the color wheel, adjusting the lightness to maintain constant luminance while changing hue; `values` is a number representing the angle between hues, in degrees. For the shorthand `hue-rotate()`, you need to specify the angle unit explicitly.

- `type="luminanceToAlpha"` performs a conversion like the one used in luminance masks, converting colors to degrees of transparency; `values` is ignored.

- `type="matrix"` performs complex color manipulations using matrix algebra; `values` is a list of 20 numbers.

For any filter primitive element that adjusts colors, the color-interpolation-filters property (or presentation attribute) can change the calculations. To get consistent results with the equivalent shorthand filters, set it to sRGB (the default is linearRGB). The property is inherited, so you can set it once on a <filter>, or even on the <svg> as a whole.

The final colors in Firefox (version 54, anyway) are noticeably different for some color effects, regardless of whether you use the longhand or shorthand formats, or whether you set color-interpolation-filters. The problem shows up most noticeably on the hue-rotate, saturate, and grayscale filters.

You can also chain filter operations together when you are using shorthand filter functions, by giving a list of functions as the filter value. So in shorthand notation, the blur-desaturate filter can be written in one line:

```
filter: blur(2px) saturate(30%);
```

You can also include url() references to SVG markup filters within the filter operations list.

Or at least, you can when more browsers support both the new shorthand filter syntax and SVG markup filters on the same elements...

There is no formal limit to the number of filter operations you can chain together in a row, although browsers may have their own practical limits. But at a certain point, there's not much more you can do to the graphic by adding another filter function to the chain that you couldn't do by changing one of the other functions earlier in the list.

Chaining outputs to inputs is the *default* behavior. For the shorthands, it's the only behavior: a straight chain from the original graphic appearance, through the filter list, to the final result.

For SVG markup filters, however, you can mix things up.

Mixing and Merging

By default, the input to the first filter primitive is the **source graphic** —the rendered result of whatever element has the `filter` property. That includes all its child elements, layered together, after any filters, clipping, and masking are applied to them.

The default input to every *other* filter primitive is the output (result) from the previous primitive.

You can change the input to a filter primitive by giving it an **in attribute**. So this primitive blurs the `SourceAlpha` layer:

```
<feGaussianBlur stdDeviation="2" in="SourceAlpha" />
```

The value of in is either a predefined keyword *or* a name you have given to the result of a previous primitive in the filter.

There are two keyword inputs that are currently supported in all web browsers:

- `SourceGraphic` is the painted result of the element being filtered, before any filters are applied (in other words, the default input for the first primitive).

- `SourceAlpha` is the source graphic with all colors set to black, so only the transparency outline remains.

The other keywords defined in the specifications are `BackgroundImage`, `BackgroundAlpha`, `FillPaint`, and `StrokePaint`. None of them are currently supported reliably cross-browser. Internet Explorer and Microsoft Edge support the background inputs (but they are buggy in IE).

If you're using filters generated by Adobe Illustrator or Inkscape, make sure they aren't using these inputs. Browsers either treat unknown keywords as a transparent black layer (sometimes not too bad a result) or as an error stopping filter processing (a very bad result: the filtered element disappears).

 The keyword names are case-sensitive, and don't follow the normal camel-casing rules. `in="sourceGraphic"` won't work.

The other option for naming inputs is to use a custom named output from a previous step.

You give a filter output a name by setting it in a **result attribute**. So the output of the following primitive would be named "blur" for the purpose of other primitives' inputs:

```
<feGaussianBlur stdDeviation="2" result="blur" />
```

The `result` name is a case-sensitive identifier. It should be unique within a given `<filter>`, but doesn't have to be unique within the document.

The Filter Effects module says it should be a valid CSS identifier (no whitespace, and doesn't start with a number), but browsers seem to accept any string. Just don't use any of the keywords as your custom `result` names—even the keywords that don't have good browser support.

Using named inputs and outputs, we can rewrite the `blur-desaturate` filter from the previous section, but with the inputs made explicit:

```
<filter id="blur-desaturate">
    <feGaussianBlur in="SourceGraphic"
                    stdDeviation="2"
                    result="blur" />
    <feColorMatrix  in="blur"
                    type="saturate" values="0.3"
                    result="final" />
</filter>
```

If all filter primitives were like `<feGaussianBlur>` and `<feColorMatrix>`, and only accepted one input, the ability to name your inputs and results wouldn't be that interesting. The usefulness comes from the filter primitives that accept a *second* input, indicated with an **in2 attribute**.

Three filter elements use an `in2` attribute; we'll have examples of each later in the chapter:

- **`<feBlend>`** combines the two inputs by performing mathematical operations on the color channels (red, blue, and green) on each pixel, after adjusting for opacity of that pixel.

- **<feComposite>** combines the inputs based on opaque versus transparent areas, or by applying a specified set of mathematical calculations to all four channels (red, green, blue, and alpha) equally.
- **<feDisplacementMap>** moves the pixels in one input by an amount determined by the color of the pixel from the other input, creating distortion effects.

If in2 isn't specified, the default input for the element is used, so you often only need to specify either in or in2.

In addition, the **<feMerge> primitive** combines *any* number of inputs, each of which is specified with the in attribute on a child **<feMergeNode> element**. If any <feMergeNode> *doesn't* have an in attribute, it gets the default input for its parent <feMerge> primitive.

The different inputs to <feMerge> are layered together from bottom to top, just as if they were sibling images in the document.

Example 16-2 uses <feMerge> to create a filter that merges the source graphic over the top of multiple copies of a blurred version of its alpha channel shadow. The filter is then applied to our heart icon, drawn 180px tall, as shown in Figure 16-4.

Figure 16-4. A heart surrounded by a dark shadow

Example 16-2. Creating a blurred shadow by merging filter layers

```
<svg xmlns="http://www.w3.org/2000/svg" xml:lang="en"
     xmlns:xlink="http://www.w3.org/1999/xlink"
     viewBox="0 0 200 200" width="2.5in" height="2.5in">
    <title>Dark Blurred Halo</title>
    <filter id="halo-dark">
        <feGaussianBlur in="SourceAlpha" stdDeviation="5" />
        <feMerge>
            <feMergeNode />
            <feMergeNode />
            <feMergeNode />
            <feMergeNode in="SourceGraphic" />
        </feMerge>
    </filter>

    <use xlink:href="../ch10-reuse-files/suits-symbols.svg#heart"
         fill="mediumVioletRed" filter="url(#halo-dark)"
         x="10" y="10" width="180" height="180"/>
</svg>
```

The result is the original shape surrounded by a blurred black shadow. The extra layers make the shadow darker than the blur would have otherwise created.

The size of the icon matters, because the standard deviation of the blur is (by default) measured in user-space units.

When the filter is applied on a reused symbol like this, the user space is that of the <use> element with the filter, not of the scaled <path> inside—because a filter is a layer effect, applied to the <use> directly.

To finish off the discussion of inputs, there are a few primitives that ignore their in value, creating completely new image layers:

- **<feFlood>** creates a uniform layer of a single color, based on its flood-color and flood-opacity presentation attributes.

- **<feImage>** loads a separate image file (or, with limited support, clones an element from the document) as a new filter layer.

- **<feTurbulence>** creates pseudorandom patterns of swirling color.

You can then blend or composite these onto your source graphic or other filter primitive results, to add colors or textures.

Example 16-3 adds an `<feFlood>` and `<feComposite>` filter primitives to Example 16-2, to turn that dark shadow into a golden glow. Figure 16-5 shows the result on a dark background.

Figure 16-5. A heart with a golden glow

Example 16-3. Creating a golden glow by compositing a flood color on a shadow layer

```
<filter id="halo-gold">
    <feGaussianBlur in="SourceAlpha" stdDeviation="5"
                    result="blur" />
    <feFlood flood-color="#fe7" />
    <feComposite in2="blur" operator="in" />
    <feMerge>
        <feMergeNode />
        <feMergeNode />
        <feMergeNode />
        <feMergeNode in="SourceGraphic" />
    </feMerge>
</filter>
```

By default, `<feComposite>` acts like `<feMerge>` with only two inputs, layering the in on top of in2. The **operator attribute** defines how those two layers are combined, or **composited**, together. The default operator, over, means the first layer on top of the second.

Using `operator="in"` turns the compositing step into an alpha-masking operation: you get the first input (the yellow layer from `<feFlood>`) masked by the alpha channel of the second input (the blurred shadow). In other words, you turn the shadow gold, making the heart appear to glow from behind.

The `in` operator name stands for inside—you get the colors of the first layer, but only when they are inside the opaque regions from the second layer. Try not to confuse it with the `in` and `in2` attributes (which are in*puts*).

With the addition of the **`<feOffset>` filter primitive**—which translates the filter input layer according to distances set in its `dx` and `dy` attributes—you have all the makings of a drop-shadow filter. Drop shadows are so common that there's a shorthand `drop-shadow()` function for that—and a new `<feDropShadow>` primitive to match. But the same techniques can be applied to less common solutions.

Building a Better Blur

The basic all-direction blur we introduced in Example 16-1 blurs both the colors within a graphic and the edges of the graphic. Figure 16-6 shows the results again, so you don't have to flip back to the beginning.

Figure 16-6. A basic blur filter applied to SVG text and an embedded photo

The text is indeed "fuzzy," and the edges of the `<image>` reveal that this is a blurred image element, and not just a blurry photograph.

Sometimes this is the effect you want. Sometimes it isn't.

The "dissolving edges" result of blurring a photograph is such a common complaint that the Filter Effects module adds a new edgeMode attribute that allows you to control it. A value of duplicate would pad the edges with the nearest color. A value of wrap would treat the input graphic as if it were a pattern tile, and blur from one tile to the next. The shorthand blur() function is *supposed* to use duplicate mode.

At the time of writing, WebKit/Safari is the only browser to have implemented edgeMode, and they treat "wrap" as equivalent to "duplicate."

So we'll have to fix the blurry edges ourselves.

We can use the <feComposite> in operation to remove the blurred bits that have strayed outside the outline of the original graphic:

```
<filter id="blur-trimmed">
    <feGaussianBlur stdDeviation="1.5" />
    <feComposite in2="SourceAlpha" operator="in" />
</filter>
```

Figure 16-7 shows what that looks like.

Figure 16-7. A blur filter on SVG text and a photo, with the result trimmed to the original alpha outline

It's better, but the edges are still a little fuzzy. We've cleaned up the blurred color that spilled off the edges, but we haven't replaced the color that was lost.

One option would be to composite our blurred layer on top of a copy of the source. That looks pretty good for the text outlines. But in a photo, especially with a large blur radius (or if you zoom in), it can be obvious that the edges aren't as blurry as the rest.

Example 16-4 shows another possible solution, using an <feMorphology> filter to pad the edges of the blur result, before trimming it to fit within the original outline. Figure 16-8 shows the final result.

Figure 16-8. Text and a photo in which the edges have been reconstructed after blurring

Example 16-4. Blurring colors but not edges

```
<filter id="blur-trimmed-filled">
    <feGaussianBlur stdDeviation="1.5" result="blur"/>  ❶
    <feMorphology radius="3" operator="dilate" />  ❷
    <feMerge>
        <feMergeNode />  ❸
        <feMergeNode in="blur" />
    </feMerge>
    <feComposite in2="SourceAlpha" operator="in" />  ❹
</filter>
```

❶ The first step is still a basic blur of the source graphic (as the default in to the first primitive). However, we now give the result a name (blur) so that we can reference it later in the filter.

❷ The result of the blur is also passed to the following <feMorphology> filter primitive (which does not specify an in attribute). An <feMorphology> filter with the dilate operator— among other effects—causes transparent pixels to become solid if they are within radius units of a solid pixel. Here, the radius is twice the blur stdDeviation, so we should more than compensate for the dissolved edges.

❸ An `<feMerge>` primitive layers the `<feMorphology>` result (as the default `in`) underneath the original `blur` (identified by name).

❹ Finally, an `<feComposite>` `in` operation clips those combined layers to include only the pixels that are within the original alpha outline.

Even when `edgeMode` is fully implemented—and able to preserve edges when filtering *rectangular* shapes, like the embedded photo— the `<feMorphology>` approach would still be useful to reconstruct edges of text and vector shapes.

How does it work? The name "morphology" refers to the change in shape. But an `<feMorphology>` filter is a very *particular* change in shape, created by expanding pixels into rectangles.

The `<feMorphology>` element has two modes, which are specified as the value of its **operator attribute**:

- `erode` (the default) sets each pixel to its darkest or most transparent neighbor, as measured separately for the red, green, blue, and alpha channels. This causes shapes to crumble away at the edges, while still maintaining—approximately—strokes around the edge.

- `dilate` sets each channel of each pixel to match the brightest or *least* transparent value from its neighbors. This causes edges to expand into transparent areas.

The amount of erosion or dilation (the distance at which a pixel is considered a "neighbor") is set by a **radius parameter**, as a number of user units (px). Similar to the standard deviation in blurs, you can give two radius numbers to have different horizontal and vertical values.

Although it's called a `radius`, the effect is rectangular, not elliptical. Whether eroding or dilating, the result of applying `<feMorphology>` to a finely detailed image tends to look like someone painted a portrait using a paint roller, with lots of big blocks of color and very few fine details, as shown in Figure 16-9.

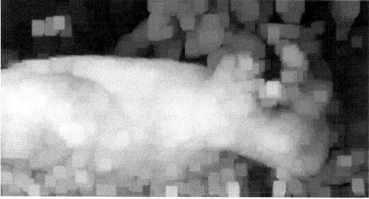

Figure 16-9. A photo modified with an <femorphology> filter: (top) with an erode operator, (bottom) with a dilate operator

Note that both `<image>` elements in Figure 16-9 are the same size, before filtering.

When `<feMorphology>` is applied to smooth gradients and blurs, the effect is more subtle. Edges and bright spots expand or contract, without changing the intermediary colors too much.

Morphology applied to photographs creates a very specific effect, with not a lot of subtleties. But it's the only option we have in filters for scaling up or down a shape—as rough as it is—so it's not surprising that it has many uses.

Morphing Shapes into Strokes

SVG strokes can create many effects (have you read Chapter 13 yet?), but they can't do everything. One limitation of strokes is that there is no "group" stroke effect, to stroke the composite outline of a set of shapes.

For text, this ruins many desired effects. Each letter in a text element is stroked individually. Under normal circumstances, characters with strokes that are brought closer to each other will overlap, not merge. If you have cursive letters that are supposed to look continuous, stroking them reveals the seams.

Even paint-order can't help you, as individual letters are still painted one after the other in most browsers. You could merge all the letters into a single <path> in graphics software, but that ruins the accessibility and editability of the text.

By using <feMorphology> to dilate the joined letter shapes and then compositing the results back with the original, we can create a rough outline around the combined shape. Example 16-5 gives the code applied to some comic-book text, and Figure 16-10 shows the result.

Figure 16-10. Merged letters with a shared "stroke"

Example 16-5. Creating a group outline with <feMorphology>

```
<svg xmlns="http://www.w3.org/2000/svg" xml:lang="en"
     viewBox="0 0 120 60" width="4in" height="2in">
    <title>Merge Stroke with feMorphology</title>
    <filter id="outline">
```

```
        <feMorphology in="SourceAlpha"
                      operator="dilate" radius="3"/>  ❶
        <feComposite in="SourceGraphic"/>  ❷
    </filter>
    <style>
        @font-face { /* omitted */ }
        text {
            font-size: 60px;
            font-family: BadaboomBB, Impact, sans-serif;
            text-anchor: middle;
        }
    </style>
    <rect fill="aqua" width="100%" height="100%" />
    <text fill="yellow" filter="url(#outline)"
          x="50%" y="50%" dy="0.35em"
          dx="0, -10, -10, -12">                        ❸
        BOOM
    </text>
</svg>
```

❶ The filter starts with the SourceAlpha outline of the filtered shape (which will be the unstroked text). The dilation morphology filter converts any transparent pixels that are within 3px (in the scaled coordinate system) of the shape's edge into opaque pixels.

❷ The <feComposite> primitive, with the default over operator, layers two inputs over one another. The primary (in) input (here, the SourceGraphic) goes on top of the secondary (in2) input. Since in2 isn't specified on the element, it defaults to the result of the previous primitive—the expanded alpha outline.

❸ The <text> that we are filtering is styled to use a web font, but the really important detail is the dx attribute. The negative values cause subsequent letters to be pulled back from their normal relative position, so that they overlap.

Filters on text, like this, are particularly useful due to the fact that the text remains readable, selectable, and accessible for both users and search engines. The visual effect itself remains easily editable if you need to change the text. This makes the technique far more powerful and adaptable than "baked in" effects created in an image editor and saved as a bitmap image or SVG paths.

For text in particular, filters are also an improvement over many vector effects that rely on <use> copies. Multiple <use> copies of text can be interpreted as repeated words by screen readers, or when copying and pasting. Within the filter, you can copy the image of the text as many times as you require, without duplicating the text itself.

For best support, only apply filters on complete <text> elements (or their parent groups). Although most browsers support filters on <tspan> and <textPath> elements, this was not allowed in the SVG 1.1 specs and—at the time of writing—is not yet supported in Firefox.

Filters in CSS layout apply to both inline and block elements.

Nonetheless, filters have their limitations. Because this "group stroke" is a *pixel* effect, not a true SVG stroke, it can create a pixelated edge, especially with large dilation radius values. The stroke in Figure 16-10 is noticeably blocky at the corners. You could use additional filter operations to smooth it out, but you can't recreate the precise geometry of a true stroke, let alone all the other functionality of SVG strokes.

Figure 16-11. Changing the color of "stroke"

The outline in Example 16-5 is black because it is derived from the colorless SourceAlpha input. You could color the outline by compositing it with an <feFlood> layer, in the same way we colored the glow shadow in Example 16-3. Example 16-6 shows the code for an indigo outline; Figure 16-11 shows the result.

Example 16-6. Coloring the group outline

```
<filter id="outline-indigo">
    <feMorphology in="SourceAlpha" result="expanded"
                  operator="dilate" radius="3"/> ❶
    <feFlood flood-color="indigo" /> ❷
    <feComposite in2="expanded" operator="in" /> ❸
    <feComposite in="SourceGraphic"/> ❹
</filter>
```

❶ The expanded outline is created with the same `<feMorphology>` primitive. It's now given a name (`expanded`) so we can access it later.

❷ The `<feFlood>` creates a continuous indigo layer.

❸ The first `<feComposite>` takes that infinite color layer (as the default `in` input) and clips it to only include the pixels that are inside the `expanded` shape.

❹ The second `<feComposite>` layers the original `SourceGraphic` over the colored expanded shape from the previous step (as the default `in2` input).

A filter like that in Example 16-5 is exactly the use case for the `StrokePaint` input. The idea of `StrokePaint` (and `FillPaint`) is that your filter could access the continuous "wallpaper" of the color, gradient, or pattern used to stroke the filtered shape. Instead of hardcoding the outline color in the filter, you would be able to apply a `stroke` value on the `<text>` (but with zero stroke width), then create the outline shape in the filter, and use it to clip the `StrokePaint` wallpaper.

Unfortunately, not only is `StrokePaint` not supported anywhere yet, but Firefox currently treats it as an error of the sort that causes the filtered element to disappear. (Other browsers treat it as a black input, so the results look the same as Figure 16-10.)

Sigh. The good news is that `flood-color` (on an `<feFlood>` element) is a presentation attribute, so you can set it with CSS rules. You can also use `currentColor` or CSS variables to quickly change the color your filter applies. The bad news is that when you change the color, you change it for *all* elements that use that filter. You would need a separate filter for a separate color.

Drawing Out of Bounds

Blurs, dilation morphology, and a few other filters can create graphical effects that are *larger* than your input. Is there a limit to how big you can get?

There is. But there's also a way to control it.

We're Going to Need a Bigger Boom

Like masks, filters require the browser to construct temporary image layers, which can use up memory. For that reason, the results of the filter are limited to a rectangular **filter region**, outside of which everything is clipped.

Just like with masks, the default filter is the object bounding box plus 10% padding. The exact dimensions are set by rectangular attributes on the `<filter>` element: x and y default to -10%, and width and height default to 120%. These are bounding-box units by default; you switch them to userSpaceOnUse with the filterUnits attribute.

There are the usual reasons for modifying the default dimensions, or switching away from bounding-box units completely:

- The bounding box is based on the fill region only; if your graphic has thick strokes or large markers, it may extend more than 10% beyond its box.

- If the bounding box has zero height or width (straight horizontal or vertical lines), bounding-box calculations will cause an error. And errors with filters usually mean that the filtered element disappears.

In addition, filters (unlike masks) can create an output result that is larger than the input, so certain filters will always need larger bounds, regardless of which element you apply them to.

Example 16-7 provides a variation on the text-outline filter from Example 16-5. To really emphasize a "BOOM!" sound effect, we're going to add visible "echoes" of the text offset from the center.

Figure 16-12 shows what happens if we apply this filter (as written in Example 16-7) to the "BOOM!" text from Example 16-5 (but in an SVG with a larger viewBox).

Figure 16-12. Offset filter layers, clipped to the filter region

Example 16-7. Adding duplicate, offset layers with a filter

```
<filter id="outline-echo">
    <feFlood flood-color="darkRed" />                                    ❶
    <feComposite in2="SourceAlpha" operator="in" result="echo" />
    <feOffset in="echo" dx="-45" dy="-25" result="echo-1" />
    <feOffset in="echo" dx="-40" dy="+30" result="echo-2" /> ❷
    <feOffset in="echo" dx="+45" dy="+25" result="echo-3" />
    <feOffset in="echo" dx="+40" dy="-30" result="echo-4" />

    <feMorphology in="SourceAlpha" result="expanded"
                  operator="dilate" radius="3" />                        ❸
    <feMerge>
        <feMergeNode in="echo-1" />
        <feMergeNode in="echo-2" />
        <feMergeNode in="echo-3" />     ❹
        <feMergeNode in="echo-4" />
        <feMergeNode in="expanded" />
        <feMergeNode in="SourceGraphic" />
    </feMerge>
</filter>
```

❶ A dark red copy of the original text is created with <feFlood> and <feComposite>.

❷ Four named copies of the red text are created with <feOffset>, each one offset to left or right, up or down, with different dx and dy values.

❸ The expanded outline is created with the same <feMorphology> primitive.

❹ All the red copies are layered together, then the expanded black outline, and finally the original graphic, in an <feMerge> stack.

As we warned—and as Figure 16-12 clearly demonstrates—the default filter region is not big enough for all the offset layers in Example 16-7. We're going to need a bigger filter region.

But how much bigger? And how do we specify it?

The final size of our filter result is the full bounding-box size, plus 30px above and below, and 45px to the left and right. If you're used to working with CSS, you may be thinking that now is a good time to reach for your trusty calc() function:

```
x="-45px"
width="calc(100% + 2*45px)"
y="-30px"
height="calc(100% + 2*30px)"
```

That would be a great idea, if we could use calc() in SVG filter attributes. But we can't. (Not yet, anyway.)

So, instead, we have to roughly estimate (and, to be sure, *over-estimate*) how much the absolute-distance offsets will be as a percentage of the bounding box:

```
<filter id="outline-echo"
        x="-50%" y="-50%" width="200%" height="200%" >
```

That gives us enough room for all the "echo" copies of the text, as shown in Figure 16-13. But if you applied the same filter to a much smaller element, you might still get clipping.

Figure 16-13. Offset filter layers, in a filter region that is large enough to contain them

For this particular SVG, where the filtered element takes up most of the SVG dimensions (but doesn't overflow them), a simpler solution is to switch to user-space dimensions:

```
<filter id="outline-echo" filterUnits="userSpaceOnUse"
        x="0" y="0" width="100%" height="100%" >
```

You could even skip the x, y, width, and height attributes, leaving them as their default 10% padding around the box—which in this case is the SVG's viewBox.

Despite the problems with bounding-box units, avoid creating excessively large filter regions, especially if you will be animating content within the filter. It consumes extra memory, and more pixels means more processing time.

User-space coordinate systems are not without their own issues, of course. In most browsers, you cannot easily predefine the graphical effect in one <svg> in an HTML document and use it elsewhere, because percentages will be misinterpreted. And if your SVG uses a viewBox with a centered coordinate system, you'll need to change the x and y attributes to match, or else your filter will only cover the bottom-right corner of your SVG.

You mostly only need to worry about the filter region when it is too small, to avoid clipping. It can sometimes be useful to make it fit tightly against the bounding box to clip overflowing blur or dilation, by setting the `<filter>` element's x and y to 0, and width and height to 100%. But if you want to do any creative clipping, you'll usually use a `<clipPath>`. (Remember that clipping paths are applied *after* filters on the same element.)

In contrast, it is often useful to clip the output from a particular *step* in the filter chain.

Half-and-Half Filter Effects

Each filter primitive works with input image layers and output image layers. These layers, like the filter as a whole, are defined by rectangular boundaries.

By default, the layers match the filter region set on the `<filter>` element. However, you can specify **filter primitive regions** for each layer. Once you do, each subsequent layer matches the previous one unless you give it different dimensions.

You set the dimensions of the filter primitive element with x, y, width, and height attributes on that element. These cause that primitive's result to be clipped to the specified rectangle. The rectangle dimensions are measured according to the **primitiveUnits** (*not* filterPrimitiveUnits) value for the `<filter>` element, which is userSpaceOnUse by default.

In addition to x, y, width, and height, the primitiveUnits setting controls most length-based attributes on filter primitives, including:

- stdDeviation on `<feGaussianBlur>`
- radius on `<feMorphology>`
- dx and dy on `<feOffset>`

You *can't* change the primitiveUnits for individual filter primitives, let alone individual attributes. This means, if you switch to objectBoundingBox units, you need to redefine every blur radius and offset distance to match. That's an awful bother, so pick your primitiveUnits carefully.

Example 16-8 makes use of the filter primitive regions to apply a filter to *part* of an element, without having to duplicate it with <use> and apply a clipping path. Instead, the two halves will be clipped with filter region attributes, and then merged back together after processing, as shown in Figure 16-14.

Figure 16-14. Photo-filled text in which the bottom half is given a wave distortion effect

The example makes use of two of the more exotic SVG filter primitives, **<feTurbulence>** and **<feDisplacementMap>**, to apply a wavy distorted effect to the filtered section of the text. For now, though, just focus on the inputs, outputs, and filter-region attributes.

Example 16-8. Applying filter effects to a subregion of the element

```
<svg xmlns="http://www.w3.org/2000/svg" xml:lang="en"
    xmlns:xlink="http://www.w3.org/1999/xlink"
    viewBox="0 0 285 65" width="4in">
  <title>Wave-Filtering Half of an Element</title>
  <pattern id="beach" patternUnits="userSpaceOnUse"
          width="285" height="65">                           ❶
      <image x="0" y="-50" width="300" height="200"
          xlink:href="hawaii-beach.jpg"
          transform="rotate(0.5)" />
      <!-- photo by Daniel Ramirez, licensed CC-BY
        https://www.flickr.com/photos/danramarch/6225153931 -->
  </pattern>
```

```
        <filter id="hawaiifilter">                              ➋
            <feOffset result="top" y="0" height="36px" />        ➌

            <feTurbulence y="30px" height="40px" result="waves"
                         type="turbulence" baseFrequency="0.01 0.1"
                         numOctaves="1" seed="53" />             ➍
            <feDisplacementMap in="SourceGraphic" in2="waves"
                              y="36px" height="29px"
                              scale="4"
                              xChannelSelector="G"
                              yChannelSelector="B" />            ➎
            <feGaussianBlur result="bottom"
                            y="34px" height="32px"
                            stdDeviation="0.4" />                ➏
            <feMerge>
                <feMergeNode in="top" />
                <feMergeNode in="bottom" />                      ➐
            </feMerge>
        </filter>
        <style>
    svg text {
        font-family: Arvo, Rockwell, sans-serif;
        font-weight: 700;
        text-transform: uppercase;
        font-size: 64px;
        fill: url(#beach) azure;
        stroke: darkSlateGray;
        stroke-width: 3px;
        filter: url(#hawaiifilter);
    }
        </style>
        <style>
@import url(https://fonts.googleapis.com/css?family=Arvo:700);
        </style>
        <rect width="100%" height="100%" fill="lightSkyBlue" />
        <rect width="100%" y="36px" height="30px"
              fill="lightSeaGreen" />                            ➑
        <text x="50%" y="56" text-anchor="middle"
              dx="-1 2 -7 -7 2 2">Hawaii</text>                  ➒
</svg>
```

➊ The text will be filled with a photograph of water and sky, using a `<pattern>`. The pattern tile is defined in user-space units, and scaled to completely cover the SVG. The photo inside is scaled and positioned to reveal the parts we want to use. A half-degree rotation straightens the horizon line between sea and sky. If this were the only place in the website using this photo, it would be a good idea to crop it ahead of time, to save on file downloads. But here, the hidden overflow of the pattern crops it for us.

❷ The filter will be applied to the same element as the pattern, and it's important that we *haven't* changed the default user-space primitiveUnits. That means that the y and height attributes on the filter primitives are defined in the user space.

❸ The output from the first <feOffset> primitive will therefore be clipped to the area from the top of the SVG to the line where $y = 36px$. And 36px just happens to be the height of the horizon line in the photo after we positioned it in the user-space <pattern>. The <feOffset> itself doesn't do anything without dx or dy, so the effect of this element is just to clip and set aside the top half of our element as a named filter layer.

❹ The next filter primitive, <feTurbulence>, generates a wavy pattern of colors from a mathematical algorithm. The y and height attributes ensure that the output color will be slightly larger than the bottom half of our SVG.

❺ The <feDisplacementMap> filter primitive takes our original SourceGraphic as input, then distorts it according to the waves generated by the <feTurbulence>. The distorted image is precisely clipped to the bottom of our SVG, starting from $y = 36px$.

❻ An <feGaussianBlur> softens the distorted image slightly, using a slightly larger filter primitive region so that the blurred top edge isn't clipped.

❼ Finally, an <feMerge> combines the top and bottom sections back together.

❽ The visible parts of the SVG consist of two colored rectangles and our <text> element. The bottom, sea-green rectangle is precisely positioned to start at that $y = 36px$ horizontal horizon line.

❾ The text itself is mostly styled with CSS, using a web font. However, the letter spacing is manually tweaked with dx, to leave extra space for the strokes while also tightening up the kerning around the "AWA" part of the word.

This example isn't as DRY as we normally like. The magic number 36 (calculated from the photograph itself) appears in multiple places. But it is defined so that it can easily be reused. The alignment between the photo pattern and the filter layers is measured entirely in user-space units, so neither has to be adjusted if you change the text content, or even the text `font-size`, as shown in Figure 16-15.

Figure 16-15. The same paired photo pattern and filter effect, on different text

You *can* even make the text editable, by placing the SVG inline in an HTML element with the `contenteditable` attribute. But it's a little buggy: if the user completely erases the text and then types new material to replace it, the extra text gets added as a sibling to the `<svg>`, instead of being included in the SVG `<text>`. So you'd need a bit of JavaScript to make it work nicely.

Although some browsers (MS Edge and IE) support `contenteditable` directly on SVG elements, it is not defined in the SVG specs, and isn't supported elsewhere.

In an ideal world, you could replace the "magic number" in the filter, at least in part, by accessing the `<rect>` element behind the text as a separate filter input, the `BackgroundAlpha` layer. Then you could use it (with `<feComposite>`) to mask the above- and below-water sections of the text. And it wouldn't even have to be a rectangle: since you'd be masking according to the alpha region of the shape, it could be a wavy path instead.

But web browsers don't (yet) support access to the backdrop from within your filter. The relevant part of the filters spec has been redefined—to fix the most problematic parts from SVG 1.1—so hopefully this will change in the future. But in the meantime, we can be glad of the one area where implementations *have* moved ahead: blend modes.

Blending with the Backdrop

If you use graphics software that is built around "layers" (such as Adobe Photoshop or GIMP), you may be familiar with **blend modes**, which control how the pixels on different layers interact with and influence the resulting color that is shown for that portion of your screen.

Blend modes allow you to create many unique color effects, making your images look like light being projected onto a screen instead of layers of paint on paper.

SVG 1.1 defined blend modes as a filter operation. The new Compositing and Blending module redefines them as a separate graphical effect, applied using the `mix-blend-mode` property. There's also a `background-blend-mode` property for CSS layered backgrounds, and in the future there may be similar properties for layered SVG strokes and fills.

Blending Basics

We've already used blend modes, in a way. The type of blending that is used everywhere in SVG and CSS is known as **normal blending**.

With normal blending, layers in an image are combined as if they were physical prints (sometimes on transparent film) stacked together, and you were looking down from above. If the top layer is completely opaque, it completely obscures any elements that it overlaps.

Blend modes take things much further, allowing the pixels of an element to "read" the color of the pixel underneath them, and calculate the result based on a particular set of algorithms.

Even normal blending—also known as alpha blending—has some math hidden in the implementation. If the top layer is semitransparent, the final color of each pixel is calculated as a combination of the color for that pixel in the top layer and the cumulative color of the layers stacked below. Blend modes change the formula for that calculation.

In SVG filters, blend modes are used in the **<feBlend> filter primitive**. It blends its primary (in) input layer over the top of the secondary (in2) input. By default, it uses normal blending, and is therefore the same as <feMerge>, or the default operator for <feComposite>. You change the default by setting the **mode attribute**.

SVG 1.1 defined four other blend modes for <feBlend>, in addition to the default mode="normal". The exact mathematical formulas can be found in the Compositing and Blending specification (*https:// drafts.fxtf.org/compositing-1*). But *conceptually* this is how they work for fully opaque layers:

screen
> Imagine that the two image layers are being displayed by two different projectors shining on the same screen. The only areas that stay dark in the final result will be those that are dark in *both* pictures. Light tones overlapping will combine to make the result *lighter* than either input. Colors will combine like they do in the RGB model, so that red plus green will create yellow.

multiply
> Imagine a single slide projector shining light through two different slides, stacked together. For light to reach the display, it must pass through both images: the only areas that will be light in the final result are those that are light in both pictures. Dark sections overlapping will make the result *darker* than either of the inputs. Opposite colors (like red and green) will cancel each other out to create black.

`darken`

This mode can't be imagined by a physical process, but is much easier to think of mathematically. For each channel (red, green, and blue), on every pixel where the two layers overlap, select the *smaller* (darker) value from either the top layer or the cumulative bottom layer. This means that opposite colors again cancel out (red + green = black), but equal colors don't get any darker or lighter.

`lighten`

Not surprisingly, this mode is the opposite of `darken`: for each color channel, for each pixel, take the *larger* (brighter) value from either the top layer or the backdrop.

For semitransparent layers, all the blend modes are adjusted so that you see more of the original backdrop color in the final blend, proportional to the amount of transparency in that pixel on the top layer. The alpha channels themselves are not calculated with the same formulas as the color channels.

 Note the spelling of `darken` and `lighten`; they are often confused as "darker" and "lighter."

If you misspell a `mode` name, the attribute will be ignored and you'll get normal blending. Which…is better error handling than most errors with filters, actually.

The Compositing and Blending spec defines 11 additional modes: `overlay`, `color-dodge`, `color-burn`, `hard-light`, `soft-light`, `difference`, `hue`, `saturation`, `color`, `luminosity`, and `exclusion`. The names and definitions are all based on blend modes used in other graphical software.

More Online

A reference with descriptions for all the blend modes is available in the "Blend Modes" guide:

https://oreillymedia.github.io/Using_SVG/guide/blend-modes.html

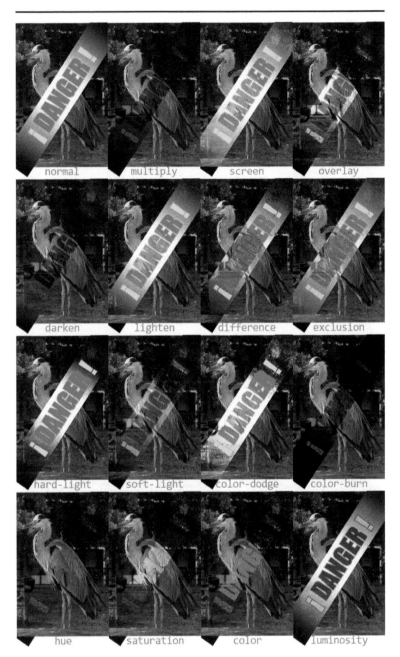

Figure 16-16. The 16 blend modes, when applied to a vector graphic layer over the top of a photo layer

The newer blend modes are supported for <feBlend> in all the latest browsers, but might not be recognized in older browsers (e.g., Internet Explorer) or other software.

Figure 16-16 shows all 16 blend modes, including normal, applied to a vector graphic (red and cyan SVG text on a white-to-black gradient rectangle) over the top of a photograph.

Example 16-9 provides the code for creating Figure 16-16 with <feBlend>. Only the markup for the normal and multiply mode is included. All the others are the same except for the filter id, <svg> offsets, and the mode attribute on <feBlend>. Note that we've set color-interpolation-filters to sRGB, so that color calculation will use the standard color model used in browsers and most graphics software.

Example 16-9. Blending a vector graphic onto a photo, with filters

```
<svg xmlns="http://www.w3.org/2000/svg" xml:lang="en"
    xmlns:xlink="http://www.w3.org/1999/xlink"
    viewBox="0 0 240 390" width="4in">
    <title>Blending Modes Compared</title>
    <style>
        filter {
            color-interpolation-filters: sRGB;
        }
        .label {
            font: 7px Consolas, monospace;
            text-anchor: middle;
            fill: royalBlue;
        }
        .warning {
            font: 16px impact, sans-serif;
            text-anchor: middle;
            fill: red;
            stroke: orange;
            paint-order: stroke;
        }
        .warning tspan {
            fill: cyan;
            stroke: darkCyan;
        }
    </style>
    <defs>
        <linearGradient id="b-w-b">
            <stop offset="0" />
```

```
        <stop offset="0.4" stop-color="white" />
        <stop offset="0.6" stop-color="white" />
        <stop offset="1" />
    </linearGradient>
    <g id="warning" transform="rotate(-56 30,45)">
        <rect fill="url(#b-w-b) white"
              x="-25" width="110" y="35" height="20" />
        <text class="warning" x="30" y="45" dy="0.6ex"><tspan
              >¡</tspan> DANGER <tspan>!</tspan></text>
    </g>
</defs>
<svg width="60" height="25%">
    <filter id="blend-normal" filterUnits="userSpaceOnUse">
        <feImage xlink:href="heron.jpg"
                 x="0" y="0" width="60" height="90" />
        <feBlend in="SourceGraphic" mode="normal" />
    </filter>
    <use xlink:href="#warning" filter="url(#blend-normal)" />
    <text class="label" y="95" x="50%">normal</text>
</svg>
<svg width="60" height="25%" x="60">
    <filter id="blend-multiply" filterUnits="userSpaceOnUse">
        <feImage xlink:href="heron.jpg"
                 x="0" y="0" width="60" height="90" />
        <feBlend in="SourceGraphic" mode="multiply" />
    </filter>
    <use xlink:href="#warning" filter="url(#blend-multiply)" />
    <text class="label" y="95" x="50%">multiply</text>
</svg>
<!--...and the rest...-->
</svg>
```

There's an important limitation of using <feBlend> to merge two
graphics like this. The image file is directly incorporated in the filter,
using **<feImage>**. That means you can't change the photo or its position within the SVG without creating a new filter. The photo is also
not an accessible element in the document. You can't add a <title>
or aria-label to it to provide an accessible description. And it can't
be interactive—as far as the browser is concerned, the entire photo
is just a decoration on the warning label.

Ideally, the <feImage> element would only be used when you want
to import a small bitmap for creating a textured effect within a filter,
and not as a substitute for actual document content.

The <feImage> element, as defined in the specs, can be used for both importing image files (like <image>) and for duplicating sections of the current document (like <use>). However, the second case wasn't very well defined, and has never been implemented in Firefox.

For cross-browser support, only use <feImage> for importing complete image files (or data URI images).

The *logical* way to create this graphic would be to use an <image> element to draw the photo as a direct child of our SVG, before drawing the #warning label on top. We would then set the warning label to blend with its backdrop.

The original SVG filter specs used the term *background* to refer to all the graphics behind an element. But that's confusing when you are working with CSS layout boxes, which can have their own background as part of the element itself.

This chapter therefore follows the terminology of the Compositing and Blending spec: the graphics behind an element are the *backdrop* for it.

The BackgroundImage input would have supported this directly in filters, among many other interesting backdrop-filtering effects. Most browsers aren't yet ready to support general filter access to the backdrop, but they have implemented blending into the backdrop—just with a very different approach.

Premade Mixes

The new **mix-blend-mode property** allows you to apply blend modes without filters. The blend mode is calculated as part of the browser's process of compositing an element on its backdrop.

This means that `mix-blend-mode` applies after all filters, clipping, and masking. It isn't part of how this element is painted, but of how this element is combined with other elements.

The `mix-blend-mode` property is a layer effect, like filters and masking. It applies to the combined image layer created by this element and all its children, and creates a stacking context. It therefore does not inherit by default. The value of `mix-blend-mode` is one of the 16 blending mode keywords, with the default being `normal`.

At the time of writing, WebKit/Safari does not support the `hue`, `saturation`, `color`, and `luminosity` values in CSS blend modes. These four are unique because pixel values can't be calculated for red, green, and blue channels separately, and therefore they aren't as easily optimized.

Microsoft Edge has not implemented CSS blending support at all. It and older browsers will ignore `mix-blend-mode` completely.

Consider fallbacks carefully, and use CSS `@supports` tests if required.

To redefine Example 16-9 to use `mix-blend-mode`, you would create an `<image>` element in each `<svg>` to embed the photograph of the heron, as the prior sibling to the group containing the warning text. Then you would remove the `filter` property from the warning group and instead set the `mix-blend-mode` property.

Example 16-10 provides the modified code for the `multiply` blend. The end result in supporting browsers would still look like Figure 16-16. In unsupporting browsers, all versions would look like `normal` blending—which, in this case, is an acceptable fallback appearance.

Example 16-10. Blending a vector graphic onto a photo, with mix-blend-mode

```
<defs>
    <image id="heron" xlink:href="heron.jpg"
           width="60" height="90" />
</defs>
<svg width="60" height="25%" x="60">
    <use xlink:href="#heron" />
    <use xlink:href="#warning"
         style="mix-blend-mode: multiply" />
    <text class="label" y="95" x="50%">multiply</text>
</svg>
```

No more extra filter markup; only one keyword to change to change the blend mode. The `color-interpolation-filters` property is also no longer required: CSS blend mode properties, like the shorthand filter functions, are always calculated in the color space used for compositing, which is usually sRGB.[1]

Isolating the Blend Effect

The separation of blending from filters means you can use and modify filters and blending separately. It is also closer to how it works in Photoshop and other software. And it is absolutely essential when you're using shorthand functions as filters, as they do not have any way of merging multiple inputs in the first place.

The compositing-stage timing of `mix-blend-mode` is also designed to make it easier for browsers to optimize blend modes, just like they optimize normal compositing of semitransparent layers, using the GPU.

 But not all GPUs support blend modes, so beware that blend modes (like filters) can use up a lot of processing power.

---

1 GPU-optimized blending on a newer system with a high color-depth monitor might use a different color space, but it will likely be closer to sRGB than to linearRGB.

But the order of operations for blend modes can cause some confusion. You need to remember that the colors you see aren't part of one element or the other, but are instead generated from the combination of the two. So if you want to use a filter to tweak that blended color (changing its saturation or brightness, for example), the filter needs to be applied on a group that contains *both* layers that you are blending.

A `filter` is one way to create an **isolation group** for blend modes. This is similar to how filters create a flattening effect for 3D transforms and `z-index` stacking.

When a container element is isolated from its backdrop, its child elements do not "see" the greater backdrop. Instead, they are blended as if the isolated container created a new image layer, starting from transparent black.

 An isolated container element can itself have a blend mode, but all of its children will be blended together first, to create a combined image layer that will be blended with the backdrop.

Blending modes, whether in CSS or in Photoshop layers, are applied cumulatively, from bottom to top. The second layer is blended into the bottom layer to create a cumulative result. The third layer is blended into that combined result, without needing to know that the result was created from two other layers. The only way you can change the order that your blends are applied is by grouping elements in the DOM and isolating them.

Most "layer effect" properties create an isolation group, including `opacity`, `filter`, `mask`, and `mix-blend-mode` itself, when any of them is set to its nondefault value. Three-dimensional transformations also force isolation. In CSS layout, so do 2D transforms and anything else that creates a stacking context, including `z-index`.

But those are all side effects. In order to control isolation directly, you can set the `isolation` property to `isolate`. The default value for the property is `auto`, reflecting all the other properties that can automatically isolate an element.

Firefox is currently buggy about `isolation`, isolating groups that shouldn't be isolated, including SVG elements with 2D transforms and those that are direct children of an element with `viewBox` scaling.

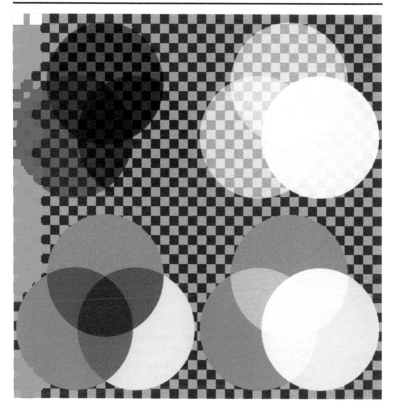

Figure 16-17. Venn diagrams created from colored circles with mix-blend-mode: (top row) without isolation, (bottom row) where each diagram is an isolated group; (left column) blending uses multiply mode, (right column) blending uses screen mode

Example 16-11 demonstrates the use of isolation to create a group of elements that blend with each other but not with their backdrop. Figure 16-17 is the result: the top pair of Venn diagrams are not isolated, so they blend with the checkered backdrop. The bottom set are contained in isolated groups. The samples on the left use multiply blending; those on the right use `screen`. CSS variables are used to pass the different blend mode options through the `<use>` element trees, since `mix-blend-mode` itself isn't inherited.

Example 16-11. Using isolation to limit the impact of blend modes

```
<svg xmlns="http://www.w3.org/2000/svg" xml:lang="en"
     xmlns:xlink="http://www.w3.org/1999/xlink"
     viewBox="0 0 400 400" width="4in" height="4in" >
   <title>Blend Modes and Isolation</title>
   <style>
      #venn use { mix-blend-mode: var(--mode); }
      .multiply { --mode: multiply; }
      .screen   { --mode: screen; }
      .isolate  { isolation: isolate; }
      .left     { fill: royalBlue; }
      .right    { fill: lightGreen; }
      .top      { fill: paleVioletRed; }
   </style>
   <pattern id="checks" width="20" height="20"
            patternUnits="userSpaceOnUse">
      <rect fill="#aaa" width="20" height="20" />
      <rect fill="#444" width="10" height="10" />
      <rect fill="#444" x="10" y="10"
            width="10" height="10" />
   </pattern>
   <rect width="100%" height="100%" fill="url(#checks)" />
   <defs>
      <circle id="c" r="11.5" />
      <svg id="venn"
           width="200" height="200" viewBox="-18 -22 36 34">
         <use xlink:href="#c" x="-6" class="left" />
         <use xlink:href="#c" x="6" class="right" />
         <use xlink:href="#c" y="-10" class="top" />
      </svg>
   </defs>
   <use xlink:href="#venn" class="multiply" />
   <use xlink:href="#venn" class="screen" x="200" />
   <use xlink:href="#venn" class="isolate multiply" y="200" />
   <use xlink:href="#venn" class="isolate screen" x="200" y="200" />
</svg>
```

The `isolation` property replaces the `enable-background` property (or presentation attribute) from SVG 1.1 filters.

There were two problems with `enable-background`:

- The `enable-background` syntax did not translate well to non-SVG contexts. It used a `viewBox`-like parameter to specify the region of an element that needed to be remembered. Even the name is confusing in a CSS context.

- `enable-background` was required to be specified at some point in order for child elements to use backgrounds in filters. That resulted in many SVG tools automatically adding it to the root SVG, whether it was needed or not. So it ceased to be useful as a hint to browsers about whether or not it needed to keep a copy of the graphical layer in memory.

Microsoft browsers support `enable-background: new`, but not the `viewBox`-style qualifications on the enabled background size. Unfortunately, when Adobe Illustrator adds `enable-background` presentation attributes, it always adds the extra parameters. So if you decide to use `BackgroundImage` to polyfill `mix-blend-mode` in Microsoft browsers, keep this in mind!

If both `isolation` and `BackgroundImage/BackgroundAlpha` were supported in the same browser, the nearest isolation group would also limit the background used for those inputs.

Future Focus
Filtering the Backdrop

Blend modes only address one set of effects for which you'd want to access the backdrop. What if you want to blur the backdrop in the parts where the current element overlaps it? Or desaturate it, without blending it with the foreground?

The Filter Effects level 2 module introduces a `backdrop-filter` property that would enable these effects. Its value would be a filter function list (the same as for `filter`). There's an experimental implementation in Safari, but expect the details to change as the spec is developed.

The filter functions would apply on the composited backdrop layers, but only in the sections that are within the bounds of the element with the `backdrop-filter` property. *Which* bounds is not currently clear in the spec.

Summary: Filters and Blend Modes

The set of filter primitives available in SVG is very extensive, as are the effects that can be achieved with them. There are, however, three problems with filters that limit their utility in complex web applications.

One issue, which is thankfully fading, is lack of support: when this book was started in 2011, no browser supported the full set of SVG filter features. Over the years since then, that situation has changed dramatically: basic filter support (SVG filters on SVG elements) is available in all modern browser versions, although there are still areas that need improvement, and bugs that need fixing.

A second problem with filters is that they can be expensive in terms of performance. This is because they are render-time operations, and a filtered object may require several layers of rasterizing and then pixel manipulations. This becomes especially costly if filter operations occur when you're animating the elements that make up your source graphic.

The final problem has more to do with the SVG standard itself. The primitive operations are, taken together, fairly comprehensive, but their effects—and the syntax used to create them—are far from obvious, even to people who are relatively familiar with computer graphics theory. This means that becoming proficient with filters requires a little bit of math and a whole lot of experimentation.

The new shorthand filter functions and the `mix-blend-mode` property directly address the authoring complexity issue, making it simple to specify simple filter effects. The shorthands don't replace SVG markup filters, however. Complex effects still need the full filter capability.

The shorthands and newer approach to blend modes are also designed to improve the performance issues, by making it easier for browsers to use the GPU in their implementations.

Hopefully, with more developers experimenting with filters, we'll also see an improvement in the remaining browser bugs and support limitations.

More Online

The filter elements and their attributes are summarized in the "Filter Elements" section of the markup guide, including a few we didn't have room for in this chapter:

https://oreillymedia.github.io/Using_SVG/guide/markup.html#filters

The shorthand filters are listed for easy reference in a "Shorthand Filter Functions" guide:

https://oreillymedia.github.io/Using_SVG/guide/filter-functions.html

The blend mode keywords are defined in the "Blend Modes" guide:

https://oreillymedia.github.io/Using_SVG/guide/blend-modes.html

PART V

SVG as an Application

The final few chapters of the book consider SVG on the web as an interactive application. They explore how you can add extra information to your graphic to make it more accessible to both human beings and computers, and how you can manipulate your graphic to make it interactive or animated. It is only a brief introduction to the full possibilities of SVG applications, however: web development with SVG is as large and diverse a topic as web development in general.

Chapter 20 ends the book with a summary of tips and best practices for creating SVG code that will be easier for you to work with—and easier for all users to appreciate.

CHAPTER 17

Beyond the Visible

Metadata for Accessibility and Added Functionality

SVG on the web is more than just a picture. It's a structured document that can contain structured information about what the graphic represents.

This chapter looks at the metadata elements and attributes available in SVG to make your graphic more accessible, or to annotate it with information that will be used by your own scripts or by other software.

Titles and Tips

The most commonly used metadata element in SVG is the `<title>`. We've used titles throughout the book—in fact, unless we've messed up, there should be a `<title>` (either SVG or HTML) in every complete example.

As we mentioned back in Chapter 1, a `<title>` is used to provide a name for a web page or document as a whole. It is used in your browser history list and bookmarks, among other places.

For SVG, a `<title>` behaves this way if it is the first child of the root `<svg>` in a *.svg* file, like this (which is the code from Example 6-1 in Chapter 6):

```
<svg xmlns="http://www.w3.org/2000/svg" xml:lang="en"
     height="20px" width="20px">
  <title>Diamond</title>
  <path fill="red"
        d="M3,10 L10,0 17,10 10,20Z
           M9,11 L10,18 V10 H15 L11,9 10,2 V10 H5 Z" />
</svg>
```

The actual title ("Diamond") is given in the text content of the
<title> element. The language of the title text is determined by the
nearest ancestor element with an xml:lang attribute—here, en
(English) is set on the root <svg>.

If you don't set a language anywhere in the document, the browser
will assign its own default, usually based on the user's language settings. This can result in very strange pronunciations by screen readers if the guess is incorrect, so always set languages in your web
documents, whether SVG or HTML.

This type of document title is consistent with the <title> element
in HTML. However, the <title> element in SVG isn't used only for
the title of the document as a whole. It is also used to set titles on
parts of a graphic.

Example 17-1 shows the code to add titles to each individual light in
our stoplight graphic from Chapter 1 (specifically, the version from
Example 1-6). The new <title> elements are direct children of the
<use> elements that draw each light.

Example 17-1. Labeling parts of a graphic with <title> elements

```
<svg xmlns="http://www.w3.org/2000/svg" xml:lang="en"
     xmlns:xlink="http://www.w3.org/1999/xlink"
     height="320px" width="140px" >
  <title>Stoplight with Titled Lights</title>
  <defs>
      <circle id="light" cx="70" r="30" />
  </defs>
  <rect x="20" y="20" width="100" height="280"
        fill="blue" stroke="black" stroke-width="3" />
  <g stroke="black" stroke-width="2">
      <use xlink:href="#light" y="80" fill="red">
          <title>Red means Stop</title>
      </use>
      <use xlink:href="#light" y="160" fill="yellow">
          <title>Yellow means Slow</title>
      </use>
      <use xlink:href="#light" y="240" fill="#40CC40">
```

```
    <title>Green means Go</title>
    </use>
  </g>
</svg>
```

You can add a `<title>` to any graphical element in SVG: shapes, `<use>`, `<image>`, and also `<g>` or nested `<svg>`. The `<title>` element should always be the first child of the element it is naming. If the title is for a group, it applies to all content within that group, except for parts that have their own title.

Why would you add extra `<title>` elements for parts of a graphic? Three reasons:

- Titles are used by screen readers and other assistive technology to describe the image to their users. For complicated graphics and diagrams, you can provide much more useful alternative text if you break it down into meaningful parts, which the user can listen to or skip over depending on their interests. At the same time, titles can help reduce the need to comment your code.

- If any parts of the graphic are interactive, a title for that part is essential, to clearly explain to assistive technology users what will happen after interaction.

- Titles are used in most desktop browsers as tooltips (pop-up labels) for that section of the graphic. When a mouse-user hovers over that section of the graphic, the tooltip will display. Good titles can therefore help many users—not just screen-reader users—understand what they are looking at.

The tooltip behavior of the `<title>` element in SVG matches the behavior of the `title` attribute in HTML.

Titles and other alternative text within the SVG markup are only available for *interactive* SVG (inline SVG or SVG as an embedded object). When SVG is used as an image, the alternative text (`alt` attribute) for the `<img>` element is used instead.

Or at least, that's how it's supposed to work. As we've warned previously, some versions of Web-Kit browsers combined with the Apple Voice-Over screen reader expose the titles from the SVG file for SVG in an `<img>`, *ignoring* the `alt` text. You can force them to follow the standard behavior by adding `role="img"` to the `<img>` element.

There are nonetheless some important limitations with `<title>` as it is currently supported in web browsers:

- Keyboard and touchscreen users cannot currently access title tooltips in most browsers. (Microsoft Edge displays tooltips for elements that receive keyboard focus, but it is currently the only major browser to do so.) Browsers also disagree about whether to create tooltips for titles that are direct children of inline `<svg>` elements in HTML (Firefox does; others don't).

- The dual nature of `<title>`, as alternative text and as a tooltip, can make it difficult to come up with a title that is appropriate both for users looking at the graphic and for users hearing it described by a screen reader.

- Many browsers currently do not reliably use `<title>` elements for the accessible description of the document that is given to screen readers, unless additional ARIA attributes are provided.

The only solution to the first issue—not all users can access tooltips —is to make sure that the text in the `<title>` is an *enhancement* to the graphic, not essential information. If you want to use `<title>` tooltips to expose data for a chart, make sure that the same data is available in another way.

You can avoid the dual nature of `<title>` with ARIA attributes. The `aria-label` attribute provides an accessible name for an element *without* creating a tooltip. It's especially useful when you're adding alternative text to text that has been converted to a path:

```
<g aria-label="Welcome" role="img">
  <!-- paths in the shape of the letters W-E-L-C-O-M-E -->
</g>
```

Visual users get the meaning from the shape of the paths; a tooltip would be a redundant distraction. But the label is essential for assistive technology users.

If an element has both `aria-label` and a child `<title>` element, `aria-label` will be used as the accessible name, but `<title>` will still form a tooltip. So you can use `aria-label` to give a bit more context than is needed in the tooltip.

For example, in a chart the colors, patterns, and positioning of elements might be enough for visual users to match the data with its category label, but they could benefit from the exact numerical values being available as a tooltip. Assistive technology users would need both values:

```
<path d="..." aria-label="Monday: $72">
    <title>$72</title>
</path>
<path d="..." aria-label="Tuesday: $68">
    <title>$68</title>
</path>
```

A tooltip that isn't used as the main label *should* be exposed to assistive technology as an additional description or help text—but you currently can't rely on browsers and screen readers to correctly convey that extra information to the user. So repeat the tooltip in the label, and (as always) make important data available in other formats.

When you're using `<title>` as the main alternative text, two changes can help maximize the likelihood that browsers will correctly pass your accessible names to screen readers:

- Use the `aria-labelledby` attribute to connect the graphic element to its `<title>`: give the `<title>` a unique `id` and repeat it in the graphic's `aria-labelledby` attribute.
- Give the named element a `role` attribute.

Neither *should* be necessary, but at the time of writing, browsers aren't very good at making SVGs accessible by default. Combining both fixes together looks something like this:

```
<path d="..." role="img" aria-labelledby="Canada-title">
    <title id="Canada-title">Canada</title>
</path>
<path d="..." role="img" aria-labelledby="USA-title">
```

```
<title id="USA-title">USA</title>
</path>
```

If unique IDs are problematic, repeat the title text in an `aria-label` attribute instead.

Note that the attribute `aria-labelledby` uses British spelling rules, with a double *l*.

The `role` attribute is also needed in some browsers when `aria-label` is used on SVG shapes and groups (or HTML `<div>` and `<span>`, for that matter).

We'll discuss `role` in more detail in "Roles and Relationships" on page 663. For simple noninteractive graphics, the most useful roles are `img` and `group`:

- Use `role="img"` for individual shapes, or for groups or `<svg>` elements that should be treated as a single image, with no interactive or accessible child content.

- Use `role="group"` to add names to elements with child content that should also be accessible: `<g>` elements and nested `<svg>` that have labeled or interactive child content, or text elements that need a label in addition to the accessible text.

Avoid using `role="group"` on the `<svg>` that defines the graphic as a whole. Instead, leave it unspecified if you aren't explicitly changing it to `img`.

Browsers assign a graphics-specific role to this element, which doesn't have a well-supported ARIA equivalent. The latest SVG accessibility specs define this as the `graphics-document` role, but any browser that would recognize that role name should also get the default correct!

Finally, you sometimes need to explicitly tell the browser to ignore parts of your SVG markup when it is building the accessible representation of the document. There are two ways of doing this, which are *not* interchangeable:

- `role="presentation"` tells the browser that this *particular* element is not meaningful, but its child content might be. Specifically, it says that this element is used for styling and layout of the child content.
- `aria-hidden="true"` tells the browser that, for accessibility purposes, this element *and* all its child content should be treated as if they had `visibility: hidden`.

Most of the time, neither attribute *should* be required. You should only need `aria-hidden` when you have duplicated text that needs to be ignored (like when we reused a `<text>` element to draw its shadow in Example 11-11). You should only need `role="presentation"` when an element that normally has a role is instead being used for decorative effect (like when an SVG is used to style text inside an HTML heading, and the `<svg>` element itself is really just a styling hook for the text content).

But browsers aren't very good at holding up their side of the "shoulds" of SVG accessibility, so developers sometimes need to make up the difference.

You don't need to use either hiding method when a parent element has `role="img"`: the children of an element with the `img` role are automatically hidden from assistive tech—which is why it's really important that `img` is not used when child content should be accessible.

Putting it all together, Example 17-2 enhances Example 17-1 with `role` and ARIA attributes, so that most browser and screen reader combinations correctly read the three titles. If the graphic and titles were a little more interesting to start out with, this would be a huge help to screen reader users.

Example 17-2. Improving accessibility of SVG titles with ARIA attributes

```
<svg xmlns="http://www.w3.org/2000/svg" xml:lang="en"
     xmlns:xlink="http://www.w3.org/1999/xlink"
     height="320px" width="140px"
     aria-labelledby="title-main">
```

```
<title id="title-main">Stoplight with Titled Lights,
    Redundant Cross-Browser Compatibility Edition
</title>
<defs aria-hidden="true">
    <circle id="light" cx="70" r="30" />
</defs>
<rect x="20" y="20" width="100" height="280"
    fill="blue" stroke="black" stroke-width="3"
    aria-hidden="true" />
<g stroke="black" stroke-width="2" role="presentation">
    <use xlink:href="#light" y="80" fill="red"
        role="img" aria-labelledby="title-red">
        <title id="title-red">Red means Stop</title>
    </use>
    <use xlink:href="#light" y="160" fill="yellow"
        role="img" aria-labelledby="title-yellow">
        <title id="title-yellow">Yellow means Slow</title>
    </use>
    <use xlink:href="#light" y="240" fill="#40CC40"
        role="img" aria-labelledby="title-green">
        <title id="title-green">Green means Go</title>
    </use>
</g>
</svg>
```

As with all things related to browser support, you will need to run your own tests and decide for yourself whether you need the extra compatibility fixes from Example 17-2, or whether you want to rely on the standard approach in Example 17-1. Browser support for SVG `<title>` (and SVG accessibility in general) is improving, and is much better than it was a few years ago. But it lags far behind the accessibility of standards-compliant HTML.

Future Focus
Multilingual Titles

Many websites offer text content in multiple languages, but reuse the same image assets for each. Including alternative text directly in the image code complicates this: the titles need to be translated every time you use the SVG code.

SVG 2 proposes a solution: multiple `<title>` elements, one for each language used. The language of each title would be set with the `lang` attribute (the namespace-free replacement for `xml:lang`). A conforming browser (none yet) would pick the best title based on the user's language preferences, and would use that for both tooltips and accessibility:

```
<use xlink:href="#light" y="80" fill="red">
    <title lang="en">Red means Stop</title>
    <title lang="fr">Rouge signifie Arrêter</title>
    <title lang="es">Rojo significa Detener</title>
</use>
```

Of course, this assumes that browsers natively understand and correctly use SVG `<title>` elements in the first place. The `aria-labelledby` hack doesn't have any way to switch languages.

Since SVG 1, there has been a similar language switch option for visual graphics: the `<switch>` element and the `systemLanguage` attribute. For example, this would switch the visible labels in Example 1-9:

```
<switch fill="red" stroke="darkRed">
    <text x="140" y="100"
          systemLanguage="en">Stop</text>
    <text x="140" y="100"
          systemLanguage="fr">Arrêtez</text>
    <text x="140" y="100"
          systemLanguage="es">Detener</text>
</switch>
```

(Note that this only works for switching complete `<text>` elements or graphics; you cannot use `<switch>` to swap individual `<tspan>` elements.)

If a multilingual SVG tooltips are important, you can therefore use `<switch>` and `<use>` to swap different elements with different titles:

```
<switch fill="red">
  <use xlink:href="#light" y="80" systemLanguage="en">
    <title xml:lang="en">Red means Stop</title>
  </use>
  <use xlink:href="#light" y="80" systemLanguage="fr">
    <title xml:lang="fr">Rouge signifie Arrêter</title>
  </use>
  <use xlink:href="#light" y="80" systemLanguage="es">
    <title xml:lang="es">Rojo significa Detener</title>
  </use>
</switch>
```

Note that you need *both* `systemLanguage` attributes (to trigger the switch) and `xml:lang` attributes (to trigger the correct pronunciation by screen readers, with the `xml` prefix for browser compatibility). All in all, it is not a very DRY solution: lots of repetition is required.

 You *cannot* use `<switch>` for switching individual `<title>` elements within a shape—or at least, no browser implemented it this way. That is why the simpler `lang` switch option was introduced in SVG 2.

The `<switch>` element was also designed for feature-support switches, similar to the CSS `@supports` rule. However, these were never well designed and have limited uses on the web.

The system-language switch has good support (if you can accept the repetitive markup), but remember: neither you or your user can control which language gets shown. The browser selects an option based on the user's language settings for the browser itself.

Linking Labels

Using `aria-labelledby` to associate a `<title>` with its parent is a bit of a hack, and shouldn't be required. The intended use of `aria-labelledby` is to link an element with a *visible* text label.

 For inline SVG, the element referenced by `aria-labelledby` can be an HTML element in the same document, instead of SVG text.

The value of `aria-labelledby` is usually the `id` of a single other element (without any # URL formatting). However, it can also be a whitespace-separated list of multiple element IDs, which are combined—in order—to form the accessible label.

For example, consider the grouped bar chart in Figure 17-1. Each bar has three labels: the category on the x-axis, the date series from the legend, and finally its own text label, which gives the data value. The final `aria-labelledby` attributes for the bars look like this:

```
<rect aria-labelledby="group-label-Vancouver
                       series-label-2013
                       value-label-Vancouver-2013"
      ...other rect attributes... />
```

With matching id values on the correct <text> elements, that bar should be read out as "Vancouver, 2013, 56%." If you updated the visible text, the alternative text would be automatically updated, too.

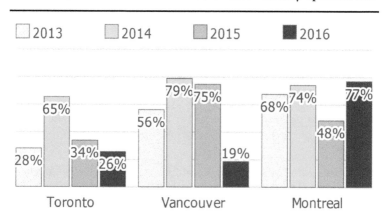

Figure 17-1. An SVG bar chart, where the full meaning of each bar is generated from three different labels

You can even reference an element's *own* id to concatenate its normal name (from <title> or aria-label) with a separate label, such as a category value. For example, in a scatterplot the shape and color of symbols might match visible labels in a legend, but the individual data values would be conveyed only by position on an axis, without a matching label:

```
<use id="data-A-13" aria-label="June 13: 36cm"
     aria-labelledby="legend-category-A data-A-13"
     class="data-point category-A" xlink:href="#symbol-A" />
<!-- ...somewhere else in the document... -->
<text id="legend-category-A">Variety A</text>
```

The final name of the <path> would be "Variety A, June 13: 36cm."

Of course, if you use <title> instead of aria-label, it is better for browser support to give the <title> element its own id, and use that in the aria-labelledby value.

Example 17-3 shows a complete (but simpler) example of using `aria-labelledby` in a labeled SVG diagram. The code is for the comparison of `stroke-linejoin` values in Figure 13-5 in Chapter 13. The `<text>` elements are grouped separately from the graphics, to share inherited styles, but the `aria-labelledby` attributes make the connections.

Example 17-3. Associating visible labels with graphics

```
<svg xmlns="http://www.w3.org/2000/svg" xml:lang="en"
     xmlns:xlink="http://www.w3.org/1999/xlink"
     width="390px" height="130px" viewBox="0 0 300 100">
    <title>Strokes with Different Linejoin Options</title>
    <symbol id="shape" viewBox="-18 -12 36 24">
        <path d="M-5,-10 H5   V-5 H10   L15,0  L10,5   H5  V10
                 H-5 V5   H-10 L-15,0 L-10,-5 H-5 V-10 Z" />
    </symbol>
    <g fill="deepskyblue"
       stroke="blueViolet" stroke-width="4" stroke-opacity="0.8">
        <use xlink:href="#shape" width="100" height="75"
             stroke-linejoin="round"
             role="img" aria-labelledby="round-label" />
        <use xlink:href="#shape" width="100" height="75" x="100"
             stroke-linejoin="bevel"
             role="img" aria-labelledby="bevel-label" />
        <use xlink:href="#shape" width="100" height="75" x="200"
             stroke-linejoin="miter"
             role="img" aria-labelledby="miter-label" />
    </g>
    <g fill="blueViolet"
       font-family="Consolas, monospace" font-size="20"
       text-anchor="middle">
        <text id="round-label" x="50"  y="95">round</text>
        <text id="bevel-label" x="150" y="95">bevel</text>
        <text id="miter-label" x="250" y="95">miter</text>
    </g>
</svg>
```

If you review the code for other figures in the book, you'll notice that we don't usually use `aria-labelledby` for visible labels. Partly that was to keep the code simple when we were discussing other topics. But it is also because `aria-labelledby` is often more trouble than it's worth for noninteractive graphics.

A screen reader reading the code from Example 17-3 would read something like: "Graphic: Strokes with Different Linejoin Options; round image; bevel image; miter image; round; bevel; miter." The text labels get read twice, once as the name of the graphic they are labeling, and then again for themselves.

You could use `aria-hidden` to hide the labels themselves, but that would cause its own problems: a screen-reader user wouldn't be able to select and copy the text. So it is often easiest—for *noninteractive* labeled diagrams—to let the visible labels be the accessible objects, and let the shapes be ignored as decorative content.

This recommendation is based on current screen readers, which don't do anything with graphics except read out their names and descriptions.

In future, as technology gets smarter, it will become more important to correctly link graphics and labels. For example, someone with partial sight (or full sight but difficulty reading) might want to tap on a graphic on a touchscreen device and have the correct label read out. Other tools like screen magnifiers might zoom in on a labeled item, and also move its label to be visible in the magnified view.

Hopefully, part of "getting smarter" will be not reading labels twice by default, so that will no longer be a concern.

Where `aria-labelledby` is essential is for *interactive* graphics. If users need to click (or keyboard-activate) a graphical element, then they and their assistive tech need to be able to correctly associate that element with its visible label.

Roles and Relationships

If you are creating custom interactive components—with SVG or HTML—in web pages, you should probably learn the basics of the Accessible Rich Internet Applications (ARIA, or WAI-ARIA) set of attributes.

The core of ARIA is the **role attribute**; we've already seen a couple of examples of `role` in action. It is supplemented by various other **ARIA attributes**. The others all have names that start with `aria-*`; we've discussed a few of them, too!

The role of role, and of ARIA as a whole, is to let assistive technology correctly communicate the structure and function of web pages, when it can't be fully expressed by the native **semantics**—the meaning, as opposed to the syntax—of the markup elements (HTML or SVG). It is most important when you're using JavaScript to create custom widgets and form elements.

ARIA roles are divided into the following categories:

- Landmark roles, like main and navigation, identify the major regions of a web page so that assistive-tech users can quickly jump to where they need to go.

- Document structure roles describe finer-grained web page structure, like tables, lists, article feeds, and figures.

- Widget roles describe form elements and other interactive controls.

- Live region roles identify sections of the web page that will change often, indicating why they are changing and therefore how important changes are to the user: changing text in a countdown timer is less important than new text in an error warning!

 A role only changes how an element is *communicated* to assistive tech users, not how it behaves. Setting role="checkbox" means that a screen reader will announce an item as a checkbox, but it's up to the web page author to make sure it also *behaves* like a checkbox: that it can receive keyboard focus, and that clicking or pressing the space bar causes it to toggle between checked and unchecked states.

In HTML5, the role attribute (and ARIA in general) shouldn't be used very often. Most roles are equivalent to an HTML element that should be used instead: use <main> instead of <div role="main">; use <button> instead of <a role="button">. As the *Using ARIA* guide (*https://w3c.github.io/using-aria/*) recommends, never use ARIA when HTML will do.

But SVG markup is inherently presentational, not semantic: elements and attributes describe what the content *looks* like, not what it *means*. So if your SVG document has complex structure—and especially if it contains interactive widgets—ARIA can help assistive technology users understand how all the individual labeled graphics are related to each other.

The ARIA attributes (including role) were only officially added to SVG in SVG 2, but they have fairly good browser support, at least in inline SVG. We've already shown examples of using the good ARIA support to compensate for poor support for native SVG accessibility.

We've already discussed the two most common roles you'll use:

- img is for indivisible and noninteractive parts of the graphic.
- group is for a section of the graphic that should have a shared label, but also have accessible parts inside it.

For more complex graphics, consider adding the following document structure roles:

- heading indicates that SVG text is equivalent to an HTML heading. Use the aria-level attribute to indicate *which* heading element: its value is 1, 2, 3, and so on, to represent <h1>, <h2>, <h3>:

  ```
  <text role="heading" aria-level="1">The Invention</text>
  <text role="heading" aria-level="2">Before</text>
    <!-- graphical diagram with labels -->
  <text role="heading" aria-level="2">After</text>
    <!-- a different graphical diagram with labels -->
  ```

  However, if the heading text is the *only* content in an inline SVG, consider using an HTML heading element wrapped around the SVG instead:

  ```
  <h1><svg role="presentation"><text>...</text></svg></h1>
  ```

- region identifies large parts of the graphic that are more important than a regular group, similar to an HTML <section>. A region must have a name, and is often aria-labelledby an element with a heading role:

  ```
  <g role="region" aria-labelledby="before-heading">
      <text id="before-heading"
            role="heading" aria-level="2">Before</text>
  ```

```
        <!-- graphical diagram with labels -->
    </g>
```

- list (on a `<g>`) and listitem (on individual graphics inside that `<g>`) can turn a group of items into an organized list, equivalent to `<ul>` or `<ol>` and `<li>` in HTML.

    The benefit of a list over a group is that most screen readers announce how many items are in the list, and which item they are currently reading, so that it is easier for screen-reader users to keep track of where they are. It's therefore recommended whenever a group has more than four or five labeled graphics within it, if they are all similar items (such as data points in a chart):

    ```
    <g role="list" aria-label="2017 data">
        <use xlink:href="#icon-1" role="listitem"
            aria-label="January: $15.3K" x="20" y="17" />
        <use xlink:href="#icon-1" role="listitem"
            aria-label="February: $12.1K" x="40" y="13" />
        <!-- and 10 more, for the rest of the months -->
    </g>
    ```

- contentinfo is used for "footer" information, such as credits and sources.

For interactive graphics, you'll need to use the full suite of ARIA roles and other attributes (*https://w3c.github.io/aria/aria/aria.html*). Remember that the role doesn't change behavior: you still need to use JavaScript to make your graphics keyboard accessible, in a way that matches the role.

Future Focus
Roles for Graphical Documents

The original set of ARIA roles wasn't designed for structured graphics. The only graphical role was img, which explicitly cannot have any structure inside it.

Describing parts of a graphic as groups or lists can help convey structure, but it does so by ignoring the *graphical* nature of the content. There's nothing to tell the user—or their software tools, which only see the processed accessible view of the web page, as created by the browser—that the content is really a data chart, and not just a bulleted list of text. This doesn't help the development of smarter assistive technology for navigating charts, maps, and other complex graphics.

The WAI-ARIA Graphics module tries to address this limitation by defining graphics-specific document structure roles. The first version of the spec only covers basic structural roles:

- `graphics-document` for the `<svg>` that defines the canvas
- `graphics-object` for a section of a graphic that represents a single, multipart thing (as opposed to a *group* of distinct items)
- `graphics-symbol` for an individual component that isn't divisible but also isn't really an image on its own, such as the symbols used for points in a chart or on a map

Future versions of the module are expected to include more specific roles for common graphical structures like chart axes, legends, data points, and data lines.

At the time of writing, browsers don't recognize the new role names. Guidelines haven't been finalized for mapping the roles to the APIs used by assistive tech such as screen readers. And a complete set of roles for data visualization and mapping is still years away.

1,000 Words Are Worth a Picture

A short `<title>` may tell you what you are looking at, but it doesn't tell you much about what it *looks* like.

The SVG `<desc>` (or description) element is designed for providing more comprehensive alternative text, either about a particular element, or about the SVG document overall. Just like `<title>`, a `<desc>` applies to its parent element.

> As with `<title>`, SVG 2 allows you to provide multiple descriptions in different languages. But that isn't currently supported in any software.

Ideally, the content of the `<desc>` element would be available to users of screen readers and similar tools as an optional description, that they can either read or skip over. Unfortunately, support for <desc> is currently even worse than support for <title>. Support for the aria-describedby attribute isn't much better.

If you want to be sure that the extra descriptive content is available to screen-reader users, you can use the aria-labelledby attribute to concatenate the description after the title. For example, in a line chart you might use the <desc> to provide an accessible description of the shape of the line:

```
<path d="..."
    aria-labelledby="title-3 desc-3">
    <title id="title-3">Average Monthly Precipitation</title>
    <desc id="desc-3">
        Values peak at more than 90mm in July, dropping to
        half that in May and September, and stay below 20mm
        between November and March.
    </desc>
</path>
```

You should, of course, make the data available as a table, too. Not only are tables easier for screen-reader users to navigate, but they are very useful for anyone else who wants to see the exact numbers! But the prose description of the key patterns in the data is a more direct equivalent to the information that a sighted user gains from a quick look at the chart.

The lack of native accessibility support doesn't mean that <desc> is *completely* ignored by software today. Certain tools, such as Inkscape, may use it to provide summary information, and websites such as Open Clip Art take their descriptions from the primary SVG <desc> element.

Unfortunately, this has meant that some authoring tools use <desc> to provide their own metadata—of the "Made with Software X" variety—which isn't very helpful as an image description.

An interesting feature of <desc> is that the element can contain markup content from other namespaces, particularly HTML. The markup *isn't* used (or expected to be used) in accessible descriptions. It's allowed as part of a strategy for SVG fallback in browsers that didn't support SVG graphics—you could use paragraph tags and other structured HTML in the <desc> and in <title>, too:

```
<p> The following diagram shows the steps: </p>
<svg>
    <title><h3>Step-by-step instructions</h3></title>
```

```
<g>
    <title>Step 1</title>
    <desc><p>Take the widget with the do-hicky
        and attach it to the something-or-other
        <em>carefully</em>
        ...</p>
    </desc>
    <path d="..."/>
</g>
```

This can be a functional fallback for inline SVG in older browsers, which will ignore all the elements they don't recognize. But beware: by default those old browsers will treat the `<title>` element like an HTML `<title>`, and not display it (although you can change this with CSS).

For inline SVG that is processed by a modern HTML parser, content inside `<desc>` is parsed like content in the main HTML document, meaning it is treated as HTML elements unless it is a `<math>` (or a `<svg>`). Only HTML "flow" elements are allowed: no sectioning content or landmarks.

For SVG processed by an XML parser, HTML elements require correct namespacing.

To create markup that works with either parser, use an `xmlns` attribute to change the default namespace, instead of an XML prefix—which won't be recognized by the HTML parser.

The browsers may not use complex content inside a `<desc>`, but you can always enhance a graphic with JavaScript to display the titles and descriptions, for all users.

Example 17-4 uses an SVG `<foreignObject>` element to display the alternative text for a section of the graphic when that region is moused-over, focused, or tapped by the user. The script directly clones the HTML markup inside the `<desc>`, so there is no duplication of content. Figure 17-2 shows one description displayed.

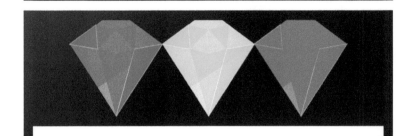

Green

Green is the color of growing grass and leaves, of emeralds, and of jade. In the continuum of colors of visible light, it is located between yellow and blue. It is the color of the wavelength of light from approximately 520–570nm on the electromagnetic spectrum.

Figure 17-2. SVG title and description, displayed by cloning content into HTML elements

Example 17-4. Associating visible labels with graphics

```
<svg xmlns="http://www.w3.org/2000/svg" xml:lang="en"
    xmlns:xlink="http://www.w3.org/1999/xlink"
    viewBox="0 0 400 400">
    <title>Displaying Titles and Descs
        with Scripting and foreignObject</title>
    <style type="text/css">
#display {
    background: white;
    padding: 1em;
    box-sizing: border-box;
    overflow: auto;
}
    </style>
    <defs>
```

```
<g id="gem">
    <polygon points="0,25 35,0 65,0 100,25 50,100" />
    <g fill="white" fill-opacity="0.3">
        <polygon points="0,25 30,30 50,100" />
        <polygon points="100,25 30,70 50,100" />
        <polygon points="28,5 35,0 65,0 72,5 50,10" />
        <polygon points="50,10 30,30 50,35 70,30" />
        <polygon points="72,5 70,30 100,25" />
    </g>
    <g stroke="white" stroke-opacity="0.5" fill-opacity="0.5">
        <polygon points="100,25 70,30 50,100" />
        <polygon points="28,5 30,30 0,25" />
    </g>
</g>
</defs>
<linearGradient id="background" y2="100%">
    <stop offset="0" stop-color="#446" />
    <stop offset="0.3" stop-color="#333" />
    <stop offset="0.8" stop-color="#333" />
    <stop offset="1" stop-color="#456" />
</linearGradient>
<rect fill="url(#background)" width="100%" height="100%" />
<g>
    <use xlink:href="#gem" x="50" y="10" fill="red"
        class="gem" tabindex="0" role="img">
        <title>Red</title>
        <desc>
            <p xmlns="http://www.w3.org/1999/xhtml">
            <span style="color:red">Red</span> is the color
            of blood, rubies and strawberries. It is the color
            of the wavelength of light from approximately
            620-740nm on the electromagnetic spectrum.
            </p>
        </desc>
    </use>
    <use xlink:href="#gem" x="150" y="10" fill="limeGreen"
        class="gem" tabindex="0" role="img">
        <title>Green</title>
        <desc>
            <p xmlns="http://www.w3.org/1999/xhtml">
            <span style="color:green">Green</span> is the color
            of growing grass and leaves, of emeralds, and of
            jade. In the continuum of colors of visible light,
            it is located between yellow and blue. It is the
            color of the wavelength of light from approximately
            520-570nm on the electromagnetic spectrum.
            </p>
        </desc>
    </use>
    <use xlink:href="#gem" x="250" y="10" fill="blue"
        class="gem" tabindex="0" role="img">
```

```
            <title>Blue</title>
            <desc>
                <p xmlns="http://www.w3.org/1999/xhtml">
                <span style="color:blue">Blue</span> is the color
                of the clear sky and the deep sea. On the optical
                spectrum, blue is located between violet and green.
                It is the color of the wavelength of light from
                approximately 450-495nm on the electromagnetic
                spectrum.
                </p>
            </desc>
        </use>
    </g>
    <foreignObject width="380" height="260" x="10" y="120" id="fo">
        <div xmlns="http://www.w3.org/1999/xhtml" id="display"
            style="max-height: 260px"></div>
    </foreignObject>
    <script>//<![CDATA[
window.onload=function(evt){
    var gems = document.getElementsByClassName("gem"),
        fo = document.getElementById("fo"),
        display = document.getElementById("display"),
        displayedElement;

    for (var index=0; index < gems.length; index++){
        var gem = gems.item(index);
        gem.addEventListener("mouseover", showTitle);
        gem.addEventListener("focus", showTitle);
        gem.addEventListener("touchStart", showTitle);
    };
    function showTitle(evt){
        var element = evt.currentTarget,
            title = element.getElementsByTagName("title")[0],
            desc = element.getElementsByTagName("desc")[0];
        if (displayedElement) {
            displayedElement.removeAttribute("aria-describedby");
        }

        display.innerHTML = "<h2>"+title.textContent+"</h2>";
        display.appendChild( desc.firstElementChild.cloneNode(true) );
        displayedElement = element;
        element.setAttribute("aria-describedby", "display");
        forceRepaint();
    }
    function forceRepaint() {
        fo.style.width = fo.style.width;
    }
};
//]]></script>
</svg>
```

Something about the HTML elements in the `<desc>` causes Chrome to stop parsing CDATA markup correctly, if you copy and paste this example into an HTML file. The HTML elements themselves parse fine, and CDATA is *usually* fine within inline SVG markup.

That was causing the script to break, since the `<!` `[CDATA[` part was being treated as the first line of the script. The solution was to add JavaScript comments (`//`) before the CDATA markup.

The benefit of this approach is that you keep your descriptions of the diagram organized directly with the SVG content that they describe. Imagine a much more complicated technical diagram with multipart instructions, and then imagine having to update that diagram to add a new step, and you can understand why it would be easier to keep both graphic and text together.

Here, we aren't using much HTML formatting (only a colored span), but the description could just as easily contain multiple paragraphs or numbered lists. However, when using complex markup, remember that the normal SVG `<desc>` behavior for screen readers (even where supported) is to just read the plain text. For screen readers that do correctly support long descriptions, the `aria-describedby` attribute is updated whenever we display the descriptions as HTML text, so that they can prompt users to jump to the formatted version of the text.

If you were using inline SVG, the `display` HTML region could easily be a regular HTML element, outside of the SVG markup, instead of HTML inside a `<foreignObject>`. (And thereby gain support in Internet Explorer, which doesn't support `<foreignObject>`.) The benefit of `<foreignObject>` is that it can be positioned and scaled within your SVG coordinate system.

The *downside* of `<foreignObject>` is that they tend to be a bit buggy. The extra `forceRepaint` method addresses one of those bugs. It contains a seemingly redundant statement:

```
fo.style.width = fo.style.width;
```

The `<foreignObject>` contents are essentially an escape hatch out of the SVG, but in many cases this means that the SVG renderer and

HTML renderer need to coordinate which one is responsible for rendering a certain section of the screen. In older versions of Chrome, the <foreignObject> wasn't properly refreshing after it was changed. Resetting the width was enough to poke the browser to clean up the screen correctly. It's not pretty, but it worked.

Machine-Readable Metadata

There is one last metadata element defined in SVG. It has the terribly creative name <metadata>.

The SVG **<metadata> element** differs from <title> and <desc> in one critical way. While those elements are designed for providing human-readable descriptive content for the SVG drawing or application, the <metadata> element exists primarily to provide machine readable annotations.

The SVG specifications don't define anything more about <metadata>. Instead, it is a container for content from other XML namespaces. There are a number of XML metadata schemes that are used in digital publishing and on the web, any of which can be embedded inside an SVG <metadata> block.

The HTML parser does not do anything special for <metadata>. It does not accept foreign-namespaced XML content, nor even HTML <meta> elements.

If you want to add machine-readable metadata to inline SVG content, use HTML metadata elements and attributes elsewhere in the page.

At its simplest, the <metadata> tag can be used to store publishing information about a given drawing—its creator, its title, when it was created and last updated, and so forth. This information is typically contained within the Dublin Core namespace (*http://dublincore.org*), using a publishing standard that has been around for several years. More context-specific metadata can use the Resource Description Framework (RDF) (*https://www.w3.org/RDF/*) metadata system.

Many SVG-creating software programs generate <metadata> sections automatically or based on document properties that can be set by the author using the software's graphical interface. You can also add <metadata> by hand or script later.

Example 17-5 shows one possible structure, containing different types of metadata commonly used for graphics.

Example 17-5. A sample SVG license and other metadata

```
<svg xmlns="http://www.w3.org/2000/svg" xml:lang="en"
    xmlns:rdf="http://www.w3.org/1999/02/22-rdf-syntax-ns#"
    xmlns:dc="http://purl.org/dc/elements/1.1/"
    xmlns:cc="http://web.resource.org/cc/">
    <title>SVG with Metadata</title>
<metadata>
<rdf:RDF>
    <cc:Work>
        <dc:format>image/svg+xml</dc:format>
        <dc:type
rdf:resource="http://purl.org/dc/dcmitype/StillImage"/>
        <cc:license
rdf:resource="http://creativecommons.org/licenses/publicdomain/"/>
        <dc:publisher>
            <cc:Agent rdf:about="http://openclipart.org/">
                <dc:title>Open Clip Art Library</dc:title>
            </cc:Agent>
        </dc:publisher>
        <dc:title>A Sample Picture</dc:title>
        <dc:date>2013-10-08T04:31:22</dc:date>
        <dc:description>This is a picture
                of a sample object.</dc:description>
        <dc:source>http://example.com/detail/sample_picture
        </dc:source>
        <dc:creator>
            <cc:Agent>
                <dc:title>jane_doe</dc:title>
            </cc:Agent>
        </dc:creator>
        <dc:subject>
            <rdf:Bag>
                <rdf:li>thing</rdf:li>
                <rdf:li>sample</rdf:li>
                <rdf:li>object</rdf:li>
            </rdf:Bag>
        </dc:subject>
    </cc:Work>
    <cc:License
rdf:about="http://creativecommons.org/licenses/publicdomain/">
        <cc:permits
rdf:resource="http://creativecommons.org/ns#Reproduction"/>
        <cc:permits
```

```
rdf:resource="http://creativecommons.org/ns#Distribution"/>
    <cc:permits
rdf:resource="http://creativecommons.org/ns#DerivativeWorks"/>
  </cc:License>
  </rdf:RDF>
</metadata>
<!-- actual SVG code here -->
</svg>
```

In this case, the metadata defines three distinct namespaces: the RDF (Resource Description Framework) namespace, which gathers metadata; the Creative Commons (CC) namespace, which contains license information; and the Dublin Core (DC) namespace, which provides information about titles, creators, and agents. Each metadata scheme has its own documentation about how to use the elements and attributes.

 The Creative Commons logos are themselves available in SVG (*http://creativecommons.org/about/downloads*). These can help people identify quickly what use can be made of a given piece of artwork or other intellectual work.

Integrating metadata directly in the SVG file helps keep your documents organized but still easy to edit. The information is useful for applications that query generic XML/RDF content. SVG editors can read this content to determine the provenance of any given file. But remember: easy to edit means easy to remove. Someone can always copy the file and remove your license and other metadata, the same as for any other file format. Furthermore, when you are optimizing SVG files for the web, you will need to decide for yourself whether the extra data is worth the extra bytes.

On the web, properly formatted metadata may be used by search engines to index files. Many social media tools also look for metadata in the form of HTML <meta> elements when creating previews for a linked document. Just like other metadata elements, the HTML <meta> elements (when correctly namespaced) can be included within an SVG <metadata> section in an SVG file—but you'll have to test to see whether the social media sites you are trying to support actually look inside the SVG file to find them.

Summary: Metadata for Accessibility and Added Functionality

Metadata elements and attributes allow you to enhance your SVG graphic with structured information about what it means. You can embed any XML-compatible metadata in a `<metadata>` block, and you can add titles and descriptions for sections of the graphic as well as for the SVG as a whole. ARIA roles and attributes allow you to further annotate the structure and function of different elements, and are particularly important for interactive graphics.

Software support for SVG accessibility, however, has lagged behind support for HTML accessibility. Even where it is supported, there isn't an established framework for how browsers should describe complex graphical structures (like data charts and maps) to assistive tools like screen readers. Things are slowly getting better, but ensuring optimal accessibility currently requires a lot of redundant ARIA attributes.

More Online

The markup guide has a short reference to the metadata elements:

https://oreillymedia.github.io/Using_SVG/guide/markup.html#metadata

---

For deciding on ARIA roles, you'll want to return to the list in "Roles and Relationships" on page 663. For further information, consult these guides for website authors:

- *Using ARIA* (*https://w3c.github.io/using-aria/*)
- *WAI-ARIA Authoring Practices* (*https://w3c.github.io/aria-practices/*)

CHAPTER 18

Drawing on Demand
Interactive SVG

If you only think of SVG as a replacement for raster image formats like PNG and JPEG, then you're only scraping the surface of what SVG can be on the web.

Sure, static SVG has its benefits: small files that are easily updated, accessible text and structured alternative text, crisp curves at any scale or resolution. If that's all you want, you are still making good use of SVG.

But comparing SVG to static graphics is like comparing HTML websites to printed articles. There is so much that the web can do that print can't. The web is a dynamic, interactive medium. Web pages can be static content documents, but they can also be software applications, or any combination of the two. And that's just as true for SVG as for HTML.

This chapter explores the potential for using SVG in interactive web content. It is not in any way a comprehensive discussion of the topic: interactive SVG is as complex a topic as interactive HTML. We cover the main ways in which you can enable and react to user actions—what you do with that is up to you. Interactive SVG can be used in web application interfaces, games, and explorable data visualizations, among many other possibilities.

As we've mentioned various times throughout the book, the capabilities of SVG differ depending on how you add that SVG to your HTML. If you use an SVG file as an image, in an `<img>` tag or as a

CSS image type, it will behave as an image. None of the components will be interactive.

To add interactive SVG to a web page, you need to either use inline SVG markup or embedded SVG objects (with `<object>` or `<iframe>`). Alternatively (and especially for testing), you can open the SVG files directly as the main web page—which becomes much more practical once you include links from that SVG web page to other pages on the web.

Linking It All Together

Hyperlinks are the threads that hold the World Wide Web together. To be a true web document language, of course SVG has links.

The link in SVG looks familiar to most web developers: it's created with an **`<a>` (anchor) element**. The only catch is that (in SVG 1, at least) the link's target is set with an **`xlink:href` attribute**, instead of `href` like in HTML.

 Like every other use of `xlink:href` in SVG, the attribute has been simplified to plain `href` in SVG 2, and in most new browsers. But keep using the `xlink` prefix for now, for support in Safari and older versions of other browsers.

Since SVG 1.1, the SVG `<a>` also accepts the familiar **target attribute** to indicate whether the linked page should replace the SVG document (`target="_self"`, the default), replace a higher-level document in the same tab (`_parent` or `_top`, useful for when the SVG is an embedded object but you want the link to replace the entire web page), or open in a new tab (`_blank`). As we mentioned in Chapter 9, link targets can also be named `<iframe>` or `<object>` elements in the same web page, or a named new tab.

 As we mentioned in Chapter 9, Microsoft browsers don't currently support named `<object>` contexts as a link target.

SVG 2 also adopts the `download`, `rel`, `hreflang`, and `type` attributes from HTML. SVG 1 had used various `xlink`-namespaced elements for similar purposes (but they never had any effect in browsers).

For anyone used to HTML hyperlinks, the most familiar use of links in SVG would be to create linked text. You can do that. The `<a>` element can be nested inside a `<text>` to turn a span of text into a hyperlink. The text inside the link inherits any SVG text layout from the surrounding elements, just like a `<tspan>` with no layout attributes. You can also set any CSS styles on the link that would apply to a `<tspan>`, such as different fonts or fill styles.

Example 18-1 shows an example of using links inside an SVG `<textPath>`, to create a curved navigation menu; Figure 18-1 shows the result, when the final link is focused. The complete SVG code could be copy-pasted as inline markup in the header of an HTML file for the bestest blog navigation ever.

Figure 18-1. Links in SVG text used as website navigation

Example 18-1. Adding hyperlinks to SVG text layouts

```
<svg xmlns="http://www.w3.org/2000/svg" xml:lang="en"
    xmlns:xlink="http://www.w3.org/1999/xlink"
    width="400px" height="200px" viewBox="0 0 400 200">
    <title>SVG Navigation Links</title>
    <defs>
        <path id="p" d="M30,220 C50,40 350,40 380,220" />
    </defs>
    <style>
    svg {
```

```
        background: #222;
        margin: 0 auto;
    }
    text {
        font: bold 28px Pacifico, sans-serif;
        text-anchor: middle;
        fill: orangeRed;
    }
    svg a:link, svg a:visited {
        text-decoration: underline;
        fill: royalBlue;
    }
    svg a:focus {
        outline: none;
        stroke: lightSkyBlue;
        stroke-width: 2px;
        paint-order: stroke;
    }
    </style>
    <style>
@import url('https://fonts.googleapis.com/css?family=Pacifico');
    </style>
    <text x="200" y="30"
        role="heading" aria-level="1"
        >Welcome<tspan x="200" y="180">
    to my website! </tspan></text>
    <text role="navigation">
        <textPath xlink:href="#p" startOffset="50%">
            <a aria-current="page">Home</a>
            <a xlink:href="/archives.html">Archives</a>
            <a xlink:href="/about.html">About Me</a>
        </textPath>
    </text>
</svg>
```

 This particular layout is broken in MS Edge and Internet Explorer. When a `<textPath>` has multiple element children (links or `<tspan>`), only the first element is used to determine the text-anchor alignment.

Also, Internet Explorer and Safari don't leave spaces between the links.

In other words, if you want to use SVG text layout for a creative website navigation, be prepared to do a lot of testing and fussing to get everything working correctly in every browser.

Unlike with HTML links, there are no default link styles for SVG. In order for users to know that something is a link, you need to add underline, color change, or other styles yourself. Similarly, default focus styles are often missing or are problematic. Without focus styles, keyboard users are lost, unable to tell *which* link will be activated if they hit Enter.

The link styles in Example 18-1 are applied with the `:link` and `:visited` CSS pseudoclasses, so they only apply to `<a>` elements that are valid links, and not to the placeholder `<a>` element for the current page in the navigation. The **aria-current** attribute conveys the same meaning as the style change to supporting screen readers.[1]

 Any styles set with `a:link` *should* also apply to visited links, unless an `a:visited` selector overrides them. But Firefox doesn't implement it that way, which caused the blue link color to disappear once a link had been visited, without the second selector.

The link selectors in Example 18-1 are qualified to only apply to descendents of an `<svg>` element, to minimize style clashes if the SVG was copied inline. Alternatively, namespace-sensitive CSS selectors could be used to ensure that the styles only applied to SVG-namespaced `<a>` elements, and not to HTML links.

More Online

We briefly mentioned namespace-sensitive CSS selectors in Chapter 3; there is a longer discussion in the extra article "XML Namespaces in CSS":

https://oreillymedia.github.io/Using_SVG/extras/ch03-namespaces.html

---

1 For more on `aria-current` usage and support, see "Using the aria-current attribute" by Léonie Watson (*https://tink.uk/using-the-aria-current-attribute/*).

The keyboard focus styles, set with the :focus pseudoclass, are similarly qualified, to only apply to the links within the SVG. The normal default focus style for links (and other focusable objects) in a web page uses the outline property. But that created two issues: Firefox couldn't draw an outline around a span within a <textPath> at all; in browsers that did draw the outline, it was drawn as a large rectangle, ignoring the curve of the text.

So the default outline is explicitly turned off in the focus rule, and a stroke is used instead. It's not perfect. Stroking cursive text emphasizes the edges between letters, and in the case of underlined text on a path, it also emphasizes the edges between the underline sections. But it is, above all, functional. And function is what focus styles are all about.

Interactive Style Switches

The CSS pseudoclasses are a simple way in which a graphic can be made interactive. You don't need to click a link for something to change in Example 18-1: simply tabbing through the links (that is, changing the keyboard focus by using the Tab key) will change the styles set with the :focus pseudoclass.

There are three pseudoclasses that are specifically defined by user interaction states:

- :focus applies to the element that currently has keyboard focus.
- :hover applies to an element that currently has the mouse pointer positioned over a clickable region, and also to any of its ancestor elements.
- :active applies to an element that is in the process of being activated, meaning it is currently being clicked, during the time when the mouse is being pressed. For HTML elements that are normally activated by the space bar (buttons, checkboxes, and radio buttons), it also applies if the space bar is being held down while the element has focus.

These selectors can apply to any graphical SVG element, not just links. But links are the only element in SVG that are by default keyboard-focusable. Also remember that touchscreen users or keyboard users won't be able to trigger :hover and may not be able to trigger :active states.

There are other CSS pseudoclasses that can be used to create inter-active effects, with a little more work. In "Targeting the Interaction" on page 698, we'll discuss using the :target pseudoclass, in combination with same-document links. And as we demonstrated in Chapter 2, the form-status pseudoclasses, like :valid or :checked, can be used to control inline SVG elements that are child or sibling to HTML form elements.

A Better Image Map

Links on text are all very well, but SVG is all about graphics. Can you create a hyperlink out of a <path> or a <use> or other graphic? Of course!

The <a> element can be used to wrap any SVG graphical elements—shapes, images, entire <text> elements, or reused icons:

```
<a xlink:href="home.html"
   aria-label="Acme Company Home Page">
   <use xlink:href="#acme-logo">
       <title>Acme Co.</title>
   </use>
</a>
```

In this context, the link element (<a>) behaves much the same as a <g> for styling and layout purposes.

 Do not use the <a> element within a <defs> section or inside a <symbol> or other unrendered element. Many browsers still allow the unrendered element to receive keyboard focus. Reused copies of graphics containing the link may or may not be functional, depending on the browser.

When a link's contents are entirely graphical, instead of text, be sure to add a meaningful name to the link element itself or to its child content, using the methods described in Chapter 17. The best-supported method for screen readers would be to use an aria-label attribute on the <a> element itself, but a <title> that is a direct child of the link also has fairly good support. Using a <title> has the benefit of adding tooltip hints for visual users on a device with hover support.

Elements with certain ARIA roles, including `button`, are treated as if they don't have any children. That means that if you use `aria-label` to *replace* the name that would normally be generated from the child content, that content (whether plain text or alternative text on child elements) is no longer accessible.

This problem is not SVG specific, but it may show up more often in SVG because of the more frequent need to use `aria-label` for alternative text.

Graphical links, known as image maps, have been a part of HTML since the 1990s. In brief, HTML image maps are defined by a `<map>` element containing `<area>` elements representing the individual links as vector shapes. The map is then applied to an `<img>` element as a cross-reference in the `usemap` attribute. The map and link areas are themselves invisible; they only serve to define the hyperlinked "hotspots" on the visible image.

There are several problems with traditional HTML image maps:

- The map hotspots cannot easily be made responsive: they are defined in pixels, and cannot scale to match the image size. This means that you cannot adjust the image size to match the available screen size, because then the invisible linked areas will be misaligned.

- Loading a large image (especially for navigation) often delays the page. And browsers currently do not provide functional links if the image cannot load at all.

- It's difficult to add interactive feedback or hover effects to an image map. Browsers show basic focus outlines around link areas, but you cannot alter them with CSS like you can for normal focus outlines.

- It can be challenging to generate the markup for the invisible hotspot areas, as very few tools output the correct code.

You can eliminate all of these disadvantages by using linked regions in interactive SVG. When correctly set up, all of the elements in an SVG are responsive; you can load extra image files, but (if carefully designed) your SVG can still be functional without them; you can use :hover and :focus styles to give interactive feedback; and it's easy to add <a> elements to SVG markup generated from graphical editors—or however else you usually create SVG.

But what if the image you want to use as a map isn't a vector image? What if it's a photograph? Can you make *parts* of a photograph hyperlinks to different destinations?

You can't, but you can.

You can't make only parts of an SVG <image> element clickable. If the <image> is a child of an <a> element, all of the image (after clipping) will be clickable. There is no way to have multiple <a> elements associated with the embedded image, equivalent to the <map> and <area> elements in HTML.

But what you *can* do is draw your <image> as a backdrop, and then draw transparent SVG <path> (or other shape) elements, each one inside a different link, as invisible hit regions over top.

Defining a <path> element to match a feature in a photograph is exceptionally difficult to achieve by hand. If you are *only* creating a link hotspot, it doesn't need to be super-precise (a rough polygon will do), but if you want to add visual enhancements then you usually want a close match between the curves of your path and the objects in the photo.

The regular solutions for converting images to vectors—using "Trace" in Adobe Illustrator, for example—provide sketchy edges, not overall shape outlines. A better solution is to load the image into Adobe Photoshop or GIMP and use the advanced selection tools ("Magnetic Lasso" tool in Photoshop, or "Intelligent Scissors" in GIMP) to select the region you want. Selections can then be converted into paths within the software, and those paths can be exported as SVG.

For this example, we're using the photograph of a skateboarding crew from Figure 18-2. The goal is to create an image map where each person in the photograph is a link to their biography page. SVG paths for each person were created with Photoshop selections.

Figure 18-2. The photograph to use in the image map

To add a little more interactivity, emphasizing the clickability of the shapes, we want to turn most of the photograph black and white, but with the skater under inspection—a link that is hovered, touched, or focused—remaining in color, as shown in Figure 18-3.

There are a number of ways to achieve this effect, some simpler than others. The approach we use relies on multiple copies of the photograph:

- The bottom layer is the grayscale backdrop, created with a desaturating filter effect.

- For each link, there is a color version of the photo, clipped to the desired person's outline, which will be faded into view when that link is hovered or focused. The clipping paths use copies of the same outline paths used for the hotspot regions.

- A final color copy of the photo provides the main color view when no links are hovered. It will be faded in and out (with `opacity` changes), so that the color doesn't instantly disappear and reappear when the clipping path is changed.

Figure 18-3. The final result, when one link is focused

Example 18-2 provides part of the code. To keep it readable, we only show the elements for one of the 11 linked skateboarders in the image, and we skip the actual path data.

Example 18-2. Creating an interactive image map with SVG links and clipping paths

SVG Markup:

```
<svg xmlns="http://www.w3.org/2000/svg" xml:lang="en"
    xmlns:xlink="http://www.w3.org/1999/xlink"
    viewBox="0 0 2074 1382">
    <title>Color-transitioning Image Map Links</title>
    <style>
        /* styles could be in the file or linked */
    </style>
    <defs>
        <image id="team-photo" width="2074" height="1382"
            xlink:href="team-photo.jpg" />                    ❶
    </defs>
    <filter id="grayscaleFilter"
            x="0" y="0" width="100%" height="100%">
        <feColorMatrix type="saturate" values="0"/>
    </filter>                                                 ❷
    <use xlink:href="#team-photo" filter="url(#grayscaleFilter)" />
```

```
    <a class="hotspot" id="konni"
       xlink:href="/team-bios/konni.html">                         ❸
       <title>Konni</title>
       <path id="konni-mask-path" d="..."/>
       <clipPath id="konni-clip">
           <use xlink:href="#konni-mask-path" />               ❹
       </clipPath>
       <use class="clip" xlink:href="#team-photo"
           clip-path="url(#konni-clip)" />
    </a>
    <!-- and 10 other links with paths and clipped images -->

    <use id="fade" xlink:href="#team-photo" />                  ❺
</svg>
```

❶ The <image> is defined once, within a <defs> section, and will
  be reused as required. It and the SVG viewBox are sized in the
  image's original high-resolution pixel size, to match the path
  data generated by Photoshop.

❷ The base copy of the image is made grayscale with an
  <feColorMatrix> filter effect.

❸ The links come next, one for each person in the photograph,
  arranged left to right so that keyboard focus moves in a predictable order. Each link has a <title> to create a tooltip and an
  accessible name.

❹ The <path> element within each link outlines that person's position in the photograph. The path is then reused in a matching
  <clipPath> element, which creates a clipped color version of
  that person's shape in the photograph.

❺ Finally, at the end of the document is the unclipped color copy
  of the photo that will be faded in and out.

CSS STYLES:

```
.hotspot path {
    fill: none;
    pointer-events: visibleFill;                    ❶
}

#fade {
    pointer-events: none;                           ❷
}
#fade, .clip {
```

```
    transition: opacity 400ms ease-in-out;   ❸
}
.hotspot:hover ~ #fade,
.hotspot:focus ~ #fade,
.hotspot:active ~ #fade { opacity: 0; }       ❹

.clip { opacity: 0; }
.hotspot:hover .clip,
.hotspot:focus .clip,
.hotspot:active .clip { opacity: 1; }          ❺

.hotspot:focus {
    outline: none;                             ❻
}
.hotspot:focus path {
    outline: skyBlue 3px solid;
    outline-offset: 20px;                      ❼
}
```

❶ The `<path>` elements inside each `hotspot` link have no `fill` (and by default, no stroke either); however, the `pointer-events` value ensures that the fill region is sensitive to mouse events so long as the path element is itself visible.

❷ The `#team-photo` element—and all its `<use>` copies—are made transparent to clicks and taps, with `pointer-events: none`.

❸ The opacity changes on the `#fade` color layer (the top, unclipped image) and all of the clipped color images will have smooth transitions.

❹ The `#fade` color layer will normally be visible, but will transition to transparent whenever one of the hotspot links is hovered or focused or activated by touch.

❺ The `.clip` clipped color images will normally be invisible, but will be made visible when the user is interacting with the image's parent link.

❻ The color changes will provide an indication of keyboard focus, but color alone is not an accessible distinction—some people can't see color well, and some devices can't display color well. To ensure focus is always clear, a standard focus `outline` is also used. However, if the `outline` was drawn around the link, it would be drawn around the combined bounding box of all its children, including the *unclipped* dimensions of the <image>. Because that would mean that every link would have the same bounding box, it's not very useful. So, that outline is turned off, and an outline specifically around the <path> element is used instead.

❼ Browsers that support the outline-offset property will position the outline 20px outside the bounding box of the path, keeping it from looking too cramped.

To be able to use the :hover pseudoclass on the <a> elements to affect the top color photo layer, the complete photograph must come later in the document than the links. That means it will be drawn on top of the links (because of the lack of z-index support for SVG), and would normally grab all the mouse hover, click, and tap events. That not only would ruin the interactive effect, it would mean that the links couldn't be opened!

The pointer-events property is used to ensure that the invisible paths in the links are sensitive to clicks, but that the images drawn on top are not.

More Online

We also used clipping paths, images, and links in "Clipped Clicks", an extra example for Chapter 15:

> *https://oreillymedia.github.io/Using_SVG/extras/ch15-imagemap.html*

In that case, we were relying on the clipping paths themselves to control pointer events, which doesn't have as good browser support: Microsoft Edge and Internet Explorer do not clip the pointer-events region when they clip an image.

The invisible "hit region" approach was also used for displaying interactive text labels on hover in "Interactive Text," an extra example for Chapter 7:

> *https://oreillymedia.github.io/Using_SVG/extras/ch07-interactive-labels.html*

Getting the Point(er) Across

The **pointer-events** property is one of those SVG features that has spread into CSS-styling of other web content. But the standard CSS version only includes a narrow slice of the SVG property's function. Many web developers have thrown pointer-events: none on an element to fix a user interface, without any idea of all the SVG-specific options for the property.

The pointer-events property determines whether an element receives mouse and touch events that pass over its region of the screen. When there are multiple elements in the same region, the topmost layer (i.e., the last element in the DOM for SVG elements) normally receives the event. If that element isn't sensitive to pointer events, the event gets passed to a lower layer.

There are *nine* different pointer-events options for SVG shapes. They control whether the fill region and/or the stroke region of the shape is sensitive to pointer events, and whether the hit region is affected by the visibility, fill, and stroke properties. The pointer-events setting is inherited.

The fill region is the shape that would be colored if fill were a solid-color value, and is affected by fill-rule.

The stroke region is the shape that would be colored if stroke were a solid-color value, and is affected by stroke-width, stroke-dasharray, stroke-dashoffset, stroke-linejoin, stroke-linecap, and stroke-miterlimit. In other words: it includes dashes and line caps/line joins, but not gaps in a dashed stroke.

Using pointer-events, you can make unpainted or hidden elements, or sections of elements, sensitive to pointer events (like we did in Example 18-2).

The values have the following meanings:

visiblePainted

If the element has `visibility` set to `visible`, then the fill region is sensitive *unless* `fill` is `none`, and the stroke region is sensitive *unless* `stroke` is `none`.

visibleFill

If the element has `visibility` set to `visible`, the fill region is sensitive (whether it is painted or not); the stroke region is never sensitive.

visibleStroke

If the element has `visibility` set to `visible`, the stroke region is sensitive (whether it is painted or not); the fill region is never sensitive.

visible

If the element has `visibility` set to `visible`, both the fill region and the stroke region are sensitive, regardless of whether or not they are painted.

painted

The fill region is sensitive *unless* `fill` is `none` and the stroke region is sensitive *unless* `stroke` is `none`, regardless of the `visibility` value.

fill

The fill region is sensitive, regardless of whether it is painted or not, and regardless of the `visibility` value; the stroke region is never sensitive.

stroke

The stroke region is sensitive, regardless of whether it is painted or not, and regardless of the `visibility` value; the fill region is never sensitive.

all

Both the fill region and the stroke region are sensitive, regardless of whether they are painted or not, and regardless of the `visibility` value.

No parts of the element are sensitive to pointer events.

As mentioned in Chapter 15, the pointer-sensitive region of an element can also be restricted by clipping paths (but this isn't yet supported in Microsoft browsers). Hidden overflow also clips the clickable region.

An element that has display: none is never sensitive to pointer events, regardless of the pointer-events property.

The default pointer-events value is visiblePainted, which means that the shape is sensitive to mouse events only in the places where it is filled and stroked, and only if it is visible. Fill regions with no fill, stroke regions that are unstroked, and hidden elements do not receive clicks, taps, or hover events.

However, even with the default pointer-events, you can still create invisible hit regions. The opacity, fill-opacity, and stroke-opacity properties never affect pointer sensitivity. Neither does the transparency of patterns, gradients, or colors used for fill or stroke.

This means, if you can't remember all the keywords, you can always leave pointer-events as the default and create transparent fill or stroke hit regions using the opacity properties.

The one thing you *can't* fake with opacity is having a section of an element that is visible but *not* interactive. For that, you always need pointer-events. In addition to turning off pointer sensitivity altogether with the none option, you may find it useful to ensure that shapes have a consistent hover shape regardless of whether or not they are being stroked.

Example 18-3 shows a simplified case. The shapes in the graphic are given a hover effect that causes the stroke-width to increase from 0 to 24px wide (as shown in Figure 18-4). With the default pointer-events option, this would cause the size of the hoverable region to change underneath the mouse pointer, making the hover effect flicker on and off for certain mouse positions. By making pointer events only sensitive in the fill region, the changing stroke width does not affect the hoverable shape, preventing any flickering feedback loops.

Figure 18-4. The hoverable shapes, with the second circle hovered

Example 18-3. Maintaining predictable hover regions despite changing strokes

```
<svg xmlns="http://www.w3.org/2000/svg" xml:lang="en"
    viewBox="0 0 400 200" width="400px" height="200px">
    <title>Hover Effects that Don't Affect Hover Regions</title>
    <style>
        circle {
            fill: currentColor;
            stroke: currentColor;
            stroke-width: 0px;
            pointer-events: visibleFill;
            transition: all 0.5s;
        }
        circle:hover {
            stroke-width: 24px;
            fill-opacity: 0.3;
        }
    </style>
    <circle color="crimson" cx="75" cy="75" r="60" />
    <circle color="springGreen" cx="200" cy="125" r="60" />
    <circle color="royalBlue" cx="325" cy="75" r="60" />
</svg>
```

Turning off stroke pointer events to avoid flickering hover effects can also be useful if you are animating a stroke dash pattern. The stroke region for pointer events only includes the dash shapes, not the gaps, so animated dashes means flickering hover effects. Again, you'd want to use the `visibleFill` value to ignore the shifting stroke sections.

On the other hand, a `visible` value (forcing both the fill *and* the stroke region to be clickable, even if they are set to `none`) can be useful to create an invisible—but still clickable—stroke region around the outside of shapes. With a large `stroke-width` value, this can increase the clickable size of links or buttons in an SVG interface, making it easier to use.

Think you've got a handle on `pointer-events`? Maybe? It gets worse. Everything we've said so far only applies to SVG *shape* elements. Other elements have their own rules.

For SVG text elements, `pointer-events` does not distinguish the fill region and stroke region. Instead, the sensitive region is always based on the character cell (em-box) rectangles: rectangles around each character, where each rectangle is 1 em tall and as wide as the normal spacing for that letter.

With the `visiblePainted` and `painted` values for text, the complete character cells are sensitive if the text has *either* fill or stroke. With the other values (including `fill` and `stroke`), the character cells will be sensitive even if the text is not painted at all—although `visibility` continues to have its normal effect on the `visible*` values.

For `<image>` elements, the `fill` and `stroke` settings have no effect, but `visibility` does. So all the `visible*` values are equivalent: the element will be sensitive to pointer events so long as it is not `hidden`. Similarly, `fill`, `stroke`, and `painted` are all equivalent to `all`. For images, the sensitive region is the rectangular shape of the `<image>` element.

> The SVG specs suggest that images should only be considered "painted" for pixels that aren't fully transparent. No browsers implement this behavior: all treat an image as a rectangular element, regardless of transparency.

For CSS layout boxes, `pointer-events` behavior isn't specified anywhere. The browsers, however, all act as if there are only two possible values: visible and none. Any value other than none causes a CSS layout box to be sensitive to pointer events over its entire border-box region (after adjusting for radiused corners), but only if it has visibility: visible.

There is no way to make a CSS layout box sensitive to pointer events when it has visibility: hidden. You can hide it with opacity: 0, since opacity never affects pointer events. But with opacity, you can't *un*hide a specific child element, like you can with visibility.

 Inline <svg> elements, and the root <svg> element in an SVG file, have CSS layout boxes and behave like other CSS boxes, not like SVG graphics. That means they are pointer-sensitive over the entire border-box region, unless visibility is hidden *or* pointer-events is none.

Within SVG layout, pointer-events only applies directly to graphical elements that actually draw content to the screen. Groups, links, <use> elements, and nested <svg> elements don't directly capture pointer events. However, containers will match the :hover class if any of their child elements are hovered, and other pointer events will bubble up the DOM tree (or shadow DOM tree) from children, which by default inherit the container's pointer-events setting.

Targeting the Interaction

Before we get to DOM events and JavaScript interaction, there is one more important type of declarative (nonscripted) interaction: links! Again! This time, not links to a *different* web page, but links within the same web page.

In other words, a link where the destination is a target fragment: a # followed by an element's id.

Same-page web links are used all the time in HTML, to allow the user to jump to a different part of a long document. If you have a number of small inline SVG graphics within an HTML page, you can use this type of same-page links to jump to the graphic from a table of contents, or from a cross-reference in the main text.

When most browsers scroll to an SVG element within an HTML document, they scroll to the *top* of the `<svg>` that contains it, not to the specific element's position. If your SVG is too large to fit on the screen, this can mean that your desired element is still offscreen.

If the SVG is already fully in view, jumping to a particular element with a same-page link *doesn't* cause a scroll effect. So why would you want to do it? Because you can create other effects in response to the change in the web page's target.

There are two SVG-specific ways to change the graphic by using link targets:

- SVG views, which we introduced in Chapter 9. By including links to views within the SVG, you can zoom in and out of the graphic dynamically. Unfortunately, you can't currently make that zoom effect transition *smoothly*; you'll get a sudden switch from one view to the other.

- SVG animation elements, which we'll introduce in Chapter 19. When an animation element is the target of a link, that animation effect is started when you trigger the link.

A final interaction option is to use the CSS `:target` pseudoclass selector to change styles on the targeted element or a sibling/child. Although not SVG-specific, it can be put to good use within interactive SVG.

Example 18-4 uses `:target` styles to create an interactive version of our `stroke-linejoin` comparison from Chapter 13 (Figure 13-5). Rather than show the three `stroke-linejoin` values side by side, there is one large sample shape, and three links for the three possible values. The targets are the links themselves, which has the benefit of not losing the keyboard focus position when a link is activated. The shape is then restyled according to which sibling `<a>` element matches the `:target` pseudoclass.

Figure 18-5 shows one possible state, after the round value has been set (but focus has been shifted to the next value).

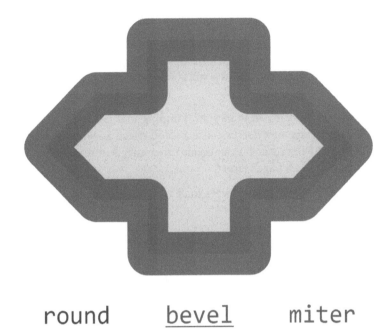

round   <u>bevel</u>   miter

Figure 18-5. An interactive SVG style sample, after the first link has been activated (but the second link is focused)

Example 18-4. Using same-page links and :target to create a style switch

```svg
<svg xmlns="http://www.w3.org/2000/svg" xml:lang="en"
     xmlns:xlink="http://www.w3.org/1999/xlink"
     width="390px" height="338px" viewBox="0 0 300 260">
    <title>Strokes with Interactive Linejoin Options</title>
    <desc>
        Selecting one of the stroke-linejoin options
        will apply that effect to the sample shape.
    </desc>
    <style>
        svg {
            font: 20px Consolas, monospace;
            text-anchor: middle;
        }
        .shape {
            fill: deepSkyBlue;
            stroke: blueViolet;
            stroke-width: 4px;
```

```
            stroke-opacity: 0.8;
    }
    #round:target ~ .shape { stroke-linejoin: round; }
    #bevel:target ~ .shape { stroke-linejoin: bevel; }
    #miter:target ~ .shape { stroke-linejoin: miter; }
    .option { fill: indigo; }
    text { fill: blueViolet; }
    .option:focus, .option:hover {
        outline: none;
        text-decoration: underline;
    }
    .option:target text { fill: inherit; }
</style>
<symbol id="shape" viewBox="-18 -12 36 24">
    <path d="M-5,-10 H5   V-5 H10   L15,0  L10,5   H5   V10
                  H-5 V5   H-10 L-15,0 L-10,-5 H-5 V-10 Z" />
</symbol>
<a id="round" class="option" xlink:href="#round">
    <text x="50"  y="250">round</text></a>
<a id="bevel" class="option" xlink:href="#bevel">
    <text x="150" y="250">bevel</text></a>
<a id="miter" class="option" xlink:href="#miter">
    <text x="250" y="250">miter</text></a>
<use class="shape"
     xlink:href="#shape" width="300" height="225" />
</svg>
```

There are a few limitations to using :target styles for interactive
graphics. You can only alter CSS-stylable properties, not XML
attributes. And you can only have one target at a time, so you can
only have a single set of options to pick from.

The Big Event

There's only so far you can go with interactivity using just CSS and
links. You can go a little further with animation elements (albeit
with worse browser support), but you're still going to hit barriers.
For flexible interaction, you need JavaScript.

We've used JavaScript in scattered examples throughout the book to
build SVG documents, but haven't touched on interactivity yet.

Interactive scripting on the web uses an **event model**. The user (or
sometimes the browser, behind the scenes) does something, which
creates an **Event object**. The event is associated with a particular
DOM element, the event's **target**. For example, when you click the

mouse or tap the screen, the target is the element under your pointer that receives the pointer event.

After creating an event, the browser looks for any JavaScript instructions you—the web page author—set for what to do with an event of that type. Those instructions could be set as event handler functions (using the onclick attribute or property, for example) or event listener functions (set using an element's addEventListener() function). Depending on the type of the event, those handlers or listeners could be set directly on the target or on one of its ancestors in the DOM tree.

Most things about JavaScript event handling work the same for SVG as they do for HTML. So we're not going to discuss them in detail here. Instead, we're going to review a few cases where SVG gets a little more complicated.

Back in Chapter 2, we reviewed some of the trickier aspects of scripting and SVG, mostly related to XML namespaces. All of that still applies here. Thankfully, event objects don't have namespaces. The complications come from switching to the SVG layout model, from dealing with <use> shadow-DOM elements, and from working around the fact that SVG doesn't have native input elements like HTML does.

Counting Clicks

For our basic event-handler demo, we're going to build a simple SVG game. We'll draw a bunch of circles (confetti pieces) on the screen, and run down a timer, and the user has to click as many circles as possible before the time runs out. We won't worry about keyboard interaction right now, which will keep things simpler.

Example 18-5 provides the JavaScript. We haven't included the matching markup here, because the script is designed to work with many different structures, either inline SVG or standalone. The requirements:

- an <svg> element in the document with an id of gameboard, to which the click targets will be added, and which is styled to have a dark background (although the script could easily be tweaked for a different color scheme)

- text elements (SVG or HTML) with the IDs of timer and scoreboard, with appropriate styles on them, whose text content will be overwritten as the game progresses

Additional style changes should be triggered by the clicked class on the circles and the game-over class on the document root element; we'll show one possible stylesheet in Example 19-1 in Chapter 19.

Figure 18-6 shows a version of the game in progress.

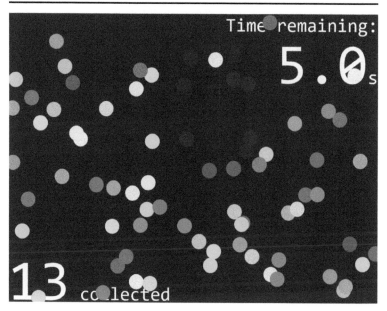

Figure 18-6. An SVG game using click events on colored circles

Example 18-5. Using click events to create an SVG game with JavaScript

```
(function(){
/* constants */                        ❶
var width = 400,  //viewBox width in px
    height = 300, //viewBox height in px
    nShapes = 80,  //number of confetti pieces to draw
    timeLimit = 15,    //total time in seconds,
    gameboard = document.getElementById("gameboard"), //the SVG
    timer = document.getElementById("timer"), //for time remaining
    scoreboard = document.getElementById("scoreboard"), //counter
    svgNS = gameboard.namespaceURI;
```

```
var score = 0; //number of pieces collected so far

/* initialize */
gameboard.setAttribute("viewBox", [0,0,width,height]);          ❷
for (var i=0; i<nShapes; i++) {
    var circle = document.createElementNS(svgNS, "circle");     ❸
    circle.setAttribute("class", "clickable");
    circle.setAttribute("r", 8); //fixed size
    circle.setAttribute("fill", randomColor() );                ❹
    circle.setAttribute("cx", Math.random()*width);
    circle.setAttribute("cy", Math.random()*height);
    gameboard.appendChild(circle);
}
var endTime = Date.now() + timeLimit*1000;
updateTime();                                                   ❺
var timerInterval = setInterval(updateTime, 100);
updateScore();
gameboard.addEventListener("click", checkClick);                ❻

function randomColor() {
    /* returns a random color with at least 50% saturation
       and 50-80% lightness (for drawing on dark background) */
    var hue = Math.random()*360,
        sat = 50 + Math.random()*50,                            ❼
        light = 50 + Math.random()*30;
    return "hsl(" + hue+"," + sat+"%," + light+"% )";
}
function updateTime() {
    var timeLeft = endTime - Date.now();
    if (timeLeft <= 0) {
        endGame();                                              ❽
        timeLeft = 0;
    }
    timer.textContent = (timeLeft/1000).toFixed(1);
}
function updateScore() {
    scoreboard.textContent = score.toFixed(0);
}
function endGame() {
    clearInterval(timerInterval);
    gameboard.removeEventListener("click", checkClick);         ❾
    document.documentElement.setAttribute("class", "game-over");
}
function checkClick(event) {
    var element = event.target;
    if (element.getAttribute("class")=="clickable") {           ❿
        element.setAttribute("class", "clicked");
        score++;
        updateScore();
    }
}
```

```
}
})();
```

❶ Customizable game-play constants are set at the top of the script, including the size of the board, the number of confetti pieces to create, the initial time for the countdown, and the IDs of the elements we'll be modifying.

❷ The `viewBox` of the gameboard `<svg>` is updated to match the dimensions that will be used in the script. The value is set using an array of four numbers, which will automatically be converted into a string as a comma-separated list.

❸ For each confetti piece, we create a new `<circle>` element, using the namespace-sensitive `createElementNS` method and a namespace URI string we extracted from the `<svg>` element.

❹ Each circle is given the same class name, a fixed radius, and then a random color (using a function we define later in the script) and a random position within the gameboard. The `Math.random()` method returns a value between 0 and 1, so multiplying it by `width` returns a value between 0 and `width` (and similarly for `height`). The circles are then appended as children of the gameboard `<svg>` element.

❺ With the confetti in place, it's time to start the timer. `Date.now()` returns a timestamp from the system clock, measured in milliseconds. Since our `timeLimit` is measured in seconds, we need to multiply it by 1,000 to convert. The `updateTime()` function will update the timer display and also check if we've run out of time. We call it once to start and then tell the browser to call it repeatedly on a 100ms interval.

❻ An `updateScore()` function sets the initial score display; changes to the score, however, won't come at predictable intervals, but based on user events. We add the event listener to the gameboard `<svg>` element, so that it can react to click events from all the child confetti elements.

❼ The `randomColor()` function uses `Math.random()` and CSS `hsl()` color notation to create random colors that will still be bright and easy to see on our dark gameboard.

❽ The updateTime() function uses Date.now() again, comparing it against our saved value, in order to calculate how many milliseconds remain in the game. After checking whether the endGame() method needs to be called, it updates the onscreen timer, using the *Number*.toFixed(*digits*) method to format the time nicely.

❾ The endGame() function is fairly simple: it turns off the timer using the clearInterval() method, removes the event listener that was counting clicks, and then sets the game-over class on the document, which will trigger additional changes in the CSS. The class is changed using setAttribute(), not classList, to avoid issues on Internet Explorer and other older browsers that don't support classList for SVG—but beware that this will replace any other classes on the element. If using inline SVG in a more complex HTML document, you may want to switch to a more robust method.

❿ The final method, checkClick(), is our event listener. The browser calls it with the MouseEvent object as a parameter. The event object's target property is a reference to the element that initially received the click. If that element is one of our confetti circles, it will match our clickable class. We switch it to the clicked class (again, using backward-compatible methods) so that the CSS can change the styles and then update the score.

The styles used in Figure 18-6 make the clicked confetti pieces almost transparent (with opacity). We can also make those pieces fully transparent to further click events using pointer-events: none, although the changed class means we will ignore those clicks anyway:

```
.clicked {
    opacity: 0.1;
    pointer-events: none;
}
```

We don't, however, remove the <circle> elements completely. That makes it easy to switch styles when the game is over, to highlight the pieces that *were* collected, as shown in Figure 18-7. The unclicked pieces are turned to black with another style rule that overrides the fill presentation attributes on the individual circles:

```
.game-over .clickable { fill: black; }
.game-over .clicked {
    opacity: 1;
    filter: drop-shadow(0 0 3px gold);
}
```

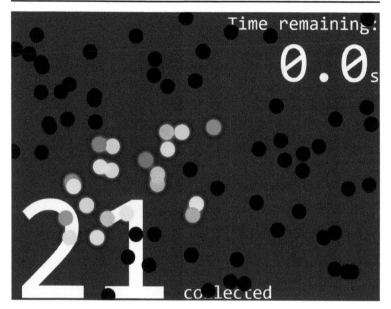

Figure 18-7. A completed version of the confetti game

Although this game isn't keyboard accessible, we still want to make it accessible to screen readers and other assistive tech. (After all, it could be played on a touchscreen even if your eyesight wasn't perfect.) Frequently updating text can be a distraction with screen readers, so appropriate ARIA roles are needed to tell the browser to be more polite:

```
<div class="count" role="timer" aria-atomic="true"
    >Time remaining: <span id="timer">00.0</span>s</div>
<div class="count" role="status" aria-atomic="true"
    ><span id="scoreboard">0</span> collected</div>
```

The ARIA attributes would be the same if you used SVG <text> elements; this version is HTML to minimize the number of *other* attributes you need.

For the score count, the `status` role tells screen readers that the user probably wants to know the changed value, and it should be read out the next time there is a break in speech.

Adding `aria-atomic="true"` to the parent element indicates that the changed value makes more sense if read out in context of the entire element—for example, "13 collected" instead of just "13."

For the timer, the `timer` role indicates that the value is changing automatically and doesn't normally need to be read out. However, we might want to give the user a warning when time is almost up; the `aria-live` attribute can be changed to indicate that the timer is a bit more important.

To add that to our script, we would add a new game variable, and then add one more check in the `updateTime()` function:

```
if ((!last5seconds)&&(timeLeft <= 5000)) {
    //less than 5 seconds left
    timer.setAttribute("aria-live", "polite");
    last5seconds = true;
}
```

Because we don't want to reset the attribute every tenth of a second, we use a Boolean variable to record the fact that we've already passed the 5-second warning point.

The `polite` value for `aria-live` switches the timer to the same behavior as the `status` role: the screen reader mentions the updated value whenever it has a break in speech, counting down the last few seconds on the timer. In contrast, the default behavior for a timer is equivalent to `aria-live="off"`.

Finally, to give visual users the same warning, you could change the color of the timer text when it matches the `[aria-live]` attribute selector.

Bubbling Out of Shadows

The confetti collector game is all very well. But what if you wanted to collect something more interesting than confetti? For example, maybe we would like to use the gemstone shapes from Example 17-4 in Chapter 17, creating a game that looks like Figure 18-8.

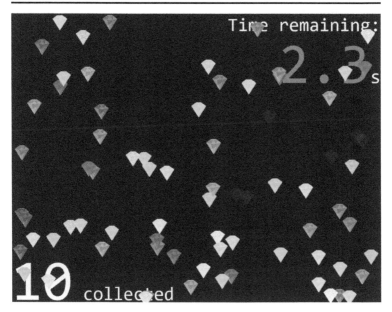

Figure 18-8. An SVG game using click events on colored gems made from <use> elements

There are a few changes to the code required. For starters, we'll want to predefine our gemstone shape as a graphic we can reuse. Although we could define it as a <symbol>, we're going to instead define it as a nested <svg> so we can set a default size and offset the position:

```
<defs>
    <svg id="gem" viewBox="0 0 100 100"
        x="-8" y="-8" width="16" height="16">
        <polygon points="0,25 35,0 65,0 100,25 50,100" />
        <g fill="white" fill-opacity="0.3">
            <polygon points="0,25 30,30 50,100" />
            <polygon points="100,25 30,70 50,100" />
            <polygon points="28,5 35,0 65,0 72,5 50,10" />
            <polygon points="50,10 30,30 50,35 70,30" />
            <polygon points="72,5 70,30 100,25" />
        </g>
        <g stroke="white" stroke-opacity="0.5"
            fill-opacity="0.5">
            <polygon points="100,25 70,30 50,100" />
            <polygon points="28,5 30,30 0,25" />
        </g>
```

```
    </svg>
  </defs>
```

The x, y, width, and height attributes on the gem <svg> set it to be approximately the same size as our confetti circles, and similarly centered on our reference point. That way, gems will never be more than half-outside our gameboard, in either direction.

In the script, we switch the code for creating circles to instead create <use> elements. The only extra hassle is having to use namespace-sensitive methods for setting xlink:href:

```
for (var i=0; i<nShapes; i++) {
    var use = document.createElementNS(svgNS, "use");
    use.setAttribute("class", "clickable");
    use.setAttributeNS("http://www.w3.org/1999/xlink",
                       "href", "#gem");
    use.setAttribute("fill", randomColor() );
    use.setAttribute("x", Math.random()*width);
    use.setAttribute("y", Math.random()*height);
    gameboard.appendChild(use);
}
```

The randomColor() method could be tweaked slightly to create brighter fill colors, since the gemstone drawing adds white tints anyway. The x and y attributes on the <use> are directly equivalent to the cx and cy attributes on the circles.

For most browsers, that's all you have to change.

But not for all browsers.

What's the confusion? The problem is that a <use> element doesn't receive click events directly. Instead, the cloned <polygon> shapes that draw the graphic receive the clicks. The SVG 1 specs defined a special DOM object for these cloned shapes, SVGElementInstance. An SVGElementInstance wasn't a full DOM Element, but it was a valid EventTarget object in the DOM event model.

In browsers that implement the SVG 1 model for the <use> element DOM, therefore, when we access the event.target object in our checkClick() event listener, we *won't* get the <use> element that we need to modify. Instead, we'll get one of these SVGElementInstance objects for the cloned polygons.

In Internet Explorer, MS Edge up to EdgeHTML 14, and older versions of Blink and WebKit, the event.target of click events on <use> elements is an SVGElementInstance object in the <use> element's shadow DOM.

Firefox never implemented the SVG 1 <use> element shadow DOM; the target is always the <use>.

Blink, WebKit, and MS Edge 15+ have switched to a model where event listeners in the main document receive a modified Event object, where the target has been switched to point to the <use> element.

In the newer browsers (and in the SVG 2 specs), when the click event "bubbles" out of the shadow DOM and into the regular DOM, it is **retargeted**, so that all events that start in the shadow DOM instead appear to come from the <use> element directly. This is part of the encapsulation model of web components' shadow DOM, but it also makes SVG event handling easier for most cases.

The implementation details aren't entirely consistent between the different browsers and the spec yet, but the main result is the same: in an event listener attached to the <use> element or one of its ancestors, event.target points to the <use> element, not to the shadow DOM.

But what can we do about the older browsers? We can make use of the fact that the SVGElementInstance interface includes a property that points to its host <use> element. If the event target has a value for that property, it will point to the <use> element. Otherwise, the event target is already a real-DOM element, and we can use it directly.

The Boolean OR (||) operator in JavaScript can be used to collapse the two options. The result of an OR operation between two Java-Script objects is the first object if it exists or the second object otherwise:

```
function checkClick(event) {
    var element = event.target.correspondingUseElement
                  || event.target;
    if (element.getAttribute("class")=="clickable") {
        element.setAttribute("class", "clicked");
```

```
        score++;
        updateScore();
    }
}
```

This works in all the browsers—but Firefox is a little flaky about whether it registers a click event at all. The problem seems to be that if the mouse pointer shifts from one polygon to another between mouse-down and mouse-up, it does not register as a "click" on either element. Changing the event listeners to use mouseup (instead of click) solves that problem.

A tap on a touchscreen should create mouseup and click events. However, there may be a slight delay (as the browser waits to see if you're doing a complex touch gesture).

You can listen explicitly for the touchend event instead—but then be sure to call prevent Default() on the touch event, so you don't get a mouse event as well.

Doing anything more complicated with <use> element shadow DOM—actually trying to detect which shadow element was clicked, for example—cannot currently be done in a cross-browser way. If you need to make the individual elements within a clone interactive, use the *Element*.cloneNode(true) DOM method to create the clones, instead of cloning with <use> elements.

Measuring Mouse Positions

A nice feature about the code in Example 18-5 is that we never have to worry about *where* the user's mouse—or finger—is on the screen. All we need to focus on is *which* element was underneath it. The browser takes care of converting from (*x,y*) locations to element positions.

But often, when handling pointer events in a graphical interface, you *do* need to know exactly where the pointer is. And that requires some extra work.

The MouseEvent interface used for click and mouseup events (including those created by touch taps) has properties to help you figure out pointer coordinates. In fact, they have multiple different versions. In modern browsers, mouse events can give you screenX and screenY coordinates, clientX/Y, offsetX/Y, or pageX/Y. Each pair is calculated relative to a different reference frame.

What we *want* for SVG is usually SVG user-space coordinates, for however the coordinate system is scaled and transformed for the current element. For example, for our clicking game we might want to draw a symbol at the location of each "miss": places where the user clicked, but not on a clickable element. In order to position the symbols correctly, we need to know the (*x,y*) position of that click within the SVG viewBox.

Unfortunately, none of the MouseEvent options currently serve that purpose.

 For offsetX and offsetY, you don't even get consistent results cross-browser for SVG elements.

So we're going to need a little math, to convert mouse coordinates into SVG coordinates. Luckily, the SVG DOM has some helper functions for us.

Every SVG element that can take a transform (basically, all the graphical elements except <textPath> and <tspan>) has a **getScreenCTM()** method. The CTM stands for *cumulative transformation matrix*. It's a matrix in the sense of a matrix transformation function. We mentioned cumulative matrices in Chapter 11 when discussing how the many transformation functions in a list can be compiled into a single matrix.

The *screen* CTM is that and more. It defines how you can convert points in that element's coordinate system back into the original, unscaled, untransformed coordinate system of the document window. It includes transformations on this element and its ancestors, plus viewBox scaling.

Internet Explorer 9 also included the transformation from browser zoom in the CTM—which breaks the mouse-conversion method in IE9 if the user has their browser set to anything other than 100% zoom.

Here's the confusing part: the coordinate system of the document window is *not* the coordinate system used to measure the screenX/Y mouse positions. But it *is* the coordinate system used to measure the clientX/Y mouse positions. So getScreenCTM() should really be called getClientCTM(). But it isn't.

Using the getScreenCTM() transformation matrix, we can convert between our local SVG coordinate system and the client coordinate system used by mouse events.

How do we convert the coordinates? Do we need to do the matrix math ourselves? Thankfully, no.

There is an **SVGPoint object** (now renamed **DOMPoint** in the latest browsers) that can do the math for us. Here's how it works:

1. Create an SVG/DOMPoint object with the createSVGPoint() method of any <svg> element. (The name of the method doesn't change, even if the object is now called DOMPoint.)

2. Set the x and y properties on the point object to the values of the *x,y* position you want to convert.

3. Call the point object's **matrixTransform(*matrix*) method**, where *matrix* is a transformation matrix object like the one returned by getScreenCTM() (an SVGMatrix or DOMMatrix, depending on the browser).

   The resulting value is a *new* point object, whose x and y properties represent the transformed position of your point.

There's just one more complication. The transformation matrix returned by getScreenCTM() is the matrix for converting *from* SVG coordinates *to* mouse-client coordinates. We want to do the reverse transformation.

Or more precisely, we want to do the *inverse* transformation. Inverting a matrix reverses its effect. And luckily for us, the transformation matrix object has an **inverse()** **method** that does just the job.

So, let's put it all together to add the "miss" shapes to our game.

First, we'll edit our markup to add an extra group to hold these shapes:

```
<g id="misses"></g>
```

The group should be layered above (meaning, after in the DOM) any backdrop elements and optionally the text, but below (before) our gemstones, which will be added by the script at the end of the gameboard SVG.

In the constants section of the script, we'll grab that element by its ID for easy reference:

```
var misses = document.getElementById("misses");
```

And then we'll modify our checkClick() event listener to react to both hits and misses. Example 18-6 provides the new function code.

Example 18-6. Creating new elements when click events do not hit a target

```
function checkClick(event) {
    var element = event.target.correspondingUseElement
                  || event.target;
    if (element.getAttribute("class")=="clickable") {
        element.setAttribute("class", "clicked");
        score++;
        updateScore();
    }
    else {
        /* create a point for the click location */
        var clickPoint = gameboard.createSVGPoint();
        clickPoint.x = event.clientX;
        clickPoint.y = event.clientY;

        /* convert it to the coordinate system
           of the `misses` group element */
        var missPoint = clickPoint.matrixTransform(
            misses.getScreenCTM().inverse() );

        /* add a circle element centered at that point */
        var circle = document.createElementNS(svgNS, "circle");
        circle.setAttribute("class", "miss");
        circle.setAttribute("r", 4);
```

```
        circle.setAttribute("cx", missPoint.x);
        circle.setAttribute("cy", missPoint.y);
        misses.appendChild(circle);
    }
}
```

You'll also want to add some styles for elements with the `miss` class. For our demo, we used a thick semitransparent stroke to create a bull's-eye effect, and added CSS animations that cause the elements to fade away (to zero opacity) a few seconds after they are added to the document. The animation code—and the rest of the CSS for this example—is included as Example 19-1 in Chapter 19.

The end result (for a player with rather poor aim) looks like Figure 18-9.

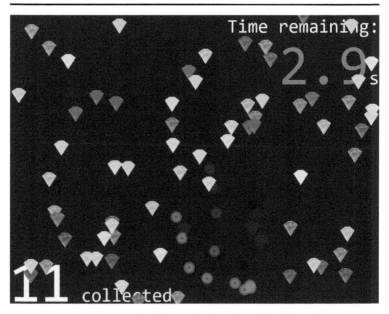

Figure 18-9. A game with additional elements added based on mouse-click positions

You could, of course, also keep count of the number of misses, or generate a net score of some sort. It's a game—get creative. And be glad that the DOM handles so much of the math for you.

Capturing the Keyboard with JavaScript-Enhanced Links

For the click-counter games, we have been ignoring keyboard accessibility. For certain gameplay structures, keyboards just don't make sense. But for general website interactivity, keyboard input is essential.

SVG 1 had no ability to handle keyboard controls—none. OK, well, there was an access key feature for the animation elements, but none of the browsers implemented that.

Because SVG 1 had full DOM support, you *could* react to keypress events, just like you could react to any other event. But you couldn't control keyboard focus so that those key strokes were directed at a particular element.

The browsers, or most of them, at least added basic keyboard access to links. Keyboard users could tab to the link and activate it with the Enter key.

 Safari, by default, does not make links keyboard accessible—in SVG or HTML. The user needs to turn on an accessibility setting to allow tabbing to links. Most users who prefer keyboard access will know about this, but not all.

Because links can receive focus, and scripts can receive keyboard events from the focused element, you can turn any valid link into a widget that listens for particular keyboard inputs. Just be sure to update the `role` and any other ARIA attributes so that all users clearly understand how the element functions, and make sure that you're listening for the correct keyboard actions for that role.

We can therefore adapt Example 18-4 (the interactive `stroke-linejoin` demo) to reflect that the interactive links used to set the `:target` styles were really behaving more like buttons (changing the current document) instead of like links (moving to a different location).

The normal keyboard behavior of a button is as follows:

- You can reach each button by pressing the Tab key.
- You can activate each button by pressing *either* the space bar or Enter.

The links have the Tab behavior (in every browser except Safari), and can be activated with Enter. So all we need to add (for most browsers) is space-bar activation.

 To get the correct behavior in Safari, you also need to add the `tabindex="0"` attribute, which we'll discuss in the next section.

If the script runs, making the links behave like buttons, it should also add the corresponding ARIA role, so assistive tech will know to *call* them a button. Example 18-7 provides the additional JavaScript for the demo.

Example 18-7. Making links behave like buttons, with JavaScript event handlers

```
var xlinkNS = "http://www.w3.org/1999/xlink";

var options = document.getElementsByClassName("option");   ❶
for (var i=0, n=options.length; i<n; i++){
    options[i].addEventListener("keypress", spaceActivation );  ❷
    options[i].setAttribute("role", "button");                  ❸
}

function spaceActivation(event) {
    if (event.charCode == 32) { //spacebar               ❹
        var option = event.currentTarget;                ❺
        var href = option.getAttribute("href")           ❻
                || option.getAttributeNS(xlinkNS, "href");
        if (href) {
            location.assign(href);                       ❼

            event.preventDefault();
            return false;                                ❽
        }
    }
}
```

❶ The elements with class `option` are the links that we are going to turn into buttons.

❷ Each is assigned the same event listener to detect space-bar key-presses; the listener function will check the event object each time to determine which link received the event.

❸ Once the listener is assigned, we can update the `role` of the elements to `button`.

❹ The `spaceActivation()` function gets called for *any* keypress, but only does anything for space bars. The script doesn't need to respond to the Enter key (or, for that matter, to mouse clicks or touch taps) because the regular link behavior already works in that case.

❺ The `currentTarget` of the event is the element that had the event listener added to it; in other words, the option link that received the keyboard event.

❻ The function looks up the `href` value for that link, checking first the default-namespace version of the attribute (in case we switch to SVG 2–style links), and then the `xlink` version.

❼ If either attribute returned a valid reference, we update the `location` object (part of the global scope for the window) accordingly.

❽ Finally, because we've successfully handled the space-bar press, we cancel the browser's normal space-bar behavior (scrolling the web page), using both the modern standard method (`preventDefault()`) and the older compatibility approach (`return false`).

Of course, now that you have the keypress-capturing script ready, you could do whatever you want with it, not just activate a link. This means you could create general-purpose link buttons that create interactive effects directly, instead of using `:target` styles to react to the click. Just remember to still give the `<a>` element a valid target (even if it is just `xlink:href="#"`) so that it is recognized as a functional, focusable link.

You could extend the same method to other types of inputs.

For example, you could create a range slider by listening for arrow keys instead of the space bar. Of course, the ARIA role would be different (slider), and you would probably want to add other ARIA attributes to explain the possible values. And of course you'd also want the slider to be accessible to mouse and touchscreen users, which means more event listeners and JavaScript to detect drag actions.

So, it would be considerably more code. But the basic idea is the same: a dummy link element grabs the keyboard focus, so that you can listen for keyboard inputs.

One limitation, however, is that we are still relying on the links and tab order to control focus in the first place. That means we can't create proper *radio* buttons, which is what the buttons in Example 18-4 really should be: a set of choices in a group. But the proper behavior of radio buttons is to use Tab to move focus in and out of the group as a whole, and use arrow keys to switch focus between the individual options. Links cannot (by default) do that.

Controlling the Keyboard with tabindex and focus()

Using links as buttons, with a bit of JavaScript help, solves many use cases—but it is a bit of a hack, and it doesn't support more complex keyboard-focus control options. Proper control of keyboard focus has long been a requested feature for SVG.

The aborted SVG 1.2 spec added a focusable attribute, with three values: true, false, and auto (the default), meaning do what the browser normally does. However, focusable was only ever implemented in Internet Explorer (and later MS Edge).

Currently, the main use of focusable is to turn *off* focusability on inline <svg> elements. In Internet Explorer, every <svg> is focusable by default, which can be annoying when that SVG is a noninteractive graphic, and can be really problematic when it is a hidden element used for definitions of symbols, gradients, and so on.

 To fix keyboard focusability in Internet Explorer, add focusable="false" to noninteractive inline <svg> elements, especially hidden SVGs.

SVG 2 deprecates focusable and instead adopts the HTML tabindex attribute. The behavior is the same as HTML: a value of 0 adds an item to the regular tab order; a positive integer value puts it in a priority tab order (not recommended); and a value of -1 makes it focusable by scripts but not by tabbing.

You focus an element from scripts by calling the element's focus() method (also added to SVG 2). Scripted focus control is used for creating widgets where focus is controlled by the arrow keys, similar to the native behavior of radio button groups or drop-down lists. A tabindex of -1 is also used to deactivate normally focusable elements (links, in SVG) to create a disabled state.

Where supported, these features all work in SVG the same as HTML. So if you want to create custom interactive widgets (such as radio buttons) within a graphic, look up design pattern guidelines for creating keyboard-accessible widgets in HTML, and work from there.

But remember: support is not yet universal, so even well-coded SVG widgets will not be keyboard-accessible everywhere.

Internet Explorer and other older browsers do not support tabindex and focus() for SVG elements.

MS Edge supports tabindex in inline SVG but not in embedded or standalone SVG files (as of EdgeHTML version 15), and doesn't yet support focus().

If you *do* look up recommendations for making accessible interactive widgets in HTML, the first advice you will (hopefully) find is to use native HTML elements whenever possible. HTML <button>, <input>, and related interactive elements should have keyboard accessibility built in, making your scripts much simpler.

SVG doesn't have any native input elements other than <a>. But that doesn't mean that you need to always script your own input widgets, one keypress at a time.

To create the illusion of proper text inputs, drop-down lists, and other inputs in SVG—without having to code all the interaction yourself—you can often borrow fully functioning input elements from HTML and then hide them.

In this approach, the HTML elements are clipped, transparent, or drawn offscreen, but they still handle keyboard (and screen reader) accessibility. You then listen for events on the HTML, and update the SVG display to match. For mouse and touch events, you handle the events directly on the graphic elements, and then update the current value of the HTML elements, if required.

More Online

The simplest version of using HTML inputs to control SVG doesn't even require JavaScript. CSS pseudoclasses can instead be used to transmit the HTML element's state to an adjacent SVG element. We used pseudoclasses like this in Chapter 2 to turn our stoplight graphic into form-validation feedback.

Read more about using interactive HTML and CSS to control SVG, including the final radio-button version of our `stroke-linejoin` demo, in "Borrowing Ready-Made Widgets from HTML":

> *https://oreillymedia.github.io/Using_SVG/extras/ch18-hidden-input.html*

Summary: Interactive SVG

SVG is so much more than an image format. When used on the web, it can be a fully interactive web document. This means you can use it to build games, educational demos, or graphics-heavy web applications of all types.

Unlike HTML, SVG doesn't come with built-in form input elements. But you can do a lot with the one interactive element you do have—the `<a>` link—and CSS pseudoclasses. You can do even more by adding JavaScript or by integrating your SVG with interactive HTML elements.

There are pitfalls to watch out for. Browser support for full keyboard focus control is still not great in SVG. The `<use>` element shadow DOM is not implemented in a cross-browser-compatible way. And the coordinates used by mouse and touch events need to be converted into SVG coordinates using extra DOM methods. But you can work around those obstacles if you plan for them from the beginning.

More Online

An element and attribute reference for the SVG `<a>` element is included in the "Document Structure Elements" section of the markup guide:

https://oreillymedia.github.io/Using_SVG/guide/markup.html#structure

A reference for the DOM methods we've used is in the "Select SVG DOM Methods and Objects" guide:

https://oreillymedia.github.io/Using_SVG/guide/DOM.html

CHAPTER 19

Transitioning in Time

Animation

An interactive web graphic is, by definition, animated, in the sense that it changes over time. But not all changes are created equal.

The interaction examples in Chapter 18 mostly involved simple switches between different states: one moment, the graphic was in one state, and the next moment, it had changed. Although this is technically animation, it skips the most interesting aspects of animated SVG graphics: the ability to show a transition *between* two states. This transition (also known as tweening or interpolation) can greatly enhance the user's understanding of a change, making it easier to comprehend a new state or fresh information.

Even without interaction, animation can enhance many graphical elements, focusing the user on one area of the screen, or emphasizing the relationships between different components. Extend those little animated moments and connect multiple animations together, and you can create a complete animated short film in SVG.

We've used animation in a few examples so far, but have not really discussed what it means to animate a vector graphic, or how to plan a project that involves animation.

This chapter runs through your options for creating animated SVG. It is neither a detailed look at designing dynamic graphics, nor a comprehensive introduction to any of the animation techniques. Instead, it tries to lay out the options so you can decide which approach is appropriate for the project at hand.

Even more than any other aspect of web design, planning for performance becomes particularly important in animation. If a browser takes too long to update a graphic, the transition between states can stutter and jerk, exhibiting **jank**, to use the animator's term. Rather than enhancing your website, a janky animation can make it look broken—distracting and irritating your users instead of captivating them.

To avoid the dreaded jank, you'll need to plan—and test—your animations carefully. There are often many ways to code a given effect, but browsers can optimize certain operations better than others.

Scalable Vector Animations

Animation adds a new dimension to web design: time. Not only do you need to know where to draw a given shape or piece of text, you need to know *when* to draw it.

Traditional film animation—the type pioneered by Walt Disney and other fledgling animation studios in the 1920s—involves drawing individual pictures (stills, or **frames**) for each moment in the animation. When the film roll switches from one frame to the next in quick sequence, you create the illusion of life and movement.

Animation frames are to time what pixels are to space: the smallest units of the graphic. Traditional animation and film are the time equivalents of a raster image. They divide up continuous time into a fixed number of intervals, and specify exactly what the image should look like at each point. Just like raster graphics have a fixed spatial resolution, so frame-based animation has a predefined temporal resolution, known as the **frame rate**.

You know by now that *vector* graphics are different from raster. Vector graphics specify paths in a theoretical mathematical coordinate space, and let the rendering engine (the web browser) convert that into pixels at whatever resolution they need.

Vector graphics define a path through space; it was only a short step to apply the same concept to describe a path through time. Specify the points—in space and time—that a graphic should pass through, and let the rendering engine calculate the individual frames.

The vector approach to animation on the web was first used successfully by Jonathon Gay in the mid-1990s for FutureSplash, which later became Flash. Taking a series of PostScript (vector) drawings, FutureSplash would calculate the transitional stages between the graphics, and render the interpolated states quickly via an animation engine.

Although it was a controversial decision at the time, the original SVG specs adopted vector animation principles in the form of dedicated animation elements. This set up SVG as an interactive, dynamic graphics language—and a competitor to Flash—rather than the static visual description it was originally conceived to be.

This "vector animation" approach is more commonly known as **declarative animation**. You *declare* in your code what you want the browser to do, and let it figure out how to make it so.

Declarative animation provides information on where and how an animated element should appear, but does not define every step. The code usually specifies the start and end points of an animation, and may set some rules for how to get from one to the other, but it relies on the browser to calculate the individual frames in between. For that reason, this approach is also known as **tweening**.

The concept is similar to the assembly-line approach Disney took later in his animation career, where **keyframes**—frames containing major poses—were drawn by lead animators. When the keyframes were complete, the work of drawing the remaining, in-between frames was handed off to apprentices. In declarative animation, the values you set in your code are the keyframes, and the computer is the apprentice.

 There are now two distinct syntaxes for declarative web animation: the SVG/SMIL animation elements, and CSS animations and transitions.

We'll review the main pros and cons of both in this chapter, but with a focus on the CSS approach, which has better browser support. The supplementary material has additional information about SVG/SMIL.

Within computer graphics, the opposite of declarative animation is often known as **procedural animation**. Procedural animation provides explicit, step-by-step instructions for how an animated graphic should look at each point in time.

That doesn't mean that you need to draw every frame ahead of time, like in a film or video. Procedural animation computer programs usually condense the drawing instructions by creating animation loops. An **animation loop** is any function that runs at regular intervals and updates the graphic to create an animated effect. For example, the function might add 1px to the x-position of a graphic every few microseconds. All the positions aren't saved ahead of time, but the code still provides an explicit instruction to the graphic at every step.

SVG has also always had procedural animation, in the form of Java-Script loops and callbacks that can modify the document at regular intervals. However, it's no coincidence that many JavaScript animation libraries abstract away the procedural details, allowing you to declare your animations in parameters to the library's methods. The library code becomes your apprentice, drawing the in-between frames and updating the DOM accordingly.

Similarly, the new Web Animations API is a declarative animation language that you can access from JavaScript. In addition to being built in to the browser, the API will have the benefit that it is the browser—not someone else's JavaScript code—that calculates the individual frames. That means that the frames can be updated independently from other JavaScript code and event-handling processes.

Smoothly Switching Styles

A few examples so far have included animation, in the form of **CSS animations or transitions**. The CSS syntax is easy to add as an enhancement, with just a few lines of code—perfect for when the animations were secondary to the main topic of an example. The CSS animation properties are also now familiar to many web developers, and they are fairly well supported in browsers.

Fairly well supported, but not universally. Particularly not for SVG.

 CSS animations and transitions aren't supported for SVG-specific properties in Internet Explorer (and aren't supported at all prior to IE10). Pre-2017 versions of MS Edge and Firefox did not support them in SVG embedded as images. Older versions of Blink and WebKit browsers (up to Safari 8) required a `-webkit-` prefix.

For detailed discussions of all the CSS animation and transition options, you'll need a dedicated book on the topic. Sarah Drasner's *SVG Animations* and Kirupa Chinnathambi's *Creating Web Animations* (both from O'Reilly) are good places to start. There's also good documentation on MDN.

This section will be a quick overview, and then a discussion of the pros and cons for animating SVG, compared to the other animation methods we'll be discussing in this chapter.

CSS animations come in two varieties, transitions and keyframe animations. Transitions are the simpler version, so we'll start with them.

CSS Transitions

CSS transitions tell the browser to apply any changes to specified style properties progressively, over a set period of time. The transition only applies if some other factor causes the style to change. Transitions don't change the styles themselves.

CSS transitions are applied to an element with the **transition shorthand property** or by longhand properties of the form `transition-*`:

- **transition-property** sets the name of the style property to transition, if its value is changed. It can be `all` for transitioning every property (but be careful of this getting out of hand), or `none` (the default) to not apply any transitions.

  The `transition-property` can also be a comma-separated list of property names. All the other transition properties can either be given in matching lists, or as a single value that will apply to all properties.

- **transition-duration** sets the length of time over which each property will be changed, in seconds (`s`) or milliseconds (`ms`). It's 0s by default, so no visible transition will be applied.

- **transition-delay** specifies an amount of time the browser should wait after the time when a new style value applies (for example, a `:hover` rule is triggered by a mouse-over), before starting the transition duration. It is useful for staggering changes to multiple properties, especially if one property cannot be smoothly transitioned.

- `transition-timing-function` describes the rate of change of the property value over the transition duration. There are various keyword values (including the default `ease`) and a `cubic-bezier()` function that allows you to specify the control points for a curve from (0,0) to (1,1).

  If none of the keywords create the effect you want, there are a number of websites that have copy-and-paste cubic Bézier functions, and Chrome and Firefox now both have visual timing-function editors in the dev tools.

The shorthand `transition` property sets all the values at once. For the timing values, the delay is always specified *after* a duration; other values can be set in any order, or omitted (which sets it to the default value). For a list of different transitions, each item in the list sets all the values for a particular transition property.

There are no SVG presentation attributes for any of these properties, or for the animation properties described in the next section. None of them are inherited by default.

In Chapter 7, we used transitions to smooth out `font-size` change for text labels that were resized based on media queries (Figure 7-4):

```
svg text { transition: font-size 0.5s; }
```

Not all properties can be smoothly transitioned through a set of continuous values, like `font-size` can. There is no halfway point between `font-family: Arial` and `font-family: Times`. Keyword values and other properties with no valid mid-point will flip from the old to the new value when the transition timing function passes the midway position.

Originally, the CSS Transitions spec had a limited list of transitionable properties, and `font-family` was not on it. The spec has since been updated so that nearly all properties can be animated, using the midway "flip" rule.

In browsers that don't support transitioning a given property, the change will apply immediately, instead of at the mid-point of the transition duration.

At the time of writing (mid-2017), Chrome and Firefox support the new rules, but Safari and MS Edge do not. Also beware: most resources on the web still refer to the old rules when discussing "animatable" CSS properties.

Even in the browsers that have updated, transitioning the transition-* properties doesn't work, and you can't transition the display property, either. Animations and transitions are only calculated for elements that are currently being displayed.

You can't transition to display: none, but you can transition to visibility: hidden. In SVG, the two are mostly equivalent, so visibility should be used if you want to add a transition effect before hiding an element. It works even in browsers that haven't been updated to the latest spec—visibility was always a transitionable property.

For example, to fade out an element, you could transition opacity to 0 over a 0.5s duration, and transition visibility to hidden with a 0s duration but 0.5s delay. That way, you get the accessibility benefits of properly hiding the element—so it can't receive keyboard and pointer events—but still have a smooth fade-out transition.

 You can't use 0 without units for duration and delay times; the CSS parser won't accept it as a valid declaration. Instead, always specify 0s or 0ms.

The following CSS would create that transition to apply whenever you added the aria-hidden="true" attribute to an element with JavaScript:

```
.may-be-hidden {
    transition-property: opacity, visibility;
    transition-duration: 0.5s, 0s;
}
.may-be-hidden[aria-hidden="true"] {
    opacity: 0;
    visibility: hidden;
    transition-delay: 0s, 0.5s;
}
```

The `transition-delay` for `visibility` is only applied *when* the element is in its hidden state. That means, when we *un*hide the element (remove the `aria-hidden` attribute), the delay won't apply anymore. The `visibility` will immediately turn back on, so that you can actually see the `opacity` transition.

In general, if you want a different transition—or no transition at all—for different directions of a state change, you change the transition properties as part of the same style rule that changes the values.

CSS Keyframe Animations

CSS animations are applied to an element with the **animation short-hand property** or by longhand properties of the form `animation-*`.

CSS animations are more specifically known as CSS keyframe animations, and also require an **@keyframes rule**. Animations apply a series of new property values to an element. The timing of the animation cycle is set in the animation properties on the element, but the new style values are defined in the `@keyframes` rule set.

The `@keyframes` rule set is identified by a custom name, which is followed by curly braces (`{}`) containing CSS rules. So the following defines an animation effect named `flicker`:

```
@keyframes flicker { /* keyframe rules go here */ }
```

You have a lot of flexibility in the names you can use (only CSS-wide keywords like `inherit` and `initial` are forbidden). However, try to avoid picking a name that could be confused for an animation-related keyword (like `alternate` or `backwards`), or your shorthand `animation` declarations might not work as expected.

Inside an `@keyframes` rule set, the individual rules mostly look like normal CSS style rules, but with one key (ahem) difference: keyframe selectors don't identify elements in the DOM, they identify positions in the animation cycle, as percentages of the animation duration time.

 The keywords `from` and `to` are also valid keyframe-rule selectors, where `from` equals 0% and `to` equals 100%.

To set the same style properties to apply at multiple points in the cycle, you can use a comma-separated selector list. This means that these rules define the flicker effect as one that starts and ends at full opacity but applies zero opacity at the halfway point:

```
@keyframes flicker {
    from, to { opacity: 1; }
    50%      { opacity: 0; }
}
```

If you don't specify the 0%/from or the 100%/to keyframe, both default to the current values on the element. So if your elements start at full opacity, this @keyframes rule is equivalent to the last one:

```
@keyframes flicker2 { 50% { opacity: 0; } }
```

In the original CSS animation draft—where only certain properties were animatable—nonanimatable properties specified in @keyframes rules were ignored completely. Under the latest spec, these properties "flip" from one value to the next when the timing function crosses the mid-point value, the same as for transitions.

The latest Chrome and Firefox support the new rules; other browsers ignore keyframe declarations for many properties that only have keyword values.

However, animation properties and display still can't be animated. If you use a CSS variable in an animation property, you also cannot animate that CSS variable. Otherwise, CSS variables are animated using the mid-point flip rule, since the browser doesn't know what the intermediate values should be.

Declaring @keyframes does not have any effect on its own. To actually make an element flicker with that animation, you would need to reference the name of that keyframe set in the element's animation properties.

There are eight longhand properties for animations:

- **animation-name** is the name you specified in the @keyframes rule (e.g., flicker), or a comma-separated list of multiple keyframe rules to apply. If it is a list, then you can give each animation its own distinct timing values, by giving the other properties as matching lists.

- **animation-duration** is the total time for one run of the keyframe cycle, from 0% to 100%.

- **animation-delay** is a wait time to apply from the time the animation rule applies to an element *or* the time the element is displayed in the document until the start of the first duration.

  The delay can be negative, which causes the animation to begin right away, partway through the animation cycle. We used negative animation delays for the stoplights in Example 1-8, so that the lights would be staggered, turning on at different times.

- **animation-direction** sets whether to apply the keyframes in normal order (0% to 100%), reverse order (100% to 0%), or to alternate back and forth in each iteration.

- **animation-timing-function** sets the transition timing function to be used between each keyframe value (that is, each rule in the @keyframes block). It defaults to ease.

  This is the only animation property that can be set within the keyframes rules, to give a unique timing function for the transition from that keyframe to the following one (in normal direction). So the following code creates alternating "in" and "out" eases between each keyframe:

```
.ball {
  animation-name: bounce;
  animation-duration: 5s;
  animation-timing-function: ease-in;
    /* default for each keyframe transition */
}
@keyframes bounce {
  /* start high, then each bounce is smaller */
  0% { transform: translateY(-50px); }
  20% { transform: translateY(-40px); }
  40% { transform: translateY(-30px); }
  60% { transform: translateY(-20px); }
  80% { transform: translateY(-10px); }
  10%, 30%, 50%, 70%, 90%, 100% {
    /* the bottom of each bounce */
    transform: translateY(0px);
    animation-timing-function: ease-out;
      /* applies to transition _after_ this state,
         i.e., for the upwards bounces */
  }
}
```

- **animation-iteration-count** is a number for how many times to repeat the keyframes cycle (default 1), or the keyword **infinite**.

- **animation-fill-mode** allows you to extend the final values of an animation after the animation is complete (**forwards**), to apply the initial values during the delay period before the animation starts (**backwards**), **both**, or **none** (the default).

- **animation-play-state** allows you to pause and restart an animation without resetting the values; the value is either **running** (the default) or **paused**.

You can also set all of the longhands using the **animation** shorthand, which takes a comma-separated list of complete animation descriptions. Just like with transitions, the duration time must always be given *before* the delay time, but otherwise the values can be given in any order. Any of the subproperties can also be omitted from any animation in the list, which sets it to the default value.

The stoplight animation from Chapter 1 (Example 1-8) used the following code to define the keyframes, the shared animation properties, and then the negative delays that cause each light to start at a different point in the cycle:

```
@keyframes cycle {
    33.3% { visibility: visible; }
    100%  { visibility: hidden;  }
}
.lit {
    animation: cycle 9s step-start infinite;
}
.red    .lit { animation-delay: -3s; }
.yellow .lit { animation-delay: -6s; }
.green  .lit { animation-delay:  0s; }
```

That **animation** shorthand is equivalent to the following longhands:

```
.lit {
    animation-name: cycle;
    animation-duration: 9s;
    animation-timing-function: step-start;
    animation-iteration-count: infinite;
    animation-delay: 0s; /* re-set to initial */
    animation-direction: normal;   /* re-set */
    animation-fill-mode: none;     /* re-set */
```

```
    animation-play-state: running;  /* re-set */
}
```

The `step-start` timing function forces all frame changes to be discrete switches from one value to the next. For `visibility`, that would happen anyway—since it can only take discrete values—but `step-start` forces the switch to happen at the beginning of each transition period instead of at the mid-point.

We also used CSS animations for some of the stroking examples in Chapter 13 and its supplementary material. In Example 13-8 (which cycled chain-link dashes around the shape) we used the following code:

```
    animation: cycle 0.5s 20 linear;
```

The `linear` timing function was essential to create the appearance of continuous movement, without any speeding up or slowing down during the 20 iterations.

In contrast, in the supplementary line-drawing example, we used an `ease-in` timing function, which caused the transitions (drawing the path and fading in the fill color) to start slowly but end sharply.

Although we didn't include the CSS code in Chapter 18, we also used CSS animations and transitions to enhance the confetti and gem collection games. Example 19-1 provides the CSS used in the final version of the figures (Figure 18-9). It assumes SVG text elements, but could easily be adapted for HTML elements.

Example 19-1. Enhancing a scripted SVG game with CSS animations and transitions

```
#gameboard {
    max-height: 100vh;
    max-width: 100%;
    background: #224;
}
.count { /* class for all the text elements */
    fill: lightYellow; /* or use `color` if using HTML text */
    font: 20px Consolas, monospace;
}
#timer, #scoreboard { /* the specific numbers being updated */
    font-size: 300%;
}
#scoreboard {
    transition: font-size 1s;           ❶
}
```

```css
.clicked {
    opacity: 0.1;
    pointer-events: none;
}
.miss {
    color: #88f;
    stroke: currentColor;
    stroke-width: 4px;
    stroke-opacity: 0.5;
    fill: currentColor;
    fill-opacity: 0.5;
    animation: flicker-fade ease-in-out 3s forwards;          ❷
}
@keyframes flicker-fade {
    from { opacity: 1;
        animation-timing-function: ease-out;                 ❸
    }
    60%  { opacity: 0.2; }
    70%  { opacity: 0.3; }
    80%  { opacity: 0.1; }
    90%  { opacity: 0.2; }
    to   { opacity: 0.0; visibility: hidden; }
}
#timer[aria-live] {
    animation: flash-color 0.3s alternate infinite;          ❹
}
@keyframes flash-color { /* again, use `color` for HTML text */
    to { fill: tomato; }                                     ❺
}

.game-over #scoreboard {
    font-size: 800%;
    animation: flash-color 0.5s 16 alternate;                ❻
}
.game-over .clickable { fill: black; }
.game-over .clicked {
    opacity: 1;
    filter: drop-shadow(0 0 3px gold);
}
```

❶ The first animation effect is a transition on font-size applied
to the scoreboard. The transition kicks in when we later change
the font-size is by adding the game-over class to the document.

❷ The elements with class miss were the circles adding to mark a
click that missed the game pieces. The animation (flicker-
fade) makes them fade to transparent a few seconds later, but
with a little bit of flickering before they disappear completely.

The `forwards` fill mode ensures that after the animation is complete they stay hidden indefinitely.

❸ Most of the keyframes in the `flicker-fade` set use the `ease-in-out` timing function set on the circles, but the first transition uses `ease-out` so that the very beginning of the animation sequence starts without any easing.

❹ In the JavaScript, during the last five seconds of the countdown we add the `aria-live` attribute to the timer. An attribute selector is used to add a matching visible `flash-color` effect, which alternates for as long as the `[aria-live]` selector matches the `#timer` element.

❺ Because we use `alternate` in the animation property, the keyframe effect itself is very simple, only setting the `to` frame. The animation therefore starts from the element's original `fill` color, transitions to `tomato` fill, and then transitions back in the next iteration.

❻ The same `flash-color` keyframe set is used to flash the scoreboard color after the game is over (starting while the scoreboard `font-size` is transitioning to 800%). This time, the flashes are a little slower (each on-off cycle taking 1s total, 0.5s in each direction), and there are a finite number of flashes (16 iterations).

By defining all the animation effects in the game using CSS, the JavaScript code was able to focus on the game logic and event handling. The classes and attributes set by the script are meaningful (semantic), not specific to particular styles. The entire game could be restyled, including the animation effects, without the JavaScript being changed.

Benefits and Limits of Animating SVG with CSS

Animating SVG—or any other web content—with CSS has a number of benefits. CSS transitions, in particular, are wonderful in their simplicity, often only requiring a single line of code to enhance an existing interactive project. Keyframe animations have a slightly more complicated syntax, but they are still fairly simple to write compared to the complexity of the effects you can create.

CSS animation effects also have performance benefits. Because the effects are declarative, the browser knows what future changes will be required, and can optimize rendering calculations to avoid repeating all the work every time it repaints the screen. It can also skip calculations entirely if it knows that an element is currently off-screen. And it can adjust the repaint frequency to prioritize other processing tasks, such as event handling. In many cases, the animation updates can run on a separate processor thread than JavaScript and events—or even on a separate processor, the GPU instead of the CPU.

You can usually create acceptable unanimated fallback in browsers that don't support CSS animations. If transitions are not supported, you just have instantaneous value changes. If keyframe animations are not supported, you get whatever base value you set on the element, with the keyframe declarations ignored. So the only extra effort is to ensure that those base values create an acceptable appearance and a functional website.

But CSS animations and transitions have their limitations. Limitations that are important for animated SVG include:

- They can only animate CSS properties. For SVG, that leaves out many attributes that you often want to animate. The possibilities will improve once there is better browser support for SVG geometry and transforms in CSS, but there is no spec yet for converting many SVG attributes to CSS properties.

  SVG features you *can't* animate with CSS, even in SVG 2, include `viewBox`, polygon/polyline `points`, filter parameters, and geometric attributes on text and graphical effects elements.

- Although an element can have multiple animations, you must set all animations (or all transitions) in the same property declaration. If you apply a different `animation` (or `transition`) property to the same element with a different CSS selector, one *replaces* the other. If you have two classes that apply independent animation effects, you'll need a separate rule for the combination of both classes:

```
.flicker { animation: flicker 0.3s infinite alternate; }
.grow    { animation: grow 5s forwards; }
.flicker.grow {
    animation: flicker 0.3s infinite alternate,
               grow 5s forwards;
}
```

If you do create a graphic with multiple interactive animations being set and removed by different classes, be sure to test carefully. There are now rules in the spec for how it should behave, but browsers may not have caught up.

- Similarly, there is no way for changes made by one animation effect to *add* to changes from another animation. If both animations are changing the opacity or the transform property on the same element, CSS cascade rules apply, and the last animation (in the animation-name list) wins out.

  To create a cumulative effect, you often need to add extra nested elements (e.g., <g> groups) to your DOM, one for each animation effect.

- You can't easily coordinate one animation effect to start after another animation finishes. You either need to string them all together in a single @keyframes rule set, or adjust the animation-delay on the second effect to always match the duration on the first effect—and then adjust the delay on a third effect to match the sum of durations of the first two effects, and so on.

  CSS variables and calc() will make this easier, but it can still be fussy for long animation sequences.

- You cannot set an animation to repeat at regular intervals with a delay between repeats; you need to incorporate the delay into the percentage values used in the @keyframes rule set.

- You cannot precisely coordinate animations on different elements. The animation timeline for each element starts (or restarts) when that element is added to the DOM, when it is given a display other than none, or when the animation effect is applied. If anything delays DOM or CSS parsing (or scripted execution), some elements will get a head start compared to others.

- You can pause animations easily, but trying to fast-forward or rewind animations by adjusting CSS properties is fussy and awkward.

In other words: CSS animations and transitions are wonderful for many effects, but they are not the solution for all your animation needs on the web.

Future Focus
Additive CSS Declarations

There are new proposals for creating a CSS syntax that would allow one declaration (such as in an animation) to add on to, or otherwise modify an underlying value. If implemented this would address some of the limitations mentioned in this section. However, this is still tentative, and it's not yet clear what this might look like, if it ever gets adopted.

Animations as Document Elements

The original syntax for declarative animation in SVG didn't use style properties to describe animations. Instead, each animation effect was an XML element of its own; the element's attributes define what should happen and when.

The SVG animation elements have features that solve some of CSS animation's limitations—but, of course, they also have limitations of their own.

SVG animation elements are based on **SMIL**, the Synchronized Multimedia Integration Language. SMIL was part of the flurry of XML language proposals from the late 1990s. It was orginally conceived as a way to coordinate on-screen events with music (thus the name), but evolved over time to become a declarative way to indicate when specific animation events should occur.

 You *don't* need to worry about a new XML namespace to use the SVG/SMIL animation elements. The relevant elements were all redefined in the SVG namespace.

The SVG version of SMIL provides a somewhat more limited subset of the full specification, but it provides enough for handling reasonably simple animation and even a certain degree of interactivity.

The biggest limitation for SVG animation elements is browser support. Internet Explorer and MS Edge have never supported them. The wider, non-SVG version of SMIL never caught on. And as CSS animations become popular, the Chrome team announced that they would be deprecating SVG/SMIL. Starting in Chrome 45, web pages using the elements showed warnings in the Chrome developer's console.

The Chrome team have since put deprecation on hold, and the browser still runs the animations without complaint. But the temporary deprecation was enough to ruin any chance (for now) to get SVG/SMIL support in MS Edge. Optimizations and improvements in existing browser implentations are also low priority, as are any new spec proposals.

This doesn't mean that an SVG element that incorprates SMIL animation won't show in IE or Edge: only that the *animation* won't be shown. The initial, default state of the SVG will still be seen in Microsoft browsers.

SMIL is very powerful, but its lack of support relegates it to the "interesting, useful, but probably not for production in most websites" category. There are JavaScript polyfills, but none that can compare to the performance of the best JavaScript animation libraries.

For the web, only use SVG/SMIL animation elements for nonessential enhancements to your graphics. In particular, use it when CSS animations cannot create your desired effect, and when scripting isn't a practical option (such as for SVG used as an image).

The following sections, and the online supplementary material, provide a basic introduction to the syntax, with a focus on features that can't be achieved with CSS animations and transitions.

Animating Attributes, Declaratively

The primary SMIL animation element, conveniently named `<animate>`, can modify nearly any attribute or style property on another SVG element. It can switch instantly between values or transition smoothly between them, and can do it at a fixed time, in response to a DOM event, or chained after another animation.

In the simplest case, `<animate>` provides an interpolation service. You specify the attribute or style property you want to change, the value you want to change it to, and the duration (length of time) it should take to get there.

The browser determines in-between values between the "base" value set on the shape and the to value set in the animation, and updates the attribute for every frame as the animation proceeds. This is the same as CSS transitions, except that the attribute you're changing does not need to have a CSS equivalent.

For instance, suppose that you wanted to show a circle that grows from a dot to a certain size. That would be animating the r attribute from 0 to the full size. The code for defining that animation with `<animate>` is given in Example 19-2.

Example 19-2. Simple animation using <animate>

```
<svg xmlns="http://www.w3.org/2000/svg" xml:lang="en"
    xmlns:xlink="http://www.w3.org/1999/xlink"
    width="100%" height="100%" viewBox="-200 -200 400 400">
    <title>Animated Circle</title>
    <circle r="0"
            fill="darkOrchid" stroke="plum" stroke-width="16">
        <animate attributeName="r" to="190"
                 dur="5s" fill="freeze" end="10s"/>
    </circle>
</svg>
```

The `<animate>` element, by default, animates its *parent* element. So we include it as a *child* of the `<circle>` element.

Alternatively, you can give an explicit target element for the animation by using an xlink:href attribute to cross-reference the target's id. The examples in the supplementary material include this approach.

Most of the attributes on the <animate> in Example 19-2 are mostly self-explanatory:

- **attributeName** specifies the name of the attribute we want to change (here, r, the circle's radius). The "attribute" can also be a style property.

- **to** specifies the new value that we want to transition the attribute to.

- **dur** defines the duration of the animation (here, 5 seconds). Durations are by default infinite, which means that if you don't specify a duration, nothing will change in your lifetime. Durations can be in seconds (s), milliseconds (ms), or even minutes (min) or hours (h), or a combination like 03:30 (3 minutes, 30 seconds).

The confusing attribute in Example 19-2 is probably fill="freeze".

This **fill attribute** comes from SMIL, not SVG, and has nothing to do with the fill color of the circle. Instead, it tells the browser how to "fill up" any extra time after the duration of the animation completes. The freeze value says to keep the last value of the animation "frozen in time" indefinitely, unless another animation replaces the value.

 The SMIL fill is therefore the equivalent of the CSS animation-fill-mode property, although the allowed values are different.

The default for SMIL's fill is remove, which means that once the animation is over, the animated effect is removed. The attribute reverts to the base value set on the element. Here, that would revert our circle down to nothing.

And that's a problem. Freezing the value is all very well for browsers that applied the animation, but without SVG/SMIL support Example 19-2 is a picture of an empty screen.

To design animations with acceptable fallback, you need the base values to create an acceptable static graphic. This usually means setting the base value to whatever value you were going to "freeze" in place anyway.

Then, how do you create an entry or reveal animation? With the **from attribute**, which gives an explicit starting value for the animation:

```
<circle r="190"
        fill="darkOrchid" stroke="plum" stroke-width="16">
    <animate attributeName="r" from="0" to="190"
             dur="5s" />
</circle>
```

Note that the to attribute on <animate> is still required. Unlike in CSS, to in SVG/SMIL does not default to the base value.

Complex Animations

A single from-to <animate> effect isn't terribly impressive. But you can create complex combinations of different animation elements, animating the same or different properties, on the same or different elements, simultaneously or in sequence. An individual <animate> element can also have multiple values (similar to CSS keyframes) and repeats.

More Online

The wide variety of SVG/SMIL animation options are controlled by interacting sets of attributes, which offer numerous ways to define the timing and progression of each animation effect.

Read more, including examples of building complex animations from multiple interacting animation elements, in "Using SVG/SMIL Animation Elements":

https://oreillymedia.github.io/Using_SVG/extras/ch19-SMIL.html

In addition to <animate>, there are three other SVG/SMIL animation elements:

- **<set>** applies a discrete change, *setting* an attribute to a different value for a specified duration.

- **<animateTransform>** applies a specific transformation function (translate, rotate, scale, skew, or matrix).

- **<animateMotion>** applies a complex transformation, defined not with transformation functions but by the route, or **motion path**, that you want the element to follow as it moves. The motion path can reference an existing SVG <path> element, by using a child <mpath> element to create the cross-reference.

The <animateMotion> effect is one of the highlights of SVG/SMIL, allowing the creation of elegant effects with a simple, declarative format.

Example 19-3 uses <animateMotion> to create an infinitely repeating animation, such as you might use for a loader image (a placeholder image for when you are loading other content). It also demonstrates a few more of the SVG/SMIL animation timing attributes. Figure 19-1 shows three different stages of the animation —but you'll need to run the code to get the full effect.

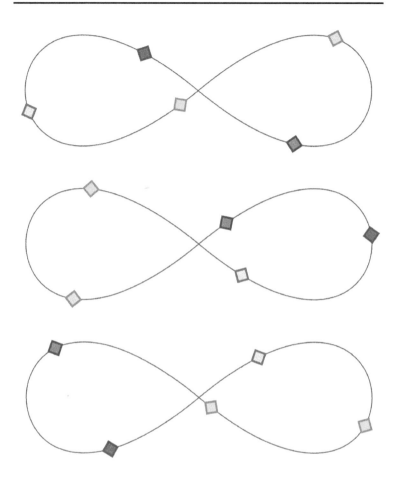

Figure 19-1. Three stages of an infinite animation of shapes moving around a path

Example 19-3. Animating motion along a path

```
<svg xmlns="http://www.w3.org/2000/svg" xml:lang="en"
    xmlns:xlink="http://www.w3.org/1999/xlink"
    viewBox="0 0 400 160" width="4in" height="1.6in">
    <title>Motion on a Path, with &lt;animateMotion&gt;</title>
    <defs>
        <polygon id="bead" points="-8,0 0,-8 8,0 0,8"
                stroke-width="2" />                        ❶
    </defs>
    <path id="track" fill="none" stroke="dimGray"
```

```
        d="M200,80 C-50,280 -50,-120 200,80
                  C450,280 450,-120 200,80Z" />          ❷
<use xlink:href="#bead" fill="orchid" stroke="indigo">
    <animateMotion dur="5s" repeatDur="indefinite"
                rotate="auto">                            ❸
        <mpath xlink:href="#track"/>                      ❹
    </animateMotion>
</use>
<use xlink:href="#bead" fill="gold" stroke="tomato">
    <animateMotion dur="5s" repeatDur="indefinite"
                rotate="auto" begin="-1s">                ❺
        <mpath xlink:href="#track"/>
    </animateMotion>
</use>
<use xlink:href="#bead" fill="springGreen" stroke="seaGreen">
    <animateMotion dur="5s" repeatDur="indefinite"
                rotate="auto" begin="-2s">
        <mpath xlink:href="#track"/>
    </animateMotion>
</use>
<use xlink:href="#bead" fill="skyBlue" stroke="mediumBlue">
    <animateMotion dur="5s" repeatDur="indefinite"
                rotate="auto" begin="-3s">
        <mpath xlink:href="#track"/>
    </animateMotion>
</use>
<use xlink:href="#bead" fill="indianRed" stroke="firebrick">
    <animateMotion dur="5s" repeatDur="indefinite"
                rotate="auto" begin="-4s">
        <mpath xlink:href="#track"/>
    </animateMotion>
</use>
</svg>
```

❶ The objects that we're going to move along the path will be
<use> copies of a predefined <polygon> "beads." The polygon is
a square centered on the origin and rotated so that the corners
of the square are positioned on the x- and y-axes.

❷ The path (which we'll move the beads along) consists of two
teardrop-shaped cubic Bézier curve segments on either side of
the center point. The result is a sideways figure 8, otherwise
known as an infinity symbol. The path is drawn visibly in the
SVG, with a thin gray stroke.

❸ Each <use> copy of the bead contains an <animateMotion> element that defines a 5-second animation that loops indefinitely.
By default, the animation duration will be the time it takes to

complete a full loop of the path. The `rotate` attribute tells our beads to rotate to match the path.

❹ The `<path>` element is referenced from the `<mpath>` element within the `<animateMotion>`.

❺ The subsequent beads are similar, except for different colors on the `<use>`, and a different `begin` value on the animation element. Just like with CSS animations, negative start times can be used to start an animation partway through its cycle.

The code for Example 19-3 amply demonstrates a significant limitation of the SVG/SMIL syntax: it is not DRY at all. Each `<animateMotion>` element is almost identical, but the attributes and child `<mpath>` element all need to be repeated. There is no equivalent to the cross-references used in SVG patterns and gradients to make one effect a template for another.

OK, theoretically there's a way to reduce repetition, by using custom XML DOCTYPE declarations to set default attribute values for elements of a given tag name. But if you don't already know what that means, you probably don't want to.

For `<animateMotion>` in particular, an important limitation is that you can't easily include a fallback static position for unsupporting browsers. The extra transformation from the motion effect is *added* to whatever position or transformation the element already had; it doesn't replace a base attribute. Without SMIL support, all the beads are drawn centered over the origin of the SVG.

We'll consider another—cross-browser compatible—way to create this effect in the section on scripted animations.

CSS Versus SVG
Motion Paths in CSS

Motion along a path is one of the most popular features of SVG/SMIL. In order for CSS animations to compete, there needed to be a way to do the same with CSS.

The CSS Motion Path module defines a series of properties:

- `offset-path` and `offset-position` define the path to use as the motion path, and position it within the parent container or SVG coordinate system.

- `offset-distance` specifies how far along the path the current element should be positioned.

- `offset-anchor` defines the position in the current element that should be positioned exactly on the path (similar to `transform-origin`, or the `refX` and `refY` attributes of markers).

- `offset-rotate` sets whether to autorotate the element to match the angle of the path.

- `offset` is a shorthand that sets all of the above.

The actual *motion* would come from animating the `offset-distance` property, using the regular CSS animation or transition syntax. However, the same `offset` properties could be used to create *static* layouts of elements positioned along a path.

> The original draft of the spec used property names starting with `motion-*`. They were changed to `offset-*` to reflect the fact that the properties themselves describe static positions, not motion.

Drawing shapes at offset distances along a path is also included in the new SVG Markers proposals. The difference with `offset-path` is that the positioned objects would be fully accessible and interactive elements, not decorations on the path. For example, you could position highway-sign labels on a map, and still have the highway number be accessible text.

At the time of writing, there is an experimental implementation of the `offset` properties in Chrome, although it does not support the full spec.

Benefits and Limits of SVG/SMIL Animation Elements

The SVG/SMIL animation elements have a number of capabilities that CSS animations and transitions don't, some of which we've covered here and some of which we describe in the supplementary material:

- They can animate attributes, not only styles.
- Many independent animations can be set on the same element, and animations of the same property can be additive.
- Progressive animations can be defined as accumulative repeats.
- Animations on the same *or* different elements can be synchronized or chained together, optionally with time offsets.
- By tying an element's begin time to its own end time, plus an offset, you can create animations that repeat after a delay.
- You can specify the number of repeats in terms of the total animation time instead of as a repeat count.
- Animation times are coordinated for the entire document; with JavaScript, you can pause or reset all animations in sync.
- Animations (or <set> changes to any value) can be triggered by any DOM event, not only the ones that create CSS pseudo-classes.
- You can animate the display property (although, for SVG, display is only a benefit relative to visibility if you are hiding and showing text spans).

However, the syntax also has some limitations compared to CSS:

- Each animation element can only animate a single target element, and there's no easy way to copy attributes from one animation to another. This means a *lot* of repeated code for many designs.
- There is no shorthand way to create alternating animations, or animations *from* a specified value to the base value specified on the element, so you end up repeating values.
- There are no keyword easing (timing) functions, there's no way to create bounce/overshoot easings without adding extra values, and there is no way to specify that the same easing

should apply for multiple transitions in a `values` list. Overall, the easing syntax is just painful to use compared to CSS.

- Applying a backward fill to a delayed animation requires a separate `<set>` element.

- You cannot easily pause individual animation effects in process.

- Transitions to and from a state that can last an indefinite amount of time (e.g., a hover effect, or a toggle button) are very difficult to coordinate using the event-triggered timing model.

But of course the biggest limitation of the animation elements is the lack of support in Microsoft browsers. This limits their practical use on the web, which means that other browsers don't have a strong incentive to improve their implementations. Bugs accumulate and performance is ignored.

The solution in most cases is JavaScript, which we'll discuss in the next section.

But JavaScript does not work in SVG used as images, or in some non-web SVG applications. And it is often overkill for simple decorative animations that can be defined in a few lines of SVG/SMIL code.

That means there is still a use for SVG/SMIL on the web, but not as the centerpiece of an animated web interface.

Scripting Every Frame

Anything you can do with SVG/SMIL and CSS animations you can do with JavaScript, because JavaScript can modify every attribute and style property on any element. JavaScript can also animate text content, not only its visibility. Scripts can create or delete elements, and can rearrange the order of elements in the DOM, which is needed—for now—to simulate `z-index` changes in SVG.

The downside—for now—is that your script needs to tell the browser what to draw at every single frame of the animation, not only at the keyframes. And those calculations normally run in the main JavaScript thread, which can conflict with other code that you have running.

At its most basic, animating your document with JavaScript is just updating attributes or style properties to new values. We've already done that in many different examples. But in order to transition those changes, like you can with CSS and SMIL animations, you don't want the full change to happen all at once. Instead, you need to spread out those updates over the duration of the animation.

To create the appearance of *continuous* change, the updates need to be made faster than the human eye can detect the individual changes. Just like the difference between a slideshow and a film, the secret to creating moving pictures is to change the graphic frequently, but only a little bit each time.

 The accepted standard for "continuous" animation on the web is 60 frames per second (fps), or about 16ms betweeen updates. But this is only a rough approximation.

If the updates from one frame to the next are subtle, you can get away with a lower frame rate (that is, longer time between updates) and it will still look continuous. However, if the updates involve significant changes—like moving long distances across the screen—even 60fps can look jumpy. You may need to soften the change with a motion blur effect, to create the appearance of smooth motion.

Continuous scripted animations therefore require repeated code that runs at regular intervals, updating values a little bit at each iteration. That means we need two things:

- an animation update function that will keep track of all the in-progress animations, and calculate and apply the current values based on the current time
- a timer function that will call our update function at regular intervals

Together, these create our animation loop.

The animation update functions can be as simple or as creative as you like. We'll give some basic examples, but we can't cover all the possibilities. But the timer functions are what drive your custom JavaScript animation, and there are only a few options for them.

Future Focus
Declarative Scripted Animations

The Web Animations API aims to address some of the main limitations of Java-Script animation. It allows you to create animation effects in JavaScript, with a declarative syntax that is logically similar to CSS and SMIL animations. The browser would then calculate the individual frames on its own, the same as it does for declarative animation. Your JavaScript code would have full control over *when* the animations run, but the API includes chaining options and universal timeline control, similar to SMIL.

The Web Animations API was inspired by the syntax of existing JavaScript animation libraries, which nearly all provide declarative API methods. Those animation libraries also do their best to optimize the frame-by-frame code for you —some more successfully than others.

But even the best JS libraries have limitations compared to a native browser API. They don't have access to the dedicated browser-rendering threads, and the library code requires extra resources to download and process.

The Web Animations API is part of a larger Web Animations specification (*https://w3c.github.io/web-animations/*), which aims to provide a consistent underlying model for *all* the native web-browser animation options: CSS, SMIL, and JavaScript.

At the time of writing, the Web Animations API only includes animation of CSS style properties. An earlier syntax for animating attribute values was dropped from the level 1 spec (but might be reintroduced later). Future levels of Web Animations are also expected to include ways to link animation progression to scroll or touch-gesture events, instead of requiring fixed time durations.

As of mid-2017, the core `animate()` method has been implemented in Chrome/Blink and in Firefox. You currently need a polyfill (*https://github.com/web-animations/web-animations-js*) for support in WebKit and IE/Edge, and for more advanced methods.

Triggering Regular Updates

In Chapter 2, we used JavaScript to animate our stoplight graphic. It wasn't a *continuous* animation, but it was an animation. The update function (`cycle()` in Example 2-2) changed which versions of the lights were visible to create the effect of one light switching off and another light switching on.

To trigger our cycle updates once every 3 seconds, we used the `setInterval()` **JavaScript function**. We also used `setInterval()` in Chapter 18, to update the countdown timer in our game.

The `setInterval()` function is a core JavaScript function. It takes two parameters: a function object and a time in milliseconds. The browser will then run that function repeatedly until the interval is cancelled, with a delay between runs of approximately the number of milliseconds you specify.

 You cancel a previously set interval with the `clearInterval()` method, passing it the token that was returned when you initially called `setInterval()`. Example 18-5 includes a `clearInterval()` after the timer is complete.

`setInterval()` and the similar, but nonrepeating `setTimeout()` used to be the only options available for regularly updating Java-Script animations.

If you're creating a discrete animation that only updates every few seconds—like the stoplight—then `setInterval()` is still a great choice.

The problem comes when you want to update your animation frequently, like every 16ms for a 60fps continuous animation. `setInterval()` is a little too bossy. The browser will try to keep up with that interval even if it has other code to run, and even if the web page is currently in a nonactive browser tab (although browsers are changing both behaviors, to keep interval-based code from locking up your computer completely).

Even the every-100ms update we used for the timer in Example 18-5 (10fps) is getting a little too frequent for `setInterval()`.

If the timer code were more complicated, and the game were inline in a web page with a lot else going on, there could be noticeable lags. If the timer ran indefinitely—instead of for max 15 seconds—it could slow down your browser if you left it open in a background tab.

Modern browsers have a better solution for triggering animation updates: `requestAnimationFrame()`.

The **`requestAnimationFrame()` method** asks the browser to run a function—which you specify as a parameter—the next time the browser is ready to update the visual rendering of this web page.

If the web page is currently in a nonactive browser tab, the function won't run until the user switches back to view the page. When the page is visible, the browser will adjust how frequently it updates, to provide a balance between animation smoothness and overall performance.

`requestAnimationFrame()` is supported in most browsers you need to worry about, but you may want to add a polyfill script for Internet Explorer 9 and Android 4.3 and under—for example, Paul Irish's version (*https://gist.github.com/paulirish/1579671*).

A polyfill converts your modern code into `setTimeout()` loops for the older browsers.

The behavior of `requestAnimationFrame()` is closer to `setTimeout()` than `setInterval()`: by default, it runs the function only once. If you want the animation to continue, your update function itself needs to request another frame.

Because you don't know exactly *when* your function will run, or how frequently, you'll need to check the current time in your update code. You could do this by grabbing the `Date.now()` system timestamp, but the browser passes a dedicated animation timestamp as a parameter to your update function.

The timestamps passed to animation functions are *not* interchangeable with the system time used in `Date.now()` timestamps. Instead, they are measured since the document was loaded or refreshed.

If you have multiple animation functions, they'll all get the exact same timestamp value for the same animation frame.

The following code adapts our timer code in Example 18-5 to use animation frames instead of fixed intervals, and to use the animation timestamp instead of Date.now():

```
var endTime;
requestAnimationFrame(updateTime);
function updateTime(t) {
    if (!endTime) {
        endTime = t + timeLimit*1000;
    }
    var timeLeft = endTime - t;
    if (timeLeft <= 0) {
        endGame();
        timeLeft = 0;
    }
    else {
        requestAnimationFrame(updateTime);
    }
    timer.textContent = (timeLeft/1000).toFixed(1);
}
```

The initial request (outside of the update function) starts the animation running. The function then requests additional animation frames until the time expires.

The timer won't run in the background if you switch to a different browser tab, but the time will be correct if you switch back to this tab.

However, because we are now relying on the animation loop itself for the timestamps, our timer only starts when the first frame of the animation is painted, not when the initial request was made. If you need an independent start time, you can use the performance.now() method to get a compatible timestamp outside of the animation loop.

Browser support for the performance object isn't quite as good as for requestAnimationFrame(). If you use it, you may need to polyfill it as well.

As before, the updateTime() function checks whether the time has run out. The request for the new animation frame only runs if that *isn't* true, so the loop will stop automatically when the timer reaches 0. Note also that the new request isn't the last line of the function. It doesn't need to be; it is only queuing the request to run later.

There is also a `cancelAnimationFrame()` **method**, which you can use instead of adding an `if` test in your animation loop. Similar to `clearInterval()`, it requires a token value that is returned when you call `requestAnimationFrame()`:

```
/* in the updateTime() function... */
frame = requestAnimationFrame(updateTime);

/* separately */
function stopTimer() {
    if (frame) { cancelAnimationFrame(frame); }
}
```

`requestAnimationFrame()` isn't perfect. It only runs if the browser is repainting the web page, but it doesn't include a check for whether the *part* of the web page you're updating is currently visible. If you've got many inline SVGs within a large web page, you'll want to add your own check to determine which ones are onscreen and therefore need updating.

Beyond that, the main limitation of `requestAnimationFrame()` animations—compared to CSS, SMIL, most JS animation libraries, or the future Web Animations API—is that you need to write your own code to calculate the updated graphic at each frame. That makes it incredibly flexible. But it can be easy to get tangled up in all that flexibility.

Calculating the Current Value

Broadly speaking, there are two main approaches to calculating animation progression:

Interpolation
Interpolation animation is the type of tweening animation used by CSS animations and transitions, SVG/SMIL, and the Web Animations API (level 1, anyway). The animation is defined by the amount of change that you want to apply, and the amount of time that it should take.

To create your own interpolation function, you convert the current time into a proportion of the animation duration, and then convert that into a proportion of the distance between your initial and final values. The conversion from time percentage to value percentage can be **linear** (one-to-one, the easiest choice), or it can use an **easing function**, equivalent to the timing functions used in CSS animations and transitions.

Physics-based animation
Used primarily for motion, physics-based animation defines the properties of the moving objects (particularly their speed and acceleration), and calculates their motion from that. The "physics" used in the animation calculation can be as realistic or as simplistic as you want. How long it takes the objects to reach a given position is determined entirely from the calculations you use.

Physics-based motion is preferred in games, where you don't want everything to be predetermined. In games, you will often change the properties of the objects—such as their speed or their direction—based on user interaction or randomization.

There is really no end to the possible calculations you could integrate into an animation loop. So we're not going to try to discuss them here. There are plenty of other good resources on game and animation design if you are interested.

Instead, as a simple example of a JavaScript animation loop, we're going to recreate our motion-along-a-path graphic from Example 19-3.

This is an interpolated animation, since we know exactly how we want the "bead" elements to move, and how long they should take. Specifically, we are interpolating the *distance* along the path. Each bead should move the same distance along the path in the same time period, completing a full loop every 5 seconds (which was the dur in our <animateMotion> elements).

To transform our beads into the correct position, we therefore need to figure out the (*x,y*) position of a point that is a certain distance along the path. That sounds like a lot of math, but luckily the browser does it for us.

The <path> element has a method called **getPointAtLength()**. (In SVG 2, all the other basic shape elements will have the method, too.) You pass in a distance in user units (px), and you get back a point object with x and y properties for the coordinates of that point on the path.

The point object is the same as the ones we used in Chapter 18 to calculate transformations on mouse-click points. Depending on the browser, the object will either be called SVGPoint or DOMPoint.

We also want to *rotate* our beads to match the angle of the path. Unfortunately, there is no getAngleAtLength() method for paths. So we need to do a *little* bit of math ourselves.

By getting two different points from the path—close to each other but not identical—we can calculate the approximate rate of change of the curve at that point. The relative *x* and *y* change can then be converted to a tangent angle, using a little bit of trigonometry (an arc-tangent function, to be precise).

Example 19-4 provides the code. The visual result is the same as Figure 19-1.

Example 19-4. Animating motion along a path, with JavaScript

```
<svg xmlns="http://www.w3.org/2000/svg" xml:lang="en"
    xmlns:xlink="http://www.w3.org/1999/xlink"
    viewBox="0 0 400 160" width="4in" height="1.6in">
    <title>Motion on a Path, with JavaScript</title>
    <defs>
        <polygon id="bead" points="-8,0 0,-8 8,0 0,8"
                stroke-width="2" />
    </defs>
    <path id="track" fill="none" stroke="dimGray"
        d="M200,80 C-50,280 -50,-120 200,80
                C450,280 450,-120 200,80Z" />            ❶
    <use xlink:href="#bead" fill="orchid" stroke="indigo" />
    <use xlink:href="#bead" fill="gold" stroke="tomato" />
    <use xlink:href="#bead" fill="springGreen" stroke="seaGreen" />
    <use xlink:href="#bead" fill="skyBlue" stroke="mediumBlue" />
    <use xlink:href="#bead" fill="indianRed" stroke="firebrick" />
    <script><![CDATA[
(function(){
var track = document.getElementById("track"),        ❷
    trackLength = track.getTotalLength(),
    beads = document.querySelectorAll("[*|href='#bead']"),   ❸
    nBeads = beads.length,
    dur = 5000; //duration of one loop of track, in ms

function update(time) {
    var t = (time % dur)/dur, /* position in repeat cycle */   ❹
```

```
        distance, /* distance along the path for this bead */
        point,    /* SVGPoint for that distance */
        point2;   /* SVGPoint for a slightly different distance */
    for (var i=0; i<nBeads; i++) {
        distance = trackLength * ( (t + i/nBeads) % 1 );        ❺
        point = track.getPointAtLength(distance);               ❻
        point2 = track.getPointAtLength((distance+2)%trackLength);
        angle = Math.atan2( (point2.y - point.y),
                            (point2.x - point.x) );             ❼
        beads[i].setAttribute("transform",
            "translate(" + [point.x, point.y] + ")"
            + "rotate(" + angle*180/Math.PI + ")" );            ❽

    }
    requestAnimationFrame(update);      ❾
}
requestAnimationFrame(update);          ❿
})();
]]> </script>
</svg>
```

❶ The markup is the same as Example 19-3, except that we've removed all the animation elements. The <use> elements are by default all drawn centered on the origin; we will be transforming them into place.

❷ We save the track path in a variable, since we'll need it for the distance calculations, but we also save its total length in a variable, since the path itself isn't changing. The getTotalLength() method is the same one we used in Chapter 13 for calculating dash lengths.

❸ We also select the bead elements ahead of time, using the namespace-insensitive version of a CSS attribute selector. Since the number of beads isn't changing, we save that to a variable, too, to save us one more step in each loop of our update function.

❹ The first step of each update() is to convert the timestamp into a value between 0 and 1, representing the proportion of the animation cycle. Because it's an infinitely repeating animation, we don't have to worry about exact start times. Instead, the modulus (%) operator finds the amount by which the timestamp exceeds an even number of dur cycles. Division converts that to a proportion.

⑤ The remainder of the calculations are done separately for each bead. The beads are evenly staggered along the track, so that bead number 4 out of 5 is 4/5 farther along the path than the first bead. The modulus operator again comes in handy to handle wraparounds, for beads that are so far ahead they are behind again. The saved `trackLength` scales up the proportions of the path to actual px distances.

⑥ Once we have the calculated distance, we can get the point object from the `<path>` element—and then we get the point 2px farther ahead (with modulus for the wraparound), so we can calculate the tangent angle.

⑦ The `Math.atan2()` function calculates a tangent angle (in radians) from two parameters: the change in y-value and the change in x-value (in that order).

⑧ Using our primary point and our calculated angle, we can therefore set the `transform` attribute on our bead: first a translation to the correct point, then a rotation to the correct angle. Because the `transform` attribute needs angles in degrees (but the JavaScript trigonometry functions use radians), we need a little more math to do the conversion: 180° equals π radians.

⑨ At the end of the `update()` function, we request that the browser do it all again at the next frame.

⑩ Finally (and most importantly), we start the loop running by requesting the first animation frame, from our main procedure function.

This version of the animation runs in every browser, including MS Edge and Internet Explorer. But if you want to use it as a loader, remember to embed it with `<object>`, not `<img>`, or copy it as inline SVG: the script won't run at all in SVG used as an image.

More Online

There are many different ways to approach the same animation—how do you choose? Browser support is one factor, but browser performance is equally important. Just because the browser understands your animation instructions does not mean that it will render the animated effect smoothly.

Read more about performance considerations, and planning your animation, in "Planning for Performance":

> *https://oreillymedia.github.io/Using_SVG/extras/ch19-performance.html*

It includes an introduction to the `will-change` property and a practical example of redesigning an animation to create smoother transitions.

Summary: Animation

SVG used in web browsers is dynamic, able to change over time. Animated SVG can consist of predetermined, noninteractive loops —the vector equivalent of animated GIFs. But animated SVG can also be part of complex interactive games and documents, giving feedback to user actions and providing continuity through content changes.

CSS animations and transitions are now the first choice for many simple animations. They have an easy-to-use syntax and are fairly well supported in browsers—and familiar to many web developers. However, they cannot be used to animate many SVG attributes, or for complex animation sequences.

The SVG/SMIL animation elements are incredibly flexible for defining animations, including attribute animations, synchronized sequences of animations, and complex motion animations. However, they have never reached full cross-browser support, and can be buggy even where supported.

For complex interactive animations, and for anything where browser support is essential, you can animate your SVG document with JavaScript. If you're adding a lot of animation, there are dedicated JavaScript libraries to help you do so efficiently. The Web Animations API also makes simple animations easier, although it still requires a polyfill library for complete browser support.

However you choose to animate your document, you'll need to consider the design of your animation carefully to ensure good performance.

You also need to design your animations carefully to consider usability. We haven't discussed design and usability in this chapter, but we cover a few points as part of our best practice guidelines in Chapter 20.

More Online

The SVG/SMIL animation elements and their attributes are summarized in the "Animation Elements" section of the markup guide:

https://oreillymedia.github.io/Using_SVG/guide/ markup.html#animation

The DOM methods used in this chapter are included in the "Select SVG DOM Methods and Objects" guide:

https://oreillymedia.github.io/Using_SVG/guide/DOM.html

For CSS animations, refer back to "Smoothly Switching Styles" on page 728, or consult the CSS specifications (*https://drafts.csswg.org/*) or MDN (*https://developer.mozilla.org/en-US/docs/Web/CSS*).

CHAPTER 20

Good Manners

Best Practices for SVG

An image is more than just a collection of details, and a complex SVG document is more than just a series of independent elements and styles. When you are starting a project, it is worthwhile to take some time to plan your approach.

This chapter summarizes some of our best advice for managing SVG on the web. If you are building an important website component using SVG, a little bit of up-front strategy and analysis can help save time and frustration later.

Planning Your Project

Got a great idea for a design, a game, an unusual interface widget? Wonderful! Time to bring it to life!

But before you start writing code—even before you start drawing in Illustrator or Sketch—make a plan. You aren't just creating a picture, you're building a product. It needs to work for your end users, and it needs to be maintainable and adaptable for future design changes.

Does Your Project Need SVG at All?

It may seem strange to ask this question in a book devoted to SVG, but, as much as we love vector graphics, we also understand that it isn't applicable to absolutely *everything* in web design and development.

If your diagram can be represented as colored squares on a web page, it's usually easier to create it using HTML elements with a little CSS, rather than using an inline SVG. You can even make the elements quickly scalable by using % or vw units for width and height.

When SVG first became available in web browsers, it replaced 1px-wide repeating raster images as the best solution for background gradients. It was also the easiest solution for rounded rectangles and circles. But CSS gradients and `border-radius` have rightly replaced both use cases.

Throughout the book, we've been comparing SVG and CSS-only solutions so you can make better decisions about which tool to use. If your all-CSS approach involves multiple nested elements, transforms, and hidden overflow to draw a shape that could be defined with a simple SVG `<polygon>`, this is a good time for SVG.

But if you can create the effect with well-supported CSS properties on the elements you've got, you can skip the SVG. We won't be offended.

While SVG's abilities extend well beyond those of CSS-only graphics, SVG must be considered as part of the *continuum* of web technologies, never as a sole answer.

Similarly, once an SVG drawing is started, there's a tendency to create *everything* inside it. But the best solution may sometimes be a hybrid one. Create a graph in SVG, but add text labels as HTML elements. Or use multiple separate `<svg>` elements and then combine them with CSS layout so they can be easily rearranged. You've now got a firm handle on a new tool for your toolbox, but that doesn't mean it should be the only tool you use.

Identify Your Browser Support Requirements

When building for the web, you are designing for an uncertain environment. The code you generate will be rendered differently depending on which web browser views it, in which device.

Throughout the book, we've warned you about browser quirks and support limitations. And while those warnings can be discouraging, they should have also clarified that things *are* getting better. Newer browsers have better support and fewer SVG bugs.

But not everyone who visits your website will be on the newest browser. You need to decide early on which older browsers you will be trying to support. There's little point in developing a site heavily infused wih SVG only to learn later that the client wants it to work in Internet Explorer 6.

If you have analytics data for the website you're working on, wonderful. But even if you don't, you can find general data about browser usage for your country, and adjust it based on your website's audience. If you're only interested in tech-savvy users with plenty of spending cash, you might only code for fairly recent software. But for many businesses, and especially for public services or health care, you need to consider a much broader audience who might be using much older computers or phones.

Once you've identified the browsers and devices you need to support, ask: does your graphic need to look the same in every browser? Or are some graphical effects optional enhancements, for which fallbacks are acceptable? If you are willing to accept compromises on older browsers, you can use more of the new features and shorthand options that simplify your code—and reduce file sizes—for the browsers that do support them.

For supporting really old browsers (Internet Explorer 8 or under, and Android versions under 4), you have to accept that some users won't have SVG at all. That means planning for plain-text fallbacks or alternative image formats.

A related decision is the **performance budget** for your site and for the graphics in particular. How many kilobytes are acceptable? How much battery power is that animated effect worth? How many seconds will users wait for this graphic to load? A good starting point might be "three seconds on 3G": every page should be ready to read and use in less than three seconds on a third-generation mobile data connection.

There are no hard-and-fast rules for how fast and lean a website has to be, or for how to make it so. Your standard should be negotiated to balance the needs of the web development team, your client or boss, the expected audience, and other stakeholders. But by having standards—based on real user data whenever possible—you have benchmarks against which you can test your work, and make adjustments as you go.

SVG often means a smaller file size than alternative graphics formats, but not always. SVG can also mean more processing on the end device. Some features, like filters and animation (and especially animated filters), use much more processing power than others. By testing your works-in-progress against preset performance budgets, you can identify when you need to change strategies.

Decide How SVG Will Integrate in Your Website

SVG on the web doesn't exist in isolation; it nearly always will be integrated in a larger website. We've discussed, in many chapters, the differences in SVG behavior that relate to *how* the SVG is integrated with HTML. Inline SVG has different requirements and possibilities than SVG as an image.

For this reason, it helps to plan early on for the embedding method. To recap, the three options and their key differences are as follows:

SVG as an image
> SVG embedded with `<img>` or as a CSS background image will be limited in its animation and interactivity. CSS inside the SVG document will be used for styling vector elements in the document itself, but these styles cannot be read or manipulated from the outside. Scripts, interactivity, and alternative text written inside the SVG will be ignored. There are also currently limitations in browser support for declarative animation.
>
> The primary advantage of SVG-as-image is its *encapsulation*: just like a bitmap image, the SVG is contained in a single file that will behave predictably when it is embedded across multiple pages.

SVG as an embedded object
> SVG embedded with `<object>` or `<iframe>` also has encapsulation and reusability, but it can have interactivity and scripting. It is often a good compromise solution, but it isn't used as much these days, which means it isn't tested as thoroughly. New bugs in scaling, sizing, and accessibility sometimes pop up in browsers.

Inline SVG

Inline SVG is also fully interactive and scriptable, but as part of the larger document. One of the biggest benefits is that SVG elements can be dynamically styled as part of the main document's stylesheets. One of the biggest limitations is that those styles can cross over even when you don't want them to. Inline SVG also currently has the best browser support for keyboard and screen-reader accessibility.

All other factors being equal, inline SVG will usually load faster than a separate file reference, but at the cost of more complicated maintainability. For most websites, you will need content management systems and/or build tools that can integrate the SVG markup in your HTML. If the same SVG code needs to be reused across pages, you'll usually require server-side includes or similar technologies to share the same source file between them. The repeated code also needs to be downloaded for each page, slowing down subsequent page loads compared to cached image files.

Sometimes you'll be able to decide on the embed method that best suits your project, while other times you'll be restricted by the structure of your existing codebase. Whichever approach you use, development of the SVG code will be easier if you know up front what the final capabilities will be.

Design for *All* Users

Very few graphics are *purely* decorative. They exist as part of the content of your website, to communicate meaning or mood. SVG content is often also a functional, interactive part of the website.

It is therefore essential that the meaning and the function is available to all users, even those who experience the web quite differently from how you do.

We've discussed SVG accessibility in Chapter 17 with regards to alternative text and ARIA roles, in Chapter 18 with regards to keyboard controls, and in scattered other locations with warnings and suggestions.

The best approach to creating an accessible website is to design it that way from the beginning. Extra code added at the last minute will always be awkwardly trying to patch holes, when those holes maybe could have been avoided altogether.

Designing for accessibility also means designing for performance. Large downloads and high CPU requirements are other ways in which users can be blocked from accessing your content or using its function. Similarly, building in solid fallbacks for older devices, and considering a diversity of screen sizes and input methods, both help increase the number of people who can use your website. But some users have requirements that go beyond the experience of switching to an older or smaller device.

As you're (literally or figuratively) sketching out your design, here are a few situations to keep in mind:

Color blindness
Color blindness is the most common visual limitation that cannot be corrected with eyeglasses. Frequently, it means an inability to distinguish red from green, but other versions of the disorder cause difficulties with different colors.

Use color to enhance meaning conveyed by shapes, text, or luminance changes, but never use color as the only source of meaning.

Not sure if your design works without color? Apply a `grayscale(100%)` filter on the root element and show it to a colleague. If they can't figure it out, you've got more work to do.

Limited contrast sensitivity
Viewing computer screens in bright sunlight makes it difficult to distinguish subtle changes in brightness in the image. Various eyesight conditions, often exacerbated by age, have the same effect.

The Web Content Accessibility Guidelines (WCAG) include minimum standards for the contrast of text against their background (*https://www.w3.org/TR/UNDERSTANDING-WCAG20/visual-audio-contrast-contrast.html*). Apply the same standards for important graphical details that affect the meaning of the content.

Extreme zoom
Small screen sizes don't leave a lot of room to draw text-heavy graphics, so users may need to zoom in and pan around a

diagram. Even on larger screens, some users will need to zoom in considerably (using browser zoom tools or dedicated screen magnification software) to be able to read it clearly.

The scalability of SVG only applies to the resolution of the zoomed graphics, not to their content. The two-dimensional nature of SVG—and of graphics in general—does not make it easy to reformat content for smaller viewports. Create responsive versions if you are able, but recognize that some users will only be seeing part of your graphic at a time.

Whenever possible, position labels in a diagram close to the graphic, so that users don't have to scroll back and forth. Label individual data points in a chart if you have the room, instead of requiring users to scan across to measure the value on an axis.

Style overrides

As an alternative to zooming in the entire graphical layout, some browsers allow users to override the `font-size` setting. Similarly, some users will override `font-family` choices to force the use of a font that is easier to read. Browsers and operating systems also have options that allow users to force the use of certain color schemes, usually in the context of creating better contrast.

You can't anticipate every possible style variation that might be applied to your website. But you can try to build more robust content that will be functional in a variety of situations.

Be especially careful of minimum font-size settings in browsers, as these can break SVG even when it isn't an accessibility issue. Scaling may mean that `font-size: 4px` will be drawn in 1-inch-tall letters, but it might still get adjusted to 16px or 20px. Consider this when deciding on your `viewBox` for a graphic with text; pick a scale that is close to the size it will be displayed (and yes, we know there are examples in this book that don't follow that guideline). If possible, make sure the layout won't break completely if text doubles in size.

To create graphics that automatically adapt to color overrides, consider using `currentColor` to inherit the text color instead of assuming that it will be black (or whatever value you set in the design). Internet Explorer, MS Edge, and Firefox on Windows also all support a limited subset of the CSS system color (*https://*

www.w3.org/TR/2010/PR-css3-color-20101028/#css2-system)
keywords to allow you to access the modified values of other
colors from Windows High Contrast Mode. The Microsoft
browsers (although not Firefox) also support a media query to
detect if custom colors are being applied.

No sound

Although SVG is a visual format, it is often used in the context
of audiovisual applications. Remember that many users will
have sound turned off, and some users don't have the option of
turning sound on—because they could not hear it anyway.
Warning or notification sounds need visual equivalents; video
and audio need captions or transcripts.

Missing context for symbols

SVG is often used for iconography. But icons are a language
unto themselves, and not everyone speaks it. Unlabeled icons
assume that your user shares a certain cultural training into
what the symbols mean. People from a different background (or
age range) than you may interpret them differently. Neurologi-
cal differences, including autism, can also change how someone
interprets the visual metaphors inherent in icons. Include text
labels for icons whenever you can.

Confusing text

Don't go overboard with text instructions, however. Too much
text is another usability problem. Long text is an obstacle for
users working in a second language, for users with reading difficulties such as dyslexia, and for anyone who is too tired, busy, or
distracted to read every word.

Distracting animation

An even worse culprit for distraction is animation or video that
plays when the user is trying to focus on something else. For
some users, animation goes beyond a distraction to become a
health risk, triggering nauseating vertigo or even epileptic
seizures.

Whenever you're using extreme graphical effects, such as
strobes or immersive 3D animation, give users a warning before
it starts. For all animations and sound, give users a way to pause
or control the effect. Consider also using new features like the

`prefers-reduced-motion` media query[1] to adjust your defaults. And provide a way to bypass the animation to get straight to the main function of the website.

Alternative inputs
> With the wide adoption of touchscreens, more developers have become aware of alternative inputs. But creating larger buttons for finger-sized touch taps is only the start. Any interactive content needs to work with touchscreens, mouse, or keyboard. Other input devices usually mimic one of these controls in the events they pass to the browser—but they may not allow fine or fast control. In addition, screen readers and voice controls rely on having clear and consistent names for all interactive elements.

If the meaning *and* function of your design can survive all these conditions, you're doing better than many. But a checklist will only get you so far: the real measure of your site's accessibility will come from testing with real users.

Working with Graphical Editors

Graphical editors, such as Adobe Illustrator and Inkscape, are a huge part of creating SVG for the web. But these tools were built primarily with print design in mind. Certain defaults and settings need to be tweaked for better code output. Creating a graphic that is optimized for animation, interactivity, and dynamic styling requires a little bit of planning ahead.

In Chapter 4, we gave some application-specific tips for a few of the most common programs, particularly regarding SVG export settings. This section outlines some general tips, applicable to most drawing tools.

Regardless of which software suite you use, there are some common steps that should be part of your project to help you get the result you want. Be aware that the terms used for specific features (such as Adobe Illustrator referring to the drawing space as the "Artboard") will change from one application to the other.

---

1 `prefers-reduced-motion` is discussed in the online supplementary example "Clipping on the Outside, with a Mask" (*https://oreillymedia.github.io/Using_SVG/extras/ch15-video-mask.html*).

Some of these strategies, like creating carefully structured groups, also make it much easier to work with the drawing while it is still *in* the graphical editor. They're also good ideas if you're creating a graphic by writing code yourself.

Most of the items in this section, in contrast, are more about changes you can make in the visual editor to help with later coding. They may be less obvious to designers who only work with the visual graphic—but they will make a huge difference to developers working with the exported code.

In addition, as we discussed in Chapter 4, you will often want to run your exported code through a dedicated optimization tool (although graphics software is getting better at optimizing code on export).

Define Your Artboard or Drawing Size

The first step of creating a graphic should be to choose the right reference system for your work in your application of choice. While vector shapes are indifferent to size and scale, it's logical to use measurements that mirror the purpose of your SVG file. For the web, this usually means pixels.

Although SVG is scalable, it helps to start with an idea of how large the graphic will be displayed. That way, you can make sure that text and stroke sizes are appropriate.

Using pixels is particularly important for small SVG icons, where the pixelation of the display becomes more obvious. If curves and lines do not neatly line up with screen pixels, the end result can have a blurred effect (as we discussed in "Anti-Anti-Aliasing for Crisp Lines" on page 492 in Chapter 13).

Snapping path points to the pixel grid can also help in larger graphics, by ensuring that coordinates can be represented by integers—and therefore with fewer characters in the code.

Of course, if your work is a precise illustration of a real-life object, you might prefer inches, centimeters, or millimeters, to match your source data. Just beware that many SVG export settings convert these to px, anyway. And even if they don't, a browser rendering won't necessarily be true to the real-life scale.

For most software and export options, the size you choose for your drawing region (artboard) will be reflected in the final SVG viewBox, width, and height. (Double-check your export options to make sure you get all three attributes in the final code!) An oversized artboard may be convenient in the editor, but it will leave whitespace around the final graphic, potentially ruining the layout. You can always change the artboard size after initially setting it.

Many programs allow you to crop the view on export to just fit the current selection or visible drawing. This can cause its own problems. Curved shapes that touch the very edges of the SVG image may appear to be trimmed in the final display, because anti-aliasing effects (which help "smooth" curves on raster screens) get cropped off. Leaving one or two pixels from the edge of the viewBox to any nonrectangular SVG elements is usually a good idea.

Of course, if the SVG export results in incorrect cropping, you can always manually adjust the viewBox in the exported code.

Structure Your Graphic

When you draw in SVG you're not just making images: you're creating *data*. A well-organized design file will create a well-organized SVG.

Whether you're creating your graphic with code or in a visual editor, you'll want to create meaningful groups that make it easier to transform substructures as a unit, and which can be given meaningful alternative text or ARIA roles.

In many graphical editors, you can have both groups and layers, but they are just groups inside groups within the final SVG. Use both features wisely. You don't want too many extra <g> elements in the final code, but you do need structured groups for applying transformations and effects like filters and masking. If you decide to reposition part of a diagram later, you want to be able to move the entire logical section with a single attribute or style property.

The most extreme version of grouping is merging multiple subpaths into a single <path> element. That ensures that all the parts will always stay together and be styled together—but at the expense of not being able to easily separate them later.

If you are going to animate your design, or reorganize it for different screen sizes, it helps to sketch out the possibilities before you start drawing. That way, you'll know which parts need to be grouped and which parts need to be separate elements.

You will sometimes have to break logical groups across layers to accommodate the lack of z-index support to alter the layering between groups. For example, text labels often need to be in a separate layer group (to prevent other shapes from overlapping the text) instead of being grouped with the shapes they label. But make sure you have a clear reason for these compromises.

Name Things

It's a well-worn joke that "naming things" is one of the hardest problems in computer science. It's still worth the effort.

Give elements names—in the form of class or id values—that will mean something to you later. For classes, focus on the common connections: *why* are these elements styled the same way?

If you are drawing shapes in a visual editor, name elements (shapes, groups, and layers) as you draw, using the software's object properties. Most applications export these layer or group names as the id attribute of SVG elements. But double-check your export and optimization settings: id values that aren't used in cross-references are sometimes removed during export.

 For best results, avoid using any spaces (separate words with - hyphens), so the name can be directly converted into a valid id attribute. Avoiding uppercase letters can also help prevent case-sensitivity issues when you're switching between SVG, HTML, and JavaScript.

It's much easier to create these references during visual editing, rather than later. When you're working with the markup code, one <path> looks much like another. Names can make it much easier to find the one you need.

Set Up Color Preferences for Web Use

Many vector illustration applications were originally designed for print, and therefore have their color space set to CMYK. In contrast, computer displays use RGB (specifically sRGB). RGB has a wider gamut (range of colors) than CMYK, so converting colors at the end of the design process is suboptimal; set the color mode before you begin drawing.

Of course, if your SVG is also expected to be used in *print*, the reverse is true: if you use RGB colors, some colors may not be accurately represented in the final printing. However, even if you are designing with CMYK palette, be aware that tools will usually remap your color selections into equivalent RGB or hexadecimal values during SVG export.

 As mentioned in Chapter 12, there are old and new proposals for alternative color profile support in SVG. CSS Color Module Level 4 also includes a cmyk() color function. However, as of this writing, no web browser yet supports these options.

Simplify Paths

In most SVG drawings, the largest contribution to file size is the path data or polygon points that describe complex drawing shapes.

You can significantly reduce the file size by using a reasonable viewBox scale and snapping points to exact pixel values (so that it takes fewer digits to specify each coordinate), and by reducing the total number of points in each path.

You can make both changes after the fact, by rounding down decimal precision on export, and by "smoothing" or simplifying paths using your editor's commands. However, you can often get better results by planning for simple paths from the beginning.

Drawing with the *least* possible number of points for each shape means fighting against the common instinct to *add* points to a curve whenever you need to tweak the shape. Instead, try to get as far as you can by adjusting the points and control points on the curve sections you already have.

Working with control points takes some practice. But it can make shapes *easier* to control in the end, particularly if you're trying to create symmetrical shapes.

As an illustration, let's consider drawing a simple heart shape. The heart icon that we've been using throughout the book was created (in Chapter 6) by carefully calculating coordinates and path data. But most designers prefer to work with a visual editor when drawing icons.

A first sketch at the path might use eight points, as in Figure 20-1. The shape is shown as it appears when selected in Adobe Illustrator, showing the on-path points (but not control points) and the bounding box.

Figure 20-1. A heart drawn in Illustrator using eight curve segments

To make this heart symmetrical, you need to adjust three pairs of points (and their control points) to be perfect matches on either side of the center axis. Remove extra points, and you have fewer points that you need to synchronize.

At its most extreme, you can create a heart shape with only two vertex points and two symmetrical cubic curves connecting them, as shown in Figure 20-2, which now shows the control points that create the shape.

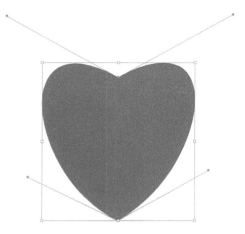

Figure 20-2. A heart drawn using two cubic Bézier segments

This may be too extreme, and may limit your ability to create just the right curve you want. But until you try it, you won't know how much nuance you can create just by adjusting those control-point handles.

Another way to keep your path data compact is to make use of strokes, instead of drawing both the inside and outside outlines of shapes. For example, a circular donut shape *could* be drawn as a path with a cutout subpath. But it can also be drawn as a thick stroke around a much simpler path (or around a <circle>).

 If you start by drawing a shape with stroke outlines, and later decide that you need it as an independent fill region, most graphical editors have a single-click option to convert the current stroke region into its own path definition.

Remember that thick strokes can have significantly different appearances depending on the stroke-linecap and stroke-linejoin options. With a little creativity and careful planning, you can use strokes to create clean geometric shapes that don't appear at first glance to be an outline at all.

Figure 20-3 shows a very different way of drawing a heart shape, as a thick stroke with round line caps on a three-point polyline.

Figure 20-3. A heart drawn as a round-capped stroke on a V-shape open-ended path

The blue rectangle in Figure 20-3 is the bounding-box outline that highlights the shape in Illustrator. Note that it is now much smaller than the visible shape, and remember that this can cause problems with objectBoundingBox graphical effects. Also beware of inconsistent browser rendering when a stroke curves in on itself.

A final path simplification option is to *merge* shapes that will always be styled and transformed as a whole. The more advanced graphical editors have multiple merge options. The simplest version concatenates all the shapes into a multipart path, keeping all the data. Other options recalculate the path data to represent the merged outline of overlapping (or intersecting, or cutout) shapes.

For example, you might draw a cloud shape as a series of overlapping circles, but then merge them into a single path representing the united outline. With a solid fill, the result looks the same, but with much less data required to define it. And now you can also switch to semitransparent fill or stroke, without the appearance breaking apart into individual circles.

Test Text Fallbacks, or Convert to Paths

Within your graphical editor, you have full control of the fonts used for your SVG text. Out on the web, less so. Try out your design with reasonable fallback fonts, and make adjustments to the text-anchor and other text layout properties to ensure that a font substitution doesn't completely break your layout.

You'll also need to add the fallback font-family lists and/or @font-face rules. Currently, the main SVG editors don't have tools to do this; you'll need to edit the CSS yourself, as described in Chapter 7.

If precise text rendering is more important than editability—for example, in a logo—many programs allow you to convert styled text elements into graphical shapes for each letter. Adobe Illustrator will also provide you with the option to convert type to shapes when you export the SVG file.

It's a bit more work, but a compromise option is to *duplicate* the text elements, convert the lower layer into paths, and then make the upper text layer transparent (but still accessible to search and to screen readers).

Of course, the approach you choose should depend on how you will be embedding the SVG. Text inside SVG used as an image isn't accessible in the first place, so might as well be converted to paths.

Consider the Backdrop

An SVG image only covers up the sections on which you explicitly draw elements. By default, the background is transparent. Graphical editors may allow you to change the background color in the display, but it is usually not automatically included in the export.

To add a background color to an SVG, you have three choices:

- Apply a background style to the element (<img>, <object>, or inline <svg>) that you use to embed the SVG in the web page.

- Add a background-color to the root <svg> element in the SVG file (that you'll be including as an image or embedded object). This is supported in all web browsers, although the background color is not used by most graphical editors.

- Include a colored backdrop shape as the rearmost layer in the SVG itself, usually a `<rect>` that covers the entire `viewBox`.

Many of the examples in this book use a `<rect>` backdrop, because it guarantees a consistent rendering when the SVG is viewed on its own. However, you get much greater flexibility by leaving the backdrop transparent and styling it when you embed it. Solid or see-through, consistent or flexible: you need to decide based on the needs of your website.

"Unset" Styles

If you're creating icons or other symbols that should inherit styles when they are used, try to remove style settings from the individual elements before export.

Inkscape has an "unset" option for both `fill` and `stroke` (represented as a question-mark icon), so that the shape will inherit styles wherever it is used. Illustrator has export options that will treat black fill as equivalent to `inherit`.

The SVG export options of the main software tools are also getting better at *not* including unnecessary style declarations for every element. However, if you do end up with SVG code that has dozens of inline styles for each element, an SVG optimizer can usually remove a lot of it.

Learn the Limits of Your Tool's SVG Output

One common theme of this book is that there is often more than one way to create a certain visual result with SVG. Different code structures may *appear* to have the same effect, but they create different possibilities for animation, scripting, and restyling.

If you're working with a graphical editor, take some time to look at the code it produces, so that you know when you need to intervene to get the result you want.

Many editors use `<path>` elements even when they could use one of the basic shapes. When you copy graphics, the default is usually to copy them as independent elements, not as `<use>` clones. Gradients might be always defined as independent user-space effects, instead of references to a shared bounding-box gradient that stretches to fit each shape.

This doesn't make their SVG export "wrong" or "bad" neccessarily. So long as the SVG visually renders correctly, it's good enough for most use cases.

The important thing is that you understand these limitations if you are going to be using the exported code in more complex projects. If the precise appearance is "baked" into the SVG, you'll often need to make changes in the original file in the original editor, and re-export the result, rather than being able to change things easily at the code level.

Many of these choices are defaults only, and can be changed if you fully investigate the software's options. For example, both Illustrator and Inkscape can use symbols and `<use>` if that's what you need.

Alternatively, you can take the approach of using the SVG output of the drawing tool as a *starting point* for your work, enhancing and modifying the code by hand to take advantage of features that the tool is not yet aware of. Draw individual bits and pieces in the editor, then copy and paste them into a separate file in your code editor, where you have full control of the document structure. In this way you can build up `<symbol>` and `<pattern>` elements from simple drawings, and use them in turn to create more complex work.

Learn the Limits of SVG, Compared to Your Tool

On the other side, a big problem with exporting SVG from graphical editors is that some editor features cannot be directly represented in standard, well-supported SVG. Each of the editors has different ways of handling SVG's limitations in its export.

For example, many editors support inset/outset strokes, instead of strokes centered over the edge of the path. SVG can't (yet) draw them directly. So there are a few possible outcomes of export:

- The inset/outset stroke feature is ignored, and the end result is an SVG that doesn't quite match the design.
- The stroke is converted to a separate path that draws the outline of the stroke shape.
- The path dimensions are adjusted slightly so that the centered SVG stroke matches the inset/outset stroke on the original shape.

Every option has pros and cons. But your preference might not match your editor's default.

If you know you are creating designs for use as SVG on the web, the best solution is to avoid using unsupported features in the first place. But if you've already got a design ready to go, the next step is to understand the export and whether you can control it.

For some effects that can't be represented in compatible SVG code, the result of export is a *raster* image of the editor's current rendering. For example, if you create a mesh gradient in Adobe Illustrator and then export as SVG, you will currently get a JPEG image, converted to a base-64 data URI, and then embedded in an SVG file. If the mesh gradient was the primary content of your graphic, it will be much easier—and a smaller file size—to just export it as JPEG directly.

Rasterized images are also used by Adobe Illustrator for many of its non-SVG-compatible filter effects. If you never look at the generated SVG markup, the only clue that you've got a raster image—and not a vector filter effect—will be the surprisingly large exported SVG file size.

 Adobe Illustrator has *two* types of filter effects. Only the "SVG filters" get exported as SVG filters; other effects are rasterized.

Figure 20-4 is an example that Dudley recently came across in a student's work. The vector diagram included a drop shadow created with one of Illustrator's default effects. The export had turned the shadow into its own data URI image layer.

Now, as we discussed in Chapter 16, a drop shadow does not need fancy graphics software. It can be created with SVG filter effects, or with shorthand filter functions in the latest browsers.

Figure 20-4. An SVG illustration with CSS drop-shadow filter

For this project, recreating the drop shadow involved applying CSS shorthands to the `<img>` elements that embedded the SVG, as it rendered faster than the equivalent longhand SVG filter effect. Since the affected images always had a filename that ended with *product.svg*, an attribute selector could be used to apply the drop shadow from the HTML file:

```
img[src$="product.svg"] {
    filter: drop-shadow(12px 12px 7px rgba(0,0,0,0.5));
}
```

This change helped to reduce the file size of the image from hundreds of kilobytes to a little over 4KB, after the base-64 image was removed and the remaining code was optimized.

Coordinating Code

Some parts of SVG development can't be completed in a graphical editor. When you switch to working with the code itself, you open up much more flexibility in what you create—which means many more opportunities to create confusing, difficult-to-maintain code.

In large projects with many developers, consider using style guides and pattern libraries to ensure consistency in the final product and efficiency in your workflow. SVG components should be integrated in those guidelines along with your HTML, CSS, and JS.

In addition, here are a few SVG-specific considerations for code organization.

Structuring Styles

SVG style properties can be set as presentation attributes, as inline styles, as CSS rules in a `<style>` section, or (except for SVG-as-image) as linked stylesheets. Which should you use?

If you're creating SVG in a graphical editor, it will usually give you the option of using presentation attributes or inline styles for export. In addition, recent versions of Adobe Illustrator can also create styles assigned by classes and rules in a `<style>` section.

At the time of writing, you have no control over the class names that Illustrator generates. The names it picks, such as `.cls-6`, aren't terribly imaginative. The result *looks* fine, but reading through the CSS later doesn't make it clear which styles refer to what. This can be improved with a little find-and-replace in your code editor, but it does mean extra work.

For other software—or for more complex CSS—you're going to need to edit the styles yourself to create a `<style>` section. Exporting your SVG with inline styles may be a useful first step, since at least it means you can cut and paste the `property: value` pairs as is.

Other than cut and paste, there are few benefits of inline styles over presentation attributes. As the examples in this book demonstrate, the `style` attribute is mostly only useful for new CSS properties that don't have presentation attribute versions, or for setting CSS variables.

So the main question is: should you use presentation attributes mixed in the markup, or CSS rules organized separately? The usual HTML/CSS rules about separating markup and styles rarely apply to SVG, where markup and styles are intertwined to create the graphical content.

Instead, here are some practical considerations when deciding how to organize your styles:

Preprocessors and build systems
If you're working within a larger project with CSS preprocessors, linters, and other build tools, you may prefer linked (external) stylesheets for your SVG code, so you can use those tools. However, remember that linked stylesheets don't work in SVG-as-image, and that same-document `url()` references won't work cross-browser if the styles are set in an external stylesheet.

Loading time
Linked stylesheets can be cached and reused by many pages, but they are slower; you'll sometimes see a "flash of unstyled SVG" (large, black SVG icons) while waiting for the stylesheet to be downloaded and parsed. At the very least, add `width` and `height` presentation attributes if you're using linked stylesheets.

Even inline `<style>` blocks can be slowed down by an `@import` rule at the top of the block, which is why we often used a separate `<style>` block later in the document to import Google font declarations.

Style computation time
If a document does not have *any* stylesheets or `<style>` sections, the browser can skip a lot of the style computation (selector matching and cascading different values from different rules). This means that presentation attributes and inline styles can be faster. But this only applies for independent SVG files; for inline SVG, the browser still needs to parse and scan all the stylesheets from your HTML, so using presentation attributes in the SVG won't save any style computation time.

Authoring convenience
For many authors, presentation attributes are simply easier, meaning no headaches about CSS selector specificity, with one value overriding another. This is a valid reason to stick with attributes. (Of course, if you *really* want to avoid unintentional

overrides from your document stylesheet, you would use inline style attributes.)

For many SVG drawings, each shape is uniquely styled, or shared styles can be applied by inheritance from a group. In those cases, classes and style rules add complexity without reducing the total amount of code.

But be careful not to get so stuck in the habit that you use presentation attributes even when they cease to be practical. If you do have multiple elements that should be styled the same, and which can't be easily grouped, repeating the style values as attributes on each element ruins the DRY-ness of your code, making it difficult to maintain.

Scripting efficiency

Presentation attributes are easy to read and modify from JavaScript with `getAttribute()` and `setAttribute()`. Inline styles are even easier (using the `element.style` object). In contrast, reading CSS set with stylesheets requires the (slower) `getComputedStyle()` approach; modifying CSS stylesheet rules means working with the CSS OM, and there's currently no easy way to access all the rule objects that apply to a given element.

But the computed style is more comprehensive, covering styles set in any method, including inherited styles, so use it whenever you *really* need to find out the current style value (like the actual width and height of an `<svg>`), especially if styles may come from a mix of sources.

DOM performance

CSS rules can reduce the total amount of style data the browser needs to keep in memory, even separate from the size of file downloads. Setting attributes or inline styles on each element, whether from markup or from script, means that the CSS text string has to be parsed and stored for each. When you have large numbers of elements (hundreds or more), this can be an important performance hit compared to creating shared style rules and setting classes on the elements.

There's no hard-and-fast answer, and you might choose to use a combination of different methods. Presentation attributes can be used as defaults that can be reset by CSS, or they can be used for unique features of a given element while shared styles are set with classes.

Sharing SVG Assets

When you have inline SVG components shared across multiple web pages, you need to think about the most practical way to manage shared SVG assets, so that everything stays coordinated.

In an ideal world, you'd create shared asset files and access each symbol or graphical effect as you need it. But if you've read the rest of the book, you know that SVG on the web is far from an ideal world. So: do you use server-side includes or build tools to add the same SVG markup to every page, or do you use a client-side AJAX (asynchronous JavaScript and XMLHttpRequest) solution to import them?

For simple cross-file `<use>` references, where the referenced element is a symbol that will be styled entirely by inheritance, browser support is getting to be pretty good. Add an AJAX solution like SVG4Everybody (*https://github.com/jonathantneal/svg4everybody*) to cover older browsers, and you're good to go.

But for more complex cross-references, the browser support isn't there (and can't easily be detected by the SVG4Everybody script). This includes `<use>` references to files with `<style>` sections, as well as references to patterns, gradients, masks, clipping paths, filters, and markers. For all of these cases, you currently need the elements to be in the same document for decent browser support.

The one exception: if you're using SVG masks, clipping paths, and filters applied to *non*-SVG elements, then the browser support for external file references is pretty close to the browser support for using the effect in the first place. So you might as well directly reference the separate asset file from your style declaration.

Just be sure to have fallback plans for the browsers that don't support either feature.

So how do you get the SVG into the HTML?

If you're already using a markup templating system—whether a static-site generator, server-side scripting, or a client-side framework—it is often easiest to use it to include your SVG markup as well. However, a custom AJAX solution may sometimes make sense as an enhancement to a server-side build routine, if the shared SVG files are very large, and you're confident most users will visit multiple pages. In those cases, adding the SVG markup to every page can slow down every download compared to AJAX-ing a cached asset file.

At this point—once you are using templating tools to copy your code into each HTML file—you'll also want to consider if it still makes sense to use <use>.

The <use> element is mostly an *authoring* convenience to keep your code DRY—but a templating system does the same thing. A <use> also reduces file size—but the difference is small if you're compressing your files with Gzip or Brotli (as you should). As currently implemented in most browsers, <use> shadow-DOM trees require as much or more memory and processing as the graphics they represent. So unless you need the live copies in the browser to all stay in sync as they are modified, it may make sense to just copy the raw markup where you need it, instead of creating symbol definitions and reusing them.

Selecting a JavaScript Library

The JavaScript examples in this book have all been of the "vanilla" variety, using standard JS methods and the DOM APIs available directly in the browser. However, we recognize that most complex scripted SVG on the web is built on one JavaScript library or another.

There are three reasons we chose the vanilla approach:

- We wanted to emphasize that you *can* script SVG directly, so long as you watch out for XML namespaces.
- We didn't want to get too distracted discussing the specifics of any particular library. SVG JavaScript libraries are huge topics unto themselves, and deserve books devoted to the subject.
- All our examples were fairly simple anyway.

If you're creating an interactive SVG that goes beyond what CSS pseudoclasses can do, or if you're building complex maps and charts from data files, it is worth taking a moment to assess whether using someone else's ready-made code will make your job easier.

That's not to say you always need to use a JS library. Library code is most often useful in four situations:

- You prefer a declarative interface for describing animations (that is, describing animations based on the desired outcome, instead of frame-by-frame calculations), but need better cross-browser support or performance than is currently available with CSS and SMIL animation.

- You want to create abstract drawing code that could be rendered using either SVG or the HTML Canvas2D API.

- You need your SVG code to play nicely with a JavaScript framework used for the rest of your website.

- You are building a complex—but not unique—data visualization and don't want to waste time reinventing the wheel…or the pie chart…or the radial-tree organizational diagram.

Some things to consider when selecting a library:

- How large a file size is the library code? Can you easily create a subset of only the methods you are using? Large libraries slow down your website both for the time to download and for the time and memory required to parse the JavaScript.

- Is the library API intuitive to use for what you want to use it for? If you have to hack around the API's limitations to create the desired effect, you're probably better off just hacking it together from vanilla JS.

- Is it optimized for your use case, particularly when it comes to tricky aspects like animation performance or asynchronous event handling?

- Does it include extra functions, such as complex mathematical or text-parsing methods, which you'd have to recreate anyway?

- Does it handle cross-browser compatibility issues for you?

If you do choose to use a JavaScript library, make sure it is designed to work with SVG, so that it uses the correct XML-namespaced

DOM methods "under the hood." We listed a few common SVG-related libraries in Chapter 4.

Test, Test, Test!

Planning ahead for browser support issues is important, and the warnings in the book should help with that. Build in compatibility as you go by working around known support limitations, or by integrating fallbacks.

But nothing replaces thorough testing of your own code.

You will often encounter "gotchas" or bugs that you did not expect or plan for. This is particularly true when your work is shown on mobile plaforms, where browsers become even more fragmented. But it is true of the major desktop browsers as well. We've filed dozens of browser bug reports while working on this book. Many of those were for weird intersections of multiple features, where the bug wouldn't show up in unit tests for support of one feature or the other.

For this reason, cross-browser and cross-platform testing is particularly important. You can *develop* your SVG-infused site using any browser you wish, but before *publishing* the work you need to check that it works.

And don't wait until you're done before testing. Regularly check your assumptions.

It's much easier to address problems as they occur, rather than having to go back and fix things after the work is otherwise complete. For this reason, it's important to check your work as you go: if possible, test in all the major rendering engines, meaning Chrome, Firefox, Safari, Edge, and Internet Explorer. If you can, test different operating systems as well: Windows, macOS, iOS, Android, and Linux.

That's quite a bit of ground to cover. Broadly speaking, there are three ways of dealing with it, from best to worst:

Test each browser in its native operating system
    The ideal testing situation is to test real browsers running on real devices. This will mean multiple machines and multiple displays, all connected to your testing server.

To avoid having to manually refresh each browser to visually check the results of code changes, you can use a tool like BrowserSync (*https://www.browsersync.io/*) or CodeKit; many integrated development environments (IDEs) now have similar capabilities. All of them work on similar principles, running a server in the background that pushes refresh requests to browsers looking at a particular URL, whenever the code is updated.

Use emulators and virtual machines
You may not have access to an extensive device lab of different phones and computer operating systems. Even if you have the correct OS, some browsers are tied to operating system upgrades, so you can't run multiple versions of the same browser on the same device.

Virtual machines can help. That means loading an entire operating system in a separate application window, sandboxed from the main system in which it is running. Using this approach, you can (in theory) run as many instances as you wish, each with its own browser version. The most common virtualization software is VirtualBox (*https://www.virtualbox.org/wiki/Virtual Box*), and Microsoft offers virtual machines for all versions of Internet Explorer and MS Edge (*https://developer.micro soft.com/en-us/microsoft-edge/tools/vms/*), starting with IE8.

There are also virtual machines (emulators) for the major mobile operating systems, in which you can run the preinstalled stock browsers and compatible versions of other major browsers. Emulation is never quite the same as having a real device, but it can identify major support issues.

A slightly less ideal option is software emulation without recreating the full operating system. Most browser developer tools can now recreate different screen sizes and resolutions, and many can simulate touch support on a desktop. But this isn't the same as recreating the full mobile versions of those browsers. In addition, Internet Explorer 11 dev tools can emulate earlier IE versions, turning off features that weren't supported in earlier versions and recreating many (but not all) of their quirks.

Use online multibrowser testing services
The final option is to mostly rely on online testing and emulation services like CrossBrowserTesting (*https://crossbrowsertest ing.com/*), BrowserStack (*https://www.browserstack.com/*), and

BrowserLing (*https://www.browserling.com/*). Microsoft also offers free online access to its IE and Edge virtual machines, via BrowserStack. Being online, they tend to be slower in response, and take more time to update, but they are still very useful. (The browser support warnings in this book owe quite a lot to Cross-BrowserTesting.)

Depending on your subscription option, you may be able to automate the testing process, running your site on many browsers and screen size, retrieving screenshots, and comparing them against reference images to see if anything is broken. However, remember that screenshots only capture *some* of the possible ways a browser can break your website: interactive features still need to be tested directly.

Don't assume that the same version of a browser is equivalent across platforms. While features are usually the same for a browser release across different platforms, there can be surprising support gaps or rendering inconsistencies.

Many browsers (particularly Firefox and Chrome) will use different low-level graphics rendering libraries depending on the operating system and the type of GPU available.

Also remember that *all* browsers on iOS devices use WebKit code for rendering web page content, including SVG.

Just because your graphic looks perfect in a specific version of a browser on Windows does not mean it will yield the same result in the same browser version on macOS or Android. Trust us—we've been caught by this exact problem when building demos for this book!

Final Thoughts

This book has been a fairly major undertaking, passing from one author to the next and filling up free time over many years.

When Kurt first began the book in 2011, SVG was just beginning to achieve practical browser support. Many things were simply not possible with SVG on the web. Since then, support for core SVG 1 features has improved incredibly—but numerous new features have also been added, with their own support issues.

The final book is the result of various tradeoffs between wanting to be exhaustive and wanting to be instructive, between wanting to make examples clear and simple and wanting to make them realistic and interesting.

Scalable Vector Graphics is a powerful document language, but its flexibility creates great complexity. Until SVG, there was generally a clear division between word and picture on the web, and the web consequently was very rectilinear: always divided into boxes. With SVG, that division breaks down. SVG has helped usher in a new era in which web interfaces have become more gamelike, immersive, and adaptive, where graphics can be interactive and dynamic, and therefore much more informative.

The final book is much more exhaustive than originally planned, but cannot hope to cover all possible quirks and complications you will discover when working with SVG. We hope that the explanations and the examples have inspired you to imagine new possibilities. We encourage you to make use of the online reference sections, as you continue to learn through experimentation.

Most of all, have fun, and don't be afraid to play.

Index

coordinate system dimensions, 259
on filter, 624
on filter primitives, 628
geometry properties, in SVG 2, 154
in graphical editors, 284, 775
on img, 321
on mask, 578
on pattern, 462, 467, 470
on rect, 149
on svg element, 7, 283, 710
on symbol, in SVG 2, 341
on use, 333
hexadecimal color values, 412
:hover selector, 604, 684, 692
(see also selectors)
href attribute
a element in SVG vs HTML, 680
CSS selectors for, 78
on marker, proposal, 545
vs xlink:href, 21, 249, 337, 449, 680, 719
hreflang attribute, 681
hsl color function, 412, 705
hsla color function, 423
HTML
elements in SVG
alternative text, 668
foreignObject, 63, 669
link and meta, 80, 676
media embeds in SVG 2, 360
embedding SVG in, 56-69
HTML5, 43, 61
parser, 5-7, 10, 63, 247, 669, 674
bugs, 673
creating elements with innerHTML, 49
element depends on context, 51
XML namespaces and inline SVG, 63, 66
vs SVG, 43
timeline, 45
WHATWG vs W3C, 62
HTMLUnknownElement DOM object, 48
HTTP headers

for cross-origin files, 348
for file types, 5
for SVGZ files, 112
HTTP/2, and multiple file requests, 94
HTTPS, 300, 348, 350
hue-rotate filter function, 608
hyperlinks (see a element)

I

Iconic library, 112
id attribute, 22, 97, 776
ARIA attributes, 655, 660
URL targets, 299, 698
iframe element, 61
(see also objects, SVG embedded as)
browsing contexts and SVG views, 301
sandboxing, 305
scaling SVG in, 304, 309
in SVG 2, 360
image element, 221, 351-359
alternative text, 359
autosizing, in SVG 2, 352
cropping, 356, 582
fallback behavior and src, 354
image maps, 687
in a pattern, 467, 518, 630
image maps, HTML vs SVG, 686-692
Images module (see CSS3 modules)
images, SVG embedded as, 56-60, 679, 768
autosizing, 59, 281
backgrounds and borders on root element, 141
embedding with CSS, 87-93
icons sprites with views, 316
limitations, 60, 79, 213, 223, 312
media queries, 86
vs use elements, 346, 350
img element, 56
(see also images, SVG embedded as)
alternative text, 653
fallback for object, 61
image as synonym, for fallback, 354

About the Authors

Amelia Bellamy-Royds is a freelance writer and web developer whose primary interest is scientific and technical communication— in words or in graphics. She is best known in web design circles for her work with SVG. In addition to explaining SVG and related web standards, she tries to make them better; Amelia is an Invited Expert on the W3C's SVG, ARIA, and CSS Working Groups.

Amelia's interest in SVG stems from work in data visualization, and builds upon the programming fundamentals she learned while earning a B.Sc. in bioinformatics. From there, she moved to work in science, health, and environmental policy research, and then to a Master's degree in journalism. Amelia currently lives in Edmonton, Alberta, Canada. This is the fourth book on SVG she has co-authored for O'Reilly Media.

Kurt Cagle is the founder of Semantical, LLC, a smart data company, and uses SVG for data visualizations and web application development. He is also author or coauthor of more than twenty books on web technologies, data modeling, and knowledge management. He lives in Issaquah, WA, with his wife, daughters, and cat, who helps edit his manuscripts.

Dudley Storey has been making web pages for almost the entire life of the web. An accomplished teacher, writer, and designer, he is also the author of *Pro CSS Animation* (Apress, 2013). Dudley is also a contributing editor at *Smashing Magazine*, and writes web development articles on his blog, *theNewCode.com*.

Colophon

The animal on the cover of *Using SVG with CSS3 and HTML5* is a blue-fronted lorikeet (*Charmosyna toxopei*). This bird is exclusively found on the Indonesian island of Buru. Buru was part of the Dutch East Indies colony from 1658 to 1942, and Lamburtus Johannes Toxopeus (born in Java, but of Dutch nationality) was the first European scientist to describe and capture this lorikeet species. His name thus became part of the bird's Latin name.

These birds are primarily green in color, with blue heads and bellies. They are small members of the parrot family, growing to about 6 inches (16 cm) long. Blue-fronted lorikeets live in pairs, occasionally forming small groups up to 10 birds. Their preferred habitat is lowland forest with plenty of flowering trees to provide them with their diet of nectar and soft fruit.

The blue-fronted lorikeet is critically endangered due to logging activity in its already limited range. Two protected areas have been established on the island to help preserve the bird's habitat.

Many of the animals on O'Reilly covers are endangered; all of them are important to the world. To learn more about how you can help, go to *animals.oreilly.com*.

The cover image is an illustration by Karen Montgomery, based on an antique engraving from *Shaw's Zoology*. The cover fonts are URW Typewriter and Guardian Sans. The text fonts are Adobe Minion Pro and Myriad Pro Light; the heading font is Adobe Myriad Condensed; and the code font is Dalton Maag's Ubuntu Mono.

Learn from experts.
ind the answers you need.